SOCIAL DYNAMICS
Models and Methods

QUANTITATIVE STUDIES IN SOCIAL RELATIONS

Consulting Editor: Peter H. Rossi

UNIVERSITY OF MASSACHUSETTS
AMHERST, MASSACHUSETTS

In Preparation

Michael D. Maltz, **RECIDIVISM**

Published

Nancy Brandon Tuma and Michael T. Hannan, **SOCIAL DYNAMICS: Models and Methods**

Peter Schmidt and Ann D. Witte, **AN ECONOMIC ANALYSIS OF CRIME AND JUSTICE: Theory, Methods, and Applications**

Alexander Basilevsky and Derek Hum, **EXPERIMENTAL SOCIAL PROGRAMS AND ANALYTIC METHODS: An Evaluation of the U. S. Income Maintenance Projects**

Walter R. Gove and Michael Hughes, with contributions by Omer R. Galle, **OVERCROWDING IN THE HOUSEHOLD: An Analysis of Determinants and Effects**

Ronald S. Burt, **CORPORATE PROFITS AND COOPTATION: Networks of Market Constraints and Directorate Ties in the American Economy**

Peter H. Rossi, James D. Wright, and Andy B. Anderson (Eds.), **HANDBOOK OF SURVEY RESEARCH**

Joan Huber and Glenna Spitze, **SEX STRATIFICATION: Children, Housework, and Jobs**

Toby L. Parcel and Charles W. Mueller, **ASCRIPTION AND LABOR MARKETS: Race and Sex Differences in Earnings**

Paul G. Schervish, **THE STRUCTURAL DETERMINANTS OF UNEMPLOYMENT: Vulnerability and Power in Market Relations**

Irving Tallman, Ramona Marotz-Baden, and Pablo Pindas, **ADOLESCENT SOCIALIZATION IN CROSS-CULTURAL PERSPECTIVE: Planning for Social Change**

Robert F. Boruch and Joe S. Cecil (Eds.), **SOLUTIONS TO ETHICAL AND LEGAL PROBLEMS IN SOCIAL RESEARCH**

The list of titles in this series continues at the end of this volume

SOCIAL DYNAMICS
Models and Methods

NANCY BRANDON TUMA
MICHAEL T. HANNAN

Department of Sociology
Stanford University
Stanford, California

ABIGAIL E. WEEKS MEMORIAL LIBRARY
UNION COLLEGE
BARBOURVILLE, KY 40906

1984

ACADEMIC PRESS, INC.
(Harcourt Brace Jovanovich, Publishers)

Orlando San Diego San Francisco New York London
Toronto Montreal Sydney Tokyo

COPYRIGHT © 1984, BY ACADEMIC PRESS, INC.
ALL RIGHTS RESERVED.
NO PART OF THIS PUBLICATION MAY BE REPRODUCED OR
TRANSMITTED IN ANY FORM OR BY ANY MEANS, ELECTRONIC
OR MECHANICAL, INCLUDING PHOTOCOPY, RECORDING, OR ANY
INFORMATION STORAGE AND RETRIEVAL SYSTEM, WITHOUT
PERMISSION IN WRITING FROM THE PUBLISHER.

ACADEMIC PRESS, INC.
Orlando, Florida 32887

United Kingdom Edition published by
ACADEMIC PRESS, INC. (LONDON) LTD.
24/28 Oval Road, London NW1 7DX

Library of Congress Cataloging in Publication Data

Tuma, Nancy Brandon.
  Social dynamics.

  (Quantitative studies in social relations)
  Bibliography: p.
  Includes index.
  1. Sociology--Research. 2. Sociology--Methodology.
I. Hannan, Michael T. II. Title. III. Series.
HM48.T85   1983   301'.072   83-25856
ISBN 0-12-703670-9 (alk. paper)
ISBN 0-12-703672-5 (pbk. : alk. paper)

PRINTED IN THE UNITED STATES OF AMERICA

84 85 86 87   9 8 7 6 5 4 3 2 1

Contents

Preface xi

Acknowledgments xvii

PART I INTRODUCTION

1 Why Dynamic Analysis? 3

    1.1 Static Analysis for Studying Change   4
    1.2 Dynamic Analysis for Studying Static Relationships   7
    1.3 Other Obstacles to Dynamic Analysis   14
    1.4 Conclusions   15

2 Varieties of Temporal Analysis: Overview and Critique 17

    2.1 Observation Plans   18
    2.2 Panel Analysis of Qualitative Outcomes   23
    2.3 Event-History Analysis   28
    2.4 Panel Analysis of Quantitative Outcomes   33
    2.5 Time-Series Analysis   38
    2.6 Conclusions   39

PART II QUALITATIVE OUTCOMES

3 Fundamentals of Event-History Analysis 43

    3.1 Event-History Data   45
    3.2 Terms for Populations of Event Histories   49
    3.3 Conclusions   77

4 Models of Change in Qualitative Variables   78

4.1 Reasons for Continuous-Time Stochastic Models   79
4.2 Models of Event Histories   91
4.3 Implications of Semi-Markov Models   96
4.4 Particular Models   101
4.5 Conclusions   114

5 Estimation Using Censored Event Histories   116

5.1 The Censoring Problem   118
5.2 Maximum-Likelihood Estimation   119
5.3 ML Estimation of Right-Censored Event Histories   122
5.4 ML Estimation of Left-Censored Event Histories   128
5.5 ML Estimators for a Single Constant Rate   135
5.6 Two Pseudo-ML Estimators   139
5.7 A Moment Estimator   140
5.8 Monte Carlo Results on Effects of Censoring   140
5.9 Measurement Error in Dates   145
5.10 Monte Carlo Results on Measurement Error   147
5.11 Markov Models with Multiple Outcomes   151
5.12 Conclusions   154

6 Models for Heterogeneous Populations   155

6.1 Parameterizing Observed Heterogeneity   157
6.2 An Example: NIT Effects on Marital Stability   165
6.3 Incorporating Unobserved Heterogeneity   174
6.4 An Example: Unobserved Heterogeneity in Job-Shift Rates   179
6.5 Misspecification of the Disturbance's Distribution   184
6.6 Conclusions   186

7 Time Dependence: Parametric Approaches   187

7.1 Sources of Time Dependence   189
7.2 Periodic Shifts in Parameters and Causal Variables   197
7.3 Linearly Changing Causal Variables   208
7.4 Time as a Proxy for Unobserved Change Processes   220
7.5 Conclusions   231

8 Time Dependence: A Partially Parametric Approach   232

8.1 Proportional Rates   233
8.2 Partial Likelihood   235
8.3 Monte Carlo Study of PL and ML Estimators   239
8.4 PL Estimation of a Hazard Function Illustrated   244

To
George, Katie, and Clare from NBT,
and to
Chris, Kevin, and Tim from MTH

Contents

- 8.5 Handling of Ties 247
- 8.6 Intermittently Measured Explanatory Variables 248
- 8.7 Estimating the Nuisance and Survivor Functions 250
- 8.8 Sources of Variation in the Nuisance Function 252
- 8.9 Multiple Outcomes 254
- 8.10 PL Estimation of Transition Rates Illustrated 256
- 8.11 Repeatable Events 259
- 8.12 Conclusions 263

9 Systems of Qualitative Variables 265

- 9.1 Modeling Strategies 266
- 9.2 An Example: Marital Status and Employment Statuses 268
- 9.3 Consequences of Ignoring Interdependence 276
- 9.4 Conclusions 294

10 A Comparison of Approaches 296

- 10.1 Cross-Sectional Analysis 297
- 10.2 Event-Count and Event-Sequence Analysis 304
- 10.3 Panel Analysis 305
- 10.4 An Example: Formal Political Structure 307
- 10.5 How Well Do These Models Fit? 321
- 10.6 Conclusions 327

PART III QUANTITATIVE OUTCOMES

11 Linear Deterministic Models 331

- 11.1 Linear Models for Rates of Change 332
- 11.2 Time Paths of Changes: Integral Equations 341
- 11.3 An Example: Organizational Growth and Decline 346
- 11.4 Linear Systems 352
- 11.5 Integral Equations for Linear Systems 355
- 11.6 Qualitative Stability 359
- 11.7 Organizational Growth and Decline Reconsidered 370
- 11.8 Conclusions 380
-      Appendix 381

12 Linear Stochastic Models 384

- 12.1 Need for Stochastic Models 385
- 12.2 Stochastic Differential Equations 388
- 12.3 Complicating the Noise Process 397
- 12.4 Diffusion Processes 400
- 12.5 Boundary Behavior 406

12.6 Systems of Equations   410
12.7 Conclusions   416

13 Estimation of Linear Models   418

13.1 Time-Series versus Panel Data   418
13.2 Two Ways to Estimate a Dynamic Model   422
13.3 Scalar Models   424
13.4 Autocorrelation of Disturbances   430
13.5 Pooled Cross-Section and Time-Series Estimators   431
13.6 Monte Carlo Studies of Pooled Estimators   447
13.7 Measurement Error   455
13.8 Unequally Spaced Observations   459
13.9 Linear Systems   461
13.10 Conclusions   464

14 Deterministic Nonlinear Models   466

14.1 Scalar Models   466
14.2 Models of Systems   477
14.3 Competition Models   478
14.4 Exact Discrete Approximations   485
14.5 An Example: National Expansion of Education   495
14.6 Qualitative Stability   501
14.7 Cyclic Behavior: Predator–Prey Interactions   506
14.8 Conclusions   509

15 Stochastic Nonlinear Models   510

15.1 Stochastic Integrals: The Nonlinear Case   512
15.2 Geometric Brownian Motion   520
15.3 The Itŏ Transformation Formula   522
15.4 Conclusions   526

16 Coupled Qualitative and Quantitative Processes   528

16.1 Quality and Quantity   529
16.2 Approaches   531
16.3 Conclusions   538

References   539

Author Index   565

Subject Index   573

Preface

Once again the study of social change—how and why social systems and actors within systems change over time—is moving to center stage in sociology. This shift in substantive concerns has placed new demands on sociological methodology and on the practice of sociological research. Although the structural-equation and log-linear models routinely used in empirical sociological research are exceedingly useful for the study of statics (i.e., relationships at a point when change is not occurring), they are ill equipped to accommodate the renewed interest in social dynamics. Of course, models and methods for static analysis may be extended to provide a basis for dynamic analysis. But such extensions are neither as simple nor as obvious as they may seem as first glance. Basic principles must be reconsidered, and old prejudices and intuitions reexamined. Then standard techniques need to be revised or replaced.

Some progress toward these extensions has already occurred. Our survey of current practice and recent developments (reported in Chapter 2) suggests, however, that progress toward the satisfactory analysis of change has been very uneven. We believe that without a broad framework for thinking about and conducting quantitative, empirical studies of social change processes, most advances will remain isolated and idiosyncratic. This book is the result of our efforts to build such a framework.

Any attempt at forging a systematic framework for the empirical study of social change must confront two issues. One involves the development of *dynamic* models—models that describe the time paths of change in phenomena. The other involves the development of *causal* models—models that describe how change in some properties induces change in still other properties. Sociologists have rarely used models that deal with *both* of these issues, that is, dynamic models that reflect arguments about causal relationships. We try to move in this direction. In doing so we rely heavily on the use of formal models to guide attempts at testing hypotheses about the processes and causes of change.

One barrier to progress in developing procedures for the empirical study of social change is the common failure in sociology to distinguish *models* from *methods* and *data* from *observation plans*. By a *model* we mean an abstract image of reality whose construction has been guided by theory, empirical generalizations from past research, and perhaps hunches. In contrast, *method* refers to the set of procedures used to estimate and evaluate a model from data. An *observation plan* is a scheme for systematically collecting information pertinent to the phenomenon being studied. The adverse consequences of failing to distinguish models from methods have been compounded by inattention to the fact that multiple observation plans can be used to collect data in order to estimate and evaluate a model. When models and methods are not distinguished, there is a tendency to view a hybrid of a method and a model (e.g., least-squares regression) as a universal tool for data analysis rather than to see a model as a picture of reality that can be tested by *various* methods using data collected under *many* different observation plans.

In our opinion one consequence of the blurring of these distinctions has been that sociologists have tended to rely heavily on discrete-time models of change. Discrete-time models are certainly appropriate for describing phenomena that change only at fixed, discrete time intervals (e.g., consequences of an annual budgetary process, job changes in labor markets in which annual contracts are universal, political party dominance in a system with regular elections). But such phenomena are much less common than ones in which changes can occur at any moment. True, a discrete-time observation plan is used almost always in the case of quantitative (metric) outcomes and quite often in the case of qualitative (discrete) outcomes. Still, as an image of reality, a model should mirror the way changes *can* occur, not the way data are collected. The relative rarity of phenomena that can change only at discrete time points, coupled with our belief that models should attempt to fit reality and not be dictated by the observation plan used to collect data, led us to concentrate on a framework that is unconventional in sociology: continuous-time models. In any case, discrete-time models are simply a special case of continuous-time models, and good treatments of discrete-time models are already available.

Another obstacle to a broad treatment of dynamic models and methods is the very different treatment given to qualitative and quantitative outcomes in the extant literature. Sociologists routinely apply stochastic models in modeling change in qualitative outcomes. In contrast, they invariably use deterministic models of change in quantitative outcomes, with randomness entering only at the estimation stage. We think that much can be gained from treating both types of outcomes consistently. In particular, this consistency seems necessary to develop models of change in coupled qualitative and quantitative outcomes. Therefore, we again depart from sociological convention: we propose a *stochastic* treatment of both discrete and metric outcomes.

Thus, we had four main goals in writing this book:

1. To clarify and develop models and methods for causal analysis of dynamic social processes
2. To formulate continuous-time models of change in both quantitative and qualitative outcomes and to develop suitable methods for estimating these models from the kinds of data commonly available to sociologists
3. To develop a stochastic framework for analyzing both qualitative and quantitative outcomes
4. To alter the way that sociologists think about the empirical study of social change processes

We think we have made a promising start in meeting the first and second goals. We have formulated a variety of continuous-time causal models of change in both quantitative and qualitative outcomes, and we have also indicated how to estimate these models from event histories (in the case of qualitative outcomes) or panel data (in the case of quantitative outcomes). We wish that we had been more successful in the development of methods for estimating continuous-time causal models of change in *qualitative* variables from panel data, but this problem is a thorny one. We decided to say very little at all about this topic rather than present methods that we consider unsatisfactory.

The third objective has also been tougher to achieve than we had hoped. Our treatment of change in qualitative outcomes is completely stochastic. But because of the complexity of stochastic models of change in quantitative outcomes, we also include an extensive discussion of deterministic models of such outcomes. We have sketched possible extensions of these models to the stochastic case, but we have done little more than scratch the surface of potential applications. Still, we hope that the strategy we have outlined will strike a responsive chord and stimulate further work on the important problems involved in developing continuous-time stochastic models of change in quantitative outcomes.

We cannot judge how well we have achieved our fourth main goal; only our readers can decide that. Our own thinking about the study of social change has certainly been transformed as we have pondered and written about the topics covered in this book. We hope that after reading this book, others will also gain a new perspective on how and why to study social dynamics.

This book is addressed primarily to sociologists interested in the empirical study of social change, but other social scientists with similar concerns should also find it germane. Although the material in this books appears, at least at first glance, to be very technical by current sociological standards, it is directed at *all* sociologists involved in quantitative empirical research, and not just the narrow circle of "mathematical sociologists." The key points of the book are contained in the verbal discussions of the social-scientific motivations for the various models and methods that we discuss, and these are illustrated, wherever possible, by applications from our own research. These include studies of job mobility, impacts of negative income tax programs on marital and employment stability, growth and decline processes in organizations, organizational mortality, changes in political structures, and expansion of national systems of education. In using earlier versions of this manuscript in sociology classes at Stanford and Berkeley, we found that students can acquire a basic understanding of our approach by studying these empirical applications even if they are unable to master all technical details.

We admit, however, that some parts of this book contain

Preface

fairly complicated material, especially Chapters 9, 12, 14, and 15. But most sections presume only a background in applied social statistics, elementary probability theory, matrix notation, and the calculus. Some familiarity with ordinary differential equations is also helpful in places. To help readers from getting bogged down by mathematical complexities, we have placed an asterisk before the titles of sections containing the more mathematically complicated discussions; these may be skipped without loss of continuity.

Since our potential audience also includes mathematically sophisticated scientists who are interested in applications of stochastic models to sociological problems, we must also make clear that we proceed rather informally. We make no pretense to mathematical rigor: we state important results without proof and refer to standard technical treatments. Insofar as technical, mathematical, and statistical matters are concerned, we view this book as an introduction and an orientation to a huge and growing technical literature. Anyone who wishes to gain a deeper understanding of the technical aspects of the models and methods that we discuss should consult the numerous works to which we refer.

This book is divided into three parts. Part I provides a general background for what follows; it includes both a discussion of the substantive importance of dynamic analyses in sociology and a review of models and methods previously used by sociologists interested in the empirical study of social dynamics. Part II contains eight chapters on models and methods for analyzing change in qualitative outcomes; it concentrates mainly on methods based on analysis of event-history data. Part III contains six chapters on comparable models and methods for analyzing change in quantitative outcomes; it focuses primarily on methods based on analysis of panel data. Although some of the chapters in Part III build on the material covered in Part II, Part III can largely be read independently of Part II.

Readers of books with more than one author often like to attribute different parts of a book to one author rather than the other(s). Often this attribution is justified. But, although some sections of *Social Dynamics* were first drafted by Tuma and others were first drafted by Hannan, each of us revised and rewrote—sometimes extensively—what the other had drafted first. We want readers to consider all chapters of this book as written by both of us, and not to think of some chapters as Tuma's and others as Hannan's.

Finally, we wish to note that the ordering of our names on the title page was decided by a coin toss, as we had decided when we first planned this book. We believe that this is appropriate given the nature of our collaboration and our firm commitment to probabilistic methods.

Acknowledgments

Since we began work on this book in 1978, we have recevied invaluable assistance from many people and organizations. We would like to acknowledge this assistance and express our thanks.

Our greatest debt is to the many people with whom we have discussed the issues raised in this book. Several of these deserve special mention. Our work on this book began when we were deeply involved in analyzing data gathered in the Seattle and Denver Income Maintenance Experiments (SIME/DIME), and our conversations with the others sharing in this task were an important context for our work on this book. In particular, numerous discussions with Lyle Groeneveld concerning how best to analyze the marital histories gathered in these experiments had considerable impact on Part II of this book. We thank Lyle for sharing his ideas with us and also for suggesting the title of this book. Our discussions with Lyle and Burton Singer concerning how to analyze interdependencies between changes in marital status and changes in family income using marital histories and monthly reports on family income were a major impetus to Part III of this book. Part III was also motivated by Hannan's collaboration with John Freeman on the study of growth and decline in sizes of school personnel components (see Chapter 11). Our earlier work with François Nielsen and Alice Young on estimation of discrete-time models of change in quantitative variables proved to be very useful when our attention turned to continuous-time models of change in such variables (see Chapter 13). Glenn Carroll and Lawrence Wu are two others with whom we discussed extensively the issues raised throughout this book. We wish to acknowledge especially Glenn's earlier work on nonlinear models of change in quantitative variables, which was the primary factor leading us to devote a whole chapter to this topic (see Chapter 14). Finally, examples from our substantive research over the past decade are scattered throughout this book, and we wish to acknowledge our collaborators' contributions to these examples and also to our general ideas about models and methods for studying social dynamics. These individuals include: Stephen Beaver, Glenn Carroll, Mary Fennell, John Freeman, Lyle Groeneveld, Philip Robins, Gary Sandefur, Louise Smith-Donals, Aage Sørensen, Barbara Warsavage, and Katherine Yaeger.

We also wish to express our thanks for the expert research assistance that we received from Linda Jean Cutshaw, Charles Denk, Sonalde Desai, Linda Drazga, Helen Garrison, Beverly Lauwagie, Katherine Lyman, Camille Marder, John McClure, Edward Mendelssohn, Susan Olzak, John Peterson, Carlisle Shoemaker, Evan Tanner, Peggy Thoits, Marlos Viana, and Joseph Waight. Douglas Crockford and subsequently David J. Pasta made significant contributions through their programming of RATE (see Tuma, 1979), the computer program used to estimate all models in Part II. François Nielsen provided a program for applying Henderson's method, which we used in the empirical examples in Chapter 11.

Donna Mar did an expert job of typing the first draft. We then decided to produce camera-ready copy using Donald Knuth's (1979, 1984) marvelous TEX, a computer program for typesetting books and other documents, on the Stanford Computer Science Department's SAIL computer. This book also uses type fonts developed by Don Knuth (1979) with his METAFONT computer program. Once this decision had been made, Katie Tuma spent many hours preparing the text to be read by TEX, as well as incorporating our numerous editorial changes. Katie's amazing accuracy and willingness to work at odd hours for long periods of time has earned our deepest appreciation. Camille Marder helped us decipher how to typeset tables using TEX, and Clare Tuma helped put the references in a format that TEX could read. At a still later stage we decided to produce most of the figures for the book using the interactive plotting program developed by Ivor Durham of Carnegie-Mellon University. We are extremely grateful to Ivor not only for adapting his

Acknowledgments

program to meet our precise requirements but also for making these changes quickly over a holiday weekend. Finally, George Tuma proofread the penultimate version of the manuscript when our energies had vanished.

Many people helped us by commenting on drafts of one or more chapters: Glenn Carroll, James Coleman, François Nielsen, Susan Olzak, David Rogosa, Rachel Rosenfeld, Ann Swidler, Barbara Warsavage, and Anatoli Yashin. Burton Singer read a complete early draft and helped us reorganize the book in many ways. Lawrence Wu read a complete later draft, identified a number of inconsistencies and errors, and suggested many improvements that we found particularly useful.

We also owe a great debt to our colleagues in the Stanford sociology department. They have set an extremely high standard of sociological scholarship and have provided superb collegial support.

We received financial support from several sources. These include grants from the National Science Foundation (SOC–78–12315 to Hannan, Freeman, and Tuma; SOC–81–09381 to Hannan and Freeman; ISI–82–18013 to Freeman and Hannan; and SOC–80–23542 to Tuma) and the National Institute of Education (NIE–G–76–0082 to Hannan and Tuma). In the early stages of writing, Hannan was a fellow at the Center for Advanced Study in the Behavioral Sciences and was supported by National Science Foundation grant (BNS–76–22943). In the late stages of our work, both Tuma and Hannan spent time as visiting research scientists at the International Institute for Applied Systems Analysis in Laxenburg, Austria. As we mentioned earlier, some of the work reported in this book was developed in the course of analysis of data from SIME/DIME. We would like to acknowledge the research support to SIME/DIME provided by the United States Department of Health and Human Services and the supportive research atmosphere of the Center for the Study of Welfare Policy at SRI International under the direction of Robert Spiegelman. Finally, the Dean of Humanities and Sciences and the Dean of Graduate Studies at Stanford University generously supplemented our computer funds whenever outside funds ran short.

We would also like to express our appreciation for permission to reproduce and adapt portions of our previously published papers. An earlier version of Chapter 2 appeared in the *Annual Review of*

Sociology, Volume 5 (Hannan and Tuma, 1980). We drew heavily on Tuma's (1982) chapter in *Sociological Methodology 1982* in preparing Chapters 3 and 8, on Tuma and Hannan's (1978) chapter in *Sociological Methodology 1979* in preparing Chapter 5, and on Tuma's (1980a) chapter in *Sociological Methodology 1980* in preparing Chapter 9. Section 9.2 summarizes work first reported in Tuma, Hannan, and Groeneveld (1980). Section 6.2 summarizes results in the volume by Groeneveld, Hannan, and Tuma (1983). Section 7.4.2 gives a condensed version of work reported by Freeman, Carroll, and Hannan in the *American Sociological Review* (1983). Section 10.1 reports findings from a paper in the *Journal of Human Resources* by Robins, Tuma, and Yaeger (1980). Sections 10.2 and 10.5 are adaptations from a paper in the *American Journal of Sociology* (1979) by Tuma, Hannan, and Groeneveld. Section 10.4 is based on a paper in the *American Sociological Review* (1981) by Hannan and Carroll. Section 13.6 draws on the chapter by Hannan and Young (1977) in *Sociological Methodology 1977* and a paper by Tuma and Young (1976). Glenn Carroll has given us permission to reproduce two tables from his unpublished (1979) paper in Section 14.5.

Part I

Introduction

1

Why Dynamic Analysis?

Sociological theories have become increasingly concerned with social change, and temporal data are becoming widely available. Yet empirical social research still addresses primarily questions about static relationships (associations among phenomena at a single time point) and focuses mainly on cross-sectional analysis. Even when time-series or panel data are analyzed, their temporal structure is often ignored—the data are treated as though they are cross-sections with some additional methodological complications involving autocorrelations. That is, the focus is on change from one equilibrium level to another, as measured, for example, by levels of variables at successive waves of a panel.

The current distribution of effort in sociology might suggest that there is no pressing need for methods for studying change. But current practice is a poor indicator of need. The paucity of dynamic analysis may reflect a lack of information about how to study change empirically as much as a lack of interest in change.

In subsequent chapters we consider models and methods for analyzing the actual time paths of change in attributes of individuals and social systems. These models and methods are useful for answering questions about the detailed structure of social change processes. Since the most convincing evidence of the value of dynamics analysis comes from research practice, subsequent chapters discuss applications in which the use of dynamic models and methods seems to have enhanced our capacity to formulate and test sociological arguments.

These applications illustrate both how to think about the study of social dynamics and how to do it.

Even though many sociologists are already convinced of the need to study social change processes, there is by no means a consensus. And those who do perceive this need do not always agree on the reasons. Because of these disagreements, this chapter discusses the value of dynamic models and methods in general terms. Naturally we hope that those who currently do not see the value in dynamic analysis will come to appreciate it. But we also hope that those who already appreciate it will acquire an expanded understanding of its value.

Since models and methods are selected partly because they mesh with theoretical concerns, we find it useful to distinguish between theories dealing with static relationships and those dealing with social change. The former attempt to describe and explain why various attributes of social actors or social systems are associated in particular ways at some moment. The latter try to describe and explain how an individual or social system changes over time.

It seems clear that explanations of social change are studied best by dynamic analysis. Section 1.1 reviews some of the theoretical emphases in sociology that seem to mandate dynamic analysis wherever possible. At first glance dynamic analysis may seem irrelevant to those interested in explaining static relationships. In Section 1.2 we challenge this view. Having stated as forcefully as we can in Sections 1.1 and 1.2 why dynamic analysis is valuable, in Section 1.3 we try to counter common objections to dynamic analysis when its intrinsic value is not disputed.

1.1 Dynamic Analysis for Studying Change

Although realism of description is one element controlling choice of models and methods, their fit to larger theoretical objectives is another. It is not surprising that the corpus of modern quantitative methodology in sociology is static—it was developed in a period in which static images of social structure dominated American sociology. However, theoretical currents have shifted toward a greater concern with processes of change. The standard static methods are ill equipped to address questions about the time-paths of change. Thus one reason for pursuing the study of dynamic models and methods is to adapt research practices to important theoretical concerns of the discipline.

The classical sociological theorists struck a reasonable balance between problems of order and problems of change. Because these theorists wrote at a time when industrial capitalism was transforming western Europe, not surprisingly they devoted considerable attention to the forces that created industrial capitalism, to those that shaped its institutional forms (state bureaucracy, factory enterprise, and so forth), and to the effects of rapid social change on individuals. Although their attitudes toward the changes accompanying industrialization varied, most of the classic theorists placed problems of social change at center stage.

Subsequent sociological theorists, especially in the United States, tended to emphasize order and to deemphasize change. The stress on problems of order was so complete during the heyday of functionalist theory that "social change" became identified as a substantive subfield on a par with institutionally defined subfields such as political sociology, sociology of the family, and sociology of religion. That is, change was not a major focus; instead it was one possible outcome to be explained within the context of an overarching theory based on the notion of an equilibrium.

The dominance of structural–functional theory broke down during the late 1960s. Since then new theoretical perspectives have multiplied. Some new theoretical directions retain a strong emphasis on equilibrium; others emphasize disequilibrium and change.

One important development exemplifying the former is the effort to apply the framework of neoclassical price theory to a broad range of social behavior. Initial steps in this direction were made by sociologists; two important examples are Emerson's (1962) and Blau's (1964) theories of power and social exchange. Subsequent developments have seen economists applying neoclassical price theory to traditional sociological subjects, such as marriage and family life (Becker, 1981). In fact, during the 1970s convergences between sociology and microeconomics began to occur—compare the role of schooling in the status attainment model developed by Blau and Duncan (1965) and refined by Duncan, Featherman, and Duncan (1972) with Becker's (1975) theory of human capital, or Hannan, Tuma, and Groeneveld's (1978) model of marital dissolution with Becker's (1981) theory.

At first glance the development of a sociological perspective built on a synthesis of sociology and microeconomics would seem to keep the equilibrium assumption at the core of sociological theory. Within the social sciences, the faith in equilibrium analysis has been nowhere stronger than in microeconomics. The assumption that markets function efficiently, so that social systems are almost always in equilibrium, has often directed attention away from a serious interest in processes of change in the social system. Nevertheless, the interest of many sociologists and some radical economists in multiple labor markets acts as a force against this. Moreover, whatever the view of system-level change, the long-standing interest of sociologists in social mobility clearly fosters concern with change processes on the individual level. And microeconomists working within the neoclassical framework (e.g., see Ghez and Becker, 1975; Heckman and Willis, 1976; MaCurdy, 1981) have done some sophisticated research on life-cycle patterns of individual behavior.

The recent interest in the life course of individuals in general and in their careers in particular also gives hope that an infusion of microeconomic theory into the study of individual behaviors is unlikely to stress static analysis. The notion of a life course or a career suggests a focus on the dependencies among the successive states occupied by an individual. For example, an employment career is more than a list of the jobs held by an individual. It consists of the sequence and timing of the various jobs and their association with other events, such as changes in marital status and geographical residence. Thus studies of careers (or the life course) focus on the contingencies that pertain to the possible transitions in a career line. For example, sociologists and economists have begun to explore how characteristics of early employment and unemployment affect future employment (Corcoran, 1979; Panel on Youth, 1973; Spilerman, 1977). Others have investigated how changes in husbands' and wives' labor force behavior unfold over time (Tuma, Robins, and Smith-Donals, 1980). Although the rapidly proliferating research on the life course and individual careers has a variety of substantive foci, it reveals a common interest in studying individual histories.

Many contemporary sociological theories emphasizing change are not based on an equilibrium perspective at all. American sociologists' renewed attention to Marx in the late 1960s has been a major force promoting the development of theories that stress change and

⟨1⟩ **Dynamic Analysis for Studying Static Relationships**   7

its historical context. Although most Marxist and neo-Marxist sociologists are hostile to positivist research and prefer a case-oriented historical approach, standard quantitative methods have been used to address some of the issues prominent in this theoretical tradition (for some examples, see Meyer and Hannan, 1979). Some of this research is static; it concerns the *absence* of much change in capitalist social structures to date. But some emphasizes processes of societal change; for example, see Paige (1975).

    Theoretical developments on social movements have also begun to emphasize dynamics. Tilly (1978) and Skocpol (1979) have been especially prominent in redirecting attention to the organizational bases of collective protest and revolution. Rejecting the assumption that collective violence occurs when social structures are falling apart, both argue that local social organization is crucial in understanding these manifestations of social unrest. Collective violence is not an aberration but a natural by-product of social organization whose forms change as the distribution of power changes. Forces that challenge and perhaps overturn the existing order can arise even when a system is apparently stable. Such shifts place theoretical emphasis squarely on dynamics. For example, a key theoretical problem is understanding how changes in the strength of contending groups, the repressive power of a state, and the nature of the relations of a state to its neighbors affect collective violence and social revolution. Understanding the timing of collective protest and its changing forms requires dynamic analysis.

    The theoretical trends sketched above, along with many others concerned with change, are fairly recent. Moreover, interest in explaining how and why social actors and social systems change over time seems to be gaining momentum. What some view as disarray in contemporary sociology may partly reflect the pluralism and struggle involved in moving from questions and arguments about static relationships to the interrelated forces for change. If movement continues in this direction, as we think it will, the need for dynamic models and methods will grow.

1.2   Dynamic Analysis for Studying Static Relationships

    As we mentioned at the outset, sociologists who wish to explain static relationships—associations among properties of social actors or social system at a point in time—may believe that they can safely forego the effort of learning and applying dynamic models and methods. In this section we argue that this belief is erroneous for two main reasons.

First, explanations of static relationships almost always assume that these relationships are unchanging, but this assumption is usually implausible, as we argue below. In such situations, static analysis can be misleading. Since dynamic models have implications for relationships at a point in time, dynamic analysis is of great value to those who wish to explain static relationships but suspect that these are not in equilibrium during the period for which data are collected.

Second, dynamic analysis has several methodological advantages over cross-sectional analysis that mean this powerful analytic tool has value for studying static relationships, even if a steady state does exist. The remainder of this section is organized around a discussion of these two themes.

1.2.1 How Often Does an Equilibrium Occur?

Two types of situations must be considered. In one, the phenomena to be explained does not appear to have a nontrivial stable equilibrium, and change is continual.[1] In the other, a stable equilibrium may exist, but the fraction of time spent near it is small. Generalizing about relationships at some moment on the basis of cross-sectional analysis is apt to be very misleading in either case.

Case 1: **Continual Change.** As an example of the former, consider the relationship among various attributes of individuals—their family background, schooling, income, marital status, health, happiness, and so forth. Both socially and physiologically, the human individual is continually changing—first growing rapidly and expanding its many capacities and and activities; then declining rather gradually until death. Norms usually specify how the social lives of individuals should change over the life course. Anthropologists (e.g., Foner and Kertzer, 1978) report that age-related rites of passage occur in almost every society they have studied. In modern industrial societies individuals move from the parental home to school to employment to retirement to death in a well known fashion, despite

---

[1] By nontrivial we mean an equilibrium that is scientifically interesting. For example, death of a person or extinction of a species are stable but trivial equilibria.

⟨1⟩ **Dynamic Analysis for Studying Static Relationships**

deviations from the normative order (Hogan, 1978, 1980; Winsborough, 1978). That change is an enduring and important feature in studying characteristics of individuals is demonstrated by the almost universal finding of age as an important explanatory variable, no matter what personal characteristic or behavior is considered.

Change seems to be the rule rather than the exception for other kinds of phenomena studied by sociologists. Most businesses are organized around efforts to increase sales and profits, which indirectly lead to an expanded work force in most instances. Many churches try to win converts as well as socialize children of adult members. Cities (at least in the United States) not only actively promote growth in population size and territory but typically regard stability as a sign of incipient decay (another form of change); see Molotch (1976). Historically many states have also tried to expand in population size and territory. Modern states typically seek to increase literacy, educational levels, health, and overall economic development (Meyer, 1980). Indeed, many social organizations of all types seem organized around a program of growth and expansion, not stability. Naturally such a program is not always successful, but with such manifest goals it is advisable to be cautious about assuming that an equilibrium currently exists.

Case 2: **Stability May Exist.** Persistence over time does seem prevalent in some realms of social life, suggesting that a steady state is possible. For example, the culture of primitive societies is widely regarded as being intrinsically conservative, that is, designed to reproduce itself and to resist innovation. (But at least some aspects of the culture of modern societies seem far from stable.) The power and class structures of societies often seem to change relatively slowly, and it is tempting to interpret persistence as a steady state. (However, Marx's forecast of cataclysmic change for the class structure under capitalism and Pareto's notion of cyclical shifts in the composition of elites alert us to be watchful for change in these social institutions.)

In areas in which we observe considerable persistence over time, the key methodological question is, What fraction of time are the phenomena being studied very near an equilibrium? If the fraction is close to unity, then dynamic analysis is not essential. But if the fraction is small, the choice between static and dynamic analysis matters a great deal. Even sociologists who wish to address static arguments are well advised to conduct dynamic studies and infer static relationships from them.

A system is unlikely to spend much time near an equilibrium when it confronts a volatile environment and adapts slowly to changed circumstances. Above we mentioned several aspects of the modern world that seem organized to promote change and which indeed seem to be changing rapidly. During this century the world's population has grown enormously; the speed of communication and transportation has increased substantially; and boundaries among societies that were formerly relatively isolated have been weakened. In short, not only has the pace of change quickened, but interdependencies have increased. As Simon (1978, p. 4) put it,

> When the system is complex and its environment is continually changing (i.e., in the conditions under which biological and social evolution actually take place), there is no assurance that the system's momentary position will lie anywhere near a point of equilibrium, whether local or global.

By itself the observation that social phenomena change continually does not vitiate static analysis. If typical changes are either small or predictable, adaptations may occur rapidly and readily so that departures from equilibrium are brief. What matters is the *pattern* of change, especially the magnitude and regularity of change.

Large, irregular (and therefore unpredictable) changes are especially significant because an extended period of disequilibrium is likely to follow them, which limits sharply the value of static analysis. Consider, for example, the situation of positions at the bottom and top of organizational hierarchies. Those at the bottom are usually specialized to deal with small, repetitive, and predictable changes; in contrast, those at the top deal with less certain, larger, and less frequent changes (Barnard, 1938; March and Simon, 1958). Thus, static models might describe well the activities of clerical and industrial workers, but not the activities of chief executive officers and other top managers.

The speed of response of social actors and social systems also affects the value of steady-state analysis. If adjustments to changed circumstances are quick, even large disturbances may produce only short periods of disequilibrium. Although we know little

⟨1⟩ **Dynamic Analysis for Studying Static Relationships**   11

about speeds of adjustment, existing theory does give some clues about the forces that constrain responsiveness. Two broad classes of intertial forces are factors that reflect *costs* of change and those that reflect *institutional mechanisms*.

Economic theorists stress the former. One common argument is that the uncertainty associated with the potential gains from radical change seldom offset the fairly certain costs of change in terms of additional resources consumed and time spent searching for an optimum.

Sociologists tend to emphasize institutional constraints—tacit assumptions about goals, rights, and rules of action. A social structure is highly institutionalized when its its members take rules as given in formulating and and making choices. Because institutionalization reduces greatly the costs of surveillance, coordination, and control of action, it can increase the efficiency of collective action. But it is a two-edged sword. When a structure is well suited to prevailing conditions, institutionalization promotes efficiency in collective activities. If conditions change, however, institutionalized structures can serve as a powerful brake on attempts at changing rules and patterns of action.

In sum, inertial forces are commonplace. Sometimes the costs of change hinder change more than institutional constraints, and at other times the opposite is true. In either case the speed of response to alterations in the social and physical environment are often slow. Consequently, it seems reasonable to think that many phenomena possessing an equilibrium are not observed near it. Then dynamic analysis is called for.

1.2.2 The Value of Dynamic Analysis in a Steady State

Although we have stressed the comparative rarity of the existence of a steady state for most phenomena studied by sociologists, surely some phenomena not only have a steady state but also are observed near it. Static and dynamic analyses are likely to agree about broad patterns in such cases, even if they differ in detail. Hence it may seem that investigators studying static relationships in a steady state certainly can afford to ignore dynamic models and methods in their empirical investigations. In this section we mention some advantages of dynamic analysis over cross-sectional analysis that apply to this situation. Of course, these apply as well to studies of change and to studies of static relationships out of equilibrium, but we have already indicated even stronger reasons for dynamic analysis in such situations.

The first advantage of temporal analysis is that it is the only way to tell whether a steady state currently exists. There may be sound arguments why some phenomenon *should be* in equilibrium, but only an analysis of temporal data can demonstrate that there actually *is* stability over time. Moreover, dynamic analysis can be used to tell whether a steady state is possible, as we discuss in Chapters 11 and 14, and how rapidly a feasible steady state will be reached, as we illustrate in Chapter 10.

A second advantage is that dynamic analysis, despite its apparent complexity, can actually simplify the study of complicated problems. In at least one crucial respect the study of change is *simpler* than the study of relationships at a point in time. In cross-sectional data everything often seems to depend on everything else. The apparent density and complexity of webs of causal relations pose a formidable obstacle to modeling and analysis. Nonexperimental research methods are sorely taxed in such situations. Analysis of systems of simultaneous structural equations, which provide one way to represent such relationships, involves difficult statistical and methodological challenges. Dynamic models and methods are no more complex in most instances, and often they are simpler.

In Chapter 11 we illustrate this advantage in an application dealing with organizational demography. Much research has addressed the relationship of organizational size to the size of the administrative staff from a static perspective (see Scott, 1975). At a given time point it is difficult to distinguish effects of several fundamental processes, in particular, the consequences of administrative rationality for allocations of staff from the results of the political processes by which occupational groups defend and extend their domains. In Chapter 11 we examine how the sizes of various personnel components are affected by each other and by exogenous changes separately in organizations experiencing growing and declining demand for their services. We find that the process of change in the administrative staff under declining demand differs from the process under growing demand in a way that agrees with a political theory of organizational demography. Far from complicating things, the shift from cross-sectional analysis to dynamic analysis simplifies

⟨1⟩ Dynamic Analysis for Studying Static Relationships 13

the task of evaluating evidence in this case. We believe that this simplification is not unusual.

A third advantage of dynamic analysis is that it is more informative than cross-sectional analysis. The example in Chapter 11 mentioned above demonstrates this point because it tells about the growth and decline of personnel components under different environmental conditions, as well as about relationships at a point in time. An empirical application presented in Chapter 10 also illustrates this advantage. Economic theory clearly predicts that the probability of family heads working at any moment is lower when a guaranteed annual income is available to families with low potential income. Both cross-sectional analyses and dynamic analyses reported in Chapter 10 support this prediction; however, the dynamic analysis provides much more information than the cross-sectional analysis. In particular, it reveals that a guaranteed annual income has rather small effects on the tendency of working family heads to leave their jobs, but that it greatly retards the tendency of nonworking family heads to find employment.

Fourth, dynamic analysis expands our ability to test arguments. Since every static model is a special case of at least one dynamic model, a dynamic model is more general. A more general model not only provides a fuller explanation of a phenomenon (and is therefore a more satisfying theory) but also increases our empirical leverage. That is, dynamic models have more abundant implications that allow them to be tested in multiple ways.

For example, it has been known for over 80 years that the Pareto distribution fits well the upper tail of several empirical distributions, including the distributions of family income and the size of firms. That is, a simple static model fits both empirical distributions, which are known to have changed fairly little over time and so can be regarded as close to a steady state. Simon (1955) proved that the Pareto distribution is the steady-state of a simple birth and death process in an open system (see Chapter 4). Many consider his reformulation of this problem to be a major advance because it shows how the Pareto distribution may arise. More pertinent to our present discussion, a birth and death process has a number of other properties that can be tested directly, which means increased avenues for evaluating this argument.

Moreover, because temporal data contain more information

than does a single cross-section, standard errors of coefficients of explanatory variables tend to be smaller in dynamic analyses than in the comparable cross-sectional analysis, as our empirical example in Chapter 10 illustrates. Finally, our ability to test arguments is also greater with dynamic analysis because one can correct for various confounding influences, such as unobserved heterogeneity. We develop this point further in Chapters 6 and 13.

Fifth, new research questions are more likely to arise out of dynamic analysis than out of cross-sectional analysis. This advantage largely follows from some of the other advantages mentioned above. For example, because dynamic analysis tell more about phenomena than does cross-sectional analysis, there are more relevant features of social life about which to ask questions.

1.3 Other Obstacles to Dynamic Analysis

If analysis of time-paths of change is so important for studying both change and static relationships, why is it so rare in empirical sociology? Several obstacles to dynamic analysis are often mentioned, even by those who value it in principle.

It is sometimes said that the major obstacle to dynamic analysis is the lack of appropriate data. Whereas static analysis can be conducted on data gathered at a single moment in time, dynamic analysis demands data on the same units over time. Cross-sectional data are much more common than temporal data for several reasons. First, it is expensive to follow people over time because they migrate, change jobs, lose interest in participating in the survey, and so forth. It is much cheaper to take a single snapshot or a series of snapshots on different samples (as in the National Opinion Research Center's "General Social Survey"). Second, the length of time needed to address some research questions is so long that stable data collection procedures cannot be maintained (because of the vagaries of research funds, shifts in an investigator's research interests, instability in measures,[2] and so forth).

Although we grant that temporal observation plans are often more expensive than a cross-sectional plan, we doubt that lack of

[2] Measures can be unstable even when the same instruments are used. For example, the same questions might continue to be asked in a survey but the meaning of the terms may change.

data explains the scarcity of dynamic analysis for two reasons. First, much sociological research now uses archival data that follow actors such as organizations or countries over time. Yet dynamic analysis is scarcely more common in these fields than elsewhere in sociology. Second, the availability of data reflects at least partly the interests of social scientists. Individual researchers collect and distribute data, and social scientists advise government agencies about what sorts of data should be collected. That relatively few temporal data sets have been available in the past may have been as much a consequence as a cause of the dominance of static analysis. As we indicate in the next chapter, temporal data are becoming widely available in many fields of sociology. While data availability may once have been a major constraint on the spread of dynamic models and methods, it appears to be so no longer.

A second obstacle to empirical dynamic analysis in the eyes of some people is its complexity. Many sociologists assume that dynamic analysis is much more complex than static analysis. We do not doubt that empirical analysis of social dynamics is subtle and at times difficult. The chapters that follow discuss a number of unsolved conceptual and methodological problems. Moreover, a serious application of the dynamic models and methods we propose will surely unveil additional complications.

This does not mean, however, that meaningful static analysis is simpler. We are certainly less familiar with the empirical study of change than with the study of static relationships. But we should not confuse unfamiliarity with difficulty. It is true that a mastery of dynamic models and methods is likely to involve some new mathematics for most sociologists; however, some aspects can be learned with only small extensions of the mathematical knowledge common among sociologists currently doing quantitative empirical research. Moreover, as in learning most things, mastery is acquired gradually. Even a long road can be traversed by many small steps. This book, we hope, will help to speed sociologists' journey towards this goal.

1.4 Conclusions

If empirical research is to clarify theoretical issues, research strategies must fit substantive problems. We have argued that contemporary sociological theory has begun to explore systematic sources of change. Sociologists increasingly study phenomena that are not in equilibrium, such as the life course of individuals, political attitudes, gender roles, class and ethnic conflict, mass political violence, evolution of organizational forms, and structural changes in national and world systems.

The static methods still dominant in sociological research are not well suited to the study of these phenomena and to the evaluation of modern and classical theories of them. As long as empirical sociological research relies solely on the familiar static methods, quantitative research will appear irrelevant to these concerns. However, by building dynamic models and estimating them with appropriate methods, we can bring quantitative methods to bear on a much broader range of problems and theories than in the past.

We also argue that dynamic analysis can be helpful in the study of static relationships—associations among attributes of social actors or social systems at a single time point. If one wishes to make generalizations about static relationships to time points other than those at which data are collected, static analysis must assume that the phenomena being explained are in equilibrium. Yet many phenomena of interest to sociologists do not seem to possess an equilibrium. Still others may have one but not spend much time near it. Dynamic analysis is clearly called for in these cases.

Dynamic analysis also has considerable value in studies of phenomena that *are* in equilibrium. It is the only way to tell whether or not an equilibrium currently exists. In addition, it is more informative, more powerful, more provocative, and sometimes even simpler than static analysis. Thus, whatever one wishes to explain, dynamic analysis can be beneficial.

Ample motivation for dynamic analysis exists; therefore the paucity of empirical studies of change in the sociological literature cannot be explained by its lack of worth. We think that the primary problem is methodological. The literature on methods for analyzing data on change over time is both fragmentary and disorganized, and it tends to emphasize potential pitfalls of temporal analysis (such as autocorrelation bias) rather than to emphasize its advantages. Clear guidelines concerning alternative designs, models, and estimators are lacking. This book is intended to help fill this void. Having discussed reasons for dynamic analysis, we now turn to the methodological issues that have impeded progress in studying change. We begin by surveying common approaches to the analysis of temporal data.

2

Varieties of Temporal Analysis: Overview and Critique

Although most sociological research in the 1960s and 1970s relied on cross-sectional analysis, the field has a long history of interest in temporal analysis. The traditional interest derives mainly from a concern that causal inferences cannot be made dependably from a cross-section because such data cannot show that one variable affects *change* in another. This concern has frequently been accompanied by exaggerated claims for the power of temporal analysis. The older literature abounds with assertions that temporal analysis is always superior to cross-sectional analysis. As we discuss at length in Chapter 13, analyses of cross-sections can give sounder results than temporal analyses when confounding influences vary more over time than over individuals. As a result of this knowledge, a much more tempered view of the methodological value of temporal analysis currently prevails in sociology.

As we noted in the previous chapter, current enthusiasm for temporal analysis stems more from substantive concerns than from methodological prejudice. Macrosociology has begun to focus on issues of structural change. Likewise, development and careers have loomed progressively larger in studies of individuals. Sociologists of many stripes have come to emphasize change, and whatever its other benefits, temporal analysis is indispensible for the study of change.

There are at least two largely separate literatures on temporal analysis, one dealing with qualitative outcomes (including both categorical and ordinal variables), the other with quantitative (i.e., cardinal or metric) outcomes. Developments in one area have diffused only slowly into the other. Progress on specifying the probabilistic mechanisms has been greater in the study of categorical outcomes; explicit stochastic models underlie many sociological studies of change in such variables. On the other hand, studies of change in quantitative variables evidence an ad hoc approach to underlying stochastic mechanisms but usually provide a much more systematic treatment of causal effects.

In this chapter we review major perspectives on the study of change in both qualitative and quantitative outcomes. We intend this review to be both a statement of the current state of the art of temporal analysis in sociology and an overview of the issues pursued in subsequent chapters. It provides the context for our general strategy—development of continuous-time models estimated from event-history data in the case of qualitative outcomes and from panel data in the case of quantitative outcomes.

2.1   Observation Plans

Traditionally sociological methodologists have stressed problems of estimation and testing rather than broader issues of research design. In particular, because of the overwhelming predominance of cross-sectional data there has been rather little concern with the opportunities and constraints provided by different observation plans, that is, the various schemes that can be used to collect systematic information pertinent to some phenomenon of interest. Of course, exceptions exist. The trade-offs of experimental and nonexperimental designs have been treated extensively, and there is a smaller but substantial literature dealing with problems of sampling design. Within the realm of temporal analysis, however, options provided by different observation plans seem less well understood. Consequently, we begin by reviewing major alternatives.

2.1.1   Qualitative Outcomes

Data on changes in qualitative variables typically come in one of four forms: panel, event-count, event-sequence, or event-history data. Sociologists have relied mainly on **panel** data, which record state occupancy of sample members at two or more points in time. Lazarsfeld, Berelson, and Gaudet's (1944) voting study is the prototype: individuals in a sample disclose their voting intentions in a sequence of surveys preceding an election. Panel surveys are often the only possible observation plan when studying changes in cognitive and affective states.

Panel data can also be gathered retrospectively when interest focuses on change in a qualitative variable whose timing may be recalled accurately. The classic example is data on social mobility gathered from information on a person's occupation currently and at some earlier time (first job, father's job on respondent's sixteenth birthday, and so forth). When recall is good, the accuracy of a retrospective panel compares favorably with that of a prospective panel, which records outcomes contemporaneously. But they differ greatly in one respect: the sampling plan. A prospective panel selects a sample or population and follows members forward in time; a retrospective panel selects a sample and works backward in time. As Duncan (1966) pointed out for analyses of mobility, a retrospective panel systematically misrepresents earlier populations because it does not include men from earlier generations who did not father sons or whose sons died or emigrated. Thus, it yields biased samples of earlier populations. One way around the problem, as Duncan noted, is to consider a father–son mobility table as a characterization of the status origins of sons. But the problem is not resolved if the *process* of change is the primary interest.

Event-count data contain more information than a panel: they record the number of different types of events in an interval. When an individual can be in only one of two states (e.g., married or not married), they give simply the number of times each state is left (e.g., the number of marriages and marital dissolutions) in a period. When there are several states (e.g., $1 \equiv$ not in the labor force, $2 \equiv$ unemployed, and $3 \equiv$ employed), event-count data may record the number of episodes (or spells) in each state for each individual. Still more usefully, they may give the number of transitions between pairs of states (e.g., changes from 1 to 2 may be distinguished from changes from 1 to 3). Event-count data are comparatively rare in sociology, except for counts of a single kind of event, for example, riots, lynchings, and hospitalizations. Methods developed specifically for analysis of event counts are still rarer (but see Hausman, Hall, and Griliches, in press), and our discussion below touches only briefly on methods for analyzing such data. Sociological methodology is ripe for a study of what can be learned about change processes from event-count data as compared either with panel data or with data from observation plans that supply even more information on temporal ordering.

Event-sequence data record the sequences of states occupied by each sample member. This observation plan can be viewed as an elaboration of the event-count plan. Suppose the possible states are 1, 2, and 3, as above. An individual's record might be (2, 1, 3, 2) for some period of time. Singer (1980) argued that event-sequence data provide the minimal necessary information for studying careers and showed that such data provide considerably more information than the more common panel. This type of observation plan is far from new in sociology (e.g., see Form and Miller, 1949), but interest in it has reawakened (e.g., see Spilerman, 1977; Hogan, 1978). We do not review literature on this observation plan in a separate section because it is customary to analyze event sequences using techniques for panel analysis; this approach assumes that the timing of events is irrelevant. Undoubtedly this assumption does not always hold in reality, but sociological methodologists have not yet considered the ramifications of such a violation of assumptions.

Event-history (or **sample path**) data provide the most complete information: they tell the timing of all moves in a sequence. Many laboratory studies of small group interaction provide event-history data. Due to the opportunity to observe a group continuously, experimenters may record the timing of transitions among structural types. In nonexperimental studies, event histories are necessarily retrospective. Nonetheless, they may differ markedly in the length of the recall period. The Coleman–Rossi life history study (Coleman et al., 1972) recorded dates of all job entries and exits in each respondent's career from the age of 14 years to the date of the interview. The Seattle and Denver Income Maintenance Experiments obtained such information as well. But in this study respondents needed to recall their event histories for only 4-month periods because they were interviewed three times a year over the study period.

Perhaps the best opportunity for collection of event-history data is in research using archival data. For example, Charles Tilly's (see references) pioneering study of trends in collective violence in small French political units used data containing the dates of all events of collective violence greater than some minimal scope. That Tilly typically aggregated over units (to the nation) and over time

⟨2⟩ Observation Plans

(to the year) in his analysis should not obscure the fact that the data consist of event histories for a population of small areal units. Numerous other studies of collective violence have used a similar observation plan.

The four observation plans described above are ordered in terms of the extent of detail on the process of change. Sociologists show a very strong preference for the simplest, the panel. In some situations a panel is the only feasible temporal observation plan. However, sociologists often forego opportunities to collect and use data on sequences and timing of events. We suspect that this tendency reflects uncertainty regarding the value of such information. Thus it is important to consider whether observation plans giving information on sequences and timing of events confer any important advantages.

If we are to make systematic comparisons among different observation plans, we must be clear about the *timing* of measurements in panel studies. Does the measurement interval reflect some fundamental periodicity in the process under study? If so, we cannot easily compare the various observation plans. If, however, the timing of measurements is largely arbitrary and events may occur at any time, the appropriate mathematical specification of the process generating the data is that of a **continuous-time, discrete-state stochastic process.** The continuous-time Markov process, introduced to sociologists by Coleman (1964a), provides an important baseline process of this type.

Observation plans differ in their ability to discriminate among classes of continuous-time stochastic models. The classic two-wave panel is very weak in terms of its ability to reject classes of models (Singer and Spilerman, 1976a). For example, one may test whether the data could have been generated by a time-stationary Markov process, but one cannot distinguish among many different classes of time-inhomogeneous processes. A third wave of observations permits a test of the Markov property, but it does not allow, for example, Markov and semi-Markov processes to be distinguished. Data on event-counts and event-sequences permit stronger inferences, and event-history data completely solve the so-called embedding problem (Singer, 1980; Tuma, Hannan, and Groeneveld, 1979). That is, information on the timing of events together with event-sequences makes it possible to test for very narrow classes of models. These analytic results tell a very important lesson in design: whenever possible one should collect data on both the sequences and the timing of changes. For this reason we concentrate on event-history analyses of changes in qualitative variables in this book.

2.1.2 Quantitative Outcomes

Some metric outcomes change more rapidly than they can ordinarily be measured, for example, size of large organizations and hours of work of individuals. Levels of other quantitative outcomes (e.g., prestige or wage rates associated with a job) change infrequently. For the latter, event-history data that record both the *dates* of jumps and the *sizes* of the jumps are appropriate. In mathematical terms, the underlying stochastic process is a jump process in which one set of parameters governs the length of time in a state and another set controls the average height of a jump. Both sets of parameters may be treated as functions of exogenous variables. Though this framework appears natural for much sociological research, we are not aware of any sociological applications. We discuss possible applications in Chapter 16.

When sociologists study changes in metric variables, they typically make measurements intermittently. This is the only feasible observation plan for rapidly changing outcomes. It is customary to distinguish three such observation plans. **Panel** data refer to a collection of a short time series (as few as two time points) on many individuals. Such data have been used widely: in the study of individual social psychology (e.g., Kohn and Schooler, 1978), status attainment (Kelley, 1973), organizational structure and demography (Meyer, 1975), and change in national social structure (Meyer and Hannan, 1979). **Time-series** data record the level of the outcome at many dates for one member of a population. Such data have been collected and analyzed largely in macrosociological research. Examples include studies of levels of collective violence (Snyder and Tilly, 1972), changes in voting patterns (Doreian and Hummon, 1976), crime rates (Land and Felson, 1976; Cohen and Land, 1979; Berk et al., 1981; and Nelson, 1981), and studies of variations over time in labor organization and activity (Shorter and Tilly, 1970). **Multiple time-series** data refer to data collected on a small number of individuals at many dates. Multiple time-series and panel data differ primarily in the relative amount of temporal variation versus intraunit variation, which affects the kinds of questions that can be addressed effectively with one rather than the other. Since the difference between the two observation plans is a matter of the extent of various kinds of information rather than a qualitative difference, we give little attention to multiple times series data, which are less common than panel data in sociological research. Although sociologists have begun to contrast time series for different systems [e.g., Tilly, Tilly and Tilly's (1975) comparisons of rates of violent protest in France, Germany and Italy for 1830–1930], they have not yet fully exploited multiple time-series data.

The sociological literature contains little guidance on the relative merits of time-series and panel analyses. If one includes all relevant causal variables and specifies the model properly, replications over time are, in principle, just as useful as replication over individuals. In practice, the choice between the two hinges on judgments about confounding factors. If the confounding factors vary more over time than among members of a population at a point in time (e.g., prices in world markets), panel analysis has the edge. If the confounding factors vary across members of a population more than over time (e.g., national culture), time-series analysis is preferable. We discuss this issue further in Chapter 13.

To this point we have focused on the broadest implications of different observation plans. We turn now to consideration of the details of various strategies, discussing strengths and weaknesses of alternative approaches to modeling.

2.2 Panel Analysis of Qualitative Outcomes

Lazarsfeld (1940, 1948) appears to have been the first sociologist to propose panel analysis of qualitative variables. He noted that data studied by social scientists often pertain to an association between two variables, X and Y. Analysts sometimes want to know whether X induces change in Y, or Y induces change in X. Observations on X and Y at a single point in time cannot tell this. Lazarsfeld suggested measuring X and Y at two times, t_1 and t_2. If X and Y are dichotomous, then there are four possible response patterns at each time, for example, $(0,0)$, $(0,1)$, $(1,0)$, and $(1,1)$. Arraying responses at time t_1 by those at time t_2 gives the famous 16-fold table. How should one analyze such a table (or one like it but with more waves, more variables, or more possible responses for each variable) to determine the extent to which change in one variable affects another?

Sociologists have used several approaches. One treats panel data on J qualitative variables at N points in time as a problem in analyzing a contingency table with JN variables. Another applies ordinary linear regression analysis, treating a change between successive waves as a dichotomous dependent variable. Both of these strategies implicitly assume that changes occur at discrete points in time or that the timing of changes is irrelevant to answering questions concerning the determinants of change. Another strategy assumes that changes can occur continuously in time, even though data happen to be recorded at discrete times.

2.2.1 The Contingency-Table Strategy

A revived interest in contingency-table analysis began in the early 1970s. Various authors, especially Goodman (1972a,b, 1973) and Bishop, Fienberg, and Holland (1975), have developed a set of powerful methods for estimating and testing log-linear models of the entries in a contingency table. These models can be used for any number of discrete variables and any number of categories per variable. We do not attempt to summarize the main features of these models because by now they are well known to sociologists.

These techniques can be viewed as natural extensions of Lazarsfeld's earlier work on panel analysis of qualitative outcomes. Goodman (1973) discussed and illustrated application of these models and methods to analysis of panel data. A variety of other sociological applications to panel data have followed. Papers by Hauser et al. (1975) and Rosenfeld (1978) on occupational mobility contain especially clear statements of the model and good illustrations of how to interpret results based on it.

The advantages of log-linear analysis of contingency tables are the wide range of substantively interesting questions for which it provides an answer and the comparative ease with which it can be used. One disadvantage is that all variables included in the analysis must be discrete. An added disadvantage, partly arising from the total reliance on polytomous variables, is the practical problem of finding a sufficiently large sample to fill all cells of the contingency table. This is especially troublesome when a large number of variables must be considered. Another possible disadvantage concerns the value of these methods in situations in which the outcomes being studied can change *continuously* in time, as discussed in more detail below.

2.2.2 The Regression Strategy

The regression strategy treats a change between two waves as a dichotomous (0–1) dependent variable in a regression on a set of independent variables. Sociologists usually assume the regression is linear in the independent variables, but nonlinear approaches (see below) are often used in other fields.

Spilerman (1972a) suggested this strategy as a way to incorporate independent variables into a Markov model. Duncan and Perrucci (1976) took this approach in studying whether or not couples migrated between two waves of a panel. Bumpass and Sweet (1972) used this method to investigate effects of causal variables on marital dissolution.

This strategy has several advantages and at least as many (if not more) disadvantages. Its main advantages are ease of application and comparatively low cost. In addition, unlike the log-linear models discussed under the contingency-table strategy, a regression approach allows both quantitative and qualitative independent variables to be included in the analysis. Consequently, the "empty-cell" problem mentioned under the contingency-table strategy is not likely to occur unless a great many interaction terms are included.

Some of the disadvantages of this strategy result from assuming that a dichotomous dependent variable is linear in the independent variables. These disadvantages include heteroscedasticity of disturbances, inefficiency of ordinary least-squares estimators, and the possibility that predicted probabilities of a change lie outside the (0–1) range (Goldberger, 1964). These deficiencies of the linear model can be overcome by estimating one of several nonlinear regression models, for example, a multivariate probit or logit model, or by use of the generalized least-squares estimation for the linear probability model, as proposed by Grizzle, Starmer, and Koch (1969).

A potentially more disturbing disadvantage of the regression approach—one shared by the contingency-table approach—arises because the timing of changes is ignored. Both approaches implicitly assume that the timing of changes is irrelevant to identification of the true underlying structure generating change. Timing is, indeed, irrelevant if changes can only occur at the times of the waves of the panel. This can happen when changes occur at discrete intervals known by the investigator, and data are collected at this interval. But usually it is false, either because the lag is unknown or because changes can occur continuously in time.

Little is known about the consequences of applying either regression or contingency-table strategies to panel analysis when the assumption mentioned above is false. Tuma (1973) noted that effects of independent variables vary both in magnitude and in statistical significance as the length of the time period varied in linear-regression analysis of job changes. Singer and Spilerman (1976a,b) discussed a more fundamental problem. As we discuss below, identification of structural parameters in continuous-time models of change in qualitative outcomes is problematic with panel data. Moreover, these problems cannot be evaded by treating the underlying processes as occurring at discrete intervals. These disturbing conclusions give added force to suggestions that investigators collect information about change in the qualitative outcome being studied that is as detailed as is feasible. Recognition of these problems has also promoted a renewed interest in panel analysis of qualitative outcomes using a strategy based on continuous-time models; for example, see Cohen and Singer (1979) and Singer and Cohen (1980).

2.2.3 Continuous-Time Strategies

Coleman (1964a) is the first sociologist to have argued persuasively for basing panel analysis of qualitative outcomes on the assumption of an underlying stochastic process in which changes may occur *continuously* in time. His elaborations of this strategy are often based on the discrete-state, continuous-time Markov model mentioned above. The simple Markov model rarely fits data well, but various improvements have been proposed to remedy this. Coleman (1964a,b, 1981) contributed many ideas for doing this, and his suggestions are often quite mathematically sophisticated. However, his empirical applications usually involve comparatively simple situations, for example, two waves of observations on two endogenous dichotomous variables or on one dichotomous dependent variable and one dichotomous exogenous variable. Even models describing these rather simple interrelationships give estimation equations that are not trivial to implement. Other sociologists (e.g., Mayer, 1972) have also constructed continuous-time stochastic models that are more realistic than the simple Markov model, but they have not been able to develop satisfactory methods of estimating parameters from panel data.

Singer and his collaborators (Singer and Spilerman, 1974, 1976a,b; Cohen and Singer, 1979; Singer and Cohen, 1980a,b; Singer, 1981) have begun to clarify what can be learned from panel data when the outcome of interest is generated by a continuous-time stochastic process. These authors have emphasized the development of tests for choosing among broad classes of models (compare the second strategy discussed under event-history analysis). Among their findings are the following.

First, observations on the proportion of transitions among states of the qualitative outcome being studied, which gives an estimate of the matrix of transition probabilities, cannot always be embedded in (described by) a (simple) Markov process. Moreover, sampling error can sometimes cause panel data to be unembeddable, even though they are actually generated by a Markov process. Second, even if the data are embeddable in a Markov process, there may not be a unique set of parameters that could have generated the data. Singer and Spilerman (1976a) detailed a procedure for finding an exhaustive set of possibilities, but sometimes the final choice must be made on substantive grounds. Third, small changes in an observed matrix of transition probabilities (which can occur because of sampling variability) can lead to a quite different set of possible processes. These problems can be reduced through appropriate design of the observation plan, for example, by spacing waves of a panel irregularly and by shortening the interval between waves. In short, the more closely panel data resemble event-history data, the fewer the problems in analysis.

Despite this research, it is still the case that panel analysis of qualitative outcomes is a methodological mine field—if changes can occur continuously in time. While mathematical and statistical invention may clarify what can be learned from panel analysis, all questions that sociologists like to ask cannot be answered by analyzing panel data. For these reasons, we do not pursue the panel strategy for qualitative outcomes in this book. We focus instead on event-history analysis, which avoids most of these problems but, surprisingly, has received much less attention.

2.3 Event-History Analysis

2.3.1 Strategies

Three main strategies for analyzing event-history data have been used and/or discussed in sociological research. The first—by far the most common—neglects some information in event histories and analyzes the data as if some other observation plan had been used. Palmer's (1954) *Labor Mobility in Six Cities* provides a good illustration of the many outcomes that can be obtained from event histories. The data consist of work histories for the years 1940–1950 for roughly 13,000 people. Some of Palmer's findings could have been collected by a series of cross-sections (e.g., the distribution of employment status for a series of years) or by a panel (e.g., occupational status in 1950 by status in 1940). She also reported event counts (e.g., number of jobs held) in different periods. Although the range of outcomes reported is impressive, her analysis does not make clear what (if anything) was gained by collecting event histories that could not have been learned from another observation plan.

More recent analyses of event-history data have also tended to ignore much of the information contained in these data. They rely on a smaller range of outcomes than Palmer did, but control for a larger number of variables, primarily through multivariate techniques. Ordinarily information on the dates of events is used only to compute counts of events in some period. Then these counts are analyzed as a metric variable measured either at one "time" (i.e., in one period) or at a series of "times." In short, event-history data are treated as event counts.

For example, Inverarity (1976) obtained the total number of lynchings in a period from newspaper reports on the dates of lynchings. Then he estimated a multiple-indicator, multiple-cause model of this variable using a procedure developed by Jöreskog (1970). The analysis is indistinguishable from that usually performed on cross-sectional data. Similarly, Snyder and Tilly (1972) computed the count of annual collective disturbances in France from archival information on dates of violent outbreaks. Unlike Inverarity, they then used time-series analysis to investigate the relation of these counts to other time-varying characteristics of France.

The second and third strategies use the information in event histories on the timing and sequence of events, as well as information on the number of events. These strategies resemble one another in assuming that a stochastic process generates events and that events may occur continuously in time. The two strategies differ in their additional assumptions and in the questions they ask of the data.

The second strategy takes an exploratory approach to data. It avoids making any additional assumptions about the process. This strategy has two forms.

One form asks what classes of stochastic processes could have generated the data and what classes are unlikely to have generated them. The goal is to reject types of models, that is, to narrow the class of possible models rather than to accept any particular model. For example, after appropriate analysis, one might conclude that the data are inconsistent with a time-homogeneous Markov process. However, it still may be impossible to pin down the class of model that did generate the data. Singer (1980, 1981), Singer and Spilerman (1976b), and Singer and Cohen (1980) provided preliminary ideas on this strategy. Because methods for implementing this strategy are still in an early state, we do not attempt to review these techniques further in this book.

The second form of the exploratory strategy is concerned less with identifying the class of model generating the data than with detecting whether certain characteristics of population members or certain features of the environment affect the change process. One may want to ask whether the same process holds for two (or more) subgroups, for example, a treatment group and a control group in an experiment, or organizations with different structures of authority. But one may be willing to make only minimal assumptions about the nature of the change process. Or one might want to test whether the data are consistent with a process in which the probability of an event per unit of time *increases* with the length of time since the last event (where an event could be, e.g., a job change). But one may not wish to make any particular assumptions about the mathematical form of this increase. We describe some ways of implementing this strategy in Chapter 3.

The third strategy is a model-testing approach. It assumes some simple stochastic process, estimates its parameters, and then tests whether some of the model's implications fit the data. More complex models are introduced either to test an argument or to improve fit. This strategy resembles the one that most sociologists use in analyzing cross-sectional data. It mainly differs from conventional model-testing approaches in the kinds of models that are assumed. We emphasize this strategy in this book because it is consistent with our goal of developing theories of change and of making full use of the information in the available data.

A comparatively simple stochastic model often assumed to describe change in qualitative outcomes is a first-order, discrete-state, continuous-time Markov process, which includes the familiar Poisson model for the number of events in a period and the general birth-and-death model as special cases. A simple Markov model (i.e., one that assumes transition rates are constant across time and over members of a population) has been applied to a wide variety of phenomena: labor mobility (e.g., Blumen, Kogan, and McCarthy, 1955), changes in attitudes (e.g., Coleman, 1964a), outbreaks of collective violence (e.g., Spilerman, 1970), and changes in friendship networks (e.g., Sørensen and Hallinan, 1977). We discuss this and other useful models of change in qualitative variables in Chapter 4.

2.3.2 Extensions

Unfortunately, the simple Markov model rarely fits sociological data well. This lack of fit has motivated various revisions and extensions of the model. It is convenient to distinguish among three types: (1) those assuming the population studied is heterogeneous, (2) those postulating time-dependence in the process, and (3) those focusing on reconceptualizing the process being studied in terms of "latent states."

1. Population heterogeneity. Population heterogeneity has been introduced in two main ways. One approach assumes that the fundamental parameters of the Markov process—the instantaneous rates of change from one state to another—depend on *observable* variables in some specified way. Coleman (1964a) proposed an extension in which rates of change are linear functions of exogenous variables, and Tuma (1973, 1976) estimated such a model. The assumption that transition rates are linear in observables can lead to a mathematically impossible situation— namely, that transition rates are negative. It seems to be both mathematically and empirically more satisfactory to assume that transition rates are log-linear functions of exogenous variables. This approach was also suggested by Coleman (1973), and it has been applied to a variety of problems, as we discuss in Chapters 6 and 10. An extended example of this strategy appears in Section 6.1.

A second approach assumes that the fundamental parameters of the Markov model have some postulated probability distribution with unknown parameters. For example, in their study of industrial mobility, Blumen, Kogan, and McCarthy (1955) postulated that there are two kinds of people, movers and stayers. In effect, they assumed a Bernoulli distribution on the parameters of the Markov process: a fraction p of the population move according to a Markov model, and the rest $(1-p)$ do not move at all. Spilerman (1972b) and Singer and Spilerman (1974) assumed that the rate of leaving a state has a gamma probability distribution but that the conditional probability of each move is the same for everyone in the population. This way of introducing heterogeneity into Markov models has a major disadvantage. It does not permit the investigator to make inferences about the *determinants* of changes in qualitative outcomes. We consider this approach in more detail in Section 6.2.

2. Time Dependence. According to the social process being studied, authors have suggested that parameters of the Markov model depend on age (e.g., Mayer, 1972), duration in a state (e.g., McGinnis, 1968; Tuma, 1976), experience (e.g., Sørensen, 1975; Flinn and Heckman, 1982), and/or experimental time (e.g., Tuma, Hannan, and Groeneveld, 1979). Both fully and partially parametric strategies [especially Cox's (1972) partial likelihood estimator] have been used to deal with time dependence, though the latter is rare. To the best of our knowledge, only DiPrete (1981), Hannan and Carroll (1981), and Coleman (1981) have yet reported use of the partially parametric strategy in sociological research. Menken et al. (1981) used it in a demographic analysis of divorce rates, and Trussell and Hammerslough (1983) used it in studying mortality rates. Use of Cox's partial-likelihood approach also plays a central role in Coleman's (1981) extension of his earlier work on stochastic modeling of changes in qualitative outcomes. Within the fully parametric strategy, the most common tactic has been to assume that the fundamental parameters are a specific function of time, for example, exponentially declining over time (e.g., Mayer, 1972; Sørensen, 1975; Sørensen and Tuma, 1981; Carroll and Delacroix, 1982). Alternatively one may divide the time axis into periods and assume that parameters are constant within periods but vary across periods (e.g., see Tuma, Hannan, and Groeneveld, 1979). The first tactic usually requires that fewer additional parameters be estimated. However, the second can be useful when little is known about the form of time-dependence. We discuss the fully parametric strategy in detail in Chapter 7 and the partially parametric strategy in Chapter 8.

3. Latent States. In typical applications of Markov models, observed outcomes are assumed to be identical to the states of the Markov process. For example, if the data tell only whether people hold a job, the states are assumed to be "holding a job" and "not holding a job." An improved conceptualization can sometimes make the application of the simple Markov model more appropriate. For example, observed states may be assumed to be related to unobserved (latent) states in a given way. If change among the latent states is truly a Markov process but the observed and latent states are not perfectly correlated, then observed changes are generally *not* describable by a simple Markov model. We consider three cases.

First, suppose true states correspond to probabilities of making an unobservable response, and change from one probability to another is Markovian. This is the basic idea underlying Coleman's (1964b) *Models of Change and Response Uncertainty*. Again, change in observed responses is not Markovian, even though the latent process is. This ingenious formulation has not been widely applied, perhaps because of its mathematical complexity.

Second, suppose change is Markovian but the true state for each episode is not always recorded accurately. If the error structure can be described, then observed changes can be expressed as a function of the true underlying Markovian process. To the best of our knowledge, this conceptualization has not yet been applied in sociological research. We mention it because it resembles the errors-in-measurement models discussed in the literature on linear models of quantitative variables.

Third, suppose each observed state is composed of several unobserved states, and movement among the latent states is Markovian. Since each observed state is associated with two or more unobserved states, the observed process of change will not be Markovian. But an extended model may retain the stationary Markov framework and still fit the data. For example, Herbst (1963) proposed a model of interfirm mobility in which "belonging to a firm" (what the data recorded) consists of four states: undecided, temporarily committed, permanently committed, and decided to leave. Mayer (1972) proposed a similar kind of model in which the data record occupational categories, but each category is composed of two latent states, one that can be left (analogous to Herbst's temporary commitment) and one that cannot (analogous to Herbst's permanent commitment). In Chapter 9 we consider similar models, which we view as attempts to describe and explain change in a system of qualitative variables.

2.4 Panel Analysis of Quantitative Outcomes

2.4.1 Strategies

The two-wave panel has also become a standard tool for the study of change in metric variables. But the problem of casting substantive arguments in operational terms within this framework is far from settled. Investigators analyze panel data for diverse reasons. Consequently, there is no single methodology of panel analysis. We find three broad approaches to panel analysis in the sociological literature.

The first strategy follows Lazarsfeld (1940, 1948) in seeking an approximation to experimental design. Lazarsfeld argued that one could approximate the study of experimentally induced changes by isolating certain classes of changes in a turnover table (such as the 16-fold table). According to this view, panel analysis is a special tool for detecting causal effects. The goal is to choose between two competing hypotheses: X causes Y, or Y causes X. This perspective has been taken over literally into the study of changes in quantitative variables by Campbell (1963) and Pelz and Andrews (1964). They reasoned that one might use **cross-correlations**—the correlation of $X(t_1)$ with $Y(t_2)$ and the correlation of $X(t_2)$ with $Y(t_1)$—to choose between the two competing hypotheses. If the correlation of $X(t_1)$ with $Y(t_2)$ is greater than the correlation of $X(t_2)$ with $Y(t_1)$, then choose the hypothesis "X causes Y," and so forth. This has become a standard procedure for choosing among rival explanations in psychological research (e.g., see Crano, Kenny, and Campbell, 1972).

Kenny (1973, 1975) explicated the logic of this procedure as a test for spuriousness. He actually specified a particular covariance structure among measured and unmeasured values of X and Y and argued that **cross-lag correlations** can be used to test certain meaningful restrictions on the covariance structure. In particular, if the covariance structure does not contain "causal effects" relating X and Y, and if a number of other strong conditions hold (such as constant variances of unmeasured and measured variables over time), the cross-lag partial correlations are zero on the average.

The test for spuriousness depends on a particular specification of the covariance structure—in short, on a model. Moreover, some of Kenny's conditions appear not to hold in many situations, for example, when X and Y have very different stabilities over time. In many reasonable situations, tests on cross-lag correlations give exactly the wrong answer, that is, they suggest that X causes Y when the reverse is true (Rogosa, 1980a).

Many of the difficulties that beset cross-lag correlation analysis can be traced to the main question, Does X cause Y *or* does Y cause X? This question presumes that only one effect exists; it does not anticipate that both effects may hold.

The structural-equation approach to panel analysis permits systematic treatment of more general questions. Instead of viewing panel analysis as a special tool for testing hypotheses, it focuses on estimating parameters of the joint distribution of variables measured at two or more points in time. The sociological literature identifies simple models embodying the various alternative causal structures relating X and Y (Duncan, 1969). Panel analysis may thus be treated as a special case of the usual nonexperimental cross-sectional analysis. Then, as Goldberger (1971) argued, there is no need for any special theory of estimation and testing for panel analysis. Standard methods for structural-equation analysis apply.

The view that panel analysis is a special case of structural-equation methods seems to be widely held in sociology. However, a third view disputes this claim. This perspective, advocated by Coleman (1964a, 1968), follows Lazarsfeld in emphasizing *change*. But it agrees with the structural-equation perspective that inferences concerning change cannot be model-free. It argues that explicit dynamic models are needed if panel analysis is to yield meaningful substantive results. In one sense the usual structural-equation models for panel analysis fit these criteria because the equations may be considered stochastic difference equations. But if change in most social processes may occur at any instant and not just at fixed intervals, as we argued earlier, the proper specification is a *continuous-time* process. The structural relations should be expressed as time-differential equations. The usual panel regressions can then be viewed as integral equations—the solutions of particular time-differential equations governing the process. The relation between integral equations and panel regressions permits use of data with discrete spacing to estimate the parameters of a process changing continuously in time. We argue below that this perspective has considerable advantages. This approach has been used to study organizational demography (Freeman and Hannan, 1975; Hummon, Doreian, and Teuter, 1975; Doreian and Hummon, 1976; Hannan and Freeman, 1978), school effects on learning (Sørensen and Hallinan, 1977), income growth (Rosenfeld, 1980), and ethnic mobilization (Nielsen, 1980) among other topics. We discuss the strategy in depth in Chapters 11 through 15.

2.4.2 Identification and Estimation

The sociological literature contains treatments of special complications that arise in the various approaches to panel analysis. In some cases, these developments tell cautionary tales; in others they suggest alternative estimation strategies.

Duncan (1969) raised a fundamental objection to the view, then widely held, that panel analysis obviates the need to use a model in making inferences, and so provides a "free lunch." He considered a two-wave, two-variable (2W2V) panel and supposed that the analyst assumes that relations are linear-additive but wishes to remain agnostic concerning the direction of causation. The most general linear-additive model then applies by default:

$$\begin{aligned} X(t_2) &= \gamma_0 + \gamma_1 Y(t_1) + \gamma_2 X(t_1) + \gamma_3 X(t_2) + \epsilon, \\ Y(t_2) &= \delta_0 + \delta_1 X(t_1) + \delta_2 Y(t_1) + \delta_3 X(t_2) + \nu, \end{aligned} \quad (1)$$

where ϵ and ν are random disturbances. Notice that this model contains both lagged effects ($\gamma_1, \gamma_2, \delta_1, \delta_2$) and instantaneous effects (γ_3, δ_3). It is easy to show that there are more parameters than covariances when data come from a 2W2V panel; consequently, none of the parameters are identified. Because the parameters cannot be estimated uniquely from data, numerical calculations do not tell anything definite about the fundamental causal structure.

Sociologists rarely estimate models like (1). Instead they typically use models with *only* lagged effects, such as

$$Y(t_2) = \gamma_0 + \gamma_1 Y(t_1) + \gamma_2 X(t_1) + \eta, \quad (2a)$$
$$X(t_2) = \delta_0 + \delta_1 X(t_1) + \delta_2 Y(t_1) + \xi, \quad (2b)$$

where η and ξ are random disturbances. As long as η and ξ are uncorrelated with the regressors (which can happen when there is no instantaneous reciprocal causation), all parameters of (2) may be identified from a 2W2V panel. Of course, the identifying restrictions may be wrong. If so, interpretations based on the restricted model with only lagged effects may be very misleading.

So identification, the fundamental issue in panel analysis, turns on the problem of using the "right" lag structure. Heise (1970) discussed some consequences of using the wrong lag. The problem, of course, is that social scientists rarely (if ever) have enough information about a process to specify the true lag exactly (Davis, 1978). As long as one focuses on discrete-time processes, lack of such knowledge is a massive obstacle to analysis.

The continuous-time specification has several advantages. It frees the substantive model from the timing of observations. Moreover, at least for linear differential-equation models, the identification problem that concerned Heise (1970) and Davis (1978) does not arise. Consider the following simple case. Let the rate of change in both X and Y depend linearly on X and Y:

$$\frac{dY}{dt} = a_0 + a_1 Y(t) + a_2 X(t),$$
$$\frac{dX}{dt} = b_0 + b_1 X(t) + b_2 Y(t). \qquad (3)$$

The integral equations corresponding to this system have the form

$$Y(t_2) = \alpha_0 + \alpha_1 Y(t_1) + \alpha_2 X(t_1),$$
$$X(t_2) = \beta_0 + \beta_1 X(t_1) + \beta_2 Y(t_1), \qquad (4)$$

where the α's and β's are complex functions of the parameters in (3) and of the elapsed time between t_1 and t_2. Inspection of these functions (discussed at length in Chapter 11) shows that the spacing of observations is taken into account in a perfectly natural way. Moreover, it is possible to compare estimates from studies with different intervals between waves of observations. Thus the continuous-time perspective solves two of the major practical difficulties in conventional quantitative panel analysis: choosing a lag and comparing findings from analyses with different lags.

⟨2⟩   Panel Analysis of Quantitative Outcomes   37

Identification issues aside, the most troublesome feature of quantitative panel analyses concerns the specification of the omitted factors, whose effects are summarized in the disturbance term. The usual practice of applying ordinary least-squares (OLS) estimators to models such as (2) implies that errors are uncorrelated over time. But if these factors are stable over time, that is, autocorrelated, the disturbance term cannot be uncorrelated with the right-hand-side variables in the conventional model in (2). Consequently, OLS estimators of the parameters of the conventional two-wave panel model are biased whenever the disturbance is autocorrelated. Evidence that autocorrelation bias is large in the research situations favored by sociologists has accumulated rapidly. Thus progress in analysis of sociological panels depends critically on solutions to the problem of autocorrelation.

The main obstacle to progress has been the heavy reliance on the two-wave panel with a single measure of each variable. Reasonably satisfactory solutions to the problem can be achieved by either increasing the number of waves or by using multiple measures of each variable. In each case, there is enough information both to estimate structural parameters and to adjust for some types of autocorrelation. Each development requires moving beyond ordinary least-squares estimators, as we discuss below.

The use of multiple measures of unobserved (or latent) variables in analysis of panel data first attracted attention in sociology as a framework within which to cope with measurement error (Blalock, 1970; Duncan, 1972). This early literature recognized that structural parameters could still be identified in some such models, even when measurement errors are autocorrelated. More recent work has shown that disturbances associated with the latent variables may also be autocorrelated without destroying identification if the model has sufficient restrictions.

Most work in this tradition has focused on efficient estimation and model testing. The key innovation is Jöreskog's (1970) development and implementation of procedures for "full information" maximum-likelihood (ML) estimation of systems of linear structural equations. The advantages of this approach were discussed by Jöreskog and Sorbom (1976) and Wheaton et al. (1977). It does, however, rely strongly on the assumption of joint normality, which is not always appropriate in studies of change. This procedure has been implemented in empirical research by Bielby, Hauser, and Featherman (1977), Kohn and Schooler (1978), and Esmer (1979), among others.

An alternative strategy involves pooling waves of a multi-wave panel. The result, called analysis of pooled cross-section and time-series data, tacitly assumes that the same process operates in each pair of adjacent waves. If so, the information in excess of that generated by a two-wave panel can be used to estimate the parameters of a postulated autocorrelation process. One promising specification of the autocorrelation process uses the classical model of variance components. It assumes that the disturbance consists of two (or more) unrelated components: one component is pure random noise; the other component is a constant summarizing enduring features of a member of the population (e.g., genetic composition, stable aspects of personality, and features of a constitutional system.) Under this specification, the disturbances are autocorrelated only because of these individual-specific components. If the latter are considered to be fixed effects, pooled within-individual regressions eliminate autoregression bias. If the individual-specific effects are treated as random variables drawn from some distribution, one may use generalized least-squares estimators that have good large sample properties and reasonably good small sample properties as well. Chapter 13 contains an extensive discussion of properties of estimators for pooled models.

2.5 Time-Series Analysis

We indicate only briefly the main lines of development of time-series analysis in sociological research. Many issues pertaining to both strategy and estimation parallel those already discussed for panel analysis. Moreover, the statistical theory is far more codified for time-series analysis than for panel analysis.

The time-series literature, especially in economics, has often focused on questions similar to those posed by Lazarsfeld. In an influential paper, Granger (1969) defined direction of causality in terms of predictability in multiple time series. He proposed that one time series $\{X(t)\}$ causes another $\{Y(t)\}$ if current values of Y can be predicted from past values of X, controlling for the effects of past values of Y. This conception resembles that underlying cross-lag correlation analysis—with the important exception that Granger

⟨2⟩ Conclusions

explicitly included the possibility of joint causation.

It turns out that translating Granger's criterion for causation into two-wave panel format does not give a cross-lag correlation test. Instead, it implies that X causes Y if the structural cross-lag parameter labeled γ_2 in equation (2a) is nonzero, and that Y causes X if δ_2 in (2b) is nonzero (Rogosa, 1979, 1980b).

Continuous-time dynamic models of quantitative variables are sometimes estimated from time-series data; for examples, see Doreian and Hummon (1976). However, the structural-equation perspective, with discrete lags, is applied more often to sociological time series. Then the standard econometric literature on time series with its focus on autocorrelation of disturbances applies. This literature stress two forms of autocorrelation, autoregressive and moving-average processes. Much recent work follows Box and Jenkins (1976), who constructed models with a disturbance process that is a very general mixture of these two processes. This strategy has swept the field of applied time-series analysis but has just begun to penetrate sociological research. Hibbs (1977) discussed the potential value of the Box–Jenkins approach to the study of policy interventions when long time series are available. Vigderhous (1977) illustrated its value in forecasting social trends, and Loftin and McDowell (1982) used it to assess the relationship between police strength and crime rates. Finally, much theoretical work on time series uses a spectral representation of the series that transforms from a time domain to a frequency domain. The goal is to decompose a long series into components of different frequency just as sound may be so decomposed. One may wish to smooth high-frequency (or short-period) waves so as to achieve a clearer representation of the longer cycles of the process [see Mayer and Arney, (1974)]. Spectral analysis has been applied in sociological research on income dynamics (Parker, 1982) and on organizational demography (Stevenson, 1982).

2.6 Conclusions

The notion that temporal analysis automatically yields conclusive inferences dies hard. However, the thrust of most recent methodological developments has been to argue cogently against this view. We have emphasized that the stock tools of temporal analysis in sociology, the two-wave panel for qualitative and quantitative outcomes, admits multiple interpretations. In the qualitative case, when changes may occur at any time, one cannot identify structural parameters from only two waves of panel data. Event counts, event sequences and event histories permit much finer model testing and should be used more often in sociological research. The identification problem plagues the quantitative case as well. If the model assumes a discrete-time process, one must know the timing of the causal lags. Overall, these methodological developments reemphasize the importance of substantive theory and models for making good use of temporal data.

    The situation is not wholly bleak, however. Sociologists have begun to devote more attention to *modeling* change processes. We propose that such developments, particularly the use of continuous-time stochastic models of change, will permit a much richer use of temporal data than in past sociological research. Not only will such models enrich sociological analysis, they also focus attention squarely on change processes. They emphasize that temporal data are not just like cross-sectional data, but that they contain information on the manner in which change comes about. The chapters that follow attempt to illustrate these advantages in concrete terms.

Part II
Qualitative Outcomes

3

Fundamentals of Event-History Analysis

This is the first in a series of chapters dealing with models and methods for studying change in qualitative variables by means of event-history analysis. As we stated in Chapter 2, event-history data allow researchers to seek answers to a far more extensive set of questions than can be answered with more conventional types of data, such as cross-sectional and panel data. Despite the advantages of event histories, comparatively few sociologists are familiar with models and methods for analyzing them. Yet the availability of event histories is increasing. They form part of the information in several existing data sets, and are being collected in a number of other surveys in progress (e.g., the 1979 National Longitudinal Survey of Youth Behavior; the High School and Beyond Study). We have chosen to focus almost solely on event-history analysis in Part II of this book because this mode of analysis offers a wide range of possibilities and because available treatments of this subject (e.g., Gross and Clark, 1975; Elandt-Johnson and Johnson, 1980) are not aimed at social scientists. However, after explicating event-history analysis, we return in Chapter 10 to both analytical and empirical comparisons of event-history analyses with analyses of more familiar forms of data, in particular, cross-sectional and panel data.

We have two main objectives in this chapter. First, we want to introduce readers to a language for discussing event histories and ways of analyzing them. This chapter provides terminology for later chapters and describes various symbolic and notational conventions that we maintain (insofar as possible) throughout the remaining chapters. Section 3.1 contains a detailed description of an event history and definitions of basic terms. Section 3.2 presents fundamental concepts pertaining to a population of event histories and a variety of descriptive statistics applicable to a sample of event histories.

Our second goal is to show how even the elementary concepts defined in this chapter can be useful in event-history analysis. The descriptive statistics discussed in Section 3.2 should be intrinsically interesting to readers who are concerned mainly with summarizing the information contained in a collection of event histories. These statistics also serve as valuable tools in exploratory analysis of event-history data and in preliminary investigations whose ultimate aim is to construct, estimate, and test explicit models of a change process. To achieve our second purpose, we illustrate most concepts using two sets of data. These two sets of data also form the basis for many of our examples in Part II.

One set of data consists of the marital histories of low-income adults who participated in the Seattle and Denver Income Maintenance Experiments (SIME/DIME). These marital histories were collected to provide an answer to the question: How would a negative income tax (NIT) program affect the marital stability of the U.S. population, especially the low-income population that is the typical target of public welfare programs? Before these data were collected and analyzed, opinions were divided, and two main answers were proposed. According to one view, a small-scale, short-term experiment would not affect marital stability because marital behavior depends primarily on social and cultural institutions that resist change. According to the other view, an NIT program would increase marital stability (even in an experimental setting) because a husband need not desert his wife and children for them to receive income supplements. Even the simple descriptive statistics reported later in this chapter indicate strongly that both views are wrong.

The other set of data consists of job histories of a national sample of black and white men aged 30–39 in 1968, collected by James S. Coleman and Peter R. Rossi. (For a description of these data, see Coleman et al., 1972.) We use these data to investigate how individuals in the United States improve their socio-economic positions. An extensive body of literature (see Blau and Duncan, 1967; Duncan, Featherman, and Duncan, 1972; Sewell, Hauser, and Featherman, 1976) reveals that a person's schooling has a potent

⟨3⟩ **Event-History Data** 45

effect on his prestige and income at a later point in time. To what extent do job changes rather than on-the-job wage increases generate this well-documented relationship? Is the underlying process the same in all segments of the economy, at all ages, for both races? We address these and other questions as we use the Coleman–Rossi job histories to illustrate the topics covered in this chapter.

3.1   Event-History Data

An event history describes the values of a qualitative variable, $Y(t)$, within some observation period running from τ_1 to τ_2:

$$\omega[\tau_1, \tau_2] \equiv \{y(u); \tau_1 \leq u \leq \tau_2\}. \qquad (1)$$

(Throughout this book we follow the common convention of denoting a random variable by a capital letter and its realization by the corresponding lower-case letter.) The set of all distinct values that $Y(t)$ can take is called the **state space** of Y. The number of distinct values that Y can take is called the **size** of the state space, which we denote by Ψ.

We concentrate on qualitative variables that have a **countable** number of states. Countable means that each element in the state space can be associated with an integer. Since variables for which Ψ is very large are usually treated as quantitative, we focus on phenomena for which Ψ is fairly small. For simplicity, we always associate elements in Y's state space with integers varying from 1 to Ψ—in increasing order if Y is ordinal.

To fix ideas, assume that available data give the marital history of a person between τ_1 and τ_2. We assume that a person must occupy one of three categories: $1 \equiv$ not married, $2 \equiv$ married, and $3 \equiv$ dead. Figure 3.1 gives a graphical display of a marital history of a typical individual. The horizontal axis represents time; the vertical axis gives the person's status at a particular time, $y(t)$. In this particular example, the person is not married at time τ_1 [$y(\tau_1) = 1$] and is married at time τ_2 [$y(\tau_2) = 2$]. The person's status at any other time between τ_1 and τ_2 can be determined from Figure 3.1.

Events refer to changes in $Y(t)$. For example, in Figure 3.1 the first event is a change from state 1 to state 2. The term **event**

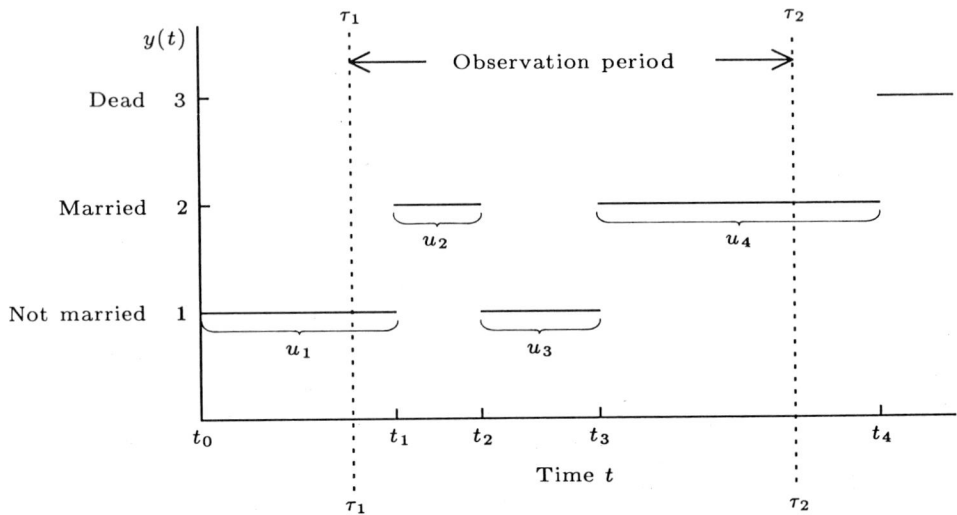

Figure 3.1. Hypothetical marital history of a typical person. Adapted with permission from Tuma (1982).

count refers to the number of events in some interval of time. We denote the total number of events in the interval[1] $(s, t]$ by the random variable $N(s, t]$.[2] Usually the interval is chosen to be the observation period, τ_1 to τ_2. In Figure 3.1, $n(\tau_1, \tau_2] = 3$. The random variable T_n stands for the time of the nth event. In Figure 3.1, the three observed events occur at times t_1, t_2, and t_3. We arbitrarily call the starting time of the process t_0 and call the start of the process "the 0th event."

We refer to the state occupied just after the nth event by the random variable Y_n, which is equal to $Y(t_n + \Delta t)$ where Δt is positive but infinitesimal. In Figure 3.1, $y_1 = 2$, indicating that the first event consists of a move to state $2 \equiv$ married. The state

---

[1] In referring to intervals of a variable (usually time), a parenthesis indicates that the endpoint of a range is excluded from the interval and a bracket indicates that the endpoint is included in the interval. Thus, $(s, t]$ denotes all time points between s and t, including t but excluding s.

[2] If the observation period begins at the moment of an event, this event is not included in a count of events occurring in this period, that is, events are counted over the period $(s, t]$, and not $[s, t]$.

⟨3⟩ **Event-History Data**

occupied at the start of the process is $y_0 \equiv y(t_0)$.

The term **episode** or **spell** describes the period of time between successive events. The nth episode refers to the period between the $(n-1)$th and nth events. The length of time from event $n-1$ until event n is called the **waiting time** to the nth event and is represented by the random variable U_n, which equals $T_n - T_{n-1}$ by definition. In Figure 3.1, the waiting time to the second event is $u_2 \equiv t_2 - t_1$.

Sometimes one is especially interested in the length of time between successive events, $n-1$ and n, given the outcome of the nth event, $k \equiv y_n$, and the outcome of the previous event, $j \equiv y_{n-1}$. We refer to this interval as the **holding time** in state j prior to a transition to state k, denoted by U_{njk}. The idea of a holding time is similar to that of a waiting time, except that a holding time is conditioned on the outcome of the next event while the waiting time does not. The concept of a holding time plays a key role in the literature on semi-Markov processes, as we indicate in Section 4.3.

Figure 3.1 tells the completed length of spells two and three. However, the completed lengths of the first and fourth episodes are unknown because there is no information on the person's marital history before τ_1 and after τ_2. When $y(t)$ actually has values for time t less than τ_1 or greater than τ_2, but these values are not observed, event-history data are said to be **censored**. Censoring describes a feature of a particular sample of *data* rather than a characteristic of the population.[3]

When data on $Y(t)$ are lacking for time t less than τ_1, the data are said to be **left-censored**. When data are lacking for time t greater than τ_2, they are said to be **right-censored**. Event-history data available to sociologists are almost always censored on the right (we do not know what will happen in the future); often they are censored on the left too. Censoring presents special problems in analyzing event-history data. Right-censoring turns out to be a manageable problem (see Tuma and Hannan, 1978); left-censoring is far more difficult to handle. In Chapter 5 we discuss both right- and left-censoring and some ways of dealing with them.

[3] According to Kendall and Buckland (1971, p. 20), "A sample is said to be censored when certain values are unknown (or deliberately ignored) although their existence is known."

The start and end of an observation period frequently fall in the middle of an episode. When the beginning or end of the observation period falls in the middle of the nth episode, we denote the observed, censored length of this episode by the random variable V_n. For example, in Figure 3.1 the time of the fourth event is not observed because it falls outside the observation period. The observed, censored length of the fourth episode is $v_4 = \tau_2 - t_3$. The completed length of the fourth spell, u_4, must be longer than v_4, but just how much longer is unknown. Similarly, unless τ_1 happens to coincide with the time of an event, the length of the first observed episode is also censored. For simplicity, in this chapter we assume data are censored on the right but not on the left, that is, $\tau_1 = t_0$.

A graphical display like Figure 3.1 is one way of describing an event history. A more compact way consists of recording for each case: the state occupied at the beginning, $y_0 \equiv y(t_0)$; the number of events that occur in the observation period, $n \equiv n(t_0, \tau_2]$; the timing of each of the n events $\{t_1, \ldots, t_n\}$ or equivalently the waiting time to each event $\{u_1, \ldots, u_n\}$; and the state entered at each event $\{y_1, \ldots, y_n\}$. From this information one can infer what state each case occupies at every moment in the observation period. Thus

$$\omega[t_0, \tau_2] = \{t_0, y_0, t_1, y_1, \ldots, t_n, y_n\}. \tag{2}$$

A complete history of state occupancies and times of changes, such as expression (2), is often referred to as a **sample path**. What we call event-history methods could as well be called sample-path methods.

Because we refer often to the history from t_0 to t_n (the time of the nth event), we introduce the notational abbreviation:

$$\omega_n \equiv \omega[t_0, t_n] = \{t_0, y_0, t_1, y_1, \ldots, t_n, y_n\}. \tag{3}$$

Despite their apparent similarity, expressions (2) and (3) are not the same unless $\tau_2 = t_n$. For $\tau_2 > t_n$, $\omega[t_0, \tau_2]$ tells not only the information in ω_n, but also that the $(n+1)$th event did not occur in the interval $(t_n, \tau_2]$. When $n = 0$, expression (3) becomes $\omega_0 \equiv \{t_0, y_0\}$, the initial conditions of the process. Finally, note that

$$\omega_{n-1} = \{\omega_{n-2}, t_{n-1}, y_{n-1}\}. \tag{4}$$

A number of equations in Part II are written in terms of ω_{n-1} instead of $\{\omega_{n-2}, t_{n-1}, y_{n-1}\}$ for notational compactness.

3.2 Terms for Populations of Event Histories

So far we have considered only information about the sample path of a single case (observational unit). Now we turn to concepts pertaining to a population. Except for occasional parenthetical remarks, in this section we assume that members of the population are homogeneous on all causal variables, including the initial conditions, ω_0. Later chapters introduce heterogeneity.

3.2.1 State Probabilities

Because $Y(t)$ has different values for different members of the population, knowledge about the value of $Y(t)$ within the population is summarized in terms of a set of **state probabilities**:

$$p_y(t) \equiv \Pr[Y(t) = y],$$

where y takes the values 1 to Ψ. If, as required earlier, the state space of Y contains the exhaustive and mutually exclusive values that Y can take, then

$$\sum_{y=1}^{\Psi} p_y(t) = 1 \qquad (5)$$

for every t.

There may exist certain values of t such that $p_y(t)$, $y = 1, \ldots, \Psi$, is not changing over time. The distribution of state probabilities at such times is called a **stationary, steady-state,** or **equilibrium distribution**. In later chapters we discuss stochastic models that have implications for the distribution of state probabilities. Some of these models have steady-state distributions; however, not all stochastic models generate equilibrium distributions.

Empirical estimates of state probabilities are routinely estimated from cross-sectional and panel data, as well as from event histories. The number of cases with $Y(t) = y$ divided by the size of a simple random sample, I, gives an unbiased, efficient estimate of $p_y(t)$. This estimator requires no assumption about the process generating $Y(t)$ for these optimal properties to hold. However, state probabilities tell little about the process of change in Y; they can only signal the existence of some sort of change if the distribution of state probabilities varies over time. Because state probabilities are relatively uninformative about the change process and because sociologists estimate them so often, we do not bother to illustrate them here.

3.2.2 Transition Probabilities

A transition probability tells the probability of a particular change in Y between two points in time, conditional on the history of the process at still earlier times.[4] Let $j \equiv y(s)$ and $k \equiv y(t)$. Then the **transition probability** $p_{jk}(s, t \mid \omega[t_0, s))$, $s \leq t$, is

$$p_{jk}(s, t \mid \omega[t_0, s)) \equiv \Pr[Y(t) = k \mid Y(s) = j, \omega[t_0, s)].$$

A transition probability is a *conditional* probability—the probability of being in state k at time t, conditional on being in state j at time s and having some prior history $\omega[t_0, s)$. Note that the sum of $p_{jk}(s, t \mid \omega[t_0, s))$ over all values of k equals unity because a sample member can be in one and only one state k at time t.

Sometimes one is interested in transition probabilities that do not condition on the previous history, that is, on $p_{jk}(s, t)$. This is simply

$$p_{jk}(s, t) = \sum_{\omega[t_0, s)} p_j(s \mid \omega[t_0, s)) \, p_{jk}(s, t \mid \omega[t_0, s)). \tag{6}$$

Definitions in the rest of this chapter condition on the previous history (sample path) to avoid the erroneous impression that some form of Markov property must be assumed in event-history analysis. An equation analogous to (6) can always be written to give the corresponding concept that does not condition on previous history.

Sociologists routinely estimate transition probabilities from panel data, that is, data on the values of Y at a series of discrete points in time. A maximum-likelihood (ML) estimate of $p_{jk}(s, t)$ is just the number of cases that have $y(s) = j$ and $y(t) = k$ divided by the number of cases that have $y(s) = j$. Because panel data do not supply information on a case's previous history $\omega[t_0, s)$, one cannot use them to estimate $p_{jk}(s, t \mid \omega[t_0, s))$, the transition probability that controls for previous history. However, this transition probability can be estimated from event-history data. An ML estimate of

---

[4] The term "transition probability" has two meanings in the literature on stochastic models of change in discrete variables. To avoid confusion, we limit usage of this term to the one most familiar to sociologists. We have created the term "event transition probability" (see below) for the other meaning.

⟨3⟩ Terms for Populations of Event Histories   51

$p_{jk}(s, t \mid \omega[t_0, s))$ is the number of cases with $y(s) = j$, $y(t) = k$, and previous history $\omega[t_0, s)$, divided by the number with $y(s) = j$ and previous history $\omega[t_0, s)$. It seems unnecessary to say more here about estimation of transition probabilities since sociologists often estimate them from panel data.

3.2.3 *Mean Number of Events

Another useful way of describing change in Y refers to the average number of events in a period, typically the observation period $(\tau_1, \tau_2]$. We denote the population **mean number of events** by $E[N(\tau_1, \tau_2]]$ and the sample mean by $\overline{n}(\tau_1, \tau_2]$.

Sometimes counts of events in a period are distinguished on the basis of the state initially occupied because the initial state seems likely to affect the mean number of events in a period. For example, a sample of initially unemployed people usually has more changes in employment status in a 6-week period than a sample of initially employed people (even if members of the two samples are identical in all other respects) because unemployment spells are shorter than employment spells on the average. For many phenomena the dependence of the mean number of events in a period on initial status falls as the length of the period increases. The mean number of changes in employment status in a 20-year period, for example, is apt to be about the same whether sample members are initially employed or unemployed, as long as they are otherwise homogeneous. Often it is also useful to distinguish counts of different kinds of events. For example, a researcher might want to obtain separate counts of the number of changes to employment and unemployment. We let the random variable $N_{jk}(\tau_1, \tau_2]$ represent the number of times state k is entered (visited) in the interval $(\tau_1, \tau_2]$ when state j is occupied at time τ_1. We denote the mean in the population by $E[N_{jk}(\tau_1, \tau_2]]$ and the corresponding sample mean by $\overline{n}_{jk}(\tau_1, \tau_2]$. Empirical estimates of the mean number of events can be obtained in the usual way, that is, by summing $n_{jk}(\tau_1, \tau_2]$ for all cases in the sample and then dividing by the number in state j at τ_1.

3.2.4 Survivor Function

Consider the first event for a population in state $j \equiv y_0$ at time t_0. The **survivor function** for the first event is the probability that this event occurs after time t, given the initial conditions, ω_0:

$$G_j(t \mid \omega_0) \equiv \Pr[T_1 \geq t \mid \omega_0].$$

Because $U_1 \equiv T_1 - t_0$, an equivalent expression is

$$G_j(u \mid \omega_0) \equiv \Pr[U_1 \geq u \mid \omega_0].$$

For example, $G_j(t \mid \omega_0)$ could be the probability that a firm founded at time t_0 with structural type $j \equiv y_0$ does not fail before time t. The survivor function is unity at the starting time t_0. It is strictly nonincreasing and tends to fall towards zero as time elapses. For an infinite value of t, $G_j(t \mid \omega_0)$ is usually (but not necessarily) zero.

In most sociological applications, more than one event can occur: people may have several marriages, countries may change their political structure several times, and so forth. The definition of a survivor function is easily generalized to such cases. In general, the survivor function for the nth event depends not only on t_{n-1} and y_{n-1}, but also on the history from the start of the process at t_0 to the time of the $(n-1)$th event, $\omega_{n-1} \equiv \omega[t_0, t_{n-1}]$:

$$G_j(t \mid \omega_{n-1}) \equiv \Pr[T_n \geq t \mid \omega_{n-1}], \tag{7}$$

or equivalently,

$$G_j(u \mid \omega_{n-1}) \equiv \Pr[U_n \geq u \mid \omega_{n-1}]. \tag{8}$$

The key nonparametric approach to estimating the survivor function (and also all other probabilistic functions defined in this section) from event-history data derives from Kaplan and Meier's (1958) proposal for obtaining a "product-limit" estimator of the survivor function when data are right-censored. The product-limit estimator is the ML estimator for the survivor function when *no* assumption is made about its functional form.[5] In this sense it is a nonparametric estimator. Because of the excellent properties of the Kaplan–Meier estimates, this procedure has become one of the most common ways of estimating empirical survivor functions.

The basic idea of the **Kaplan–Meier estimator** can be summarized as follows. Suppose that a sample of I cases with previous history ω_{n-1} (including a move to state $j \equiv y_{n-1}$ at time t_{n-1}) are

---

[5]Other ML estimators can be obtained if one is willing to make *some* assumptions (even if very weak ones) about the functional form of the survivor function; for example, see Tarter (1979).

observed from t_{n-1} to τ_2. Let I^* denote the number of cases whose nth event occurs in $(t_{n-1}, \tau_2]$, $I^* \leq I$. Arrange the I^* cases observed to have events in the *order* of the occurrence of the events. Label the time of the first event in the sample $t_{(1)}$, the time of the second $t_{(2)}$, and so forth; these are usually called the **order statistics** for the sample. Label the case with the first observed event (1), the case with the second observed event (2), and so forth; these are usually called the **rank statistics** for the sample.

Assume that $G_j(t - \Delta t \mid \omega_{n-1})$ has been estimated and that one wants to estimate $G_j(t \mid \omega_{n-1})$ where Δt is small and positive. Clearly,

$$G_j(t \mid \omega_{n-1}) = G_j(t - \Delta t \mid \omega_{n-1}) \, p_{jj}(t - \Delta t, t \mid \omega_{n-1}).$$

This equation provides a recursive formula for calculating the estimated survivor function. One needs to know only how to estimate $p_{jj}(t - \Delta t, t \mid \omega_{n-1})$ for every t and Δt to calculate $G_j(t \mid \omega_{n-1})$.

To estimate the transition probability $p_{jj}(t - \Delta t, t \mid \omega_{n-1})$, two situations must be considered: no case has an event in $(t - \Delta t, t]$, and $\kappa > 0$ cases have events in $(t - \Delta t, t]$. If no case has an event in $(t - \Delta t, t]$, the estimate of $p_{jj}(t - \Delta t, t \mid \omega_{n-1})$ is unity. Consequently, only a time interval in which an event occurs shifts the estimated survivor function, that is, $G_j(t \mid \omega_{n-1}) = G_j(t - \Delta t \mid \omega_{n-1})$ if no event occurs in $(t - \Delta t, t]$. On the other hand, if κ events occur in $(t - \Delta t, t]$, $p_{jj}(t - \Delta t, t \mid \omega_{n-1})$ equals the number still in state j at time $t - \Delta t$ minus κ, divided by the number still in state j at time $t - \Delta t$.

Summarizing this procedure formally, we obtain that the Kaplan–Meier estimator of the survivor function for the nth event at time t is

$$\widehat{G}_j(t \mid \omega_{n-1}) = \prod_{t_{(i)} < t} \frac{I - (i) - c(t_{(i)})}{I - (i-1) - c(t_{(i)})}, \tag{9}$$

where, as defined earlier, I is the size of the sample in state y_{n-1} with previous history ω_{n-2} at t_{n-1}, $(i-1)$ the number of events that occurred before $t_{(i)}$, (i) the number (rank) of the event that occurs at $t_{(i)}$, and $c(t_{(i)})$ the number of sample members lost from the sample before $t_{(i)}$ because of right censoring. Note that the survivor function is undefined for every time t after the last moment that a member of the sample is observed in state j.

The usefulness of the Kaplan–Meier estimator of the survivor function is enhanced by the fact that Kaplan and Meier (1958) provided a formula for estimating the asymptotic sample variance of the survivor function:

$$\text{Var}\big[\widehat{G}_j(t \mid \omega_{n-1})\big] \approx \big[\widehat{G}_j(t \mid \omega_{n-1})\big]^2$$

$$\cdot \sum_{t_{(i)} < t} \frac{1}{\big[I - (i) - c(t_{(i)})\big]\big[I - (i-1) - c(t_{(i)})\big]}.$$

The estimated variance allows tests of hypotheses about the equivalence of the survivor functions in different populations. (For another approach to such tests, see Peto and Peto, 1972.)

Sparsity of data commonly precludes estimation of empirical survivor functions quite as detailed as suggested above, except in the case of first events. Investigators usually ignore many aspects of previous history ω_{n-1}. Advocates of cohort analysis may wish to retain the starting time t_0, which defines a cohort of population members whose histories begin at the same time. In some analyses it may be substantively important to note the number of past events. For example, in analyses of birth rates it is important to control parity (number of previous births). Often people ignore the number of the event, assuming that the survivor function for second events is like that for first events, and so forth. Sometimes analysts also ignore the timing of the previous event, or at least group together cases whose previous event occurred at roughly the same time. However, survivor functions are usually distinguished on the basis of the state j that is being left. For example, the survivor functions for leaving employment and for leaving unemployment surely differ.

We use the Coleman–Rossi job histories for black and white men to illustrate the Kaplan–Meier estimator of a survivor function. In this example the event is "leaving the first full-time job in the civilian nonagricultural labor force (CNALF)," where "full-time" means the job is held for at least 35 hours per week. Figure 3.2 displays a plot of the Kaplan–Meier estimate of the survivor function versus duration in the job. When duration in the job is zero, the survivor function equals unity. As duration in the job increases, the survivor function tends to fall toward zero. No one in the sample of 477 black (537 white) men is observed to hold the first full-time job in the CNALF for longer than 24 years and 7 months (22 years and 4 months). Moreover, at least one member of each sample has still not left the first full-time job at the end of the observation period. Consequently, the survivor function cannot be estimated at durations longer than 24.6 (22.3) years.

The right-hand side of Figure 3.2 gives an enlarged picture of the survivor functions for the first 5 years. Notice that the curves for black and white men are very similar for the first 2 months; however, after 3 months the curve for white men drops precipitously, whereas the curve for black men declines gradually. As we show below, this unanticipated drop at 3 months for white men makes it difficult to fit standard parametric models to these data. Thus, this plot demonstrates the value of examining Kaplan–Meier estimates of survivor functions even when estimation of a parametric model is the ultimate goal. The fact that this sharp drop occurs at 3 months suggests that the first full-time job is more likely for white men than for black men to be a summer job ending with a return to school. Evidence given below supports this hypothesis.

3.2.5 *Waiting-Time Distribution Function

Change in Y can also be described in terms of the distribution of waiting times—the lengths of the intervals between successive events. Typically one wants to consider the waiting-time distribution for the nth event, given that the $(n-1)$th event consists of a move to state $j \equiv y_{n-1}$ at time t_{n-1}. In general, the cumulative distribution function (CDF) for the waiting time to the nth event depends on the entire previous history ω_{n-1}, and not just t_{n-1} and $j \equiv y_{n-1}$:

$$F_j(u \mid \omega_{n-1}) \equiv \Pr[U_n < u \mid \omega_{n-1}]. \tag{10}$$

A comparison of (8) and (10) indicates that the CDF for the waiting time is the complement of the corresponding survivor function:

$$F_j(u \mid \omega_{n-1}) = 1 - G_j(u \mid \omega_{n-1}). \tag{11}$$

Often analysis is done, not with the CDF, but with the probability density function (PDF) of the waiting time, which is the derivative of

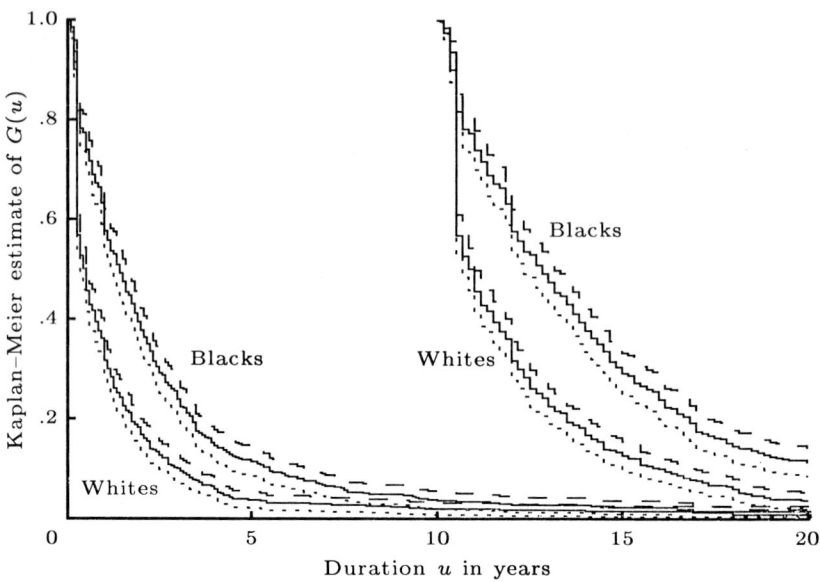

Figure 3.2. Kaplan–Meier estimate of the survivor probability $G(u)$ for the first full-time job in the CNALF versus duration u, by race. Number of events/cases: 468/477 (blacks); 528/537 (whites). The solid curve denotes the Kaplan–Meier estimate of $G(u)$; the dashed and dotted curves denote the upper and lower 95% confidence intervals, respectively.

the CDF with respect to u [and, based on (11), minus the derivative of the survivor function]:

$$f_j(u \mid \omega_{n-1}) = \frac{\mathrm{d}F_j(u \mid \omega_{n-1})}{\mathrm{d}u} = -\frac{\mathrm{d}G_j(u \mid \omega_{n-1})}{\mathrm{d}u}. \qquad (12)$$

With a trivial modification, the Kaplan–Meier procedure for estimating the survivor function also gives an estimate of the CDF for the waiting time. Merely insert the Kaplan–Meier estimate of the survivor function into (11).

The mean and the variance of the waiting time are conceptually useful ways of summarizing the information in a waiting-time distribution. The mean waiting time to the nth event, given previous history ω_{n-1} (including $j \equiv y_{n-1}$), is defined as the first moment of U_n:

$$\mathrm{E}[U_n \mid \omega_{n-1}] \equiv \int_0^\infty u f_j(u \mid \omega_{n-1})\, du. \tag{13}$$

The variance (the second moment of U_n about the mean) is equivalent to

$$\mathrm{Var}[U_n \mid \omega_{n-1}] = -\{\mathrm{E}[U_n \mid \omega_{n-1}]\}^2 + \int_0^\infty u^2 f_j(u \mid \omega_{n-1})\, du. \tag{14}$$

The most obvious way of estimating the mean waiting time from a sample of event histories consists of summing the observed waiting times and dividing by the number of episodes. However, usually some fraction of the episodes in a sample is censored. What should be done with censored waiting times—drop them, or include them as if they were uncensored? We delay detailed discussion of the censoring problem until Chapter 5. Here we mention only that censoring makes it impossible to obtain a nonparametric estimate of the mean (and variance) of the waiting time from a sample of event histories.

3.2.6 Hazard Function

A concept closely related to the survivor function is the **hazard function** or **failure rate**. In the case of the first event for the population in $j \equiv y_0$ at starting time t_0, the hazard function is defined as[6]

$$h_j(t \mid t_0) \equiv \lim_{\Delta t \downarrow 0} \frac{G_j(t \mid t_0) - G_j(t + \Delta t \mid t_0)}{G_j(t \mid t_0)\, \Delta t} \tag{15a}$$

$$= -\frac{d \log G_j(t \mid t_0)}{dt} = \frac{f_j(t \mid t_0)}{G_j(t \mid t_0)}. \tag{15b}$$

As the limit of the ratio of two positive quantities [see (15a)], a hazard function is necessarily positive. However, unlike a probability, it can exceed unity. The hazard function is the inverse of Mills'

---

[6] A downward arrow ($\downarrow$) indicates that Δt approaches zero from the right, that is, that Δt is never negative.

(1926) ratio according to the definition in (15b) (see Johnson and Kotz, 1970).

The hazard function is the instantaneous probability of "failing" (i.e., having an event) at time t, given that failure has not occurred before t. An intuitive understanding of this key concept can be gained by considering the discrete-time analogue, the proportion who have not failed by t, but fail between t and $t + \Delta t$. By definition, this proportion is the number in j at t_0 who fail in the interval $(t, t + \Delta t]$, divided by the number at risk of failure at time t. If both the numerator and denominator are divided by the number at risk of failing at time t, this proportion is unchanged. The denominator becomes the proportion at risk of failure, which is analogous to $G_j(t \mid \omega_0)$. The numerator gives the proportion who fail between t and $t + \Delta t$, which is analogous to $G_j(t \mid \omega_0) - G_j(t + \Delta t \mid \omega_0)$. Note that $G_j(t \mid \omega_0) - G_j(t + \Delta t \mid \omega_0)$ is positive because $G_j(t \mid \omega_0)$ cannot increase as time passes. Thus the proportion of those who have not failed by t, but who do fail between t and $t + \Delta t$, is

$$\frac{G_j(t \mid t_0) - G_j(t + \Delta t \mid t_0)}{G_j(t \mid t_0)}. \tag{16}$$

What happens to (16) if Δt is divided by 2? The denominator will be the same, but the numerator will be roughly half as large, assuming Δt is small. Thus the proportion in (16) depends on Δt. To obtain a measure of the likelihood of failing that is independent of the length of Δt, divide the expression in (16) by Δt and let Δt become smaller and smaller, that is, take the limit as Δt approaches zero. The result is the hazard function in (15).

Because the hazard function is the limit of the ratio of two positive quantities, as (15) indicates, it is necessarily positive. However, unlike a probability, a hazard function can be greater than unity. In fact, there is nothing intrinsic requiring it to be finite. Special problems that arise when the hazard function is infinite are dealt with in the mathematical literature on this subject. We ignore these problems because the assumption of finite hazard functions seems reasonable in sociological applications.

The hazard function for the nth event, like that for the first event, is defined in terms of the corresponding survivor function. In general the hazard function for the nth event, like the survivor function for this event, depends on the time and outcome of the previous event and on previous history:

$$h_j(t \mid \omega_{n-1}) \equiv \lim_{\Delta t \downarrow 0} \frac{G_j(t \mid \omega_{n-1}) - G_j(t + \Delta t \mid \omega_{n-1})}{G_j(t \mid \omega_{n-1})\Delta t}$$

$$= -\frac{\mathrm{d}\log G_j(t \mid \omega_{n-1})}{\mathrm{d}t}$$

$$= \frac{f_j(t \mid \omega_{n-1})}{G_j(t \mid \omega_{n-1})}, \tag{17}$$

where $j \equiv y_{n-1}$. The relationship in (17) plays an important role in estimating hazard functions from event-history data, as we show below. It implies that

$$A_j(t \mid \omega_{n-1}) \equiv -\log G_j(t \mid \omega_{n-1}) = \int_{t_{n-1}}^{t} h_j(s \mid \omega_{n-1})\,\mathrm{d}s. \tag{18}$$

Thus specification of the hazard function for a process defines the survivor function, and vice versa. This expression also makes plain why the logarithm of the survivor function is often called the integrated or cumulative hazard function.

According to (17), a hazard function can be estimated empirically from an estimated log survivor plot. The estimated hazard function at some time t is the negative of the slope of the estimated log survivor function at this time. Consequently, any graphical or analytic technique for evaluating this function's slope is a possible method for estimating the hazard function.

Thus the logarithm of the Kaplan–Meier estimator can be used as an estimator of the hazard function. Since the logarithm is a monotonic transformation and the large-sample properties of ML are preserved under monotonic transformations, this will give good asymptotic estimates of the hazard function. But, due to the nonlinearity of the transformation, there is a bias in small samples. That is, the log of the Kaplan–Meier estimator gives biased estimates of the hazard function in small samples. Aalen (1978) used martingale theory to derive a better estimator.[7] His nonparametric estimator

---

[7] His estimator turns out to be the same as one proposed by Nelson (1972).

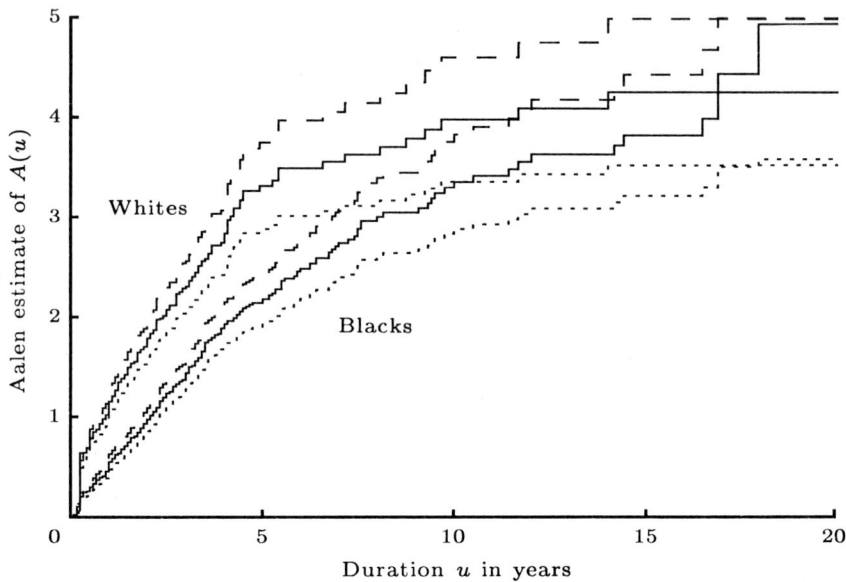

Figure 3.3. Aalen estimate of the cumulative hazard function $A(u)$ for the first full-time job in the CNALF versus duration u, by race. Number of events/cases: 468/477 (blacks); 528/537 (whites). The solid curve denotes the Aalen estimate of $A(u)$; the dashed and dotted curves denote the upper and lower 95% confidence intervals, respectively.

for the cumulative hazard function is

$$\widehat{A}_j(t \mid \omega_{n-1}) = \sum_{t_{n-1} \leq t_{(i)} < t} \frac{1}{I - (i) - c(t_{(i)})}. \tag{19}$$

This estimator is unbiased, consistent, and asymptotically normal. An associated estimator of the variance of the cumulative hazard function is

$$\mathrm{Var}\big[\widehat{A}_j(t \mid \omega_{n-1})\big] = \sum_{t_{n-1} \leq t_{(i)} < t} \frac{1}{[I - (i) - c(t_{(i)})]^2}.$$

Figure 3.3 plots the Aalen estimate of the cumulative hazard function displayed in Figure 3.2 versus duration in the job. The slope of the curve at a given duration gives the estimated hazard function for leaving a job after that duration. In Figure 3.3 the slopes of the curves for both black and white men become noticeably less steep as duration in the job increases, suggesting that the hazard function is a declining function of duration.[8]

One way of estimating the hazard function (under smoothing assumptions) is to regress the estimated log survivor probabilities on some function of duration. To illustrate this approach, we estimated two sorts of models:

$$h(u) = \alpha + \beta u + \gamma u^2 + \delta u^3,$$

and

$$h(u) = \alpha u^{\beta - 1}.$$

In the first, sometimes called a generalized Rayleigh model (see Gross and Clark, 1975), the hazard function is a polynomial function of u, the duration in the job. The second is the hazard function for a Weibull model. When $\beta = \gamma = \delta = 0$ in the first, or when $\beta = 1$ in the second, these models reduce to a single term, α, which implies that duration is exponentially distributed. Substituting these functions in (18) and solving for $A(u)$ yields the following expressions:

$$-A(u) = \alpha u + \beta \frac{u^2}{2} + \gamma \frac{u^3}{3} + \delta \frac{u^4}{4},$$

and

$$\log A(u) = \log \alpha + \beta \log u,$$

where $u > 0$ and $A(u) > 0$. These equations can be estimated by ordinary linear regression. Although the resulting estimators do not have optimal properties, they provide a quick and inexpensive method of checking the fit of these models.

Table 3.1 reports the estimated unstandardized coefficients from such regressions using the same data plotted in Figure 3.3. (Observations were weighted by the inverse of the width of the 95%

---

[8]Variation in the hazard function over time may also result from heterogeneity in the sample, which we are ignoring here, as we indicated at the outset of this section.

Table 3.1. Estimated parameters and R^2 for several models of the rate of leaving the first job in the CNALF for black and white men

	R^2	α	β	γ	δ
Polynomial					
1. Black men	.9539	0.384			
White men	.8876	0.642			
2. Black men	.9974	0.522	−0.017		
White men	.9830	0.967	−0.054		
3. Black men	.9985	0.561	−0.028	0.001	
White men	.9910	1.137	−0.121	0.005	
4. Black men	.9989	0.523	−0.009	−0.002	0.0001
White men	.9920	1.233	−0.182	0.014	−0.0004
Weibull					
Black men	.9719	0.534	0.846		
White men	.8670	1.038	0.728		

confidence interval to adjust for the known heteroscedasticity in $A(u)$ as a function of u.) At first glance the R^2 values for all five models (see Table 3.1) seem quite high. Yet addition of each higher-power term in t in the polynomial model improves fit significantly at the .001 level.

Panels (a) through (e) of Figure 3.4 show the residuals from the five estimated models versus duration in the job, along with the 95% confidence intervals for the estimated log survivor functions. If absolute fit of an estimated model is good, the residuals should not only be small but within the 95% confidence intervals. The polynomial hazard function with a single term clearly does not fit the data well for either black or white men [see panel (a) of Figure 3.4]. The Weibull model gives a much better fit for small durations but fits badly for durations above 7–10 years in the job [see panel (e) of Figure 3.4]. The polynomial hazard function with two terms fits the log survivor function fairly well for black men for durations under 18 years, which encompasses the large majority of the observation period for this sample; however, it does not fit well for white men [see panel (b) of Figure 3.4]. Undoubtedly the data on white men are difficult to fit because of the marked drop in the survivor function after 3 months, as we noted in the discussion of Figure 3.2. Addition of a third and then fourth term to the polynomial hazard function [see panels (c) and (d) of Figure 3.4, respectively] improves fit for both black and white men, but even the hazard function with four terms does not predict the log survivor function for white men well for durations under a year. Overall it seems that a fairly simply parametric model of the hazard function can describe these data reasonably well for black but not white men.

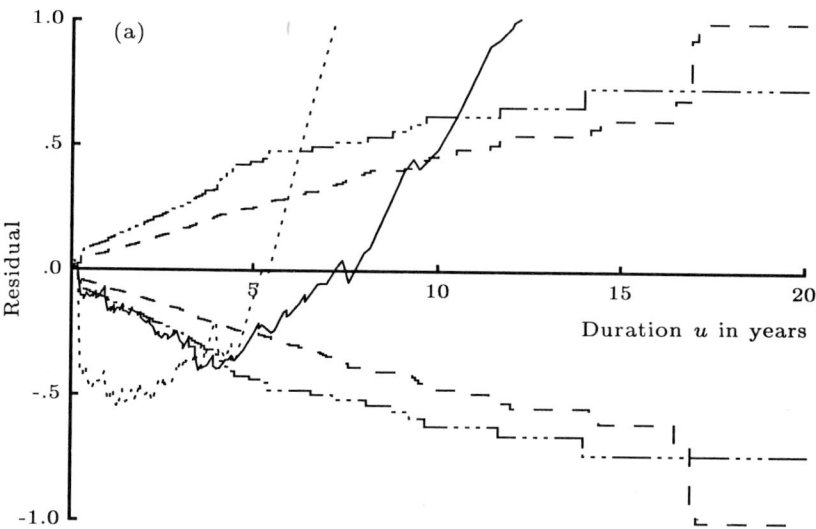

Figure 3.4. Residual ≡ (Aalen estimate minus the predicted value of $A(u)$) versus duration u, by race: (a) $h(u) = \alpha$; (b) $h(u) = \alpha + \beta u$; (c) $h(u) = \alpha + \beta u + \gamma u^2$; (d) $h(u) = \alpha + \beta u + \gamma u^2 + \delta u^3$; (e) $h(u) = \alpha u^{\beta-1}$. The solid and dotted curves denote the residual for blacks and whites, respectively; the dashed and dot-dot-dot-dashed curves denote the difference between the Aalen estimate of $A(u)$ and the 95% confidence intervals for blacks and whites, respectively.

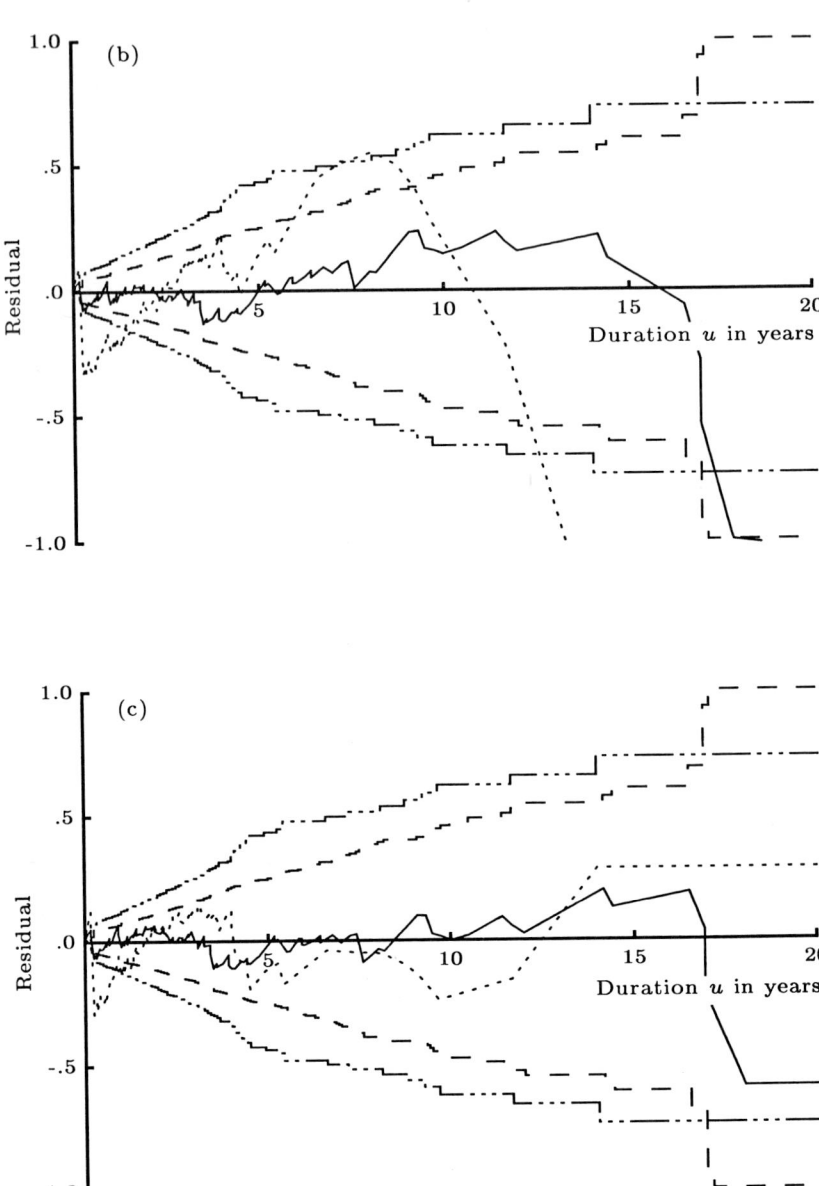

Figure 3.4. (*Continued*)

⟨ 3 ⟩   Terms for Populations of Event Histories

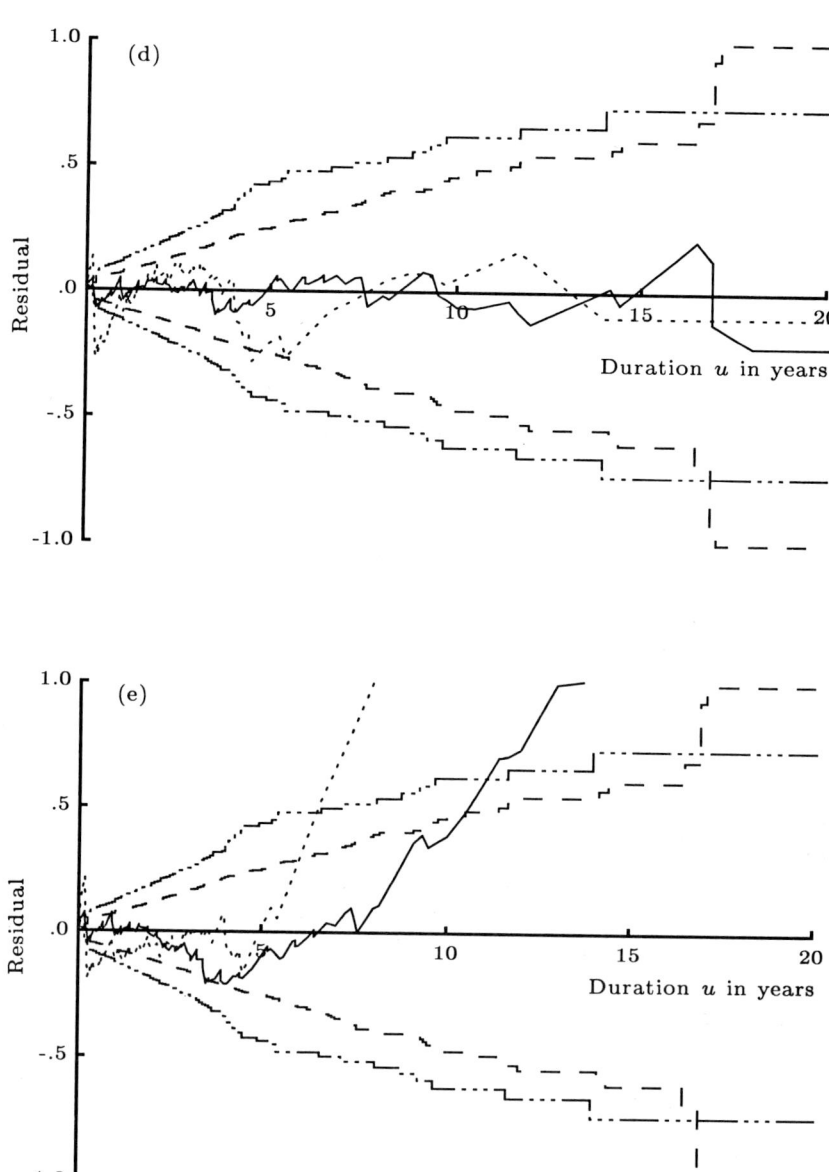

Figure 3.4. (*Continued*)

3.2.7 Conditional Transition Probabilities

When different kinds of events may occur, a useful concept is the conditional transition probability for the nth event at time $t = t_n$ (or after waiting time $u = u_n$), which may be defined in either of two equivalent ways:

$$m_{jk}(t \mid \omega_{n-1}) \equiv \Pr[Y_n = k \mid T_n = t,$$
$$T_{n-1} = t_{n-1}, Y_{n-1} = j, \omega_{n-2}]; \quad (20a)$$

$$m_{jk}(u \mid \omega_{n-1}) \equiv \Pr[Y_n = k \mid U_n = u,$$
$$T_{n-1} = t_{n-1}, Y_{n-1} = j, \omega_{n-2}]. \quad (20b)$$

These expressions give the probability that the nth event is a move to state $k \equiv y_n$, given that this event occurs at time t (waiting time u) and given previous history $\omega_{n-1} = \{t_{n-1}, y_{n-1}, \omega_{n-2}\}$. If Y's state space contains Ψ elements, there are Ψ^2 conditional transition probabilities for every moment in time. Note that

$$\sum_{k=1}^{\Psi} m_{jk}(t \mid \omega_{n-1}) = 1, \qquad (21)$$

because one and only one state k can be entered when any state j is left.

The terms "conditional transition probability" and "transition probability" are easily confused. The term transition probability refers to the probability of being in state k at a given time t, given that state j is occupied at an earlier time s (see Section 3.2.2). The two times s and t may be close together or far apart. Moreover, the number of events between s and t is unspecified. The individual may have changed from j to one or more intermediate states before moving to k. The term conditional transition probability refers to the probability of entering some state k, conditional on the event occurring at time t (waiting time u) to an individual in state j. The main thing to remember is that conditional transition probabilities are associated with the *occurrence of a particular type of event* (a change from j to k) *at a particular time*.

⟨3⟩ Terms for Populations of Event Histories

To estimate conditional transition probabilities, count the number of cases in a sample that have the history ω_{n-1} and move to state k at time t_n; then divide by the number of cases with the history ω_{n-1} that have *any* event at time t_n. The only practical problem is that the sample size must be quite large in order to have a reasonable number of cases whose nth event occurs at a given time t, let along enough with the same history ω_{n-1}. Consequently, empirical estimates of conditional transition probabilities often assume that these probabilities do not depend on previous history except for $j \equiv y_{n-1}$ and do not vary over time or with the number of the event. That is, it is common just to estimate m_{jk}. The assumption that conditional transition probabilities are independent of time and of past history is a necessary (though not a sufficient) condition for a time-stationary Markov process; see Section 4.2.

In our discussion of Figure 3.2, which displays a plot of the Kaplan–Meier estimate of the survivor function for black and white men in their first full-time job in the CNALF, we pointed out that the curve for white men drops sharply at 3 months. We suggested that this might come about because the first full-time job for many young men is a summer job that they hold only until school begins again. If this is so, we expect the conditional transition probability of returning to school (as opposed to leaving a job for any other reason) to be much higher for a job held 3 months than for one held for a shorter or longer time.

These ideas can be examined empirically by estimating conditional transition probabilities. Of all exits from the first full-time job in the CNALF, the estimated probability of returning to school is .122 for blacks and .398 for whites. By themselves, these figures are deceiving because the estimated conditional transition probability depends markedly on the duration in the job. When the duration is 3 months, the estimated conditional transition probability rises to .722 for blacks and to .837 for whites. On the other hand, for other durations, the estimated conditional transition probability is .035 for blacks and .135 for whites. Thus, an exit from the first full-time job is much more likely for whites than for blacks to be followed by a return to school, no matter how long the job has been held. Moreover, both blacks and whites are very likely to return to school after 3 months in the job and not very likely to return to school at other times.

3.2.8 *Event Transition Probabilities

We use the term **event transition probability**[9] to refer to the probability that the nth event consists of a move to state $k \equiv y_n$, given the previous history ω_{n-1}, including $j \equiv y_{n-1}$:

$$q_{jk}(\omega_{n-1}) = \int_{-\infty}^{\infty} f_j(s \mid \omega_{n-1}) \, m_{jk}(s \mid \omega_{n-1}) \, ds. \qquad (22)$$

An event transition probability bears obvious conceptual similarities to a conditional transition probability. However, a conditional transition probability refers to the probability of a particular transition at a *given time* whereas an event transition probability refers to the probability that the transition *ever* occurs. If conditional transition probabilities are time invariant, then they equal the corresponding event transition probabilities (assuming that *some* event eventually occurs with probability one). But, as we illustrated in Section 3.2.7, conditional transition probabilities are not constant over time for all substantively interesting processes.

Censoring generally prevents us from obtaining good empirical estimates of event transition probabilities. The outcome of events that have not yet occurred cannot be foretold—except for those processes known to have only a single possible outcome, for example, death. Consequently, the concept of an event transition probability is important primarily because of its role in constructing models of change (see Section 4.3), and not because of its utility in empirical analysis.

3.2.9 Conditional Survivor Function

The concept of a **conditional** (or **outcome-specific**) **survivor function** arises only when there are multiple outcomes, which are traditionally called **competing risks** in the biometric literature. Consider the population in state $j \equiv y_{n-1}$ at time t_{n-1}. Imagine that

---

[9]As noted in footnote 4, what we term an "event transition probability" is typically called a "transition probability" in portions of the literature on discrete-state stochastic processes, while what we term a "transition probability" is sometimes called an "interval transition probability" (e.g., see Howard, 1971).

there are Ψ independent[10] latent random variables, U_{jkn}^*, $k = 1$ to Ψ, giving the waiting time in state j until a transition to k. (The subscript n on U shows that it refers to the nth event.) These random variables are said to be **latent**, symbolized by the superscript $*$ on U, because the realization of U_{jkn}^* is unobserved unless it is less than the realization of every other latent variable, that is, unless $u_{jkn}^* < u_{jk'n}^*$, for all $k' \neq k$. This conceptualization is sometimes pictured as a race between competing independent processes in which only the first-place winner's name (k) and time (u_{jkn}^*) are recorded.

For example, consider a cohort of first marriages. Eventually each marriage ends, either because one spouse dies or because the couple divorces. There is a race between Death and Divorce, so to speak. The winner (why the marriage ends) and the winning time (the date it ends) can be observed, but usually not the finish time of the loser.

As its name suggests, a conditional survivor function is related to a survivor function. If the nth event has not occurred by some u, one may infer that $U_{jkn}^* > u$ for all k. Consequently, *if* the Ψ processes are independent,

$$G_j(u \mid \omega_{n-1}) = \prod_{k=1}^{\Psi} G_{jk}(u \mid \omega_{n-1}), \qquad (23)$$

where

$$G_{jk}(u \mid \omega_{n-1}) \equiv \Pr\bigl[U_{jkn}^* > u \mid \omega_{n-1}\bigr]$$

is defined as the conditional survivor function for the transition from j to k.

The conditional survivor function can be estimated with only a few simple modifications to the Kaplan–Meier procedure for estimating the (unconditional) survivor function. First, only the I^* events that consist of a move from state $j \equiv y_{n-1}$ to state $k \equiv y_n$ are counted in ordering the times of events in the sample. Thus, $t_{jk(1)}$ is the time of the first move to k among those in the sample with previous history ω_{n-1}, including entry into $j \equiv y_{n-1}$ at time

---

[10]Although the notion of Ψ latent competing independent processes is a useful conceptual device, it is important to note that statistical independence of such latent processes is not identifiable (see Tsiatis, 1975).

t_{n-1}. There may be moves from state j to states other than k (and moves from states other than j), but these are ignored in determining $t_{jk(1)}$ and the other ordered times. One treats any member of the sample in state j that has a transition to any state other than k as if it is censored at the time of its event. Thus, any member of the sample with a move from j to any state other than k before $t_{jk(1)}$ contributes to $c(t_{jk(1)})$. With these redefinitions of quantities, (9) provides an estimate of $G_{jk}(t \mid \omega_{n-1})$.

3.2.10 *Holding-Time Distribution Function

When an episode can end with one of several different events, it can be useful to describe change in Y in terms of the **distribution of holding times**—the lengths of episodes in state j that end with a transition to state k. The CDF of the holding time for a transition from state j to state k at the nth event, given previous history ω_{n-1}, $F_{jk}(u \mid \omega_{n-1})$, is defined as the probability that the waiting time in state j is less than u, given that the nth event consists of a move to state $k \equiv y_n$:

$$F_{jk}(u \mid \omega_{n-1}) \equiv \Pr[U^*_{jkn} < u \mid \omega_{n-1}]$$
$$= \Pr[U_n < u \mid Y_n = k, \omega_{n-1}].$$

Frequently, analysis is done with $f_{jk}(u \mid \omega_{n-1})$, the PDF of the holding time, rather than the CDF; by definition,

$$f_{jk}(u \mid \omega_{n-1}) = \frac{\mathrm{d}F_{jk}(u \mid \omega_{n-1})}{\mathrm{d}u}.$$

The concept of a holding-time distribution function can seem counterintuitive if causality is attributed to the condition. It may seem as though the outcome of an event (i.e., the kind of transition) has a causal effect on the length of time until the event occurs. In most social-scientific applications, such a causal interpretation is inappropriate. Instead the kind of transition should be regarded as a piece of information that may affect predictions about the waiting time in a state.

For example, assume that there are data on the length of marriages of men and women born in 1900 who first married in 1920. Suppose that the data are divided into two batches—one of marriages that end voluntarily (i.e., by separation, divorce, or desertion) and another of marriages that end involuntarily (i.e., with one spouse's death). Will the distribution of the length of marriage look the same in the two groups? Almost surely not! We expect the distribution to be highly skewed to the right with a mode under 5 years for the voluntarily ended marriages but to be skewed to the left with a mode over 30 years for the involuntarily ended marriages. In making these predictions, we are certainly not claiming that the outcome of marriage is ordained at its beginning. Rather, we are suggesting that knowing how a marriage ended improves predictions about how long it lasted.

Given the conceptual similarity between a waiting time and a holding time, and the simple relationship between the (unconditional) survivor function and the waiting-time distribution function, one might expect an equally simple relationship between the conditional survivor function and the holding-time distribution function. But though the two are related, the relationship is not a particularly simple one. In particular,

$$F_{jk}(u \mid \omega_{n-1}) \neq 1 - G_{jk}(u \mid \omega_{n-1}).$$

The holding-time distribution function is not easily estimated from empirical data because censoring prevents us from observing all cases that eventually make a transition from j to k. Like the concept of event transition probability, the holding-time distribution function is important primarily in constructing models of change in Y (see Section 4.3).

3.2.11 Instantaneous Transition Rates

In much of the discussion in the rest of Part II we focus on the concept of an **instantaneous transition rate**, or simply **rate** for short. We choose this focus because instantaneous transition rates and initial conditions determine state probabilities, transition probabilities, the mean number of events in an interval, and other attributes of an event history. On the other hand, knowing the state probabilities at any given time or transition probabilities for any pair of times s and t does not uniquely determine transition rates, except in special cases.

Instantaneous transition rates can be defined in several ways; all build on concepts discussed above. One way defines an instantaneous transition rate as the limit of a transition probability when the time interval is infinitesimal:

$$r_{jk}(t \mid \omega_{n-1}) \equiv \lim_{\Delta t \downarrow 0} \frac{p_{jk}(t,\, t + \Delta t \mid \omega_{n-1})}{\Delta t}.$$

Another way defines an instantaneous transition rate as the product of a hazard function and a conditional transition probability:

$$\begin{aligned} r_{jk}(t \mid \omega_{n-1}) &\equiv h_j(t \mid \omega_{n-1})\, m_{jk}(t \mid \omega_{n-1}); \\ r_{jk}(u \mid \omega_{n-1}) &\equiv h_j(u \mid \omega_{n-1})\, m_{jk}(u \mid \omega_{n-1}). \end{aligned} \qquad (24)$$

It follows from (21) and (24) that

$$\begin{aligned} \sum_{k=1}^{\Psi} r_{jk}(t \mid \omega_{n-1}) &= \sum_{k=1}^{\Psi} h_j(t \mid \omega_{n-1})\, m_{jk}(t \mid \omega_{n-1}) \\ &= h_j(t \mid \omega_{n-1}) \sum_{k=1}^{\Psi} m_{jk}(t \mid \omega_{n-1}) \\ &= h_j(t \mid \omega_{n-1}). \end{aligned} \qquad (25)$$

Thus the rate of leaving state j (i.e., entering any state k) is identical to the hazard function for state j.

According to (18), the hazard function determines the survivor function. Equation (25) implies that transition rates determine it too. Substitution of (25) into (18) followed by exponentiation yields

$$G_j(t \mid \omega_{n-1}) = \exp\left[-\int_{t_{n-1}}^{t} \sum_{k=1}^{\Psi} r_{jk}(s \mid \omega_{n-1})\, ds\right]. \qquad (26)$$

Rearranging (26) gives

$$G_j(t \mid \omega_{n-1}) = \prod_{k=1}^{\Psi} \exp\left[-\int_{t_{n-1}}^{t} r_{jk}(s \mid \omega_{n-1})\, ds\right]. \qquad (27)$$

But by (23),

$$G_{jk}(t \mid \omega_{n-1}) = \exp\left[-\int_{t_{n-1}}^{t} r_{jk}(s \mid \omega_{n-1})\, ds\right], \qquad (28a)$$

⟨3⟩   Terms for Populations of Event Histories   73

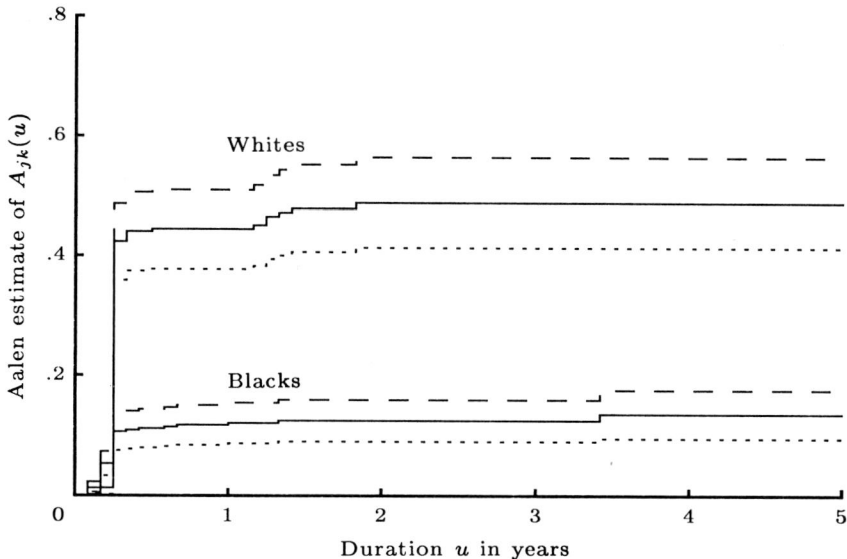

Figure 3.5. Aalen estimate of the cumulative transition rate $A_{jk}(u)$ for $j \equiv$ (the first full-time job in the CNALF) versus duration u, by race; $k \equiv$ return to school. Number of events/cases: 52/477 (blacks); 183/537 (whites). The solid curve denotes the Aalen estimate of $A_{jk}(u)$; the dashed and dotted curves denote the upper and lower 95% confidence intervals, respectively.

or

$$A_{jk}(t \mid \omega_{n-1}) \equiv -\log G_{jk}(t \mid \omega_{n-1}) = \int_{t_{n-1}}^{t} r_{jk}(s \mid \omega_{n-1})\,\mathrm{d}s, \quad (28b)$$

implying

$$-\frac{\mathrm{d}\log G_{jk}(t \mid \omega_{n-1})}{\mathrm{d}t} = r_{jk}(t \mid \omega_{n-1}). \quad (29)$$

Thus, estimating the instantaneous rate of a transition from j to k from Kaplan–Meier estimates of the conditional survivor function is exactly like estimating the hazard function from an estimated survivor function. According to (29), the slope of $A_{jk}(t \mid \omega_{n-1})$ at time t gives an estimate of the transition rate $r_{jk}(t \mid \omega_{n-1})$. Moreover,

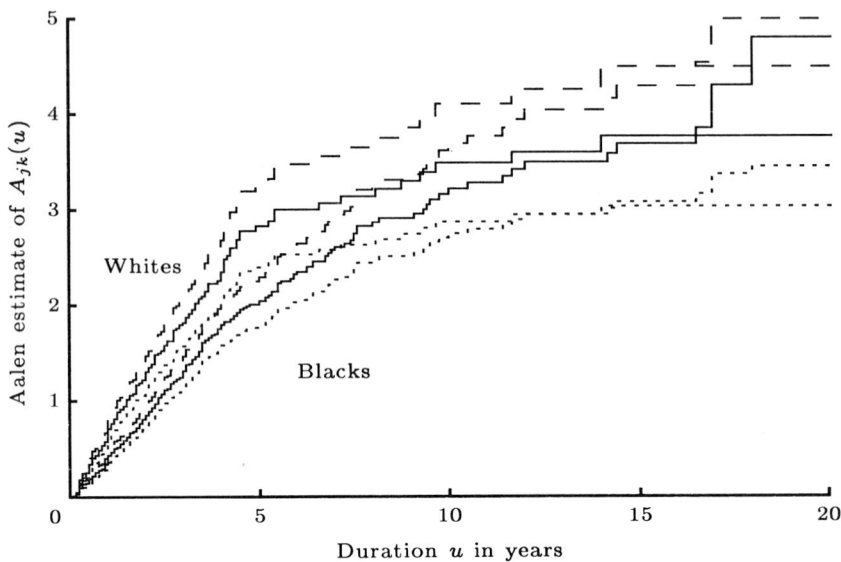

Figure 3.6. Aalen estimate of the cumulative transition rate $A_{jk}(u)$ for $j \equiv$ (the first full-time job in the CNALF) versus duration u, by race; $k \equiv$ all other activities. Number of events/cases: 416/477 (blacks); 345/537 (whites). The solid curve denotes the Aalen estimate of $A_{jk}(u)$; the dashed and dotted curves denote the upper and lower 95% confidence intervals, respectively.

Aalen's estimator in (19) is readily extended to provide an estimator of $A_{jk}(t \mid \omega_{n-1})$, the cumulative transition rate.

Figures 3.5 and 3.6 display plots of u, the duration in a job, versus $A_{jk}(u)$, where j stands for the first full-time job in the CNALF; they are based on the same data analyzed in Figure 3.3. In Figure 3.5, $k \equiv$ return to school; in Figure 3.6, $k \equiv$ all other activities (in most cases, a new job). The solid curves show the estimated cumulative transition rates; the dashed and dotted curves show the corresponding upper and lower 95% confidence intervals, respectively. The slope of a curve provides an estimate of the transition rate for the particular sample.

Notice first that the curves for black and white men are much more similar in both of these figures than in Figure 3.3. In Figure

⟨3⟩   Terms for Populations of Event Histories   75

3.5, the curve jumps at 3 months for each sample; the jump is just much larger for white than black men. The curve for each sample is extremely flat after 3 months, indicating that the rate of returning to school after 3 months in a job is almost nil. Clearly the rate of returning to school is strongly time dependent. In Figure 3.6, the curve for each sample is almost linear for the first 5 years; after that, the slope declines. Although the rate of leaving a job for a reason other than to return to school is smaller for black than white men, the curves for the two samples are clearly much more similar in Figure 3.6 than in Figure 3.3. These curves indicate that the rate of leaving the first job in the CNALF mainly differs for black and white men because the former are so much less likely to return to school after 3 months in the job.

Our final empirical example in this chapter concerns the effects of the NIT programs in SIME/DIME on marital stability. Panels (a) and (b) of Figure 3.7 display plots of the estimated cumulative marital-dissolution rate $A_{jk}(u)$ versus length of time on the experiment u, where j denotes "married" and k denotes "not married." Each panel contains two solid curves, one for couples with an NIT treatment and another for couples in the control group. The dashed and dotted curves give the upper and lower 95% confidence intervals, respectively. The solid curve for the treatment group lies outside the 95% confidence interval for the control group after roughly 0.50 years on the treatment for both black and white couples. At almost every time the slope of the solid curve is steeper for the group with the NIT treatment than for the control group, which means that the group with the NIT treatment has a higher rate of marital dissolution. Thus these plots suggest that the marital-dissolution rate of both blacks and whites is related to an exogenous variable—the NIT program.

Notice also that the slope of each solid curve varies slightly with the length of time on the experiment. Time variation in the slope is especially noticeable in the case of black couples with the NIT treatment [see panel (a) of Figure 3.7]. The curvature of these curves implies that the marital-dissolution rate of both couples in the control group and couples with the NIT treatment is time dependent, although not markedly so.

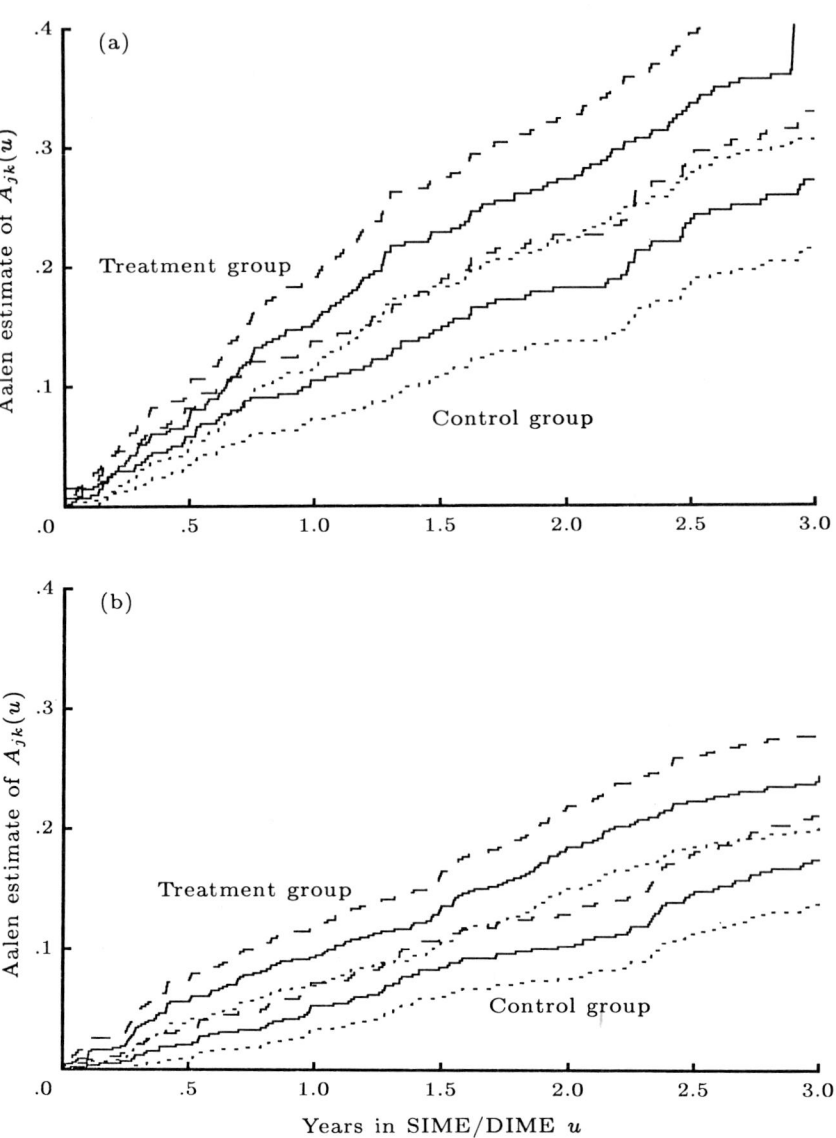

Figure 3.7. Aalen estimate of the cumulative marital-dissolution rate of (a) black couples and (b) white couples, $A_{jk}(u)$, versus years in SIME/DIME u, by treatment. The solid curve denotes the Aalen estimate of $A_{jk}(u)$; the dashed and dotted curves denote the upper and lower 95% confidence intervals, respectively.

3.3 Conclusions

In this chapter we have concentrated on defining, explaining, and illustrating fundamental terms and concepts appearing throughout Part II of this book. The terms considered in Section 3.1 describe various features of a single entity's event history (sample path), while those covered in Section 3.2 deal with features of a population or random sample of event histories.

As our examples show, the descriptive statistics discussed in Section 3.2 are highly useful in exploratory analyses of temporal data. Given appropriate data, various descriptive statistics can be computed within classifications of key explanatory variables, which often provides insight into potential sources of change in the phenomenon being studied. To pursue an exploratory approach to temporal analysis further, these statistics can be calculated within finer and finer classifications (and cross-classifications) of more and more exogenous variables and of past history. The sample size needs to be quite large to proceed very far with this approach, however. As one cross-classifies by more explanatory variables, any particular statistic measures the population value less precisely.

Since theory commonly guides our empirical analyses, we favor modeling the change process by parameterizing the dependence of transition rates on exogenous variables, time, and past history. The next chapter begins our discussion of this strategy.

4

Models of Change
in Qualitative Variables

Many valuable insights about change in qualitative variables can be gained by examining the simple descriptive statistics discussed in the previous chapter. But explicit stochastic models of the change process are equally valuable, perhaps more so. Henceforth we concentrate on explicit models and limit discussion to continuous-time models of transition rates. Our reasons for these choices are presented in Section 4.1.

Exactly what type of model should be used depends, of course, on the substantive application. Theory often suggests the broad qualitative features of a model and sometimes even has very specific implications. Although we cannot restrict discussion to a particular model outside the context of a given substantive problem, we can identify several classes of stochastic models that seem likely candidates for sociological applications. Section 4.2 contains a fairly nontechnical description of the main features of some of these.

Section 4.3 outlines how to derive implications of the classes of models discussed in Section 4.2 for some of the quantities defined in Chapter 3—the survivor function, the mean length of an episode, the mean number of events in a period, transition probabilities, and state probabilities. This section is addressed to readers who have a particular model in mind and wish to derive its mathematical implications for various quantities used to summarize event-history data. It presents some useful results and provides a guide to the technical literature that derives and discusses them.

Section 4.4 describes some important special cases of the classes of models considered in Section 4.2. It also summarizes the implications of these special cases for various outcomes. This section serves primarily to introduce particular models encountered in subsequent chapters. It also reports analytical results used in later empirical analyses.

4.1 Reasons for Continuous-Time Stochastic Models

All chapters in Part II except the previous one deal with explicit, continuous-time stochastic models of transition rates. Why do we pay so much attention to explicit models and so little to exploratory methods? And, given a focus on models, why do we limit discussion to continuous-time stochastic models? Lastly, why do we base these models on transition rates, which cannot be observed directly, rather than on some directly measurable quantity, such as the length of episodes or the count of events in a period? This section contains our answers to these questions.

4.1.1 Why Emphasize Explicit Models?

Most social scientists believe that construction, estimation, and testing of explicit models lie at the heart of social research, although they rely on a type of model (some form of linear model) quite different from those discussed in Part II of this book. Due partly to a dearth of explicit sociological theories, this approach to social research has been questioned by many advocates of "exploratory data analysis," developed by Tukey (1977). [For a balanced view on the value of confirmatory and exploratory approaches, see Tukey (1980).] Consequently, it seems desirable—even necessary—to review reasons for using explicit models. Advocates of exploratory data analysis make several claims, most of which we support. Since we do not oppose exploratory data analysis, we first note areas of agreement.

Supporters of exploratory data analysis claim that analysts should not rely *unthinkingly* on the normal (Gaussian) distribution.[1] We concur; in particular, we think that models based on the normal distribution are not usually the most natural way to approach

---
[1] Indeed, they object to unthinking reliance on any *particular* distribution.

the study of change in qualitative variables.[2] Consequently, Part II of this book does not discuss any models based on the normal distribution. On the other hand, the normal distribution does play a key role in our discussions of stochastic models of change in metric variables in Part III. In short, we believe that social scientists should neither automatically select nor invariably reject models based on the normal distribution; they should scrutinize the problem at hand to see whether or not such models seem appropriate.

Another claim is that social scientists would gain valuable insights by investigating more features of their data than has been customary in the Fisherian era. Means, variances and covariances are important summarizing statistics, but other features of data—order statistics (e.g., medians, quartiles, and "hinges"), the shape of a distribution, properties of outliers, and so forth—give useful information and have been neglected excessively in social research. This claim is somewhat related to the first. Means, variances, and covariances are sufficient statistics for multivariate normal distributions, that is, knowing them completely specifies such a distribution. But other attributes of data (e.g., the median) may be better ways of summarizing features of data (e.g., its central tendency) when the distribution is not normal. "Better" is used in the statistical sense of being more resistant (e.g., to outliers) and more robust (to variations in the distribution in the population).

Having agreed with the first claim, we can scarcely disagree with the second. We encourage those analyzing event-history data to utilize some of the ways of summarizing these data that were described in Chapter 3, especially log-survivor plots, which show the shape of the sample distribution of waiting times.

A third assertion is that analysts should pay more attention to the implications of models that they do estimate, and not rely so

---

[2] We are not claiming that continuous-time, discrete-state stochastic models cannot be constructed from normal distribution theory. In fact, implications about movement among discrete states can be derived from a continuous-state, continuous-time model driven by a normally distributed noise process (e.g., see Lancaster, 1972). However, it is almost always more complicated to build various realistic features (e.g., state dependence, duration dependence) into such models than for those treated in Part II of this book. In Chapter 16 we discuss the strategy of using continuous-state models to derive implications for certain qualitative outcomes.

heavily on a single summary measure of a model's fit, for example, the value of R^2. They should examine residuals to see in what ways (if any) the model's predictions deviate systematically from the data and use this information to build still better models.

This advice is sound, indeed central, to scientific procedure. Though several fairly simple classes of models are useful baselines in studying change in qualitative variables (see Section 4.2), we agree that one must address the question, How well does this model fit the data? Space limitations prevent us from pursuing this issue for all empirical analyses presented in this book. However, we do consider this question in detail for one particular case (see Section 10.6); we use this case to illustrate some ways of tackling this question for the kinds of models discussed in Part II. But improved methods for diagnosing a model's fit are certainly needed.

We disagree with at least one assertion currently popular with many (by no means all) champions of exploratory methods of data analysis. This is the claim that, We don't have anything but our data; consequently, our main task as analysts is to summarize the main features of data and to uncover patterns of relationships apparent within those data.

The popularity of this view with statisticians is understandable. But social scientists are not just social statisticians (in the original sense) preparing compendia of social facts. Social *scientists* have more information available than just the data at hand. First, there may be information about the main characteristics and patterns found in similar data on previous occasions. This provides a basis for predicting what will be found in the future. Moreover, social scientists may have formulated explanations for these empirical generalizations, which lead to specific hypotheses about what a particular body of data will reveal.

Sound social theories are the ultimate objective of social-scientific research. We do not believe that this objective can ever be reached if social scientists do not attempt to go beyond their immediately available data: to propose competing models, to estimate these models, to compare the predictions of these models with the data at hand and with other data (if possible), and finally to attempt to either extend or improve these models.

We are not overly sanguine about the level of development of social-scientific explanations and theories in many areas; they tend to be fragmentary, imprecise, and sadly lacking in generality. However, we think that explicit models have a place, even in areas at the frontiers of sociological knowledge, where understanding is so rudimentary that predictions are little more than vague hunches. In such situations exploratory comparisons of the descriptive statistics described in Chapter 3 may absorb much of the research effort. It may be informative to compare descriptive statistics within finer and finer classifications (and cross-classifications) of more and more explanatory variables and of past history. But a sample must be exceptionally large to proceed very far with this strategy. Consequently, after preliminary exploration of the data, it can be useful to formulate and estimate an explicit model that summarizes the main features and patterns observed in the exploratory phase of the analysis. We view such an inductively constructed model as a higher form of descriptive statistic because the model has implications that reproduce a variety of sample statistics closely, if not exactly. Obviously one cannot reach firm conclusions about a model constructed to fit patterns found in exploratory data analysis. But social research is a collective enterprise, and inductively built models guide subsequent research so that social scientists do not behave like naive rats in separate mazes.

In sum, we regard explicit models as both a valuable tool for the latter phases of exploratory research and as ways of encapsulating the best current explanation(s) of a particular phenomenon. Like other potent tools, models can be dangerous if one disregards instructions for using them. In particular, one must take care to check whether a model really fits the data well and be willing to refine or replace it when a model's predictions exhibit systematic discrepancies from the data.

4.1.2 Why Choose Continuous-Time Stochastic Models?

Many readers may find our emphasis on explicit models easier to swallow than our steadfast attention to continuous-time stochastic models. With a few notable exceptions, most sociologists choose discrete-time models, whether investigating change in qualitative or quantitative outcomes. What are the advantages of one type of model over the other?

The paramount reason for using continuous-time models is realism. Most outcomes studied by sociologists can change at any

⟨4⟩ **Reasons for Continuous-Time Stochastic Models**   83

moment, and not just at fixed intervals. Riots and wild-cat strikes can erupt at any time. People decide to marry, change jobs, and move from one geographic location to another without regard to any fixed time schedule. Of course, some transitions mainly occur at certain fixed intervals. For example, the political party of elected officials in the United States (though not in parliamentary systems) mainly changes at elections that occur at fixed intervals established by law.[3] Similarly, certain social psychological experiments are designed to proceed in a sequence of "trials," which are typically regarded as processes unfolding at discrete time intervals, even though the intervals are rarely equally spaced in real time. But we are hard pressed to identify *many* social phenomena that can only change at certain fixed intervals. For most social processes, continuous-time models seem more realistic than discrete-time models.

If continuous-time models are more realistic, why choose discrete-time models? Such models must possess advantages not shared by continuous-time models if they are preferred even when continuous-time models are more realistic. But to the best of our knowledge, discrete-time models have no noteworthy intrinsic advantages over continuous-time models. Yet even if discrete-time models are not intrinsically preferable to continuous-time models, they are certainly more familiar to social scientists, and methods for estimating and testing them are much more widely available. From a pragmatic viewpoint, these are important reasons why social scientists continue to rely on discrete-time models. Innovations are costly. Quite aside from the difficulty of overcoming social inertia, the long-run gain from an innovation must compensate for the costs of learning and implementing it. So if we are to make a convincing case for switching to continuous-time models, we must identify definite disadvantages to discrete-time models.

We begin by considering what some supporters regard as advantages of discrete-time models. Then we point out some of their disadvantages, which seem not to have been considered too carefully

---

[3]Note that even in this example there may be changes between the fixed time points, for example, an official who dies in office may be replaced by someone belonging to a different party. In treating party changes as a discrete-time process, we implicitly assume that intraterm changes are very infrequent and substantively unimportant.

in the past. We stress that we advocate the use of discrete-time models when the process being studied can only change at fixed time intervals. The discussion that follows pertains solely to situations in which continuous-time models are substantively more appropriate.

Advocates of discrete-time models usually cite *simplicity* as the main advantage of such models. Different authors seem to mean different things by this.

Some claim that discrete-time models are easier to work with mathematically. It is true that development of continuous-time models and derivation of their implications benefits from an elementary knowledge of the calculus. But we question whether the calculus is intrinsically any more difficult than the infinite-series expressions arising in discrete-time formulations. In fact, one of the major side-benefits of continuous-time models is their ability (in many instances) to summarize rather complicated dependencies over time with a comparatively simple mathematical function. Indeed, even in sciences in which discrete-time models are more realistic (e.g., many areas of population genetics), continuous-time models are used almost universally as approximations because they simplify the process of deriving implications.

For some authors, simplicity seems to mean that they believe social scientists will find discrete-time models easier to understand. If, as we argued above, continuous-time models often lead to expressions that are mathematically simpler than comparable ones for discrete-time models, this assertion (however kindly it is sometimes meant) can only be regarded as a derogation of the intelligence of social scientists. Surely social scientists can learn mathematical tools that thousands of physical scientists and engineers use routinely.

Another assertion often garbed in the cloak of simplicity is that discrete-time models make data analysis easier. Proponents of this position usually point out (correctly) that all data-collection schemes aggregate over time to some extent. They allege that it is simpler to build models based on the smallest unit of time distinguishable in the data. In short, they advocate that event histories (data on dates and outcomes of changes in Y) be converted into panel data (data on the value of Y for each of the minimally distinguishable units of time) and analyzed with standard discrete-time models of change in a qualitative variable Y. From a purely pragmatic viewpoint, following this advice tends to magnify the complexity and cost of analysis. More importantly, it can distort inferences. We begin with the pragmatic aspects of this issue.

For illustrative purposes, consider the marital histories collected in the Seattle and Denver Income Maintenance Experiments (SIME/DIME); these record the dates of changes in marital status to the nearest day for 5 years (1825 days ignoring leap years) for roughly 4500 women. These data supply over 8 million daily observations; however they contain only about 9000 different episodes (of marriage and singleness). Is it truly easier and less costly to analyze the former than the latter? We suspect that most social scientists will agree that it is not. Of course, the practical difficulties that arise in managing data do not depend only on the total number of observations (the sample size multiplied by the number of waves), but experience with very large social panels (e.g., the Michigan Panel Study of Income Dynamics and the National Longitudinal Surveys) has shown that total size is an important factor. Similarly, the cost of analysis is not determined solely by the total number of observations, but usually there is a rough correspondence.

Faced with detailed event histories, die-hard defenders of discrete-time panel models are likely to make two arguments. One is that a huge number of observations, though indeed difficult to manage and costly to analyze, greatly sharpens our ability to reject null hypotheses. So, for example, there should be no difficulty in measuring very precisely the impact of negative income tax (NIT) programs on marital stability, given the availability of over 8 million (daily) observations. The other point is that one can, if it seems desirable, avoid these costs by aggregating observations over time, for example, from days to months, months to years, and so forth. In short, there are always trade-offs between the quantity of information analyzed and the cost of the analysis. By choosing to use discrete-time models to analyze the panel data embedded within event histories, one can choose to purchase whatever amount of information one can afford.

Each argument involves a half-truth—it is true in a narrow sense, but dangerously misleading because of what it overlooks. For purposes of discussion, we assume that research funds are so generous that there is no concern with the cost of analysis, which we previously mentioned as a disadvantage of the panel approach. We also assume that the sample size is fixed because the value of a large sample is not under debate.

The first argument emphasizes the value of a large number of waves in a panel for estimating and testing alternative models. We do not dispute the general principle that more waves increase the information content of data on changes over time. However, we wish to challenge the implicit assumption that the number of waves by itself tells very much about the information value of a panel.

Consider again the case of SIME/DIME, which tells the marital status of each person on 1825 occasions (days). Would the information value of the data be as great if marital status was measured for 1825 seconds (about 30 hours), 1825 weeks (roughly 35 years), or 1825 years? The answer is clearly no.

Surely one would not choose the first design. Within a randomly selected 30-hour period, it is quite possible that none of the 4500 women would experience a change in marital status. The data's value as a panel would be nil—no greater than that of a cross-section. Neither would one choose the last design (1825 years) because sample members would be in a theoretically uninteresting state (dead) for roughly 95% of the observation period.

Observations for either 1825 days or 1825 weeks (35 years) are highly informative. For many purposes the latter is preferable. Weekly observations would let one study life-cycle aspects of marital formation and dissolution, effects of shifts in societal norms about marriage and family life, and so forth. For other purposes daily observations are preferable. One can maintain stable data-collection procedures more readily and report results sooner. Moreover, daily information may aid in untangling the temporal ordering of related processes, such as changes in a husband's and wife's employment statuses.

In sum, a large number of waves has value partly because it often means that the data cover a longer time span. But whether the overall observation period is too short or too long can only be decided within the context of a substantive problem, that is, by knowing the typical rates of change. By itself, the number of waves tells little about the information content of a panel.

The value of more waves is often expressed in another guise. If the total time span is fixed, more waves mean a smaller spacing between observations. Thus, both social-scientific and policy considerations dictated that SIME/DIME last about 5 years. Given this overall length, are not 5 waves (annual measurements) preferable to

⟨ 4 ⟩   **Reasons for Continuous-Time Stochastic Models**   87

2 (observations at the beginning and end of the experiment)? 60 waves (monthly) to 5? 1825 waves (daily) to 60? 160 billion waves (each second) to 1825?

Of these different designs, the two-wave panel has the least value, as is well known. With only two waves, many models that one might want to estimate and test are seriously underidentified, especially with regard to hypotheses pertaining to variation in the change process over time. Moreover, inferences about time-stationary models depend heavily on what one assumes is the true interval at which changes can occur. No one would maintain that people can change their marital status only at 5-year intervals; therefore, such a spacing in the data must surely be some multiple of the true spacing. As we mentioned in Chapter 2, Singer and Spilerman (1976b) indicated that what one postulates to be the true spacing can affect conclusions about the sort of model that could have generated the data. They illustrated their results for a two-wave panel with data on two states. They showed that for a given set of data, a very simple model—a time-stationary Markov chain—can be acceptable for a certain spacing, unacceptable for a closer spacing, again acceptable for a still closer spacing, and so forth. Additional waves aid in discriminating among different classes of potential models, and in this sense provide valuable information.

Now we turn to the other extreme of the designs mentioned above. Are 160 billion waves (measurements each second for 5 years) more valuable than 1825 waves (daily observations)? In particular, are they 86,400 (the number of seconds in a day) times as informative? Though the gain from measuring marital status to the nearest second (assuming it were possible) is surely positive, it is probably negligible. We have confidence in such a statement because a person is extremely unlikely to change marital status several times in a single day. Within any arbitrarily selected interval, measurements to the nearest second rather than the nearest day would increase only slightly the accuracy in measurements of the number of changes in marital status and in the length of stay in any episode. In fact, one would probably lose very little information if marital status were measured to the nearest week, and only a little more if it were measured to the nearest month.

Changing to annual observations would mean a serious (if not fatal) loss of information, however. The main gain from decreasing the space between observations is that it lets one distinguish sample members with zero or one change within an interval from those with multiple changes. With annual measurements, those who remain married the entire year cannot be distinguished from those initially married who separate and then remarry. Of those in SIME/DIME whose marriages broke up, roughly 20% remarried within a year. So unless the models used to analyze the data are chosen carefully, annual measurements would lead to an underestimate of the degree of "marital mobility" in the sample. Moreover, the information loss from annual measurements would not affect all sample members equally. Among those who separate, those with a high propensity to change their marital status are more likely to remarry within the year than those with a low propensity to change. Consequently, the information loss is related to the outcome being studied, a situation that invariably leads to biased inferences—unless the model estimated explicitly recognizes that multiple transitions may have occurred between waves.

Thus we conclude that there is value in having more waves in a panel covering a fixed period, that is, in having measurements spaced more closely together. The major benefit comes from choosing the spacing between waves to be sufficiently small that the probability of two or more changes between measurements is small. Further increases in the number of waves adds little.

One issue remains. Is there a gain, a loss, or no difference in using discrete-time rather than continuous-time models to analyze the panel observations embedded within event histories? Advocates of discrete-time models sometimes imply that one advantage is the substantial increase in the total number of observations. But do the 8 million daily observations in SIME/DIME contain any information not present in the 9000 episodes in these same data? Clearly they do not, since either type of data can be constructed from the other. In fact, unless one is very careful, treating these data as 8 million daily observations can be highly misleading: it exaggerates the information content of the data.

4.1.3 Why Model Transition Rates?

Some readers may question our formulation of models in terms of transition rates instead of quantities that can be observed directly, for example, the length of the waiting time in a state, the

⟨4⟩ Reasons for Continuous-Time Stochastic Models   89

number of events in a period, and the sequence of states occupied at a series of points in time. Traditional social-scientific research formulates linear (or sometimes nonlinear) regression models for one or more observable variables. Most social scientists seem to regard such models as "natural" and find it easy to translate their diffuse intuitions into testable hypotheses about properties of such models.

Consider, for example, how different analysts might use job histories to study labor mobility. Some would build a model of the length of jobs or of episodes of unemployment. Others might construct a model of the number of jobs held during a particular period. Others yet might analyze changes over time in the proportion of the sample that is employed. And still others might model the probability that those out of work find jobs or that those working leave their jobs within a given interval.

We have no objection to different analysts focusing on different aspects of a problem. However, it is important to recognize that these outcomes are not independent, as we stated informally in Chapter 3 and indicate formally in Section 4.3. For example, if the number of events in a period of given length increases, then the average of the observed time between successive events must decline.

The models typically used by social scientists ignore the interdependencies among different measurable outcomes. For illustrative purposes, assume that there are data giving histories of strikes in various industries and also data on a vector of explanatory variables, $\mathbf{x}$, describing each industry's internal social organization and environment. The most common methodological tool in social-scientific research is linear regression analysis, and many analysts would use it with these data too. One approach to analyzing event histories, proposed by Morrison (1970) in a study of migration, is to use them to define a dummy variable for each industry i, z_i, that equals 1 if any strike occurs within any arbitrarily selected period of length τ_z and otherwise equals zero, and then to regress z_i on $\mathbf{x}_i$, which assumes that $\mathrm{E}[Z \mid \mathbf{x}, \tau_z] = \boldsymbol{\beta}_z' \mathbf{x}$. A second approach that some find equally natural (e.g., see Feigl and Zelen, 1965; Felder, 1975) is to use event histories to define u_i, the waiting time between successive strikes in industry i, and then to regress u_i on $\mathbf{x}_i$, which assumes that $\mathrm{E}[U \mid \mathbf{x}] = \boldsymbol{\beta}_u' \mathbf{x}$. Still a third possibility (e.g., see Jorgenson, 1961) consists of measuring the total number of strikes within any arbitrarily selected period of length τ_n for each industry i, n_i, and then regressing n_i on x_i, which assumes that $E[N \mid x, \tau_n] = \beta'_n x$.

Though not widely recognized, each of the linear regression models implies that a Poisson process governs the occurence of strikes in industry i in a way that depends on i's value of x. The first linear regression approach implies that the hazard function h is given by

$$h = -\frac{\log[1 - \beta'_z x]}{\tau_z}.$$

But this equation implies that

$$E[U \mid x] = -\frac{\tau_z}{\log[1 - \beta'_z x]};$$

$$E[N \mid x, \tau_n] = -\frac{\tau_n}{\tau_z} \log[1 - \beta'_z x].$$

On the other hand, the second approach implies that

$$h = \frac{1}{\beta'_u x},$$

which in turn implies that

$$E[Z \mid x, \tau_z] = 1 - \exp\left[-\frac{\tau_z}{\beta'_u x}\right];$$

$$E[N \mid x, \tau_n] = \frac{\tau_n}{\beta'_u x}.$$

Finally, the third approach implies that

$$h = \frac{\beta'_n x}{\tau_n}.$$

However, this implies that

$$E[Z \mid x, \tau_z] = 1 - \exp\left[-\frac{\tau_z}{\tau_n}(\beta'_n x)\right];$$

$$E[U \mid x] = \frac{\tau_n}{\beta'_n x}.$$

⟨4⟩ Models of Event Histories   91

In short, if the same data are analyzed in all three instances, then each of these traditional linear regression approaches implies that the other two are wrong—all three cannot be true simultaneously. Which should one choose, and on what basis? This question has no simple answer. In fact, our purpose is not to answer it, but to insist that it be addressed. We argue that social scientists *must* consider the implications of their models for outcomes other than those used in estimation.

By formulating models in terms of transition rates, one can derive implications for each of the observable variables mentioned above, so that the linkages between different outcomes are made explicit. It is valuable to know these linkages for many reasons. From the theorist's viewpoint it means that a comparatively few basic postulates yield deductions pertaining to a wide range of observable outcomes—a few general statements replace many particularistic ones. The explicit linkages are also highly useful to the empirical analyst. They mean that the same model can be estimated and tested using various kinds of data. Consequently, analysts are less tied to particular sources of data and can compare their findings to those of investigators with different types of data. Finally, explicit linkages have advantages for social forecasters, who can use them to make predictions about the consequences of planned and unplanned alterations in social environments for outcomes other than those observed directly.

We must acknowledge that knowing these explicit linkages is a two-edged sword. A model with such global properties tends to make more stringent assumptions than a series of models for different observable outcomes. Hence it may fit data on any particular outcome less well than a model designed specifically to predict that outcome. On balance we think that the advantages of modeling transition rates—especially when one succeeds in explaining several different outcomes reasonably well—greatly outweigh this potential disadvantage. In fact, from our perspective even this apparent disadvantage is an asset: it increases leverage in assessing a model's fit and in diagnosing areas in which the model needs improvement.

4.2 Models of Event Histories

In the interest of parsimony we seek to use simple models. In this section we outline the main features of three broad classes of simple stochastic models. We begin with the most restrictive, binomial and multinomial models, which we regard as intrinsically unrealistic. We then turn to more complex models—continuous-time Markov and semi-Markov models. Even these are undoubtedly too simple to be very realistic in many situations, but they often provide a good starting point.

4.2.1 Binomial and Multinomial Models

In discrete-time analyses of categorical variables, investigators commonly begin with a model based on the assumption that the probability of being in a given state at one time point does not depend on the state occupied at the previous time point. Stated differently, this assumption means that a sample member's location in the state space at one moment gives no clues about its probable location at any future time—including the next moment. The discrete-time model resulting from this assumption is called the binomial model when there are two states and the multinomial model when there are three or more states. Given the widespread use of these models in discrete-time analyses, their continuous-time analogues may appear to be promising bases for event-history analysis. For the moment we simply assert that the continuous-time analogues of these models are almost always unrealistic; we show why in Section 4.4. Instead we focus on slightly more complex classes of models, which allow much richer and more realistic kinds of analyses.

4.2.2 Markov Models

Markov models assume that a sample member's location at some future time depends on its present location, but not on the path taken to reach the present state, that is, its past history. One way of stating the key assumption of a Markov model is that the instantaneous rate of a transition from state $j \equiv y_{n-1}$ to state $k \equiv y_n$ at a given time t depends only on j, k, and t—and not on the entire previous history ω_{n-1}:

$$r_{jk}(t \mid \omega_{n-1}) = r_{jk}(t), \qquad k \neq j. \tag{1}$$

Markov models also forbid self-transitions: $r_{jj}(t) = 0$.

Though this "history-free" assumption is not very realistic for sociological applications, it can be modified so that it is less restrictive than it seems at first, as we explain later. The Markov

⟨4⟩   Models of Event Histories   93

assumption obviously improves on the assumption underlying the binomial and multinomial models. Whether referring to the marital status of a person, the type of political regime of a nation, or the number of riots that a city has had, no social scientist would argue that knowledge of these outcomes at one time does not give valuable information for predicting them at a later time.

Applications of Markov models in the social sciences usually make the additional assumption that instantaneous transition rates are time-stationary:[4]

$$r_{jk}(t) = r_{jk}. \qquad (2)$$

The assumption of time stationarity greatly simplifies derivation of the implications of a Markov model. This simplification is important to the analyst who wants to estimate explicit stochastic models from panel or event-count data, but it rarely proves necessary in analyzing event-history data. Time stationarity plays a useful role in event-history analysis mainly when one needs to derive the implications of an empirically estimated model for various other observed quantities. This need may arise, for example, in social forecasting or in attempting to evaluate the fit of a model to the data (see the discussion in Section 10.6).

A simple conceptual device called **operational time** permits an elementary form of time variation in transition rates to be retained along with the mathematical simplicity of a time-stationary Markov process. Operational time $w(t)$ refers to a transformation of the natural time scale t in such a way that a Markov process which is not stationary in time t becomes stationary in time w. For example, suppose that time t refers to age and that all transition rates decline exponentially as age increases, that is, $w(t) = e^{-bt}$, where b is ordinarily an unknown parameter to be estimated. If change is a time-stationary process in w-time but not in t-time, one can derive various implications about changes in w-time using the simpler mathematics of time-stationary Markov processes and then convert to the natural time scale t through the substitution that $t = -\log w/b$. Sociologists who have used operational time to draw conclusions about

---

[4]Time homogeneity is another term that is sometimes used instead of time stationarity. We prefer the term *time stationarity* to avoid possible confusion between *population homogeneity* and *time homogeneity*.

certain kinds of time nonstationarity include Sørensen (1975) and Spilerman (1970).[5]

Unfortunately, operational time does not handle all forms of time nonstationarity. Although the transformation of time, $w(t)$, may have any mathematical form (for instance, it need not be a monotonic function), all transition rates must change over time in the same way. Operational time cannot handle situations in which some transition rates increase over time and others decrease. As a consequence, operational time is useful especially in dealing with age dependence in transition rates because a wide variety of individual behaviors appear to occur with declining frequency as age increases. For example, with increasing age, people seem to become less likely both to marry and to divorce, and less likely both to be fired (or laid off) and to leave a job voluntarily (until the age of retirement approaches). On the other hand, operational time is less useful in handling variation in transition rates over historical (calendar) time because some rates seem to increase when others decrease. For instance, in recent decades marital dissolution rates have risen dramatically while rates of marriage have stayed about the same or declined. When the business cycle improves over time, jobholders are both more likely to quit and less likely to be laid off. Consequently, it is almost always unrealistic to postulate a transformation of calendar time in which rates of change in marital status and in employment status are time invariant.

4.2.3 Semi-Markov Models

Semi-Markov models, also known as **Markov renewal models** in the technical literature, bear important similarities to Markov models. Like Markov models, semi-Markov models assume that transition rates (or equivalently, hazard functions and conditional transition probabilities) are independent of previous history. Unlike Markov models, they allow transition rates to depend on the duration in a state, that is, the length of time since the previous event, as well as on calendar time. Unlike Markov models, they also permit successive states to be the same. For example, they let one model the situation in which a person goes from one job in a given occupation to another job in the same occupation with no intervening

---

[5]Neither author used the phrase "operational time," however.

⟨4⟩ Implications of Semi-Markov Models

period in some other state. We can state the assumptions of a general semi-Markov model formally in either of the following equivalent ways:

$$r_{jk}(t \mid \omega_{n-1}) = r_{jk}(t \mid t_{n-1}),$$
$$r_{jk}(u \mid \omega_{n-1}) = r_{jk}(u \mid t_{n-1}),$$
(3)

where $j \equiv y_{n-1}$, $k \equiv y_n$, $u \equiv t - t_{n-1}$, and ω_{n-1} stands for past history. For a good introduction to the general form of semi-Markov model specified in (3), see Hoem (1972).

In general, the dependence of transition rates on the duration in state j may have any mathematical form. The particular form that is chosen varies, of course, with the substantive application. We introduce a few of the common choices in Chapter 7. Because of this duration dependence, transition probabilities in semi-Markov models generally depend on previous history, unlike the case of Markov models (see remarks in Section 4.3).

Because there are many mathematical challenges involved in deriving implications of semi-Markov models that assume transition rates depend on both the time of the previous event t_{n-1} and the duration in the state u, virtually all applications of semi-Markov models (and many general treatments, e.g., Pyke, 1961a,b and Howard, 1971) assume that transition rates depend only on duration and not on the time of the previous event, that is,

$$r_{jk}(u \mid t_{n-1}) = r_{jk}(u).$$
(4)

Through the device of operational time, discussed above, one can still allow certain elementary forms of dependence of transition rates on time t (Ginsberg, 1971). In particular, suppose that transition rates have the form in (4) in operational time $w(t)$, which transforms the natural time scale. One can then derive implications of the semi-Markov process in w-time and finally convert back into the natural time scale in order to draw conclusions about the process in t-time. As we commented earlier, operational time is useful especially for handling age dependence in transition rates. So through the device of operational time, one can construct semi-Markov models that include both duration and age dependence in transition rates. Consequently, for most social-scientific applications, semi-Markov models are considerably more realistic than time-stationary Markov models, which have usually been used in previous social-scientific applications.

4.3 Implications of Semi-Markov Models

In Section 4.1 we argued that an important advantage of explicit, continuous-time models of transition rates is that they have implications for a wide variety of directly measurable quantities. We now want to show how to derive a variety of implications for those classes of models that are the most promising candidates for immediate sociological applications—namely, those described in Section 4.2. To avoid redundancy, we focus on the implications of the semi-Markov model specified by (4), which includes binomial and multinomial models, renewal models, discrete-time Markov models, and time-stationary Markov models as special cases.

We concentrate on five main outcomes: the survivor function for a given state, the mean of the waiting time in a given state, the mean of the number of events in a given period, transition probabilities, and state probabilities. (For definitions of these terms, see Section 3.2.) These represent only a fraction of all outcomes that can be derived from semi-Markov models. But it is not our intent to provide an encyclopedic account of all derivable quantities or even to show how to derive the expressions that we have chosen to consider. Rather, we have two main objectives. First, we want to provide readers with a guide to a literature[6] that is oriented mainly to the interests of mathematicians and statisticians and secondarily to the concerns of physical scientists and engineers. Buried within this hoard of information are some genuinely useful—and surprisingly simple—nuggets that we want to call to the attention of the social-scientific community. Second, by revealing the intrinsic simplicity of these relationships, we hope to encourage more social scientists to try to formulate explicit continuous-time models of social processes.

Matrix notation greatly simplifies the expressions pertaining

---

[6]For a brief and lucid introduction to renewal models (a simple form of semi-Markov model), see Cox (1962). Cox and Miller (1965) gave a good introduction to both discrete-time and continuous-time Markov models with discrete states; they also included a very brief (pp. 350–356) treatment of semi-Markov models that provides a useful summary and simple illustration of some important results. Finally, for an exceptionally clear and extensive discussion of semi-Markov models, see Howard (1971), who stated results for many quantities other than those mentioned in this section.

⟨4⟩ Implications of Semi-Markov Models

to several quantities discussed below. So before turning to the results for particular outcomes, we define several matrices. All of the matrices are dimensioned Ψ by Ψ, where Ψ is the size of the state space of $Y(t)$. The key matrix (in the sense of defining the stochastic process) is the matrix of transition rates[7] $\mathbf{R}(u)$, whose jkth element is $r_{jk}(u)$, where u is the waiting time in state j:

$$\mathbf{R}(u) \equiv \begin{pmatrix} r_{11} & r_{12} & \cdots & r_{1\Psi} \\ r_{21} & r_{22} & \cdots & r_{2\Psi} \\ \vdots & \vdots & & \vdots \\ r_{\Psi 1} & r_{\Psi 2} & \cdots & r_{\Psi\Psi} \end{pmatrix}. \tag{5}$$

As indicated in (10) below, $\mathbf{R}(u)$ defines the matrix $\mathbf{G}(u)$, which has the survivor function $G_j(u)$ in every element of the jth row:

$$\mathbf{G}(u) \equiv \begin{pmatrix} G_1(u) & G_1(u) & \cdots & G_1(u) \\ G_2(u) & G_2(u) & \cdots & G_2(u) \\ \vdots & \vdots & & \vdots \\ G_\Psi(u) & G_\Psi(u) & \cdots & G_\Psi(u) \end{pmatrix}. \tag{6}$$

Next we define the so-called core matrix $\mathbf{C}(u)$ as

$$\mathbf{C}(u) \equiv \mathbf{G}(u) \# \mathbf{R}(u), \tag{7}$$

where $\#$ denotes the Hadamard product.[8] This means that the jkth element in $\mathbf{C}(u)$ is

$$c_{jk}(u) \equiv G_j(u) r_{jk}(u). \tag{8}$$

Equivalent definitions of $c_{jk}(u)$ (preferred by some authors) are

$$c_{jk}(u) \equiv f_j(u) m_{jk}(u) \equiv f_{jk}(u) q_{jk}, \tag{9}$$

---

[7] We stress that $\mathbf{R}(u)$ is the matrix of *transition rates*. It is *not* the so-called infinitesimal generator or intensity matrix sometimes mentioned in the literature on Markov processes. The latter is similar to $\mathbf{R}(u)$ except that the main diagonal contains the negative of the hazard function instead of the rate of the self transition.

[8] The Hadamard product of two matrices $\mathbf{A}$ and $\mathbf{B}$, though not very familiar to sociologists, is the simplest form of matrix product. By definition, c_{jk}, the jkth element of $\mathbf{C} \equiv \mathbf{A} \# \mathbf{B}$, equals $a_{jk} b_{jk}$. Note that $\mathbf{A}$ and $\mathbf{B}$ must have identical dimensions to form their Hadamard product.

where $f_j(u)$ is the PDF of the waiting time in state j, $m_{jk}(u)$ is the conditional probability of a transition from state j to state k after waiting time u, $f_{jk}(u)$ is the PDF of the holding time in state j before a transition to state k, and q_{jk} is the event transition probability from state j to state k (see definitions of these terms in Section 3.2).

4.3.1 Survivor Function

Recall from Section 3.2 that the survivor function is the probability that those with previous history ω_{n-1}, including entry into state $j \equiv y_{n-1}$ at time t_{n-1}, are still in state j after a waiting time u; it is denoted by $G_j(u \mid \omega_{n-1})$. Although we gave the expression relating the survivor function to transition rates in (20) in Chapter 3, it deserves repetition because of its central role both in estimation equations and in expressions for other quantities derivable from a semi-Markov model:

$$G_j(u \mid \omega_{n-1}) = \exp\left[-\int_0^u \sum_{k=1}^{\Psi} r_{jk}(s \mid \omega_{n-1})\,ds\right]. \qquad (10)$$

Since transition rates in a semi-Markov model do not depend on previous history [see (3)], equation (10) reduces to the following for a semi-Markov model:

$$G_j(u \mid \omega_{n-1}) = \exp\left[-\int_0^u \sum_{k=1}^{\Psi} r_{jk}(s \mid t_{n-1})\,ds\right], \qquad (11)$$

and this simplifies still further in the class of semi-Markov models in which transition rates do not depend on the time of the previous event, t_{n-1} [see (4)]:

$$G_j(u \mid \omega_{n-1}) = \exp\left[-\int_0^u \sum_{k=1}^{\Psi} r_{jk}(s)\,ds\right]. \qquad (12)$$

For time-stationary semi-Markov models, transition rates do not depend on time [see (2)], so that we obtain

$$G_j(u \mid \omega_{n-1}) = \exp\left[-u \sum_{k-1}^{\Psi} r_{jk}\right]. \qquad (13)$$

⟨4⟩ Implications of Semi-Markov Models   99

4.3.2 *Mean of the Waiting Time

By definition the mth moment of U_{jn}, the waiting time in state j between the $(n-1)$th and nth events, given that $j \equiv y_{n-1}$ is entered at time t_{n-1} and previous history ω_{n-1}, is

$$\mathrm{E}[U_{jn} \mid \omega_{n-1}] = \int_0^\infty u^m f_j(u \mid \omega_{n-1}) \, du. \tag{14}$$

But

$$f_j(u \mid \omega_{n-1}) = G_j(u \mid \omega_{n-1}) \sum_{k=1}^{\Psi} r_{jk}(u \mid \omega_{n-1}). \tag{15}$$

Therefore,

$$\mathrm{E}[U_{jn} \mid \omega_{n-1}] = \int_0^\infty u^m G_j(u \mid \omega_{n-1}) \sum_{k=1}^{\Psi} r_{jk}(u \mid \omega_{n-1}) \, du. \tag{16}$$

In particular, the mean (or first moment) is

$$\mathrm{E}[U_{jn} \mid \omega_{n-1}] = \int_0^{\Psi} u\, G_j(\omega_{n-1}) \sum_{k=1}^{\Psi} r_{jk}(u \mid \omega_{n-1}) \, du. \tag{17}$$

For a time-stationary Markov model, the above simplifies to

$$\mathrm{E}[U_{jn} \mid \omega_{n-1}] = 1 \Big/ \sum_{k=1}^{\Psi} r_{jk}. \tag{18}$$

4.3.3 *Mean of the Number of Events in a Period

Recall from Section 3.2 that the number of changes to state k in the period $(s,t]$, given $j \equiv y(s)$, is denoted by the random variable $N_{jk}(s,t)$. One would like to know the moments of this random variable, especially its mean. These moments are difficult to derive for a general semi-Markov model except when $s = t_0$. Therefore we focus on this case, assuming for simplicity of notation that $t_0 = 0$.[9]

---

[9] For a time-stationary semi-Markov model, the expression for $\mathrm{E}[N_{jk}(s, s+t)]$ is identical to that for $\mathrm{E}[N_{jk}(0,t)]$.

Let $N(0, t]$ denote the Ψ by Ψ matrix that has $N_{jk}(0, t]$ as its jkth element and let $E[N(0, t]]$ denote the matrix whose jkth element is the mean (first moment) of $N_{jk}(0, t]$. Howard [1971, pp. 736–740, especially his equation (11.12.13)] showed that

$$E^*[N(0, v]] = [I - C^*(v)]^{-1} - I, \qquad (19)$$

where a superscript * denotes the Laplace transform of the function.[10] (The left-hand side of (19) denotes the Laplace transform of the expected value of $N(0, t]$, and *not* the expected value of the Laplace transform of $N(0, t]$.) Howard also gives an expression for the variance of $N(0, t]$—see his equation (11.12.21)—and describes how to find higher moments of $N(0, t]$.

4.3.4 *Transition Probabilities

We denote the probability of a transition from state j at time s to state k at time t by $p_{jk}[s, t]$ and the matrix of transition probabilities by $P[s, t]$. It turns out to be quite complicated to derive an expression for transition probabilities in a semi-Markov model unless s equals the time of an event. So we assume that $s \equiv t_n$, where n may have any permissible value.[11] Then [see Howard, 1971, equation (11.5.6) on p. 710],

$$P^*(t_n, t) = [I - C^*(v)]^{-1} [G^*(v) \# I]. \qquad (20)$$

Howard (1971, pp. 741–745) also discussed the more general case in which s does not refer to the time of an event.

[10] Let $g(t)$ be a function of t (usually time in our applications) such that $g(t) = 0$ for $t < 0$. We denote the Laplace transform of $g(t)$ by $g^*(v)$ and define it as:
$$g^*(v) \equiv \int_0^\infty e^{-vt} g(t) \, dt.$$
Because of their wide usage in mathematical problems, Laplace transforms of common functions are tabulated extensively; see especially the Bateman Manuscript Project (Erdelyi, 1954). For a very short but clear introduction to Laplace transforms, see Cox (1962, pp. 7–15) or Howard (1971, pp. 695–709).

[11] For a time-stationary semi-Markov model, the expression is the same, however, whether or not s equals the time of an event.

4.3.5 *State Probabilities

Given the matrix of transition probabilities, the distribution of state probabilities $\mathbf{p}(t)$ is easily shown to be

$$\mathbf{p}(t) = \mathbf{p}(t_n)' \mathbf{P}(t_n, t). \tag{21}$$

Notice that in general one can write an expression for $\mathbf{p}(t)$ only if its value at an earlier time is known, which we have specified to be the time of the nth event, t_n, for consistency with our expression for transition probabilities.

Some semi-Markov models have a so-called steady-state or equilibrium distribution, usually denoted by $\mathbf{p}(\infty)$ to indicate that this distribution is reached in the long run. When an equilibrium distribution exists,

$$p_k(\infty) = \lim_{\Delta t \to \infty} p_{jk}(0, \infty), \tag{22}$$

for all j and k.

4.4   *Particular Models

In this section we consider several special cases of a general semi-Markov model. Most arise in discussions of topics in later chapters. All but the first are actually continuous-time Markov models, which assume that transition rates do not depend on either time or past history, and that a state left cannot be immediately reentered. Despite these restrictions, the particular models that we treat are still fairly general and provide useful benchmarks for a wide variety of substantive applications in the social sciences. However, only a few have yet been used by social scientists to any great extent.

Our discussion of each model has three main parts: (1) a formal statement of its assumptions, (2) a brief review of its past and potential applications, and (3) a report of its implications for two of the many quantities derivable from its assumptions (see Section 4.3). The two quantities are the mean number of events in a period $(0, t]$ and transition probabilities. Since all models considered in this section have time-stationary transition rates, we do not repeat the equations for the survivor function, which is given by (13); the mean waiting time, which is given by (18); or the distribution of state probabilities, which is a simple function of the transition probabilities [see (21)]. This section is intended primarily to provide reference materials for topics in subsequent chapters.

4.4.1 Flow Diagrams

Figure 4.1 gives an overview of the models discussed in this section; it describes each model in terms of a **flow diagram**. Like the causal diagrams that sociologists so often use to depict causal relationships among variables, flow diagrams ordinarily provide a better intuitive idea of a model's key assumptions than the corresponding mathematical statements. (The mathematical statements are necessary, however, to derive a model's implications.) As a piece of abstract artwork, a flow diagram closely resembles a causal diagram. However, interpretation of symbols in the two types of diagrams is entirely different.

As in a causal diagram, the two main components of a flow diagram are boxes and arrows, each of which is usually labeled in some way. In a flow diagram, a **box** represents a *state* or possible value of Y, and not a *variable*. A flow diagram contains Ψ boxes, one for each of Y's states. (Recall that Ψ is the size of Y's state space.) Suppose $Y(t)$ is a dichotomous variable denoting a person's marital status at time t, and $1 \equiv$ unmarried and $2 \equiv$ married. Then a flow diagram describing change in marital status would have two boxes, one labeled either "1" or "unmarried" and another marked "2" or "married."

The second main component of a flow diagram is an **arrow**, which indicates a *permissible* transition or flow from the box at the arrow's tail to the box at the arrow's head, and not a *causal* relationship. Thus, an arrow from box 1 to box 2 shows that a member of the population who happens to occupy state 1 *may* move directly to state 2. The absence of an arrow from box j to box k shows that a direct transition from state j to state k may not occur—it has probability zero. In general, semi-Markov models allow direct transitions from state j to state j (self transitions); this is indicated in a flow diagram by an arrow that both starts and ends in box j. Continuous-time Markov models do not allow transitions from state j to state j. Note that only the first model in Figure 4.1 [panel (a)] has an arrow from a box to itself.

The symbol over an arrow denotes the *instantaneous rate* of a *transition* from the state at the tail of the arrow (j) to the state at the head of the arrow (k), and *not a path or regression coefficient*. In general, such a transition rate is labeled $r_{jk}(t)$. However, the subscripts are usually dropped in models in which many transition

⟨4⟩ *Particular Models 103

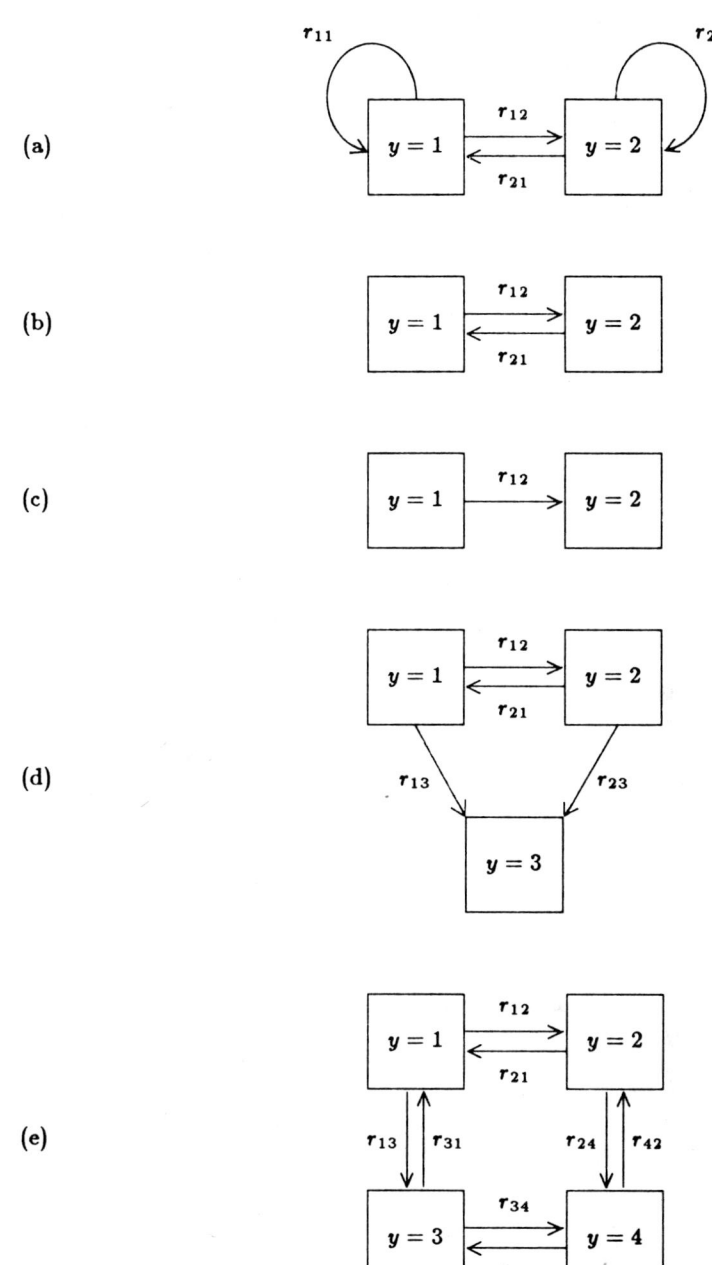

Figure 4.1. Flow diagrams for models discussed in Chapter 4.

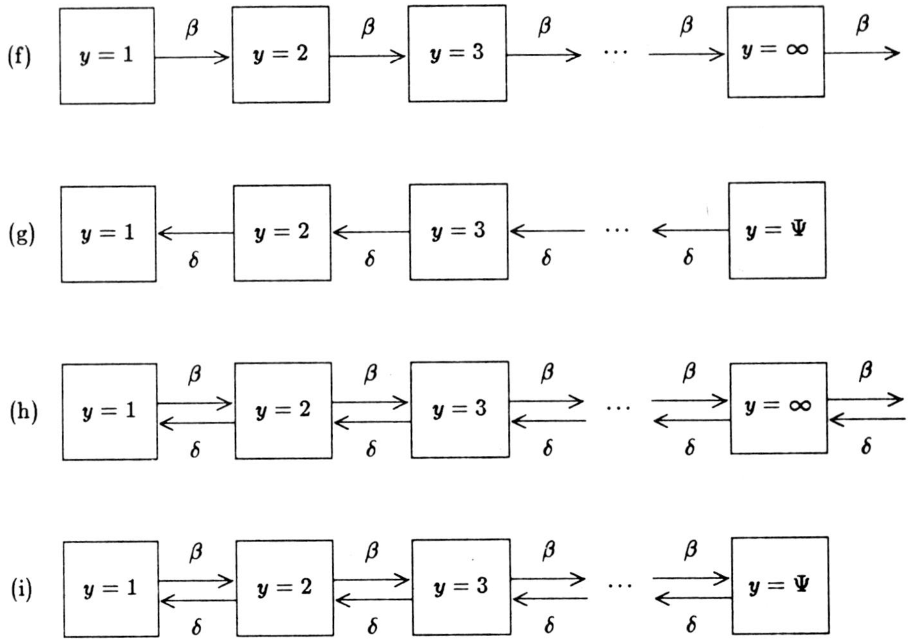

Figure 4.1. (Continued)

rates are identical. For example, in the pure growth (Poisson) model in panel (f) of Figure 4.1, only a direct transition to state $j+1$ is possible for any given state j. Moreover, $r_{j,j+1}$ has the same value for every j, so for simplicity we denote it by β.

4.4.2 Two-state Semi-Markov Model

As depicted in panel (a) of Figure 4.1, this model assumes that $Y(t)$ is dichotomous. Following our convention of labeling states of Y from 1 to Ψ, we label the states of Y by 1 and 2. The model allows both self-transitions and transitions from each state to the other. The matrix of transition rates corresponding to this model is

$$\mathbf{R}(u) = \begin{pmatrix} r_{11} & r_{12} \\ r_{21} & r_{22} \end{pmatrix}. \tag{23}$$

Given the widespread usage of dichotomous variables in social research, the two-state, time-stationary semi-Markov model would appear to have broad applicability. To the best of our knowledge, however, the most general version of this model has not yet been applied in empirical social research. Most social scientists (e.g., Singer and Spilerman, 1974) commenting on this (and other) semi-Markov models have viewed self-transitions as unrealistic. This is certainly true in some instances—people do not move from unmarried to unmarried, or from unemployed to unemployed. But in some social settings self-transitions do occur: sometimes an event occurs (e.g., a person changes jobs, a country changes political regimes), and some dichotomous attribute has the same value before and after the event. The "event" consists of an observed change or decision point, but the new status does not differ appreciably from the prior status. We believe that models incorporating self-transitions should not be dismissed out of hand. Imaginative sociologists may yet discover that such models provide meaningful analogues for various aspects of social systems.

Let $h_1 \equiv r_{11}+r_{12}$, $h_2 \equiv r_{21}+r_{22}$, $A \equiv r_{12}+r_{21}$, $B \equiv 1-e^{-At}$, and $k \equiv 3-j$, where $j = 1, 2$. Then the implications of the two-state, time-stationary semi-Markov model are as follows:

Mean Number of Events in Period $(0,t]$—

$$E[N_{jj}(0,t]] = \frac{r_{kj} h_j At + (r_{jj} r_{jk} - r_{jk} r_{kj}) B}{A^2};$$

$$E[N_{jk}(0,t]] = \frac{r_{jk} h_k At + r_{jk}(r_{jk} - r_{kk}) B}{A^2}.$$

(24)

Transition Probabilities—

$$p_{jk}(0,t) = 1 - p_{jj}(0,t) = p_j(\infty) B, \qquad (25)$$

where

$$p_j(\infty) = \frac{r_{kj}}{A} \equiv \frac{r_{kj}}{r_{12}+r_{21}}. \qquad (26)$$

It is interesting to note that transition probabilities for the two-state, time-stationary semi-Markov model do not depend on the values of r_{11} or r_{22}, the rates of the self-transitions. This fact means that the rates of self-transitions for this model cannot be estimated from panel data.

4.4.3 Alternating Renewal Model

The alternating renewal (AR) model is one of the simplest and potentially most useful continuous-time stochastic models. It is the special case of the previous model in which direct transitions from 1 to 1 and from 2 to 2 are not permitted. Thus $r_{11} = r_{22} = 0$ by assumption. [See panel (b) of Figure 4.1.] The term "alternating" arises because an event signals a move from one state to the other, so that every population member alternates between the two states over time.

One of the first sociologists to have discussed the AR model (though not by this name) is Coleman (1964a, Chapter 5), who proposed it as a model of voting intentions and other individual attitudes. More recently it has been used as a baseline model of changes in marital status (Hannan, Tuma, and Groeneveld, 1977a), of changes in employment status (Tuma and Robins, 1980), and of conformity to peer influence (Drazga, 1978). Given the popularity of dichotomous dependent variables among social scientists and improved methods of estimating the AR model (see Chapter 5 and also Singer and Spilerman, 1974), usage of the AR model by social scientists seems likely to increase.

The implications of the AR model for the mean number of events in a period and for transition probabilities are obtained by setting $r_{11} = r_{22} = 0$ in equations (24) and (25), respectively. Note that for given values of r_{12} and r_{21}, the AR model has exactly the same transition probabilities as the more general two-state, time-stationary semi-Markov model. Therefore, panel data cannot be used to distinguish the AR model from the more general two-state, time-stationary semi-Markov model. However, the mean number of events is smaller for the AR model, as one would expect intuitively. Thus data on counts of events allow the two models to be distinguished empirically.

4.4.4 Loss Model

The loss (L) model, which we also sometimes call the model of a single nonrepeatable event, is the special case of the AR model in which one state (say, 2) cannot be left, once it is entered. Any state with this property is commonly called an absorbing state (or occasionally a trapping state). This property of state 2 is depicted in the flow diagram for the L model [see panel (c) of Figure 4.1] by

⟨4⟩ *Particular Models

the absence of any arrows with tails in box 2; it is stated formally as $r_{2k} = 0$ for all k.

We call this the "loss" model because state 2 typically denotes some form of loss, for example, death of a person, failure of a firm, or demise of a social movement. The first sociologist to mention this model again seems to have been Coleman (1964a, Chapter 8). Social scientists have not used it widely, perhaps because of the unrealistic assumption that r_{12} (e.g., the mortality rate) does not depend on time.

The implications of the loss model are found by setting $r_{11} = r_{21} = r_{22} = 0$ in the corresponding equations for the two-state, time-stationary semi-Markov model.

4.4.5 The Binomial Model Reconsidered

Earlier we claimed that binomial and multinomial models almost never provide a realistic baseline for social-scientific applications of continuous-time models of change in qualitative variables. We argued that time-stationary Markov processes are considerably more realistic, especially when extended in ways outlined in Chapters 5 through 9. To buttress this claim, we consider the circumstances under which the AR model reduces to the still simpler binomial model. We could make a similar point about the multinomial model for Ψ possible outcomes using a time-stationary Markov model with Ψ states.

Binomial and multinomial models assume that the probability of being in a given state (say, k) at one time is independent of the state occupied at any previous time point. We can state this formally in the following way:

$$p_{jk}(0, t) = p_{kk}(0, t).$$

In the case of the two-state model, the above equation means that for the binomial model to apply, it must be the case that

$$p_{12}(0, t) = p_{22}(0, t).$$

Substitution of (25) into the above equation gives

$$\frac{r_{jk}}{A} e^{-At} = 1 - \frac{r_{kj}}{A} e^{-At}.$$

Straightforward algebraic manipulation yields

$$e^{-At} \equiv e^{-(r_{12}+r_{21})t} = 0. \qquad (27)$$

For (27) to hold in general it must be true that $r_{12} + r_{21}$ is infinite, that is, that the rate of change from one state to the other is infinitely rapid, implying that the mean duration in a state is zero. For virtually all commonly encountered social processes, the average duration in a state seems to have a positive, nonzero length. We note, however, that panel studies in which the interval between waves of the panel are long (i.e., t is large relative to the mean waiting time in a state), may *appear* to be generated by a binomial model. To us this suggests a deficiency of the panel design when the spacing between waves is large rather than the intrinsic realism of the binomial model. Consequently, we do not pay further attention to binomial and multinomial models in the chapters that follow.

4.4.6 Alternating Renewal and Loss Model

At least one assumption of the AR model makes it extremely unrealistic for social-scientific applications: it assumes that every member of the population alternates between states 1 and 2 forever. But change in a dichotomous dependent variable is often interrupted by some form of loss or attrition of sample members. For example, people selected to participate in a panel study cannot always be followed for the entire observation period. Some die; others move and cannot be located; still others get exasperated with the deluge of questions and refuse to be interviewed any more. Sample attrition also occurs in following other social units, for example, firms, and countries. By combining the AR model with the L model, one can model change in a dichotomous dependent variable *and* the process of sample attrition simultaneously. Combining the AR and L models is especially helpful when sample attrition or other losses are related to the value of Y, that is, when the rate of transition to state 3 (lost) depends on the value of y, $r_{13} \neq r_{23}$. We can state the assumptions of the alternating renewal and loss (ARL) model formally in terms of the matrix of transition rates:

$$\mathbf{R}(u) = \begin{pmatrix} 0 & r_{12} & r_{13} \\ r_{21} & 0 & r_{23} \\ 0 & 0 & 0 \end{pmatrix}. \tag{28}$$

Panel (d) of Figure 4.1 gives the flow diagram for the ARL model.

The ARL model has been applied by Tuma, Hannan, and Groeneveld (1979) to the process of changing marital status when

⟨4⟩ *Particular Models

couples may also drop out of an experiment. It has also been discussed by Tuma and Robins (1980) as a way of investigating changes in employment status when respondents leave the observed sample at a rate dependent on their employment status.

The implications of the ARL model are:

Mean Number of Events in Period $(0, t]$—

$$\mathrm{E}\big[N_{jj}(0,t]\big] = \frac{r_{12}\,r_{21}\,(B_1\,\lambda_2 - B_2\,\lambda_1)}{C}; \tag{29a}$$

$$\mathrm{E}\big[N_{jk}(0,t]\big] = \frac{r_{jk}\left[B_2\,\lambda_1\,(h_k + \lambda_2) - B_1\,\lambda_2\,(h_k + \lambda_1)\right]}{C}; \tag{29b}$$

$$\mathrm{E}\big[N_{j3}(0,t]\big] = \frac{1}{C}\big[B_2\,\lambda_1\,(r_{jk}\,r_{k3} + r_{j3}\,h_k + r_{j3}\,\lambda_2)$$
$$\qquad - B_1\,\lambda_2\,(r_{jk}\,r_{k3} + r_{j3}\,h_k + r_{j3}\,\lambda_1)\big]; \tag{29c}$$

where

$$h_j \equiv r_{jk} + r_{j3}, \qquad k \equiv 3 - j;$$
$$\lambda_1 \equiv -\frac{1}{2}\left[h_1 + h_2 + \sqrt{(h_1 - h_2)^2 + 4r_{12}\,r_{21}}\right];$$
$$\lambda_2 \equiv -\frac{1}{2}\left[h_1 + h_2 - \sqrt{(h_1 - h_2)^2 + 4r_{12}\,r_{21}}\right]; \tag{30}$$
$$B_j \equiv 1 - e^{\lambda_j t};$$
$$C \equiv \lambda_1\,\lambda_2\,(\lambda_1 - \lambda_2).$$

Transition Probabilities—

$$p_{jj}(0,t) = \frac{(1 - B_1)(h_k + \lambda_1) - (1 - B_2)(h_k + \lambda_2)}{\lambda_1 - \lambda_2}; \tag{31a}$$

$$p_{jk}(0,t) = r_{jk}\,\frac{B_2 - B_1}{\lambda_1 - \lambda_2}; \tag{31b}$$

$$p_{j3}(0,t) = 1 - p_{jj}(0,t) - p_{jk}(0,t); \tag{31c}$$

$$p_{33}(0,t) = 1; \tag{31d}$$

$$p_{3j}(0,t) = 0; \tag{31e}$$

where $j = 1, 2$, and $k \equiv 3 - j$.

4.4.7 Model of Coupled Dichotomous Variables

As suggested by its name, this model is usually used to represent change in two dichotomous variables, only one of which may change in any infinitesimally small moment of time [see panel (e) of Figure 4.1]. Because each dichotomous variable has two states, this model as $4 = 2 \cdot 2$ states. The matrix of transition rates for this model is

$$\mathbf{R}(u) = \begin{pmatrix} 0 & r_{12} & r_{13} & 0 \\ r_{21} & 0 & 0 & r_{24} \\ r_{31} & 0 & 0 & r_{34} \\ 0 & r_{42} & r_{43} & 0 \end{pmatrix}. \tag{32}$$

Coleman (1964a) is apparently the first sociologist to have proposed this model. In fact, his *Introduction to Mathematical Sociology* probably devotes more attention to this model than to any other. In Coleman's applications of this model, the two dichotomous variables are usually either two attitudes or else one attitude and one behavior. More recently Holland and Leinhardt (1977) and Wasserman (1977) used a special case of this model to describe change in affective ties between members of a dyad.[12] This model should receive more attention as social scientists begin to study coupled changes in qualitative variables, for example, linked changes in marital status and employment status. We discuss this application and model at length in Chapter 9.

4.4.8 Pure Growth (Poisson) Model

Probably the most famous continuous-time stochastic model is the Poisson model, which is illustrated in panel (f) of Figure 4.1. We prefer to call it the pure growth model because a population member in state y can only grow, namely, make a transition to state $y + 1$. In most models discussed in Part II, Ψ is finite and indeed quite small, as we noted at the beginning of Section 3.1. The pure growth model is one of two models that we mention in which Ψ is infinite. However, in most applications the largest observed value of Y tends to be fairly small, mainly because analysts usually treat $Y(t)$ as a metric variable when observed values of Y are large (see discussion in Part III). The matrix of transition rates for the pure

---

[12]The special case treated by these authors assumes that $r_{12} = r_{34}$, $r_{21} = r_{43}$, $r_{13} = r_{24}$, and $r_{31} = r_{42}$.

⟨4⟩ *Particular Models*

growth model is

$$\mathbf{R}(u) = \begin{pmatrix} 0 & \beta & 0 & \cdot & \cdot & \cdot & 0 \\ 0 & 0 & \beta & 0 & \cdot & \cdot & 0 \\ 0 & 0 & 0 & \beta & \cdot & \cdot & 0 \\ 0 & \cdot & \cdot & 0 & \beta & 0 & 0 \\ 0 & \cdot & \cdot & \cdot & 0 & \beta & 0 \\ 0 & \cdot & \cdot & \cdot & 0 & 0 & \beta \end{pmatrix}, \qquad (33)$$

where β is the rate of change from y to $y+1$.

Somewhat surprisingly, one of the earliest applications of the pure growth model involved a social-scientific question, namely, Did the frequency of an unfortunate rare event (deaths by kicks of a horse) in a social organization (a company in the Prussian army) reflect differences in luck or differences in organizational effectiveness? [The data suggested luck; see Bortkewitsch (1898) as cited by Coleman (1964a, pp. 291–292).] More recently, Spilerman (1970) used the pure growth model to investigate whether the differential incidence of riots in cities could be explained by chance. (On this occasion the data suggested that cities actually differ in their propensity to have riots.) The pure growth model is a likely baseline for many other comparatively infrequent events that occur repeatedly to a given social unit over time, for example, strikes in an industry, and lynchings in Southern counties.

The implications of the pure growth (Poisson) model are:

Mean Number of Events in Period $(0, t]$—

$$E[N_{jk}(0,t]] = 1 - e^{-\beta t} \sum_{n=1}^{k-j} \frac{(\beta t)^m}{m!}, \qquad m \equiv k-j > 0; \qquad (34)$$

$$E[N_{jk}(0,t]] = 0, \qquad k \leq j.$$

Transition Probabilities—

$$p_{jk}(0,t) = \frac{(\beta t)^m \, e^{-\beta t}}{m!}, \qquad m \equiv k-j \geq 0; \qquad (35)$$

$$p_{jk}(0,t) = 0, \qquad k < j.$$

4.4.9 Pure Decline (Bounded Growth) Model

This model is extremely similar to the pure growth model, as can be seen by comparing panels (f) and (g) of Figure 4.1. The main formal difference is in the value of Ψ, which is assumed to be infinite in the pure growth model but finite in the pure decline model. This is the reason for calling the pure decline model the "bounded growth" model. It is customary to arrange the matrix of transition rates so that the only nonzero elements correspond to transitions from state y to state $y - 1$ (a decline). Thus, the matrix of transition rates of the pure decline model is

$$\mathbf{R}(u) = \begin{pmatrix} 0 & 0 & 0 & \cdot & \cdot & \cdot & 0 \\ \delta & 0 & 0 & 0 & \cdot & \cdot & 0 \\ 0 & \delta & 0 & 0 & \cdot & \cdot & 0 \\ \cdot & \cdot & \cdot & \cdot & \cdot & \cdot & \cdot \\ \cdot & \cdot & \cdot & \delta & 0 & 0 & 0 \\ \cdot & \cdot & \cdot & 0 & \delta & 0 & 0 \end{pmatrix}, \tag{36}$$

where δ is the rate of change from $y + 1$ to y.

The pure decline model is typically applied to two sorts of problems. First, it is used to model the diffusion from a fixed source of a given item (e.g., a piece of information, adoption of some behavior) through a group of size $\Psi - 1$. Second, it is used to model independent losses from a group of size $\Psi - 1$, hence the name "pure decline" model. When Ψ is very large, $Y(t)$ is customarily treated as a metric variable, as noted in Section 11.1. The implications of the bounded growth model are similar to those for the pure growth model.

4.4.10 Growth and Decline Model

This model, usually called a simple birth and death model, combines the pure growth and pure decline models, as shown in panel (h) of Figure 4.1. Like the pure growth model, a sample member in state y can grow (move to state $y+1$). Like the pure decline model, a sample member in state y can decline (move to state $y-1$). All other direct transitions from state y are impossible. We can represent this model formally by the matrix of transition rates:

⟨4⟩ *Particular Models

$$\mathbf{R}(u) = \begin{pmatrix} 0 & \beta & 0 & \cdot & \cdot & \cdot & 0 \\ \delta & 0 & \beta & 0 & \cdot & \cdot & 0 \\ 0 & \delta & 0 & \beta & \cdot & \cdot & 0 \\ \cdot & \cdot & \cdot & \cdot & \cdot & \cdot & \cdot \\ \cdot & \cdot & \cdot & \delta & 0 & \beta & 0 \\ \cdot & \cdot & \cdot & 0 & \delta & 0 & \beta \end{pmatrix}, \qquad (37)$$

where the parameters β and δ denote the growth and decline rates, respectively.

Several slightly more complex versions of this model have received attention. In the most general of these, which is usually called the general birth and death model, each of the permissible transition rates is distinct from every other. This model is too general to be useful in scientific applications because an infinite number of parameters need to be estimated. But all data sets are finite, allowing only a finite number of parameters to be estimated. In a more useful generalization of the (simple) growth and decline model, the growth and decline rates are assumed to be linear functions of y. Many authors have discussed this model; for example, see Chiang (1968), Cox and Miller (1965), Keiding (1975), Çinlar (1975), and Karlin and Taylor (1975).

The bounded growth and decline model is still another version of this model [see panel (i) of Figure 4.1]; it differs from the simple growth and decline model only in having a finite state space Ψ. The value of this model for sociological applications does not yet seem to be widely recognized. However, it should be widely applicable, given the popularity of ordered categorical scales (e.g., of political conservatism, of one person's liking for another, or of organizational complexity). It can also be used to model diffusion from a fixed source of some item in a group of size $\Psi - 1$, when defections can occur as well as adoptions.

As its name suggests, the growth and decline model is ordinarily applied to the process of independent gains and losses in the size of some group. When the observed values of $Y(t)$ are very large, most analysts treat $Y(t)$ as a metric variable and use the models discussed in Part III. In fact, the growth and decline models discussed in Part III can be derived as limiting cases of the corresponding discrete-state growth and decline models.

An implication of the bounded growth and decline model is:

Transition Probabilities—

$$p_{jk}(0, t) = \frac{\theta^k(1-\theta)}{1-\theta}$$

$$+ \frac{2}{\Psi} \sum_{y=0}^{\Psi-1} \frac{\theta^{\frac{k-j}{2}} \exp\left[-(\beta+\delta)t + 2t\sqrt{\beta\delta}\cos(y\pi/\psi)\right]}{1 + \theta - 2\sqrt{\theta}\cos(y\pi/\psi)}$$

$$\cdot \left\{ \sin\left[\frac{jy\pi}{\psi}\right] - \sqrt{\theta}\sin\left[\frac{(j+1)y\pi}{\psi}\right] \right\}$$

$$\cdot \left\{ \sin\left[\frac{ky\pi}{\psi}\right] - \sqrt{\theta}\sin\left[\frac{(k+1)y\pi}{\psi}\right] \right\}, \qquad (38)$$

where $\beta \neq \delta$ and $\theta \equiv \beta/\delta$. Equation (38) comes from Takacs (1962), who noted that transition probabilities for the case in which Ψ is infinite can be obtained from (38) by taking the limit as Ψ approaches infinity. He also gave an expression for the case in which $\beta = \delta$.

4.5 Conclusions

This chapter concludes our two-part introduction to basic ideas used in event-history analysis. Unlike the previous chapter, which considered only descriptions of event histories, the present chapter introduced explicit stochastic models that might guide sociological forays into event-history studies. The chapter began by arguing the case for using explicit models. Beyond noting that much sociological research is devoted to testing specific theories and that model-testing is a routine aspect of such work, we point out that explicit models have implications for diverse observable quantities. Thus even in descriptive or exploratory research, explicit stochastic models can sometimes be used to unify a broad set of concrete empirical findings. In this sense, use of models can sharpen understanding of a body of empirical results and suggest nonobvious ways of testing their implications.

Our use of stochastic models in event-history analysis has two controversial features: we specify continuous-time models, and we concentrate on unobservable transition rates. Many sociologists find it more natural (and believe it is simpler) to use discrete-time models for observable outcomes. We argue at length that this is not so for most sociological processes. Not only does the use of a continuous-time model add realism, but it also simplifies analytic work and

⟨4⟩ Conclusions

makes empirical analysis more economical (because data are stored very compactly). Though transition rates (like probabilities) cannot be observed directly, they can be easily estimated, as we noted in Chapter 3. Once one knows (or has estimated) transition rates for a process, one can derive many other interesting features of a process: mean waiting times, the mean number of events in a period, and so forth.

The second half of the chapter gives useful analytic results for several stochastic models that have already served usefully in event-history studies and have much untapped potential. We concentrate especially on semi-Markov models, which generalize the better-known Markov model by allowing transition rates to depend on duration in a state and by permitting direct transitions from a state to itself. We cite results that express five quantities (introduced in Chapter 3) as functions of the transition rates for a semi-Markov process: (1) the survivor function, (2) the mean waiting time in a state, (3) the mean number of events in a period, (4) transition probabilities, and (5) state probabilities. Then we show how these general results specialize for particular cases of possible substantive interest. We consider two- and three-state models with both recurrent and absorbing states; models with pure growth, pure decline, and both growth and decline; and a model of coupled dichotomous variables. The analytical results for these models are used in various places in the remaining chapters of Part II.

Having concluded the ground work for event-history analysis with explicit models, we now consider the details for actually implementing this strategy. We turn first to the problem of estimating explicit models from censored event histories.

5

Estimation Using Censored Event Histories

As we noted in Chapter 2, sociologists rarely make full use of event histories. Instead, their analyses typically use only a portion of the information in their data. Ignoring information on the timing of events is often justified on grounds of convenience. Occasionally there are substantive reasons too. For example, White (1970) argued that the duration of job vacancies can be ignored because of their brevity relative to the typical length of time that a person holds a job. However, many analysts probably make incomplete use of the information in event histories because the literature on sociological methodology provides little guidance on how to analyze such data. Moreover, some investigators probably do not realize the potential value of the information in event histories.

In this chapter we lay out the essential details of a feasible strategy for utilizing all of the information in event histories. We emphasize estimation of parameters in explicit stochastic models by the method of maximum likelihood (ML) and devote attention to both large- and small-sample properties of such estimators.[1] Rather than begin with a general treatment of such estimators, however, we focus first (in Section 5.1) on a special methodological problem that arises in event-history analysis: the problem of censored observations. By organizing much of the discussion of estimators in later sections around the censoring problem, we can best relate statistical

[1] In Chapter 8 we describe estimation of stochastic models that are partially parameterized and partially left unspecified.

issues to considerations involving research design.

Section 5.2 discusses basic principles of ML estimation and reviews procedures for testing models estimated by ML. Section 5.3 outlines a general scheme for ML estimation of right-censored event histories. We show how ML estimation neatly handles the problem of right-censoring.[2] In Section 5.4 we raise the troublesome problem of left-censoring and sketch some strategies for dealing with it. None of these is completely satisfactory—each requires highly restrictive assumptions and some information on past history. Moreover, each is much harder to implement than the strategy for dealing with right-censored data. Consequently, subsequent discussion concentrates on estimation of models using right-censored event histories.

Sections 5.5 through 5.7 concentrate on estimators for the Poisson model. Although the assumptions of this model are highly restrictive, it lets us develop in detail the general ML estimation scheme presented in Sections 5.2 through 5.4. In addition, it allows us to pursue a number of issues that arise in estimating more complex models and to compare several different kinds of estimators. We derive several ML estimators for this model in Section 5.5, discuss two pseudo-ML estimators that adjust for censoring in an ad hoc way in Section 5.6, and describe a widely known moment estimator in Section 5.7. We report findings from a Monte Carlo study of the quality of different estimators for the Poisson model in Section 5.8.

Section 5.9 introduces another common problem in event-history analyses: measurement error in the dates of events. We indicate how the imposition of arbitrary observations periods can create what we call false censoring and false events when the dates of events are measured unreliably. Section 5.10 gives the results from a Monte Carlo study of the effects of two types of measurement error in dates: errors whose variances are time-independent and errors whose variances increase with time (either the length of the episode or the distance from a point in time, such as the date of a survey).

Finally, in Section 5.10 we return to a more general model—the time-stationary Markov model. Unlike the Poisson model, this model includes multiple kinds of events and several different transition rates. We illustrate ML estimators for a three-state Markov

---

[2] To the best of our knowledge, Boag (1949) first reported the use of ML estimation to deal with the censoring problem.

model and compare them with pseudo-ML estimators that are constructed like those discussed in Section 5.6. We show that conclusions about estimation approaches for this more complicated model are qualitatively similar to those for the Poisson model.

5.1 The Censoring Problem

The problem of censoring is not new to social scientists. Sørensen (1977) discussed it in the following context. Suppose a survey at a point in time collects information on the dates on which the I individuals in a sample entered and left a certain state, such as employment. To avoid recall errors, one may want to analyze only data pertaining to either a recent time period (e.g., the past 2 years) or the current state occupied by each individual. The problem is that the ending date of the current state is generally unknown. That is, the data are right-censored. For example, in a study of unemployment, some individuals will be unemployed at the time of an interview. Persons can be asked how long they have been unemployed, but the total, completed duration of the current episode of unemployment cannot be determined. Information on events prior to some point in time, for example, a respondent's employment history prior to the current episode of unemployment, may be lacking or may not be trustworthy. Such data are said to be left-censored. Thus it is important to learn how to use incomplete event histories.

Exactly the same problem arises with archival data. For example, organizational analysts studying the failure rate of organizations face this problem because public records sometimes cover limited time periods. Official records may tell which organizations exist in a certain year, but not when they were founded. Further, in any observed year, some organizations existing in a previous year will "die" and others will not. Observations on the life span of organizations are censored—almost always on the right, occasionally only on the left, and often on both the left and the right.

Panel studies that obtain retrospective data on the periods between waves of interviews lead to the same problem. For example, in the Seattle and Denver Income Maintenance Experiments (SIME/DIME), family heads were interviewed several times a year. Each interview recorded the dates of all intervening changes in jobs and in marital status. During the experiment some people dropped out of the study and others could not be found. At the end of the

⟨5⟩ Maximum-Likelihood Estimation 119

experiment some family heads had not yet changed their jobs or marital status. Both types of observations involve a form of censoring. What should be done with information on such cases?

There are at least three possible approaches to the censoring problem: (1) ignore censored observations and analyze only those episodes with observed starting and ending dates; (2) treat censored observations as though events occur when the observation period starts and ends; or (3) use a method of estimation that adjusts for censoring under the assumption that the same stochastic model applies to all episodes, whether or not observations on them are censored. Though social scientists sometimes use the logic of the second strategy inadvertently, it probably has few defenders. Recoding censored observations in this way is the same as recoding nonevents as events. The first strategy, ignoring censored observations, is more common, especially when caused by attrition. [For example, almost all panel studies of change in marital status do this—see the discussion in Hannan, Tuma, and Groeneveld (1976).] In the next three sections we develop and discuss the third approach, first in general terms and then within the context of a particular model. In Sections 5.6 and 5.11 we compare a statistically sound method with the two ad hoc procedures mentioned above. We show that the ad hoc procedures lead to biased estimates of parameters of the models considered. Equally important, the procedure with good properties is no more difficult to implement than the ad hoc ones.

5.2 Maximum-Likelihood Estimation

In Chapter 4 we reviewed several classes of continuous-time stochastic models that serve as useful baselines in event-history analysis. We also discussed advantages of estimating such models (or extensions of them) rather than limiting analyses solely to the exploratory and descriptive methods outlined in Chapter 3. But we did not attempt to describe how these models might actually be estimated or tested. In this section we explain the fundamental principles involved in estimating and testing such models by the method of ML. We begin by commenting briefly on reasons for focusing on this method of estimation.

5.2.1 Advantages of ML Estimation

Maximum-likelihood estimation of a model from event-history data has several main advantages over more commonly used methods such as least-squares and moment estimation. First, ML estimators have excellent properties in large samples under fairly weak regularity conditions on the probability distribution function of a random variable—asymptotically (i.e., as the sample size I becomes infinitely large), they are unbiased and normally distributed and have minimum variance (e.g., see Dhrymes, 1970). So in a sufficiently large sample, ML estimation may be relied on to produce good estimates, as long as the assumptions of the model being estimated hold. Sometimes least-squares and moment estimators share these properties, but there is no general theorem guaranteeing the excellence of these estimators for nonlinear models like those we consider.

Second, the commonly cited advantages of moment and least-squares estimation—convenience and computational ease—rarely apply in the case of continuous-time stochastic models. At worst, ML estimation tends to be no more difficult or costly than other methods giving poorer estimates.

Third, ML estimation allows censored observations to be used in estimating parameters, thereby avoiding biases that result from various ad hoc procedures designed to cope with censoring, as we show in Sections 5.6 and 5.11. Moment and least-squares estimators that deal with censoring can sometimes be developed (e.g., see Miller and Halpern, 1981), but are not readily available. Moreover, modifying these methods to deal with censoring tends to require as much effort as ML estimation, and sometimes more.

5.2.2 Basic Principles of ML Estimation and Testing

The likelihood function $\mathcal{L}$ is defined as the joint probability (or joint probability density) of sample observations. When observations on different sample members are statistically independent, the likelihood is just the product of the contribution of each sample member i raised to the power of its sampling weight w_i:

$$\mathcal{L} = \prod_{i=1}^{I} \mathcal{L}_i^{w_i}. \tag{1}$$

In a simple random sample each sample member has a weight of 1. In stratified random samples and in multistage random samples, which are common in survey research, different sample members tend to have different sample weights. As long as the sample weights are

⟨ 5 ⟩ Maximum-Likelihood Estimation

known, these more complex sample designs can be easily incorporated into the likelihood equation, as shown above.[3]

Finding ML estimates of parameters in a model involves two steps. First, write an individual's contribution, $\mathcal{L}_i$, in terms of the parameters in the model and the data on i. Second, find the values of the parameters that make $\mathcal{L}$ in (1) largest for a given set of data. Sometimes equations for ML estimators can be written as explicit functions of the data. But for most models considered in Part II, this is impossible, and ML estimates must be found by numerical methods. Usually this involves first taking a logarithmic transformation of (1):

$$\log \mathcal{L} = \sum_{i=1}^{I} w_i \log \mathcal{L}_i.$$

Since a logarithm is a monotonic function, parameters that maximize $\log \mathcal{L}$ also maximize $\mathcal{L}$. Ordinarily an optimization procedure based on the Newton–Raphson method is used to maximize $\log \mathcal{L}$. Rather than discuss optimization procedures, which rarely concern social scientists trying to find ML estimates of parameters, we refer interested readers to one of the many treatments of this subject, for example, Murray (1972). Instead, we concentrate on the first step.

The form of $\mathcal{L}_i$ depends on both the assumptions of the model being estimated and the type of data available. In our discussion of change in qualitative variables, we treat a wide variety of models but concentrate on event-history data. We outline the general form of $\mathcal{L}_i$ that applies for right-censored event histories in Section 5.3 and for left- and right-censored histories in Section 5.4. We not only state conclusions but also show how likelihood functions are derived. We include these derivations because we think they foster understanding of important issues in the design and analysis of event histories. However, Sections 5.3 and 5.4 are fairly technical, and some readers may wish to skim them at first reading. The key results, which we refer to often in subsequent chapters, can be found in equations (7), (8), (15), and (16).

Before turning to ML estimators for right-censored event histories, we briefly discuss testing of models when ML has been used

---

[3] See Hoem (1983) for a discussion of the usage of weights in event-history analysis.

to estimate parameters. Analysts commonly perform two kinds of statistical tests: (1) a test of a hypothesis about a *single* parameter and (2) a test of a hypothesis about a *set* of parameters. Maximum-likelihood estimation provides information that can be used for both types of tests.

An estimate of the lower bound of the variance–covariance matrix of $\boldsymbol{\theta}$, a vector of parameters estimated by ML, is given by

$$\left[\frac{\partial^2 \log \mathcal{L}}{\partial \boldsymbol{\theta}^2}\right]^{-1}$$

(see Dhrymes, 1970). The diagonal elements of this matrix, which is usually calculated routinely when numerical methods are utilized to maximize $\mathcal{L}$, tell the estimated variances of parameters. Thus, information is readily available from which to calculate the standard error of a single parameter and so to test hypotheses about it.

Hypotheses about a set of parameters can be tested by means of a likelihood ratio test, which is discussed in virtually all basic statistics texts (though rarely in those written for sociologists). Let $\mathcal{L}_1$ and $\mathcal{L}_0$ represent the likelihood $\mathcal{L}$ for two models: one with no constraints on its parameters (the alternative hypothesis) and one with k constraints (the null hypothesis), respectively. Usually the k constraints are that k parameters are zero, but any k equality constraints may be tested. The likelihood ratio λ is defined as $\max(\mathcal{L}_0)/\max(\mathcal{L}_1)$. For a sufficiently large sample size, $-2\log\lambda$ has a χ^2 distribution with k degrees of freedom under the null hypothesis. We illustrate both kinds of tests on numerous occasions in subsequent chapters.

5.3 ML Estimation of Right-Censored Event Histories

In general, the contribution of the ith sample member to the likelihood $\mathcal{L}_i$ is simply the joint probability of i's observed values on the endogenous variables, conditional on i's observed values of the exogenous variables. To specify $\mathcal{L}_i$ for right-censored event histories, we must first indicate exactly what data are assumed to be available. Then we must indicate which variables are regarded as "exogenous" and which ones as "endogenous." Distinguishing between exogenous and endogenous variables is occasionally obvious but often merely conventional. It always involves substantive decisions that should not be made automatically. We point out aspects of these decisions that deserve special care.

We assume that right-censored event histories describe the complete history or sample path on each individual i from $\tau_{i1} = t_{i0}$ to τ_{i2}, that is, $\omega[\tau_{i1}, \tau_{i2}] = \omega[t_{i0}, \tau_{i2}]$. Recall that for qualitative variables this history can be summarized by the following information: t_{i0}, the time of the start of the process for sample member i; $y_{i0} \equiv y_i(t_{i0})$, i's value of Y at the start of the process; $N_i \equiv n_i(t_{i0}, \tau_{i2}]$, the number of events that have occurred to i by time τ_{i2}; $\{t_{1i}, t_{2i}, \ldots, t_{N_i i}\}$, the times of the events that occur to i in the observation period; and $\{y_{1i}, y_{2i}, \ldots, y_{N_i i}\}$, i's values of Y immediately after each of i's observed events. Sometimes it is convenient to count events with an indicator variable D_{in}, which equals 1 if the nth event occurs in the observation period and zero otherwise. Clearly $N_i = \sum_{n=1}^{\infty} D_{in}$. Because we focus solely on the contribution of a single i to the likelihood in the rest of this section and in the next, we suppress the subscript i on all variables except $\mathcal{L}_i$ to simplify the notation.

Sometimes there is also information on assorted variables thought to affect the process of change in $Y(t)$. Although we do not discuss specific models containing explanatory variables until Chapter 6, we set the stage for these later discussions by showing how a vector of explanatory variables, x, enters into the likelihood equation. The vector of explanatory variables may contain metric or dummy variables (or both). Throughout Part II we treat x as exogenous.

We generally assume that each sample member's entire history must be regarded as endogenous, except possibly for the initial conditions ω_0. As a consequence, not only does the likelihood for a portion of a sample member's history, say that spanning τ_1 to τ_2, depend on the history from t_0 to τ_1, but the history from t_0 to τ_1 is also something to be explained by the exogenous variables. This assumption has important consequences for the likelihood function for event-history data. However, it only causes serious complications when histories are censored on the left, as we explain in Section 5.4.

Deciding whether the initial conditions ω_0 are exogenous is often problematic. Social scientists regard them as exogenous on some occasions and as endogenous on others. For example, in an analysis of marital histories, t_0 is usually the date of birth, and y_0 is single (not married). In this case it often seems reasonable to treat t_0 and y_0 as exogenous. In a study of organizational mergers, t_0 is typically the date of founding of an organization, while y_0 may describe its initial structure and form. In this case the initial structure and form y_0 might well be regarded as an outcome to be explained by the founding date t_0 and by environmental conditions at that time $\mathbf{x}(t_0)$. Some analysts may even wish to treat the date of founding, t_0, as something to be accounted for by some set of explanatory variables. For instance, analysts may wish to explain why many new organizations are launched in certain historical periods and few in others (see the discussion in Stinchcombe, 1965).

In this section we treat the initial conditions, $\omega_0 \equiv \{t_0, y_0\}$, as well as the values of the explanatory variables $\mathbf{x}$, as exogenous. Therefore, we write $\mathcal{L}_i$ as follows:

$$\mathcal{L}_i = \Pr\big[\omega(t_0, \tau_2) \mid \omega_0, \mathbf{x}\big]. \qquad (2)$$

To treat the initial conditions as endogenous, simply multiply the right-hand side of (2) (and other equations derived from it below) by $\Pr[\omega_0 \mid \mathbf{x}] \equiv \Pr[t_0, y_0 \mid \mathbf{x}]$.

To use (2) in actual analyses, it must be translated into concepts that can be derived from a particular model. In describing this translation, we distinguish event histories consisting of data on a single episode from those containing data on multiple episodes. We begin by discussing the simpler case of the likelihood for data on first episodes. However, the exposition of this likelihood is not merely a didactic exercise. In many research contexts the likelihood for first episodes is directly useful. Sometimes event-history data contain information on only a single episode, either because the event is nonrepeatable (e.g., death of a person, failure of a firm), or because the observation plan ignores all episodes but the first (e.g., the survey gathers information only on the date of a person's first marriage). And sometimes there is information on multiple episodes, but the data on the first episode are more reliable (e.g., see the discussion in Section 10.4).

5.3.1 A Likelihood for First Episodes

When data describe event histories for the first episode only, an individual's event history contains only two pieces of information in addition to the initial conditions t_0 and y_0: whether or not the

⟨5⟩ ML Estimation of Right-Censored Event Histories

first event occurs before τ_2, and the date t_1 and the outcome y_1, if the event does occur. If the first event is not observed, that is, the length of the first episode is censored, (2) can be written as

$$\mathcal{L}_i = \Pr\bigl[T_1 > \tau_2 \mid \omega_0, \mathbf{x}\bigr]. \tag{3a}$$

If the first event is observed, (2) becomes

$$\mathcal{L}_i = \Pr\bigl[T_1 \in [t_1, t_1 + \Delta t], Y_1 = y_1 \mid \omega_0, \mathbf{x}\bigr], \tag{3b}$$

where $\Delta t \downarrow 0$ in this and all subsequent similar expressions in Section 5.3.

The first expression [equation (3a)] is the survivor function [compare (5) in Chapter 3]:

$$\Pr\bigl[T_1 > \tau_2 \mid \omega_0, \mathbf{x}\bigr] = G_{y_0}(\tau_2 \mid \omega_0, \mathbf{x}). \tag{4}$$

The second, (3b), can be decomposed into the product of two terms:

$$\Pr\bigl[T_1 \in [t_1, t_1 + \Delta t], Y_1 = y_1 \mid \omega_0, \mathbf{x}\bigr] = \Pr\bigl[T_1 \in [t_1, t_1 + \Delta t] \mid \omega_0, \mathbf{x}\bigr]$$
$$\cdot \Pr\bigl[Y_1 = y_1 \mid t_1, \omega_0, \mathbf{x}\bigr]. \tag{5}$$

The first term on the right of (5) is the probability that the first event occurs at time t_1, conditional on the initial conditions ω_0 and the explanatory variables $\mathbf{x}$. This is just the probability density function for the waiting time to the first event, $f_{y_0}(t_1 \mid \omega_0, \mathbf{x})$, which equals the product of the corresponding hazard and survivor functions according to (10b) in Chapter 3:

$$\Pr\bigl[T_1 \in [t_1, t_1 + \Delta t] \mid \omega_0, \mathbf{x}\bigr] = h_{y_0}(t_1 \mid \omega_0, \mathbf{x})\, G_{y_0}(t_1 \mid \omega_0, \mathbf{x}).$$

The second term on the right-hand side of (5) is the conditional transition probability for the outcome of the first event—compare (14) in Chapter 3:

$$\Pr\bigl[Y_1 = y_1 \mid t_1, \omega_0, \mathbf{x}\bigr] = m_{y_0 y_1}(t_1 \mid \omega_0, \mathbf{x}).$$

Therefore (3b) is equivalent to

$$\Pr\bigl[T_1 \in [t_1, t_1 + \Delta t], Y_1 = y_1 \mid \omega_0, \mathbf{x}\bigr]$$
$$= m_{y_0 y_1}(t_1 \mid \omega_0, \mathbf{x})\, h_{y_0}(t_1 \mid \omega_0, \mathbf{x})\, G_{y_0}(t_1 \mid \omega_0, \mathbf{x})$$
$$= r_{y_0 y_1}(t_1 \mid \omega_0, \mathbf{x})\, G_{y_0}(t_1 \mid \omega_0, \mathbf{x}). \tag{6}$$

It is convenient to combine the expressions in (4) and (6) into a single equation. Let D_i denote a dummy variable that equals 1 if the first event is observed for case i and otherwise equals zero. Then i's contribution to the likelihood for first episodes is

$$\mathcal{L}_i = G_{y_0}(\tau_2 \mid \omega_0, \mathbf{x})^{1-D_i} \left[r_{y_0 y_1}(t_1 \mid \omega_0, \mathbf{x}) \, G_{y_0}(t_1 \mid \omega_0, \mathbf{x}) \right]^{D_i}, \quad (7)$$

where i continues to be suppressed on the right-hand side for clarity.

If a time-stationary Markov process governs change in Y, the survivor function is given by equation (13) in Chapter 4. Then (7) simplifies to

$$\mathcal{L}_i = \left\{ \exp\left[-v_1 \, r_{y_0}(t_0, \mathbf{x})\right] \right\}^{1-D_i} \left\{ r_{y_0 y_1}(t_0, \mathbf{x}) \exp\left[-u_1 \, r_{y_0}(t_0, \mathbf{x})\right] \right\}^{D_i}, \quad (8)$$

where u_1 is the length of a completed first spell and v_1 is the length of censored first spells. This equation serves as the basis for several estimators discussed later in this chapter.

5.3.2 *A Likelihood for Multiple Episodes

Construction of i's contribution to the likelihood when event histories contain observations on multiple events parallels the steps above, but is somewhat more complicated. First we write an expanded version of (2):

$$\mathcal{L}_i = \Pr\big[T_{N+1} > \tau_2, \, T_N \in [t_N, t_N + \Delta t], Y_N = y_N,$$
$$\ldots, \, T_1 \in [t_1, t_1 + \Delta t], Y_1 = y_1 \mid \omega_0, \mathbf{x}\big]. \quad (9)$$

Then, using the rule that

$$\Pr[A \text{ and } B] = \Pr[A \mid B] \cdot \Pr[B],$$

where A and B denote any two outcomes, we rewrite the above expression for $\mathcal{L}_i$ as the product of $(N+1)$ terms:

$$\mathcal{L}_i = \Pr\big[T_{N+1} > \tau_2 \mid \omega_n, \mathbf{x}\big]$$
$$\cdot \Pr\big[T_N \in [t_N, t_N + \Delta t], Y_N = y_N \mid \omega_{n-1}, \mathbf{x}\big]$$
$$\cdot$$
$$\cdot$$
$$\cdot$$
$$\cdot \Pr\big[T_1 \in [t_1, t_1 + \Delta t], Y_1 = y_1 \mid \omega_0, \mathbf{x}\big],$$

or

$$\mathcal{L}_i = \Pr[T_{N+1} > \tau_2 \mid \omega_N, \mathbf{x}] \prod_{n=1}^{N} \Pr[T_n \in [t_n, t_n + \Delta t] \mid \omega_{n-1}, \mathbf{x}]. \tag{10}$$

The first term handles right-censoring. It tells the probability that the $(N+1)$th event has not occurred by τ_2, the end of the observation period. This term is just the survivor function for the $(N+1)$th event, conditional on previous history and the vector of explanatory variables [see (5) in Chapter 3]:

$$\Pr[T_{N+1} > \tau_2 \mid \omega_N, \mathbf{x}] = G_{y_N}(\tau_2 \mid \omega_N, \mathbf{x}). \tag{11}$$

Each of the other N terms gives the probability of the time and outcome for one of i's observed events. Steps paralleling those leading to (6) above yield

$$\Pr[T_n \in [t_n, t_n + \Delta t], Y_n = y_n \mid \omega_{n-1}, \mathbf{x}] = r_{y_{n-1} y_n}(t_n \mid \omega_{n-1}, \mathbf{x}) \cdot G_{n-1}(t_n \mid \omega_{n-1}, \mathbf{x}) \tag{12}$$

Substitution of (11) and (12) into (10) yields the following general expression for i's contribution to the likelihood for multiple episodes and right-censoring:

$$\mathcal{L}_i = G_{y_N}(\tau_2 \mid \omega_N, \mathbf{x}) \prod_{n=1}^{N} r_{y_{n-1} y_n}(t_n \mid \omega_{n-1}, \mathbf{x}) G_{n-1}(t_{n-1} \mid \omega_{n-1}, \mathbf{x}). \tag{13}$$

Equation (13) is the foundation for constructing ML estimators of the parameters in most of the models discussed later in this chapter and in subsequent chapters. Note that it is very general and applies to non-Markovian processes as well as to Markov and semi-Markov processes.

If either a Markov or semi-Markov process governs change in $Y(t)$, then (13) becomes still simpler because the terms of $\mathcal{L}_i$ do not depend on previous history:

$$\mathcal{L}_i = G_{y_N}(\tau_2 \mid t_N, \mathbf{x}) \prod_{n=1}^{N} r_{y_{n-1} y_n}(t_n \mid t_{n-1}, \mathbf{x}) G_{y_{n-1}}(t_{n-1} \mid t_{n-1}, \mathbf{x}). \tag{14}$$

Moreover, as we noted in Chapter 4, both in time-stationary Markov and semi-Markov models, the survivor function for the nth event in state y_{n-1} does not depend on the exact time of the previous event, t_{n-1}, but only on the length of time that has elapsed since the previous event, $u \equiv t - t_{n-1}$:

$$G_{y_{n-1}}(t \mid t_{n-1}, \mathbf{x}) = G_{y_{n-1}}(u \mid \mathbf{x}).$$

Therefore, (14) becomes

$$\mathcal{L}_i = G_{y_N}(v_{N+1} \mid \mathbf{x}) \prod_{n=1}^{N} r_{y_{n-1} y_n} G_{y_{n-1}}(u_n \mid \mathbf{x}), \qquad (15)$$

where $v_{N+1} \equiv \tau_2 - t_N$ is the censored length of the last (i.e., $N+1$th) episode. Given a time-stationary Markov model, which assumes that transition rates are time invariant, the survivor function is [compare (13) in Chapter 4]:

$$G_{y_{n-1}}(u \mid \mathbf{x}) = \exp[-u_n r_{y_{n-1}}(\mathbf{x})],$$

so that (15) can be simplified still further, yielding

$$\mathcal{L}_i = \exp[-v_{N+1} r_{y_N}(\mathbf{x})] \prod_{n=1}^{N} r_{y_{n-1} y_n}(\mathbf{x}) \exp[-u_n r_{y_{n-1} y_n}(\mathbf{x})].$$
$$(16)$$

Equation (16) is the basis for estimation of most models discussed in the rest of this chapter and in Chapter 6; equation (15) is the starting point for estimation of the time-dependent models in Chapter 7.

5.4 *ML Estimation of Left-Censored Event Histories

The expressions for $\mathcal{L}_i$ given in the previous section are correct for right-censored event-history data, that is, when $\omega[t_0, \tau_2]$ is observed. In general they are incorrect if data are censored on the left as well as on the right.

To show the consequences of left-censoring, we begin with the simple case of a single nonrepeatable event. We rely heavily on a concrete example to communicate the main points. After discussing the issues and developing $\mathcal{L}_i$ for first episodes, we turn to the case of multiple outcomes and repeatable events. The same problems and solutions occur as in the simpler case. But in practice it is much more difficult to implement these solutions when multiple episodes can occur.

⟨5⟩ *ML Estimation of Left-Censored Event Histories 129

5.4.1 A Likelihood for First Episodes

To illustrate the problems arising in constructing $\mathcal{L}_i$ for left-censored first episodes, we assume that the objective is to estimate mortality rates using data on a random sample of the U.S. population in $\tau_1 = 1960$, who are followed until $\tau_2 = 1970$. Thus we have event-history data from 1960 to 1970, with the event of interest being death. We observe that some sample members are still alive in 1970; these are right-censored cases. Others die during the observation period, and we record the date of death of each of these cases. But we do not know the history of any sample member prior to 1960; all cases are left-censored. In particular, we do not have information on the initial conditions ω_0, including the birth date of each sample member.

Two new problems arise in constructing the likelihood for left-censored event histories. The first problem, often called "sample selection bias," occurs whenever a sample is selected in terms of an endogenous variable (see Heckman, 1979). In terms of our example, it means that parameter estimates are usually biased if the likelihood ignores an important piece of available information, namely, that all sample members are alive in 1960. Bias is a potential problem because the distribution of the explanatory variables, $\mathbf{x}$, at the start of the process (t_0) differs from that in a sample of cases selected so that $y(\tau_1)$ has a particular value (or values). As the duration in a state increases, the proportion of cases with $\mathbf{x}$'s associated with lower rates increases. Consequently, the average number of events in the interval τ_1 to τ_2 tends to be less than it would be if we observed the original distribution of $\mathbf{x}$'s. For example, because females have a lower mortality rate than males at almost any given age, the proportion of women in any given age group in a sample of those still living tends to rise with age. More broadly, the older a sample member is, the more likely he or she possesses characteristics favoring longevity. As a result, for any given birth cohort, we tend to observe fewer deaths during our observation period than if the sample contained the distribution of $\mathbf{x}$'s at birth. A likelihood for left-censored event histories must correctly take into account the probability of occupying the observed state at the start of the observation period in order to avoid sample selection bias. In terms of our example, each individual's contribution to the likelihood must take into account that death did not occur before 1960.

The second problem happens when there are missing data on the initial conditions for the observed cases. The practical problem is how to compensate for our ignorance of previous history. In the case of first episodes, the piece of previous history that we lack is the initial conditions ω_0. In general we cannot treat the start of our observation period as though it is the start of the process. If the hazard rate increases (decreases) monotonically with the duration in a state, the average number of events in an interval of length $\tau_1 - \tau_2$ tends to increase (decrease) as $\tau_1 - t_0$ increases. For example, if mortality rates increase with age, then on the average a higher proportion of sample members die between 1960 and 1970 when we take a random sample of those alive in 1960 than when we take a sample of those born in 1960. If we wish to estimate and test models in which the rate of an event depends on the length of time since t_0, we must take care that the likelihood for left-censored event histories does not treat τ_1 as if it were t_0.

We begin with the problem of sample selection bias, which arises whenever one focuses on a segment of event histories that do not begin at t_0. We assume initially that we observe $\omega[t_0, \tau_1)$ as well as $\omega[\tau_1, \tau_2]$, the actual period being studied. We can then write individual i's contribution to the likelihood as

$$\mathcal{L}_i = \Pr\big[\omega[\tau_1, \tau_2] \mid \omega[t_0, \tau_1), \mathbf{x}\big]; \tag{17a}$$

$$\mathcal{L}_i = \Pr\big[\omega[\tau_1, \tau_2] \mid \omega_0, \omega(t_0, \tau_1), \mathbf{x}\big]. \tag{17b}$$

In (17a), we let the history in the interval τ_1 to τ_2 depend not only on the explanatory variables $\mathbf{x}$, but also on the previous history $\omega[t_0, \tau_1)$. In (17b), we decompose the previous history into two pieces. One piece, ω_0, is the initial conditions—a person's birthdate in our example. The second piece, $\omega(t_0, \tau_1)$, is the history between the start of the process and the start of the observation period, τ_1. This second piece consists of the information that the first event did not occur before τ_1, for example, that the person is still alive in 1960.

Using the definition of a conditional probability, we can write (17b) as

$$\mathcal{L}_i = \frac{\Pr\big[\omega(t_0, \tau_2] \mid \omega_0, \mathbf{x}\big]}{\Pr\big[\omega(t_0, \tau_1] \mid \omega_0, \mathbf{x}\big]}. \tag{18}$$

⟨5⟩ *ML Estimation of Left-Censored Event Histories

For the research design described in our example, that is, a random sample of the (living) U.S. population in 1960, the above equation is equivalent to

$$\mathcal{L}_i = \frac{\Pr[\omega(t_0, \tau_2] \mid \omega_0, \mathbf{x}]}{G(\tau_1 \mid \omega_0, \mathbf{x})},$$

where $G(\tau_1 \mid \omega_0, \mathbf{x})$ is the survivor function. If the person is still alive in 1970, this reduces to

$$\mathcal{L}_i = \frac{G(\tau_2 \mid \omega_0, \mathbf{x})}{G(\tau_1 \mid \omega_0, \mathbf{x})}.$$

If the person dies at t, where $\tau_1 < t \leq \tau_2$, it becomes

$$\mathcal{L}_i = \frac{r(t \mid \omega_0, \mathbf{x}) \, G(t \mid \omega_0, \mathbf{x})}{G(\tau_1 \mid \omega_0, \mathbf{x})}.$$

Combining these two expressions gives

$$\mathcal{L}_i = \frac{[G(\tau_2 \mid \omega_0, \mathbf{x})]^{1-D_i} \, [r(t \mid \omega_0, \mathbf{x}) \, G(t \mid \omega_0, \mathbf{x})]^{D_i}}{G(\tau_1 \mid \omega_0, \mathbf{x})}. \qquad (19)$$

Thus, if the hazard and survivor functions can be expressed in terms of $\mathbf{x}$ and $\omega_0 \equiv \{t_0, y_0\}$ (which we temporarily assume is observed), the observation period need not begin at the start of the process. We stress that *(19) reduces to the likelihood for right-censored event-history data if (and only if) the hazard function is time invariant.*

Now we consider the second problem—lack of information on the initial conditions ω_0. In attempting to deal with this data gap, we assume that individual i's contribution to the likelihood $\mathcal{L}_i$ can be written as in (19). That is, we assume that the model lets the hazard and survivor functions be expressed in terms of ω_0 and $\mathbf{x}$. For the moment suppose that we know that 60% of the sample was born in 1930 and 40% in 1920, but do not know any particular person's birthdate. Since (19) gives us a formula for $\mathcal{L}_i$ for any t_0, it seems reasonable to take a weighted average of the values of $\mathcal{L}_i$ for the two birthdates. That is, we give a weight of .6 to the value of $\mathcal{L}_i$ calculated when $t_0 = 1930$ and a weight of .4 to the value of $\mathcal{L}_i$ calculated when $t_0 = 1920$. We take the weighted sum as i's contribution to the likelihood.

The same idea can be used even if there is no information about the distribution of birthdates in the sample. It is necessary to know the probability of each possible value of the initial conditions, conditional on $\mathbf{x}$: $\Pr[\omega_0 \mid \mathbf{x}]$. Then $\mathcal{L}_i$ can be calculated for each possible value of ω_0 as in (19) and multiplied by $\Pr[\omega_0 \mid \mathbf{x}]$. The sum of these products is an individual's contribution to the likelihood. Essentially this procedure takes advantage of the familiar relationship

$$\Pr[A] = \sum_k \Pr[A \mid B_k] \Pr[B_k].$$

We can write the result formally as

$$\mathcal{L}_i = \int_{\omega_0} \frac{\left[G(\tau_2 \mid \omega_0, \mathbf{x})\right]^{1-D_i} \left[r(t \mid \omega_0, \mathbf{x}) G(t \mid \omega_0, \mathbf{x})\right]^{D_i} \Pr[\omega_0 \mid \mathbf{x}]}{G(\tau_1 \mid \omega_0, \mathbf{x})} \, d\omega_0. \tag{20}$$

This strategy is sometimes referred to as **integrating out** the unobservables.

Though complicated in appearance, this procedure is not too difficult to implement as long as $\Pr[\omega_0 \mid \mathbf{x}]$ is known. There are two sources for this set of probabilities. The first source is existing empirical data. Sometimes, as we suggested in our example, the marginal distribution of ω_0 in the sample is known, even though the value of the initial conditions cannot be identified for particular sample members. More frequently, there is independent information on the distribution in the population. In our example, for instance, we might estimate the distribution of birthdates from the age distribution reported in the 1960 U.S. Census of the Population. The other way of obtaining $\Pr[\omega_0 \mid \mathbf{x}]$ is to derive it from a model. For example, following Gompertz (1825), one might assume that the mortality rate increases exponentially with age and also that the birth rate in the U.S. has some particular functional form over historical time. Together these two assumptions allow derivation (quite possibly with some effort) of the distribution of birth dates of those living in 1960. Not surprisingly, an empirical estimate of $\Pr[\omega_0 \mid \mathbf{x}]$ tends to be more accurate than one derived from a model. However, empirical estimates are not available in all substantive problems.

5.4.2 A Likelihood for Multiple Episodes

In constructing a likelihood for multiple episodes, the same two problems that occur in the case of first episodes arise again. There is the potential problem of sample selection bias. Even if one does not select a sample on the basis of occupying certain states at the start of the observation period but takes a random sample of the whole population at time τ_1, the distribution of sample members *across* various states at τ_1 and of the x's of those *within* a particular state generally differs from the distribution at t_0. To prevent biased estimates, $\mathcal{L}_i$ must be constructed in a way that takes these differences into account.

Once again, a second problem involves compensating for the missing data on each sample member's history prior to τ_1, the start of the observation period. In the case of data on multiple episodes, information may be lacking not only on the initial conditions, but also on the times and outcomes of events between t_0 and τ_1. Even the number of previous events may be unknown. This missing information tends to limit the kinds of models that can be estimated and also to complicate estimation of those models that can be estimated.

Again we begin with the problem of sample selection bias. We assume temporarily that we wish to construct a likelihood for the history from τ_1 to τ_2, but also have data on each sample member's history from t_0 to τ_1. Because the expressions for $\mathcal{L}_i$ in (17) and (18) contain nothing specific to first episodes, they apply equally well to multiple episodes. Subsequent equations differ, however.

Note that both the numerator and denominator of (18) are identical in form to (2), our starting point in constructing i's contribution to the likelihood in the case of right-censored event histories. Steps parallel to those that we took in going from (2) to (10) to (13) let equation (18) in the case of multiple episodes be written as

$$\mathcal{L}_i = \frac{\overline{G}_{y_{M+N}}(\tau_2 \mid \omega_{M+N}, \mathbf{x}) \prod_{n=1}^{M+N} r_{y_{n-1}y_n}(t_n \mid \omega_{n-1}, \mathbf{x}) G_{y_{n-1}}(t_n \mid \omega_{n-1}, \mathbf{x})}{G_{y_M}(\tau_1 \mid \omega_M, \mathbf{x}) \prod_{n=1}^{M} r_{y_{n-1}y_n}(t_n \mid \omega_{n-1}, \mathbf{x}) G_{y_{n-1}}(t_n \mid \omega_{n-1}, \mathbf{x})}$$

or

$$\mathcal{L}_i = \frac{G_{y_{M+N}}(\tau_2 \mid \omega_{M+N}, \mathbf{x})}{G_{y_M}(\tau_1 \mid \omega_M, \mathbf{x})}$$

$$\cdot \left\{ \prod_{n=M+1}^{M+N} r_{y_{n-1}y_n}(t_n \mid \omega_{n-1}, \mathbf{x}) \, G_{y_{n-1}}(t_n \mid \omega_{n-1}, \mathbf{x}) \right\}.$$

As in the case of first episodes, the expression for $\mathcal{L}_i$ depends only on transition rates and survivor functions. If they can be expressed in terms of $\mathbf{x}$ and the initial conditions, there is no obstacle to allowing the observation period to begin after t_0.

We now turn to the second problem—missing information on the history prior to τ_1. The formal solution to the problem is the same as it is in the case of first episodes. Recall that our strategy was to calculate $\mathcal{L}_i$ for a particular value of the unobserved history (ω_0 in the case of first episodes) and multiply it by the probability that the unobserved history has this particular value. We then took the sum of all possible products as i's contribution to the likelihood.

In applying this strategy to first episodes, we lacked only *one* piece of information, the initial conditions. As we discussed earlier, often the probability distribution of the initial conditions can be estimated empirically or inferred from a model. In the case of multiple episodes, analysts usually lack *several* additional pieces of information. In the worst situation, information is lacking not only on the initial conditions but also on the times and outcomes of events between t_0 and τ_1, including the number of events that have occurred prior to τ_1. In this case it is very difficult to estimate the probabilities of different possible past histories empirically or to derive them from a model unless restrictive assumptions are made (e.g., change in Y is governed by a Markov or semi-Markov process). Even if these probabilities can be estimated or predicted, "integrating them out" is difficult analytically and expensive to do computationally (via numerical integration). Moreover, estimates obtained by maximizing the resulting likelihood function are sure to be imprecise (i.e., to have large standard errors) as compared to those obtained from maximizing the corresponding likelihood for right-censored event histories. In short, much work is apt to yield disappointing results.

To be fair, we should emphasize that this statement is our informed opinion and is not based on analytic results or Monte Carlo investigations. For certain substantive problems it may be possible to obtain good empirical estimates of the distributions of different histories or to predict them from a simple but realistic model. But this fortunate circumstance does not occur in those substantive problems that interest us, so we have a dismal view of the possibility of dealing effectively with left-censored event histories when multiple episodes occur.

We should also mention that it is fairly common for fragments of the history prior to τ_1 to be recorded. Each piece of added data aids in identifying which possible past histories are more likely. Consider, for example, marital and work histories of individuals. It is rare not to know the birthdates of sample members (and their spouses). Quite frequently analysts also know the date of the most recent event—surveys often ask respondents to tell the date that their current job (or marriage) started, even if they do not obtain complete retrospective life histories. This information is extremely helpful in estimating models in which transition rates depend on the duration in a state. And it is not too uncommon for surveys to gather data on how many events have occurred in the past (e.g., how many times the person has previously been married, how many jobs have been held in the past). Each additional piece of information boosts an analyst's chances of estimating realistic models, even when some details of sample members' past histories are missing.

In the rest of this book we do not attempt to construct likelihood functions for specific models that are applicable to left-censored event histories. This omission does not mean that we believe that left-censoring is a rare or unimportant problem. In part, this decision reflects the fact that we have extensive ground to cover quite aside from this topic. In part, it results from the difficulty of implementing the approaches that we have outlined in this section. Our intent has been to alert readers to the problems raised by left-censoring, to encourage them to collect event histories that are *not* censored on the left if at all possible, and to stimulate methodological investigations of this challenging and important problem.

5.5 ML Estimators for a Single Constant Rate

Sociologists are seldom interested in modeling processes in which there is a single, constant rate of an event. Ordinarily the main objective is to explain variations in rates over time, among members of a population, across different states, and perhaps across different episodes. Nonetheless, in the rest of this chapter our discussion of ML estimation of continuous-time, discrete-state stochastic models from event-history data concentrates mainly on one of the most restrictive models—the pure growth or Poisson model.[4] The simplicity of this model lets us explicate the details of ML estimation more clearly than do complicated models. At the same time, it permits us to pursue many of the issues that arise in estimating more complex and realistic models.

Recall (see Section 4.4) that in a pure growth model the state space of $Y(t)$ consists of the nonnegative integers and that the instantaneous rate of change in $Y(t)$ is given by

$$r_{jk} = \begin{cases} \beta, & k = j+1, \\ 0, & k \neq j+1, \end{cases}$$

so that the hazard function h_j also equals β. Since a transition can only occur to the next higher integer, $Y(t)$ is a nondecreasing function of time t and increases by at most 1 in any infinitesimal interval of time. In fact, $Y(t)$ is identical to the count of events that have occurred by t, $N(t)$.

To obtain the contribution of the ith sample member to the likelihood when change in $Y(t)$ is governed by a Poisson process, simply replace r_{jk} in (16) with β. This yields

$$\mathcal{L}_i = e^{-\beta v_{i,N+1}} \prod_{n=1}^{N_i} \beta\, e^{-\beta u_{in}}.$$

Recall that $e^\alpha\, e^\beta = e^{\alpha+\beta}$. This rule lets the above equation be rewritten more simply as

$$\mathcal{L}_i = \beta^{N_i} \exp\left[-\beta\left(v_{i,N+1} + \sum_{i=1}^{I} u_{in}\right)\right]. \tag{22}$$

Now insert (22) into (1) and again collect terms. This gives

$$\mathcal{L} = \beta^N\, e^{-\beta(V+U)}. \tag{23a}$$

---

[4] The Poisson model does serve as a common and useful baseline in modeling riots, lynchings, criminal victimizations, outbreaks of war, strikes, and so forth.

⟨5⟩   **ML Estimators for a Single Constant Rate**

Notice that the likelihood function for the whole sample depends only on β; the total number of events in the sample,

$$N \equiv \sum_{i=1}^{I} N_i \equiv \sum_{i=1}^{I} n_i(\tau_{i1}, \tau_{i2}],$$

and the total time that the sample is observed, $U + V$, where

$$U \equiv \sum_{i=1}^{I} \sum_{n=1}^{N_i} u_{in};$$

$$V \equiv \sum_{i=1}^{I} v_{i,N+1}.$$

Further, it must be the case that

$$\tau_i \equiv \tau_{i2} - \tau_{i1} = v_{i,N+1} + \sum_{n=1}^{N_i} u_{in},$$

which means that $\mathcal{L}$ in (23a) can be expressed as

$$\mathcal{L} = \beta^N e^{-\beta \tau}, \tag{23b}$$

where $\tau \equiv U + V$. Thus the likelihood depends only on β, τ, and N, the total count of events in the sample.

The likelihood in (23) happens to be one that yields an explicit equation for the ML estimator of β. To find the ML estimator, differentiate the logarithm of $\mathcal{L}$ with respect to β, and then set this derivative equal to zero (because a derivative must equal zero at the maximum or minimum of a function):

$$\frac{\partial \log \mathcal{L}}{\partial \beta} = \left\{ \frac{1}{\beta} \sum_{i=1}^{I} N_i \right\} - \sum_{i=1}^{I} \tau_i = 0.$$

The only value of β satisfying this equation is

$$\beta = \frac{N}{U+V} = \frac{N}{\tau}. \tag{24}$$

This is the ML estimator of β for the Poisson model. Below we refer to the estimator in (24) as the all-spell ML estimator because it uses information on all observed episodes, whether censored or not.

We also refer below to the ML estimator that uses information on the first episode only. This likelihood function is obtained by replacing $r_{y_0 y_1}$ in (8) with β and substituting $\mathcal{L}_i$ in (1):

$$\log \mathcal{L} = \sum_{i=1}^{I} (1 - D_{i1})(-\beta v_{i1}) + D_{i1}(-\beta v_{i1} + \log \beta).$$

The likelihood above gives what we term the first-spell ML estimator:

$$\beta = \frac{D_1}{U_1 + V_1}, \qquad (25)$$

where the number of individuals in the sample with first events is

$$D_1 \equiv \sum_{i=1}^{I} D_{i1},$$

the total length of completed first episodes is

$$U_1 \equiv \sum_{i=1}^{I} u_{i1},$$

and the total length of censored first episodes is

$$V_1 \equiv \sum_{i=1}^{I} v_{i1}.$$

Information on the last (as well as the first) episode may be used to obtain a ML estimator for β. For the Poisson model, the ML estimator that uses data only on the last, censored episode is the same as the first-spell estimator. We refer to the ML estimator that uses only data on the last episode as the last-spell ML estimator. This estimator can be regarded as the consequence of looking backward in time from the end of the observation period. The last observed event is the *first* event when one looks backward in time. The ability to look backward or forward in time (so-called time reversibility) is a unique characteristic of time-stationary Markov processes.

5.6 Two Pseudo-ML Estimators

ML estimation makes it easy to express the consequences of inadequately dealing with the censoring problem. We consider the two alternatives introduced in Section 5.1. The most common procedure is to ignore censored observations. The likelihood function formed under this procedure is

$$\mathcal{L} = \prod_{i=1}^{I} \prod_{n=1}^{N_i} \beta\, e^{-\beta u_{in}},$$

giving the following pseudo-ML estimator of β:

$$\beta^* = \frac{N}{U}. \tag{26}$$

A second alternative is to recode censored observations so that events are assumed to occur at the end of the observation period. This gives a pseudo-ML estimator with the form

$$\beta^\dagger = \frac{N+I}{U+V}. \tag{27}$$

Clearly, the true ML estimator in (24) is lower than either of these estimators for any given set of data. This can be seen from the ratio of the ML estimator to the pseudo-ML estimators. In the case of (26), the estimator that ignores censored observations, β/β^* equals $U/(U+V)$, the proportion of the total observation time spanned by uncensored spells. In the case of (27), the estimator that recodes censored spells, $\beta/\beta^\dagger$ equals $N/(N+I)$, the fraction of spells that are not censored. Thus, the greater the number of censored spells and the longer the observation time spanned by them, the larger the pseudo-ML estimators relative to the true ML estimator. Since the ML estimator is unbiased in large samples, these ad hoc procedures give upwardly biased estimates in large samples. Furthermore, as we discuss below, the ML estimator is slightly upwardly biased in small samples. Because the ad hoc procedures give still higher estimates, they do not improve on the ML estimator in small samples either.

5.7 A Moment Estimator

Moment estimators, that is, estimators that replace population moments (e.g., means, variances) with sample moments, can also be applied to event histories. Several alternatives, many of which are identical to the ML estimator discussed above, are discussed by Sørensen (1977) and Tuma and Hannan (1978). Here we mention only one moment estimator that has circulated in the methodological subculture of sociology for some time and was finally proposed in print by Sørensen (1977).

Sørensen wanted to estimate β from all episodes and to correct for censoring. He considered and correctly rejected the inverse of the mean length of all spells (censored as well as uncensored), $(N+I)/(U+V)$, as upwardly biased [see equation (27)]. Instead he proposed

$$\beta_s = \frac{N+I}{U+2V}, \tag{28}$$

in which the lengths of all censored episodes are doubled. His reasoning depended on the fact that the expected length of a censored episode is twice the expected length of an episode ending in an event (see Feller, 1971). Doubling the observed length of censored episodes (i.e., V) is intended to compensate for the difference in the expected length of censored and uncensored episodes. The line of thinking that generates this estimator is sound, but the quality of this estimator is poor, as we report below.

5.8 Monte Carlo Results on Effects of Censoring

Though the estimators discussed above use different information about events within a period of time, all but those in (26), (27), and (28) are ML estimators, which are asympotically normal, unbiased, and efficient under quite general conditions. In other words, in large samples these estimators cannot be improved on. However, for small samples the ML estimator in (25) is known to be slightly upwardly biased and to have a nonnormal distribution (Bartholomew, 1957, 1963; Mendenhall and Lehman, 1960).

Below we report results of a Monte Carlo study that investigated how sample size and censoring affect the properties of various ML estimators. These results are useful for showing that in small

⟨5⟩ Monte Carlo Results on Effects of Censoring

samples the upward bias is quite small and that the large-sample theory is a good approximation for the types of situations confronted by most sociologists. It also shows the costs of ignoring information on certain episodes. Finally, it lets us contrast the ML estimators with the non-ML estimator that doubles the length of censored spells.

In all phases of the Monte Carlo study, we examined samples of size 25, 50, 100, 250, and 500 and chose the true value of β to equal 1 per unit of time. (For expository purposes we assume that time is measured in years.) For each sample member we used the relationship

$$\log G_j(u_n) = \log\left[e^{-\beta u_n}\right] = -\beta u_n \tag{29}$$

to simulate u_n, the waiting time between events $n-1$ and n. For each sample member we drew a pseudo-random number from a (0,1) uniform distribution and called this $G(u_n)$; then we used (29) to calculate u_n. For each sample size we generated 100 data sets.

We begin with the results for (25), the first-spell ML estimator. Table 5.1 reports the mean of the estimate of β in the 100 data sets of each sample size. If the estimator is unbiased, the mean in the 100 data sets should approximately equal 1, the true value of β. With no censoring, the mean of β for $I = 25$ is 5.5% higher than the true value. However, the percentage bias declines to 1.5% for $I = 50$ and is negligible for the larger sample sizes. This result is encouraging because the relative bias seems quite small for sample sizes that sociologists usually consider small.

Next we consider the effect of censoring. First, we chose the length of the observation period τ so that the probability of no event prior to τ, that is, the level of censoring, was .2, .5, .8, and .9. Then we used an expression like (29) to calculate τ except that τ replaced u_n. If u_1 (the length of the first episode) was greater than τ for a case, then the case was treated as censored at τ. If u_1 was less than τ, it was uncensored.

Table 5.1 reports the mean of β in 100 data sets of each sample size and censoring level. Three results are of interest. First, for medium-sized samples, censoring has a negligible effect on the bias. Second, for small samples, especially $I = 25$, censoring actually reduces the upward bias in the estimator. Finally, as we expected, censoring increases the variance of the estimator considerably. A shift from 0% to 20% censoring approximately doubles the variance;

Table 5.1. Effect of censoring on the ML estimator of a constant rate $\alpha = 1$, using data on first episodes (100 data sets for each sample size and censoring level)

Sample size	Censoring level	Mean of $\hat{\alpha}$	Variance of $\hat{\alpha}$
25	0	1.055	0.058
	.20	1.059	0.091
	.50	1.034	0.110
	.80	1.018	0.206
	.90	1.019	0.426
50	0	1.015	0.023
	.20	1.017	0.043
	.50	0.998	0.057
	.80	0.991	0.094
	.90	0.974	0.168
100	0	1.006	0.012
	.20	1.006	0.023
	.50	0.997	0.030
	.80	0.996	0.055
	.90	0.990	0.103
250	0	1.005	0.004
	.20	1.004	0.010
	.50	0.999	0.012
	.80	1.006	0.028
	.90	1.010	0.049
500	0	1.001	0.002
	.20	0.999	0.004
	.50	0.995	0.006
	.80	1.000	0.013
	.90	0.996	0.023

so does a shift from 80% to 90% censoring. Insofar as the mean-squared error is concerned, the impact of censoring on the variance actually swamps its effect on bias. For the combination of small samples and high levels of censoring, which implies few observed events,

⟨5⟩ **Monte Carlo Results on Effects of Censoring**   143

the estimator is very imprecise. However, in relatively large samples the effects of even extreme levels of censoring are modest. These results suggest that the first-spell ML estimator has good properties for small samples with slight censoring and for moderately large samples with even high degrees of censoring. We also found that the distribution of the estimates tends to be fairly symmetrical even in moderately large samples, as asymptotic theory implies.

To this point we have estimated the rate at which an event occurs from information on first episodes only. In many research contexts multiple events occur within a given observation period τ. To investigate the way information on multiple episodes affects ML estimators, we chose τ to be 1 year, so that the average number of events within the period would be 1. However, during this period some sample members have more than one event and others none.

We contrast three estimators of the rate when τ equals 1 year: (1) the ML estimator in (24), which uses data on all spells in the first year; (2) the ML estimator that uses information only on the length of the last spell in the first year; and (3) the moment estimator in (28), which doubles the length of censored spells. The findings are given in Table 5.2.

The results for the ML estimator for all spells in the first year [row (1) of Table 5.2] are very good, much better than those for the first-spell ML estimator (compare Table 5.1). For example, the average bias for $I = 25$ is only 0.5%, as compared with 5.5% to 1.8% for the first-spell ML estimator with the same sample size. This bias is remarkably small for such a small sample.

Next consider the ML estimator for the last spell in the first year [row (2) of Table 5.2]. Both the upward bias and variance are larger than for the all-spell ML estimator in row (1). So the last-spell ML estimator is clearly inferior to the all-spell ML estimator. However, it is still a reasonably good estimator and could be used if only the starting date of the last spell is known or accurate.

Now consider Sørensen's proposal—the moment estimator that doubles the length of censored spells [row (3) of Table 5.2]. It is upwardly biased by about 23%, which is much larger than the bias of any other estimator studied. Clearly, this estimator cannot be recommended.

Finally, we chose τ equal to 5 years. We compare two estimators: the ML estimator in (24), which uses data on *all* spells in the

Table 5.2. Quality of alternative estimators of a constant rate $\alpha = 1$ (100 data sets for each estimator and sample size)

Estimator[a]	Sample size	Mean of $\hat{\alpha}$	Variance of $\hat{\alpha}$
(1)	25	1.005	0.035
	50	1.005	0.021
	100	0.999	0.010
(2)	25	1.047	0.060
	50	1.040	0.041
	100	1.017	0.017
(3)	25	1.239	0.025
	50	1.236	0.016
	100	1.229	0.007
(4)	25	0.980	0.042
	50	0.975	0.018
	100	0.988	0.009
(5)	25	1.112	0.003
	50	1.110	0.001
	100	1.112	0.001

[a]Note:
(1) ≡ ML estimator for all spells in the first year.
(2) ≡ ML estimator for the last spell in the first year.
(3) ≡ Moment estimator with the last spell for the first year doubled.
(4) ≡ ML estimator for all spells in the fifth year.
(5) ≡ ML estimator for the last spell in the fifth year.

fifth year, and the ML estimator that uses data on the *last* spell in the fifth year. The former lets us examine the effects of having both left- and right-censoring. The latter lets us study β when almost all sample members have previously had at least one event.[5]

First consider the results for the ML estimator for all spells in

---

[5]Given the assumptions of the model and $\beta = 1$, the probability of no event in 5 years is less than .01. Consequently, virtually every sample member has at least one event when τ equals 5 years.

the fifth year [see row (4) of Table 5.2], in which data are censored on both the left and right. The all-spell ML estimator is slightly downwardly biased, by approximately 2%. For a given sample size the variance is about the same as for the all-spell ML estimator for the first year. On the other hand, the estimator that uses only data on the last episode during the fifth year [see row (5) of Table 5.2], has a fairly large upward bias (about 11%) but a very small variance. For small samples ($I = 25$ and 50), this estimator has a smaller mean-squared error than the all-spell ML estimator for the fifth year. With larger sample sizes, however, it has a larger mean-squared error than the all-spell ML estimator. Consequently, the choice between these two estimators is less clear than in the case of data on the first year, where data are censored on the right but not the left.

Overall, the results of the Monte Carlo study indicate that all ML estimators adjust for censoring reasonably well. In fact, except for very small samples, the quality of these estimators appears good even with extreme levels of censoring. This finding is very important for analyzing data in which the observation period is short relative to the average length of time between events, a common situation in studies of marriage and divorce, failure of organizations, and so forth. The quality of estimators based on first and last spells is generally not as good as that of estimators that use all spells during some period. However, even first-spell estimators do reasonably well, especially in moderately large samples. The only non-ML estimator investigated, the moment estimator that doubles the length of censored episodes (see Section 5.7), is much poorer than any ML estimator. We recommend that it not be used.

5.9 Measurement Error in Dates

So far we have assumed accurate measurement of the timing (or dates) of events and, by implication, of the length of episodes. Do our optimistic conclusions about the quality of ML estimators applied to event-history data still hold when dates are reported unreliably? It is important to answer this question because measurement error in dates is usually a serious concern in sociological applications of event-history analysis. Although we cannot give a general answer to this question, we have conducted a small Monte Carlo study that provides a preliminary answer for a limited class of situations. Below we report some of the main findings of the study. The full details are reported in Carroll et al. (1978b).

We used the same procedure described earlier to generate the length of episodes [see equation (29) and the related discussion]. We simulated measurement error by altering the times generated by (29). We studied two different types of measurement error, time independent and time dependent. Specifically, we calculated the length of the nth episode with measurement error u_n as

$$u_n^* = \gamma_j u_n, \tag{30}$$

where u_n denotes the true length of the nth episode generated by (29) and γ_j is a pseudo-random deviate that introduces measurement error, as described below. The true date of the nth event is

$$t_n = \sum_{m=1}^{n} u_m,$$

while the date of the nth event with measurement error is

$$t_n^* = \sum_{m=1}^{n} u_m^*.$$

In the first type of measurement error, $j = 1$ and γ_1 represents a pseudo-random deviate from a gamma distribution with a mean of 1 and with a variance of one-tenth. In the second type, $j = 2$ and γ_2 denotes a similar deviate also with a mean of 1 but with a variance of one-tenth of u_n.[6] The length of an episode with measurement error has the same expected value as the length without measurement error but has a different variance. For the time-independent error, the variance of u_n is 1.1, while for the time-dependent error the variance of u_n equals 1.6. Thus, if we measure reliability as $\text{Var}(u_n)/\text{Var}(u_n^*)$, then our simulation generates event-history data with .91 reliability (time-independent error) and .63 reliability (time-dependent error) in the observed length of an episode.

[6]We generated the gamma-distributed deviate by a rejection technique proposed by Johnk (1964) and developed by Phillips and Beightler (1972). The simulated distribution of γ is $f(\gamma) = \gamma^{\alpha-1} \exp[-\gamma/\phi]/\phi^\alpha \Gamma(\alpha)$, where γ, α and ϕ are always positive. We used $\alpha = 10$, $\phi = 0.10$ for the first type of measurement error ($j = 1$) and $\alpha = 10u_i$, $\phi = 0.10u_i$ for the second type ($j = 2$).

One additional issue must be addressed before turning to the results: the interaction between censoring and measurement error in the length of an episode. We determined τ, the length of the observation period, from the expected proportion surviving to a particular time according to the true model. We did not alter τ to compensate for effects of measurement error on the proportion surviving to τ. However, measurement error sometimes shifts the timing of an event from one side of τ to the other. For example, suppose τ is 0.5 and an individual's nth event occurs at $t_n = 0.45$. If there is no measurement error, this event is observed. However, with measurement error the time of this event may be $t_n = 0.52$, in which case it is not observed. We call this phenomenon *false censoring* because measurement error shifts events *out of* the observation period, causing them to be censored. Similarly, measurement error can also shift events *into* the observation period, creating *false events*.

Problems of false censoring and false events are likely to arise when the investigator imposes censoring levels on event-history data. For example, a sociologist studying merger activity of organizations might confine the analysis to a certain historical period. During this period certain organizations in the sample are not involved in mergers and hence are censored cases. However, some of these censored cases may have actually have been involved in a merger during the selected period, but the date of the merger may be erroneously recorded as occurring in some other period. In this case, measurement error creates false censoring. Other organizations may have mergers in an earlier or later period, but measurement error may shift these events into the selected period, creating false events. If the entire event history is used in the analysis, measurement error alters the dates of events but does not affect the actual number of events. By imposing an observation period, the investigator creates an error in the number of events observed in the period.

We were uncertain how false censoring and false events would affect ML estimators based on event-history data. Consequently, we pay special attention to this issue in the results discussed below.

5.10 Monte Carlo Results on Measurement Error

We begin by reporting the Monte Carlo results for a single, nonrepeatable event. Table 5.3 gives the mean and variance of the estimate of β in 100 data sets of each sample size and censoring level.

Table 5.3. Effect of measurement error on the ML estimator of a constant rate $\alpha = 1$, using data on first episodes (100 data sets for each sample size and censoring level)

Sample size	Censoring level	No measurement error		Time-independent multiplicative error		Time-dependent multiplicative error	
		Mean of $\hat{\alpha}$	Variance of $\hat{\alpha}$	Mean of $\hat{\alpha}$	Variance of $\hat{\alpha}$	Mean of $\hat{\alpha}$	Variance of $\hat{\alpha}$
25	0	1.082	0.048	1.273	0.078	1.364	0.089
	.20	1.048	0.075	1.319	0.112	1.366	0.116
	.50	1.040	0.116	1.371	0.172	1.330	0.161
	.80	0.973	0.269	1.382	0.422	1.115	0.344
	.90	0.999	0.482	1.367	0.751	1.051	0.524
50	0	1.028	0.023	1.227	0.038	1.282	0.048
	.20	1.021	0.035	1.302	0.043	1.341	0.052
	.50	1.023	0.052	1.320	0.050	1.291	0.065
	.80	0.987	0.092	1.338	0.106	1.136	0.110
	.90	1.003	0.209	1.374	0.272	1.037	0.221
100	0	1.009	0.010	1.201	0.016	1.243	0.024
	.20	1.016	0.017	1.293	0.027	1.324	0.022
	.50	1.032	0.023	1.325	0.033	1.298	0.029
	.80	1.013	0.063	1.376	0.081	1.139	0.067
	.90	1.003	0.109	1.358	0.135	1.095	0.116

As we expected, when there is measurement error, the quality of the ML estimator deteriorates: both the bias and the variance increase substantially, with a few exceptions. Several patterns are noteworthy. Both types of measurement error produce an upward bias in the estimated rate. This pattern reflects at least partially the parametric form used to simulate measurement error. Although the gamma-distributed error has a mean of 1 in both types of measurement error, the median is slightly less than 1. Consequently, the simulated measurement error decreases the observed length of an episode more frequently than it increases it. This may be the reason why the estimated rate is uniformly higher than the true rate.

The other interesting result in Table 5.3 concerns the effect

⟨ 5 ⟩   Monte Carlo Results on Measurement Error   149

of censoring when there is measurement error in the length of an episode. As censoring increases, bias usually increases when there is time-independent measurement error. We think the pattern of greater bias with increased censoring results from false censoring and false events, which alter the number of events observed in the period. For the time-dependent disturbance, bias first increases with censoring and then decreases as censoring becomes still greater.

Next we consider the problem of measurement error when events are repeatable. We simulated data on multiple events using the following procedure. We again used equation (29) to simulate the length of each episode, repeating this procedure for each individual i until t_{in} exceeded 5 years. We then censored observations at 5 years. Because the true rate equals 1, the expected number of events for each individual during the 5-year period is five. Of course, some have more and others fewer. Moreover, as we have already commented, false censoring and false events introduce additional noise into the number of events within the 5-year observation period.

Again both time-independent and time-dependent measurement errors are considered. We introduce time-independent errors in exactly the same way as we did above for the case of a single nonrepeatable event. We altered the form of the time-dependent error, however. Many event histories are collected retrospectively. For data collected with this design, the unreliability of the date of an event tends to increase monotonically with the distance from the survey date. So we specified that the variance of the time-dependent measurement error increases linearly with the distance from τ, the end of the observation period.[7]

Table 5.4 presents the mean and variance of several of the ML estimators considered in earlier sections. We begin with the ML estimator for all spells in 5 years. As expected, neither the mean nor

---

[7]Specifically, we used a gamma-distributed disturbance with a mean of 1 and variance $0.10(5 - t_{in})$. We constrained the process so that the order of events was fixed. Consequently, the timing of the nth event with measurement error must be later than the time of the $(n-1)$th event, which also included measurement error. For example, let $t_1 = 1$, $t_2 = 2$, and t_1^* (the time of the first event with measurement error) = 1.5. Then, t_2^* was constrained to be greater than $t_1^* = 1.5$. Thus we required $t_{y+1}^* > t_y^*$ for all values of y. When a time did not satisfy this constraint, we redrew the disturbance and recalculated t^*.

Table 5.4. Effect of measurement error on alternative ML estimators of a constant rate $\alpha = 1$, using data on multiple episodes (100 data sets for each estimator and sample size)

ML estimator[a]	Sample size	No measurement error		Time-independent multiplicative error		Time-dependent multiplicative error	
		Mean of $\hat{\alpha}$	Variance of $\hat{\alpha}$	Mean of $\hat{\alpha}$	Variance of $\hat{\alpha}$	Mean of $\hat{\alpha}$	Variance of $\hat{\alpha}$
(1)	50	0.996	0.004	0.996	0.004	0.996	0.004
	100	1.007	0.002	1.007	0.002	1.007	0.002
(2)	50	1.119	0.001	1.078	0.001	1.171	0.002
	100	1.112	—	1.082	—	1.174	—
(3)	50	1.012	0.027	1.238	0.044	1.353	0.063
	100	1.019	0.011	1.258	0.017	1.382	0.037
(4)	50	1.016	0.023	0.715	0.020	1.353	0.043
	100	1.025	0.012	0.722	0.009	1.392	0.025

[a]Note:
(1) ≡ ML estimator for all spells in 5 years.
(2) ≡ ML estimator for last spell in the fifth year.
(3) ≡ ML estimator for first spell.
(4) ≡ ML estimator for all spells in the fifth year.

the variance of the estimated rate is altered by measurement error. With this research design the total number of events is unaltered by measurement error. Consequently, the all-spell ML estimator is unaffected by measurement error. The estimator that uses only the last-spell in the fifth year fares almost as well. The percentage bias in β is roughly 8% for the time-independent error and 17% for the time-dependent error. Not surprisingly, the first-spell ML estimator has a larger upward bias. Though the gamma-distributed error has a mean of 1, it decreases more often than raises the length of an episode, as we mentioned above. The increased bias in the estimated rate for the first-spell ML estimator probably reflects this fact.

The estimator that uses all spells in the last year has an odd pattern of effects. The time-independent error leads to a downward bias in the estimated rate, while the time-dependent error induces an upward bias. A possible explanation of this can be found again in the parametric form of the disturbance, which decreases the median length of an episode and therefore tends to increase the estimated rate. However, for a given 5-year observation period the number of events is fixed. Thus the gamma-distributed disturbance shifts events to earlier points in time. Consequently, finding a lower estimated rate in the fifth year is not surprising because events have been disproportionately shifted to an earlier period. In the case of time-dependent errors, this shift is less pronounced. The disturbances are smaller in the fifth year because recent events are more accurately recalled. Therefore, the events are not shifted as much as in the first year. However, some events are still shifted out of the fifth year, leading to a lower estimated rate for the fifth-year estimator. The higher estimate of β for the estimator that uses all spells in the last year and data with a time-dependent error is an apparent anomaly.[8]

Several items pertaining to investigator-imposed censoring deserve mention. First, the combined effect of measurement error and censoring on bias are less clear with data on multiple events. On the whole, estimators tend to be upwardly biased in this situation, except for the ML estimator that uses data for the entire 5-year period. This estimator is insensitive to measurement error.

5.11 Markov Models with Multiple Outcomes

In most realistic research applications, the process of change is more complex than the discussion to this point has indicated.

---

[8]This result might be explained by the constraint requiring the order of events to remain constant. For example, if the length of an early episode is made dramatically longer by the disturbance, then subsequent events are shifted to later times by the ordering constraint. Although the disturbance lowers the median length of an episode, a single large increase in the timing of an event can cause later events to stack up near the end of the observation period. Because the time-dependent disturbance introduces greater variance into the length of earlier episodes, this phenomenon becomes more likely. Consequently, events are likely to be bunched in the fifth year more often for the time-dependent measurement error than for the time-independent error, leading to a greater upward bias in the estimated rate for the time-dependent measurement error.

Usually multiple kinds of events can occur, and not all rates are the same. We consider two examples.

Sørensen's (1977) work on censoring was motivated by an interest in the rate at which people voluntarily change jobs. Implicitly there are at least two kinds of events: voluntary and involuntary job shifts. In his empirical analysis, Sørensen (1975) ignored data on the theoretically uninteresting event—an involuntary job shift.

Our second example concerns the problem of attrition in panel studies that gather event histories for the periods between successive waves. Usually some people interviewed in earlier waves do not answer questions in later waves. So, for example, in analyzing rates of change in marital status from such data, we must consider three events: marriage, marital dissolution, and attrition from the study. Virtually all reports from panel studies ignore data on those who later leave the study.

From our foregoing analysis, it should not be surprising that excluding the observations on those with a theoretically uninteresting event (e.g., an involuntary job shift or an exit from a panel study) leads to biased estimates of the substantively interesting rates (e.g., the rate of a voluntary job shift and rates of change in marital status). We illustrate this point with a three-state model. For simplicity we consider only the first event for those initially in state 1 and assume that transition rates are time invariant. Instead of a single parameter β, we consider β_{12} and β_{13}, which denote the rates of changes from state 1 to 2 and from state 1 to 3, respectively. The rate of leaving state 1 is just $(\beta_{12} + \beta_{13})$.

Substituting these rates into the likelihood for data on first episodes when change in Y is governed by a time-stationary Markov process [see (8)] yields

$$\log \mathcal{L} = \sum_{i=1}^{I} (1 - D_{i12} - D_{i13}) \left[-(\beta_{12} + \beta_{13}) v_{i1} \right]$$

$$+ D_{i12} \log \beta_{12} + D_{i13} \log \beta_{13}$$

$$- (D_{i12} + D_{i13})(\beta_{12} + \beta_{13})(u_{i12} + u_{i13}),$$

where D_{i1k} is a dummy varible that equals 1 if case i moves from state 1 to state k in the observation period and otherwise equals

⟨5⟩ Markov Models with Multiple Outcomes 153

zero, u_{i1k} is the completed length of a spell in state 1 that ends with a move to state k, and v_{i1} is the censored length of a spell in state 1 for case i. The ML estimators are

$$\beta_{1k} = \frac{D_{1k}}{U_{12} + U_{13} + V_1}, \tag{31}$$

for $k = 2$ or 3, where the total length of completed episodes ending in a move from state 1 to state k is

$$U_{1k} \equiv \sum_{i=1}^{I} u_{i1k};$$

the total number of moves from state 1 to state k is

$$D_{1k} \equiv \sum_{i=1}^{I} D_{i1k};$$

and, as before, V_1 is the total length of censored episodes. (The subscript 1 signals that all I cases begin in state 1 by assumption.) The main point of (31) is that the estimators of *both* rates depend on the sum of *all* time in state 1, including the time in state 1 spent by those who move to what may be a theoretically uninteresting state (e.g., an involuntary job shift; attrition).

As before, we contrast the ML estimator with a pseudo-ML estimator that ignores certain observations. This time we consider the consequences of ignoring cases that move to state 3 when estimating β_{12}. The pseudo-ML estimator is just

$$\beta_{12} = \frac{D_{12}}{U_{12} + V_1}.$$

Clearly, this formula gives a higher estimate of the rate than does the ML estimator in (31). Because the latter has good statistical properties and, if anything, is slightly upwardly biased, we again conclude that the pseudo-ML estimator yields an upwardly biased estimate of the rate. This is an instance of the general phenomenon that selection of sample members in terms of endogenous variables biases estimates of causal effects. ML estimators avoid this problem.

5.12 Conclusions

Data on event histories, which record the dates of events, are likely to become increasingly common as sociologists become more aware of their value in studying change over time. These data are almost always censored, that is, information is missing on events that occur before or after a certain observation period. Unless investigators deal with censoring in a sound way, they are likely to make erroneous inferences about the change process.

We have discussed several Markov models of the occurrence of events and several approaches to estimation when event histories are censored. We considered the Poisson model at length because the methodological issues are more easily understood for this model. We showed analytically that pseudo-ML approaches to the censoring problem give biased estimates of rates. We conducted a Monte Carlo study of the small-sample properties of ML estimators for censored event histories. Our results showed that the various ML estimators have very good properties in small samples when the degree of censoring is small or in medium-sized samples even when the degree of censoring is high. Further, we found that measurement error in the length of an episode causes only moderate deterioration in the quality of the ML estimator. In fact, our studies suggest that the most pronounced effects of measurement error can be avoided if the investigator does not impose arbitrary observation periods on complete event histories. When data on the timing of natural events are available, they should be used in entirety. It appears that investigators following this advice can then place a high degree of confidence in ML estimates of the rate at which an event occurs.

6
Models for Heterogeneous Populations

The discussion in Chapters 3–5 concentrated mainly on analyzing change in a qualitative variable in a homogeneous population. But social scientists invariably think that populations are heterogeneous—that members of the population being studied vary in observed and unobserved characteristics affecting the process of change. Understanding sources of variation in the process of change within a population is almost always a fundamental goal when social scientists study change.

In Chapter 3 we described exploratory and descriptive approaches to analyzing population heterogeneity. These involved estimation of descriptive statistics pertaining to event histories within cross-classifications of explanatory variables. We illustrated this approach with plots of duration on the Seattle and Denver Income Maintenance Experiments (SIME/DIME) versus the Aalen estimates of the cumulative marital dissolution rate for white and black couples with and without negative income tax (NIT) treatments (see Figure 3.5). The slope of one of these curves provides an estimate of the marital dissolution rate in the group. The plots indicate that the slope of the curve is much steeper for those with NIT treatments than for controls. This finding suggests that the NIT treatments increased the marital dissolution rate of white and black couples.

Can analysis stop with these exploratory approaches? If we truly want to understand sources of heterogeneity in the process of change, the answer is no both in our particular example and in general. In our example, the NIT treatments are only one source of heterogeneity in marital dissolution rates. Treatments were assigned randomly within combinations of stratification variables (race, site, marital status, and normal earnings level). Consequently, NIT treatments are not statistically independent of these variables (as they would be in simple random assignment of treatments to subjects). Thus, the difference in the slopes of the curves for controls and those with NIT treatments in Figure 3.5 could result from differences in the stratification variables for those with and without NIT treatments. To obtain unbiased estimates of the treatment effects, one must control for the stratification variables.

The need to control for more than one explanatory variable is ubiquitous in social research. Explanatory variables hypothesized to affect the process of change are rarely independent of one another in nonexperimental research. To estimate the genuine effect of a particular variable, one must control for other variables with which it is correlated. There are at least two ways of doing this.

First, the exploratory strategy illustrated in Figure 3.5 can be extended by estimating transition rates within cross-classifications of explanatory variables. As we noted in Chapter 3, this exploratory strategy quickly leads to vanishingly small numbers of observations within a cell, except in huge samples. Consequently, a second approach, namely, expressing the dependence of the process of change on explanatory variables in a parametric form, has great appeal.

Two main strategies for modeling population heterogeneity in continuous-time stochastic models of change in qualitative variables have been proposed. One, introduced to sociologists by Coleman (1964a), expresses fundamental parameters of a process as functions of observed explanatory variables. Another consists of postulating that the fundamental parameters are random variables with a known probability distribution. The simplest social-scientific implementation of this strategy is the well-known Mover-Stayer model proposed by Blumen, Kogan, and McCarthy (1955). A third strategy combines the other two. It assumes that fundamental parameters are functions of observed explanatory variables and of a random disturbance with a known probability distribution. To the best of our knowledge, this last strategy was first implemented by Tuma (1978) and is still relatively undeveloped.

We consider each of these three strategies in this chapter. In Section 6.1 we begin by discussing the first strategy—explicit specification of fundamental parameters in terms of observed explanatory variables. We emphasize this strategy because it seems more consistent with the social-scientific goals of understanding the sources of population heterogeneity and testing hypotheses about causal effects than does the second strategy. We compare various specifications of the dependence of transition rates on explanatory variables. Section 6.2 presents an illustration that shows how we attempted to explain the simple treatment-control differences in marital dissolution rates seen in Figure 3.5 by parameterizing the effects of NIT treatments in a way suggested by substantive arguments.

Section 6.3 discusses issues pertaining to models that add unobserved heterogeneity to the models discussed in Section 6.2. Section 6.4 illustrates such combined models using the Coleman–Rossi data on job shifts. Finally, Section 6.5 discusses work on the effects of misspecifying the distribution of the unobserved heterogeneity.

6.1 Parameterizing Observed Heterogeneity

Several important issues confront analysts who want to parameterize the effects of observed explanatory variables on transition rates. The most pressing question is, What is the nature of the relationship between transition rates and explanatory variables? Once this question is answered, more practical issues arise. We want to know, first, how to estimate the effects of causal variables and, second, how to test whether the effects of causal variables differ significantly from certain hypothesized values. Because we included a vector of explanatory variables in our discussion of maximum-likelihood (ML) estimation of stochastic models from event-history data in Chapter 5 and also indicated how to test such models in Section 5.2, we concentrate on the first question in this section.

Obviously the form of the relationship between transition rates and explanatory variables is preeminently a substantive question. Nevertheless, certain functional relationships may have wider applicability than others. In static analysis of metric variables, for example, social scientists turn automatically to linear models. We do not condone unthinking reliance on linear models for such analyses or think that all effects on metric variables are additive. Still, this response is usually justified for two reasons. First, after suitable transformation, many nonlinear relationships become linear in parameters (if not in variables), making the linear model more general than it seems at first.[1] Second, the linear model often provides a surprisingly good first approximation to more complicated relationships.

By analogy one might expect a linear relationship between transition rates and explanatory variables to play an equally central role in analyses of change in discrete variables. Coleman (1964a) thought so—virtually all of his examples that decompose transition rates in terms of explanatory variables premise a linear relationship between transition rates and explanatory variables. It has seemed natural to others, too (e.g., see Tuma, 1973, 1976). But a linear relationship between transition rates and causal variables has disadvantages that do not arise in the standard linear model of a metric variable. As the limit of a probability measure, transition rates must be positive. But a line may extend into negative as well as positive regions of a space. Suppose we postulate a linear relationship between the transition rate r_{jk} and the vector of explanatory variables $\mathbf{x}$, for example,

$$r_{jk} = \boldsymbol{\alpha}'_{jk}\mathbf{x}, \qquad (1)$$

where $\boldsymbol{\alpha}_{jk}$ denotes a vector of parameters to be estimated. Unless appropriate constraints are placed on $\boldsymbol{\alpha}_{jk}$, we are likely to obtain the absurd result that estimated transition rates are negative for some values of $\mathbf{x}$.

This problem has a simple solution. Recall that in analyses of metric variables it is common to express the *logarithm* of a nonnegative metric variable as linear in the explanatory variables. This suggests that we posit a log-linear relationship between transition rates and explanatory variables $\mathbf{x}$,

$$\log r_{jk} = \boldsymbol{\alpha}'_{jk}\mathbf{x}, \qquad (2)$$

which implies that

$$r_{jk} = e^{\boldsymbol{\alpha}'_{jk}\mathbf{x}}, \qquad (3)$$

[1] Use of a transformation does make probabilistic analysis more complicated, however. If one assumes that the original nonlinear model has some simple, well-behaved probability structure, the probability structure of the transformed model is ordinarily very complicated.

⟨6⟩ Parameterizing Observed Heterogeneity

or

$$r_{jk} = \prod_{m=1}^{M} (\theta_{jkm})^{x_m}, \qquad (4)$$

where $\theta_{jkm} = e^{\alpha_{jkm}}$ and M is the length of the vector **x**. Outside the context of a particular substantive problem, there is no clearcut reason for choosing (1) rather than (3), other than familiarity and tradition. Most theorizing done by sociologists has been of the sort that generates hypotheses about "y rising as x increases" or "y falling as x increases," and so forth. Both (1) and (3) are consistent with such statements. Lacking any specific substantive arguments for preferring (1) over (3), we concentrate on models built on (3) because it conveniently prevents the prediction of negative rates.

Because most sociologists are relatively unfamiliar with loglinear relationships and with transition rates, we begin by discussing how to interpret the coefficients in a model like (3). For simplicity we assume that the objective is to interpret α, the coefficient of a representative variable x within the vector **x**. Since

$$e^{\alpha+\beta} = e^{\alpha} \cdot e^{\beta},$$

(3) and (4) can be rewritten in the following way, where the subscripts j and k are suppressed for simplicity:

$$r = e^{\alpha x} r^* \qquad (5a)$$
$$= \theta^x r^*, \qquad (5b)$$

where $\theta = e^{\alpha}$ and r^* is the rate when $\exp(\alpha x) = 1$, that is, when $x = 0$. We let r^* express the combined effects of all variables in **x** other than x so that these other variables do not distract us as we interpret the effect of x on the rate.

Note first that if $\alpha = 0$ (or equivalently, if $\theta = 1$), then $r = r^*$ for all values of x. In other words, a shift in x has no influence on the rate r. Of more interest is the way the rate r changes as x changes. The slope dr/dx is the change in r, dr, for a small (infinitesimal) change in x, dx. This is simply

$$\frac{dr}{dx} = \alpha e^{\alpha x} r^* \qquad (6a)$$
$$= \alpha r. \qquad (6b)$$

Because the rate r is always positive, the slope depends on the sign of α. If α is negative, r decreases as x increases; if α is positive, r increases as x increases. Equation (6) indicates that the magnitude of the change in r for an infinitesimal change in x depends on the value of r. In fact, α is simply the fractional change in r for an infinitesimal change in x. Some analysts like to multiply α by 100 and call it the percentage change in r accompanying an infinitesimal change in x.

We stress the phrase "infinitesimal change in x" because α is *not* the change in r accompanying a 1-unit change in x. If the relationship between the rate and explanatory variables were linear, this distinction would be unnecessary. For a linear relationship, the change in the outcome is a constant multiple of the change in each explanatory variable, other things being equal. *But for a log-linear relationship, the size of the change in* r *depends on the magnitude of* r. So discussing the effect of a variable requires more care than in linear models.

Define $r(x) = \exp(\alpha x)\, r^*$. Now consider the rate when x increases by 1 unit, that is, to $(x+1)$:

$$r(x+1) = e^{\alpha(x+1)}\, r^* = e^{\alpha x + \alpha}\, r^*$$
$$= e^{\alpha}\, e^{\alpha x}\, r^* = e^{\alpha}\, r(x).$$

We see that the rate $r(x+1)$ is $\theta = e^{\alpha}$ times as great as the rate $r(x)$. For example, suppose $\theta = 2$. This means that a 1-unit increase in x doubles the rate, or, phrased differently, increases the rate by 100%. To interpret the effect of x in percentage terms, one can say that a 1-unit change in x leads to a percentage change in r of $100(\theta - 1)$. This is not exactly the same as 100α, the percentage change in r accompanying an infinitesimal change in x, but the two are close if α is small:

$$\theta - 1 = e^{\alpha} - 1$$
$$= \left[1 + \alpha + \alpha^2/2! + \alpha^3/3! + \cdots\right] - 1$$
$$= \alpha + \left[\alpha^2/2! + \alpha^3/3! + \cdots\right]$$
$$\approx \alpha,$$

for α much less than 1.

⟨6⟩ Parameterizing Observed Heterogeneity

Table 6.1. Some useful transformations of a causal variable z when $r = \exp[\alpha f(z)] r^*$ and $z > 0$.

	$f(z)$	dr/dz	d^2r/dz^2
1.	z	αr	$\alpha^2 r$
2.	z^2	$2\alpha z r$	$2\alpha r(1 + 2\alpha z^2)$
3.	$\log z$	$\alpha r/z$	$\alpha(\alpha - 1)r/z^2$
4.	$-1/z$	$\alpha r/z^2$	$\alpha r(\alpha - 2z)/z^4$

We find it convenient to express the effect of a dummy variable on a transition rate in terms of θ because this quantity is the ratio of the rate for those with a value of 1 on the dummy variable to the rate for those with a value of zero when all other variables have the same values. But θ is much less meaningful when x is a metric variable; we then prefer to report the effect of x in terms of α. In the examples below, some variables are dummies; then we report the effect of a variable as θ. Other variables are metric, and we then report α.

It may seem overly restrictive to limit discussion to log-linear relationships between transition rates and explanatory variables. But, as in linear regression analysis, the term "linearity" refers to the relationship between the outcome and the parameters, rather than that between the causal variables themselves. By setting x in (5) equal to various transformations of an observed explanatory variable z, one can introduce a variety of patterns of relationships between the transition rate and the causal variable z. Table 6.1 lists four transformations that we have found useful in empirical analyses and summarizes a few characteristics of each transformation. Notice that dr/dz is positive (i.e., r increases as z increases) when $\alpha > 0$; the opposite holds when $\alpha < 0$.

Choosing one transformation rather than another may seem difficult, especially because transition rates are not directly observable. Inability to observe transition rates directly tends to hamper thinking about such transformations. To sharpen intuition about the choice of one transformation rather than another, consider the case in which transition rates are independent of time, as we assume throughout the present chapter. If $r = \exp[\alpha f(z)]\, r^*$ and $z > 0$, as in Table 6.1, the expected duration in a state equals the inverse of r [see (18) in Chapter 4]:

$$\mathrm{E}\bigl[U \mid f(z), r^*\bigr] = \frac{1}{r} = \mathrm{e}^{-\alpha f(z)}\, \frac{1}{r^*}. \tag{7}$$

Many analysts find it easier to think about the effects of causal variables on the mean duration in a state than about their effects on the rate itself. Equation (7) translates a log-linear effect of $f(z)$ on the hazard function into an effect of $f(z)$ on the mean duration.

For many social processes, the duration of an episode in some state has high positive skewness (i.e., has many values bunched near zero but a long tail). It is customary in analyzing a metric variable with such a shape to take its logarithm before analyzing it with linear regression. Equation (7) suggests that the expected value of the logarithm of the duration in a state is linear in the explanatory variables. In fact, it can be shown that

$$\mathrm{E}\bigl[\log U \mid f(z), r^*\bigr] = \gamma - \alpha f(z) - \log r^*,$$

where γ is Euler's constant $(0.5772157\ldots)$. So this common specification in linear regression analyses is exactly correct if the hazard function is a log-linear function of time-invariant explanatory variables. Thus, when using models of transition rates that are log-linear in causal variables $\mathbf{x}$, analysts may find it helpful to think in terms of the form of the relationship between the mean of the log-duration in an episode and these variables. The two forms should be approximately the same, though opposite in sign.

Figure 6.1 illustrates the relationship between a transition rate and the four transformations of a causal variable z given in Table 6.1; it displays relationships in which the rate increases as z increases. To emphasize the differences in the shapes of the various transformations, where possible we selected α in (5) so that different curves would have a point in common. In Figure 6.1 the curves for all but the fourth transformation have a rate of $2r^*$ when z equals 10. When z equals 10, the curve for the fourth transformation has a rate of $0.667r^*$.

Although the rate increases monotonically for all four transformations illustrated in Figure 6.1, the four differ in important ways.

⟨6⟩ **Parameterizing Observed Heterogeneity**

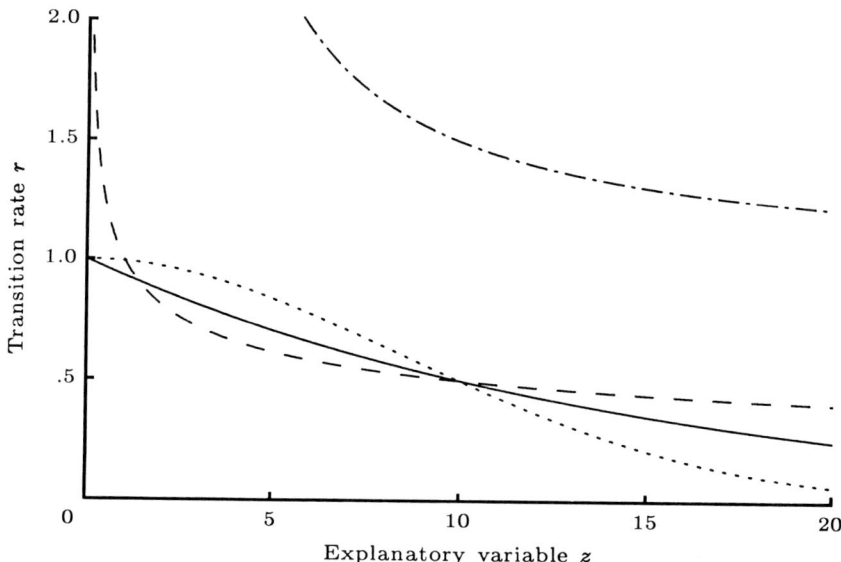

Figure 6.1. Selected relationships between a transition rate and an explanatory variable z when $r = \exp[\alpha f(z)] r^*$ and $dr/dz > 0$. The solid curve denotes $f(z) = z$; the dotted curve, $f(z) = z^2$; the dashed curve, $f(z) = \log z$; the dot-dashed curve, $f(z) = -1/z$.

First, they differ in the value that the rate takes when z ranges from zero to some large positive quantity (infinity). When z approaches infinity, the rate also approaches infinity, except in the case of the fourth transformation, where it approaches r^*. When $z = 0$, the rate equals r^* for the first and second transformations but is zero for the third and fourth transformations, *whatever the values of other variables*.

The four transformations yield relationships between the rate and z that differ in their shapes as well as in their ranges. The first and second are upward bending (accelerating functions of z). The third is upward bending when $\alpha > 1$, linear when $\alpha = 1$, and downward bending when $\alpha < 1$. The fourth is S-shaped (an accelerating function of z for small z, a decelerating function of z for large z).

Figure 6.2 shows how the mean duration varies with z for the same four transformations. Figure 6.3 shows how the mean log-

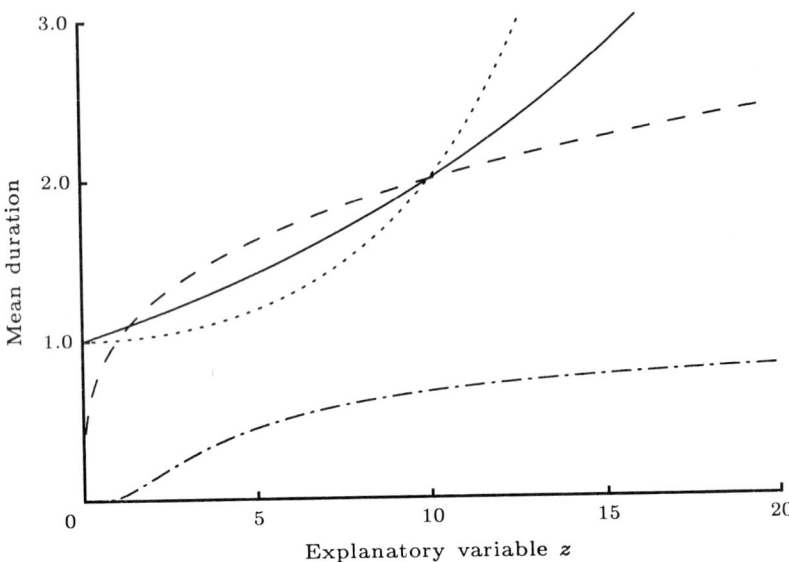

Figure 6.2. Selected relationships between mean duration and an explanatory variable z when $r = \exp[\alpha f(z)] r^*$ and $dr/dz > 0$. The solid curve denotes $f(z) = z$; the dotted curve, $f(z) = z^2$; the dashed curve, $f(z) = \log z$; the dot-dashed curve, $f(z) = -1/z$.

duration varies with z for the same transformations. Since the rate is a monontonically increasing function of z, the mean duration and the mean of log-duration are monotonically *decreasing* functions of z, as these figures show. For the third and fourth relationships, the mean duration (Figure 6.2) is large when z is small, but it decreases at a decelerating rate as z increases, approaching zero for the third curve and r^* for the fourth. For the first and second transformations, the mean duration equals r^* when $z = 0$ and then falls toward 0 as z increases. In the case of the first transformation, the decline in the rate as z increases falls gradually; in the case of the second, however, the decline in the rate has a backward S-shape. The general shapes of the corresponding curves in Figure 6.3 are roughly similar, though the ranges of values differ, of course.

These same figures can also be used to show the relationships between z and the rate, mean duration, and mean log-duration when

⟨6⟩ An Example: NIT Effects on Marital Stability   165

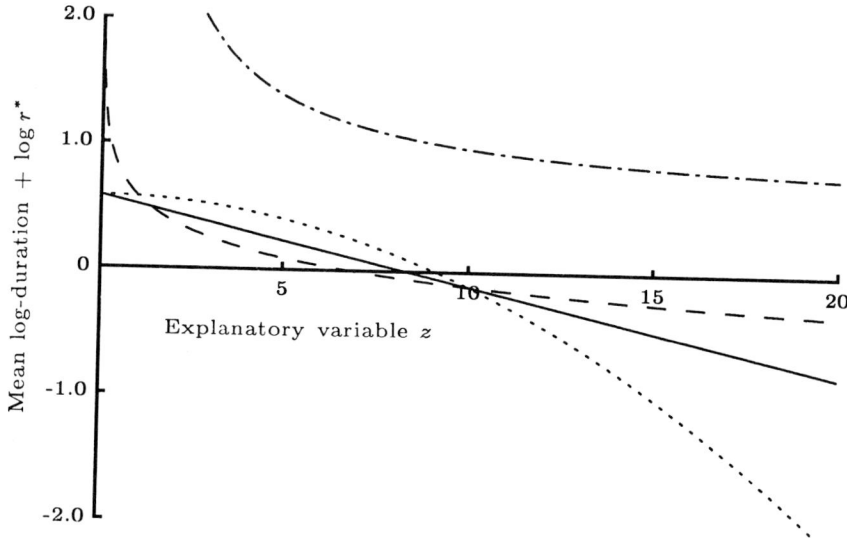

Figure 6.3. Selected relationships between mean log-duration and an explanatory variable z when $r = \exp[\alpha f(z)] r^*$ and $dr/dz > 0$. The solid curve denotes $f(z) = z$; the dotted curve, $f(z) = z^2$; the dashed curve, $f(z) = \log z$; the dot-dashed curve, $f(z) = -1/z$.

$\alpha < 0$. Recall that the rate falls as z increases when $\alpha < 0$. So by changing the sign of α, one can see the implications of the transformations in Table 6.1 when increases in z lead to decreases in the rate. Hence, when $\alpha < 0$, Figure 6.2 can be viewed as a plot of the rate versus z. It shows that when $z = 0$, the rate equals r^* for the first and second transformations and is infinite for the third and fourth transformations. When z becomes very large, the rate falls to zero except in the case of the fourth transformation, where it declines to r^*. Similarly, when $\alpha < 0$, Figure 6.1 can be viewed as a plot of the mean duration versus z, and the reflection of the plot in Figure 6.3 along a horizontal line through Euler's constant shows the mean log-duration versus z.

6.2 An Example: NIT Effects on Marital Stability

To illustrate ways of parameterizing heterogeneity in terms of explanatory variables and interpreting causal analysis of transition rates, we report results from our investigations (with Lyle Groeneveld) of the effects of an NIT program on the marital dissolution rate. We concentrate on analyses of data on white couples during the first 36 months of SIME/DIME. For a fuller discussion that includes results for blacks and Chicanos, see Groeneveld, Hannan, and Tuma (1983).

We have already noted (see Figure 3.5) that the marital dissolution rate of white (and black) couples is much higher for those with NIT treatments than for those in the control group. As mentioned in the introduction to this chapter, we need to control variables used in the stratified assignment of subjects to treatments (site and normal earnings level) because these variables are correlated with the treatments. Other variables affecting dissolution rates (e.g., the schooling of the husband and wife, the number and ages of children) are also uncontrolled in Figure 3.5. Though these variables are not appreciably correlated with the treatments, controlling for their effects should make estimates of the treatment-control differences more precise.

Finally, the displays in Figure 3.5 do not show the effects of variations in the NIT treatments—the different levels of the income guarantee (also called the income support) and of the tax rate (the rate at which benefits fall as a family's other income rises). We would like to know how such variations among the different NIT treatments affect the marital dissolution rate. Because the number of combinations of treatments and stratification variables exceeds the size of the sample (4500 families, including 1087 white couples), it is useful to introduce these controls by expressing the dissolution rate as a function of characteristics of the treatments, the stratification variables, and other relevant variables.

In the first phase of our analyses, we focused on the differences between the dissolution rates of those with various financial plans and the rate for controls with the same values on other causal variables (referred to as "comparable controls" for short). Preliminary analyses (Hannan, Tuma, and Groeneveld, 1977a) revealed systematic variations in rates across plans with different income guarantees but not across plans with different tax rates. So we concentrated on the guarantee levels in subsequent analyses.

Table 6.2 gives the ML estimates of θ for dummy variables denoting the level of income guarantee. Recall that θ gives the ratio of the rate for those with a value of 1 on the dummy variable to the

⟨6⟩ An Example: NIT Effects on Marital Stability

Table 6.2. Maximum-likelihood estimates of the effect of the level of the NIT guarantee on the marital dissolution rate of white couples with children $(I = 1007)^a$

	Model I	Model II	Model III
Low guarantee	2.06***	1.72**	1.17
Medium guarantee	1.63*	1.41	0.98
High guarantee	0.89	0.80	0.57

*Significant at the .10 level.
**Significant at the .05 level.
***Significant at the .01 level.
^{a}See footnote 2 for a list of the other variables included in all models.

rate for those with a value of zero when all other variables have the same values. In the present context, θ gives the ratio of the marital dissolution rate for those with a given income guarantee to the rate for comparable controls.

For the present we focus on the results for Model I in Table 6.2 and postpone discussion of Models II and III. Model I includes measures of various attributes of the family, its manpower treatment and the length of its treatment.[2] According to these estimates, the treatment-control difference in the dissolution rate declines as the level of the income guarantee increases. Those on the program with the guarantee that is 90% of the poverty line (the low guarantee) have a significantly higher dissolution rate than comparable controls. So do those with a guarantee 25% above the poverty line (the medium

[2] The other explanatory variables are the ages of the husband and wife, years of schooling of the husband and wife, the number of children in the family, a dummy for presence of any children less than 6 years old, a dummy for previous experience with Aid to Families with Dependent Children (AFDC), the duration of marriage at the beginning of the experiment, a dummy for the site, dummy variables for the experimental manpower treatments, a dummy variable for a 3-year treatment (rather than a 5- or 20-year treatment), the square of the level of family income, and the inverse of the wife's predicted income if she were single. The reasons for the nonlinear transformations of the last two variables are discussed in detail below.

guarantee). But the dissolution rate of those with a guarantee 40% above the poverty line (the high guarantee) is slightly *lower* than the rate for comparable controls.

This pattern may seem paradoxical: improvements in economic circumstances appear to affect the dissolution rate more when they are smaller! We cannot easily dismiss the genuineness of this pattern. It holds for a variety of specifications of the other variables in the model and for two different estimators. Moreover, it is robust with respect to possible biases due to sample attrition (Hannan, Tuma, and Groeneveld, 1976).

How can we explain this pattern? We argue that an NIT program (like many other public transfer programs) has two opposing effects on the marital dissolution rate. It tends to raise family income, which tends to stabilize a marriage. But, since all family members are eligible for NIT payments whether or not household heads are (or remain) married, it also improves the financial alternatives to marriage. Hence the dependence of spouses on their marriage declines under the NIT treatments, which tends to destabilize a marriage. Depending on the strength and forms of the two effects, an NIT program may increase the marital dissolution rate, decrease it, or leave it unchanged.

Nonpecuniary differences between the NIT treatments and the current welfare system are important in understanding this pattern. For families with a given income, benefits received under the low-guarantee treatment are financially similar to benefits available under current welfare programs (i.e., AFDC and Food Stamps). So nonpecuniary differences are necessary to explain the finding that those with the low guarantee have a substantially higher dissolution rate than comparable controls. Hannan, Tuma, and Groeneveld (1977a) identified several nonpecuniary differences, all of which suggest that income from the current welfare system is discounted in its behavioral consequences. In particular, we argued that a dollar from current welfare programs increases independence less than a dollar of earned income or a dollar from an NIT treatment.

To test these arguments, they must be translated into a particular model that can be estimated. We could choose any functional form illustrated in Figure 6.2 to represent the hypothesis that the marital dissolution rate falls as family income increases, and we could select any form depicted in Figure 6.1 to capture the idea

⟨6⟩ An Example: NIT Effects on Marital Stability

that the dissolution rate rises as independence increases. To choose among the various possibilities, we must introduce additional considerations about the relationship between the dissolution rate, family income, and independence. The critical issue is the way in which the NIT-induced changes in family income and independence affect the marital dissolution rate.

Families with NIT treatments receive payments whenever their incomes fall below a "break-even" level determined by the levels of their assigned income guarantee and tax rate (the rate at which payments are decreased as a function of wage and other nonwage income). We expect a given NIT payment to a couple, P, to have the strongest effect on the dissolution rate r at intermediate levels of family income I. When family income is high, a typical NIT payment has little impact on the family's manner of living and should have a weaker effect on r than the *same* change at lower levels of family income. At the other extreme, when family income is very low, a typical NIT payment may still leave the family destitute and do little to make married life tolerable. Consequently, the effect of P on the rate when I is very low may be less than its effect at higher levels of family income. Of the decreasing functions shown in Figure 6.2, the only one behaving in this fashion is

$$r = e^{\alpha(I+P)^2} r^\dagger, \tag{8}$$

where $\alpha > 0$ and $r^\dagger$ summarizes the effects of all measured covariates other than I and P.

We measure family income I in terms of the income reported by the family in the current month. We compute the NIT payment P as the payment that the family should receive based on their income in the month.[3]

Because NIT guarantees continue when marriages end, an NIT program generally affects the levels of independence of members of a family even when the family does not currently receive payments. One way to model this effect is to focus on the payments that spouses would receive after the marriage ended. Such potential payments generally increase levels of independence. Because financial dependence on marriage is usually more critical for wives, we

---
[3]We used calculated payments rather than values reported in interviews or in the SIME/DIME payment system to minimize missing values.

emphasize the effects of the NIT programs on the income levels of wives after a marital dissolution. We denote by P_s the payment that a wife would receive after the end of her marriage. Because individuals assigned to NIT treatments could choose between participating in their assigned NIT treatment or in the standard welfare system, it turns out to be simpler to formulate the model in terms of the change in independence due to the NIT treatments, ΔI_s, rather than P_s.

As with the income effect, we also expect a given change in independence due to the NIT treatment, ΔI_s, to have the strongest effect on r at the intermediate levels of independence I_s. When independence is very low, a typical value of ΔI_s may still leave the wife very dependent on marriage. When independence is high, a typical increase in independence, ΔI_s, may not greatly augment a wife's already satisfactory financial opportunities outside marriage and so may have a weaker effect on the rate than at lower levels of independence. The only increasing function in Figure 6.1 with a shape consistent with this pattern is

$$r = e^{\beta(I_s + \Delta I_s)^{-1}} r^*, \qquad (9)$$

where $\beta > 0$ and r^* denotes the combined effects of all measured covariates other than I_s and ΔI_s.

Measurement of I_s and ΔI_s is a little complicated. We measure independence by the wife's expected income if she were single, calculated as follows. Let E_s denote a woman's earnings if she were single (assumed to be the same as her earnings while married)[4] and N_s her nonwage income (excluding welfare benefits) if she were single. Based on the values of E_s, N_s, and the number of dependent children in the family, we calculate W_s, the value of the AFDC and Food Stamp grants that a woman could receive if she were single. To incorporate a welfare discount, we treat the discounted welfare benefit as 50% of W_s. Then independence I_s is

$$I_s = (E_s + N_s + 0.5 W_s)$$

[4]We have used two measures of the expected earnings of single women: (1) observed earnings while married; (2) predictions based on the behavior of otherwise similar single women. The present analysis uses the first strategy.

for the controls. For those with an NIT treatment, we also calculate the predicted NIT payment if the woman is single, P_s, on the basis of E_s and N_s. The change in independence due to the NIT treatments, ΔI_s, is measured as $(P_s - 0.5W_s)$ or zero, whichever is greater. Note that $\Delta I_s = 0$ for those in the control group.

Before turning to the results, we note briefly that the forms in (8) and (9) are very flexible and place few constraints on the findings a priori, except that the dissolution rate be monotonically related to family income and independence. Depending on the estimate of α in (8) and of β in (9), the effects on the dissolution rate of the experimentally induced changes in family income and independence may be small or large, and greatest near the lower or upper end of the ranges of income and independence in the sample. Moreover, if the estimate of α or of β is positive, rather than negative as posited, the entire shape of the relationship between the dissolution rate, family income, and independence will be contrary to our hypotheses. Thus, there are ample possibilities for the findings to be inconsistent with our arguments.

The actual model that we estimated was similar to the one used in calculating the estimates for Model I in of Table 6.2. However, it omitted the dummy indicators of the income-guarantee levels, used current ages, duration of marriage, and family size (rather than preexperimental levels), and included the predicted changes in family income and independence due to the NIT treatments.[5] Maximum-likelihood estimation of this model gives the following results for the two coefficients of interest[6] (with standard errors in parentheses):

$$\hat{\alpha} = -0.012 \quad (0.003);$$

$$\hat{\beta} = -2.38 \quad (0.593).$$

Both coefficients are statistically significant at the .01 level. They imply, as predicted, that the marital dissolution rate falls as family income rises and increases as independence increases.

[5] We tried a variety of discounts other than 50%. We obtained roughly the same qualitative results when the discounts ranged from 25% to 75%; see Appendix C of Hannan, Tuma, and Groeneveld (1977b).

[6] Models allowing different coefficients for I and I_s and the NIT-induced changes in these variables do not significantly improve on the models reported here.

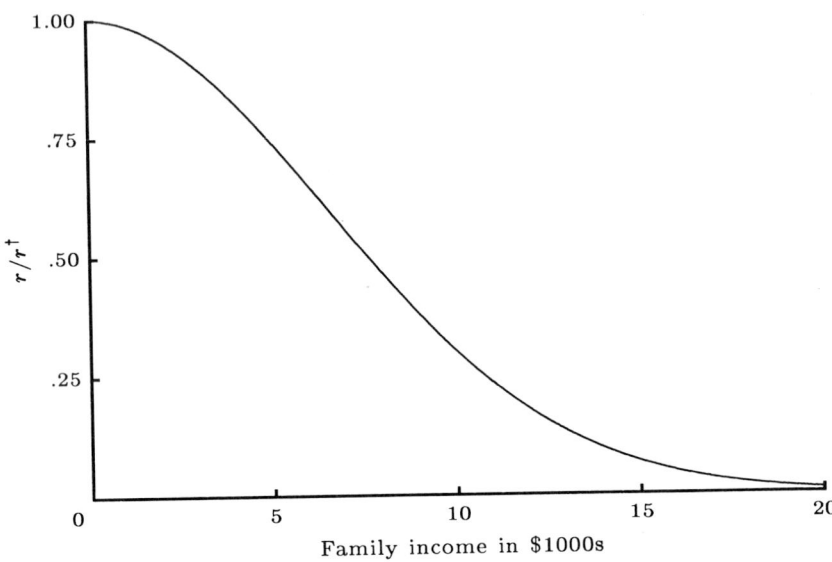

Figure 6.4. Estimated effect of family income on the marital dissolution rate of white couples with children.

To aid in interpreting these results, we plot the estimated effects of family income and independence in Figures 6.4 and 6.5. One curve shows the estimate of $r/r^{\dagger}$ versus family income; the other displays the estimate of r/r^* versus independence. These ratios depict the relationships of interest net of the other covariates in the model.

As hypothesized, the curve for family income (see Figure 6.4) has a backward S-shape within the range of family incomes in the sample. The curve declines most steeply when family income is $6450, which is slightly above the mean of family income in our sample. Thus, relatively small changes in family income can have large stabilizing effects in this population.

The curve for independence (see Figure 6.5) has an S-shape within the range of independence within the sample, as we argued. The curve rises most steeply when independence is $1400. This amount is lower than the mean of $I_s + \Delta I_s$ for those with the low guarantee and quite a bit lower than the mean for those with the medium and high guarantees.

Model I, whose estimates we have just discussed, adjusts only

⟨6⟩   An Example: NIT Effects on Marital Stability   173

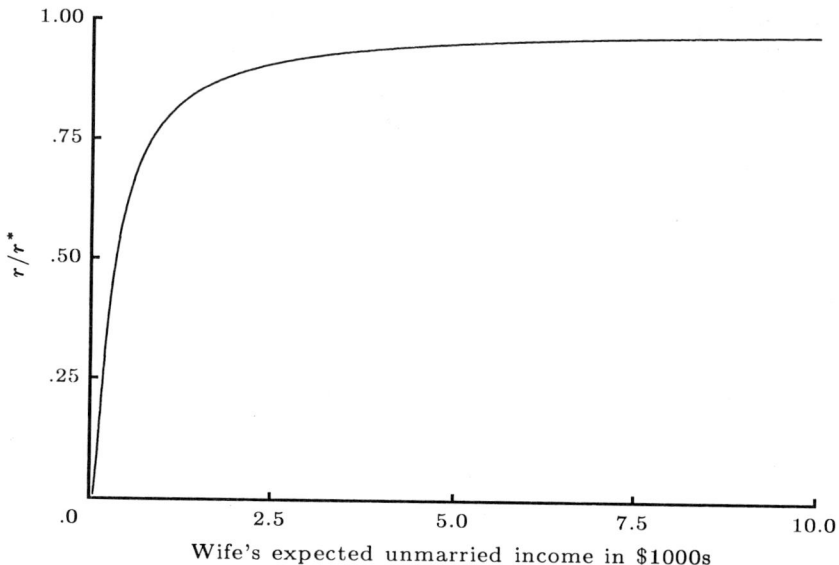

Figure 6.5. Estimated effect of a wife's financial independence on the marital dissolution rate of white couples with children.

for preexperimental characteristics of families (including income and independence), as is appropriate in assessing the total effects of the treatments. Next we want to assess to what extent each family's current income and independence accounts for the total effects. Therefore, we estimated Model II, which incorporates measures of income and independence based on the earnings and (nonexperimental) non-wage income in the current month but excludes changes in family income and independence generated by the NIT treatments, P and ΔI_s. Comparison of estimates for Models I and II (see Table 6.2) indicates that taking current behavior (including labor supply adjustments) into account lowers estimated effects of the NIT treatments only slightly.

To demonstrate that the combination of the experimentally induced changes in family income and independence can, indeed, account for the seemingly paradoxical pattern of effects of the guarantee levels, we introduce the estimated NIT-induced changes in family income and independence, P and ΔI_s, into Model II, giving Model III. If the changes in income and independence that result from the

NIT treatments can explain the findings for Model I in Table 6.2, then the estimates of θ for each guarantee should be close to unity. The estimates of θ for the treatments in Model III are, in fact, much closer to unity (within one standard error) than the corresponding estimates for Models I and II. We conclude that the pattern of estimates for Model I does reflect, at least partly, the joint operation of the impacts of the NIT treatments on family income and independence.

6.3 Incorporating Unobserved Heterogeneity

To this point we have assumed that the variation in transition rates within a population depends only on variation in the measured variables used as covariates. In other words, we have assumed that all relevant causal variables have been measured and included in the model. But this sort of assumption is never exactly true in social research, and it is rarely even approximately true. Few readers need to be convinced that operationalized models of transition rates typically exclude some sources of variation in rates.

Suppose that a transition rate varies within a population but an analyst assumes that the rate is a constant, either absolutely or conditional on a set of observed variables. What difference does this make? Perhaps the most important substantive implication of ignoring unobserved variation in transition rates of transition is that it produces spurious change over time in estimated transition rates.

The earliest work in the social sciences on unobserved heterogeneity in transition rates was motivated by an interest in showing that deviations from a stationary Markov model could be explained in terms of unobserved heterogeneity. Blumen, Kogan, and McCarthy (1955) proposed that a population of job-holders that appears to be homogeneous is actually composed of two subpopulations. They postulated that the hazard of leaving the job is nonzero for one subpopulation (the "movers") but zero for the other (the "stayers"). Suppose that a cohort of job entrants contains pI movers and $(1-p)I$ stayers. Suppose further that an analyst ignores heterogeneity in the population and assumes all individuals are alike—the distinction between movers and stayers is ignored. The hazard for the whole population begins at the level pr, where r is the rate of leaving for movers. But as time unfolds, some movers exit. Consequently, over time the set of persons still in the same job contains an increasing fraction of stayers, causing the rate of leaving a job to decline to zero as time passes. Thus, unobserved (and ignored) heterogeneity has generated spurious time dependence. When Blumen, Kogan, and McCarthy estimated p and r, they found that predictions based on these estimates fit their data better than the stationary Markov model for a homogeneous population that had been their baseline model.

Silcock's (1954) study of job mobility also relied on a model containing a parametric representation of unobserved heterogeneity in transition rates. He assumed that each job entrant sampled a rate of leaving from a gamma distribution and kept that rate for his/her entire job tenure. Like the mover–stayer model, Silcock's model implies that estimated transition rates decline with duration in a job. But it is often more realistic than the mover–stayer model because there is a distribution of nonzero rates instead of only a single nonzero rate r.

In the previous section we considered models with the form

$$r_{ijk} = \phi_{jk}(\mathbf{x}_i), \tag{10}$$

where $\mathbf{x}_i$ is a vector of measured covariates and ϕ_{jk} is a deterministic function. In particular, we concentrated on the cases in which the function relating observed covariates to the transition rate is linear or log-linear. The unobserved factors influencing the rate for the ith sample member can be summarized by the random variable ϵ_{ijk}. A potentially useful approach to including the effects of these unobserved factors is to assume that a transition rate equals the function of the observed covariates $\phi_{jk}(\mathbf{x}_i)$ in (10) multiplied by ϵ_{ijk}:

$$r_{ijk}(t \mid \mathbf{x}_i) = \phi_{jk}(\mathbf{x}_i)\,\epsilon_{ijk}. \tag{11}$$

Because transition rates must be nonnegative, ϵ_{ijk} must also be nonnegative [assuming that $\phi_{jk}(\mathbf{x}_i)$ is nonnegative]. Since ϵ_{ijk} is unobserved, it does not restrict generality to assume that it has a mean of unity, that is, $\mathrm{E}[\epsilon_{ijk}] = 1$. With this assumption, the transition rate equals the deterministic function of the observed covariates on average:

$$\mathrm{E}[r_{ijk}] = \phi_{jk}(\mathbf{x}_i). \tag{12}$$

In other words, the specification in (10) gives the expected rate. In this sense, the models discussed in this section are natural stochastic generalizations of the models discussed in Section 6.2.

The key difference is that models like (11) have a nonzero variance for fixed i, j, and k. Let σ^2_{ijk} denote the variance of ϵ_{ijk}. A reasonable goal in working with models like the one in (11) is to estimate σ^2_{ijk} and the effects of the measured variables x_i. We now consider parametric approaches to this problem. That is, we consider approaches in which an analyst specifies some particular parametric distribution $f(\epsilon_{ijk})$ for the unobserved factors.

We assume that r_{ijk} is time invariant for any i, $j = y_{n-1}$, $k = y_n$, and time of entry t_{n-1}. This implies that T_n has probability density

$$f_j(t \mid t_{n-1}, h_{ij}) = h_{ij}\, e^{-h_{ij}(t-t_{n-1})}, \qquad (13)$$

where

$$h_{ij} = \sum_{k=1}^{\Psi} r_{ijk}. \qquad (14)$$

Note that the probability density of T_n in (13) depends on the unobservable hazard function h_{ij}, which in turn depends on ϵ_{ijk} by (11) and (14). But to estimate parameters from data, one needs a probability density for T_n that depends only on observed variables. This can be obtained by multiplying the conditional density in (13) by the probability density of the hazard function and integrating over all possible values of h_{ijk} (i.e., from 0 to ∞):

$$f_j(t \mid t_{n-1}) = \int_0^\infty f_j(t \mid t_{n-1}, h_{ij}) f(h_{ij})\, d h_{ij}. \qquad (15)$$

Equation (13) provides the first term within this integral. The second term in the integral is the probability density of the hazard function for individual i in state j, which has not yet been specified.

Although it is possible to proceed with the assumption that the disturbances associated with different transition rates are correlated, this greatly complicates analysis. We use the simplifying assumption that the rates are not correlated. This assumption implies that the probability density for the hazard function factors into the

⟨6⟩ Incorporating Unobserved Heterogeneity

product of the separate densities for the transition rates from state j to all possible states:

$$f(h_{ij}) = \prod_{k=1}^{\Psi} f(r_{ijk}), \qquad (16)$$

where

$$f(r_{ijk}) = f(\epsilon_{ijk}) \frac{\mathrm{d}\,\epsilon_{ijk}}{\mathrm{d}\,r_{ijk}}. \qquad (17)$$

Similarly,

$$\mathrm{d}h_{ij} = \prod_{k=1}^{\Psi} \mathrm{d}r_{ijk}. \qquad (18)$$

Thus the single integration in (15) becomes a Ψ-fold integration under the assumption of uncorrelated disturbances.

The procedure of "integrating out the unobserved variables" requires a parametric specification of the distribution of these variables. We illustrate this procedure for the case in which the disturbance is gamma-distributed, as proposed by Tuma (1978).

6.3.1 A Gamma-Distributed Disturbance

Because it is so flexible, the gamma distribution is used commonly in contexts like the ones we are considering. Of the various tractable nonnegative probability distributions, it is perhaps the most flexible. Depending on the values of its parameters, a gamma distribution can range from a highly skewed J-shape to a nearly symmetric unimodal shape. For this reason, Silcock (1954), Spilerman (1972b), Manton and Stallard (1980), and others have specified gamma-distributed disturbances in models of hazards lacking measured covariates.

If the unobserved variable ϵ_{ijk} has a gamma distribution, then

$$f(\epsilon_{ijk}) = \frac{\lambda_{ijk}}{\Gamma(\nu_{ijk})} (\lambda_{ijk}\,\epsilon_{ijk})^{\nu_{ijk}-1}\, e^{-\lambda_{ijk}\,\epsilon_{ijk}}, \qquad (19)$$

where $\Gamma(\nu_{ijk})$ is the gamma function

$$\Gamma(\nu_{ijk}) = \int_0^\infty \varsigma^{\nu_{ijk}-1}\, e^{-\nu_{ijk}}\, \mathrm{d}\varsigma.$$

The mean of the gamma distribution in (19) is ν_{ijk}/λ_{ijk} and the variance is $\nu_{ijk}/\lambda_{ijk}^2$. To meet the restriction that ϵ_{ijk} have a mean of one, it is necessary that

$$\nu_{ijk} = \lambda_{ijk},$$

which implies that

$$\text{Var}[\epsilon_{ijk}] = 1/\lambda_{ijk}.$$

Together, (17) and (19) imply that

$$f(r_{ijk}) = \frac{(\lambda_{ijk}/\phi_{ijk})^{\lambda_{ijk}}}{\Gamma(\lambda_{ijk})} r_{ijk}^{\lambda_{ijk}-1} \exp[-\lambda_{ijk} r_{ijk}/\phi_{ijk}], \quad (20)$$

with the expected value of r_{ijk} given by (12) and

$$\text{Var}[r_{ijk}] = \phi_{jk}^2(\mathbf{x}_i)/\lambda_{ijk}.$$

Substituting (16), (18), and (20) into (15) and integrating gives an expression for the probability density of T_n that does not depend on the disturbances:

$$f_j(t \mid t_{n-1}) = \left[\sum_{k=1}^{\Psi} \frac{\phi_{jk}(\mathbf{x}_i)\lambda_{ijk}}{\phi_{jk}(\mathbf{x}_i)[t-t_{n-1}] + \lambda_{ijk}}\right]$$
$$\cdot \prod_{k=1}^{\Psi} \left[\frac{\lambda_{ijk}}{\phi_{jk}(\mathbf{x}_i)[t-t_{n-1}] + \lambda_{ijk}}\right]^{\lambda_{ijk}}. \quad (21)$$

Equation (21) implies that the survivor function for a randomly selected case is

$$G_j(t \mid t_{n-1}) = \prod_{k=1}^{\Psi} \left[\frac{\lambda_{ijk}}{\phi_{jk}(\mathbf{x}_i)[t-t_{n-1}] + \lambda_{ijk}}\right]^{\lambda_{ijk}}.$$

The unconditional rate of leaving state j at time t is related to the probability density function for T_n and the survivor function at t as follows:

$$\frac{f_j(t \mid t_{n-1})}{G_j(t \mid t_{n-1})} = h_{ij}(t \mid t_{n-1}) = \sum_{k=1}^{\Psi} r_{ijk}(t \mid t_{n-1}).$$

Therefore the hazard function for a randomly selected case is

$$h_{ij}(t \mid t_{n-1}) = \sum_{k=1}^{\Psi} \frac{\phi_{jk}(\mathbf{x}_i) \lambda_{ijk}}{\phi_{jk}(\mathbf{x}_i)[t - t_{n-1}] + \lambda_{ijk}},$$

and the transition rate for a randomly selected case is

$$r_{ijk}(t \mid t_{n-1}) = \frac{\phi_{jk}(\mathbf{x}_i) \lambda_{ijk}}{\phi_{jk}(\mathbf{x}_i)[t - t_{n-1}] + \lambda_{ijk}}. \tag{22}$$

Notice that the rate in (22) depends on the duration in the state $(t - t_{n-1})$ even though each individual's rate (conditioning on the disturbances) is fixed over time. This is an instance of the general result that unobserved heterogeneity creates spurious time dependence in transition rates.

6.4 An Example: Unobserved Heterogeneity in Job-Shift Rates

The study of job shifts illustrates the potential value of including the effects of both observed and unobserved variables. This case is especially interesting because some of the relevant factors that are difficult to measure in research are also difficult for participants to evaluate. Potential employers and potential employees must base their decisions on easily observable characteristics of individuals and jobs. But the amount of information available about individuals and jobs varies across contexts.

When a firm hires an outsider, it typically relies on a few easily observed indicators of productivity and suitability for training, such as the level and kind of schooling and prior experience. Such indicators may be screening devices, but they are poor ones. When a firm promotes an insider, it can not only use easily available indicators but can also assess the person's performance in similar (though perhaps less senior or less skilled) jobs. In an analogous fashion, a person evaluating job opportunities in outside firms must rely on easily observed indicators of job rewards, such as prestige and the wage rate. Thus, we predict that the effects of easily observed indicators of job rewards and personal resources on the rate of an upward job shift is smaller for intrafirm shifts (i.e., shifts within firms) than for interfirm shifts (i.e., shifts between firms).

Once again we use the Coleman–Rossi data introduced in Chapter 3. We concentrate on white men's transitions from fulltime jobs in the civilian nonagricultural labor force (CNALF). As measures of easily observed characteristics of employees we use education and years of employment at the beginning of the spell. Our measures of the observable characteristics of jobs include the prestige level associated with the job and its wage rate. We also include other variables that earlier research has shown to be related to prestige and income attainment: father's education and verbal ability. See Tuma (1978) for more details.

Although we are interested primarily in rates of upward job shift, it is informative to begin by estimating models for the hazard function, the rate of leaving a job. Table 6.3 reports estimates for several models. Model IA assumes that the hazard function is a constant α, which applies to all job shifts and all persons. The ML estimate of α is 0.385 for whites. Under the assumption that the exit rate is a constant, the expected completed duration in a job is the inverse of the exit rate, or 2.60 years.

Model IB assumes that the exit rate has a gamma distribution within the population from which the sample was drawn but is a constant for any job–person match. This is exactly the model proposed by Silcock (1954). Table 6.3 says that the estimated average exit rate is 0.595 and that the estimated variance is 0.507. Silcock's formula (1954, p. 435) for the average completed duration in a job implies that white men spend an average of $1/[0.595 - 0.595(0.570)] = 3.41$ years in a job. Thus, the average duration in jobs is higher according to Model IB than IA, even though the mean exit rate is higher in Model IB than in IA. This occurs because Model IB predicts that some job–person matches are extremely stable. These very stable matches raise the average completed duration more than enough to compensate for the increase in the average exit rate.

Model IA can be viewed as having the same form as IB except that a constraint has been imposed, namely, that the variance of the exit rate is fixed at zero. Thus, a likelihood ratio test comparing Models IA and IB indicates whether the exit rate varies significantly within the population. The value of χ^2 for this test (with one degree of freedom) is 386.2, implying that Model IA can be rejected at any reasonable level of significance.

Model IIA permits the exit rate to depend on the measured

⟨6⟩ An Example: Unobserved Heterogeneity in Job-Shift Rates

Table 6.3. Maximum-likelihood estimates of models of the rate of leaving a job in the CNALF for white men[a]

	A	B
Model I		
Mean rate	0.385	0.595
Variance, σ_j^2	0	0.507
χ^2 for IB versus IA	—	386.2*
(df)		1
Model II		
Intercept	−0.231	0.510
Father's education	0.016***	0.017**
Verbal ability	0.043***	0.052***
Education	−0.002	−0.017
Prestige	−0.022***	−0.025***
Wage rate	−0.070***	−0.101***
Years in jobs	−0.025*	−0.034*
Variance, σ_j^2	0	0.453
Decrease in σ_j^2		
IIB versus IB (%)	—	7.1
χ^2 for Model IIB		
versus Model IA	311.0***	706.9***
(df)	6	7
versus Model IB	—	320.7***
(df)		6
versus Model IIA	—	395.9***
(df)		1

*Significant at the .10 level.
**Significant at the .05 level.
***Significant at the .01 level.
[a]Number of men, 713; number of jobs, 3484.

characteristics of persons and jobs but does not include the effect of unobserved variables. Table 6.3 indicates that this model fits significantly better than Model IA. Finally, Model IIB, which adds the observed covariates to Model IB, fits significantly better than any other model in Table 6.3. Despite the impressive significance levels, adding the six measured covariates has reduced the estimated variance in the exit rate by only 7.1%. Thus, the improvement in fit obtained by allowing the exit rate to depend on the covariates is modest by customary standards.

Now we turn to the main substantive issue, the relative strength of characteristics that differ in ease of observability on rates of upward job shifts within firms and between firms. Table 6.4 reports ML estimates of a series of models parallel to those just discussed, except that the models in Table 6.4 pertain to upward shifts and distinguish transitions within a firm from those between firms. Model IIIA, like Model IA in Table 6.4, assumes that the rate is constant. The estimate in Table 6.4 shows that upward intrafirm moves are much less common than promotions within a firm. Allowing the transition rates to be affected by gamma-distributed disturbances, as in Model IIIB, improves the fit significantly.

The estimates for Model IVB, which adds measured covariates to Model IIIB, provide the information needed to assess the prediction that characteristics that are easy to observe have stronger effects on moves *between* firms than moves *within* firms. The global test concerns the degree to which the variance of the unobserved factor is reduced by adding the measured covariates. The results show a pattern of decreases that agree with our hypothesis: adding the covariates decreases the variance by only 42.4% for promotions within firms but by 69.4% for upward moves between firms.

Another way to evaluate the hypothesis is to consider the magnitude of the effects of various covariates. We made predictions about characteristics of both persons and jobs. The estimated effects of the two easily observed characteristics of persons, education and years in jobs, are larger in magnitude for moves between firms than for promotions, as predicted. The effects of the two easily observed characteristics of jobs, prestige and wage rates, are also larger in magnitude for moves between firms than for promotions. Finally, the effect of verbal ability, which was measured in the Coleman–Rossi study but may be hard for employers to measure, is stronger for promotions than for moves between firms. Thus, results for white men agree with our hypothesis about the relative importance of easily and difficultly observed characteristics of workers and jobs.

⟨6⟩ Misspecification of the Disturbance's Distribution

Table 6.4. Maximum-likelihood estimates of models for the rate of moving upward within a firm (In) and between firms (Out) for white men in jobs within the CNALF[a]

	Out	In
Model IIIA		
Mean rate	0.045	0.018
Variance, σ_{jk}^2	0	0
Model IIIB		
Mean rate	0.083	0.025
Variance, σ_{jk}^2	6.33	8.13
χ^2 for IIIB versus IIIA	70.5***	12.4***
(df)	1	1
Model IVB		
Intercept	−0.840	−3.43
Father's education	0.048*	0.018
Verbal ability	0.106**	0.149**
Education	0.142***	0.116***
Prestige	−0.100***	−0.075***
Wage rate	−0.838***	−0.166
Years in jobs	0.030**	0.025
Variance, σ_{jk}^2	1.94	4.68
Decrease in σ_{jk}^2		
IVB versus IIIA (%)	69.4	42.4
χ^2 for Model IVB		
versus Model IIIA	438.5***	78.5***
(df)	7	7
versus Model IIIB	368.0***	66.1***
(df)	6	6

*Significant at the .10 level.
**Significant at the .05 level.
***Significant at the .01 level.
[a]Number of men, 713; number of jobs, 3484.

6.5 Misspecification of the Disturbance's Distribution

Rarely if ever does social-scientific theory or prior research provide convincing reasons for specifying any particular distribution of the disturbance. As we mentioned in previous sections, usually distributions like the gamma distribution are used on the assumption that they are flexible enough to accomodate a diversity of unkown distributions of the actual disturbance. That is, it is assumed in practice that distributions like the gamma or log-normal approximate reasonably well the true (but unknown) distributions encountered in substantive research. But how well do they?

Unfortunately, we know very little about either the realism of any particular specification or the consequences of misspecifying the distribution of a disturbance affecting transition rates. The one study of this subject of which we are aware (Heckman and Singer, 1982a) provides a fairly pessimistic assessment of the question posed above. These researchers estimated three models of the rate of leaving unemployment. All four were similar to (11). They contained a log-linear function of measured covariates (including the logarithm of the duration of unemployment). An unobserved disturbance was also included in the log-linear function. The four models made the same assumption about the deterministic part of the model, but they differed in their assumptions about the unobserved disturbance. One assumed a normal distribution; the second, a log-normal distribution; the third, a gamma distribution.[7] The fourth made no assumption about the distribution of the disturbance. Heckman and Singer estimated the first three models by the method of ML outlined in Chapter 5. They estimated the fourth model by using a modification of the EM algorithm developed by Dempster, Laird, and Rubin (1977) for estimating models from incomplete (i.e., missing) data.[8]

Heckman and Singer's surprising result was that the estimates for the four models were quite different in some respects. One of the sharpest differences was in the estimated effect of the duration

---

[7] Based on the information given by Heckman and Singer (1982a), this specification differs from the one discussed in Section 6.4, where the gamma-distributed disturbance was a *multiplier* of the log-linear function of covariates and not an *additive* term in the log-linear function.

[8] The EM algorithm is also based on ML estimation, but it differs from what we discuss in Chapter 5.

⟨6⟩ **Misspecification of the Disturbance's Distribution**

of unemployment. The three models with parametric assumptions about the disturbance yielded estimates implying that the rate of leaving unemployment declines with increasing duration. Though the three agreed about the sign of the effect of duration, the point estimates varied widely. Thus, the distribution chosen for the disturbance made a major substantive difference in this case. Still more important, the estimation procedure making no assumption about the distribution of the disturbance gave *opposite* results. The rate of leaving unemployment actually increased as duration increased. If this estimation procedure gave reasonably good estimates, none of the three models making parametric assumptions even estimated the sign of this key relationship correctly.

What are we to make of these findings? Generalizing from one particular empirical analysis is hazardous. The sample analyzed by Heckman and Singer was small, and the data may have odd properties. The parametric part of the model could be misspecified in ways that affect variation across the four models in the estimated coefficients of covariates. Still, this is a useful cautionary tale. It warns us not to make casual decisions about distributions of the disturbance and adds urgency to ongoing research on this topic.

Some more general results on the application of the EM algorithm to this problem have been reported already. Heckman and Singer (1982b) found that the estimation procedure based on the modification of the EM algorithm was quite effective in estimating the effects of covariates in Monte Carlo simulations; however, it cannot recover the variance of the disturbance. This is an important limitation in research in which the variance of the disturbance plays a key substantive role, as in the example in Section 6.4.

Some other research relevant to the application of a modified EM algorithm to this problem has also been reported recently. In an application of hazard models to demographic data, Trussell and Richards (in press) found that conclusions can be sensitive not only to the choice of the distribution of the unobserved disturbance but also to assumptions about the nature of time dependence in the hazard functions,[9] the topic of our next two chapters. Thus, unobserved heterogeneity is not the only danger to correct inference that sociologists using these models must worry about.

---

[9]Such sensitivity is not inevitable (Manton, Stallard, and Vaupel, 1984).

6.6 Conclusions

This chapter has illustrated several ways of adapting event-history methods to the case of heterogeneous populations. We began with models that express the dependence of a set of transition rates on observed (measured) covariates. We concentrated on models that are log-linear in parameters, pointing out that such models allow considerable flexibility in addressing causal relations.

We then added a disturbance term to a model of a transition rate, introducing the effects of unobserved variables. We showed that in cases in which it is appropriate to assume that the disturbance has some particular distribution, the effect of the disturbance on the hazard function (or the transition rate) can be eliminated by integrating over the disturbance. This procedure allows the analyst both to estimate the effects of measured variables and to estimate the variance (and other parameters when they are defined) of the disturbance. We illustrated this procedure for the commonly used specification of a gamma-distributed disturbance.

The final section noted results suggesting that estimation of the effects of observed covariates may be sensitive to the distribution chosen for the disturbance. Although research on this problem has virtually just begun, the first steps have been informative, if somewhat discouraging. This issue and its possible solutions seem likely to figure prominently in the future development of event-history methods in the social sciences.

7

Time Dependence: Parametric Approaches

In this chapter we consider the second major extension of the conventional Markov model: incorporating time dependence in transition rates. Although most sociologists feel uneasy with a model that ignores causal effects (or population heterogeneity), many do not worry much about time dependence. We think that they should. The first section of this chapter discusses sources and types of time dependence in sociological research.

Currently two main approaches are used in estimating time-dependent models of change in qualitative variables. One is fully parametric: it consists of building explicit models of the way transition rates vary over time as well as over members of the population. The second approach is partially parametric: it treats population heterogeneity parametrically, but makes no assumptions about the way transition rates vary over time. This chapter develops and illustrates several versions of the fully parametric approach. Chapter 8 explains and illustrates a partially parametric approach. In principle, each approach can be used to control for any type of time dependence. Nonetheless, in practice certain strategies seem more congruent with some forms of time dependence than with others. Consequently, each approach should be part of a sociologist's repertoire for dealing with time dependence.

Developing a parametric approach to time dependence requires specifying *how* a process changes over time. We illustrate two ways of modeling time dependence parametrically. The first assumes that transition rates vary over time only because measured causal factors affecting them vary over time. This approach uses information on the time paths of exogenous variables to estimate parameters in models of transition rates. The second way assumes that some changing causal factors have not been measured. Therefore, it relates transition rates to measures of time that serve as proxies for omitted changing causal factors. Clearly, these two approaches are complementary—both measured causal variables and measures of time can be included in models of transition rates, as we illustrate.

Implementing the first approach, parameterizing the effects of time-varying causal variables, requires specification of the time paths of these variables. In general the pattern of time variation of different causal variables varies; moreover, it is usually unknown. Ignorance of the functional form of time variation in causal variables is not important (at least in principle) if they are measured continuously. Then the pattern of time dependence can be studied empirically, and the empirical findings can be summarized with some explicit mathematical function of time. Or the observed values of the causal variables at all times can be used, as described in Chapter 8.

Although many metric variables affecting transition rates *vary* more or less continuously over time, they are rarely *measured* continuously. Often they are measured only once, usually at the beginning of an episode. Sometimes they are measured several times, either at the times of waves of a panel or at the beginning and end of episodes. When explanatory variables are measured intermittently, it is necessary to make additional assumptions about how these variables change between the times of measurement. Section 7.2 discusses the case of periodic measurements on explanatory variables assumed to be constant between measurements. We illustrate this case with analyses of the effects of negative income tax (NIT) treatments on marital stability. Section 7.3 discusses the case of exogenous variables that change linearly over time when these variables are measured once, intermittently, or continuously. An analysis of age, experience, and duration dependence in job-shift rates provide an application of the models discussed.

The second approach to parametric models of time dependence uses specifications in which parameters are interpreted directly as indicators of the pattern of time variation. As we discuss below, this strategy uses measures of time as proxies for processes that are difficult to observe directly. Therefore, this strategy is especially

⟨7⟩ Sources of Time Dependence

useful for testing hypotheses about the strength of unobserved processes. Section 7.4 describes several widely used specifications of time dependence and gives an empirical illustration of a situation in which the existence of time dependence has important substantive implications. We demonstrate the value of this approach with an analysis of age dependence in disbanding and merger rates of American national labor unions.

7.1 Sources of Time Dependence

There are at least three main sources of time variation in aggregate or population-level transition rates: population heterogeneity, misspecification of the state space of the process, and temporal variation in transition rates of individual units. We regard the first two sources of time dependence as spurious because they result from misspecifying the stochastic process describing a single unit's behavior. We consider the third to be the main source of true—that is, behavioral or structural—time dependence. The models and methods discussed in this and the next chapter concentrate on this type of time variation. (The first source, population heterogeneity, is discussed at length in Chapter 6; the second source, misspecification of the state space, is treated in Chapter 9.)

The discussion in Chapter 6 assumes that each transition rate is a function of observed and/or unobserved explanatory variables and of parameters giving the effects of these variables. Throughout Chapter 6 we assume that both explanatory variables and their effects are constant within an episode, although they may change from one episode to another. Often causal variables also change over time *within* an episode as well. If they do, transition rates change within episodes too. Moreover, the *coefficients* of causal variables (and other parameters) may also change over time within episodes. We want to extend the models discussed earlier to allow either explanatory variables or parameters (or both) to vary over time.

We emphasize time variation in causal variables because it seems to be more important in sociological research than time variation in parameters. Direct measures of time, such as age and seniority, are among the most commonly used time-varying causal variables. Often a measure of time like age serves as a proxy for other time-varying causal variables that are measured intermittently but are strongly associated with this measure of time. So before turning to specific ways of introducing time dependence, we discuss some measures of time that are frequently used in sociological research.

7.1.1 Age

Transition rates seem to vary more systematically with age than with any other measure of time. As a person, firm, nation, or other social entity ages, its tendency to exhibit certain behaviors changes. Therefore transition rates associated with these behaviors tend to exhibit time dependence.

Age variation in behaviors (and in associated rates) results mainly from age variation in causal variables affecting the likelihood of these behaviors. When these causal variables are unobserved but are strongly associated with age, age serves as a useful proxy for their effects. For example, much of the strong pattern of age variation in birth rates reflects age variation in a woman's physiological capacity to reproduce, which is costly to measure. The association between reproductive capacity and age is so strong, in fact, that it is easy to forget that age does not *directly* affect fertility rates.

Transition rates also vary with age because social norms dictate how social units (especially persons) ought to behave at different ages. For example, social norms about the proper ages for women to give birth generate patterns of age variation in birth rates that differ substantially from what one would expect upon the basis of age dependence in reproductive capacity. Social norms (and sometimes laws) also regulate when people should attend school, marry, begin to work for pay, and retire. These norms produce age dependence in the rate of the corresponding events.

Sociologists often regard age as primarily a property of persons. But other social units exhibit life cycles too. There are arguments for life cycles in organizations (Stinchcombe, 1965), social movements (Gamson, 1975), nations (Almond and Powell, 1966; Lipset, 1963), and cities (Madden, 1957; Sjoberg, 1963). For example, it has been suggested (Michels, 1915/1959) that the internal flow of information tends to decline as organizations age. We also expect information flow to affect the rate at which organizations alter their behavior in response to environmental and technological changes. Given the difficulty of measuring information flows over the life span of an organization, age-dependent stochastic models become a useful vehicle for explaining rates of organizational adaptation.

7.1.2 Historical Period

Changes in environmental conditions may also cause transition rates to shift over time either for an entire population or for some subpopulation. Some aspects of social environments change continuously in time. Although some changes have only small impacts, many changes with small separate effects can have a large cumulative effect. Other changes are catastrophic; they are associated with marked differences in a wide range of variables within a comparatively brief interval. For example, social revolutions are commonly thought to generate such catastrophic changes.

Methods for handling effects of environmental variation on transition rates depend partly on the objectives of the research. Sometimes the effects of certain environmental shifts have direct sociological interest. At other times one just wants to control environmental variations so that they do not confound the study of other processes.

Methods for handling time variation in transition rates also depend partly on data availability. Sometimes, measures of important changes in environmental conditions are lacking; at other times, measures of only a few factors are available. Attempting to measure *all* relevant features of a changing environment is a hopeless task, especially in areas of social research beyond experimental control.

Because environments shift irregularly and erratically and are difficult to measure completely, it is difficult to parameterize the dependence of rates on historical time. We suggest an approach for dealing with this common situation. It involves estimating models that allow measured and unmeasured environmental variables to affect rates of subpopulations in different ways in different eras. It is appropriate when subpopulations are differentially affected by environmental variables that vary mainly from one era to another but are relatively constant within an era. The partially parametric approach discussed in the next chapter, which is based on homogeneous but unknown variation over time in rates within the population, is also suitable for dealing with unmeasured changes in the environment.

7.1.3 Cohort

Mention of age and period effects may lead readers to think of cohort effects. Analysis of cohorts (especially birth cohorts) has been advocated especially by demographers (see Ryder, 1965), but also by sociologists (e.g., Glenn, 1977), political scientists (e.g., Converse, 1976), and psychologists (e.g., Baltes and Reinert, 1969). When a cohort is defined by birth date, there is a linear dependency among period (current date), age (current date minus birth date), and cohort. Because of this linear dependency, an identification problem invariably arises whenever these three variables are postulated to have an additive effect on an outcome. Consequently, a model in which age, period, and cohort are posited to have either linear or log-linear effects on transition rates is not identified.

Strategies for identifying continuous-time models with age, period, and cohort effects are the same as those for discrete-time models. One can assume that one (or more) of these three measures of time has no effect on the outcome, impose a sufficient number of equality constraints on the model to identify it, or include measures of the causal variables for which age, period, and cohort are surrogates. Since no new issues seem to arise in identifying effects of age, period, and cohort on transition rates in continuous-time models, we do not discuss the problem further. Instead, we refer interested readers to one of the discussions of the problem within the context of discrete-time models of qualitative variables (Fienberg and Mason, 1978; Pullum, 1977).

7.1.4 Duration

Transition rates are said to depend on duration when they vary with the length of time since the previous event. Obviously, duration is identical to age for the first event. Consequently, one can distinguish duration dependence from age dependence only if an event occurs more than once, that is, if the event is repeatable. For example, in a study of the rate at which strikes occur in some industrial enterprise, one can distinguish conceptually between the dependence of this rate on the enterprise's age and its dependence on the length of time since the previous strike. In contrast, the notion that mortality rates vary with "duration" makes sense only if duration dependence is used as a synonym for age dependence.

Transition rates sometimes vary with duration because social norms say that certain events should occur after a certain length of time in a state. For example, the dependence of birth rates on the length of time since the previous birth is due partly to social norms favoring certain birth spacings. Similarly, social norms (and sometimes even regulations) concerning promotion on the basis of seniority create duration dependence in the rate of promotion from one job to another with higher status.

Reasons for duration dependence in rates center more often on the omission of causal variables that tend to vary with the duration since the previous event. In one form of misspecification, the observed states represent aggregations of several unobserved states. It is well known (e.g., see Cox and Miller, 1965) that rates of transitions among aggregated states appear to depend on duration, even if rates of transitions among the disaggregated states are time independent. For example, the time dependence of birth events, mentioned above, may also be due partly to aggregation of the state space. The interval between births involves transition among several states. At the very least, one should distinguish between "not pregnant" and "pregnant." Even if the rate of becoming pregnant and the rate of successfully completing a pregnancy were time independent (which of course they are not), the birth rate will depend on the duration since the previous birth if the states "pregnant" and "not pregnant" are collapsed into a single state.

Another form of misspecification of the state space occurs when a system of coupled quantitative and qualitative variables describes the dynamics of some phenomenon, but only change in the qualitative variable is considered. The unmeasured endogenous quantitative variable generates time dependence in the rates of change in the qualitative variable studied.

The dynamics of marital formation, dissolution, and reconciliation illustrate this point. Suppose that marital status is the qualitative variable studied and that available data give the dates when marriages begin, break up, and are reformed for some group of people. Extrapolating from the concept of "marriage-specific investments" suggested by Becker, Landes, and Michael (1977), we propose that a metric variable relevant to the dynamics of this process is "person-specific investments." By this term we mean one person's knowledge of another person's preferences and behavioral style and of various ways of managing satisfactorily a close relationship with this other person. Such knowledge is specific to the other person to a considerable degree: for example, gentle teasing may promote positive feelings with one person but make another angry. The level of person-specific investments tend to change over time. When two people first meet, these investments grow, which increases the likelihood that they marry—in short, it increases the rate of marital formation. Once married, these investments usually grow still more, especially in the early stages of marriage, making the rate of marital dissolution decline as marital duration increases. If the marriage *does* break up, each spouse's investments in the other tends to decline over time, causing the rate of reconciliation between them to decrease also. This scenario describes a system of coupled qualitative and quantitative variables. The levels of the metric variables (investments in the other person) affect the rates of marital formation, dissolution, and reconciliation. At the same time, the qualitative variable (marital status: never married, married, separated) affects the rate and direction of changes in these metric variables. If one analyzes data on marital status only, the model is misspecified and the rates of change in marital status are likely to appear to depend on the duration of the current marital status.

Parallel arguments abound. For example, the rate of a job shift is claimed to depend on duration because job-specific capital tends to increase with the duration in a job, and this sort of human capital decreases the job-exit rate (Becker, 1975; Tuma, 1976; Jovanovich, 1979a,b). The decline of migration rates with a person's duration in a geographic area is said to occur because a person's ties to a locale tend to increase with length of residence (Ginsberg, 1971). Usually a person's ties to a locale do not vanish instantly following a change in residence but decline gradually as the length of time in a new locale increases. This should lead to duration dependence in the rate of return migration also.

Similar arguments apply to macrosociological phenomena. Consider, for example, the stability of political regimes. We expect the likelihood of a shift in regime to decrease (i.e., stability to increase) as the length of time that a regime has been in power increases. It is plausible that the stability of a regime rises with the political resources of its supporters and falls with the political resources of the supporters of *other* regimes, ceteris paribus. When a new regime comes to power, the political resources of supporters of former regimes are likely to erode while resources of the supporters of the new regime are likely to grow. Testing this argument requires data both on the dates of shifts from one political regime to another and on the political resources of supporters of various regimes at

⟨7⟩ Sources of Time Dependence   195

multiple points in time. Since data on the former are available (see Section 10.4) but data on the latter are difficult to obtain, empirical analyses are likely to show that political stability rises with the length of time since the last change in regime.

The most desirable strategy in these examples is to model the system of coupled qualitative and quantitative variables and to estimate this model using measures of all variables in the system, as we discuss in Chapter 16. But information on some variables in the system is often missing. Then transition rates among states of a qualitative variable generally depend on duration, even when other sources of time dependence are controlled.

7.1.5 Experience

Experience (sometimes called exposure) refers to the cumulative time spent in a particular subset of states in the state space. Experience can be distinguished from duration in the current state only when events are repeatable; experience can be distinguished from age only when there are multiple kinds of events. Dependence of transition rates on experience is sometimes called **state dependence** (e.g., see Heckman, 1978). When transition rates depend on experience, future changes (which are governed by the transition rates) depend on past occupancy of particular states, and not just on the current state. Thus, stochastic processes governed by experience-dependent rates are not Markovian.

Arguments for effects of experience are less common than arguments for effects of age, period, and duration. However, experience does seem relevant for many sociological processes. Two substantive examples illustrate this.

First, hypotheses about the effects of experience on job-shift rates and rates of moves between employment and unemployment have been proposed. According to one perspective (e.g., see Mincer, 1974), human capital *appreciates* as work experience (time spent in employment) increases. Similarly, it may *depreciate* as time spent in unemployment increases. If the stock of human capital affects rates of shifting among jobs and between employment and unemployment, as Becker (1975), Tuma (1976), Bartel and Borjas (1977), and others have argued, such rates should depend on current experience as measured by the cumulative time spent in certain states.

Second, experience with different sorts of political regimes can affect the rate of changing from one form of regime to another. For example, some nations that currently have military rule may have had multiparty regimes in the past, while others may have previously had only one-party regimes. The rate of change from military rule to a multiparty government is presumably higher in the first group of nations than in the second, other things being equal, because the existence of a particular form of regime creates a political infrastructure and culture supporting this form of regime. Even if the form of the regime changes, the infrastructure and culture of an earlier regime are likely to persist to some degree. In other words, rates of change in political regimes are likely to depend on experience with different forms of regimes.

7.1.6 Combining Sources of Time Variation

Substantive arguments often suggest that transition rates vary with several measures of time. For example, individual i's rate of a transition from j to k at time t may depend on i's age at time t, $A_i(t)$; i's experience at time t, $E_i(t)$; i's duration in state j at time t, $D_i(t)$; and on calendar time, t:

$$r_{ijk}(t \mid t_{i,n-1}) = g\big[A_i(t), E_i(t), D_i(t), t\big]. \tag{1}$$

There is certainly nothing substantively wrong with formulating such a model. But can it be estimated?

If estimation is based on maximum likelihood (ML), the answer to this question depends on whether the components of individual i's contribution to the likelihood $\mathcal{L}_i$ can be expressed in terms of observed variables. In particular, both the rate of observed transitions at the time of their occurrence, $r_{ijk}(t_{in} \mid t_{i,n-1})$, and the log of the survivor function, $\log G_{ijk}(t \mid t_{i,n-1})$, must be expressible as functions of observed variables.

If the model in (1) is to be estimated, age, experience, and duration must be observed at some point during each episode. Without loss of generality, we can assume that the time of observing these variables is $t_{i,n-1}$, the start of the nth episode for individual i, because for $t \geq t_{n-1}$,

$$D_i(t) \equiv t - t_{i,n-1}; \tag{2a}$$

$$A_i(t) = A_i(t_{i,n-1}) + t - t_{i,n-1}; \tag{2b}$$

$$E_i(t) = E_i(t_{i,n-1}) + t - t_{i,n-1}. \tag{2c}$$

Equation (2) means that (1) can be rewritten as a function of t and of variables that are *fixed* throughout the episode:

$$r_{ijk}(t \mid t_{i,n-1}) = g[A_i(t_{i,n-1}), E_i(t_{i,n-1}), t_{i,n-1}, t]. \qquad (3)$$

Consequently, the models discussed in the remaining sections of this chapter can be written solely in terms of t without loss of generality. Our discussion assumes that models cast originally in the form of (1) are transformed into (3) and that $A_i(t_{i,n-1})$, $E_i(t_{i,n-1})$, and $t_{i,n-1}$ are absorbed into a vector of explanatory variables, $\mathbf{x}_i(t_{i,n-1})$, measured at the start of the episode. Age, duration, experience, and historical time may be among the members of the vector $\mathbf{x}_i(t_{i,n-1})$, as expression (1) indicates.

7.2   Periodic Shifts in Parameters and Causal Variables

One way of introducing time dependence allows rates to shift discontinuously at fixed dates. That is, it assumes that each transition rate is fixed within a particular time period p running from τ_p to τ_{p+1}, but may differ from the rate in every other period $p' \neq p$.

There are several motivations for this assumption. First, the explanatory variables may be fixed over time but have time-varying coefficients. If the exact form of time variation in parameters is unknown, it is reasonable to try to approximate it by a step function:

$$\log r_{ijk}(t \mid t_{i,n-1}) = \boldsymbol{\alpha}'_{jkp} \mathbf{x}_i \qquad (4)$$

for all t such that $\tau_p \leq t < \tau_{p+1}$.

Second, the explanatory variables may have constant coefficients but change over time from one exogenously determined period to another. For example, imagine a study of the rate at which bills leave Congressional committees with different kinds of outcomes (e.g., recommended for passage or killed). These rates may depend on the political power of the committee's chairperson or the number of liberals and conservative members on the committee. These explanatory variables vary not only across committees, but also from one period (session of Congress) to another. Another classic example of exogenously determined shifts in explanatory variables occurs in experiments in which subjects are rotated among different treatments over time. Scientists often wish to test hypotheses about the effects of the *order* in which treatments are administered.

In these examples the explanatory variables can vary from one period p to another, but their coefficients are assumed to be time invariant. In this case, equation (4) should be replaced by

$$\log r_{ijk}(t \mid t_{i,n-1}) = \alpha'_{jk} x_{ip} \qquad (5)$$

for all t such that $\tau_p \leq t < \tau_{p+1}$.

Finally, there is the general case in which both causal variables and parameters may vary over time. Allowing both the explanatory variables and their effects to vary from one period to another is often a reasonable way of approximating and investigating these changes. Combining (4) and (5) gives

$$\log r_{ijk}(t \mid t_{i,n-1}) = \alpha'_{jkp} x_{ip} \qquad (6)$$

for all t such that $\tau_p \leq t < \tau_{p+1}$. Notice that both the causal variables and their coefficients are subscripted by the period p. We concentrate on (6) because (4) and (5) are special cases.

In order to find the ML estimators of the α_{jkp}, one must determine the survivor function [see equation (15) in Chapter 5]:

$$G_j(t \mid \omega_{n-1}) = \prod_{k=1}^{\Psi} G_{jk}(t \mid \omega_{n-1}), \qquad (7a)$$

where

$$G_{jk}(t \mid \omega_{n-1}) = \exp\left[-\int_{t_{n-1}}^{t} r_{jk}(s \mid \omega_{n-1}) \, ds\right]. \qquad (7b)$$

This last equation must be solved in order to find ML estimates of the parameters α_{jkp}. Recall that integration is a linear operation; the integral of any function over the range s to t equals the sum of the integral of the function over the range s to $s + \Delta s$ and the integral of the function over the range $s + \Delta s$ to t, for any Δs. So to solve (7b), one just integrates over each time period and sums over the total number of time periods P:

$$\log G_{ijk}(t \mid t_{i,n-1}) = \sum_{p=1}^{P} \int_{\tau^*_p}^{\tau^*_p} r_{ijkp}(s \mid t_{i,n-1}) \, ds$$

$$= \sum_{p=1}^{P} \exp\left[\alpha'_{jkp} x_{ip} (\tau^*_p - \tau^*_{p-1})\right], \qquad (8)$$

⟨7⟩ Periodic Shifts in Parameters and Causal Variables

where by definition $\tau_{P+1} \equiv \infty$ and

$$\tau_p^* = \begin{cases} 0 & \text{if } \tau_{p+1} \leq t_{n-1} \text{ or } t_n \leq \tau_p \text{ (state } j \text{ is entered after} \\ & \text{period } p \text{ ends or } t_n \text{ occurs before period } p \text{ begins)}; \\ \tau_p & \text{if } t_{n-1} < \tau_p < t_n \text{ (state } j \text{ is entered before period } p \\ & \text{begins and } t_n \text{ occurs after period } p \text{ begins)}; \\ t_{n-1} & \text{if } \tau_p \leq t_{n-1} < \tau_{p+1} \text{ (state } j \text{ is entered in period } p), \end{cases}$$

$$\tau_{p+1}^* = \begin{cases} 0 & \text{if } \tau_{p+1} \leq t_{n-1} \text{ or } t_n \leq \tau_p \text{ (state } j \text{ is entered after} \\ & \text{period } p \text{ ends or } t_n \text{ occurs before period } p \text{ begins)}; \\ \tau_{p+1} & \text{if } t_{n-1} < \tau_p < t_n \text{ (state } j \text{ is entered before period} \\ & p \text{ ends and } t_n \text{ occurs after period } p \text{ ends)}; \\ t_n & \text{if } \tau_p \leq t_{n-1} < \tau_{p+1} \text{ (}t_n \text{ occurs in period } p). \end{cases}$$

For simplicity, equations (4) through (8) assume that the dates defining the time periods are the same for all members of the population. However, as long as the time periods are exogenously determined, it is straightforward to allow dates to vary across members of the population. To introduce this complication, we subscript each time period p by the individual i, p_i, in the equations above.

The remainder of this section shows how a model of periodic shifts in transition rates can be used in analyzing event histories gathered in a social experiment. Although such a model can be used when any exogenous variable shifts at discrete points in time, it is especially useful in analyzing experimental data because experimental treatments typically begin and end at known, exogenously determined points in time.

7.2.1 An Example: Effects of NIT Eligibility on Marital Stability

As various examples in Chapters 3 and 6 have indicated, both nonparametric and parametric analyses strongly suggest that couples with NIT treatments had significantly higher marital-dissolution rates during the first 3 years of the Seattle and Denver Income Maintenance Experiments (SIME/DIME). Do the financial–control differences found in these analyses really reflect a genuine behavioral response to the NIT treatments?

These differences in the dissolution rate could be caused by preexisting differences between controls and those with NIT treatments. Subjects were assigned to NIT treatments according to a stratified random design. Consequently, having an NIT treatment is correlated with the stratification variables (race–ethnicity, marital status, site, and normal earnings level), most of which are typically believed to be associated with rates of change in marital status.

In the parametric analyses reported in Section 6.2, we controlled for the main effects of site and normal earnings level and for the interactive effects of race–ethnicity and original marital status. (We did the latter by analyzing data on couples in separate race–ethnic groups.) As a general rule, we did not control for interactive effects of site and normal earnings level. Unfortunately, too few subjects had any particular combination of the stratification variables to control for all possible interactions among the stratification variables and the treatments.

Because there is an exogenous change in the eligibility for NIT payments, we can test the hypothesis that the differences in the dissolution rates of the control and treatment groups reflect a genuine response to the NIT programs. We simply compare the dissolution rate of controls and those assigned an NIT treatment in two periods: during the period of eligibility for NIT payments, and the period after eligibility ends. Suppose the dissolution rates of controls and those with NIT treatments differ in the same way in both periods. Then it is not clear whether the financial–control difference in this rate results from a permanent (irreversible) change in the behavior of those with NIT treatments or from preexisting differences between financials and controls in the values of the stratification variables (or unobserved variables correlated with them). On the other hand, suppose the dissolution rates of controls and those with NIT treatments differ during the period of eligibility for NIT payments, but not during the period of ineligibility. Such a finding would suggest that the financial–control difference during eligibility reflects behavioral changes induced by the NIT programs, and not just differences in preexisting values of stratification variables.

Although there are only *two* substantively interesting temporal periods (the period of eligibility and the period after eligibility), it is necessary to construct models involving *three* periods in order to test this hypothesis. Period 1 is the first 3 years of the experiment when both the 3- and 5-year NIT groups were eligible for NIT payments. Period 2 is the fourth and fifth years of the experiment; in this period the 5-year NIT group was still eligible for NIT payments, but the 3-year NIT group was ineligible for these payments. Period 3 is the sixth and seventh years; neither the 3- nor 5-year NIT group was eligible for NIT payments in this period. However, the data on the 3-year NIT group stops at the end of five years. Consequently, the third period furnishes data only on the 5-year NIT group and the control group.

To see if the effects of the NIT treatments differ during and after eligibility, we estimated two three-period models:

I. $r_p = r^* \exp[\lambda_{0p} + \alpha_1 \text{NIT3} + \alpha_2 \text{NIT5}]$,

II. $r_p = r^* \exp[\lambda_{0p} + \lambda_{1p} \text{NIT3} + \lambda_{2p} \text{NIT5}]$,

where $p = 1, 2, 3$; r^* denotes the part of the dissolution rate determined by x, a vector of background and stratification variables; and

$$r^* \equiv e^{\beta' x}.$$

β is a vector of parameters giving the effects of the variables in x; we assumed that these effects do not vary over time in order to to improve the efficiency of the estimated NIT effects. NIT3 denotes a dummy variable that equals 1 for those assigned a 3-year NIT treatment; NIT5 denotes a dummy variable that equals 1 for those assigned a 5-year NIT treatment. The α's are parameters that are constrained to have the same effect in every time period. The λ's are parameters that are allowed to vary from one period to the other. There is one important exception: λ_{21} is constrained to equal λ_{22}, which means that the effect of the 5-year NIT treatment is the same throughout the 5-year period during which this group is eligible for NIT payments.

Model I assumes that the dissolution rates of the 3- and 5-year treatment groups differ from the dissolution rate of the control group in the same way during and after the period of eligibility for NIT payments; formally, this means that $\lambda_{11} \equiv \lambda_{12} \equiv \alpha_1$ and that $\lambda_{21} \equiv \lambda_{22} \equiv \lambda_{23} \equiv \alpha_2$. If Model II improves significantly on Model I, it suggests that the financial–control differences in the dissolution rate represent a behavioral response to the NIT treatments. Furthermore, we expect λ_{11} and $\lambda_{21} \equiv \lambda_{22}$ to be significantly positive.

Table 7.1. Financial–control group differences in the marital-dissolution rate during and after eligibility for NIT payments, by race[a]

	Effect of		χ^2 (df)
	NIT3	NIT5	
Blacks ($I = 1082$)			
Model I	1.26*	1.44***	136.49 (19)
Model II			136.86 (21)
During eligibility	1.26*	1.41**	
After eligibility	1.21	1.88	
Whites ($I = 1508$)			
Model I	1.20†	1.42***	197.78 (19)
Model II			199.39 (21)
During eligibility	1.29**	1.45***	
After eligibility	0.99	1.20	

†Significant at the .15 level.
*Significant at the .10 level.
**Significant at the .05 level.
***Significant at the .01 level.
[a]The models also include the following control variables: the wife's age at enrollment, the wife's education, the number of children, as well as dummy variables for three manpower treatments, residence in Denver, presence in the family of children under 5 years of age, and receipt of AFDC in the year before SIME/DIME.

In contrast, we expect λ_{12} and λ_{23} to be less positive, and perhaps even temporarily negative, as those with NIT treatments readjust to the existing structure of public transfers [such as Aid to Families with Dependent Children (AFDC), Food Stamps, and Unemployment Insurance] after eligibility for NIT payments ends.

Table 7.1 gives the results of estimating these models from the marital histories of black and white couples in SIME/DIME. It reports the ML estimates of the α's and λ's in the two models and the results of likelihood ratio tests comparing these two models to models without any explanatory variables. The difffference in the value of χ^2 for these likelihood ratio tests, which is 0.37 for black and 1.59 for white couples (with 2 degrees of freedom), can be used to test the hypothesis that Model II improves on Model I. Clearly, Model II does not improve significantly (at the .10 level) on Model I for either black or white couples. For both black and white couples, the effects of both the 3- and 5-year NIT treatments during the eligibility period are positive and significant. During the posteligibility period, the financial–control difference in the dissolution rate for white couples is small and does not differ significantly from zero for either the 3- or 5-year NIT treatments.

Do the financial–control differences in dissolution rates of black and white couples reflect behavioral responses to the NIT treatments in SIME/DIME? Or do they reflect preexisting differences in stratification and other background variables whose effects are not included in our models? Unfortunately, the results in Table 7.1 do not provide an unarguable answer. Model II barely improves on Model I according to the likelihood ratio test, implying that financial–control differences in the dissolution rate during and after eligibility are not detectably different. This may partly be because it is difficult to estimate the financial–control difference precisely during the posteligibility period because so few marital events occur during this period. The fact that financial–control differences during the posteligibility period are statistically insignificant and smaller than in the eligibility period (except for black couples with the 5-year NIT treatment) provides some evidence that differences during the eligibility period reflect behavioral responses to the NIT treatments.

One conclusion that *can* be drawn is a methodological one: event-history data during periods differing in the presence of some variable of great substantive interest are potentially very valuable in assessing whether this variable has genuine effects.

7.2.2 An Example: Time Variation in Effects of NIT Programs on Marital Stability during Eligibility

The models estimated in the previous example assume that the effects of the NIT treatments were constant throughout the experimental period. But there are several reasons why the NIT effects might vary during the eligibility period. Treatment effects may increase in strength over the experiment because the subjects did not fully understand the treatments at first or needed to search for an opportunity to change state (e.g., to find separate housing).

Treatment effects could also be largest in the beginning of the experiment if some couples were on the verge of a marital breakup when SIME/DIME began and found that the NIT benefits made a long-desired breakup financially feasible at last. Once these fragile marriages dissolved, the effects of the NIT treatments might decline considerably or even vanish. Whatever the pattern of NIT effects in the beginning and middle of the eligibility period, NIT effects could decline near the end if couples anticipated losing their eligibility for NIT payments and having to rely on current welfare programs for assistance with long-term financial needs. Indirect treatment effects (e.g., effects of treatments on work behavior, which may in turn affect marital status) also can cause treatment effects to vary over time, but it cannot be predicted a priori whether indirect effects enhance or dampen the initial response.

In sum, there are a number of reasons for thinking that the effects of the experimental treatments might vary during the experimental period, but we cannot predict the shape of the pattern of time variation. Therefore, it is useful to divide the period of NIT eligibility into two or more subperiods and to investigate how the NIT effects vary among these subperiods.

Unlike the previous example, it is not clear how to divide the total observation period into periods. The exogenous variable of interest—the NIT treatments—do not change; rather we want to study changes in their effects. We could subdivide the period of NIT eligibility in many different ways. Most arguments about time variation in NIT effects seem to identify three qualitatively important subperiods: the early, middle, and late phases of the eligibility period. The models that we estimated to investigate time variation in NIT effects operationalized these subperiods in the following way. We defined the "early" period as the first 6 months following the start of NIT eligibility and the "late" period as the last 12 months preceding the end of NIT eligibility. The "middle" period is a residual category, the period of eligibility between the "early" and "late" periods. For couples with a 3-year NIT treatment, the middle period runs from the seventh to the twenty-fourth month; for couples with a 5-year NIT treatment, the middle period runs from the seventh to the forty-eighth month. Thus the middle period is much longer for those with a 5-year NIT treatment.

Since the early, middle, and late periods begin and end at

different dates for the 3- and 5-year treatment groups, the models that we actually estimate have five rather than three periods: 0 to 0.5 year, 0.5 to 2.0 years, 2.0 to 3.0 years, 3.0 to 4.0 years, and 4.0 to 5.0 years. Thus we estimated the following models:

I. $r_p = r^* \exp\left[\lambda_{0p} + \alpha_1 \text{NIT3} + \alpha_2 \text{NIT5}\right],$

II. $r_p = r^* \exp\left[\lambda_{0p} + \lambda_{1p} \text{NIT3} + \lambda_{2p} \text{NIT5}\right],$

where p ranges from 1 to 5, and r^*, NIT3, and NIT5 are defined as in the previous example. As in the previous example, the α's are constrained to be the same in every period p; the λ's are allowed to vary from one period p to another.

Model I lets the marital-dissolution rate vary across the five periods; however, it assumes that only the intercept λ_{0p} varies over time. Hence Model I assumes that the pattern of time variation is the same for the control group as it is for those with 3- and 5-year NIT treatments. In short, Model I recognizes that the marital-dissolution rate of *all* couples may vary over time for many unmeasured reasons—historical trends, aging of the couples, and so forth.

In its most general form, Model II assumes that the NIT effects vary across all five periods, as indicated by the time-varying coefficients of the 3- and 5-year NIT treatments, λ_{1p} and λ_{2p}, respectively. To examine the notion of "early," "middle," and "late" stages in eligibility, we also estimated a constrained version of Model that assumed $\lambda_{22} \equiv \lambda_{23} \equiv \lambda_{24}$. This assumption means that the effects of the 5-year NIT treatment are the same during the seventh through forty-eighth months of eligibility. We also estimated several other versions of Model II that imposed various other constraints, but none of these gave appreciably different results.

For blacks there is no evidence of substantial variation in experimental effects over time. Although the intercepts do differ significantly across the five periods, none of the models that permit the NIT effects to vary by period (within the 5 years of the treatments) improve significantly over Model I, which has period-varying intercepts. There is little to be learned from inspection of these estimates, and we do not report them here.

Table 7.2 gives the results for white couples. It shows that the estimated intercepts for the five periods in Model I are relatively constant during the first 3 years of SIME/DIME and then decline

Table 7.2. Maximum-likelihood estimates of models of time variation in effects of NIT treatments on the marital-dissolution rate of white couples in SIME/DIME[a]

Time period (years)	Intercept	NIT3	NIT5	χ^2 (df)
Model I				181.9 (21)
0.0–0.5	0.94	1.28*	1.45***	
0.5–2.0	1.00	1.28*	1.45***	
2.0–3.0	0.98	1.28*	1.45***	
3.0–4.0	0.88	1.28*	1.45***	
4.0–5.0	0.63	1.28*	1.45***	
Model II, constrained				188.3 (25)
0.0–0.5	0.70	1.93**	2.74***	
0.5–2.0	1.00	1.42**	1.35*	
2.0–3.0	1.18	0.92	1.35*	
3.0–4.0	0.93	—	1.35*	
4.0–5.0	0.72	—	1.17	
Model II, unconstrained				191.8 (27)
0.0–0.5	0.77	1.93**	2.74***	
0.5–2.0	1.00	1.57**	1.80***	
2.0–3.0	1.46	0.81	0.91	
3.0–4.0	1.06	—	1.26	
4.0–5.0	0.79	—	1.17	

*Significant at the .10 level.
**Significant at the .05 level.
***Significant at the .01 level.
[a]See the note to Table 7.1 for a list of the other covariates.

somewhat. These estimates imply that marital-dissolution rates tend to decrease with the passage of time, as one would expect.

The constrained and unconstrained versions of Model II, which allow the effects of NIT programs to vary over time, are much more interesting. Both the constrained and unconstrained versions improve significantly on Model I *only* if we choose the unconventionally high significance level of .20 (χ^2 = 6.4 and 9.9 with 4 and

⟨7⟩ Linearly Changing Causal Variables   207

6 degrees of freedom, respectively). Thus, the results of estimating these models do not provide a definitive answer to the question of how the effects of the NIT treatments vary over time. As our discussion below indicates, these results suggest to *us* that the NIT effects *do* vary over time, but a much larger sample would be necessary to assert this with confidence.

In general, the results for both versions of Model II suggest that the NIT effects decline with the passage of time. Both versions indicate that the NIT treatments greatly increased the marital-dissolution rate during the initial 6 months, by 93% for the 3-year group and by 174% for the 5-year group. Results for the later periods can be interpreted in more than one way. According to the constrained version of Model II, the effect of the NIT treatments is significantly positive in the middle period, though much smaller than in the early period, but it is negligible in the late period of the experiment. According to one interpretation of the unconstrained version of Model II, the NIT treatments raise the marital-dissolution rate appreciably only during the first 2 years of eligibility. This interpretation is consistent with the argument that NIT programs affect primarily those couples with "fragile" (i.e., unsatisfactory) marriages and that the effects of the NIT treatments vanish once these unstable marriages have broken up.

Still another interpretation of the unconstrained version of Model II comes from expressing the estimated NIT effects as multipliers of the rate for the control group in the second period (0.5–2.0 years). These estimates (not included in Table 7.2) indicate that the marital-dissolution rate for the 3- and 5-year NIT groups decline fairly steadily with time and are similar to the rate for the control group only in the final year of eligibility. In contrast, the dissolution rate for the control group rises and then falls, peaking in the third year of the experiment at a value twice the rate for the control group in the initial 6 months. According to this viewpoint, the odd pattern of time variations in the dissolution rate for the control group is the unexpected and (as yet) unexplained finding.

As in the example that investigated NIT effects during and after NIT eligibility, the methodological conclusions of this example are clearer than the substantive ones. This example shows that models with the form given in (6) offer a useful way of investigating how the effects of experimental treatments vary over time. For findings to be clear-cut, however, there need to be data on sufficient events in various time periods that time variations in rates can be detected.

7.3 Linearly Changing Causal Variables

In Chapter 6 we introduced heterogeneity by postulating that transition rates are log-linear functions of explanatory variables describing the environment, the state occupied, and the individual occupying the state:

$$\log r_{ijk}(t \mid t_{i,n-1}) = \alpha'_{jk} x_i, \tag{9}$$

where r_{ijk} denotes the rate of a move from j to k by individual i, α_{jk} is a vector of time-independent parameters, and x_i denotes individual i's values on a vector of explanatory variables affecting this rate. The relationship between transition rates and causal variables expressed in (9) often seems to fit data well. As we suggested in Chapter 6, it has heuristic value even when it cannot be derived from any simpler set of assumptions.

It seems natural to generalize (9) by allowing the explanatory variables to be functions of time:

$$\log r_{ijk}(t \mid t_{i,n-1}) = \alpha'_{jk} x_i(t), \tag{10}$$

where $x_i(t)$ denotes the values of the explanatory variables at time t for individual i. Equation (10) expresses formally what we previously stated in words: transition rates vary over time when explanatory variables vary over time.

Often it is convenient to assume that explanatory variables change *linearly* over time:

$$x_i(t) = x_i(\tau) + \kappa_i (t - \tau), \tag{11}$$

where τ is the time of the most recent measurement of the causal variables and κ_i is a vector of parameters describing the growth rate of these causal variables for individual i. When age, experience, duration, or historical time is one of the explanatory variables, (11) obviously holds and the corresponding element of κ_i equals 1 for all i. As Coleman (1968) suggested (see also the discussion in Chapter

⟨7⟩ Linearly Changing Causal Variables

11), the assumption of linear growth in explanatory variables can provide a useful approximation, even when the true change process is nonlinear. Naturally, a linear approximation to nonlinear change is more satisfactory when the interval between τ and t is relatively short. Such an approximation may yield quite misleading results when this interval is long.

When (11) is a reasonable approximation, one can substitute (11) into (10) to obtain

$$\log r_{ijk}(t \mid t_{i,n-1}) = \alpha'_{jk} x_i(t)$$
$$= \alpha'_{jk} x_i(\tau) + \alpha'_{jk} \kappa_i (t - \tau)$$
$$= \alpha'_{jk} x_i(t_{i,n-1}) + \alpha'_{jk} \kappa_i (t - t_{i,n-1}) \quad (12a)$$

or equivalently,

$$r_{ijk}(t \mid t_{i,n-1}) = e^{\alpha'_{jk} x_i (t_{i,n-1})} \, e^{\alpha'_{jk} \kappa_i [t - t_{i,n-1}]}, \quad (12b)$$

Equation (12b) can be expressed more compactly as

$$r_{ijk}(t \mid t_{i,n-1}) = \theta_{ijk}(t_{i,n-1}) \, e^{\gamma_{ijk} [t - t_{i,n-1}]} \quad (13)$$

where

$$\theta_{ijk}(t_{i,n-1}) \equiv e^{\alpha'_{jk} x_i (t_{i,n-1})}; \quad (14a)$$
$$\gamma_{ijk} \equiv \alpha'_{jk} \kappa_i. \quad (14b)$$

Expression (13) implies that the conditional survivor function is:

$$\log G_{ijk}(t \mid t_{n-1}) = -\frac{\theta_{ijk}(t_{n-1})}{\gamma_{ijk}} \left[e^{\gamma_{ijk} t} - e^{\gamma_{ijk} t_{i,n-1}} \right]. \quad (15)$$

According to (13), the rate of transition from j to k for case i is an exponential function of time t. Clearly, γ_{ijk} plays an important role in this model. If $\gamma_{ijk} > 0$, the transition rate becomes infinitely large as $t \to \infty$, and the conditional survivor function given by (15) approaches zero. If $\gamma_{ijk} < 0$, the transition rate approaches zero as $t \to \infty$, and the conditional survivor function is greater than zero. If $\gamma_{ijk} < 0$ for all k, then the probability that some event occurs is less than unity, even if the process is observed infinitely long. A distribution function with this property is said to be *defective*. This is a statistical term; it does not mean that the model is substantively deficient unless it is impossible for members of the population to remain in state j forever. The assumptions made in this section allow γ_{ijk} to vary among members of the population [see (14b)] but not over time. Hence, under these assumptions, it is possible that the probability of leaving state j is zero for some members of the population, but not others.

Notice that

$$\frac{\mathrm{d}r_{ijk}(t \mid t_{i,n-1})}{\mathrm{d}t} = \gamma_{ijk}\, r_{ijk}(t \mid t_{i,n-1}),$$

or

$$\gamma_{ijk} = \frac{\mathrm{d}r_{ijk}(t \mid t_{i,n-1})}{r_{ijk}(t \mid t_{i,n-1})} \Big/ \mathrm{d}t.$$

Thus γ_{ijk} can be interpreted as the instantaneous fractional change in case i's rate of a transition from j to k per unit of time.

Consider the special case of (13) in which there is a single nonrepeatable event and a homogeneous population, that is, $\theta_{ijk} = \theta$ and $\gamma_{ijk} = \gamma$ for all i and $t_{i,n-1} = t_0$. Then (13) becomes

$$h(t \mid t_0) = \theta\, e^{\gamma[t-t_0]}, \tag{16}$$

and (15) simplifies to

$$\log G(t \mid t_0) = -\frac{\theta}{\gamma}\left[e^{\gamma t} - e^{\gamma t_0}\right]. \tag{17}$$

Expression (17) implies that a log survivor plot yields a curve that is an exponential function of time t. It defines what is known as the Gompertz distribution. This distribution is named for Benjamin Gompertz (1825), who suggested that the dependence of mortality rates on age in human populations can be described well (except at very young ages) by a function in which the death rate increases exponentially as age increases. There is a substantial literature on the distribution of times implied by (16), which is called a Type-I extreme-value distribution in the statistical literature. See Johnson

⟨7⟩ **Linearly Changing Causal Variables**

and Kotz (1970, Volume I, pp. 272–295) for an excellent summary and references.

A simple transformation of the time scale t converts the Gompertz model into another well-known model, the Weibull model.[1] Let

$$t \equiv \log(s + \delta), \tag{18}$$

where δ is a scaling factor. This expression implies that $s = e^t - \delta$. Substituting (18) into (16) yields

$$\begin{aligned} h(t \mid t_0) &= \theta \, e^{\gamma \log(s+\delta) - \gamma \log(s_0+\delta)} \\ &= \theta \, (s + \delta)^\gamma \, (s_0 + \delta)^{-\gamma} \\ &= \lambda \, (s + \delta)^\gamma, \end{aligned} \tag{19a}$$

where $\lambda \equiv \theta(s_0+\delta)^{-\gamma}$ and $t_0 \equiv \log(s_0+\delta)$. If $t_0 = 0$, then $s_0 + \delta = 1$ and $\lambda = \theta$. It is straightforward to generalize this model to the case of multiple states and repeatable events: one just substitutes $r_{jk}(t \mid t_{n-1})$ for $h(t \mid t_0)$ and subscripts λ, δ, and γ by j and k:

$$r_{jk}(t \mid t_{n-1}) = \lambda_{jk} \, (s + \delta_{jk})^{\gamma_{jk}}. \tag{19b}$$

The expression in (19) has the form of a three-parameter Weibull model (see Johnson and Kotz, 1970, Volume I, Chapter 20).

Since both the rate in a Gompertz model and the transformation of time t in (18) are monotonic functions of time, the rate in a Weibull model is a monotonic function of time s. As s increases, the rate increases if $\gamma > 0$, is a constant if $\gamma = 0$, and decreases if $\gamma < 0$.

The original Gompertz model does not allow θ and γ to vary over members of a population, whereas they do in our derivation [see (14)], which can be regarded as a generalized Gompertz model. Moreover, when the causal variables change linearly as given by (11)

---

[1] Recall that in Chapter 4 we mentioned the device called *operational time*, a simple transformation of the natural time scale, which is sometimes used to simplify the apparent structure of a model. One of the most common is a logarithmic transformation, such as the one discussed here.

and t is transformed as in (18), the parameters in (19b) become $\theta_{ijk} = \alpha'_{jk}\kappa_i$ and

$$\lambda_{ijk} = \theta_{ijk}(t_{i,n-1})\left[s_{i,n-1} + \delta_{jk}\right]^{-\theta_{ijk}}$$
$$= e^{\alpha'_{jk}\mathbf{x}_i(t_{i,n-1})}\left[e^{t_{i,n-1}}\right]^{\alpha'_{jk}\kappa_i}$$
$$= e^{\alpha'_{jk}\mathbf{x}_i^*(t_{i,n-1})},$$

where $\mathbf{x}_i^*(t_{i,n-1})$ includes $t_{i,n-1}$ as well as the other variables in $\mathbf{x}(t_{i,n-1})$. Hence the transition rate in time scale s is simply

$$r_{ijk}(s \mid s_{i,n-1}) = e^{\alpha'_{jk}\mathbf{x}_i^*(s_{i,n-1})}(s + \delta_{jk})^{-\alpha'_{jk}\kappa_i}, \qquad (20)$$

where $s_{i,n-1}$ is the time of entry into j in this time scale. This model is a generalization of the three-parameter Weibull model.

As in Chapter 6, there are two possible approaches to the sources of heterogeneity in a population, denoted by $\mathbf{x}$ and $\mathbf{x}^*$ above. One can assume that all sources of heterogeneity are measured, or one can postulate that they are unobserved but have some specified probability distribution. We concentrate on the first approach. Just how one proceeds depends on the type of observation plan used to measure the explanatory variables.

7.3.1 A Single Measurement of Causal Variables

Sometimes explanatory variables are measured at only a single time τ_i for each case i. In this situation the κ_i's, the growth rates of the explanatory variables for the various members of a sample, cannot be estimated from the data and additional assumptions about them are necessary to estimate the model.

The simplest alternative is to assume that $\kappa_i = \kappa$ for all i, which implies that $\gamma_{ijk} = \gamma_{jk}$ is just a constant to be estimated. Then the rate of change in r_{ijk} with respect to time is the same for all the members of the population, either rising or falling at a single pace. When this assumption seems unreasonable, an alternative is to assume that κ_i is some specific function of a vector of variables also measured at the same time τ_i, $\mathbf{z}_i(\tau_i)$. For example, one might assume that κ_i is a linear function of the elements of $\mathbf{z}_i(\tau_i)$:

$$\kappa_i = \mathbf{\Gamma}\mathbf{z}_i(\tau_i), \qquad (21)$$

⟨7⟩ Linearly Changing Causal Variables

where $\boldsymbol{\Gamma}$ is a matrix of parameters. Substituting (21) in (14b) gives

$$\gamma_{ijk} = \boldsymbol{\alpha}'_{jk}\boldsymbol{\Gamma}\mathbf{z}_i(\tau_i) \equiv \boldsymbol{\beta}'_{jk}\mathbf{z}_i(\tau_i), \qquad (22)$$

where $\boldsymbol{\beta}_{jk} \equiv \boldsymbol{\alpha}'_{jk}\boldsymbol{\Gamma}$. The vector of parameters $\boldsymbol{\beta}_{jk}$ is identified, but the individual elements in $\boldsymbol{\Gamma}$ are not. With the specification in (22), the model for the transition rate in (12b) becomes

$$r_{ijk}(t \mid t_{i,n-1}) = e^{\boldsymbol{\alpha}'_{jk}\mathbf{x}_i(t_{i,n-1})} e^{\boldsymbol{\beta}'_{jk}\mathbf{z}_i(\tau_i)[t-t_{i,n-1}]}. \qquad (23)$$

This model appears to contain "causal" effects of both vectors **x** and **z**. However, according to the derivation of the model, the effects of **z** are not causal—they are merely indirect effects that result from the effects of the z's on the growth rate of the x's.

7.3.2 Intermittent Measurement of Causal Variables

Sometimes there are multiple (though intermittent) measurements of the explanatory variables. In this case there are more efficient ways of using the data than the one outlined above, and it is not necessary to make such restrictive assumptions.

Figure 7.1 illustrates the kinds of observation plans that we have in mind. It depicts a five-wave panel survey in which data are collected at times $\tau_1, \tau_2, \ldots, \tau_5$, depicted by the vertical dotted lines. At each wave, retrospective event histories of the discrete dependent variable are collected for the period beginning either at the time of the previous wave or at some earlier time. (For example, an individual's history from t_0 to τ_1 might be collected at the first survey.) This type of observation plan was used to collect the marital and job histories of those enrolled in SIME/DIME.

Typically each survey also collects data on metric variables believed to affect rates of transition between states of the discrete dependent variable. Panels (a) and (b) illustrate two common observation plans. In one plan [see panel (a)], the explanatory variables are measured at the beginning and end of each episode in the various states of the dependent variable. Coleman and Rossi, for example, used this kind of observation plan in their 1968 study of the lives of American men (see Coleman et al., 1972); they measured wage rates at the beginning and end of each job held by the respondents. In another observation plan [see panel (b)], the explanatory variables are measured at the times of the surveys. SIME/DIME, for example,

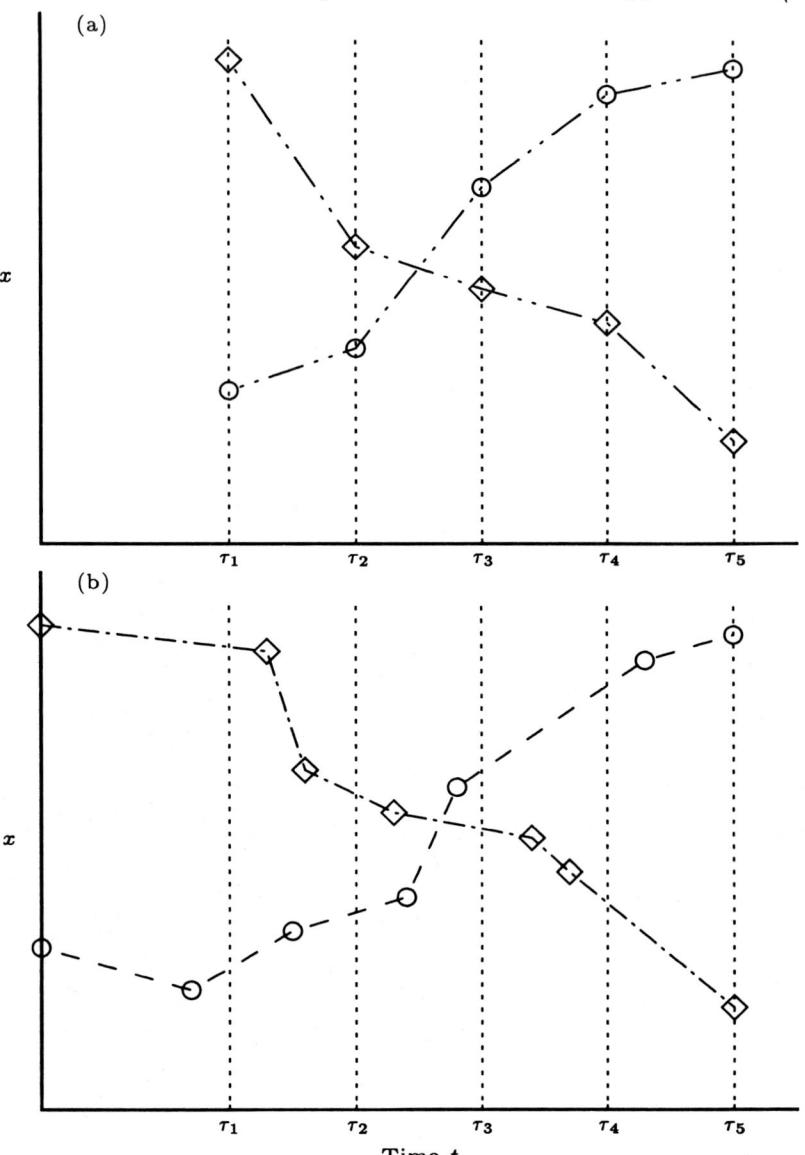

Figure 7.1. Illustrative observation plans for collecting information on a covariate x at successive times τ_1 through τ_5 (indicated by dotted lines). (a) x measured at the time of each survey; (b) x measured at the times of events and at the last survey. Diamonds and circles depict hypothetical observations on x for two persons.

⟨7⟩ **Linearly Changing Causal Variables**

used a plan similar to this in measuring a family's unearned income, such as benefits from unemployment insurance and social security.

Panels (a) and (b) show hypothetical observations for two individuals, labeled by circles and diamonds, respectively. The dashed lines connecting the circles and the dotted and dashed lines connecting the diamonds indicate that the explanatory variables are assumed to change linearly between measurements. Notice that the rate of change in the explanatory variables may vary across members of the sample. To stress this point, panels (a) and (b) of Figure 7.1 show values of the explanatory variable falling for one individual and rising for the other. Since there are multiple measurements on the explanatory variables for each sample member i, it is unnecessary to assume that $\kappa_i = \kappa$ or that κ_i is some specified function of $z_i(\tau_i)$. Instead, κ_i can be estimated directly from the data.

In the case of the observation plan depicted in panel (a), the rate of change in the explanatory variables may vary with episode n, which we indicate by κ_{in}. Its obvious estimator is

$$\kappa_{in} = \frac{\Delta x_{in}}{\Delta t_{in}} \equiv \frac{x_i(v_{in}) - x_i(t_{i,n-1})}{v_{in} - t_{i,n-1}}, \qquad (24)$$

where $v_{in} = t_{in}$ if the nth episode is uncensored and equals the time of the last observation if this episode is censored, $\Delta x_{in} \equiv x_i(v_{in}) - x_i(t_{i,n-1})$, and $\Delta t_{in} \equiv v_{in} - t_{i,n-1}$.

To obtain ML estimates of parameters, the contribution of each individual i to the likelihood $\mathcal{L}_i$ must be determined. According to (15) in Chapter 5, $\mathcal{L}_i$ depends on $r_{ijk}(t_{in} \mid t_{i,n-1})$, the rate of the observed nth transition at the time of its occurrence, and on $G_{ijk}(t \mid t_{i,n-1})$, the survivor function for each of the observed episodes, where t equals t_n if the nth event *is not* censored and equals the time of the last observation, τ_2, if the nth event *is* censored. The rate $r_{ijk}(t_{in} \mid t_{i,n-1})$ is given by (13), where (14) specifies $\theta_{ijk}(t_{i,n-1})$ and γ_{ijk}, and κ_i is given by (24). Substituting (24) into the right-hand side of (12b) and integrating gives a result analogous to (15):

$$\log G_{ijk}(t \mid t_{i,n-1}) = \frac{\Delta t_{in}}{\alpha'_{jk} \Delta x_{in}} \left\{ \exp\left[\alpha'_{jk} x_i(t_{i,n-1}) \right] \right.$$

$$\left. - \exp\left[\alpha'_{jk} x_i(t_{i,n-1}) - \alpha'_{jk}(t - t_{i,n-1}) \frac{\Delta x_{in}}{\Delta t_{in}} \right] \right\}. \quad (25)$$

Thus, by substituting (13) and (25) into the general expression for individual i's contribution to the likelihood, $\mathcal{L}_i$, given in (15) in Chapter 5, a likelihood can be constructed for this model.

To obtain the log survivor function in the case of the observation plan depicted in panel (b), one proceeds in a similar fashion as in panel (a). However, there is an estimate of κ_{in} for each time interval p between successive surveys instead of the single estimate in (24). Consequently, the result is similar in form to (25), but somewhat more complicated.

7.3.3 Continuous Measurement of Causal Variables

"Continuous" measurement of causal variables usually means that variables are measured intermittently with a very small interval between measurements. In such situations, the remarks made in the previous section apply.

In contrast, values of causal variables are truly *known* continuously, that is, at every moment in some interval, when the variables have a known growth rate. Any measure of time discussed in Section 7.1 provides an example of such a variable. Because time changes linearly with a growth rate of 1 per unit of time, its value at any point in an episode can be inferred if its value is known at one point in the episode.

Below we present an example in which age, work experience, and duration, as well as certain time-invariant covariates, are hypothesized to affect the rate of shifting jobs. Since the growth rates of age, experience, and duration within a job are known to equal 1, this model can be estimated without difficulty.

7.3.4 An Example: Time Dependence in Job-Shift Rates

In our discussion of the effects of experience on transition rates, we mentioned that several scholars have argued that human capital rises as work experience increases. How human capital affects job-shift rates depends on its type. It has been argued that, ceteris paribus, general human capital raises job-shift rates because it increases a person's opportunities for a better job, but that job-specific human capital, sometimes measured by the duration (the length of time spent) in the current job, lowers these rates (see Becker, 1975; Tuma, 1976). Although education is widely agreed to be the most important aspect of a person's general human capital, not everyone thinks that work experience augments general human capital. For

⟨7⟩ Linearly Changing Causal Variables   217

example, Sørensen (1975) argued that the gap between a person's fixed resources (such as education) and changing job rewards (such as occupational prestige) decreases as experience increases. According to Sørensen, it is the size of this gap, and not human capital in the form of work experience, that affects job-shift rates. Sørensen's argument implies that the effect of work experience on job-shift rates vanishes when a person's fixed resources and current job rewards are controlled. Thus, according to Sørensen's argument, apparent dependence of job-shift rates on experience results from misspecifying the model and not from true (i.e., structural) dependence on work experience.

Still another measure of time often hypothesized to affect job-shift rates is age. Arguments vary for this source of time variation in job-shift rates, but it is generally agreed that job-shift rates decline as age increases, until the usual age of retirement approaches. Since age and work experience are highly correlated, it is important to include age as well as work experience in a model designed to estimate the effect of work experience. Otherwise the estimated effect of work experience will be biased.

To evaluate arguments about the existence and meaning of time dependence in job-shift rates, we once again use the Coleman–Rossi data on black and white American men. These data measure several key resources of individuals, $x_1 \equiv$ {father's education, verbal ability, and own education}, and two important job rewards, $x_2 \equiv$ {the wage rate, prestige}.[2] Information in these data also let one tell the value of three other variables at any moment within a job: $D(t)$, the duration in the job at time t; $E(t)$, the cumulative work experience at time t; and $A(t)$, the person's age at time t.

We seek to estimate the following model:

$$r_{ijk}(t \mid t_{i,n-1}) = g(\mathbf{x}_{i1},\ \mathbf{x}_{i2},\ E_i(t),\ A_i(t),\ D_i(t)).$$

As in Chapter 6, we assume that $g(\cdot)$ is a log-linear function of $\mathbf{x}_i(t) \equiv \{\mathbf{x}_{i1},\ \mathbf{x}_{i2},\ E_i(t),\ A_i(t),\ D_i(t)\}$:

$$\log r_{ijk}(t \mid t_{i,n-1}) = \boldsymbol{\alpha}_1' \mathbf{x}_{i1} + \boldsymbol{\alpha}_2' \mathbf{x}_{i2} + \beta_1 E_i(t) + \beta_2 A_i(t) + \beta_3 D_i(t).$$

[2] These data give the wage rate at the start and end of each job. Since the change in the wage rate within jobs is quite small on average, we use the initial wage rate and ignore any variation over time (within a job) in the wage rate in the analysis reported below.

Using (2) [see (3)], this equation can be rewritten as

$$\log r_{ijk}(t \mid t_{i,n-1}) = \alpha_1' x_{i1} + \alpha_2' x_{i2} + \beta_1 E_i(t_{i,n-1})$$
$$+ \beta_2 A_i(t_{i,n-1}) + \gamma D_i(t), \qquad (26)$$

where $\gamma \equiv \beta_1 + \beta_2 + \beta_3$.

Table 7.3 reports ML estimates of the parameters in (26) for moves of black and white men from a job in the civilian nonagricultural labor force (CNALF) to another job whose rewards (prestige and wage rate) are at least 5% higher (upward), at least 5% lower (downward), or between 5% higher and 5% lower (lateral).[3]

The estimated effect of age on the rate of upward moves does not differ significantly from zero; however, it has a significantly positive effect on the rate of lateral moves and a significantly negative effect on the rate of downward moves. These results suggest that increasing age is not a handicap to improving job opportunities and, in fact, provides some protection against loss of job rewards. Moreover, contrary to conventional beliefs, it appears that job-shift rates do not always fall as people get older.

In contrast, the estimated effect of work experience does not differ signficantly from zero except for black men's rate of lateral moves, where it is significantly negative. On the whole, then, these results suggest that cumulative work experience is not an important aspect of human capital insofar as job-shift rates are concerned.

Finally, we consider the estimated effect of duration *net* of the effects of age and experience, that is, $\beta_3 \equiv \gamma - \beta_1 - \beta_2$. These estimates indicate that the rates of upward, lateral and downward moves of both black and white men fall significantly as the duration in a job moves. The net effect of duration (β_3) is even more negative than the total effect (γ) in the case of upward and lateral moves, but it is less negative in the case of downward moves. In all, these results indicate that the job-shift rates of black and white men depend markedly on duration. One cannot tell, however, whether the apparent duration dependence in job-shift rates arises because of the effects of job-specific human capital or for other reasons.

[3] See Tuma (1978) for detailed definitions and arguments about the effects of rewards and resources. We do not discuss these results because they are not pertinent to the patterns of time dependence being considered.

Table 7.3. Maximum-likelihood estimates of a Gompertz model of the rate of upward, lateral, and downward job shifts of black and white men[a]

	Upward	Lateral	Downward
Blacks			
Intercept	−2.315	−5.806	−2.410
Father's education	0.022	−0.037	−0.017
Ability	0.083***	−0.002	−0.040
Education	0.114***	−0.003	0.0002
Prestige	−0.076***	−0.010	0.038***
Wage rate	−0.802***	0.191***	0.192***
Age at start	0.042	0.120***	−0.105***
Experience at start	−0.009	−0.094***	0.061
Duration (γ)	−0.053***	−0.129***	−0.106***
Duration (β_3)	−0.086***	−0.155***	−0.062
Number of events	376	148	191
Whites			
Intercept	−0.944	−3.279	−0.870
Father's education	0.029**	−0.011	0.014
Ability	0.097***	0.014	−0.083*
Education	0.105***	−0.108***	−0.096**
Prestige	−0.076***	0.007	0.033***
Wage rate	−0.512***	0.051	0.131**
Age at start	−0.008	0.058**	−0.106***
Experience at start	0.027	−0.040	0.054
Duration (γ)	−0.142***	−0.167***	−0.180***
Duration (β_3)	−0.161***	−0.185***	−0.128***
Number of events	475	282	234

*Significant at the .10 level.
**Significant at the .05 level.
***Significant at the .01 level.
[a]Based on 2851 jobs for black men and on 3484 jobs for white men.

7.4 Time as a Proxy for Unobserved Change Processes

So far this chapter has taken an unconventional tack in developing models of time dependence in transition rates. Instead of simply positing the existence of time dependence, we have shown that time trends in causal variables create time dependence in rates. For example, the previous section derived a generalization of the Gompertz model as an implication of the assumption that a transition rate depends log-linearly on covariates that change linearly over time. We have stressed this strategy for incorporating time dependence in models of transition rates because it directs attention to the essential task of parameterizing causal effects and clarifies the meaning of time variation in transition rates.

But what about situations in which key causal variables are difficult to measure? Such situations call for a strategy that attaches substantive interpretation to the "effects" of various measures of time. We believe that this approach is potentially fruitful for comparative analysis of social processes. It is often a useful first step in research designed eventually to collect information on relevant causal variables and parameterize their effects. Investigation of the way that transition rates vary with various measures of time may help to suggest which classes of variables should be measured in subsequent research. This strategy can be used with any measure of time discussed in Section 7.1.

A large number of time dependent models of hazard functions and transition rates have been proposed by those taking this strategy. Usually a particular model is chosen simply because it broadly approximates the hypothesized shape of the hazard function or transition rate. Based on our previous experience (e.g., see Tuma, 1972), ML estimates of various two- and three-parameter models of hazard functions or transition rates from a given set of data usually yield predicted survivor functions that (1) fit the data surprisingly well and (2) are almost distinguishable unless the sample size is very large. Thus, it appears as though it is not too important which particular model is chosen by those adopting this strategy. Consequently, we do not attempt to discuss any particular one in detail. It seems useful to distinguish only between rates with two basic shapes in our discussion below: rates that change monotonically with time, which seems to be the more common choice, and rates that change nonmonotonically.

⟨7⟩ Time as a Proxy for Unobserved Change Processes

Table 7.4. Some common specifications in which the hazard function is a monotonic function of time t and $t_0 = 0$

Name	$h(t)$	dh/dt
Gamma[a]	$\dfrac{\lambda(\lambda t)^{\beta-1} e^{-\lambda t}}{\Gamma(\beta) - \lambda^\beta \int_0^t u^{\beta-1} e^{-\lambda u}\, du}$	$\left[\dfrac{\beta - 1 - \lambda t}{t} - h(t)\right] h(t)$
Gompertz	$\theta e^{\gamma t}$	$\theta \gamma e^{\gamma t}$
Makeham	$\psi + \theta e^{\gamma t}$	$\theta \gamma e^{\gamma t}$
Rayleigh	$\alpha + \beta t$	β
Weibull	$\lambda[t + \delta]^\gamma$	$\lambda[\gamma - 1][t + \delta]^{\gamma-1}$

[a]$\Gamma(\beta)$ denotes the gamma function, $\int_0^\infty u^{\beta-1} e^{-u}\, du$.

7.4.1 Monotonically Changing Rates

Various specifications are used when analysts suspect that a hazard function changes monotonically with some measure of time. It is neither possible nor especially useful to provide a comprehensive list and discussion of these specifications. However, as an introduction to this topic, we give the hazard function and its first derivative with respect to time for a selection of such specifications in Table 7.4.[4] Examples of the shapes resulting from these specifications and of the range of values that they take can be found in Figure 7.2.

Each can also be used as a specification of transition rates in multistate models of repeatable events. One merely substitutes $r_{jk}(t \mid t_{n-1})$ for $h(t \mid t_0)$ and subscripts the parameters in Table 7.4 with j and k. It is worth noting that one consequence of this substitution is that in general the hazard function for state j does not have the same form as the rate of transition from j to k. In fact, transition rates that are *monotonic* functions of time can yield a hazard function that is a *nonmonotonic* function of time.

To illustrate this point, assume that state 0 is entered at $t_0 = 0$ and that there are two possible moves: from state 0 to state 1 or from state 0 to state 2. Assume that a Gompertz model describes

---

[4]Two good sources of information on the implications of these specifications are Hastings and Peacock (1974) and Johnson and Kotz (1970).

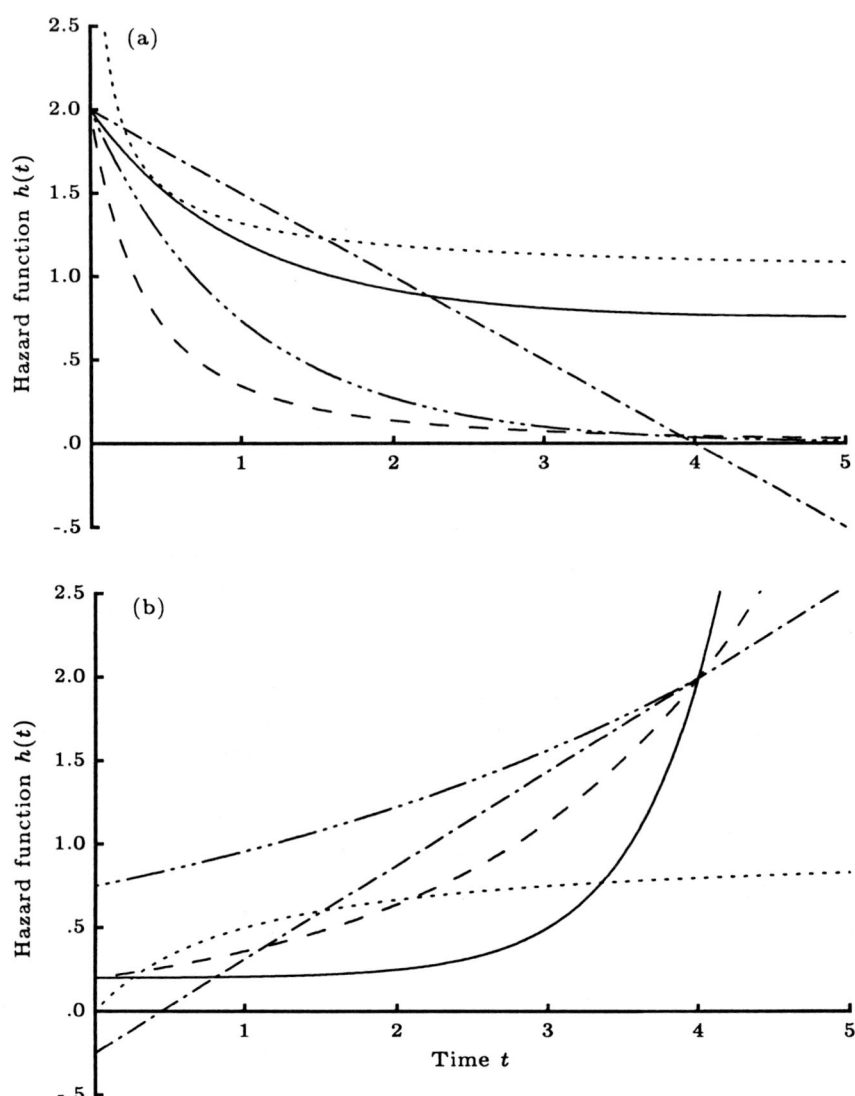

Figure 7.2. Shapes of selected specifications of a monotonically changing hazard function. (a) $dh(t)/dt < 0$; (b) $dh(t)/dt > 0$. The dotted curve denotes gamma; the dot-dot-dot-dashed curve, Gompertz; the solid curve, Makeham; the dashed curve, Rayleigh; the dot-dashed curve, Weibull.

⟨7⟩ Time as a Proxy for Unobserved Change Processes

these rates and, in particular, that

$$r_{01}(t) = \theta_1 \, e^{\gamma_1 t}, \qquad \gamma_1 > 0,$$
$$r_{02}(t) = \theta_2 \, e^{\gamma_2 t}, \qquad \gamma_2 < 0,$$

where both θ_1 and θ_2 are greater than zero. Since $h_0(t) = r_{01}(t) + r_{02}(t)$, these expressions imply that

$$h_0(t) = \theta_1 \, e^{\gamma_1 t} + \theta_2 \, e^{\gamma_2 t}.$$

Notice that

$$\frac{d h_0(t)}{dt} = \gamma_1 \, r_{01}(t) + \gamma_2 \, r_{02}(t).$$

Since γ_1 and γ_2 have opposite signs, $h_0(t)$ either falls and then rises, or rises and then falls, depending on the magnitudes of the parameters in the model.

Each specification in Table 7.4 (whether for a hazard function or a transition rate) can be generalized (with varying degrees of difficulty) to a model that includes covariates. One simply postulates that the parameters in the ordinary specification (such as one of those in Table 7.4) are some particular function of the covariates. For example, one may postulate the hazard function for a Gompertz model and assume that

$$\theta = e^{\alpha' \mathbf{x}};$$
$$\gamma = \boldsymbol{\kappa}' \mathbf{z}.$$

The result is simply (23), the equation derived from the assumption of linearly changing causal variables in Section 7.3. Similarly, one may postulate the hazard function for the Weibull model and assume that

$$\lambda = e^{\alpha' \mathbf{x}}.$$

The result is (20), which we derived in another way in Section 7.3.

7.4.2 An Example: Age Variation in Organizational Death Rates

Our example remains close to the classical models of time variation in rates, which have dealt typically with age variation in death rates. However, unlike the classical demographers who studied mortality in human populations, we study death rates of formal organizations.

It is widely claimed that organizations, like people, have high infant death rates and that death rates decline sharply with age. Stinchcombe (1965) argued that organizations suffer a "liability of newness" because they must rely on the cooperation of strangers, lack standard operating procedures, and have low levels of legitimacy. Therefore, he argued, the death rate is high initially but declines with age as legitimacy is earned and as trust and procedures become established. Unfortunately, legitimacy, trust, and stability of procedures are difficult to measure; age is a useful proxy.

Interest in age dependence in organizational death rates has increased recently as organizational theorists have turned their attention to organizational ecology and demography. The likelihood that organizations face a high liability of newness points to the value of studying the effects of environmental conditions at birth on selection in organizational populations (Carroll and Delacroix, 1982).

Although there is a long history of research on age dependence of death rates of organizations (for a review, see Carroll, 1982), it has not yet been established that death rates *do* vary with age. Most earlier research failed to use sound research designs to study this issue. Much earlier research also ignored differences among organizations in size at founding. The few studies that have analyzed jointly the effects of age and size on death rates have produced mixed results. Some have reported that death rates do vary substantially with age; others have reported that the apparent effect of age vanishes when size at birth is controlled.

The analysis reported below uses information on the life histories of 476 national labor unions in the United States during the period 1860–1980.[5] The data contain information on the dates of founding and selected subsequent events, such as disbanding or disappearance by merger. Since we assume all unions begin in the same state ($1 \equiv$ "newly founded") and can transit to two absorbing states ($2 \equiv$ "merged" and $3 \equiv$ "disbanded"), this is a three-state loss model with two nonzero transition rates. Here we summarize a portion of the results in Freeman, Carroll, and Hannan (1983).

Figure 7.3 shows Aalen estimates of the cumulative transition rates of disbanding and absorption by merger for these unions versus

[5]The data come from published compliations of births and deaths of unions and from histories of individual unions.

⟨7⟩ Time as a Proxy for Unobserved Change Processes   225

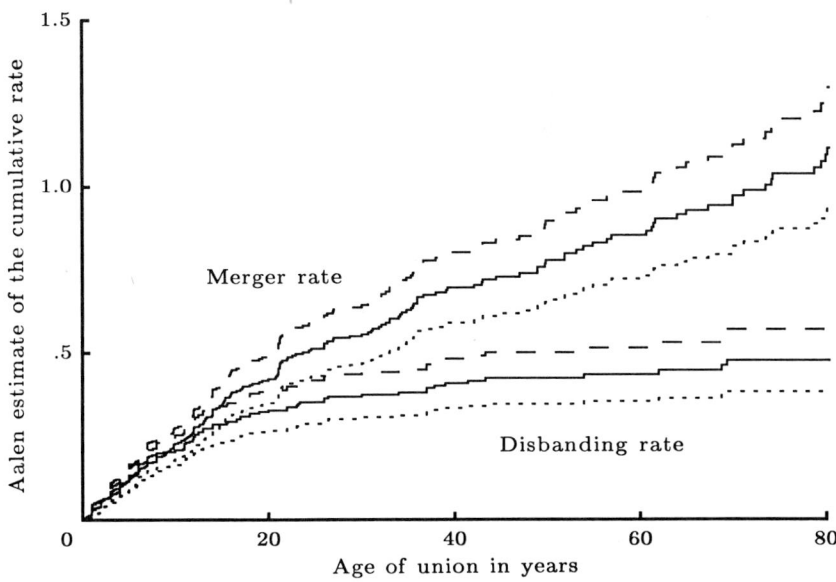

Figure 7.3. Aalen estimates of the cumulative merger and disbanding rates of national labor unions in the United States ($I = 476$). The solid curves denote the Aalen estimates; the dashed and dotted curves the upper and lower 95% confidence intervals, respectively.

age.[6] The two transition rates appear to rise in a similar fashion for the first 10 or 20 years of existence; thereafter the merger rate drops sharply relative to the disbanding rate. As we explained in Chapter 6, such curvature can be a consequence of unobserved heterogeneity. The main rival explanation to age dependence in these rates is size dependence. Therefore we concentrate on distinguishing the effects of age and size within one type of model: the Makeham model defined in Table 7.4.

Since social arrangements are unlikely to be immortal, it seems realistic to propose a model that implies a finite expected length of life for a social organization. One way of doing this is to replace the Gompertz model with the Makeham model (see Table

---

[6]Recall that the slope of the cumulative transition rate at a given age gives an estimate of the corresponding transition rate.

7.4). Notice that when γ is negative, $h(t \mid t_0)$ approaches ψ rather than zero as time passes. At t_0, the rate equals $\psi + \theta$. Since the asymptotic rate equals ψ, θ tells the extent to which the initial rate exceeds the asymptotic rate (assuming that $\gamma < 0$).

Since we are interested in comparing the effects of size and age on disbanding and merger rates, we need to generalize the Makeham model in Table 7.4 to apply to multiple outcomes and to include the effects of covariates.

The data currently available contain a measure of size (number of members) only at the time of founding. Since we are interested in evaluating the claim that new organizations face a liability of newness, using information on size only at founding is probably not a serious limitation.

When all covariates are fixed at their levels at t_0, the generalized Makeham model is

$$r_{ijk}(t \mid t_{i0}) = \psi_{jk}(\mathbf{x}_i) + \theta_{jk}(\mathbf{x}_i)\, e^{\gamma_{jk}(\mathbf{x}_i)[t-t_0]}. \tag{24}$$

The parameters in this equation have the following interpretation. The effects of the fixed covariates on the asymptotic transition rate are given by the elements of $\boldsymbol{\psi}_{jk}(\mathbf{x}_i)$. The effects of covariates on the degree to which the initial rate exceeds the asymptote are given by the elements of $\boldsymbol{\theta}_{jk}(\mathbf{x}_i)$. Finally, the effects of the covariates on the speed with which the rate declines from its initial level to the asymptote are given by the elements of $\boldsymbol{\phi}_{jk}(\mathbf{x}_i)$.

In general, analysts may want to specify that different elements of x affect different aspects of the process. We specify models in which size at founding affects the liability of newness θ_{1k} and the rate of decline in the death rate γ_{1k}, but does not affect the asymptotic death rate, ψ_{1k}. Let the initial size of the ith union be denoted by S_i. We assume that the rate of transition from state 1 ("newly founded") to state $k = 2$ or 3, has the general form

$$r_{1k}(t \mid t_0) = \psi_{1k} + \theta_{1k}(S_i)\, e^{\gamma_{1k}(S_i)[t-t_0]}. \tag{27}$$

We think that size has nonlinear effects on the death rate of organizations, which we expressed in the following way:

$$\theta_{1k}(S_i) = e^{\beta_{1k0} + \beta_{1k1} \log S_i};$$

$$\gamma_{1k}(S_i) = \gamma_{1k0} + \gamma_{1k1} \log S_i.$$

Table 7.5. Maximum-likelihood estimates of the effects of age and size on merger and disbanding rates of national labor unions[a]

	Parameter						
	ψ_{1k}	β_{1k0}	β_{1k1}	γ_{1k0}	γ_{1k1}	χ^2	(df)[b]
Merger rate							
Model I	.014***						
Model II		−4.09***		−.070**		5.0	(1)
Model III	.010***	−4.34***		−.070**		14.0	(2)
Model IV	.010***	−3.65***	−.103	−.075***		14.5	(3)
Model V	.010***	−2.04	−.358	−.281*	.029	15.7	(4)
Disbanding rate							
Model I	.009***						
Model II		−3.61***		−.056***		107.2	(1)
Model III	.002**	−3.36***		−.110***		121.6	(2)
Model IV	.002**	−1.87***	−.226***	−.104***		134.7	(3)
Model V	.002***	−1.92***	−.221**	−.100		134.7	(4)

*Significant at the .10 level.
**Significant at the .05 level.
***Significant at the .01 level.
[a] $I = 476$.
[b] Likelihood ratio test versus Model I.

(We have found that a model with a nonlinear specification fits better, in the sense of producing a larger likelihood, than a model with a linear one.) With these assumptions about the dependence of the parameters in the Makeham model on size, (27) becomes

$$r_{1k}(t) = \psi_{1k} + \theta_{1k0} \, e^{\beta_{1k0}+\beta_{1k1}\log S_i + (\gamma_{1k0}+\gamma_{1k1}\log S_i)[t-t_0]}. \quad (28)$$

Table 7.5 reports ML estimates of the parameters in (28) for the merger rate and the disbanding rate. It also contains estimates of a hierarchy of simpler models that build up to (28), along with likelihood ratio χ^2 values testing each model against the model at the next lower level of the hierarchy. The hierarchy begins with the natural baseline of a constant-rate model, called Model I. The second is the classic Gompertz model with no covariates, called Model II. The next is a Makeham model with no covariates, Model III. According to the results reported in Table 2, the pure Gompertz model improves significantly on the constant-rate model for both outcomes. The Makeham model also improves significantly on the Gompertz model. Thus we chose Model III as the appropriate baseline against which to compare the fit of models that include effects of size at founding.

Next we introduce size into the liability-of-newness term, $\theta_{1k}(\cdot)$; in particular, we estimated Model IV, which allows β_{1k1} to be nonzero. Here we see a difference between outcomes. This modification improves significantly on Model III for the disbanding rate but not for the merger rate.

Finally, we consider Model IV, the full model in (28), which allows size to affect both the liability of newness and the rate at which this liability wears off. In neither case does the fit of this model improve significantly upon the fit of Model IV (at the .10 level). Thus, within the hierarchy of models we chose, it seems clear that one does not need the full complexity of (28). The best-fitting model of the disbanding rate is Model IV; the best-fitting model of the merger rate is Model III.

We also calculated the likelihood ratio χ^2 value for a test of pooling types of outcomes (disbandings and mergers). Given our findings, the most informative test is based on results for Model IV. The χ^2 value for this test is 42.6 with 4 degrees of freedom, which means that the null hypothesis (that the parameters of the merger and disbanding rates are the same) is highly unlikely.

What have we learned? First, death rates and merger rates for national labor unions in the United States vary strongly with age. There is a liability of newness, independent of the effects of initial size; it is substantial, as we illustrate in Figure 7.4. The solid curve in Figure 7.4 shows the pattern of age variation in the merger rate implied by the estimates for Model III; the various broken curves depict age variation in the disbanding rate implied by the estimates for Model IV for four levels of size: the first, second, and third quartiles, and the maximum observed in the data ($S =$ 200, 700, 3000, and 517,000, respectively). These curves show that the rates decline rapidly over the first 10–15 years of a union's existence. Moreover, differences in disbanding rates by initial size are quite large.

We have also learned that the aging process differs by type

⟨7⟩   Time as a Proxy for Unobserved Change Processes   229

Figure 7.4. Estimated age variation in the merger and disbanding rates of national labor unions in the United States. The solid curve denotes the merger rate for all values of S_i; the dot-dot-dot-dashed curve, the disbanding rate when $S_i = 200$; the dashed curve, the disbanding rate when $S_i = 700$; the dotted curve, the disbanding rate when $S_i = 3000$; the dot-dashed curve, the disbanding rate when $S_i = 517{,}000$ (maximum observed).

of outcome. Initial size lowers the disbanding rate sharply but does not apparently affect the merger rate. This makes substantive sense: often the most successful organizations enter mergers, but only the least successful disband. In order to understand age and size variations in merger rates, one presumably needs to include the effects of changes in size after founding. It may also be necessary to specify models in which age variation is nonmonotonic. Reading the histories of labor unions gives the impression that the merger rate falls with age and then rises again as the initial founders and members turn the reins of power over to the next generation.

7.4.3   Nonmonotonically Changing Rates

As we suggested in the previous example, a hazard function

Table 7.6. Selected specifications in which the hazard function is a non-monotonic function of time t and $t_0 = 0$

Name	$h(t)$	dh/dt
Generalized Rayleigh	$\alpha + \beta t + \gamma t^2 + \cdots$	$\beta + 2\gamma t + \cdots$
Inverse Gaussian[a]	$\dfrac{\dfrac{\alpha}{\sqrt{2\pi t^3}}\exp\left[-\dfrac{(\beta t + \alpha)^2}{2t}\right]}{\Phi\left(\dfrac{\beta t + \alpha}{\sqrt{t}}\right) - e^{-2\alpha\beta}\Phi\left(\dfrac{\beta t - \alpha}{\sqrt{t}}\right)}$	$-\left[\dfrac{\beta^2 + \dfrac{3}{t} - \dfrac{\alpha^2}{t^2}}{2} + h(t)\right]h(t)$
Log-logistic	$\alpha t^{\gamma-1}\left(1 + \dfrac{\alpha t^\gamma}{\gamma}\right)^{-1}$	$\dfrac{1}{t}\left[\gamma\left(1 + \dfrac{\alpha t^\gamma}{\gamma}\right)^{-1} - 1\right]h(t)$
Log-normal	$\dfrac{\dfrac{1}{t}\exp\left[-\dfrac{(\log t)^2}{2\sigma^2}\right]}{\sigma\sqrt{2\pi} - \int_0^t \dfrac{1}{u}\exp\left[-\dfrac{(\log u)^2}{2\sigma^2}\right]du}$	$-\left[\dfrac{1 + \dfrac{\log t}{\sigma^2}}{t} + h(t)\right]h(t)$
Sickle[b]	$\alpha t\, e^{-\beta t}$	$\alpha e^{-\beta t}(1 - \beta t)$
Sum of exponentials	$\sum_{m=1}^{M} \beta_m e^{\lambda_m t}$	$\sum_{m=1}^{M} \beta_m \lambda_m e^{\lambda_m t}$

[a] $\Phi(\cdot)$ denotes the cumulative normal distribution function.
[b] See Diekmann and Mitter (1983).

or a transition rate is sometimes believed to vary nonmonotonically with time. It may be thought to fall and then rise, as in the case of age variation in human mortality rates and in organizational merger rates. Or, it may be hypothesized to rise and then fall, as has been sugggested for the case of job-shift rates (Bartholomew, 1973).

Some specifications used in such situations are reported in Table 7.6. As in the case of the specifications of a monotonically changing hazard function given in Table 7.4, each of these can be used as a model of a transition rate as well as a hazard function. Again, each can be generalized to include covariates; however, we

⟨ 7 ⟩   Conclusions   231

have not yet seen empirical applications of such generalizations. We suspect that such generalizations are likely to undergo considerable development and be applied to many substantive problems as sociologists become familiar with the value of the strategy that we have described and illustrated in Section 7.4.

7.5   Conclusions

This chapter presents the first half of our treatment of time dependence; the next chapter completes the discussion. We began by considering various substantive reasons for expecting time dependence. We argued that much of the apparent time dependence actually reflects faulty specification either of the state space of the process or of the set of explanatory variables affecting the process. Still, true behavioral (or structural) time dependence seems meaningful in certain classes of situations. These situations often involve causal variables that are either functions of time or closely related to time: age, duration, cohort, and experience. Although it may be argued that any of these variables actually serves as a proxy for other variables that are hard to measure directly, it is often useful to parameterize the change process in terms of them. Such efforts provide clues to the underlying structure and direct attention to those situations in which an intensive effort to measure more subtle latent factors is well advised.

We discussed and illustrated three types of parametric models of time dependence in transition rates. The first type assumes that transition rate are log-linear functions of causal variables that change fron one temporal period to another; effects of these causal variables may also change from period to period. This model can also be used to approximate an unknown pattern of change in causal factors. The second type of model assumes that transition rates are log-linear functions of causal variables that change linearly over time. This type of model gives a generalization of the widely known Gompertz model. With a logarithmic transformation of time, it gives a generalization of the equally well-known Weibull model. In the third type of model, time is a proxy for unknown, unobserved causal processes. Various specifications of hazard functions and transition rates are used in this situation. We mentioned two classes of specifications, one in which rates change monotonically with time and another in which they change nonmonotonically, and listed several examples of each.

8

Time Dependence: A Partially Parametric Approach

A parametric approach to time dependence is a valuable tool in empirical analysis when substantive theory or previous empirical research suggests the form of time dependence in transition rates. But such guidelines are not always available. Moreover, sometimes sociologists want to control possible confounding effects of time variation that are very difficult to parameterize—for example, assorted variables that change over time in an apparently patternless way. Often analysts would like to eliminate the effects of these confounding variables, but have no particular interest in modeling them. In such situations, an approach to event-history analysis that is *partially parametric* has considerable appeal.

There has been a rapid development of such a partially parametric approach. The key innovation in its development is Cox's (1972, 1975) partial-likelihood (PL) method of estimating models of so-called proportional hazards or proportional rates. Such models, described in detail in Section 8.1 (and in still greater detail in Kalbfleisch and Prentice, 1980), allow transition rates to depend on observed explanatory variables that have an unspecified pattern of time variation. In addition, they assume that an unspecified time-dependent nuisance function affects the rates of all members of the population in the same multiplicative way. Although it is necessary to specify the way transition rates depend on the observed explanatory variables, the approach is "distribution free" in the sense that the form of the nuisance function and the form of the time variation in explanatory variables are not specified.

⟨ 8 ⟩   **Proportional Rates**

In Section 8.2 we tell why maximum likelihood (ML) cannot be used to estimate models with an unspecified nuisance function. We also explain how to construct a partial-likelihood function and show that causal effects can be estimated by maximizing this function. The resulting method is known as partial-likelihood estimation. In Section 8.3 we report the findings of a Monte Carlo study comparing the quality of ML and PL estimators in medium-sized samples when the lengths of episodes are censored. Section 8.4 contains an empirical example of this approach.

Sections 8.5 and 8.6 take up complications that often arise in applications of PL estimation. The first, discussed in Section 8.5, is the occurrence of ties in the observed length of episodes. The second, treated in Section 8.6, concerns ways of dealing with intermittent measurement of explanatory variables. Such an observation plan presents problems because the PL function assumes that causal variables are measured at the times of all events.

The primary aim of PL estimation is to *control* for unknown forms of time variation. It does not directly provide estimates of the *form* of time variation. Section 8.7 outlines ways of estimating both the unknown nuisance function and the survivor function. We discuss sources of variation in the nuisance function in Section 8.8. We show that the nuisance function need not apply solely to variation in rates with time. It can also handle many other forms of unspecified variation in rates.

The remaining sections describe generalizations of the proportional hazards model to encompass more complex situations. Section 8.9 deals with multiple outcomes, returning to the subject of models with proportional rates, which is first raised in Section 8.1. An empirical example illustrating this application is given in Section 8.10. Section 8.11 discusses the opportunities and problems that arise when events are repeated, that is, there are data on multiple episodes.

8.1   Proportional Rates

Currently the only partially parametric approach to event-history analysis applies solely to models of proportional rates. Such models assume that each transition rate $r_{jk}(t)$ can be factored into two components. One component is an unknown, (possibly) time-dependent nuisance function $q_{jk}(t)$, which affects the rate of every member of the population in the same way. The second component, $\theta_{jk}(\mathbf{x}(t))$, is assumed to depend on a vector of (possibly time-varying) observed causal variables $\mathbf{x}(t)$, on parameters to be estimated, and possibly also on time t. Thus the proportional rate model has the form

$$r_{jk}(t) = q_{jk}(t)\theta_{jk}(\mathbf{x}(t)). \tag{1}$$

Note that the ratio of the rates for two members of the population, i and v, is independent of the nuisance function $q_{jk}(t)$ and depends only on the function of observed variables, $\theta_{jk}(\mathbf{x}(t))$:

$$\frac{r_{ijk}(t)}{r_{vjk}(t)} = \frac{q_{jk}(t)\theta_{jk}(\mathbf{x}_i(t))}{q_{jk}(t)\theta_{jk}(\mathbf{x}_v(t))} = \frac{\theta_{jk}(\mathbf{x}_v(t))}{\theta_{jk}(\mathbf{x}_i(t))}. \tag{2}$$

This relationship is the reason for calling (1) a model of proportional rates. Although it may seem rather innocuous, it is the key to the currently available partially parametric approach to event-history analysis.

A model in which the nuisance function has an additive effect,

$$r_{jk}(t) = q_{jk}(t) + \theta_{jk}(\mathbf{x}(t)), \tag{3}$$

is not a model of proportional rates because the ratio of the rates for two members of the population depends on the nuisance function $q_{jk}(t)$:

$$\frac{r_{ijk}(t)}{r_{vjk}(t)} = \frac{r_{ijk}(t)q_{jk}(t) + \theta_{jk}(\mathbf{x}_i(t))}{r_{vjk}(t)q_{jk}(t) + \theta_{jk}(\mathbf{x}_v(t))}.$$

Models in the form of (3) can be estimated by a parametric approach if $q_{jk}(t)$ is known, but not by existing partially parametric methods.

Although the partially parametric approach to event-history analysis does not require specification of $q_{jk}(t)$, it *does* require parametric assumptions about the dependence of $\theta_{jk}(\cdot)$ on the observed variables $\mathbf{x}(t)$. Customarily it is assumed that the rate of an event is a log-linear function of the current values of observed variables:

$$\theta_{jk}(\mathbf{x}(t)) = e^{\alpha'_{jk}\mathbf{x}(t)}, \tag{4}$$

where $\boldsymbol{\alpha}_{jk}$ is an unknown vector of parameters to be estimated. If, consistent with the usual notation in linear regression models, the first element in the vector of variables is unity, then the first element of $\boldsymbol{\alpha}_{jk}$ must be constrained to be zero. Otherwise it cannot be distinguished from $q_{jk}(t)$. Illustrations in this section retain the assumption in (4), which agrees with most parametric approaches to event-history analysis (e.g., see Tuma, Hannan, and Groeneveld, 1979; Sørensen and Tuma, 1981). But the approach is readily adapted to other specifications of $\theta_{jk}(\cdot)$.

To date, most interest in a partially parametric approach to event-history analysis has occurred among biometricians developing methods for studying causes of death. Consequently, the literature on this approach largely assumes that there is a single nonrepeatable event. Then $r_{jk}(t)$ equals $h(t)$, the hazard function, and (1) becomes

$$h(t) = q(t)\theta(\mathbf{x}(t)), \qquad (5)$$

where usually it is assumed that

$$\theta(\mathbf{x}(t)) = e^{\boldsymbol{\alpha}'\mathbf{x}(t)}. \qquad (6)$$

For simplicity, we begin with this case and later turn to the more general case of multiple outcomes and repeatable events.

8.2 Partial Likelihood

Unfortunately the parameters in (5) [or in (21)] cannot be estimated by ML because the specific form of $q(t)$ is unknown, which means that a parametric expression cannot be written for the survivor function, a key component of the full likelihood. Nevertheless, Cox's (1972, 1975) PL method can be used in its place. The underlying idea can be sketched as follows.

As with the Kaplan–Meier estimator of the survivor function, the data are first arranged in the order at which events occur in the sample, assuming for simplicity that only one sample member has an event at any moment. So, for example, $t_{(1)}$ denotes the time of the first event that is observed in the sample, while $\mathbf{x}_{(1)}$ denotes the value of the vector of explanatory variables for the sample member that has the first event, and so forth. Usually the times of events are observed for only some subset I^* of the sample, $I^* \leq I$. The remaining $I^c = I - I^*$ cases are right-censored; no events occur within the period during which they are observed.

Now consider the sequence of random quantities $\{E_1, C_1; E_2, C_2; \ldots; E_{I^*}, C_{I^*}\}$ where E_i contains the information that case (i) has the event at $t_{(i)}$ and C_i all information about censoring in the time interval $[t_{(i-1)}, t_{(i)})$. The full likelihood can be expressed as

$$\mathcal{L} = \Pr[E_1, \ldots, E_{I^*}; C_1, C_2, \ldots, C_{I^*}].$$

Applying the definition of a conditional probability repeatedly yields

$$\mathcal{L} = \Pr[E_1, C_1] \prod_{i=2}^{I^*} \Pr[E_i, C_i \mid E_1, C_1, \ldots, E_{i-1}, C_{i-1}]$$

$$= \Pr[E_1 \mid C_1] \prod_{i=2}^{I^*} \Pr[E_i \mid E_1, \ldots, E_{i-1}, C_1, \ldots, C_i]$$

$$\cdot \Pr[C_1] \prod_{i=2}^{I^*} \Pr[C_i \mid E_1, \ldots, E_{i-1}, C_1, \ldots, C_{i-1}].$$

Cox (1972) called the first product, that is,

$$\Pr[E_1 \mid C_1] \prod_{i=2}^{I^*} \Pr[E_i \mid E_1, \ldots, E_{i-1}, C_1, \ldots, C_i],$$

the partial likelihood, $_p\mathcal{L}$.

Knowledge of $C_1, \ldots, C_i$ and $E_1, \ldots, E_{i-1}$ lets one designate the collection of cases still at risk of experiencing the event at time $t_{(i)}$, $R(t_{(i)})$. It is customary to rewrite the partial likelihood $_p\mathcal{L}$ as

$$_p\mathcal{L} = \prod_{i=1}^{I^*} \Pr[E_i \mid R(t_{(i)})].$$

To illustrate the construction of the PL, suppose that the sample contains five cases (i.e., $I = 5$): a, b, c, d, and e. Suppose also that events are observed for four cases (i.e., $I^* = 4$) and occur at times $t_{(1)}$, $t_{(2)}$, $t_{(3)}$, and $t_{(4)}$ and that information on the fifth

⟨8⟩ Partial Likelihood

case is censored at a time between $t_{(2)}$ and $t_{(3)}$, denoted by $t_{(1)}^c$. It is convenient to label cases in such a way that case a has the event at $t_{(1)}$, b has the event at $t_{(2)}$, information on c is censored at $t_{(1)}^c$, d has the event at $t_{(3)}$, and e has the event at $t_{(4)}$. To denote random variables, their realizations and the corresponding probability functions pertaining to a particular sample member, we subscript the usual symbol with the letter representing the case. For example, T_a is the random variable standing for the time of the event for case a and t_a is its realization. The probability that the event has not occurred by time t for case a is $G_a(t)$, the probability density that it occurs at t is $f_a(t) = h_a(t) G_a(t)$, and so forth.

The risk-set at any moment is the set of individuals who can conceivably experience the event in question. There are four relevant risk-sets involved in the PL for this example. First, $R(t_{(1)}) = \{a, b, c, d, e\}$, which means that all five cases are at risk of the first event. $R(t_{(2)}) = \{b, c, d, e\}$; it excludes case a because t_a is less than $t_{(2)}$. $R(t_{(3)}) = \{d, e\}$; it excludes a and b because t_a and t_b are less than $t_{(3)}$, *and* it excludes c because c is censored at t_1^c, which is less than $t_{(3)}$. The other relevant risk-set, $R(t_{(4)}) = \{e\}$, contains only the single sample member e.

The PL for this example can be written as

$$_p\mathcal{L} = \Pr[a = (1) \mid R(t_{(1)})] \cdot \Pr[b = (2) \mid R(t_{(2)})]$$
$$\cdot \Pr[d = (3) \mid R(t_{(3)})] \cdot \Pr[e = (4) \mid R(t_{(4)})].$$

The fourth term in $_p\mathcal{L}$, $\Pr[e = (4) \mid R(t_{(4)})]$, equals unity because case e is the only member in the risk-set at $t_{(4)}$. The third term is a simple but more typical term. The probability that case d (and not e) has an event at time t, given that an event occurs at time t and that d and e are the only cases at risk of the event, is

$$f_d(t) G_e(t) = h_d(t) G_d(t) G_e(t)$$
$$= \theta(\mathbf{x}_d(t)) q(t) G_d(t) G_e(t).$$

Likewise, given these conditions, the probability that case e (and not d) has an event at time t is

$$f_e(t) G_d(t) = h_e(t) G_d(t) G_e(t)$$
$$= \theta(\mathbf{x}_e(t)) q(t) G_d(t) G_e(t).$$

Therefore, the third term is:

$$\Pr[d = (3) \mid R(t_{(3)})]$$

$$= \frac{f_d(t_{(3)}) G_e(t_{(3)})}{f_d(t_{(3)}) G_e(t_{(3)}) + G_d(t_{(3)}) f_e(t_{(3)})} \quad (7a)$$

$$= \frac{h_d(t_{(3)}) G_d(t_{(3)}) G_e(t_{(3)})}{h_d(t_{(3)}) G_d(t_{(3)}) G_e(t_{(3)}) + h_e(t_{(3)}) G_d(t_{(3)}) G_e(t_{(3)})} \quad (7b)$$

$$= \frac{h_d(t_{(3)})}{h_d(t_{(3)}) + h_e(t_{(3)})} \quad (7c)$$

$$= \frac{\theta(x_d(t_{(3)})) q(t_{(3)})}{\theta(x_d(t_{(3)})) q(t_{(3)}) + \theta(x_e(t_{(3)})) q(t_{(3)})} \quad (7d)$$

$$= \frac{\theta(x_d(t_{(3)}))}{\theta(x_d(t_{(3)})) + \theta(x_e(t_{(3)}))}. \quad (7e)$$

Each term of the numerator and denominator in (7b) contains the same product of the survivor functions, which permits cancellation of every survivor function. Consequently, the third term does not depend on the survivor function; furthermore, it does not depend on the nuisance function $q(t)$ because $q(t)$ is a common factor in each term of the numerator and the denominator in (7d), allowing its cancellation also. The fraction remaining in (7e) is an explicit function of observed variables.

The first and second terms of $_p\mathcal{L}$ are constructed in basically the same way. Analogous to (7d), they reduce to the following:

$$\Pr[a = (1) \mid R(t_{(1)})]$$

$$= \frac{h_a(t_{(1)})}{h_a(t_{(1)}) + h_b(t_{(1)}) + h_c(t_{(1)}) + h_d(t_{(1)}) + h_e(t_{(1)})};$$

$$\Pr[b = (2) \mid R(t_{(2)})]$$

$$= \frac{h_b(t_{(2)})}{h_b(t_{(2)}) + h_c(t_{(2)}) + h_d(t_{(2)}) + h_e(t_{(2)})}.$$

Again the nuisance function cancels from every term of the numerator and denominator, leaving expressions paralleling (7e).

The above discussion is readily generalized to arbitrarily large samples of size I in which I^* sample members have events. In general, the term in the PL for the event at $t_{(i)}$ is

$$\frac{\theta(\mathbf{x}_i(t_{(i)}))}{\sum_{v \in R(t_{(i)})} \theta(\mathbf{x}_v(t_{(i)}))}. \tag{8}$$

The PL for the whole sample is the product of I^* such terms:

$$_p\mathcal{L} = \prod_{i=1}^{I^*} \frac{\theta(\mathbf{x}_i(t_{(i)}))}{\sum_{v \in R(t_{(i)})} \theta(\mathbf{x}_v(t_{(i)}))}. \tag{9}$$

If $\theta(x(t))$ is given by (6),

$$_p\mathcal{L} = \prod_{i=1}^{I^*} \frac{e^{\boldsymbol{\alpha}'\mathbf{x}_i(t_{(i)})}}{\sum_{v \in R(t_{(i)})} e^{\boldsymbol{\alpha}'\mathbf{x}_v(t_{(i)}))}}. \tag{10}$$

The PL estimate of $\boldsymbol{\alpha}$ in (6) is obtained by finding the value that maximizes $_p\mathcal{L}$ in (10); one treats the PL as though it were a full likelihood. Cox (1975) claimed that the PL estimator of $\boldsymbol{\alpha}$ are consistent; Efron (1977) proved that under fairly general conditions the PL estimators are efficient (see also Oakes, 1977). Efron's proofs assume that censoring is exogenous, that is, not a consequence of the process being studied. Tsiatis (1981) proved that the PL estimators are consistent. The asymptotic variance–covariance matrix of estimated parameters $\boldsymbol{\alpha}$ can be estimated as $[\partial^2 \log_p \mathcal{L}/\partial \boldsymbol{\alpha}^2]^{-1}$. As noted in Chapter 5, the estimated variance of a parameter lets one test hypotheses about it.

8.3 Monte Carlo Study of PL and ML Estimators

The analytic results cited above indicate that PL estimators have optimal large sample properties but does not guarantee that they have good properties in the small to medium-sized samples available to most social scientists. Consequently, in collaboration with Glenn Carroll and Barbara Warsavage, we conducted a series of Monte Carlo experiments to investigate the properties of PL estimators in situations resembling those in empirical social research. Here we summarize only the main findings; a detailed description of procedures and results appears in Carroll et al. (1978a).

We concentrated on three main issues in our Monte Carlo studies of PL estimators. First, we studied the effect of censoring on PL estimators. Because greater censoring means fewer cases with observed times of events, we expected the variance of PL estimators to increase with censoring, but we were unsure of the effect of censoring on bias. Second, we compared the relative quality of PL and ML estimators when both are based on a correctly specified model. Because PL estimators use less of the information in event-history data than ML estimators, we expected PL estimators to be less efficient. However, we did not know how great the difference in efficiency would be in medium-sized samples, or how different be used to estimate parameters in a model their biases would be. Third, we compared the quality of PL and ML estimators when the ML estimator is based on an incorrectly specified model. Allowance for an unknown nuisance function is the main advantage of PL estimation. Maximum-likelihood estimation requires that the form of each rate be specified completely. Undoubtedly, empirical analyses based on ML estimation sometimes make incorrect assumptions about this form. We expected ML estimators to be inferior to PL estimators under such circumstances, but we did not have any idea how much poorer they would be.

Our Monte Carlo studies focused on the case of a single nonrepeatable event. We investigated two types of situations. In Case A, the rate of an event was a time-independent, log-linear function of two exogenously determined random variables X_1 and X_2:

$$h(t) = e^{\alpha_0 + \alpha_1 X_1 + \alpha_2 X_2} . \tag{11}$$

Case B resembled Case A except for a time-dependent nuisance function $q(t) = \exp[\beta t]$:

$$h(t) = e^{\alpha_0 + \alpha_1 X_1 + \alpha_2 X_2} e^{\beta t} . \tag{12}$$

Conditional on the values of X_1 and X_2, data on the time to an event has an exponential distribution in Case A and a Gompertz distribution in Case B.

⟨8⟩   Monte Carlo Study of PL and ML Estimators   241

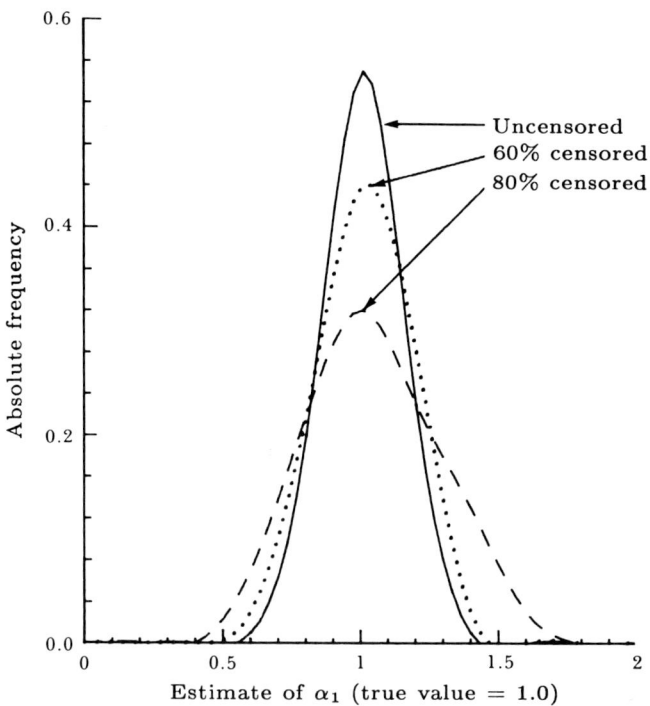

Figure 8.1. Consequences of censoring for the partial-likelihood (PL) estimator of the effect of an explanatory variable on a time-invariant rate ($I=100$; 100 samples for each level of censoring). Adapted with permission from Tuma (1982), p. 34.

We studied sample sizes of 50 and 100 and several levels of censoring. We concentrate on the results for the case in which X_1 and X_2 are uncorrelated random variables with a standard normal distribution,[1] and the true parameters are: $\alpha_0 = -4.0$, $\alpha_1 = 1.0$ and $\alpha_2 = -1.0$. For Case B, $\beta = 1.0$, we report only the results for estimates of α_1; results for α_2 are qualitatively very similar.

Figure 8.1 shows the consequences of censoring for PL estimates of α_1 in a sample of size 100 for Case A. As expected, censoring

---

[1] We also investigated the effect of the distribution of X_1 and X_2 and of a correlation between them.

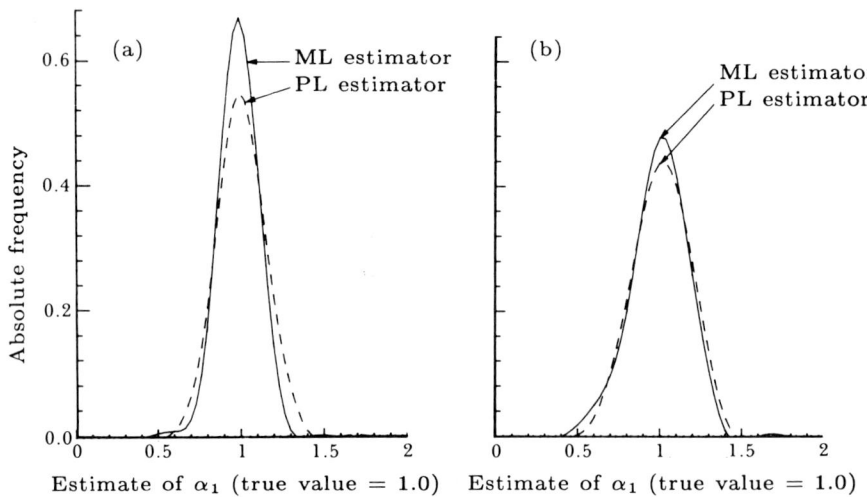

Figure 8.2. Partial-likelihood (PL) and maximum-likelihood (ML) estimators of the effect of an explanatory variable on a time-invariant rate using (a) uncensored and (b) 60% censored data ($I = 100$; 100 samples for each estimator and level of censoring). Adapted with permission from Tuma (1982), p. 35.

increases the variance of PL estimates. We found that PL estimates are usually (though not always) biased away from zero. Bias increases as either the sample size decreases or censoring increases. This pattern resembles that reported for ML estimates in Chapter 5. Overall, however, the quality of PL estimates is very high in samples of size 50 or 100, even when as many as 80% of the sample observations are censored.

Figure 8.2 compares the quality of ML and PL estimators for Case A when both estimators are based on a correctly specified model. Both ML and PL estimates have very similar distributions. However, as expected, the ML estimates are concentrated somewhat more about the true value than are the PL estimates, especially when the data are uncensored. But the mean squared errors of the ML and PL estimates differ very little, by less than .005 for all levels of censoring examined.

Figure 8.3 compares the quality of PL and ML estimators for

⟨8⟩ Monte Carlo Study of PL and ML Estimators   243

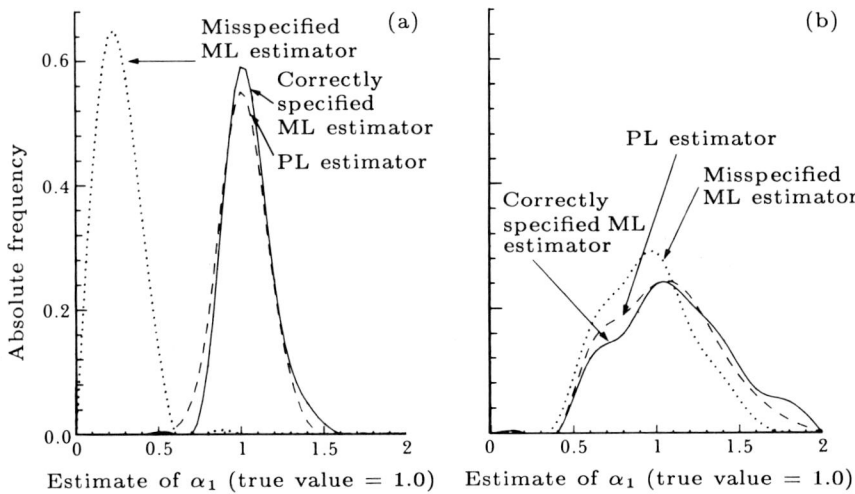

Figure 8.3. Partial-likelihood (PL) and maximum-likelihood (ML) estimators of the effect of an explanatory variable on an exponentially increasing rate using (a) uncensored and (b) 80% censored data ($I = 100$; 100 samples for each estimator and level of censoring.) Adapted with permission from Tuma (1982), p. 36.

Case B. Two sets of ML estimates were obtained, one for a correctly specified model, and one for a misspecified model, which assumes that the rate of an event is given by (11), whereas the rate is really given by (12).

When the data are not censored, the relative quality of the different estimates is similar to that expected. The misspecified ML estimates tend to be badly biased toward zero. However, the correctly specified ML estimates and the PL estimates have very similar distributions, with the PL estimates actually slightly less biased than the ML estimates for the correctly specified model.

The relative quality of the different estimates for censored data surprised us initially. When 80% of the sample observations are censored, the distribution of the misspecified ML estimates closely resembles that of the PL estimates and of the ML estimates for the correctly specified model. In fact, the bias and variance of the misspecified ML estimates are actually smaller than for either the PL or correctly specified ML estimates.

On reflection, we realized why censoring improves the quality of ML estimates for a misspecified model that assumes a time-invariant rate. Greater censoring means a shorter observation period, which in turn tends to mean that the true rate varies less over the observation period. Consequently, models with time-invariant rates approximate the data more closely when the observation period is shorter, that is, censoring is greater. Based on this reasoning, we suspect that our finding of less bias in estimates for the misspecified model when censoring is greater is not peculiar to the particular coefficients selected, or even to the particular form of $q(t)$, as long as $q(t)$ changes monotonically over time.[2] It also suggests that biases due to unknown time variation in rates can partially be avoided by design, for example, by observing a larger sample for a shorter period, as well as by an estimation approach.

8.4   PL Estimation of a Hazard Function Illustrated

Aalen estimates of the cumulative hazard functions in Figure 3.3 suggest that young black and white American men leave their first full-time job in the civilian nonagricultural labor force (CNALF) at a rate that depends on duration in the job. Black men show a pattern in which the hazard function for leaving the first job seems to decline (at a decelerating rate) as duration increases. The pattern for white men is more complicated; it resembles that for black men, except for a sharp drop in the survivor function (implying a sharp increase in the hazard function) at 3 months.

The plots in Figure 3.3 ignore variation in attributes of people and jobs commonly thought to affect job-exit rates, for example, individual resources like schooling and parental advantages, and job rewards like occupational prestige. These data contain too few cases to obtain Aalen estimates of cumulative hazard functions within categories of cross-classifications of these variables. Hence parametric and partially parametric approaches are very useful for investigating relationships between such variables and the job-exit rate.

---

[2]Censoring seems unlikely to improve the quality of estimates of a misspecified model when change in $q(t)$ is cyclical (e.g., sinusoidal).

⟨8⟩ PL Estimation of a Hazard Function Illustrated   245

To show this, we estimated three models of the rate of leaving a job:

Model A. $\quad h(t) = e^{\alpha' x},$

Model B. $\quad h(t) = e^{\alpha' x} e^{\beta t},$

Model C. $\quad h(t) = e^{\alpha' x} q(t),$

where t stands for duration in the job in years; the vector x contains measures of the person's schooling in years at the start of the job, the father's completed schooling in years, Siegel's (1970) occupational prestige score for the job, and a dummy variable equalling unity if the job began in June (i.e., was a summer job); α and β are parameters; and $q(t)$ is an unspecified nuisance function of t, the duration in the job. Based on previous analyses of job-exit rates (e.g., Sørensen and Tuma, 1981), the job-exit rate might be expected to increase with own schooling and fall with the job's prestige. The dummy variable for June may have a positive effect on the job-exit rate if summer jobs are temporary in nature. As a diffuse personal resource, father's education should have a positive but weak effect on the job-exit rate.

Based on the cumulative hazard plots in Figure 3.3, Model A's assumption about dependence of the hazard function on duration is unrealistic. We included Model A because it is a common and easily estimated baseline. Model B is fairly plausible for black men, but not white men, who have a marked (but transient) increase in the hazard function at 3 months. Clearly, Model C is the most flexible because it makes no assumption about the form of duration dependence.

We estimated Models A and B by ML and Model C by PL. Table 8.1 gives the estimated parameters. From a substantive viewpoint, the results are surprising. In particular, father's education increases the rate of leaving a job significantly for both young black and white men, whereas the status-attainment literature suggests that effects of family background on career mobility are mediated by schooling. Moreover, own education has no effect on the job-exit rate for white men, though its effect is significantly positive for black men. The status-attainment literature leads suggests that effects of own education will be stronger for white than black men. Further empirical analyses reported in Section 8.10 yield results closer to what one expects.

Table 8.1. Maximum-likelihood and partial-likelihood estimates of models of the rate of leaving the first job in the CNALF, by race [from Tuma (1982), p. 40]

	Model A (ML)	Model B (ML)	Model C (PL)
Blacks ($I = 477$)			
Intercept	-1.350	-1.021	not est'd
Father's education	0.043***	0.029**	0.029**
R's education	0.074***	0.068***	0.068***
SES of job	-0.028***	-0.024***	-0.025***
$1 \equiv$ Job began in June	0.252***	0.234**	0.247***
β	0	-0.098	not est'd
Whites ($I = 537$)			
Intercept	-0.403	0.072	not est'd
Father's education	0.075***	0.056***	0.054***
R's education	0.031	0.012	0.010
SES of job	-0.038***	-0.026***	-0.026***
$1 \equiv$ Job began in June	0.576***	0.445***	0.475***
β	0	-0.247	not est'd

*Significant at the .10 level.
**Significant at the .05 level.
***Significant at the .01 level.

From a methodological viewpoint, the degree of similarity in the estimated coefficients across the three models (and two methods of estimation) is surprising. The similarity of the coefficients for Models B and C is to be expected for black men: Figure 3.3 suggests the Gompertz model approximates their job-exit rate fairly well, and the Monte Carlo results in Section 8.3 indicate that ML and PL estimates of parameters in a Gompertz model are close when the model is specified correctly. The similarity of the estimated coefficients for Model A to those for Models B and C is the main surprise. Model A fits the survivor functions for both black and white men badly; see Figure 3.4. Moreover, our Monte Carlo study shows that ML estimates for Model A are badly biased when data are generated by a Gompertz model and are uncensored. (In these data fewer than 2% of the cases are censored.)

⟨8⟩ Handling of Ties

There are several possible explanations for the similarity of coefficients for the three models (and two methods of estimation). First, it may be due to chance. However, empirical analyses of other data have also yielded similar estimates of coefficients for these three models (and two methods), suggesting that the similarity in Table 8.1 is not mere happenstance.

Second, the duration dependence in the hazard function suggested by the Aalen plots in Figure 3.3 may have come about largely because of heterogeneity across cases. Allowing the job-exit rate to depend on these four variables may have reduced greatly the hazard function's dependence on duration. This can be only a partial explanation because the ML estimate of β is -0.109 for blacks and -0.303 for whites when all causal variables are excluded. These values are too close to those in Table 8.1 to accept this explanation.

Finally, the degree of duration dependence may be sufficiently slight that the ML estimate of the α's in Model A are not greatly biased. We did not vary the magnitude of β in our Monte Carlo experiments, so we have no evidence for or against this possible explanation. All in all, the similarity of the coefficients points to a need for further investigations of the sensitivity of the estimated coefficients of variables in proportional hazard models to the model, method of estimation, sample size, degree of censoring, and the nature and extent of variation over time in the hazard function.

8.5 Handling of Ties

The PL in (9) assumes that only one member of the sample has an event at any moment. However, the data sometimes indicate that several sample members have events at the same time. Sometimes events actually do bunch in time. Exits from school, for example, tend to be concentrated in June and occur less frequently at other times of the year. At other times ties occur because of the way the data on times of events are coded. For example, Horvath (1968) reported data on the duration of wars in terms of arbitrarily selected intervals of time (0–1 years, 1–2 years, and so forth). This procedure causes many wars to appear to be the same length although they undoubtedly had different lengths.

Several authors (e.g., Cox, 1972; Efron, 1977; Kalbfleisch and Prentice, 1978; Prentice and Kalbfleisch, 1979) have discussed ways to generalize (9) to account for ties (multiplicities) in the times of events. No clear consensus on a practical way of dealing with ties has yet emerged. The exact expression for the term of the PL corresponding to the $d(t_{(i)})$ events occurring at time $t_{(i)}$ involves taking permutations over members of the risk-set at $t_{(i)}$. If the number of ties is large, the PL becomes very complex and costly to maximize. Much of the discussion in the literature centers on feasible approximations to the exact PL. Prentice and Kalbfleisch (1979) claimed that when the fraction of tied events is small, the different approaches that have been suggested approximate the PL in (9) where the risk-set at $t_{(i)}$, $R(t_{(i)})$, includes all $d(t_{(i)})$ cases with an event at $t_{(i)}$.

8.6 Intermittently Measured Explanatory Variables

An especially valuable feature of PL estimation is that it allows an unspecified form of time variation in the measured causal variables. Moreover, the form of time variation may vary within the sample. To be useful, however, this feature requires that the analyst have the information required for the PL: measurements on the time-varying causal variables at the *time of events in the sample*. Such information is likely to be missing for metric variables unless they are measured continuously. Faced with missing data on the values of the explanatory variables at the time of the events in the sample, analysts are apt to make certain compromises.

One compromise replaces the value of the vector of explanatory variables for member v at $t_{(i)}$, the time of the ith event, $\mathbf{x}_v(t_{(i)})$—which appears in the PL but is not measured—with $\mathbf{x}_v(\tau_v)$, the values of the variables at τ_v, the time of the nearest measurement on v before $t_{(i)}$. That is, the necessary measurements, $\mathbf{x}_v(t_{(i)})$, might be approximated with the closest (in time) available values, $\mathbf{x}_v(\tau_v)$. This substitution assumes that the explanatory variables are approximately constant within intervals between measurements, or over the entire observation period if each variable is measured only once.

Other compromises may seem more realistic. We mentioned in Chapter 7 that the assumption of linear change often provides a reasonable and useful approximation to an unknown process of change in causal variables, as long as the interval between measurements is short relative to the rate of change in these causal variables. The hypothesis of linear change implies

⟨8⟩ **Intermittently Measured Explanatory Variables**

$$\mathbf{x}_v(t_i) = \mathbf{x}_v(\tau_v) + \boldsymbol{\kappa}_v[t_i - \tau_v]. \tag{13}$$

Exactly how the assumption in (13) is used depends on the observation scheme. The most common and least informative scheme is a single measurement on the explanatory variables, usually at the start of the observation period. In other schemes, the explanatory variables (especially metric ones) are measured intermittently. Explanatory variables are often measured at the dates of a panel survey, which rarely coincide with the times of events of sample members. On other occasions they are measured at the beginnings and ends of observation periods and at the times of any events *for the particular sample member* in the interim. (For example, in the Coleman–Rossi life-history data, earnings are measured at the time of entering and leaving each job.)

Given intermittent measurements on the explanatory variables, $\mathbf{x}_v(t_{(i)})$ can be predicted for each member v for the time of each event $t_{(i)}$ and inserted in the PL. There are several ways of predicting $\mathbf{x}_v(t_{(i)})$. First, given two measurements on each sample member v, say, τ_{1v} and τ_{2v}, $\tau_{1v} < \tau_{2v}$, one can interpolate linearly, predicting $\mathbf{x}_v(t_{(i)})$ as

$$\mathbf{x}_v(t_i) = \mathbf{x}_v(\tau_{1v}) + \frac{[t_{(i)} - \tau_{1v}][\mathbf{x}(\tau_{2v}) - \mathbf{x}(\tau_{1v})]}{\tau_{2v} - \tau_{1v}}. \tag{14}$$

Second, $\mathbf{x}_v(\tau_{2v})$ may be regressed on $\mathbf{x}_v(\tau_{1v})$ and perhaps other variables $\mathbf{z}_v(\tau_{1v})$:

$$\mathbf{x}_v(\tau_{2v}) = \boldsymbol{\Gamma}'\mathbf{x}_v(\tau_{1v}) + \boldsymbol{\beta}'\mathbf{z}_v(\tau_{1v}).$$

Then $\mathbf{x}_v(t_{(i)})$ may be predicted as in (14), using the value of $\mathbf{x}_v(\tau_{2v})$ predicted by the above regression rather than the actual observed value. The panel regression utilized in this second way of predicting $\mathbf{x}_v(t_{(i)})$ is not easy to implement unless the spacing of the x's is the same for all members of the sample, that is, $\tau_{2v} - \tau_{1v} = \tau_{2i} - \tau_{1i}$ for all i and v. However, it can be useful when some members of the sample have fewer than two measurements on the explanatory variables or when substantive theory suggests that the expected (rather than actual) value of a variable is the genuine causal force.

Ways of dealing with the missing information on explanatory variables are less satisfactory when they are measured only once.

Usually sample members vary in the rate of change in the explanatory variables, that is, in κ_i. With only a single measurement on each sample member, little can be done about such variation except to entertain the hypothesis that κ_i depends on other measured explanatory variables $z_i(\tau)$:

$$\kappa_i = \beta' z_i(\tau). \tag{15}$$

Suppose, for example, that the job-exit rate depends on a person's current wage rate, which is measured only at τ, the start of the job. One might hypothesize that wages grow approximately linearly over time within a job, and that the growth rate of a person's wage depends on other measured variables like schooling and race. Let $W(t)$ represent the wage rate at time t, S schooling, and R race (a dummy variable). Then one might postulate that

$$W_i(t) = W_i(\tau_i) + \left[\beta_1 S_i + \beta_2 R_i\right]\left[t - \tau_i\right].$$

Substituting the above into (6) and simplifying gives

$$\theta_i(t) = \exp\left[\alpha W_i(\tau_i) + \alpha(\beta_1 S_i + \beta_2 R_i)(t - \tau_i)\right].$$

More generally, substituting (15) into (6) yields expressions like

$$\theta_i(t) = \exp\left[\boldsymbol{\alpha}' \mathbf{x}_i(\tau_i) + \boldsymbol{\alpha}' \mathbf{z}_i(\tau_i)\boldsymbol{\beta}'(t - \tau_i)\right]. \tag{16}$$

Note that (16), unlike the previous expressions for $\theta(\cdot)$ considered in this chapter, specifies θ as an explicit function of time t, and not solely of the observed causal variables $\mathbf{x}(\tau)$ and $\mathbf{z}(\tau)$. The coefficient of time t can be identified (and is not absorbed into the nuisance function) because the time variation in (16) depends on the value of $\mathbf{z}(\tau)$ and therefore is not identical for all individuals in the sample. From another viewpoint, (16) merely illustrates a slightly different kind of time-varying explanatory variable, an interaction between time and characteristics of sample members.

8.7 Estimating the Nuisance and Survivor Functions

Maximizing $_p\mathcal{L}$ in (10) does not give any direct information about $q(t)$, the unknown function of time. It only gives estimates of the effects of observed variables on the rate of the event. Without

⟨8⟩ Estimating the Nuisance and Survivor Functions

an estimate of $q(t)$, a group's survivor function or any other observable feature of an event history cannot be predicted. Although it is enough for some research purposes to estimate the causal effects of variables, sometimes it is valuable to predict some observable quantity. The PL estimates can give, say, the percentage decrease in the school dropout rate for each 1000-dollar increase in parental income, but they do not tell what proportion of children remain in school beyond the twelfth grade for a given level of parental income.

Breslow (1974) has suggested a way of estimating $q(t)$ from the PL estimate of $\boldsymbol{\alpha}$ in (6). His method rests on the assumption that for all members of the population, $q(t)$ is a constant for all values of t between $t_{(i-1)}$ and $t_{(i)}$. This assumption is equivalent to the one discussed at length in Section 7.2, except that in Breslow's formulation time periods are defined by the events observed in the sample rather than exogenously. Given Breslow's assumption, the ML estimator of $q(t)$, conditional on the PL estimate, $\widehat{\boldsymbol{\alpha}}$, is:

$$\widehat{q}(t) = \frac{1}{[t_{(i)} - t_{(i-1)}] \sum_{v \in R(t_{(i)})}^{I} e^{\widehat{\boldsymbol{\alpha}}' \mathbf{x}_v}},$$

where $t_{(i-1)} \leq t < t_{(i)}$. A plot of $\widehat{q}(t)$ versus time t gives some notion of the kind of time variation in the rate that occurs in the sample, which may suggest reasonable parametric forms of time dependence for investigators who wish to derive other implications of the model. For example, if the hazard function is time invariant, a plot of $\widehat{q}(t)$ versus t should not vary with t within sampling variation.

Breslow also gave the corresponding (ML) estimator of the integrated nuisance function:

$$\widehat{Q}(t) \equiv \int_{t_0}^{t} \widehat{q}(s) \, ds = \sum_{t < t_{(i)}} 1 - \frac{1}{\sum_{v \in R(t_{(i)})} e^{\widehat{\boldsymbol{\alpha}}' \mathbf{x}_v}}.$$

The integrated nuisance function can be used in conjunction with the PL estimate of $\boldsymbol{\alpha}$ to predict the survivor function (or the log survivor function, as desired). By comparing a plot of the average of the PL prediction of $G(t)$ versus t with the plot of the Kaplan–Meier estimator of the survivor function [see equation (9) in Chapter 3] versus t, the fit of a model can be assessed visually. Serious discrepancies between the two plots (e.g., the first plot does not lie within the confidence interval of the second plot) suggest that important causal variables have been omitted or that the model has otherwise been misspecified, as we discussed in Chapter 4.

8.8 Sources of Variation in the Nuisance Function

What does t in the previous equations in this chapter represent? Does t represent the historical moment (calendar time) or the age of some member of the population?

As long as this question is phrased in terms of either one or the other, it cannot be answered outside a particular substantive context. Often we do not welcome having to choose between allowing for unspecified variation in rates with calendar time and allowing for unspecified variation in rates with age. For many phenomena, both sources of time variation seem important but difficult to parameterize. Consider the classic example of a nonrepeatable event: death. Certainly the rate of dying depends on a person's age. But equally well it varies with calendar time because of historical fluctuations in social and economic conditions. It would be desirable to allow death (and other transition) rates to vary with both age and historical time in an unspecified way.

Consider the following extension of the model in (5):

$$h_i(t) = q(t, A_i(t))\, \theta(\mathbf{x}_i(t)), \tag{17}$$

where t refers to calendar time, and $A_i(t)$ denotes the age of the ith member of the sample at time t. This model says that the hazard function for the ith member is an unspecified function of time t and i's age at this time, $q(t, A_i(t))$, and of some function $\theta(\cdot)$ (which must, of course, be specified) of other observed variables. We would like to construct a PL for the model in (17) in such a way that the unspecified function of calendar time and age does not enter.

Recall from the discussion in Sections 8.1 and 8.2 that the key to constructing such a PL is that the ratio of the rates for two members, i and v, depends only on $\theta(\cdot)$. For (17) this ratio is:

$$\frac{h_i(t)}{h_v(t)} = \frac{q(t, A_i(t))\, \theta(\mathbf{x}_i(t))}{q(t, A_v(t))\, \theta(\mathbf{x}_v(t))}.$$

⟨8⟩ **Sources of Variation in the Nuisance Function**

The nuisance functions for i and v cancel only if they are the same age at time t, that is, they have the same birthdate.

This observation suggests that a PL for (17) does not depend on the age- and time-dependent nuisance function if members of the risk-set at time t *not only* occupy the same state the moment before t, *but also* have the same birthdate. It is not necessary that everyone in the sample have the same birthdate. However, it must be possible to partition the sample so that in general the risk-set for an event at time t is nondegenerate, that is, contains more than one case. Few samples are large enough to yield many members with exactly the same birthdates. However, coarser groupings of sample members with similar birthdates are probably adequate except in cases of very irregular forms of age variation in transition rates.

If age is included in the nuisance function, it can no longer be included in $\mathbf{x}(t)$ because its coefficient cannot be identified. All members of a risk-set have the same value for this variable, causing it to cancel from the numerator and denominator of every term in $_p\mathcal{L}$.

The discussion above suggests that the nuisance function can depend on other variables, in addition to time and age, as long as one can identify suitable, nondegenerate risk-sets. In the extreme case, the sample could be partitioned into pairs matched on every variable but one, for example, an experimental treatment. Each risk-set would contain two members, and the observations would consist of which member of each pair had an event first. In fact, the estimation for such matched pairs would be identical to that for the familiar binary logit model with dummy variables denoting the treatments, assuming the specification of $\theta(\cdot)$ in (6) is retained.

The above discussion also points to one nuisance factor that cannot be allowed in constructing the PL: a random disturbance. Consider the following model:

$$h_i(t) = q(t)\epsilon_i(t)\theta(\mathbf{x}_i(t)), \tag{18}$$

where $\theta(\cdot)$ continues to be given by (6). The model in (18) is similar to the model with episode-specific disturbances discussed in Section 6.3. Each $\epsilon_i(t)$ can be regarded as summarizing assorted unobserved variables affecting i's hazard function. The unobserved variables may be measurement errors in the explanatory variables, time-varying transitory shocks, and so forth. The ratio of the rates for two members, i and v reduces to

$$\frac{h_i(t)}{h_v(t)} = \frac{\epsilon_i(t)\,\theta\bigl(\mathbf{x}_i(t)\bigr)}{\epsilon_v(t)\,\theta\bigl(\mathbf{x}_v(t)\bigr)}.$$

In general, the disturbances do not cancel. Furthermore, since they are unobserved, we do not have any information allowing identification of a risk-set of sample members who are identical except for $\theta(\cdot)$. We are not aware of any evidence on the consequences of ignoring episode-specific disturbances in models of proportional hazards estimated by PL.

8.9 Multiple Outcomes

Discussion on PL estimation to this point has concentrated on a model for a single, nonrepeatable event. It is important for event-history analysis to extend this approach to the case in which there are multiple kinds of outcomes ("competing risks"). Prentice et al. (1978) provided a useful survey of the issues involved in applying PL to multiple outcomes.

Holt (1978) outlined ways of generalizing the partially parametric approach to event-history analysis when there are multiple outcomes. Generalization turns out to be straightforward, as long as occurrences of the different outcomes are independent. A concrete example clarifies this crucial assumption. Consider the rate of leaving a job. One might want to distinguish between people quitting a job and being fired, assuming, for example, that the rate of leaving a job is the sum of two rates: the rate at which people quit and the rate at which they are fired. The assumption that these two rates are independent implies that if one of the two rates becomes zero (e.g., laws are passed forbidding employers from firing employees), the other rate is unaltered. In general, the validity of the assumption that rates are independent is dubious. Unfortunately, dependence among the rates cannot be identified (Tsiatis, 1975). Just as in the identification of effects of age, period, and cohort, substantive theory must guide any formulation of models incorporating dependencies among rates of different outcomes. Lacking such a theory, one can only proceed in practice as though occurrences of different outcomes are independent. However, caution must be used in extrapolating to situations with a different structure of outcomes.

⟨8⟩ **Multiple Outcomes**

Discussion in Section 8.1 began with a type of model of potentially wide applicability. In it, each transition rate $r_{jk}(t)$ is a product of two terms, as expressed formally in (1): a nuisance function $q_{jk}(t)$, and a term that depends on the explanatory variables, $\theta_{jk}(\mathbf{x}(t))$. We follow Holt (1978) in constructing the PL for this model.

As in the case of a single event, begin by ordering sample data by the observed time of events. In addition, tag the time of each event by the state left, j, and the state entered, k, giving

$$t_{jk(1)}, t_{jk(2)}, \ldots, t_{jk(I^*)}.$$

To be accurate, I^* should be subscripted by j and k; we omit this to avoid overburdening an already complicated notation. But notice that I_{jk} does not equal $I_{j'k'}$ in general; that is, different transitions generally occur with different frequencies in the sample. Similarly, note that each transition occurring in the sample has a "first" event, a "second" event, and so forth.

Once the data are ordered by the observed times of the transitions, it is necessary only to construct terms resembling the one in (8). The product of these terms is the PL. The only tricky point in constructing the PL is to identify the correct risk-set for each t_{jki}, $R(t_{jki})$. But this risk-set is just all sample members who occupy state j a moment before t_{jki}. Then the PL is (see Holt, 1978)

$$_p\mathcal{L} = \prod_{j=1}^{\Psi} \prod_{k=1}^{\Psi} \prod_{i=1}^{\Psi} \frac{\theta_{jk}(\mathbf{x}_i(t_{jk(i)}))}{\sum_{v \in R(t_{jk(i)})} \theta_{jk}(\mathbf{x}_v(t_{jk(i)}))}.$$

Under certain circumstances the nuisance function $q_{jk}(t)$ is the same for every outcome for a given origin, that is, $q_{jk}(t) = q_j(t)$ for all k. It is then possible to write a PL that uses the data more efficiently than (19). We do not give the appropriate PL for this case, which can be found in Holt (1978), because the assumption that $q_{jk}(t) = q_j(t)$ for all k seems unrealistic in most situations likely to be studied by social scientists. The assumption would mean, for example, that the unspecified time dependence in the rate of a marital dissolution is the same as the unspecified time dependence in the rate of a spouse dying.

8.10 PL Estimation of Transition Rates Illustrated

Section 8.4 reported results for PL estimates of effects of selected individual resources and job rewards on black and white men's rate of leaving the first full-time job in the CNALF. In that section, various outcomes of a job exit are not distinguished. However, the Aalen estimates of the cumulative transition rates plotted in Figures 3.5 and 3.6 suggest distinguishing two types of job exits: those followed by a return to school, and exits for all other (mainly work-related) reasons. The plots in Figures 3.5 and 3.6 indicate quite different patterns of duration dependence in the rates of these two transitions. In addition, personal resources and job rewards seem likely to affect these two rates differently. The rate of returning to school seems likely to rise with father's schooling (an aspect of educational inheritance), fall with a person's own schooling (a ceiling effect), fall with a job's prestige (as opportunity costs of schooling rise), and rise for a summer job (one begun in June). On the other hand, the rate of job exits for all other (work-related) reasons seem likely to rise with own schooling (opportunities are greater), fall with the job's prestige (better jobs are rarer), and be relatively unaffected by the month the job began and by father's education (since a voluminous literature indicates parental advantages are transmitted primarily via schooling in the United States).

To test these hypotheses and to illustrate the application of PL estimation to models of transition rates, we estimated models like A, B, and C in Section 8.4, except that the left-hand side variable was a transition rate rather than a hazard function. We again estimated Models A and B by ML and Model C by PL. The results of the analyses appear in Tables 8.2 and 8.3.

From a substantive viewpoint, results are much more plausible than those obtained for the hazard function. The rate of returning to school (see Table 8.2) is much higher for jobs begun in June. Moreover, for both black and white men, the rate of returning to school rises significantly with father's schooling and falls with the job's occupational prestige. Own schooling depresses the rate of returning to school for white men, but, surprisingly, not for black men. Such a difference could arise if the effect of own schooling was nonlinear and black men were further from the educational ceiling on average. But the contrary is true: own schooling is about 0.5 year higher for black than white men on average and its variance

Table 8.2. Maximum-likelihood and partial-likelihood estimates of models of the rate of leaving the first job in the CNALF to return to school, by race [from Tuma (1982), p. 40]

	Model A (ML)	Model B (ML)	Model C (PL)
Blacks ($I = 477$)			
Intercept	−3.747	−1.938	not est'd
Father's education	0.123***	0.079*	0.079*
R's education	0.060	0.018	0.016
SES of job	−0.094***	−0.060***	−0.060***
1 ≡ Job began in June	2.091***	1.940***	1.960***
β	0	−2.109	not est'd
Whites ($I = 537$)			
Intercept	−1.945	−0.438	not est'd
Father's education	0.172***	0.106***	0.102***
R's education	−0.093**	−0.107***	−0.108***
SES of job	−0.041***	−0.016**	−0.018**
1 ≡ Job began in June	1.952***	1.608***	1.659***
β	0	−1.938	not est'd

*Significant at the .10 level.
**Significant at the .05 level.
***Significant at the .01 level.

is about the same. Other nonlinearities might explain this finding; they could be explored by representing own schooling by a series of dummy variables.

The rate of leaving the first job in the CNALF for reasons other than to return to school (see Table 8.3) also agrees well with what one would expect on the basis of substantive theory and prior empirical research (e.g., see Tuma, 1976; Sørensen and Tuma, 1981). For example, previous literature suggests that the rate of leaving a job rises with personal resources like educational level and falls with a job's rewards such as its prestige level. The estimates for all three models (see Table 8.3) agree with these hypotheses and are statistically significant. Sometimes the father's educational level is also regarded as a personal resource that helps a person get a new job

Table 8.3. Maximum-likelihood and partial-likelihood estimates of models of the rate of leaving the first job in the CNALF for any reason other than to return to school, by race [from Tuma (1982), p. 40]

	Model A (ML)	Model B (ML)	Model C (PL)
Blacks ($I = 477$)			
Intercept	−1.465	−1.197	not est'd
Father's education	0.033**	0.022	0.021
R's education	0.075***	0.070***	0.074***
SES of job	−0.023***	−0.019***	−0.021***
1 ≡ Job began in June	0.050	0.037	0.056
β	0	−0.072	not est'd
Whites ($I = 537$)			
Intercept	−0.862	−0.524	not est'd
Father's education	0.019	0.006	0.018
R's education	0.096***	0.082***	0.081***
SES of job	−0.034***	−0.026***	−0.030***
1 ≡ Job began in June	−0.006	−0.096	−0.018
β	0	−0.139	not est'd

*Significant at the .10 level.
**Significant at the .05 level.
***Significant at the .01 level.

(see Granovetter, 1974). In contrast, the status attainment literature (which, of course, does not examine the process of changing jobs directly) leads one to expect almost all effects of father's education to be mediated by a person's own educational level. For both black and white men the estimated effect of father's educational level in Table 8.3 is positive, suggesting that it is a personal resource, but it is statistically significant only for Model A for black men. Its effect on this rate is clearly much less than the effects of the person's own educational level, as one would expect. Finally, notice that entering the job in June has no appreciable effect on this rate for either black or white men, which is plausible.

On the methodological side, these results again show a striking similarity in the three sets of estimates. Virtually every estimated coefficient in one set is within one standard error of the corresponding coefficients in the other two sets. The only exceptions are the constant terms, which are naturally affected considerably by the assumption about time dependence.

8.11 Repeatable Events

So far we have focused on nonrepeatable events, or equivalently, on the first event of a sequence of events. The case of repeated events presents a major challenge to event-history analysis because, as we noted in the previous chapter, it is rarely reasonable to assume that the rate of successive events for the same individual are independent, even after conditioning on observed causal variables.

Consider, for example, job-exit rates. A typical individual holds a series of jobs in his or her career. Though one may measure a wide range of variables affecting job-exit rates, not all of them can be measured. Some unmeasured variables describe individual characteristics that are fairly stable over time, for example, native intelligence, personal charm, and physical stamina. Let m_i stand for such variables. Other unmeasured variables may be stable attributes of jobs j and k, for example, firm-specific opportunities for occupants of a job in category j to be promoted to a job in category k. Let m_j and m_k stand for stable unmeasured attributes of elements in states j and k, respectively.[3] Still other unmeasured variables may be transitory disturbances specific to a particular episode. We denote these by $\epsilon_{ijkn}(t)$, where the subscript n indexes the number of i's particular visit to state j.

Job shift rates may also vary in unspecified ways with several measures of time: calendar time, t; i's age at time t, $A_i(t)$; i's experience at time t, $E_i(t)$, defined as the total time that i has spent in state j as of time t; and the length of time that i has spent in the current episode, $D_i(t)$. At least in principle, data on repeated events permit the separate effects of calendar time, age, experience, and duration to be identified.

A potentially interesting general model is

$$r_{ijkn}(t) = q_{ijkn}(t)\theta_{jkn}\left(\mathbf{x}_i(t)\right) m_i^{\beta_n} m_j^{\gamma_n} m_k^{\delta_n} \epsilon_{ijkn}(t), \qquad (20)$$

[3] This notation differs somewhat from earlier usage, where j and k denote states, not elements in states. A separate notation for the elements in a state seems superfluous since this is the only place we refer to them.

where $\epsilon_{ijkn}(t)$ denotes random disturbances associated with i's nth event (a transition from j to k), which may result from measurement error in the x's at time t, transitory shocks, and so forth;

$$q_{ijkn}(t) = q_{jkn}\left(t,\, A_i(t),\, E_i(t),\, D_i(t)\right); \qquad (21)$$

and, for example,

$$\theta_{jkn}\left(\mathbf{x}_i(t)\right) = e^{\boldsymbol{\alpha}'_{jkn}\mathbf{x}_i(t)}. \qquad (22)$$

We have intentionally made the expressions in (20) to (22) very general so that we can show which components of the model are barriers to PL estimation when a wide range of hypotheses are being entertained.[4]

Recall that the crucial assumption allowing construction of a PL is that the rates of any two members of some known risk-set are proportional functions of observed variables. For the model specified by (20), the ratio of the rates of any two individuals, i and v, for a transition to k at time t during the nth visit to j is

$$\frac{r_{ijkn}(t)}{r_{vjkn}(t)} = \frac{q_{ijkn}(t)\,\theta_{jkn}\left(\mathbf{x}_i(t)\right) m_i^{\beta_n} m_j^{\gamma_n} m_k^{\delta_n} \epsilon_{ijkn}(t)}{q_{vjkn}(t)\,\theta_{jkn}\left(\mathbf{x}_v(t)\right) m_v^{\beta_n} m_j^{\gamma_n} m_k^{\delta_n} \epsilon_{vjkn}(t)}. \qquad (23)$$

To form a PL in which risk-sets are nondegenerate, that is, contain at least two cases, a way must be found to choose a risk-set so that all terms in (23) cancel except $\theta_{jkn}\left(\mathbf{x}_i(t)\right)$ and $\theta_{jkn}\left(\mathbf{x}_v(t)\right)$.

As indicated in Section 8.8, an episode-specific disturbance completely blocks formation of the PL. A nondegenerate risk-set cannot be identified because $\epsilon_{ijkn}(t)$ is, by definition, both unknown and specific to the episode. So either $\epsilon_{ijkn}(t)$ must be dropped from (20) or parametric methods of estimation must be used. To show

---

[4]Both (21) and (22) could be still more complicated without affecting the discussion that follows. For instance, (21) could also include a term to represent the length of time on an experiment, and (22) could also include an additional term allowing for an interaction between the effects of the observed variables $\mathbf{x}_i(t)$ and time t, as outlined in Section 8.7. Since these added complexities would not alter the discussion that follows in any qualitative way, we ignore them.

⟨8⟩ Repeatable Events

what can be estimated by the PL approach, we drop $\epsilon_{ijkn}(t)$, that is, assume it is always unity.

Dropping only $\epsilon_{ijkn}(t)$ from (20) is not enough. To form a PL with nondegenerate risk-sets, still other restrictive assumptions must be imposed. We consider two sets of restrictions, each of which lets one construct a PL that can serve as the basis for estimating coefficients of the observed variables $x_i(t)$.

One set of identifying restrictions postulates that transition rates are not affected by any unmeasured variables, either episode-specific disturbances or stable omitted variables, including both those specific to an individual i and those specific to j and k. That is,

$$\epsilon_{ijkn}(t) = m_i = m_j = m_k = 1,$$

for all i, j, k, n, and t. Now consider the risk-set in which those entering state j for their nth visit at time t_{n-1} have identical values of age and experience at that time (and of any other sources of variation in the nuisance function). Then the nuisance function $q_{ijkn}(t) = q_{vjkn}(t)$ if both i and v are members of the same risk-set, leaving the desired result:

$$\frac{r_{ijkn}(t)}{r_{vjkn}(t)} = \frac{\theta_{jkn}(x_i(t))}{\theta_{jkn}(x_v(t))}.$$

Thus, if no unobserved variables affect transition rates, that is,

$$r_{ijkn}(t) = q_{ijkn}(t)\,\theta_{jkn}(x_i(t)), \qquad (24)$$

a PL like that in (19) can be formed, except that members of a risk-set must have additional characteristics in common. All must enter state j for the nth time at the same time t_{n-1} and have the same birthdate and experience at this time.

Equation (24) is more general than (1) in several ways. First, it allows the coefficients of the observed variables to depend on the number of visits to a state, a form of experience dependence sometimes called "occurrence dependence" (Heckman and Borjas, 1980). Second, it lets the nuisance function depend on several measures of time: calendar time, age, experience, and duration. Of course, a model as general as (24) has a price. Obviously a very large sample is needed to estimate the parameter vector α_{jkn} because of the difficulty in finding sufficient sample members with the same birthdate and experience who enter the same state at the same time. In practice, data availability may force additional restrictive assumptions (e.g., the number of the visit has no effect on the rate; the nuisance function does not depend on experience, and so forth) or approximations (e.g., the nuisance function is the same for cases within 5-year birth intervals). But such additional restrictions are not *intrinsically* necessary.

A second set of identifying restrictions was first proposed by Chamberlain (1979), who was particularly concerned with correcting for stable unobserved attributes of i, m_i. To find a risk-set in which m_i is known to be the same for all members, the risk-set may contain observations only on i. To pool observations on i into a risk-set so that unobservables cancel when computing the ratio of pairs of rates, the nuisance function may depend solely on duration, and not on historical time, age, past experience, or the number of visits to state j. In principle, transition rates can depend on stable unmeasured characteristics of j and k, m_j and m_k. However, this approach requires data on the same individual i in two or more sojourns in states j and k. For example, the same person would have to be observed holding the same job on two different occasions or marrying the same spouse twice. Such data are hard to find. So in practice m_j and m_k are apt to be excluded, that is, assumed to be unity. Ignoring such practical problems, one can write a very general model that can be estimated by PL in principle and that does include stable effects of persons and of elements in states j and k as

$$r_{ijk}(u) = q_{jk}(u)\,\theta\big(\mathbf{x}_i(u)\big)\,m_i\,m_j\,m_k, \tag{25}$$

$$\theta_{kl}\big(\mathbf{x}_i(u)\big) = e^{\boldsymbol{\alpha}'_{jk}\mathbf{x}_i(u)}, \tag{26}$$

where u is the duration in state j. Notice that the coefficients of the stable unmeasured variables included in (25) must be the same for all episodes (i.e., they cannot depend on the number of visits to state j).

Although the model in (25) can be estimated by PL, the advantages of this model are gained at a considerable price. First, the effects of time-invariant attributes of individual i (e.g., the effects of a person's sex and race or of a country's region and cultural heritage) cannot be estimated because they are confounded with m_i. Second, as mentioned above, PL estimation of (25) requires the assumption that the nuisance function does not depend on calendar time, age, experience, or the number of visits to the state. In most substantive problems concerning repeatable events, ignoring the effects of stable unmeasured attributes of individual sample members is apt to bias estimates of the coefficients of other variables. Nevertheless, it seems equally important to control variation in rates with calendar time, age, experience, and the number of visits to a state. Consequently, the solution to this problem provided by the model in (25) is not entirely satisfactory.

Third, PL estimation of (25) requires data on at least two occurrences of a given transition for each sample member used in the analysis. As Chamberlain (1979) noted, analysis of subsamples that do not have the same number of events introduces systematic biases into parameter estimates. Due to censoring, the requirement of two (or more) events for each sample member means that (25) cannot be estimated (without bias) for many data sets. For example, in Hannan, Tuma, and Groeneveld's (1978) analysis of the effects of of negative income tax plans on the marital dissolution rate, fewer than 2% of the women studied had two or more martial dissolutions within the 3-year observation period. Similarly, in the analysis of political instability described in Chapter 10, 27 of the 90 countries studied had the same political form for the entire 25-year observation period, and another 27 had only one change. None of these 54 cases could be used in PL estimation if one insisted on estimating a model that included stable unmeasured attributes of a country.

8.12 Conclusions

This chapter has discussed and illustrated a partially parametric approach to event-history analysis: Cox's (1972, 1975) partial-likelihood (PL) method of estimation of proportional rate models with an unspecified nuisance function. Such a model has two parts, one specified parametrically and one unspecified. If the unspecified part affects every member of some identifiable group in the same way, it can be eliminated from a component of the likelihood function called the PL. Parameters that maximize the PL have been shown to have excellent statistical properties, assuming that the postulated proportional rate model is valid. Although the unspecified nuisance function in a model is typically regarded as being some function of time, other observed variables can be treated as nuisances if an investigator wants to control (rather than estimate) their effects. The PL approach calls for some unusual data on causal variables—measurements at the times of events in the sample (rather than at some exogenously specified intervals). We discuss ways of dealing with this.

Partial likelihood also has some inherent limitations that investigators should recognize. Disturbances of the classical sort, that is, random errors that are independent across cases and across repeated observations on the same case, cannot be assumed. Observations on repeated events for the same case offer considerable analytic possibilities that have barely been tapped in empirical analyses. PL seems unable to take full advantage of these. The unspecified nuisance function can be allowed to depend on a wide range of observed variables—historical time, age, experience, length of time in some state, and other time-varying causal variables. Or one can estimate models with case-specific unobserved variables if one assumes the nuisance function does not depend on historical time, age, or other time-varying causal variables. Unfortunately, one cannot allow both.

9

Systems of Qualitative Variables

In earlier chapters of Part II we have concentrated on change in a single qualitative (i.e., discrete) variable, for example, a person's marital status or the type of political regime in a nation. In this chapter we discuss the problem of analyzing change in a system of coupled qualitative variables, that is, in a system of dynamically interdependent discrete variables. Dynamic interdependence means that the level of each variable in the system affects (either directly or indirectly) the likelihood of a change in the level of every other variable in the system. For example, the system might consist of two attributes of individuals, such as their marital and employment statuses. The empirical literature suggests that change in a person's employment status depends on his or her marital status and that change in marital status also depends on the person's employment status. If these hypotheses are correct, then marital status and employment status form a system of coupled variables.

Section 9.1 shows how models for a single qualitative variable can be readily extended to the case of systems of such variables. Section 9.2 illustrates such an extension to the problem of analyzing changes in employment status and marital status within the Seattle and Denver Income Maintenance Experiments (SIME/DIME).

Despite the ease of extending the scalar models and methods discussed in Chapters 3–8 to the case of multiple outcomes, models for change in systems of coupled qualitative variables are rarely discussed in sociology. This oversight may result partly from the lack of data suitable for estimating such models. But it may also result partly from inadequate information on the consequences of ignoring dynamic interdependencies among qualitative variables. Consequently, Section 9.3 focuses on two main questions: (1) When can ignoring dynamic interdependencies lead to comparatively small errors in inference? (2) Which research designs minimize errors and which ones accentuate them? We present results for several illustrative cases, each involving a bivariate system in which change in one variable is ignored.

9.1 Modeling Strategies

We consider modeling change in a system of J qualitative variables $Y_1(t), Y_2(t), \ldots, Y_J(t)$ as functions of a vector of exogenous variables $\mathbf{x}$. As long as change in the system of J variables depends only on the levels of the J variables and on the levels of the exogenous variables $\mathbf{x}$, it turns out to be simple to model change in this system. In fact, with a suitable transformation of the variables, it is identical to modeling change in a single variable.

Suppose that each variable $Y_j(t)$ can take on distinct values denoted by the positive integers ranging from 1 to Ψ_j, where Ψ_j is the size of the state space of the jth variable. We assume that Ψ_j is finite for all J variables. The value or state of the system of variables can be described by the ordered J-tuple giving the value of each of the J variables: $(y_1(t), y_2(t), \ldots, y_J(t))$. Elementary principles of combinatorics imply that the number of distinct values for this J-tuple is just

$$\Psi = \prod_{j=1}^{J} \Psi_j.$$

Because each Ψ_j is finite, Ψ must be finite too.

Knowing Ψ, we can define a new random variable $Y(t)$ that records the values of the J variables at a particular time t. We define $Y(t)$ by associating each distinct value of the ordered J-tuple given above with a particular integer value of $Y(t)$, where these integers range from 1 to Ψ. There is a large number of ways of making these associations. If a particular integer value of Y is associated consistently with a particular combination of the levels of the J variables, it is not important how the association is made, as long as neither the values of the J variables nor the values of $Y(t)$ are ordered. The

⟨9⟩ Modeling Strategies

important point is that we have a problem of modeling change in a *single* qualitative variable once we define $Y(t)$ to represent the values of the system of variables. Therefore, our earlier discussions of models for one variable apply to the problem of describing change in a system. In principle no new issues arise.

We consider a particular example that shows how a single qualitative variable can represent a system of qualitative variables. To lay the base for issues developed later, we assume that the system consists of two dichotomous variables $Y_1(t)$ and $Y_2(t)$, where $Y_1(t)$ is marital status and takes the values $1 \equiv$ not married and $2 \equiv$ married, and $Y_2(t)$ is employment status and takes the values $1 \equiv$ not employed and $2 \equiv$ employed. Since each variable has two possible values, there are $2 \cdot 2 = 4$ different states in the bivariate system. These are $(1,1) \equiv$ (not married and not employed), $(1,2) \equiv$ (not married and employed), $(2,1) \equiv$ (married and not employed), and $(2,2) \equiv$ (married and employed). The system consisting of $Y_1(t)$ and $Y_2(t)$ can be described by a new random variable $Y(t)$ that has the possible integer values ranging from 1 to 4. In particular, we associate 1 with $(1,1)$, 2 with $(1,2)$, 3 with $(2,1)$ and 4 with $(2,2)$.

One rule for defining $Y(t)$ given a system of J dichotomous variables, each with values 1 and 2, is

$$Y(t) = -2 + \sum_{j=1}^{2^J} 2^{J-j} Y_j(t).$$

In general, if Y is formed from a system of J dichotomous variables, then $\Psi = 2^J$.

Change in the system of J qualitative variables can be described by describing change in $Y(t)$. As we mentioned in earlier chapters (see especially Chapter 4), the fundamental parameters describing the change process are the $\Psi(\Psi - 1)$ instantaneous rates of transition, or, equivalently, the Ψ hazard functions and the $\Psi(\Psi-2)$ unique conditional transition probabilities.

The need to estimate $\Psi(\Psi - 1)$ rates suggests that analysis of change in a system of qualitative variables may present practical problems, even though no new analytical issues arise. Even when the number of variables in the system is small, $\Psi(\Psi - 1)$ is quite large. Therefore, event-history data must contain information on a great many events if the most general model of change in a system of qualitative variables is to be estimated.

For many phenomena it is reasonable to assume that only one of the J variables in the system can change in any sufficiently small moment of time. This simplifying assumption, which forms the basis of Coleman's (1964a) influential strategy for estimating systems from panel data (see also Sørensen and Hallinan, 1976; Holland and Leinhardt, 1977), has the advantage of reducing the number of unique transition rates that must be estimated from $2^J (2^J - 1)$ to $2^J J$, assuming all J variables are dichotomous. The decrease is drastic even when J is small. It means that there are 8 rather than 12 rates to be estimated for two dichotomous variables, 24 rather than 56 for three variables, 64 rather than 240 for four variables. We make this simplifying assumption throughout this chapter.

In addition we assume that the coupling occurs between *states* rather than between rates of change directly, which we term *state dependence*. For example, we consider the assumption that a person's rate of entering or leaving employment depends on his or her marital status. But, we assume that it does not depend on the person's *rate* of marital formation or marital dissolution. As far as we know, the problem of analyzing direct dependence between rates, what we call *rate dependence*, has not been solved. Therefore, we restrict attention to the simpler case of state dependence.

9.2 An Example: Marital and Employment Statuses

Under the assumptions stated in the previous section, it is straightfoward to use event-history data on movements among states of several qualitative variables to estimate causal effects on transition rates. In this section we illustrate this type of multivariate analysis.

In Chapter 6 we showed that the negative income tax (NIT) treatments used in SIME/DIME significantly increased rates of marital dissolution of black and white couples. These treatments also affect rates of entering and leaving employment for both husbands and wives (see Tuma and Robins, 1980; Tuma 1980b; Tuma, Robins, and Smith-Donals, 1980). These analyses of changes in employment status, like the analyses of marital stability reported in previous chapters, assume that changes in marital status and changes in employment status occur independently. But a large nonexperimental literature shows that marital status affects employment and that

⟨9⟩ An Example: Marital and Employment Statuses

employment statuses of men and women affect marital formation and dissolution. It is conceivable that the estimated effects of NIT treatments on dissolution rates reported in Chapter 6 reflect only the indirect effect of experimentally induced changes in employment statuses. In other words, the NIT treatments may not directly influence the dissolution rate but just lead to changes in the employment statuses of husbands and wives, which in turn alter the rate of marital dissolution. The only way to study the linkage between marital stability and changes in employment status is to analyze a system in which these variables are allowed to be dynamically interdependent.

A system in which employment status and marital status are coupled could be formulated in several ways. For example, one could focus on women and define the states as (married, employed), (married, not employed), (single, employed), and (single, not employed). Use of such a state space allows analysis of moves by a woman over the life cycle, showing how her characteristics affect transition rates. Alternatively, one could focus on the coupling between the employment statuses of husbands and wives, using the state space $1 \equiv$ (HU, WU), $2 \equiv$ (HU, WE), $3 \equiv$ (HE, WU), and $4 \equiv$ (HE, WE), where H and W denote the husband and wife, respectively, and E and U denote employed and unemployed (not employed), respectively. The unit of analysis for this second state space is the couple rather than the individual man or woman. Consequently, marital dissolution should be included as a fifth state to allow the possibility of a couple's marriage ending. Tuma (1980b) and Tuma and Smith-Donals (1980a,b) used such a state space to study the effects of NIT treatments on husbands' and wives' rates of changing employment status. We also use the latter state space in the example discussed below; however, we focus on transitions from each of the four states defined in terms of the husband's and wife's employment statuses to the fifth state, "marriage dissolved." In terms of Figure 9.1, we focus on the four transition rates that go from the boxes on the corners to the box in the center, rather than the eight transition rates involving only changes in employment statuses.

The SIME/DIME data provide information on the dates of all changes in employment status and marital status. These data let us define spells in each of the four possible combinations of employment statuses for every couple; they also tell us when a marriage dissolves. Thus, when we use the state space depicted in Figure 9.1,

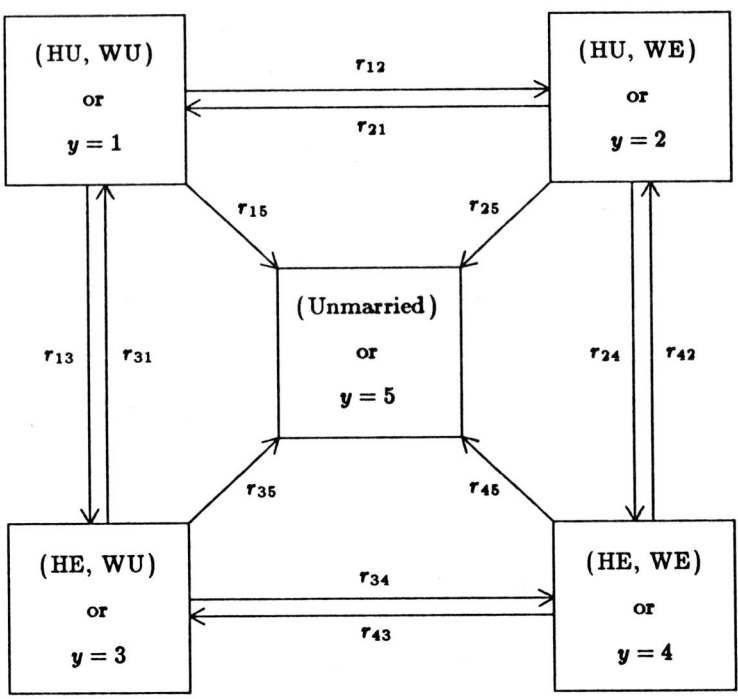

Figure 9.1. A diagram of the state space for the system consisting of employment and marital statuses.

the spells of marriage used to estimate impacts of NIT treatments in Section 6.2 are broken down more finely, producing nearly four spells per marriage on the average. We assume that unobservable heterogeneity does not persist across these new spells for the same couple and that the rates depicted in Figure 9.1 do not depend on previous history. These assumptions let us analyze the pooled spells as independent observations, conditional on the covariates included in a model of the transition rates.

We are especially interested in learning how estimates of NIT effects on the marital dissolution rate using this new state space compare with those that ignore changing employment statuses. To investigate this issue, we estimate a set of hierarchical models. The most general model (called Model I below) is

⟨9⟩ An Example: Marital and Employment Statuses

$$\log r_{j5n} = \sum_{j=1}^{4} z_{jn} \left(\alpha_{j50} + \sum_{m=1}^{M} \alpha_{j5m} x_m \right), \tag{1}$$

where j ranges from 1 to 4 and denotes one of the possible combinations of husband's and wife's employment statuses (see Figure 9.1), n denotes the number of spells (also defined by the spouses' employment statuses), r_{j5n} is the marital dissolution rate for state j and spell n, $\mathbf{x}$ a vector of M causal variables including both experimental treatments and preexperimental characteristics of the couple, and z_j a dummy variable indicating the husband's and wife's employment statuses in spell n. We let x_1, the first variable in the vector $\mathbf{x}$, denote a dummy variable indicating the NIT treatment; the coefficient of this variable, called the "NIT effect" below, interests us most. The model in (1) allows the current employment statuses of a husband and wife to have additive effects on the dissolution rate, effects that interact with each other, and effects that interact with all other covariates.

We also estimated several constrained versions of Model I. Model II lets the husband's and wife's employment statuses have additive effects and interact with the effect of the NIT treatment:

$$\alpha_{45m} = \alpha_{25m} + \alpha_{35m}, \tag{2a}$$

for $m = 0$ and 1; however, it constrains all other covariates to have the same effect for all four values of j:

$$\alpha_{j5m} = \alpha_{k5m}, \tag{2b}$$

for $j \neq k$ and $m = 2, \ldots, M$. Expression (2a) is a formal way of stating that the husband's and wife's employment statuses do not interact with each other; it states that the effect of being in state 4 in Figure 9.1 is the sum of the effects of being in states 2 and 3.

Model III also lets the husband's and wife's employment statuses have additive effects:

$$\alpha_{450} = \alpha_{250} + \alpha_{350}, \tag{3a}$$

but constrains all covariates (including the NIT treatment) to have the same effect for all four combinations of the husband's and wife's employment statuses:

$$\alpha_{j5m} = \alpha_{k5m}, \tag{3b}$$

for $j \neq k$ and $m = 1, \ldots, M$. Like Models II and III, Model IV lets the husband's and wife's employment statuses have additive effects:

$$\alpha_{450} = \alpha_{250} + \alpha_{350}. \tag{4a}$$

In addition, it lets the wife's employment status—but not the husband's—interact with the NIT treatment:

$$\alpha_{151} = \alpha_{351};$$
$$\alpha_{251} = \alpha_{451}. \tag{4b}$$

It constrains all other covariates to have the same effect for all four combinations of the husband's and wife's employment statuses:

$$\alpha_{j5m} = \alpha_{k5m}, \tag{4c}$$

for $j \neq k$ and $m = 2, \ldots, M$.

The last model, Model V, uses information only on the employment statuses occupied at the beginning of the experiment. That is, for all j and n, z_{jn} pertains to the husband's and wife's employment statuses when SIME/DIME began instead of their current employment statuses. For black couples Model V is like Model IV with z_{jn} redefined; for white couples Model V is like Model III with z_{jn} redefined. Since this model, like those discussed in Section 6.2, uses only preexperimental information to estimate experimental effects, it is an appropriate model for estimating the *total* effects of treatments, which may reflect both direct and indirect effects of treatments on dissolution rates.

9.2.1 Results

We began by estimating Model I. This model contains roughly four times as many parameters as the other models. Moreover, the number of marital dissolutions occurring within any combination of employment statuses is rather small. Consequently, estimated standand errors for Model I tend to be large, making it difficult to detect substantively important effects. For this reason, we do not report point estimates of parameters for this model; they can be found in Tuma, Hannan, and Groeneveld (1980). Moreover, a likelihood ratio test of Model II versus Model I is not significant at the .10 level

⟨9⟩ An Example: Marital and Employment Statuses

Table 9.1. Maximum-likelihood estimates of the effects of husbands' and wives' current employment statuses and the NIT treatment on the rate of marital dissolution of black and white couples in SIME/DIME (Model II)[a]

	Black couples	White couples
Husband employed	0.60	0.55**
Wife employed	0.92	1.55*
NIT treatment	0.84	1.12
Husband employed · NIT treatment	1.29	1.19
Wife employed · NIT treatment	1.77**	1.26
3-Year program	0.88	0.88
Number of spells	2872	4755

*Significant at the .10 level.
**Significant at the .05 level.
[a]Entries are multipliers of the rate. Other covariates included in the model are husband's age and education, wife's age and education, duration of the marriage at enrollment, number of children at enrollment, and dummy variables for site (Denver or Seattle), six levels of normal income, children under 5 years old at enrollment, family's receipt of Aid to Families with Dependent Children (AFDC) in the year before enrollment, and three manpower treatments.

for either black or white couples. Thus it is not essential to allow nonexperimental covariates to interact with employment statuses.

Table 9.1 reports ML estimates of Model II. It shows that employment of the husband stabilizes marriages for both white and black couples and that employment of the wife destabilizes marriages of white couples. More importantly, these results show that the effect of the NIT treatment depends strongly on the wife's employment status for black but not white couples. This conclusion is sustained in the results for Models III and IV, reported in Tables 9.2 and 9.3, respectively. Notice that the estimated effects of the NIT treatment in the model that allows only additive effects of the NIT treatment and employment status (see Table 9.2) is quite similar for black and white couples. However, Table 9.3 reveals that the NIT effect for

Table 9.2. Maximum-likelihood estimates of the effects of the NIT treatment and husbands' and wives' current employment statuses on the rate of marital dissolution (Model III)[a]

	Black couples	White couples
Husband employed	0.72*	0.62***
Wife employed	1.30*	1.79***
NIT treatment	1.38	1.40
Number of spells	2872	4755

*Significant at the .10 level.
**Significant at the .05 level.
***Significant at the .01 level.

[a]Entries are multipliers of the rate. Other covariates included in the model are the same as in Table 9.1, plus a dummy variable for the 3-year program.

black couples occurs entirely among those in which the wife is employed. While the NIT effect is stronger when the wife is employed for both black and white couples, it depends on the wife's employment status much less for white couples than for black couples.

Finally, we address the question of total versus direct effects. Table 9.4 reports the relevant estimates for Model V, which uses only preexperimental information on covariates. Notice that the estimated total effects of the NIT treatment is virtually the same as the "direct effect" from Model III. Little seems to be lost by ignoring the coupling of employment status and marital status in estimating the effects of NIT treatments on dissolution rates of the white couples.[1] The two sets of estimates differ more substantially for black couples. Only the model that uses the current employment status of the wife indicates that the NIT effects differ substantially and significantly for couples with employed and not employed wives.

A husband's and a wife's employment statuses do affect the marital dissolution rate. The dissolution rate tends to rise when husbands are not employed or when wives are employed. Since the

---

[1]Coupling is important in the study of the effects of the NIT treatments on the other variable (employment status) for reasons discussed in the next section.

⟨9⟩ An Example: Marital and Employment Statuses

Table 9.3. Maximum-likelihood estimates of the effects of husbands' and wives' current employment statuses, the NIT treatment, and the interaction of the NIT treatment and the wife's current employment status on the rate of marital dissolution (Model IV)[a]

	Black couples	White couples
Husband employed	0.71*	0.62***
Wife employed	0.91	1.55*
NIT treatment	1.01	1.27
Wife employed · NIT treatment	1.82**	1.28
Number of spells	2872	4755

*Significant at the .10 level.
**Significant at the .05 level.
***Significant at the .01 level.
[a]Entries are multipliers of the rate. Other covariates included in the model are the same as in Table 9.1, plus a dummy variable for the 3-year program.

effects of NIT treatments cause both husbands and wives to spend longer periods out of work, the indirect effects of NIT treatments on dissolution rates are unclear. By inducing longer spells out of work for husbands, the NIT treatment tends to increase the dissolution rate. But, by causing longer periods out of work for wives, the NIT treatment tends to lower the dissolution rate. Thus, the indirect effect of the NIT treatment can either stabilize or destabilize marriages. Table 9.3 shows that for white couples these two indirect effects essentially offset each other, giving a total effect of roughly the same magnitude as the direct effect. In this case qualitative conclusions are apparently unaffected by ignoring coupling between marital status and employment statuses.

The situation is more complicated for black couples. Not only do employment statuses produce indirect effects of NIT treatments on the dissolution rate, but the wife's employment status interacts directly with the NIT treatment. Indeed, virtually the entire total effect of the NIT treatment among black couples occurs when

Table 9.4. Maximum-likelihood estimates of the effects of husbands' and wives' enrollment employment statuses and the NIT treatment on the rate of marital dissolution of black and white couples (Model V)[a]

	Black couples	White couples
Husband's employment at enrollment	0.92	0.83
Wife's employment at enrollment	1.34*	1.32
NIT treatment	1.45*	1.68**
3-Year program	0.80	0.69
Number of spells	2840	4687

*Significant at the .10 level.
**Significant at the .05 level.
[a]Entries are multipliers of the rate. Other covariates included in the model are the same as in Table 9.1.

the wife is employed. Here is a case in which qualitative inferences depend strongly on allowing coupling between different qualitative outcomes.

9.3 Consequences of Ignoring Interdependence

Although it is straightfoward in principle to analyze systems of coupled qualitative variables from complete event histories under the assumptions we have made, it is often necessary to ignore some kinds of coupling. Most variables of sociological interest are dynamically interdependent with many other variables. Ordinarily not all variables believed to be interdependent can be analyzed, either because data are limited or because resources for such complicated analyses are lacking. So it is important to understand what happens when changes in some variables are ignored. If possible, we would like to learn how the structure of interdependencies and the research design affect the size and direction of biases that arise from such a simplification. If the form of the true process is known, we may be able to judge when conclusions based on analyses of misspecified models are likely to be sound. Perhaps we can even learn how to

⟨9⟩ Consequences of Ignoring Interdependence

adjust for biases contingent on such a misspecification.

It is difficult, if not impossible, to obtain general results on the consequences of ignoring dynamic interdependence in a system of qualitative variables. For this reason, and for expository purposes, we concentrate on the simplest case—two interdependent dichotomous variables, $Y_1(t)$ and $Y_2(t)$. In particular, we assume that change in $Y(t) \equiv 2Y_1(t) + Y_2(t) - 2$ is described by a time-stationary Markov process. This model, which is depicted in panel (e) of Figure 4.1, is defined by the matrix of transition rates:

$$\mathbf{R}(u) = \begin{pmatrix} 0 & r_{12} & r_{13} & 0 \\ r_{21} & 0 & 0 & r_{24} \\ r_{31} & 0 & 0 & r_{34} \\ 0 & r_{42} & r_{43} & 0 \end{pmatrix}. \quad (5)$$

Suppose that a time-stationary Markov model of change in *only one* of the two variables, $Y_1(t)$, is actually estimated and that $Y_2(t)$ is ignored. This is the alternating renewal (AR) model illustrated in panel (b) of Figure 4.2. The matrix of transition rates for this model is

$$\mathbf{R}^* = \begin{pmatrix} 0 & r^*_{12} \\ r^*_{21} & 0 \end{pmatrix}. \quad (6)$$

Throughout Section 9.3 an asterisk (*) as a superscript on a symbol refers to the misspecified univariate model in (6).

When $r_{12} = r_{34}$, $r_{13} = r_{24}$, $r_{21} = r_{43}$, and $r_{31} = r_{42}$, the rate of change in Y_1 does not depend on y_2, and the rate of change in Y_2 does not depend on y_1. In this case implications of (6) for outcomes related to Y_1 are identical to the implications of (5). But when these identities do not hold, Y_1 and Y_2 are dynamically interdependent, and the bivariate and univariate models have different implications.

9.3.1 Implications

Sociologists may find it useful to summarize knowledge about change in a qualitative variable in terms of three quantitites: (1) the probability that the variable has a particular value at some point in time, (2) the length of time that the variable (continuously) has one value rather than another, and (3) the number of times that the variable changes its value in some period of time. The implications of the univariate model, which are presented in equations (24) through (26) in Chapter 4, apply when r_{12}^* and r_{21}^* are estimated rather than the rates in (5). Below we give the solutions for the first two outcomes under the assumptions of the bivariate model. The third, which gives the expected number of events, is so complex that we do not include it here; it can be found in Tuma (1980a).

Steady-State Probability Distribution. Given the assumptions of a Markov model, the probability that $Y_1(t) = y_1$, $p_{y_1}(t)$, depends on time t and the initial distribution. To avoid arbitrary assumptions about the latter two quantities, we focus on the equilibrium (steady-state) probability $p_{y_1}(\infty)$, the value of $p_{y_1}(t)$ as t approaches infinity.[2] For the bivariate model in (5), it can be shown that for $y_1 = 2$,

$$p_{y_1}(\infty) = \{r_{12}r_{24}(h_3 + r_{43}) + r_{13}[r_{34}(h_4 + r_{43})$$
$$+ r_{12}r_{21} + r_{13}r_{31} + (h_1 + \lambda_2)(h_1 + \lambda_3)$$
$$+ (h_1 + h_3 + \lambda_2 + \lambda_3)(h_3 + \lambda_4)]\}/(-\lambda_2\lambda_3\lambda_4), \quad (7)$$

where

$$h_j = \sum_{k \neq j} r_{jk}, \quad j = 1, \ldots, 4,$$

are the hazard functions for the four states; $\lambda_1 = 0$; and λ_j, $j = 2$, 3, 4 are distinct negative nonzero eigenvalues of **R** in (5).[3]

Duration. Even when every member of a population has the same transition rates, the duration in a state has a distribution with a nonzero variance, given the assumptions of a Markov model. We

---

[2]For a finite-state, time-stationary Markov process, a steady-state probability distribution exists if states intercommunicate, that is, it is possible to move from each state to every other state in a finite number of moves (Cox and Miller, 1965). Both the bivariate and univariate models meet this condition.

[3]Eigenvalues are defined in Section 11.5. In this particular case, one eigenvalue is necessarily zero; this is defined to be λ_1. For many sociological applications, the other eigenvalues are distinct, negative, and nonzero, as we assume here. However, these assumptions are not always true; in these instances (7) has a different form, which we do not consider.

limit consideration to $E[U_y]$, the mean (or expected) duration that Y_1 continuously equals y_1. For the bivariate model in (5),

$$E[U_{y_1}] = \frac{\alpha(y_1)\left[h_b + r_{ab}\right] + \left[1 - \alpha(y_1)\right]\left[h_a + r_{ba}\right]}{h_a h_b - r_{ab} r_{ba}}, \qquad (8)$$

where $a \equiv 2y_1 - 1$, $b \equiv 2y_1 - 2$, and $\alpha(y_1)$ is the proportion of individuals for whom $Y_2(0) = 2$ when $Y_1(0) = y_1$.

Number of Events in a Period. A Markov model of change in a set of variables also implies that the number of times any given variable changes in a period has a distribution with a nonzero variance, even when everyone in the population has the same transition rates. However, it is not always possible to write this distribution as an explicit function of the transition rates except for very simple Markov models (e.g., a Poisson model). The expected number is a useful summary statistic that can be derived more readily than the probability distribution. The derivation of the equations for the bivariate model requires an additional assumption that has not previously been necessary, namely, that the process is in equilibrium. The solution is found in Tuma (1980a, Appendix).

9.3.2 Research Design

We would like to know which research design yields sample estimates closest to the true population values. Choice of a design involves many decisions, most of which we ignore. In particular, we disregard effects of the sample size I, assuming that I is so large that variations in it do not affect conclusions. Instead, we focus on two decisions that seem especially problematic when considering a misspecified model. First, what kind of data should be used to estimate parameters? In particular, should panel data or event-history data be used?[4] Second, what kind of sample design should be used? In

---

[4]In a system of J dynamically interdependent dichotomous variables, cross-sectional data provide information on $Y_j(t)$, $j = 1, \ldots, J$, for the I members of the sample and thus allow $2^J - 1$ linearly independent proportions to be calculated. However, $2^J J$ transition rates describe the change process. Because $2^J J > 2^J - 1$ for $J \geq 1$, cross-sectional data do not provide enough information for the transition rates to be estimated uniquely, even if the process is in equilibrium and the model is specified correctly. Consequently, we do not discuss cross-sectional data.

particular, should sample members be selected according to values of the omitted endogenous variable(s), such as Y_2, or should they be selected randomly, ignoring the omitted endogenous variable(s) entirely?

We consider estimation from two kinds of data on Y_1: two-wave panel data, in which $Y_1(0)$ and $Y_1(\tau)$ are observed for every member of a sample for times $t_0 = 0$ and τ, and event-history data, in which $Y_1(t)$ is observed for all t in an interval $0 \leq t \leq \tau$. For a correctly specified model, event-history analysis is superior to panel analysis as we discuss at length in the next chapter, but this advantage may not hold when the model is misspecified.

We consider two kinds of samples: a sample selected randomly from a population in equilibrium (a type r sample), and a sample selected so that everyone has the same value on Y_2 initially (a homogeneous sample). Homogeneous samples include those in which $Y_2(0) = 1$ for all I sample members (a type 1 sample), and those in which $Y_2(0) = 2$ for all I sample members (a type 2 sample). Obviously, $\alpha(y_1)$, the proportion in the sample with $Y_2(0) = 2$ when $Y_1(0) = y_1$ (which affects estimates of rates in the misspecified, univariate model), is zero in a type 1 sample and unity in a type 2 sample. In a type r sample,

$$\alpha_1 = \frac{p_2(\infty)}{p_1(\infty) + p_2(\infty)},$$

$$\alpha_2 = \frac{p_4(\infty)}{p_3(\infty) + p_4(\infty)},$$

$$p_1(\infty) = \left[(h_1 + \lambda_2)(h_1 + \lambda_3)(h_1 + \lambda_4) + r_{12}r_{21}(h_1 - h_3 - h_4)\right.$$
$$\left. + r_{13}r_{31}(h_1 - h_2 - h_4)\right]/(\lambda_2\lambda_3\lambda_4),$$

$$p_3(\infty) = \{r_{12}\left[(h_1 + \lambda_2)(h_1 + \lambda_3) + (h_1 + h_2 + \lambda_2 + \lambda_3)(h_2 + \lambda_4)\right.$$
$$\left. + r_{12}r_{21} + r_{13}r_{31} + r_{24}r_{42}\right] + r_{13}r_{34}r_{42}\}/(-\lambda_2\lambda_3\lambda_4),$$

$$p_3(\infty) = \{r_{13}\left[(h_1 + \lambda_2)(h_1 + \lambda_3) + (h_1 + h_3 + \lambda_2 + \lambda_3)(h_3 + \lambda_4)\right.$$
$$\left. + r_{12}r_{21} + r_{13}r_{31} + r_{34}r_{43}\right] + r_{12}r_{24}r_{43}\}/(-\lambda_2\lambda_3\lambda_4),$$

$$p_4(\infty) = \left[r_{12}r_{24}h_3 + r_{13}r_{34}h_2\right]/(-\lambda_2\lambda_3\lambda_4),$$

where $p_y(\infty)$ is the steady-state probability that $Y(t) = y$.

⟨9⟩ **Consequences of Ignoring Interdependence**

It may seem better to analyze type 1 and type 2 samples separately than to analyze a type r sample. Unlike the latter procedure, the former partially controls for the omitted endogenous variable Y_2. Ordinarily, analysts expect such controls to improve the quality of estimates.

Two-Wave Panel Data. Data from a two-wave panel provide information on $Y_1(0)$ and $Y_1(\tau)$ for the I members of the sample. The transition probabilities in the univariate model can be estimated from these data as

$$\widehat{p}^*_{yk}(0,\tau) = \frac{\text{Number for whom } Y_1(0) = y \text{ and } Y_1(\tau) = k}{\text{Number for whom } Y_1(0) = y},$$

for $y, k = 1, 2$. When

$$\widehat{\phi}(0,\tau) \equiv \widehat{p}^*_{12}(0,\tau) + \widehat{p}^*_{21}(0,\tau) < 1, \tag{9}$$

the unique ML estimators of the rates r^*_{12} and r^*_{21} are as follows (Singer and Spilerman, 1974, p. 392):[5]

$$\widehat{r}^*_{12} = \frac{\widehat{p}^*_{12}(0,\tau) \log\left[1 - \widehat{\phi}(0,\tau)\right]}{-\tau \widehat{\phi}(0,\tau)}; \tag{10a}$$

$$\widehat{r}^*_{21} = \frac{\widehat{p}^*_{21}(0,\tau) \log\left[1 - \widehat{\phi}(0,\tau)\right]}{-\tau \widehat{\phi}(0,\tau)}. \tag{10b}$$

To relate the estimates of the rates in the univariate model to the true rates in the bivariate process, $p_{yk}(0,\tau)$ must be expressed as a function of the rates for the bivariate process. When the sample is large, as we assume here, the sample estimate of $p_{yk}(0,\tau)$ approximately equals its true value. The latter is a function of $\alpha(y_1)$, the proportion with $Y_2(0) = 2$ given that $Y_1(0) = y_1$, which depends on the type of sample. It also depends on the matrix of the true probabilities of a change from $y_0 \equiv Y(0)$ to $y_\tau \equiv Y(\tau)$, $p_{y_0 y_\tau}(0,\tau)$:

$$\widehat{p}^*_{12}(0,\tau) = (1 - \alpha_1)\left[p_{13}(0,\tau) + p_{14}(0,\tau)\right]$$
$$+ \alpha_1 \left[p_{23}(0,\tau) + p_{24}(0,\tau)\right], \tag{11a}$$

$$\widehat{p}^*_{21}(0,\tau) = (1 - \alpha_2)\left[p_{31}(0,\tau) + p_{32}(0,\tau)\right]$$
$$+ \alpha_2 \left[p_{41}(0,\tau) + p_{42}(0,\tau)\right], \tag{11b}$$

[5]When (9) does not hold, the data are not consistent with any time-homogeneous, continuous-time, univariate Markov process.

where $p_{y_0 y_\tau}(0,\tau)$ is an element of the matrix $\mathbf{P}(0,\tau)$ given by

$$\mathbf{P}(0,\tau) = \sum_{j=1}^{2^J} \mathbf{A}_j \, e^{\lambda_j \tau}, \qquad (12)$$

$$\mathbf{A}_j \equiv \prod_{\substack{k=1 \\ k \neq j}}^{J} \frac{\mathbf{R} - \lambda_k \mathbf{I}}{\lambda_j - \lambda_k}, \qquad (13)$$

for $j = 1, \ldots, J$, where $\lambda_1 = 0$ and the other eigenvalues are distinct, negative, and nonzero.[6]

Event-History Data. Maximum-likelihood estimates of the transition rates can also be obtained from event-history data, as we discussed in detail in Chapter 5. As in Section 5.11, define the total length of completed episodes in state j as

$$U_j \equiv \sum_{i=1}^{I} u_{ij},$$

and the total number of moves from state j to k in the observation period $(\tau_1, \tau_2]$ as

$$N_{jk} \equiv \sum_{i=1}^{I} n_{ijk}(\tau_1, \tau_2).$$

Then the ML estimates of r_{12}^* and r_{21}^* are

$$\widehat{r}_{12}^* = \frac{N_{12}}{U_1}; \qquad (14a)$$

$$\widehat{r}_{21}^* = \frac{N_{21}}{U_2}. \qquad (14b)$$

Since the numerators and denominators of the right-hand sides of equations (14a) and (14b) are random variables, they vary from one

---

[6]This solution of equation (5) holds when λ_j, $j = 2, \ldots, 2^J$, are distinct, negative eigenvalues of the matrix of transition rates (Bartholomew, 1973).

⟨9⟩ **Consequences of Ignoring Interdependence**

sample to another. When the sample is large and the observation period is long, as we assume here, the right-hand side of each equation equals its expected value, that is,

$$\hat{r}_{12}^* = \frac{1}{\mathrm{E}[U_1]} \,; \qquad (15a)$$

$$\hat{r}_{21}^* = \frac{1}{\mathrm{E}[U_2]} \,. \qquad (15b)$$

To relate $\hat{r}_{12}^*$ and $\hat{r}_{21}^*$ to the rates of the bivariate model, merely substitute the values of $\mathrm{E}[U_1]$ and $\mathrm{E}[U_2]$ given by (8) into (15). Notice that $\mathrm{E}[U_1]$ and $\mathrm{E}[U_2]$ depend on α_1 and α_2 as well as the transition rates of the bivariate process.

9.3.3 Procedure

The correctly specified bivariate model gives unbiased estimates of parameters and accurate predictions of the various outcomes considered above for both research designs. A misspecified model generally has a nonzero bias.[7] When the estimated model consists of a univariate Markov process but a bivariate Markov process actually describes change in the system, the direction and magnitude of bias depends in a complicated nonlinear way on the eight unique nonzero transition rates of the bivariate process given in (5). The bias also depends on the particular outcome considered and on the research design used—the kind of data collected and the type of sample. Analytic expressions for the bias can be written, but they are so complex that they are difficult to interpret.

Because of this complexity, we decided not to study bias analytically. Instead we describe the bias numerically for conditions resembling phenomena of substantive interest. This procedure lets us see the size and direction of biases that may be encountered when dynamic interdependence in the selected phenomena is overlooked.

---

[7]If we considered sample size as a varying feature of the research design, we might be most interested in the mean squared errors associated with the misspecified model because mean squared errors depend on variance as well as bias. Because we are concentrating on situations in which the sample size is extremely large, we ignore variance, assuming in effect that it is zero.

Of course, we cannot be certain of obtaining similar patterns if the true process differs markedly from the conditions studied.

We chose to study specific conditions resembling a phenomena that interests us: the dynamic interrelationship between employment status and marital status of men and women. Partly because of data limitations and partly to avoid complicated analytical problems associated with modeling dynamic interdependencies between qualitative variables, our previous empirical research in these areas was based on models that ignored dynamic interdependencies. We undertook the research discussed in this chapter to assess the extent to which our previous research in these substantive areas may have erred because of this type of model misspecification.

We present results for two bivariate systems,[8] each consisting of two dichotomous variables, Y_s and Y_r. Pair 1 refers to a man's marital status Y_s and his employment status Y_r. Pair 2 refers to a wife's employment status Y_s and her husband's employment status Y_r. For each pair we consider the bias arising from studying Y_s (i.e., setting $Y_1 = Y_s$) and ignoring Y_r (i.e., setting $Y_2 = Y_r$) and from studying Y_r and ignoring Y_s. Y_s always denotes the more slowly changing variable and Y_r the more rapidly changing one. That is, Y_s and Y_r are defined so that the expected number of changes in Y_s is less than the expected number of changes in Y_r for any finite positive interval $[0, \tau]$.

We assigned numerical values to the transition rates in the bivariate process as follows. First we assumed that variables in each pair were independent and then chose transition rates so that the steady-state probability distribution and the mean duration in each state resemble values in empirical data that we have analyzed previously. We chose 0.10 and 0.05 for the rate (per year) of marital formation and marital dissolution, respectively. We chose 5.0 and 0.40 for the annual rate of a man's entering and leaving employment, and 1.25 and 0.80 for the comparable annual rates for a woman.

Then we built interdependence into each pair of variables. We assumed that the above rates hold when the other variable equals unity (i.e., the person is married, or employed). We set the rates when the other variable equals zero equal to the following multiples

[8]See Tuma (1980a) for more details and results on two additional bivariate systems.

of these rates:

$$r_{12} = \kappa\, r_{34},$$
$$r_{13} = \kappa\, r_{23},$$
$$r_{21} = r_{43}/\kappa,$$
$$r_{31} = r_{42}/\kappa,$$

where $\kappa > 0$. The parameter κ may be regarded as a measure of the degree of coupling betweem the pair of variables. When $\kappa = 1$, the two variables are independent. The more κ differs from one, the greater the interdependence between the two variables. For each pair we set $\kappa = 0.25, 0.50, 0.80, 1.0, 1.25, 2.0$, and 4.0, giving a total of 14 different bivariate processes.

For each of the 14 bivariate processes, 2 univariate processes may be studied, giving a total of 28 conditions. Moreover, for each condition we considered four research designs, and for each design we calculated the expected value and the bias for the following: transition rates, the steady-state probability that $Y_1 = 1$, the mean duration that Y_1 equals zero and unity, and the mean number of changes in Y_1 in a period $(0, \tau)$. We begin by summarizing what we found and then give a small fraction of all numerical results for illustrative purposes.

9.3.4 Findings

First, the results indicate that the bias in each outcome is zero for all four research designs when κ is unity, that is, changes in Y_1 and Y_2 are independent. Because we considered only asymptotic results (i.e., results for an infinitely large sample) for ML estimators, this outcome must be true mathematically. Consequently, it provides evidence of the accuracy of the computational procedure used to calculate the expected value of each outcome and the bias obtained under different research designs.

Second, the calculations show that the more κ differs from unity, the greater the percentage bias in an outcome (defined as 100 times the bias divided by the true value). In most conditions investigated, absolute bias also increases as κ increases.

Third, percentage bias in predictions based on the analysis of panel data depend on the length of time between the waves of the panel, that is, τ. We arbitrarily chose two values for τ, 2 and 5 ("years"), because these values approximate the interval in panel studies of these topics. Estimates of the mean duration and of the mean number of changes in Y_1 in a period often have much larger biases when τ is 5 rather than 2. However, a longer spacing between waves gives better predictions of the third variable, the equilibrium probability. But in this case the difference in percentage bias for 2 and 5 years is much less than is for the other two outcomes.[9] We report illustrative results for $\tau = 2$, so that the panel design can be examined in its generally more favorable condition.

Fourth, results for the univariate model of the more slowly changing variable Y_s do not depend much on the type of data or the kind of sample. More important, and quite surprising, is the finding that for every outcome considered both the absolute and percentage biases are usually small in magnitude when we study the more slowly changing variable Y_s. They are usually much smaller than those for the more rapidly changing variable Y_r. Thus, these investigations suggest that the percentage biases resulting from ignoring dynamic interdependencies are large mainly when the ignored variables change much more slowly than the variables studied.

Fifth, the pattern of biases associated with one of the four outcomes considered does not always give a good clue about the pattern of biases for another outcome, especially in studies of the more rapidly changing variable, Y_r. This necessitates a separate discussion of the biases associated with each of the four outcomes.

Transition Rates. Table 9.6 reports the true rates of change in Y_1 when $y_2 = 1$ (labeled True, $y_2 = 1$) and when $y_2 = 2$ (labeled True, $y_2 = 2$) for selected cases. It also gives estimates of the rates

---

[9] At first glance these results may seem surprising. If the interval between waves is very short, the estimated matrix of transition probabilities approximately equals an identity matrix. As the interval increases, the number of transition increases. This fact may suggest that information always increases with the length of the interval. But this reasoning ignores the fact that when the interval is infinite, every column of the estimated matrix of transition probabilities equals the equilibrium probability distribution. So if the interval is infinitely long, panel data contain no more information than cross-sectional data (see footnote 4). We can estimate the equilibrium probability distribution, but not the mean duration in an episode or the mean number of changes.

⟨9⟩ Consequences of Ignoring Interdependence 287

Table 9.5. Definitions of symbols used in Tables 9.6 through 9.9

Symbol	Definition
Y_1	The dichotomous variable that is studied
Y_2	The dichotomous variable that is ignored
Y_s	The variable in a pair that changes more slowly
Y_r	The variable in a pair that changes more rapidly
$Y_1 = Y_s$	The variable that changes more slowly is studied (and the variable that changes more rapidly is ignored)
$Y_1 = Y_r$	The variable that changes more rapidly is studied (and the variable that changes more slowly is ignored)
True, $y_2 = 1$	The true rate of change in Y_1 when $y_2 = 1$
True, $y_2 = 2$	The true rate of change in Y_1 when $y_2 = 2$
P1	Results for a two-wave panel data on a sample selected so that Y_2, the ignored variable, equals 1 at the first wave
P2	Results for the two-wave panel data on a sample selected so that Y_2, the ignored variable, equals 2 at the first wave
Pr	Results for the two-wave panel data on a random sample in equilibrium at the first wave
Pw	A weighted sum of the results for the P1 and P2 designs. The weights are the probabilities that the ignored variable, Y_2, equals 1 and 2, respectively, in equilibrium
E1	Results for event-history data on a sample selected so that Y_2, the ignored variable, equals 1 initially
E2	Results for event-history data on a sample selected so that Y_2, the ignored variable, equals 2 initially
Er	Results for event-history data on a random sample in equilibrium initially
Ew	A weighted sum of the results for the E1 and E2 designs. The weights are the probabilities that the ignored variable, Y_2, equals 1 and 2, respectively, in equilibrium

r_{12}^* and r_{21}^* of the univariate process for data from a two-wave panel (P) with $\tau = 2$ and for event-history data (E).[10] For each type of data we consider results for three kinds of samples: a type 1 sample ($Y_2(0) = 1$), a type 2 sample ($Y_2(0) = 2$), and a type r sample (a random sample from a population in equilibrium). In Table 9.6 and subsequent tables, we denote the research design by combining these

[10] See equations (10) and (14).

labels. For example, P1 denotes a panel design in which $Y_2(0) = 1$ at the time of the first wave. Table 9.5 summarizes the abbreviations used for labels in Table 9.6 and subsequent tables.

First, as mentioned above, when the more slowly changing variable Y_s is studied, estimates of the rates depend comparatively little on the type of data or sample. In addition, the estimates for all research designs fall between the two comparable true rates (labeled True, $y_2 = 1$ and True, $y_2 = 2$), as might be anticipated. They also tend toward the value of the true rate where the omitted variable has the value that predominates in equilibrium (compare Table 9.7). For example, in Pair 3 the equilibrium probability that $Y_r = 2$ for a given value of Y_s is above .5, so the estimated rates for Y_s tend to be nearer those labeled True, $y_2 = 2$ than to those labeled True, $y_2 = 1$. This indicates that the relative rates of change in the omitted variable Y_2 affect the estimated rates in the misspecified univariate model.

Second, the type of research design greatly affects estimates of the rates when the more rapidly changing variable Y_r is studied. Estimates for event-history designs are between the two comparable true rates (labeled True, $y_2 = 1$ and True, $y_2 = 2$), and the estimate for the random design (Er) always lies between those for the two types of homogeneous sample designs (E1 and E2), as might be expected. Furthermore, as in studies of the more slowly changing variable Y_s, the estimated rates tend toward the true rates associated with the value of the ignored variable that is most prevalent in the steady state.

Third, rates estimated from a panel design are almost always smaller than those from the event-history design with the same kind of sample. Sometimes these estimates are smaller than *either* of the two comparable true rates (labeled True, $y_2 = 1$ and True, $y_2 = 2$); see Pair 2 where $Y_1 = Y_r$ for an example. And, surprisingly, an estimate based on the random panel design (Pr) does not always fall between the estimates for the two homogeneous panel designs, P1 and P2; see Y_r of Pair 1, for example.

We might be tempted to conclude from these findings that estimates from an event-history design are better than those from a panel design in studies of a variable that changes more rapidly than the variable being ignored (i.e., in studying Y_r while ignoring Y_s). As we see below, this is usually the case, but not always, if better means smaller biases in the prediction of other outcomes.

⟨9⟩ **Consequences of Ignoring Interdependence**

Table 9.6. Transition rates: true values for a bivariate model and expected values for a misspecified model of Y_1 estimated by various research designs

Change from: to:	$Y_1 = Y_s$		$Y_1 = Y_r$	
	$y_1 = 1$ $y_1 = 2$	$y_1 = 2$ $y_1 = 1$	$y_1 = 1$ $y_1 = 2$	$y_1 = 2$ $y_1 = 1$
Pair 1				
True, $y_2 = 1$	0.050	0.100	2.500	0.800
P1	0.082	0.057	2.230	0.628
Pr	0.088	0.054	1.324	0.212
P2	0.090	0.053	3.020	0.291
E1	0.087	0.054	2.524	0.727
Er	0.088	0.054	3.012	0.490
E2	0.088	0.054	4.906	0.421
True, $y_2 = 2$	0.100	0.050	5.000	0.400
Pair 2				
True, $y_2 = 1$	2.500	0.400	10.000	0.200
P1	1.280	0.767	4.022	0.224
Pr	1.267	0.766	3.568	0.202
P2	1.268	0.767	4.080	0.233
E1	1.408	0.723	8.418	0.302
Er	1.272	0.768	5.446	0.318
E2	1.270	0.772	5.155	0.329
True, $y_2 = 2$	1.250	0.800	5.000	0.400

Equilibrium Probabilities. Table 9.7 gives illustrative values of the equilibrium probability that $Y_1 = 2$ and the percentage bias in predicting this probability using various research designs. The entries refer to the same conditions reported in Table 9.5.[11]

Considering the comparatively poor estimates of rates obtained from the random panel design, it is somewhat surprising to

[11] The bias for the misspecified model reported in this table is obtained by inserting the estimates in Table 9.5 in equation (21) in Chapter 4 and then subtracting the expected value, which is calculated from (7) and the rates of the bivariate process. A comparable procedure is used to calculate bias for the misspecified model in subsequent tables.

Table 9.7. The equilibrium probability that $Y_1 = 2$: true value for a bivariate model and percentage bias for a misspecified univariate model of Y_1 estimated by various research designs

	Pair 1		Pair 2	
	$Y_1 = Y_s$	$Y_1 = Y_r$	$Y_1 = Y_s$	$Y_1 = Y_r$
True	.621	.862	.623	.946
P1	−5.0%	−9.5%	0.4%	0.1%
P2	0.9	5.8	−0.0	−0.1
Pw	0.1	0.0	0.0	0.0
Pr	0	0	0	0
E1	−0.8	−10.0	6.0	3.0
E2	0.1	6.8	−0.2	−0.5
Ew	−0.0	0.5	0.1	0.8
Er	−0.0	−0.2	0.0	−0.1

find that the bias in the equilibrium probability that $Y_1 = 2$ is *identically* zero for this design. Judging from our computations, the lack of bias for this outcome and design appears to result from a mathematical identity rather than the coincidental choice of the transition rates of the bivariate process.

For both event-history and panel designs, biases in equilibrium probabilities are almost always greater for samples selected to be homogeneous in the omitted endogenous variable, Y_2, than for a random sample. Although social scientists are accustomed to thinking that control of covariates improves the accuracy of estimates, this result is not so surprising upon reflection. The value of Y_2 on which a sample is selected is *not* a fixed characteristic of members of the sample. As τ increases, the distribution of $Y_2(\tau)$ in a homogeneous sample approaches the distribution of $Y_2(0)$ in a random sample.[12]

It seems reasonable to think that the predictions based on a random sample should resemble some kind of weighted average of the predictions in the two homogeneous samples (type 1 and type

---

[12]This suggests that inferences from homogeneous and random samples differ most when the interval between waves of a panel is comparatively short.

⟨9⟩ Consequences of Ignoring Interdependence   291

2 samples). This reasoning suggests that a prediction that weights the prediction from each type of homogeneous sample by the corresponding proportion in the steady state might have even smaller biases than those in a random sample. To explore this possibility, Table 9.7 and subsequent tables also report percentage biases for such weighted predictions (labeled w).

Table 9.7 shows that biases in the weighted predictions (Pw and Ew) compare favorably in many cases to those from the random designs (Pr and Er). In fact, in a study of the more rapidly changing variable Y_r, biases in the equilibrium probability are very small for the weighted panel prediction (Pw). This pattern also holds in a study of the more slowly changing variable Y_s when the interval between the waves of the panel is 5 years; however, when the interval is 2 years, the bias for the Pw design is sometimes worse than for either the Ew or Er designs. But on the whole the percentage bias in the equilibrium probability for the weighted panel prediction is almost as good as that for the random panel prediction and usually considerably better than either the random or weighted event-history prediction. Still, the percentage biases for the Er and Ew predictions are fairly small in most instances, especially in studies of the more slowly changing variable Y_s. Thus panel analysis has a relative advantage over event-history analysis in predicting an equilibrium probability, but the size of the advantage is usually small.

Mean Duration. Table 9.8 reports the mean duration that Y_1 equals zero and unity, assuming the process is in equilibrium, for the same conditions reported in the previous table. It also reports the percentage bias.

First, the percentage bias for the random event-history design is zero because we are "predicting" the same quantity used to estimate the rates of the univariate model.

Second, the percentage bias is often much larger (although occasionally smaller) for a homogeneous sample than for the comparable weighted prediction. Sometimes the latter produces somewhat smaller biases than the former, but more often biases are much larger. This pattern suggests that mean duration should not be predicted from a particular stratum when dynamic interdependencies between the stratifying variable and the variable studied are ignored.

Weighted event-history prediction is preferable to either the random or weighted panel prediction. Interestingly, the weighted

Table 9.8. The mean duration in states 1 and 2: true values for a bivariate model and percentage biases for a misspecified univariate model of Y_1 estimated by various research designs

	$Y_1 = Y_s$		$Y_1 = Y_r$	
	$y_1 = 1$	$y_1 = 2$	$y_1 = 1$	$y_1 = 2$
Pair 1				
True	11.397	18.632	0.332	2.042
P1	6.4%	−6.4%	35.1%	−21.9%
P2	−1.9	−0.6	−0.3	68.1
Pw	−2.2	−0.6	−2.3	0.7
Pr	0.1	0.3	40.3	35.2
E1	−2.8	0.7	−43.0	39.0
E2	−0.4	0.1	−38.6	16.3
Ew	−0.2	−0.1	−16.6	−2.2
Er	0	0	0	0
Pair 2				
True	0.786	1.301	0.184	3.146
P1	−0.6%	0.2%	35.4%	42.1%
P2	0.3	0.2	33.5	36.3
Pw	0.3	0.2	34.2	38.5
Pr	0.4	0.4	52.6	57.4
E1	−9.7	6.4	−35.3	5.2
E2	0.2	−0.5	5.6	−3.4
Ew	−0.3	−0.1	−9.8	−0.1
Er	0	0	0	0

event-history prediction invariably has a negative bias, while the random panel prediction consistently has a positive bias. Thus the two predictions always bracket the expected value.

Mean Number of Changes in a Period. Table 9.9 gives the expected value of the mean number of changes in Y_1 in a period, conditional on the initial value of Y_1.[13] It also reports the percentage

---

[13] Recall that the derivation of the expected number requires the assumption that the population is in equilibrium.

⟨9⟩ Consequences of Ignoring Interdependence

Table 9.9. Mean number of changes in Y_1 in $(0, \tau)$ where $\tau = 2$: true values for a bivariate model and percentage biases for a misspecified univariate model of Y_1 estimated by various research designs[a]

	$Y_1 = Y_s$			$Y_1 = Y_r$		
	$n_{y_1 y_1}(\tau)$	$n_{12}(\tau)$	$n_{21}(\tau)$	$n_{y_1 y_1}(\tau)$	$n_{12}(\tau)$	$n_{21}(\tau)$
Pair 1						
True	0.009	0.162	0.102	0.754	1.609	0.896
P1	0.5%	−5.6%	6.1%	7.3%	−1.4%	12.8%
P2	1.3	1.8	−0.5	−40.1	−15.3	−66.2
Pw	1.2	0.8	0.4	−22.2	−10.0	−23.7
Pr	−0.2	−0.1	−0.1	−66.6	−33.2	−133.6
E1	−0.3	−1.0	0.8	26.8	7.6	24.0
E2	0.2	0.3	−0.1	−6.8	0.9	−14.6
Ew	0.2	0.1	0.1	6.0	3.5	3.9
Er	−0.0	−0.0	−0.0	−4.2	−1.7	−3.9
Pair 2						
True	0.728	1.340	1.098	0.550	1.495	0.605
P1	0.2%	0.3%	−0.0%	−32.0%	−11.6%	−41.9%
P2	−0.3	−0.2	−0.2	−29.1	−10.6	−36.3
Pw	−0.3	−0.2	−0.2	−30.2	−11.0	−38.3
Pr	−0.6	−0.3	−0.4	−39.7	−14.6	−57.2
E1	0.9	3.4	−2.7	−0.1	1.3	−3.6
E2	0.2	0.0	3.0	2.1	0.5	2.7
Ew	0.3	0.2	0.2	1.3	0.8	0.4
Er	−0.0	−0.0	−0.0	−0.3	−0.1	−0.3

[a]See text for definitions of $n_{y_1 y_1}(\tau)$, $n_{12}(\tau)$, and $n_{21}(\tau)$.

biases in these quantities for various research designs.

As previously mentioned, for the more slowly changing variable Y_s, both absolute and percentage biases are fairly small for all designs. The random and weighted event-history predictions usually produce the smallest biases, but the random and weighted panel predictions are almost as good. On the other hand, the biases for the more rapidly changing variable Y_r depend greatly on the research design. Biases for a panel design are almost always larger than those for the corresponding event-history design. The bias for the random panel design is usually the largest in magnitude; furthermore, the bias for the weighted panel prediction cannot be relied on to be smaller than the bias for a prediction from a homogeneous panel design.

The magnitude of the bias is almost always smaller for the random event-history design than for any other design; often it is much smaller. Occasionally the bias for the weighted event-history prediction is the smallest, but in these instances it is only *slightly* smaller in size than the bias for the random event-history prediction. It should be noted that the random event-history prediction always has a negative bias while the weighted event-history prediction usually has a positive bias. Together these two predictions usually give a narrow bracket around the expected value.

9.4 Conclusions

This chapter has two main themes. The first is that the models and methods discussed in Chapters 3–8 can be applied directly to the study of change in systems of coupled qualitative variables. However, this extension relies on complete event histories and on assumptions that may not always be appropriate in sociological research. Our approach assumes that the coupling occurs between observed states rather than between rates. It also assumes that different spells for the same person (or other unit) are independent observations. This means that unobserved heterogeneity does not persist across spells. When substantive models are well specified, these assumptions may be appropriate. If they are not realistic, recourse must be made to the strategy of conditioning rates on previous history, as discussed in Chapter 3.

The second main theme concerns the consequences of ignoring coupling. Although we cannot draw general conclusions about the effects of ignoring dynamic interdependencies among qualitative variables from the small number of cases examined in this chapter, we can make a few general statements that can be regarded as hypotheses to be investigated in subsequent research.

As we would expect, biases from ignoring dynamic interrelationships tend to increase with the degree of interdependence of the

⟨9⟩ Conclusions

variables. However, under some circumstances both absolute and percent biases are not large when interdependencies are ignored.

If the variable being studied changes more slowly than the ignored variable, biases are relatively small for all outcomes and research designs examined in this chapter. This is true even when the rates of changes in the two variables differ by a factor as small as 2 and the rate of change in each variable depends strongly on the value of the other variable.

Even when other outcomes are estimated poorly, estimates of equilibrium probabilities obtained from either panel or event-history data are remarkably good despite misspecification of the model. The panel prediction based on a random sample of a population in equilibrium is unbiased, in spite of the model misspecification. The prediction based on event-history analysis of a random sample is less accurate than the panel one, but is still quite good.

Biases in predicting the mean duration and the mean number of changes in a variable in a period are often fairly small when based on estimates from event-history analysis of a random sample, even though the model is misspecified.

For most outcomes event-history analysis of a sample distributed randomly across values of the ignored variable tends to give consistently smaller biases (and fewer very large biases) than event-history analysis of samples selected to be homogeneous on the value of the omitted endogenous variable. Since the latter procedure attempts to control partially for the effects of the omitted variable, this may seem somewhat surprising at first. This finding apparently reflects the fact that the omitted variables are not fixed characteristics but change over time until they eventually reach the distribution in a random sample.

10
A Comparison of Approaches

We return finally to an issue raised in Chapters 3, 4, and 9: the advantages of event-history analysis over other approaches. Obviously any comparison of alternative approaches depends at least partly on the assumptions about the process generating events. To make the comparisons concrete, we assume that events are generated by a time-stationary Markov process whose transition rates are log-linear functions of exogenous variables. We suspect, however, that the qualitative conclusions that emerge from study of the Markov model have broad applicability. Moreover, we wish to challenge the widespread view that substantive assumptions ought to be dictated by the form in which the data are collected. That is, we do not believe that sociologists ought to change their assumptions about the underlying process (their model, in our terminology) when they shift from analyzing panel data, say, to analyzing cross-sections or event histories. In our view, the strategy of formulating problems in terms of continuous-time stochastic models has a major advantage: different data structures can be used to estimate parameters of the same model. This provides a way of unifying various procedures for analyzing data.

We begin with an extended discussion of cross-sectional analysis because this has been, and will undoubtedly continue to be, the mainstay of sociological research. We then contrast event-history analysis with two other strategies that use temporal data: event-count analysis and event-sequence analysis. Our discussion of each is brief. To the best of our knowledge, event-count analysis has not

⟨ 10 ⟩ Cross-Sectional Analysis

yet been developed (let alone applied) except for the most elementary kind of Markov model, the Poisson model. We are not aware of any formal event-sequence analyses in sociology. So our comments on them are intended to encourage the development of these approaches. On the other hand, panel analysis is the standard sociological tool for analyzing change. Thus we review in some detail work on methodological problems that arise in this approach.

We also present an extended empirical illustration that shows that event-history analysis may yield substantive conclusions quite different from those of panel analysis. Finally, we discuss the fit of models for dynamic analysis in general and within the context of a particular substantive example.

10.1 Cross-Sectional Analysis

Cross-sectional data give the state that each member of a sample occupies at a particular time t. Earlier we referred to the unconditional probability of being in a state j at time t as the state probability $p_j(t)$. Given Ψ possible states, there are only $(\Psi - 1)$ unique state probabilities since the Ψ probabilities must sum to unity. But, in general, there are $\Psi(\Psi - 1)$ unique transition rates. Because $\Psi(\Psi - 1) > (\Psi - 1)$ for $\Psi > 1$, it is immediately obvious that cross-sectional analysis does not allow all parameters of a model to be identified unless $\Psi - 1$ of the transition rates can be treated as known constants, either on theoretical grounds or from a priori knowledge. With event-history analysis all $\Psi(\Psi - 1)$ parameters can be estimated. So event-history analysis is clearly preferable to cross-sectional analysis if social scientists want to understand the process fully or to predict other outcomes.

Nevertheless, under certain conditions cross-sectional analysis can supply useful information about the process that generates events. It is worthwhile identifying these conditions. We begin by considering the situation in which the process has been operating a comparatively long time so that the distribution of the population across states is in equilibrium.

For concreteness we again consider the case of a two-state model with time-stationary transition rates that are log-linear functions of a vector of observed variables, $\mathbf{x}$. The two-state model implies that the probabilities of being in each state eventually reach stable, steady-state values [see (26) in Chapter 4]:

$$p_j(\infty) = \frac{r_{kj}}{r_{jk} + r_{kj}} = \frac{e^{\alpha'_{kj}\mathbf{x}}}{e^{\alpha'_{jk}\mathbf{x}} + e^{\alpha'_{kj}\mathbf{x}}}$$

$$= \frac{1}{1 + e^{(\alpha_{jk} - \alpha_{kj})'\mathbf{x}}}, \quad (1)$$

where $j = 1, 2$ and $k \equiv 3 - j$. Of course, even when the steady states are reached, individuals continue to change from one state to the other. That is, the model implies an equilibrium probability distribution on the aggregate level; it neither assumes nor implies equilibrium on the individual level. In a large population homogeneous on $\mathbf{x}$, the proportion in a state should approximately equal the probability of being in that state.

Note that (1) implies

$$\frac{p_1(\infty)}{p_2(\infty)} = e^{(\alpha_{21} - \alpha_{12})'\mathbf{x}}; \quad (2)$$

or

$$\log \frac{p_1(\infty)}{p_2(\infty)} = \boldsymbol{\theta}'_{12}\mathbf{x}, \quad (3)$$

where $\boldsymbol{\theta}_{12} \equiv \boldsymbol{\alpha}_{21} - \boldsymbol{\alpha}_{12}$. Thus, this model implies that in the steady-state, the log of the odds of being in one state (e.g., unmarried) rather than in another state (married) is linear in $\mathbf{x}$. Equation (3) is the usual form of a binary logit model (Berkson, 1944; Theil, 1969, 1970), and if all members of $\mathbf{x}$ are dummy variables, then it is just a special case of Goodman's (1972a,b) log-linear model of the odds ratio. *Thus, when a population is in equilibrium, logit (or log-linear) analysis of cross-sectional data tells the difference in the effects of variables on the two rates, r_{12} and r_{21}*. Note that a variable can have "no effect" in the cross-sectional logit analysis because it has *equal* effects on the two rates. That is, it should *not* be taken as evidence that a variable is irrelevant to the process, only that it has no *net* effect on the steady-state distribution.

Even when the two-state process has reached a steady state so that logit and rate estimates should agree qualitatively, empirical estimates from the two procedures will normally differ. We illustrate this point with selected results from Robins, Tuma, and Yaeger's (1980) analyses of the employment histories of household

⟨10⟩ Cross-Sectional Analysis

heads in the Seattle and Denver Income Maintenance Experiments (SIME/DIME). In these analyses individuals were classified as being in one of two states, $1 \equiv$ employment and $2 \equiv$ nonemployment. Results pertaining to the effects of negative income tax (NIT) programs on employment are given in Table 10.1; further details and results pertaining to covariates used as control variables can be found in Robins, Tuma, and Yaeger (1980).

Columns (1) and (2) of Table 10.1 report the ML estimates of the effects of the NIT programs on the rates of leaving and entering employment, respectively. Note that these results indicate that the NIT programs significantly and substantially lower the rate of *entering* employment for husbands, wives, and unmarried women but usually have much smaller and often insignificant effects on the rate of *leaving* employment. These results imply that nonworking heads took much longer to return to work under an NIT program, and that working heads were prone to have somewhat shorter spells of working under an NIT program.

The estimated effects of the NIT programs on rates of entering and leaving employment reported in Table 10.1 along with the other estimated effects [see Robins, Tuma, and Yaeger (1980)] imply that a new steady state is approached closely within 2 years under a NIT program. So we contrast the effects of the NIT programs on the steady-state probability of employment that are predicted by the results in columns (1) and (2) of Table 10.1 with logit estimates of these effects based on an analysis of the cross-sectional data on employment 2 years after the start of SIME/DIME.

The steady-state probability of employment predicted by the analysis of effects of covariates on transition rates is given by equation (1) with $j = 1$ and $k = 2$. If α_{21m} is the effect of the NIT program on the rate of entering employment and α_{12m} is the effect of the NIT program on the rate of leaving employment, then the effect of the NIT program is predicted to be be $\theta_{12m} \equiv \alpha_{21m} - \alpha_{12m}$, where m stands for the variable denoting the NIT treatment. Assuming the model is correctly specified, this prediction should be asymptotically identical to the effect estimated in a logit analysis of cross-sectional data collected in the steady state. The estimated effect of the NIT program on the steady-state probability obtained from the rates, given in column (3) of Table 10.1, tends to be smaller than the logit estimate θ_{12m}, given in column (4). The logit estimates

Table 10.1. Estimated effects of an NIT program on employment of black and white husbands, wives, and unmarried female heads of families (estimated asymptotic standard errors in parentheses)[a]

	(1)	(2)	(3)	(4)
Husbands				
3-Year NIT program	0.129**	−0.109*	−0.238***	−0.330*
5-Year NIT program	0.135*	−0.493***	−0.628***	−0.721***
Wives				
3-Year NIT program	0.041	−0.356***	−0.397***	−0.527***
5-Year NIT program	0.173**	−0.343***	−0.516***	−0.450**
Unmarried female heads				
3-Year NIT program	0.189**	−0.410***	−0.599***	−0.614***
5-Year NIT program	0.108	−0.569***	−0.677***	−0.622***

*Significant at the .10 level.
**Significant at the .05 level.
***Significant at the .01 level.

[a] (1) = ML estimates of effects on the rate of leaving employment.
(2) = ML estimates of effects on the rate of entering employment.
(3) = (2) - (1) = Predicted effects on the steady-state probability of employment.
(4) = Logit estimates of effects on the probability of employment at the eighth experimental quarter.
For columns (1)–(3), $I = 2157$ for husbands, 2119 for wives, and 1617 for unmarried female heads. For column (4), $I = 1601$ for husbands, 1548 for wives, 1263 for unmarried female heads. Other covariates included in the models are predicted preexperimental net wage rate, preexperimental disposable income, weeks worked in the year prior to SIME/DIME, age in years, number of family members, number of children, years of schooling, and dummy variables for three manpower treatments, race, site, and six levels of normal preexperimental income.

range from 13% smaller to 86% larger than the predicted steady-state effects. In addition, standard errors are much larger (ranging from 49% to 107%) for the logit estimates than for the predicted steady-state effects. It is not surprising that the estimates obtained from the event-history analysis are more precise than the logit estimates because they are based on more information, the complete sample paths over 2 years.

The difference in the NIT effects on the rates of entering and leaving employment may differ from the logit estimate of the NIT effect for at least two reasons. First, the two analyses are based on somewhat different samples. The logit analysis used data on those who remained on the experiment for at least 2 years, and approximately one-fifth of the original sample had dropped out of the experiment before 2 years elapsed. Thus the sample size in the logit analysis was about 20% smaller than in the rate analyses. As we noted before, the ability to use partial information is a major advantage of event-history analysis. Second, 2 years after the start of the experiment may not be long enough for the proportion employed to reach its steady-state value under an NIT program. If so, the two analyses compare different probability measures. Based on other analyses not reported here, the second reason does not seem to be a likely explanation for the difference in the two estimated effects of the NIT program.

Is there a similar connection between the general, Ψ-state Markov model and multinomial logit analysis? Unfortunately, the answer is no, as can be proved by a single contrary case. Consider $\log[p_1(\infty)/p_2(\infty)]$ for the three-state model of marital status change with attrition, which we used in the empirical analyses reported in Chapters 6 and 7. Though both $p_1(\infty)$ and $p_2(\infty)$ are zero (because eventually everyone "attrites"), they do have a finite ratio. Inserting equation (31) in Chapter 4 into (21) in that chapter yields

$$\lim_{t \to \infty} \log \frac{p_1(t)}{p_2(t)} = \log \frac{r_{21} + p_1(0)[r_{23} + \lambda_2]}{r_{12} + [1 - p_1(0)][r_{13} + \lambda_2]}, \quad (4)$$

where

$$\lambda_2 \equiv -(r_{12} + r_{21}) - \sqrt{(r_{12} - r_{21})^2 + 4 r_{12} r_{21}}.$$

The expression on the right-hand side of (4) is quite complicated. Specifying that the rates are log-linear functions of x does not produce anything resembling a multinomial logit model.[1]

---

[1] If $r_{13} = r_{23}$, that is, attrition rates for married and unmarried women are identical, then (4) does simplify to (3).

However, an important class of Markov models—birth and death processes—do have a steady-state distribution that has the form of a multinomial logit model. In these models, states can be ordered so that only transitions between neighboring states can occur (e.g., in a three-state model transitions from 1 to 3 and from 3 to 1 are impossible). Then, for example, in a three-state model with ordered states, equations (2) and (3) continue to apply and, in addition,

$$\frac{p_2(\infty)}{p_3(\infty)} = e^{(\boldsymbol{\alpha}_{32} - \boldsymbol{\alpha}_{23})' \mathbf{x}} ; \qquad (5)$$

$$\log \frac{p_2(\infty)}{p_3(\infty)} = \boldsymbol{\theta}'_{23} \mathbf{x}, \qquad (6)$$

where $\boldsymbol{\theta}_{23} \equiv \boldsymbol{\alpha}_{32} - \boldsymbol{\alpha}_{23}$. Furthermore,

$$\frac{p_1(\infty)}{p_3(\infty)} = \frac{r_{32} r_{21}}{r_{12} r_{23}} = e^{(\boldsymbol{\alpha}_{32} - \boldsymbol{\alpha}_{21} - \boldsymbol{\alpha}_{12} - \boldsymbol{\alpha}_{23})' \mathbf{x}}. \qquad (7)$$

The similarity in form of (7) to (3) and (5) means that cross-sectional data provide no clues about how to order the states. Ordering states must be done on theoretical grounds, or else one must have event-history data, which reveal what kinds of transitions do occur. But when states are known to be ordered in a given way, cross-sectional multinomial analysis does allow conclusions about the *net* effect of a variable on transition rates between neighboring states.

If the steady state has not been reached, the logarithm of the odds of being in one state rather than another depends in a complicated way on time, the transition rates, and the initial conditions, even for the simplest two-state case.

What does it mean when variables have very different effects in cross-sectional analyses of comparable data collected two points in time? Has the underlying process changed, that is, has the relationship between variables and transition rates altered? Or has the system just moved closer to its ultimate steady-state value? These questions cannot be answered without temporal analyses of some kind.

As we discussed in Chapter 2, social scientists have been so wedded to cross-sectional analysis that they seldom seem to reflect

⟨10⟩ Cross-Sectional Analysis

on the likelihood that an equilibrium exists or on the length of time required for a system to reach a new equilibrium following some intervention or structural upheaval. We suspect that inertia greatly slows the speed with which most social systems reach equilibria. The equilibrium assumption implicit in sociological theories that were prominent a few decades ago (e.g., functionalism) began to be attacked more than a decade ago. But these criticisms have barely begun to penetrate sociological methodology.

To make our discussion of this issue more concrete, we refer to one of our empirical illustrations presented in Chapter 7, our research on the effects of NIT programs on marital stability. Many analysts faced with data on marital status during an experiment might conduct some sort of logit analysis that assumes that equilibrium is reached within the experimental period. But will the steady-state probability distribution of marital status be approached during a comparatively short experiment? As social experiments go, SIME/DIME is long—treatments last 3 or 5 years—so it might seem that equilibrium would be reached. However, according to the models we have discussed, how long it takes to approach a new steady state (say, to within .01 of its ultimate value) depends on both pre-experimental and experimental rates of marital status change. Our results imply that SIME/DIME is much too short for the steady state to be approached during the experimental period.

Marriage and dissolution rates are approximately equal to annual probabilities of forming and dissolving a marriage, respectively.[2] Among SIME/DIME's participants, who have incomes below the U.S. median, both rates are somewhat higher than in the overall U.S. population. In the environment facing the control group, $r_{12} = 0.10$ and $r_{21} = 0.05$ are fairly typical.[3] If an aggregate-level equilibrium exists at the beginning of the experiment, the initial probability of being unmarried is roughly $0.05/(0.10 + 0.05) = .333$.

---

[2]If there is no attrition, the probability of a change in marital status in Δt is $1 - \exp[-r_{jk}\Delta t]$; see equation (13) in Chapter 4. By a Taylor series expansion this is approximately $1 - (1 - r_{jk}\Delta t) = r_{jk}$. So when $\Delta t = 1$, the probability of a change is approximately r_{jk}.

[3]These numbers are obtained by rounding off the crude proportions of controls who marry (if initially unmarried) and end their marriages (if initially married) in the first year of the experiment.

Our published analyses (see Hannan, Tuma, and Groeneveld, 1977a) indicate that for whites the least generous NIT treatment in SIME/DIME had a negligible effect on marriage rates but roughly doubled the marital dissolution rate. If the dissolution rate under the NIT program is twice that of the controls, that is, if $r_{21} = 0.10$, then according to the two-state model the equilibrium probability of being unmarried under such an NIT program is $0.10/(0.10 + 0.10) = .50$. Thus the model predicts that under such conditions, the proportion of unmarried women in the population would eventually increase about 50% above its pre-NIT value (from .333 to .500). However, the proportion of unmarried women would increase only by about .04 (see Figure 10.1), or about 13%, in the first 2 years and by about .09, or about 26%, in the first 5 years. It would take nearly 19 years to be within .01 of the steady-state proportion. If data on marital status of participants at any point during the 3–5 years of the experiment are analyzed cross-sectionally, the ultimate effect of the NIT program will be greatly underestimated. As we show in the last section of this chapter (see especially Figure 10.1), the observed curves for guarantee levels do not suggest that a plateau or equilibrium has been reached within the first 2 years. The only way to decide whether a system is in equilibrium is to collect data over time and to analyze the time path of change.

10.2 Event-Count and Event-Sequence Analysis

We observed in Chapter 2 that a number of studies have analyzed the number of times that a particular event (e.g., a riot) occurs in some time period. We refer to this type of analysis as event-count analysis. Numerous surveys have asked such questions as, How many times have you been married? and How many times have you been divorced? However, we are not aware of any attempts to analyze counts of more than one type of event with a single model.

Given the Markov assumption, expressions for the expected number of different types of events in some time interval can be derived, as we outlined in Section 4.3. For example, in Chapter 4 we gave expressions for both a two-state, time-stationary semi-Markov model and for a three-state Markov model with an absorbing state. Such equations, combined with observed data on the counts of different types of events, permit transition rates to be estimated by a nonlinear regression approach. That is, rates, or the causal effects of variables on rates, can be estimated by minimizing the sum over all units of the squared deviation between the observed count of events for each unit and that predicted by the model. This approach, which we have not yet used, has one inherent limitation. We know of no theorem (comparable to the Gauss–Markov theorem in linear-regression analysis) that estimators obtained in this way have optimal statistical properties, even in an infinite sample.

ML estimators typically have optimal asymptotic properties. But to perform ML estimation one must know the probability mass function for the count of events. The expression for this function has apparently not yet been derived for a general Ψ-state Markov model. In fact, it is not even clear that it is possible to write such an expression in closed form for a general Ψ-state model.

Given these difficulties, it seems obvious that event-history analysis is preferable to event-count analysis, at least at present. Nevertheless, event-count analysis deserves further study. Under some circumstances, event counts either already exist or are feasible to collect, while event histories or panel data cannot be obtained.

When more than two states are studied, there is often more information that just event counts. For example, there may be counts of event sequences, the sequence of states through which each unit moves. The additional information on sequences is useful in testing models, as we remarked in Chapter 2. However, very little attention has been paid to methods for analyzing data gathered under this observation plan.

10.3 Panel Analysis

Panel data, which tell the states occupied by members of a sample at a series of discrete points in time, are the temporal data most often available to sociologists. Singer and Spilerman (1974, 1976a,b) and Singer and Cohen (1980) have identified a series of problems regarding estimation of transition rates in a Markov model from panel data. We pay special attention to these results. If the problems of inference are so difficult for such a comparatively simple process, surely they are worse when the underlying process is more complex.

First, sometimes panel data on categorical variables cannot be embedded in, that is, described by, a Markov process. This is not necessarily a fault if the data are not generated by such a process. However, sampling variability and measurement error can cause panel data to be unembeddable even though they are truly generated by a Markov process. We regard this as an inherent deficiency of panel data.

Second, even though the panel data may be describable by a Markov process, there may not be a *unique* matrix of transition rates that describe the data. Furthermore, the different matrices obtained in the nonunique cases may suggest substantially different qualitative conclusions (e.g., see Singer and Spilerman, 1976a, p. 31). Given proper specification of a stochastic model (an admittedly strong assumption), neither embeddability nor uniqueness is a problem in event-history analysis because ML estimators based on such data give unique estimates of rates, or of causal effects on rates.

Third, Singer and Spilerman (1976a, pp. 44–48) note that small changes in an observed matrix of transition probabilities (due to sampling variability or measurement error) can sometimes lead to very marked changes in estimates of transition rates. This is clearly undesirable. On the other hand, based on our experience in analyzing event histories, given a moderately large sample, fairly substantial errors in records on the occurrence or timing of events do not qualitatively alter estimated transition rates (see Section 10.5). Relative insensitivity to sampling and measurement error is, we believe, an important advantage of event-history analysis. Because such errors are unavoidable, the sensitivity issue clearly deserves further study—in both panel and event-history analysis.

Fourth, estimation of transition rates from panel data is also sensitive to the length of the time interval between waves of the panel. When the time interval is large, each row of the matrix of transition probabilities approaches the steady-state probability distribution [see equation (22) in Chapter 4]. In this situation there are only $(\Psi - 1)$ unique transition probabilities, rather than $\Psi(\Psi - 1)$. This means that the data contain no more information than cross-sectional data. On the other hand, if the time interval between waves of the panel is very short, almost all members of the sample are still in their original state. This is not very informative either. With event-history analysis the length of the observation period cannot be too long. It can be too short, if no events have occurred. And, as we reported in Chapter 5, rates can be estimated well when as few as

10% of the sample have had an event. We have not seen comparable results based on panel analysis, but it is unlikely to perform as well.

Fifth, we know of no way of estimating parameters from panel data when transition rates are functions of exogenous variables, as is almost always the case in problems of interest to sociologists. Singer and Spilerman (1974) reported some work on estimating parameters from panel data that are generated by a mixture of Markov processes, when the mixture is described by some specified probability distribution. This work is helpful, but it still does not permit causal inferences to be made.

A final problem with panel analysis concerns the ability to study and detect time dependence in the process generating events. This appears to present a very difficult problem for panel analysis. As we indicated in Chapters 7 and 8, various kinds of time dependence can readily be investigated through event-history analysis.

10.4 An Example: Formal Political Structure

We turn now to an empirical illustration that demonstrates further the differences between event-history analysis and the main alternatives discussed above. Unlike our previous empirical examples, this illustration concerns a *macrosociological* process: changes in formal political structure. It draws on the work of Hannan and Carroll (1981), which reports additional details. Because we know of no other applications of these methods to macrosociological issues, we consider this example at length to demonstrate the potential value of event-history analysis in the study of such issues.

We consider several arguments concerning trends toward centralist states, namely, one-party states and military regimes (Sartori, 1976). The literature on political development cites numerous causes for this trend, including both factors internal to nations and properties of the world system. Unfortunately, most research on these issues consists of case studies. We know of only one broadly comparative study that has applied multivariate methods of temporal analysis. Thomas, Ramirez, Meyer, and Gobalet (1979), whom we refer to as TRMG for short, used panel analysis to estimate the effects of measures of socioeconomic structure of nations, connections with the world system, period, and cohort on changes in centralism of state structure. The conventional methodology, used by TRMG, ignores information on sequences and timing of changes. We reanalyze the same data using the more powerful methods discussed in Chapters 4–9.

We concentrate on *formal centralism*, the degree to which formal authority is located in a single organization in society. We identify four forms of political organization:[4]

1. **Traditional no-party states**: states ruled by traditional rulers and traditional elites. These countries are usually monarchies (e.g., Libya, Jordan), and party organizations are illegal.
2. **Military regimes**: states ruled by the military, whether or not parties have been abolished. Military rule may be constitutional (e.g., Ghana) or not (e.g., Ethiopia).
3. **One-party states**: states with only one legal party represented in the legislature (e.g., China, Czechoslovakia, U.S.S.R.) and those with a single dominant party (e.g., Poland, Mexico, Iran).
4. **Multiparty states**: a residual category that includes states with two or more parties.

Data on political organization come from Banks (1977). He gave yearly reports on party structure for 140 nations and, in addition, reported the date of some changes (e.g., coups d'etat). We identify the time of a change with the year in which it occurs because finer detail on timing is available for only a fraction of all changes. The independent variables used in the analysis are:[5] gross

---

[4]The distinction between one-party and multiparty states sometimes breaks down. For example, India has been labeled a single party system (Duverger, 1968) although the opposition often mobilizes a substantial popular vote. We classified it as a multiparty state based on Sartori's (1976) suggestion that the criterion be average differences in election returns, which we took to be 40%. This same decision rule placed Iran in the one-party category. For countries in which election returns are unavailable, we used the classification given by Sartori (1976), Banks and Textor (1963), and Banks (1977).

[5]Sources for measures of these variables are as follows: per capita gross national product in 100,000 constant 1973 dollars (IBRDWT), population size in 100,000's (UNDY), ethnolinguistic diversity (Taylor and Hudson, 1971), urbanization (UNDY), educational enrollments (UNSY), and export-partner concentration (UNYITS). Recall that all variables are measured in the year beginning each episode. For episodes censored on the left, independent variables are measured in 1950.

⟨10⟩ An Example: Formal Political Structure

Table 10.2. Panel observations on political form, 1950–1975 (absolute frequency; relative frequency in the row in parentheses)

	1975				
	No party	Military	One party	Multiparty	Total
1950					
No party	1 (0.50)	1 (0.50)	0	0	2 (1.00)
Military	0	1 (0.33)	0	2 (0.67)	3 (1.00)
One party	0	1 (0.12)	6 (0.75)	1 (0.12)	8 (1.00)
Multiparty	0	9 (0.23)	2 (0.05)	28 (0.72)	39 (1.00)
Colony	1 (0.03)	14 (0.37)	15 (0.39)	8 (0.21)	38 (1.00)
Total	2	26	23	39	90

national product (GNP) per capita, population size, ethnolinguistic diversity (where a score of zero is complete homogeneity and a score of one indicates maximum possible heterogenity), urbanization, levels of enrollments in educational systems, date of independence, and export-partner concentration, a common measure of dependence in the world economy (see Chase-Dunn, 1975; Rubinson, 1976).

10.4.1 Panel Analysis

Table 10.2 presents the data in the form of a mobility table: political form in 1975 (the destination state) is cross-classified by political form in 1950 (the origin state). Over the 25-year period there is a sharp rise in the proportion of military regimes and one-party states. Indeed, 76% of the newly independent states have one of the two centralist forms in 1975.

We are mainly interested in testing hypotheses about the causes of these changes. Thus the data in Table 10.2 must be related in some fashion to measures of the various independent variables listed above. The existing literature suggests three strategies for analyzing such data.

Most current work on analyzing mobility tables like Table 10.2 uses log-linear models for counted data (e.g., see Hauser, 1977). These methods might be appropriate if our independent variables were categorical. However, our causal variables are metric, and we would lose much information by categorizing them.

The most common alternative to categorical analysis uses regression analysis or a close relative (e.g., logit analysis). Traditional procedures require that the outcome space be collapsed into dichotomies. TRMG followed this strategy. They collapsed tables like Table 10.2 in two ways. First, they created a dummy variable called state centralism, which combines states 1, 2, and 3 into one category. Second, they defined a dummy variable called military regime, which combines states 1, 3, and 4 into one category. Then they regressed each dummy variable on the lagged value of the same variable and on various measures of a country's socioeconomic structure.

This strategy has at least two defects. First, the analyses of the two dummy variables are not independent. Second, this method does not deal with the constraints on discrete outcomes (see Hanushek and Jackson, 1977, Chapter 7, for a discussion of these problems). Both defects can be remedied by using multivariate logit or probit analysis procedures for multiple, discrete outcomes (polytomies); see Nerlove and Press (1973) or Heckman (1981). We do not advocate use of this strategy for the problem at hand because of the weaknesses of panel analysis that we discussed earlier.

10.4.2 Counts of Transitions

Table 10.3 reports counts of all observed transitions. Not surprisingly, Table 10.3 gives the impression of much greater flux than Table 10.2. For instance, the counts on the main diagonal are much smaller in Table 10.3 than in Table 10.2. According to Table 10.2, 72% of the countries with multiparty systems in 1950 have the same form in 1975. Based on Table 10.3, only 49% of the states with multiparty systems in 1950 have the same form continuously. In addition, the distribution of initial forms for states becoming independent after 1950 differs considerably from their distribution in 1975 (compare the bottom rows of the two tables).

10.4.3 Event Sequences

Table 10.3 does not tell which multistep patterns of change occur most commonly. This gap is filled by Table 10.4, which records

⟨10⟩ An Example: Formal Political Structure

Table 10.3. Counts of transitions between political forms, 1950–1975 (absolute frequency; relative frequency in parentheses)[a]

	Destination				
	No party	Military	One party	Multiparty	Total
Origin					
No party	2 (0.50)	1 (0.25)	0	1 (0.25)	4 (1.00)
Military	0	22 (0.48)	7 (0.15)	17 (0.37)	46 (1.00)
One party	0	18 (0.47)	19 (0.50)	1 (0.03)	38 (1.00)
Multiparty	1 (0.01)	31 (0.39)	9 (0.11)	39 (0.49)	80 (1.00)
Colony	1 (0.03)	1 (0.03)	16 (0.42)	20 (0.53)	38 (1.00)
Total	4	73	51	78	206

[a]Observations on the main diagonal have had no change in state by 1975; these are right-censored observations.

the 30 distinct sequences that occurred in the data. The two most frequent patterns are a stable multiparty state and a change from colonial status to a multiparty state. Movements back and forth between a multiparty state and a military regime are also common.

If the parameters of the underlying stochastic process do not vary across countries, that is, countries are homogeneous, event sequences can be used directly to test among classes of models. For example, Singer (1980) showed how to test the Markov property using straightforward conditional probability arguments; see also Billingsley (1961) and Goodman (1968).

Simple calculations suggest that moves between a multiparty state and a military regime involve a higher-order state dependence. Table 10.3 reports that the probability of moving from state 4 to state 2 is .39 and that the probability of moving from state 2 to state 4 is .37. Under the Markov assumption the probability of the

Table 10.4. Counts of various sequences of political forms for the period 1950–1975, by form in 1950[a]

\multicolumn{2}{c}{No party}	\multicolumn{2}{c}{Military}	\multicolumn{2}{c}{One party}	\multicolumn{2}{c}{Multiparty}	\multicolumn{2}{c}{Colony}
#	Seq.	#	Seq.	#	Seq.	#	Seq.	#	Seq.
1	12	1	2424	5	3	22	4	1	51
1	141	1	24242	1	32	6	42	1	52
		1	2434	1	323	1	423232	8	53
				1	234	4	424	6	532
						1	4242	1	53232
						1	42423	1	5323232323
						1	42424	8	54
						1	424242	4	542
						1	4242424	1	5423
						1	43	5	543
								2	5432

[a] See Hannan and Carroll (1981) for the names of the countries with each sequence.

two-step move 4 → 2 → 4 equals .39(.37) = .14. According to Table 10.4 there are 16 such two-step moves and 31 moves from 4 to 2. Thus the empirical probability of a 4 → 2 → 4 move is 16/31 = .52, much higher than that predicted under the Markov assumption. If the population is indeed homogeneous, the Markov assumption should be rejected. However, because we think the countries are heterogeneous, the Markov property cannot be tested quite so simply. The apparent dependence on history may partially reflect the continued operation of stable causal variables. Unfortunately, there are not enough cases to test the Markov property when measures of social structure are controlled.

10.4.4 Event-History Analysis

Next we conduct event-history analysis using methods discussed in earlier chapters. We assume causal variables affect rates in the following general way:

$$r_{jk}(t) = e^{\alpha'_{jk} \mathbf{x}(\tau_0)},$$

where τ_0 denotes the first time that a country is observed. We wish to estimate α_{jk}, the effects of observed variables on transition rates.

⟨ 10 ⟩   An Example: Formal Political Structure

Our estimation procedures varied in two ways. First, we estimated causal effects using PL (see Chapter 8) as well as ML (see Chapter 5) because rates of change among political forms may well vary over historical time.[6] With the available data, however, the two sets of estimates turn out to be very similar, perhaps because of the high degree of censoring in the data (see the discussion in Section 8.3). Consequently, we report only the ML estimates here; both sets of estimates are given in Hannan and Carroll (1981). Second, we estimated models using all episodes recorded in the data and using only the first episode observed for each state. A necessary condition for pooling data on all episodes is that the Markov property hold, which seems questionable in this instance. We report analyses using data on both the first episode and all episodes because data are too scanty for extensive non-Markovian analyses. If results of the two analyses differ substantially, we conclude that qualitative conclusions regarding causal effects will be misleading unless higher-order dependencies are taken into account.[7] We find that results for the two sets of data agree broadly, though less closely than ML and PL estimates for the same set of data. Consequently, we report results for analyses of both sets of data.

10.4.5 Estimated Rates from Event Histories

We begin by reporting in Table 10.5 the ML estimates of transition rates assuming both population homogeneity and time independence to allow comparison with the proportions in Tables 10.2 and 10.3. The top half of Table 10.5 gives rates based on all episodes; the bottom half reports rates based only on the first episode. Changes from military to multiparty, from multiparty to military, and from one party to military have the highest off-diagonal entries in Table 10.3 and also in Table 10.5. The rates of flow into military (first column in Table 10.5) are relatively high, but the rates

---

[6]This comparison gives only a rough indication of the problem. If the process is indeed non-Markovian, even the analysis of first episodes is misspecified due to the omission of the relevant historical data.

[7]We also estimated models with explicit time dependence (the Gompertz model discussed in Chapter 7), which takes into account changes in levels of independent variables during spells. We do not report results of these analyses because the fit of these models was not significantly better than the fit in simpler models.

Table 10.5. Maximum-likelihood estimates of rates of transitions among political forms, assuming time-stationarity and population homeogeneity

	Destination				
Origin	No party	Military	One party	Multiparty	Any change
All episodes (192)					
No party		0.016	0	0.033	0.049
Military	0		0.028	0.071	0.099
One party	0	0.046		0.002	0.048
Multiparty	0.001	0.033	0.009		0.043
First episodes (90)					
No party		0.022	0	0.002	0.024
Military	0		0	0.077	0.077
One party	0	0.034		0	0.034
Multiparty	0	0.024	0.009		0.033

of flow out (first rows of each half) are even higher. Flows out of multiparty are larger than flows in, which are indeed quite small.

Notice that the data on timing of events affect conclusions. In Table 10.3, which ignores timing, the percentages of flows from multiparty to military and back are fairly similar. In Table 10.4 the corresponding rates are quite different; the rate of flow from military to multiparty is more than twice as large as the reverse.

Table 10.5 lets us evaluate Huntington's (1968) claims about the relative stability of political forms.[8] He argued that one-party states are inherently more stable than no-party, military, and multiparty states, which lack the institutional support necessary for stability. Huntington also claimed that multiparty states are more likely than one-party states to experience military coups. The two-wave panel data in Table 10.2 appear to support these assertions: one-party states most frequently retain their form (compare entries on

---

[8]Huntington's argument distinguishes between two-party and multiparty systems. Other analyses based on his distinction do not yield substantially different conclusions.

the diagonal) and became military regimes in 1975 only half as often as multiparty states (relative frequency of .12 versus .23). But these appearances are deceiving; they arise solely because panel data lack important information, as can be seen by comparing the results in Tables 10.2 and 10.5.

Consider first the relative stability of different political forms. Summing the rates of all types of changes for a given origin form gives the rate of *any change* in form, which is reported in the last column of Table 10.5. A higher rate of any change in a form means that the form is less stable. Not surprisingly, military regimes are much more likely to undergo a change in form than any other type. The multiparty state is the most stable based on the analysis of all episodes and the second most stable based on the analysis of first episodes. The one-party state appears to be slightly less stable than the multiparty state in both analyses, though the differences in stability are quite small. In any case, Huntington's claim for greater stability of one-party states is not supported. One-party states seem no more stable than multiparty and no-party states, and perhaps somewhat less stable.

Next consider Huntington's claim that multiparty states are more susceptible to military coups than one-party states. The results in Table 10.5 again dispute Huntington's assertion. The rate of change to a military regime is roughly 40% higher in one-party states than in multiparty states, according to both the all-episode and first-episode analyses.

The main point of these comparisons is that panel analysis and transition-rate analyses do not always lead to the same conclusions. The specific conclusions discussed above must be regarded as tentative. The number of observations is not large. More importantly, the analyses in both Tables 10.2 and 10.5 make no attempt to control for differences in the social and economic position of the countries. To rectify this deficiency, we turn next to causal analysis of transition rates.

10.4.6 Causal Analysis

TRMG sought to evaluate two alternative explanations of the sources of state centralism. One account, following the lead of Lipset (1960), focuses on the existence of cultural rules and modernizing institutions that prepare individuals for effective political participation. Institutional arrangements that produce modern political capacities include a productive industrial economy, urbanization, modern schooling, and so forth. The first account expects oppositional politics (i.e., multiparty states) to be more effective and stable in nations with such characteristics.

The second argument, favored by TRMG, focuses on institutional rules and power relations in the modern world system. It holds that modern states must increase productivity to meet expectations of the modern world system. Poor countries face intense pressure to modernize and resort to centralist strategies to speed economic growth. But according to this argument, urbanization, modern schooling, and other modernizing experiences do not affect rates of political change when per capita GNP and dependence are controlled. TRMG also argued that ethnic diversity challenges claims of a unitary national identity. The resulting "moral boundary crisis" generates the need for symbols of unitary national authority. A centralist state is one solution to such a need (see Wallerstein, 1966).

The panel regressions of TRMG reveal consistent negative effects of per capita GNP on each of their measures of state centralism. This finding does not help to distinguish between the modernization and world-system arguments because both predict that national wealth retards tendencies towards centralism. TRMG reported no evidence of other modernizing experiences (e.g., urbanization and schooling) affecting centralism. Since they found that two measures of national dependence (export-partner concentration and investment dependence) significantly increase centralism, they concluded that the data favor the world-system perspective.

Here we investigate the effects of most of the independent variables used by TRMG.[9] Like them, we study the 1950–1975 period, but we do not collapse categories of political forms. Some differences between our analysis and theirs may reflect this difference, as we discuss further below. But we think that our results diverge from those of TRMG largely because we used event-history analysis rather than panel analysis.

We begin with simple models and gradually increase complexity. First we estimate effects on overall rates of stability, ignoring

---

[9]We could not measure dependence (used by TRMG) for enough countries to include it in our analyses.

⟨10⟩ An Example: Formal Political Structure

Table 10.6. Maximum-likelihood estimates of effects of explanatory variables on the rate of any change in political form (standard errors in parentheses)

	All episodes	First episodes
Intercept	−2.765***	−1.917***
	(0.6963)	(0.3903)
Per capita GNP	−0.0023***	−0.0030***
	(0.0006)	(0.0008)
Population size	−0.0006*	−0.0012*
	(0.0003)	(0.0007)
Ethnic diversity	0.9642**	−0.0672
	(0.4727)	(0.5334)
Region	a	b

*Significant at the .10 level.
**Significant at the .05 level.
***Significant at the .01 level.

[a]Includes region effects, jointly significant at the .10 level.
[b]Excludes region effects, not jointly significant at the .10 level.

origin and destination. Then we consider effects on rates of movement *out of* particular forms (ignoring destination) and then on rates of movement *into* particular forms (ignoring origin). These analyses are less useful than a complete analysis of each kind of transition. Unfortunately, the sample is too small to estimate causal effects on twelve distinct transition rates reliably.

Effects on Instability. Only four of the variables examined had significant effects on the rate of instability: per capita GNP, population size, ethnic diversity, and region (a set of dummy variables). Table 10.6 gives the relevant findings. Both per capita GNP and population size decrease the rate of political instability. These estimated effects are quite substantial. For example, the coefficient of per capita GNP (−0.0023 in the first column of Table 10.6) implies that the rate of political instability is five times greater in a country with a per capita GNP of $300 than in one with a per capita GNP of $1000.

Comparison of analyses using first and all episodes reveal similar estimates for the effect of per capita GNP, but slightly different estimates for the effect of population size. Both effects are larger in the analysis of first episodes. Ethnic diversity has strong and significant effects in the analysis of all episodes but an insignificant effect in the analysis of first episodes. This finding suggests that ethnically diverse countries contribute disproportionately to *multiple* changes of political form. It does not, however, appear to affect the rate of *ever* changing political forms. This difference in the findings of the two analyses may also mean that the Markov assumption is not appropriate here.[10] Given this divergence of findings, we concentrate on the analysis of first episodes below.

Effects on Movement out of Specific States. Next we repeated analyses like those in Table 10.6 but distinguished between states with different forms before a change. The analysis of TRMG suggests that the effect of wealth depends strongly on the original political form. They found that richer nations are less likely to move out of noncentralist forms and more likely to move out of centralist forms. Our results, reported in Table 10.7, are quite different. High levels of per capita GNP stabilize one-party states more than multiparty states. National wealth has small and insignificant effects on rates of movement out of military regimes.

Effects on Entering Categories. Next we examine effects on flows into the four forms and ignore the initial political form. The relevant findings appear in Table 10.8. These results support the arguments of TRMG. Per capita GNP has a negative impact on rates of movement into both centralist forms, military regimes and one-party states.

The most striking effect in Table 10.8 is the impact of ethnic diversity on flows into the one-party form. Consider the smaller estimate of this effect (bottom half of table). It implies that for

---

[10] It may also mean that we misspecified the causal structure or that rates are time dependent (with some form other than the Gompertz, which we estimated). Still, the most likely explanation for the difference between first- and all-episode analyses is that political systems have "memory," that states tend to return to previous political forms, ceteris paribus. For example, countries with a multiparty regime and a history of military rule may be more likely to return to military rule. Such historical effects are inconsistent with the Markovian specification used here.

⟨10⟩ An Example: Formal Political Structure

Table 10.7. Maximum-likelihood estimates of effects of explanatory variables on the rate of change from a specific political form (standard errors in parentheses)

	Origin		
	Military	One party	Multiparty
All episodes			
Intercept	−1.159 (1.518)	−1.793** (0.7278)	−1.959*** (0.3904)
Per capita GNP	−0.0010 (0.0013)	−0.0053** (0.0024)	−0.0030*** (0.0008)
Population size	−0.0004 (0.0008)	−0.0012 (0.0013)	−0.0013** (0.0006)
Ethnic diversity	0.9231 (0.8993)	0.1191 (0.8506)	1.116** (0.5249)
Region	a	b	b
First episodes			
Intercept	c	−1.929 (1.592)	−1.839*** (0.4493)
Per capita GNP	c	−0.0040 (0.0036)	−0.0031*** (0.0010)
Population size	c	−0.0036 (0.0052)	−0.0018 (0.0009)
Ethnic diversity	c	−2.796*** (1.069)	0.7989 (0.6162)
Region	c	a	b

*Significant at the .10 level.
**Significant at the .05 level.
***Significant at the .01 level.

[a] Includes region effects, jointly significant at the .10 level.
[b] Excludes region effects, not jointly significant at the .10 level.
[c] A model with region effects could not be estimated.

Table 10.8. Maximum-likelihood estimates of effects of explanatory variables on the rate of change to a specific political form (standard errors in parentheses)

	Destination		
	Military	One party	Multiparty
All episodes			
Intercept	−2.366***	−5.332***	−4.920***
	(0.3545)	(0.9668)	(1.393)
Per capita GNP	−0.0027***	−0.0026*	−0.0016
	(0.0007)	(0.0016)	(0.8885)
Population	−0.0009*	−0.0021	−0.0004
	(0.0005)	(0.0016)	(0.0005)
Ethnic diversity	−0.0149	3.257***	1.659*
	(0.4887)	(1.200)	(0.9823)
Region	b	b	a
First episodes			
Intercept	−1.725***	−4.494***	−3.666***
	(0.4276)	(0.6401)	(0.3132)
Per capita GNP	−0.0036***	−0.0011*	0.0002*
	(0.0010)	(0.0006)	(0.0001)
Population	−0.0011	−0.0002	−0.0001
	(0.0008)	(0.0003)	(0.0002)
Ethnic diversity	−0.8696	2.023***	−0.4519
	(0.6095)	(0.8504)	(0.6041)
Region	b	b	b

*Significant at the .10 level.
**Significant at the .05 level.
***Significant at the .01 level.

[a]Includes region effects, jointly significant at the .10 level.
[b]Excludes region effects, not jointly significant at the .10 level.

countries close to the mean level of ethnic diversity (0.5), the rate of flow into a one-party form is more than 2.5 times larger than in those with complete cultural and linguistic homogeneity. For countries close to the maximum level of ethnic diversity (scores of .9), the estimated rate is 6 times larger than the rate for completely homogeneous countries (scores of zero). Apparently ethnic diversity exerts a very strong pressure to change toward one-party rule.

Discussion. Our general findings regarding the effects of per capita GNP agree with the panel regressions of TRMG in one respect but disagree in another. The two analyses agree with respect to effects on movement toward centralism. Richer countries are less likely than poor ones to move from multiparty states to one-party or military rule. However, the literature does not anticipate our findings concerning political stability. We find that countries with high per capita GNP have greater political stability, *whatever their form*. Successful countries seem to retain their political strategies. This conclusion gives a very different image of the process underlying changes in political structure and calls into question the world-system arguments advanced by TRMG. Furthermore, it contradicts Huntington's (1968) claim that sustained modernization threatens the one-party system.

Because panel regressions and event-history analysis yield qualitatively different findings for these issues, the choice between these two methods makes an important substantive difference. We think that dynamic methods make better use of available data and provide a sounder footing for substantive conclusions.

10.5 How Well Do These Models Fit?

Markov models have a reputation for fitting data poorly. But our extensions of the Markov model should have helped to improve the ability of this model to fit sociological data. In previous chapters we have used likelihood ratio tests to assess the relative fit of a series of nested models. We have learned that some models do not improve on others. Here we consider absolute fit and compare our modeling strategy with a common alternative.

Three main questions are involved in assessing a dynamic model: (1) To what extent do predictions based on the model differ systematically from observed values? (2) If there are systematic differences, are they related to observed exogenous variables, causing us to make erroneous inferences about effects of these variables on a particular outcome? (3) As compared with approaches that seek to minimize prediction errors for a single observable variable, how well does a dynamic model explain sample variation in observable outcomes related to the process being studied?

Obviously the fit of a dynamic model cannot be evaluated outside of the context of a particular substantive problem to which the model has been applied. The modeling strategies we have discussed in Chapters 4 through 9 may fit data on some phenomena well, but not fit others. Our intent here is to show that dynamic analysis based on a Markov model that includes the extensions we have suggested *can* fit data well. We focus again on our dynamic analysis of the effects of NIT programs on marital stability (see Chapter 7). The model used is an extension of the ARL (alternating renewal and loss) model described in Section 4.4, in which "married" and "not married" are two nonabsorbing states and "attrition from the sample" is a third absorbing state.

In answering the questions listed above within the context of this substantive problem, we consider three kinds of outcomes: the probability of being in a given state (e.g., single) at any moment, the expected number of marriages and marital dissolutions in any given time interval, and the probability of leaving the original marital status in some time period. The extended ARL model implies that each of these is a function of marriage, dissolution, and attrition rates [see equations (29)–(31) in Chapter 4]. Thus we can predict each woman's rates of marriage, marital dissolution, and attrition from knowledge of her guarantee level and her values on other causal variables and from the estimated effects of these variables. Using the predicted rates we can predict the kinds of outcomes listed above. We chose to consider these outcomes at two arbitrary times: 1 and 2 years after the start of the experiment. For each woman studied in our analysis of transition rates, we retrieved the observed outcomes listed in Table 10.9. These variables were not used directly in estimating transition rates; nor, of course, are they independent of those data, which is the reason for having a single model. We also predicted outcomes for each woman using the estimated effects from one-period models of remarriage and attrition and a two-period model of marital dissolution (see Tuma, Hannan, and Groeneveld, 1979, for the estimated effects). The model of dissolution was similar

⟨10⟩ How Well Do These Models Fit?

Table 10.9. Selected outcomes pertaining to marital stability of white women in SIME/DIME: observed values and those predicted by ML estimates of an ARL model of change in marital status and by linear regression [adapted from Tuma, Hannan, and Groeneveld (1979)]

Outcome[a]	Sample size[b]	Sample mean	ARL model Mean residual	ARL model R^2	Linear regression R^2	Linear regression ΔR^2
Single at $t=1$	1917	0.351	−0.005	0.675	0.664	0.011
Single at $t=2$	1917	0.350	0.002	0.500	0.481	0.019
Married at $t=1$	1917	0.598	0.011	0.631	0.627	0.003
Married at $t=2$	1917	0.540	−0.004	0.439	0.428	0.011
Attrited at $t=1$	1917	0.050	−0.006	0.008	0.010	−0.002
Attrited at $t=2$	1917	0.111	0.002	0.025	0.023	0.002
Number of dissolutions, $t=1$	1917	0.050	−0.002	0.050	0.043	0.007
Number of dissolutions, $t=2$	1917	0.109	−0.001	0.083	0.068	0.015
Number of marriages, $t=1$	1917	0.046	0.002	0.111	0.087	0.024
Number of marriages, $t=2$	1917	0.086	−0.006	0.138	0.109	0.029
Always single to $t=1$	705	0.848	0.004	0.069	0.072	−0.003
Always single to $t=2$	705	0.740	0.020	0.092	0.089	0.003
Always married to $t=1$	1212	0.885	0.016	0.022	0.029	−0.007
Always married to $t=2$	1212	0.768	0.017	0.044	0.045	−0.001

[a] The observed variables are dummy (0 or 1) variables, except for the variables giving the numbers of marital events.

[b] There were 705 initially single white women and 1212 initially married white women, giving a total of 1917 white women.

to the one discussed in Section 7.2, but the observation period was 2 years rather than 5 years.

To detect systematic differences between observed values and predictions, we report the mean residual for each outcome, that is, the mean difference between observed and predicted variables. We also report the observed mean of each outcome because the relative size of a systematic difference is of some interest too. With predictions from a linear regression model, the mean residual would be zero.

This need not be the case with predictions based on the extended ARL model. The results in Table 10.9 show that the mean residuals for predictions based on the extended ARL model are usually small in both absolute (the largest is 0.02) and relative terms. There is little indication of any overall pattern in these differences, except for the last four dummy variables, which have consistently positive mean residuals. It is well known that no change in status has tended to be underpredicted in sociological applications of Markov models (e.g., see Blumen, Kogan, and McCarthy, 1955). Our introduction of population heterogeneity has made this a comparatively small problem, but it has not erased it entirely.

Small mean residuals could hide systematic differences associated with different treatments, which is clearly undesirable if differences between outcomes for controls and for those on financial treatments are of interest. To answer the second question, we performed one-way analysis of variance (ANOVA) on the residuals for each outcome. Treatment differences in the residuals never even approached statistical significance. (The smallest probability level was greater than .50.)

In addressing the third question, we focus on a single, common, inexpensive alternative—linear regression analysis. We regressed each observed outcome on the prediction from the extended ARL model; we also regressed each of the 14 outcomes on initial marital status, treatments, and other causal variables used in our analysis of the transition rates. For both the extended ARL model and the regression model we report R^2, the square of the correlation between the observed and predicted variables. Because we expected a poorer fit from the extended ARL model than from one designed to minimize errors, we were surprised to find that the extended ARL model explains the sample variation better than the linear regression model for 10 of the 14 outcomes. Moreover, the advantage of the extended ARL model in these 10 cases tends to be larger than the advantage of linear regression in the other 4.

Though we have considered the predictions of the extended ARL model for several outcomes at two arbitrary times, we have not yet seen how well it predicts the time path of these outcomes. Computational expense forced us to examine the time path of only one outcome. We selected the proportion who were not married at time t, conditional on not having been lost through attrition by time

⟨10⟩   How Well Do These Models Fit?   325

t. We chose this outcome because it is similar to the most important policy outcome; because it should reveal whether experimental effects are confined to an initial, brief adjustment period; and because it depends about equally on estimates of marriage, dissolution, and attrition rates. Since this prediction requires estimates of all four rates of change (r_{12}, r_{13}, r_{21}, r_{23}), it provides a severe test of our method.

Figure 10.1 gives observed and predicted curves for this outcome by guarantee level. Points on the observed curve are given by $I_{j1}(t)/[1 - I_{j3}(t)]$, where $I_{j1}(t)$ and $I_{j3}(t)$ are the number in treatment j at time t who are unmarried and lost through attrition, respectively. Points on the predicted curves are calculated as

$$\frac{1}{I_j} \sum_{i=1}^{I_j} \frac{p_{ij1}(t)}{1 - p_{ij3}(t)},$$

where $I_j \equiv I_{j1}(0) + I_{j2}(0)$ (the initial number in treatment j), and $p_{ij1}(t)$ and $p_{ij3}(t)$ are calculated for each woman i enrolled in treatment j using equations (31b) and (31c) in Chapter 4, respectively. Predictions are based on the one-period models of remarriage and attrition and on the two-period model of dissolution; they assume each woman has her assigned treatment.

We begin by considering the observed (squiggly) curves. First, note that the proportion of unmarried women at the start of the experiment differs greatly from one treatment to another. These initial differences result from the use of a stratified random design in which marital status was a stratification variable. Unmarried women were more likely to be assigned to treatments with a lower guarantee level. Because of this, a comparison of "post-test" levels of marital status is clearly inappropriate.

Next, notice that the observed curve for the control group is relatively flat, suggesting that there are no important "natural" time trends (e.g., due to aging or secular change). However, the observed curves for the three guarantee levels show noticeable increases in the conditional proportion of unmarried women after 2 years (+.039 for the low guarantee, +.044 for the medium guarantee, and +.031 for the high guarantee versus +.009 for the control group). Furthermore, the proportion of unmarried women among those on the financial treatment rises fairly steadily throughout the 2-year period. This

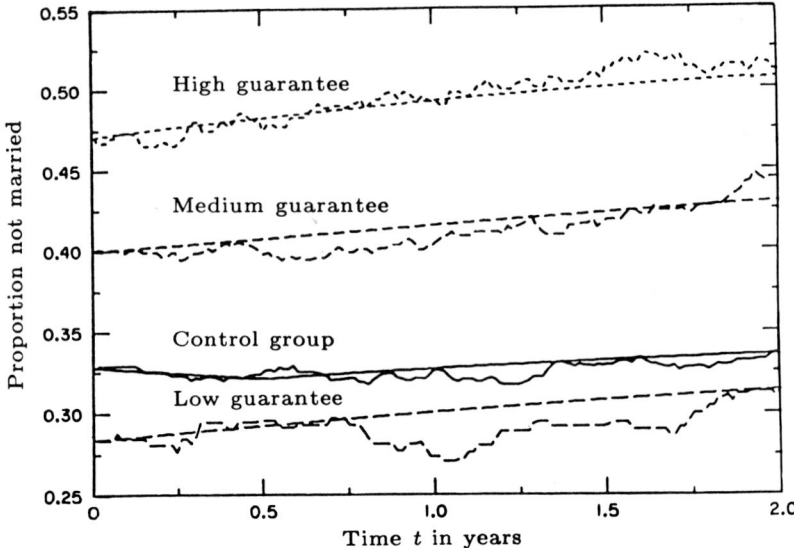

Figure 10.1. Observed and predicted proportions of white women who are not married at time t, conditional on not having been lost through attrition by time t, by the level of the NIT guarantee. From Tuma, Hannan, and Groeneveld (1979).

upward trend is quite apparent for the low and medium guarantees. It is less certain for the high guarantee, which has the fewest subjects and the most extreme fluctuations about any overall time trend. There is little evidence that the proportion of unmarried women among those on financial treatments has reached a plateau within the first 2 years of the experiment, as one would expect if an equilibrium was attained during this period. This suggests that dynamic analysis is really needed to assess experimental effects accurately.

Next consider the fit between the (smooth) curves predicted by the extended ARL model and the actual (squiggly) curves. We rely on visual inspection to compare the two sets of curves. On the whole, the fit is quite good except for the high-guarantee group, for which the actual curve is noticeably below the predicted curve. Because only 240 women are in the high-guarantee group, a change in status of a very few women makes a substantial difference in the observed curve. Hence the deviations for this group are less worrisome

⟨ 10 ⟩   Conclusions

than they would be for a large group like the controls ($I = 847$).

Our scrutiny of the implications of the extended ARL model for various outcomes at arbitrary times has revealed no major disadvantages and even some small advantages. The model's primary advantage is, of course, its ability to predict the time path of a variety of interdependent outcomes reasonably well.

10.6   Conclusions

Our conclusions are simple. Event histories provide rich opportunities for answering fundamental sociological questions. We have shown how to analyze event histories when data are available on the timing of events. The procedures we have discussed permit analysis of causal effects on the rates at which events occur and of time dependence in such rates. These procedures are simple to implement and in our empirical application they yield good predictions about a variety of observable variables.

Event-history analysis offers important advantages over other common approaches to the study of causal effects on changes in qualitative variables. In many situations it is no more difficult to obtain information on the timing of events than the count of events. Consequently, we urge that sociologists collect and analyze such data.

Part III
Quantitative Outcomes

11
Linear Deterministic Models

This is the first in a series of chapters that consider models of change in **quantitative variables**, such as wealth, academic achievement, organizational size, intensity of intergroup hostility, and so forth. The term *quantitative* denotes variables that may take on a continuum of values, usually any real number (or vector), but sometimes only a nonnegative real number (or vector). Usually sociologists have no real interest in any *particular* level of such variables. Still, following Lazarsfeld's lead, they have tended to collapse information on a continuum into a few broad categories, for example, to break the wealth distribution at the median or into quintiles. This tendency has waned as methods for analyzing models based on **linear structural equations** have become popular. Sociologists are now more prone to analyze the joint distribution of quantitative variables. The structural-equation approach has concentrated almost completely on such analyses. For an overview of structural-equation methods, see Duncan (1975).

Structural-equation methods are not inherently static. Indeed, they are routinely used to test dynamic hypotheses in the fields in which they were developed, biometrics and macroeconomics. Nonetheless, sociological applications of such methods have been almost wholly static. Even when sociologists analyze quantitative data over time, they rarely focus on the *process* of change. Instead, they tend to relate levels of variables pertaining to different time periods in much the same way that they relate variables measured at the same period.

Many sociologists use models that are implicitly dynamic to analyze panel data (e.g., they often use lagged values of dependent variables as covariates) but seek to answer only static questions. Until recently, Coleman (1964a, 1968) was the only sociologist to propose specific continuous-time models for the empirical study of change in quantitative outcomes. His strategy has now begun to influence empirical research by sociologists, as we mentioned in Chapter 2. This strategy seems to have broad applicability in sociological research. We think that it will influence sociological analysis even more if it incorporates insights and procedures from the structural-equation tradition. This and the remaining chapters in Part III attempt to join the dynamic and structural-equation perspectives. We begin with an overview of models of change in quantitative outcomes.

Ultimately we want to unify sociological methods for analyzing change in qualitative and quantitative outcomes. Here we encounter a major stumbling block. Our treatment of discrete outcomes in Part II was resolutely probabilistic: randomness enters as a defining characteristic of fundamental processes. In contrast, both static and dynamic models for quantitative variables in social scientific applications are usually deterministic; randomness enters only to account for imperfect fit or improper measurement. That is, probabilistic considerations are ignored in the model-building stage. One adds a disturbance term with some assumed probability distribution to an otherwise deterministic model only when estimation begins.

There is an obvious way to make treatment of the two kinds of variables compatible—formulate probabilistic models of change in quantitative variables. This way may be obvious, but it is certainly not simple, even for an elementary treatment. Rather than jump at once into this technical discussion, we first survey linear deterministic models. Many fundamental issues arising in stochastic models of change in quantitative variables are revealed in analogous deterministic models. In the next chapter we compare the advantages of deterministic and stochastic models and discuss some issues that do not arise in the deterministic case.

11.1 Linear Models for Rates of Change

Structural-equation analysis as practiced in sociology translates substantive propositions into **algebraic equations**, that is, equations that express the level of one variable in terms of the levels of other variables. Extensive experience in other disciplines suggests a different mathematical structure for dynamic analysis. The alternative strategy builds substantive arguments into **differential equations** (**DEs** for short), that is, equations that relate rates of change in one variable to levels (and perhaps rates of change) in others.[1] This section explores possible sociological interpretations of **deterministic differential equations** (**DDEs** for short) for quantitative variables.

To help bridge the gap between static and dynamic models, we begin with dynamic models that imply the usual structural-equation models in a steady state. In structural-equation models, the typical equation (excluding the disturbance term) has the form

$$y = \boldsymbol{\theta}'\mathbf{x}, \qquad (1)$$

where $\mathbf{x}$ is an $M + 1$ by 1 vector whose leading element is unity and $\boldsymbol{\theta}$ an $M + 1$ by 1 vector whose leading element is the intercept (constant term). A dynamic model that implies the relationship in (1) in a steady state is

$$\frac{\mathrm{d}y(t)}{\mathrm{d}t} = c\, y(t) + \mathbf{b}'\mathbf{x}. \qquad (2)$$

The relationship between the static and dynamic models, equations (1) and (2), can be seen by setting equation (2) equal to zero (the condition that holds in equilibrium—see Section 11.6) and solving for the equilibrium value, y^e:

$$y^e = -\frac{1}{c}\mathbf{b}'\mathbf{x}. \qquad (3)$$

Comparison of equations (1) and (3) shows that the parameters of the static model, $\boldsymbol{\theta}$, are composites of the parameters of the underlying dynamic model, $\mathbf{b}$ and c:

$$\boldsymbol{\theta} \equiv -\frac{1}{c}\mathbf{b}.$$

---

[1] We assume that a continuous-time framework is natural for modeling sociological processes (see the discussion in Chapters 2 and 4). If outcomes change at fixed intervals, difference equations should be used instead of the DEs discussed in this and succeeding chapters.

The relationship between the two sets of parameters is reminiscent of the relationship between reduced-form and structural parameters in a static structural-equation model.

Because we work extensively with models like equation (2), we explore its substantive interpretation in depth. This DDE holds that the rate of change in the outcome y depends linearly on its own level and on the levels of a set of exogenous variables. Though these variables affect the rate of change in y instantaneously, their implications for changes in the *level* of $y(t)$ are not realized immediately, as we show below.

The specification of instantaneous effects on rates of change may not be realistic in all sociological applications. Introducing explicit lags into the causal effects in DDEs raises no conceptual obstacles, but it does convert simple and tractable DDEs into cumbersome integro-differential equations.[2] Such a change complicates analysis as well as exposition. Few sociological arguments about change call clearly for the more complex formulation. Therefore, we focus on the specification in (2) with instantaneous effects on rates of change.

We discuss two substantive frameworks for interpreting linear DDEs: **negative feedback** and **partial adjustment**. Coleman (1968) motivated models with linear negative feedback as follows. Repeated measurements of the same individual commonly reveal that those far from the mean on the first measurement tend to be closer to the mean on the second. Such a result, called regression toward the mean, can be an artifact of random measurement error (Lord and Novick, 1968, pp. 74–76). But it can also occur when measurement is very accurate.

A more fundamental principle may be involved. If c is positive in (2), a variable that begins above the equilibrium level grows indefinitely; any that begins below the equilibrium level decays to zero. That is, a process with positive feedback is unstable. Although many social processes may be unstable, surely some are stable, as we argued in Chapter 1. Stability requires that feedback be negative (see Section 11.6). Negative feedback produces regression toward

---

[2]Models with such lags are common in treatments of population growth with delays due to maturation; they also occur in treatments of environmental effects. Cushing (1977) provided a comprehensive treatment of one class of such models.

⟨11⟩ Linear Models for Rates of Change

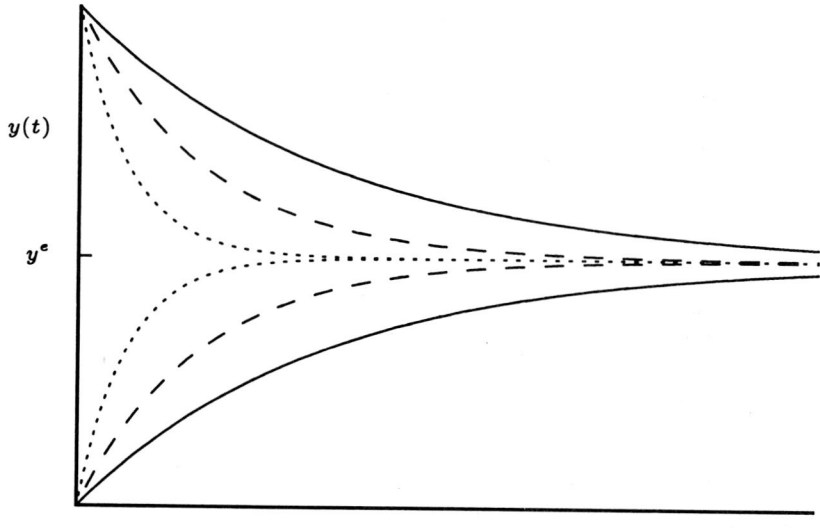

Figure 11.1. An illustrative time path for a process governed by negative feedback.

some level, perhaps the mean. When c is negative, $y(t)$ adjusts to the steady-state level given in equation (3), y^e. If $y(t)$ is above y^e, it declines over time; if $y(t)$ is below y^e, it increases over time. So $y(t)$ always moves toward the steady state. The farther $y(t)$ is from the steady state, the more rapidly it changes. Large deviations from the steady state are subject to a strong restoring force. As the process approaches the steady state, the restoring force weakens. Figure 11.1 illustrates the typical behavior of such restoring action for three levels of b when the process starts above and below the steady state.

Does negative feedback have any clear sociological meaning? Coleman offered two related interpretations. First, negative feedback may be viewed as a characteristic of equilibrating systems, as the preceding paragraph implies. In particular, the existence of negative feedback is usually considered to be a defining attribute of functional systems. Functional systems are those in which elements are retained because they have beneficial consequences (see Stinchcombe, 1968, Chapter 3, for an extended discussion of the formal structure of functional theories). Second, negative feedback may reflect cycles of causation that have been omitted from the model. That is, negative feedback might be considered the consequence of effects of y on other variables that in turn affect y. Coleman (1968, pp. 440–441) argued that the effect of $y(t)$ on the rate of change in y

> acts as a surrogate for all the variables involved in cycles leading back to itself... this approach does not aid much in the development of theory, because it obscures the relationships of which the system is composed... As the formal system becomes more complete, this [negative feedback] coefficient should approach zero. Thus the size of the coefficient allows a way of evaluating the completeness of any representation of the empirical system by a system of differential equations.

Thus negative feedback can be viewed either as a property of an equilibrating system or as a measure of our ignorance of the causal structure.

There is a second broad motivation for linear DE models of social processes. Suppose that in each period the outcome adjusts fully to the gap between its current level and some **target level** or **criterion**, $y^*(t)$. In a discrete-time perspective, full adjustment occurs when

$$y(t + \Delta t) - y(t) = \left[y^*(t) - y(t) \right].$$

This model is hardly realistic unless Δt is very long. Social systems rarely adjust fully in the short run because they are subject to numerous constraints hindering rapid change. In recognition of such constraints, social scientists usually replace the model of full adjustment with a model of partial adjustment, in which some fraction of the gap between y^* and $y(t)$ is closed in each period. In the simplest partial-adjustment model the fraction of the gap that is closed in each period is a time-invariant constant. The magnitude of this constant conveys information about the degree of responsiveness of the system to deviations from y^*. Thus, it is natural to regard the adjustment parameter as a fundamental property of the social system under study. However, the adjustment parameter depends on Δt, the length of the period. Indeed, this is an important limitation of discrete-time models whenever the length of the period is arbitrary (see the discussion of the hazard function in Section 3.2.6). To acknowledge the dependence of the adjustment parameter on Δt, we

⟨11⟩ **Linear Models for Rates of Change**   337

write the linear partial-adjustment model as

$$y(t + \Delta t) - y(t) = g(\Delta t)\left[y^*(t) - y(t)\right],$$

where $g(\Delta t)$ is a function that expresses the fraction of the gap that is closed as a function of Δt. Such discrete-time models have been used widely in the social sciences, especially in economics.

As we have stressed throughout (see especially Section 4.1), we believe that continuous-time formulations are preferable for most social processes. Linear partial adjustment is defined clearly in continuous time as well as discrete time. A continuous-time partial-adjustment model is obtained as the limit of the discrete-time model when $\Delta t \to 0$. Suppose, for example, that

$$g(\Delta t) = r\,\Delta t.$$

Letting Δt become smaller and smaller yields the continuous-time **linear partial-adjustment model**:

$$\frac{\mathrm{d}y(t)}{\mathrm{d}t} = r\left[y^*(t) - y(t)\right]. \tag{4}$$

The parameter r tells the **speed of adjustment** (per unit of time) of y to the gap between its current and target levels. When r is close to zero (but positive), y adjusts very slowly. Large values of r imply rapid adjustment. In Chapter 1 we argued that the speed of adjustment of a social unit to changed circumstances depends on social structural arrangements, such as the complexity networks of authority. Thus adjustment speeds can be interpreted as fundamental parameters of social systems.

So far the model has only two parameters, the adjustment parameter and the criterion. However, in general the criterion depends on levels of exogenous variables that vary over time.[3] For the moment we assume that this dependence is linear and time stationary:

$$y^*(t) \equiv \boldsymbol{\pi}'\mathbf{x}(t). \tag{5}$$

---

[3] For simplicity, we assume that the relevant exogenous variables have been measured. If they have not, one must adapt structural-equation methods for estimating models with unobservable variables to the dynamic case.

Substituting equation (5) into equation (4) yields a model with the same form as equation (2):

$$\frac{dy(t)}{dt} = r[\boldsymbol{\pi}'\mathbf{x} - y(t)] = r\boldsymbol{\pi}'\mathbf{x}(t) - ry(t). \tag{6}$$

Notice that (2) and (4) have the same form except that $c \equiv -r$ and $\mathbf{b} \equiv r\boldsymbol{\pi}$. Thus the negative-feedback model may also be viewed as a partial-adjustment model in which the criterion depends linearly on exogenous variables.

Nielsen (1980) and Nielsen and Rosenfeld (1981) have stressed a different implication of the linear partial-adjustment model. They considered the case in which the exogenous variables do not vary over the history of the process, $\mathbf{x}(t) \equiv \mathbf{x}$, and individuals begin with the lowest level of y at some initial time t_0 and then rise in the level of y in a manner that depends on $\mathbf{x}(t)$. For example, this situation might apply to growth in the levels of earnings or status achieved by individuals in some social system in which individuals enter at different levels. Among other things, one might be interested in how the parameters of the dynamic model determine the *persistence* of initial conditions, that is, the point of initial entry, $y_0 \equiv y(t_0)$. By solving equation (2) over the period $[t_0, t]$ (see Section 11.2), one obtains this information:

$$y(t) = e^{c\Delta t} y_0 + [1 - e^{c\Delta t}] y^e, \tag{7a}$$

or

$$y(t) = \gamma y_0 + [1 - \gamma] y^e, \tag{7b}$$

where $\gamma \equiv e^{c\Delta t} \equiv e^{-r\Delta t}$ and $\Delta t \equiv t - t_0$. If r is positititve so that c is negative, then $0 \leq \gamma \leq 1$, and the level of y at any time t is a weighted average of the initial level y_0 and the steady-state level y^e. The weight given to the origin y_0 goes to zero as t goes to ∞. Notice that the weight given to the origin also depends on the speed of adjustment. For large values of r, the effects of the origin vanish quickly. For values of r close to zero, the effects of the origin persist over a much longer period.

Although we have focused on the feedback or adjustment parameter, most sociological work with partial-adjustment models stresses the effects of causal variables. To consider such effects in a

⟨11⟩ **Linear Models for Rates of Change** 339

partial-adjustment model, we must clarify the interpretation of the criterion $y^*(t)$. Sometimes the criterion is equated with the equilibrium of the system, as in Land (1970). From equation (4) it is clear that this interpretation fits the model. That is, setting equation (4) equal to zero gives $y^*(t)$ in (5) as the equilibrium level.

Nonetheless, we think that this interpretation is not helpful in general. Treatments of scalar linear models, multivariate linear models, and nonlinear models should be as consistent as possible. As we discuss more fully in Section 11.6, it is problematic whether stable equilibria exist for systems of linear DDEs (and also for many nonlinear scalar processes). If there is no stable equilibrium, it is not useful to tie the interpetation of parameters to a steady state. Therefore, we think that $y^*(t)$ in equation (4) should be conceptualized as the level toward which causal forces are impelling y, and not necessarily as the equilibrium level of y.

There are several ways to interpret $y^*(t)$ without relying on an equilibrium conception. One generic interpretation relies on notion of the *goal* of a system. In studies of formal organizations, $y^*(t)$ may be considered an objective to which an organization is committed. Alternatively, in an interpretation based on rational utility maximization, $y^*(t)$ might be defined as the level of y giving maximum utility, given a set of preferences and objective constraints, such as prices. In either case, one assumes that purposeful individual or collective actors seek to adjust outcomes in ways that narrow the gap between the objective, $y^*(t)$, and reality, $y(t)$. Notice that this conceptualization applies even when the objective is unreachable and no equilibrium exists.

The criterion may also reflect some conscious decision-making process or unknown constraints resulting from undirected, uncoordinated social forces. For example, π in (6) may summarize the interaction of attempts at initiating action, such as changing the level of $y(t)$, and attempts at repressing such action. Over time, $y^*(t)$ may trace the dynamic balance between opposing social forces. Thus, even when the structural relations involve conflict among social units, partial-adjustment models may still be applied.

In this and the following chapters we sometimes use the ecological concept of niche. The modern approach to defining a niche distinguishes clearly between steady states and constraints due to the actions of the environment and other actors. Assume that growth of some population is constrained by M environmental factors (e.g., numbers of various competitors). The fundamental niche (Hutchinson, 1957) is the set of points in this M-dimensional space within which growth exceeds some minimum value. In many sociological applications of ecological theory, one seeks to summarize the effects of environmental variations on population growth in terms of a few parameters, such as π in (5), which are called the **niche parameters**. The value of $y^*(t)$ for given x(t) is termed the **carrying capacity** of the environment for the population; it is almost always denoted by K in this literature because it is assumed typically to be a constant rather than a function of exogenous variables.

Although the parameters r and y^* (K) are fixed in the short run for biotic populations, presumably they have evolved by natural selection. Modern evolutionary theory suggests that there are trade-offs between capacity for fast response and capacity to sustain high numbers in stable environments. Some species seem to have followed evolutionary paths that emphasize investment in the capacity to respond rapidly to fluctuating conditions and to exploit ephemeral resources. Others have specialized in the capacity to maintain large populations in intensely competitive, stable environments. These two strategies are called **r strategies** and **K strategies**, respectively.[4]

Many social groups, like biotic populations, face trade-offs between the speed of response and competitive power. This is clear in the case of firms. Some firms invest primarily in the capacity to react quickly to changing demand, which usually requires them to keep a high proportion of resources in liquid form, for example, that they subcontract work and avoid long-term labor contracts. As the demand for a product changes, such firms can shift production quickly by changing personnel, subcontractors, and so forth. The garment manufacturers who invest in the ability to copy any new fashion introduced by haute couture designers almost overnight provide a classic example.

Other firms invest in the capacity to withstand competition in stable markets. This strategy can take several forms. One involves

---

[4]See Brittain and Freeman (1980) for additional discussion of r and K strategies in industrial organization and an interesting account of the forces sustaining both types of strategies in the semiconductor industry in the United States.

commitment to producing items at lower per-unit cost than competitors. Another is to invest in developing a reputation for high quality in production and service. Both strategies require large fixed investments, in plant and equipment in the first case and in marketing and quality control in the second. Clearly such investments dampen the speed of response to changes in technology and tastes.

Both the niche parameters and the carrying capacity have clear substantive interpretations even when the dynamic system has no steady state. Tying the interpretation of these parameters to existence of an equilibrium is unnecessary; indeed, it greatly limits the generality of this analytic approach.

We think that partial-adjustment models have broad applicability in sociological analysis. As we have suggested, the notion of a criterion or target encompasses diverse social structural relations. We have devoted much attention to the sociological interpretation of parameters of DDEs because these parameters are fundamental in the continuous-time framework. But, just as in the case of the rates for qualitative outcomes considered in Part II, continuous-time rates of change in quantitative outcomes cannot be observed directly. Consequently, we now turn to the implications of a DDE for observable outcomes.

11.2 Time Paths of Changes: Integral Equations

Empirical implications of a DDE are obtained by solving the DDE subject to some boundary conditions.[5] The resulting equation, called an **integral equation** (**IE** for short), describes the time path of change in the observable outcome.

Following Nielsen and Rosenfeld (1981), some readers may wish to consider IEs as the fundamental behavioral equations because they have observable dependent variables. If social scientists seek invariant relationships, treating coefficients of IEs as the fundamental structural parameters is inadvisable because these coefficients depend on elapsed time between t_0 and t, the timing of measurements. Usually the interval between measurements is irrelevant to

---

[5]In all cases considered in this chapter, the boundary conditions include only the initial value of the process, $y(t_0)$. Knowledge of the initial value eliminates the constant of integration that arises in a general solution. Finding the solution of a DDE subject only to an initial boundary condition is called an initial-value problem in the mathematical literature.

substantive issues. More importantly, if the spacing of measurements varies among studies, the parameters of the IE are not invariant across studies, even if the parameters of the DDE are invariant.

Although we do not advocate treating IEs as fundamental behavioral equations, we do find them useful for two purposes. First, since an instantaneous rate of change is unobservable, one cannot estimate a DDE directly; estimating the parameters in the corresponding IE and then recovering the parameters in the underlying DDE provides one solution to this problem. Second, as we indicate in the next section, an IE is useful in investigating the stability of a process.

Equation (7) displays the solution to the linear DDE in (2) when the steady-state level y^f is constant over the entire observation period. This is a special case of the more general linear model:

$$\frac{dy(t)}{dt} = cy(t) + f(t), \tag{8}$$

where $f(t)$ is some function of time, and the initial value of the process is $y(t_0)$.

As we show in the appendix to this chapter, the solution to equation (8) obtained by integrating from t_0 to t is

$$y(t) = e^{c\Delta t} y(t_0) + e^{ct} \int_{t_0}^{t} e^{-cs} f(s)\, ds, \tag{9}$$

where $\Delta t \equiv t - t_0$. Depending on the functional form of $f(t)$, this equation may be simplified further. For example, if the causal factors do not vary over the observation period, and if $f(t) = \mathbf{b}'\mathbf{x}$ for all t, the integral in (9) is a linear function of $\mathbf{x}$. Then the IE may be written as

$$y(t) = e^{c\Delta t} y(t_0) + \frac{e^{c\Delta t} - 1}{c} \mathbf{b}'\mathbf{x}, \tag{10a}$$

or equivalently as

$$y(t) = \gamma y(t_0) + \boldsymbol{\beta}'\mathbf{x}, \tag{10b}$$

where

$$\gamma \equiv e^{c\Delta t};$$

$$\boldsymbol{\beta} \equiv \frac{e^{c\Delta t} - 1}{c} \mathbf{b}.$$

⟨11⟩   Time Paths of Changes: Integral Equations   343

Notice that $y(t)$ is a linear function of **x** and lagged y, but that the coefficients are complicated functions of the parameters of the dynamic model and of elapsed time. This suggests that one use equation (10b) as an estimation equation, and then use estimates of γ and β to recover estimates of the parameters of the dynamic model (see Coleman, 1968, and Chapter 13 in this volume). In the scalar case it is extremely simple to recover **c** and **b** from estimates of γ and β. The definitions of γ and β imply that

$$c = \frac{\log \gamma}{\Delta t};$$

$$\mathbf{b} = \frac{c}{\gamma - 1} \beta. \tag{11}$$

In practical applications, IEs are seldom as simple as (10) because causal variables seldom remain constant over the observation period. However, as long as their time-varying behavior can be represented by some reasonably simple function of time, equation (9) can be expressed in a form suitable for empirical analysis.

Coleman (1968) suggested that linear change in the causal variables from $\mathbf{x}(t_0)$ to $\mathbf{x}(t)$ is often a reasonable approximation, especially when $\Delta t \equiv t - t_0$ is short. This assumes that

$$\mathbf{x}(t) = \mathbf{x}(t_0) + \boldsymbol{\kappa}(t - t_0), \tag{12a}$$

or equivalently that

$$\Delta \mathbf{x}(t) \equiv \mathbf{x}(t) - \mathbf{x}(t_0) = \boldsymbol{\kappa} \Delta t, \tag{12b}$$

where $\boldsymbol{\kappa}$ is a vector of parameters telling the rate of change in $\mathbf{x}(t)$.[6] Once again the integral in equation (9) simplifies to a general form directly suitable for linear regression analysis. The trick involves performing the integration in terms of $\boldsymbol{\kappa}$ but substituting $\Delta \mathbf{x}(t)/\Delta t$ for $\boldsymbol{\kappa}$ in the last step (see appendix). The resulting IE is

$$y(t) = \gamma y(t_0) + \boldsymbol{\beta}_1' \mathbf{x}(t_0) + \boldsymbol{\beta}_2' \Delta \mathbf{x}(t), \tag{13}$$

[6]Clearly *all* elements in $\mathbf{x}(t)$ cannot change linearly over time—by construction one element of $\mathbf{x}(t)$ equals 1 for every case so that there can be a constant term in $\boldsymbol{\beta}_1$. One can view the corresponding elements of $\Delta \mathbf{x}(t)$ and $\boldsymbol{\kappa}$ as identically zero, however, in which case the results that follow still apply.

where γ retains its previous definition;

$$\beta_1 \equiv \frac{e^{c\Delta t} - 1}{c} \mathbf{b};$$

$$\beta_2 \equiv \frac{1}{c}\left(\frac{e^{c\Delta t} - 1}{c\Delta t} - 1\right)\mathbf{b} \equiv \frac{\gamma - 1 - \log\gamma}{c^2\Delta t}\mathbf{b}.$$

These definitions imply that

$$c = \frac{\log\gamma}{\Delta t}; \qquad (14a)$$

$$\mathbf{b}^{(1)} = \frac{c}{\gamma - 1}\beta_1; \qquad (14b)$$

$$\mathbf{b}^{(2)} = \frac{c^2\Delta t}{\gamma - 1 - \log\gamma}\beta_2. \qquad (14c)$$

As Coleman (1968) has noted, $\mathbf{b}^{(1)}$ and $\mathbf{b}^{(2)}$ in (14b) and (14c), respectively, provide two (possibly different) estimates of $\mathbf{b}$, the first using the estimate of β_1 and the second using the estimate of β_2.[7] The existence of two ways of estimating $\mathbf{b}$ is reminiscent of overidentification in simultaneous-equation models. If the model [including the assumption that $\mathbf{x}(t)$ changes linearly over time] is correct, the two estimators have the same asymptotic expected value. But estimates from finite samples may not agree because of sampling variability. Which is the better estimator of $\mathbf{b}$?

An estimator of $\mathbf{b}$ can be formed by averaging the two different estimates. If $\mathbf{x}(t_0)$ and $\Delta\mathbf{x}(t)$ have similar levels of variability, this is not a bad idea. But, when the two regressors have very different levels of variability, the estimators based on them differ in precision. This difference should be incorporated into estimation, perhaps by using the generalized least-squares (GLS) approach discussed in Chapter 13 (see also Goldberger, 1973), or by taking a

---

[7]Coleman also suggests using consistency of the two estimates of $\mathbf{b}$ to test the model. Note, however, that one is testing the fit of both the model of change and the approximation that $\mathbf{x}(t)$ changes linearly with time. If the two estimates of $\mathbf{b}$ do not agree closely, it may result from misspecification of the time variation in $\mathbf{x}(t)$ rather than misspecification of the functional form of the DDE.

weighted average of the two estimates in which the greater weight is given to the more precise estimate. Alternatively, one might use maximum-likelihood (ML) estimation, which pools all the information into one estimator.

Some other specifications besides linear change in $\mathbf{x}(t)$ also yield explicit solutions. Consider the case in which each element of $\mathbf{x}(t)$ changes exponentially over time:

$$x_m(t) = x_m(t_0)\, e^{\kappa_m \Delta t}, \tag{15}$$

for $m = 1, \ldots, M$. Replacing $f(s)$ in (9) with $\mathbf{b}'\mathbf{x}(s)$ where elements in $\mathbf{x}(t)$ are given by (15) yields

$$y(t) = \gamma y(t_0) + \boldsymbol{\beta}_1' \mathbf{x}(t_0) + \boldsymbol{\beta}_2' \Delta \mathbf{x}(t), \tag{16}$$

where γ retains its earlier definition;

$$\boldsymbol{\beta}_1 \equiv \left[1 - e^{c\Delta t}\right] \varsigma;$$

$$\boldsymbol{\beta}_2 \equiv \varsigma;$$

$$\varsigma_m \equiv \frac{b_m}{\kappa_m - c}.$$

These definitions imply that

$$c = \frac{\log \gamma}{\Delta t};$$

$$b_m^{(1)} = \frac{\kappa_m - c}{1 - \gamma} \beta_{1m};$$

$$b_m^{(2)} = (\kappa_m - c)\beta_{2m}. \tag{17}$$

Notice that the panel data used in estimating the IE in (16) also permit κ_m in (15) to be estimated. Given these estimates, it is simple to estimate $\mathbf{b}$ and c from the coefficients of the IE in (16) using (17). Again there are two ways to estimate $\mathbf{b}$.

11.3 An Example: Organizational Growth and Decline

We now describe an application of these methods to a sociological problem. In part we are running ahead of our discussion—we use methods discussed in Chapter 13. However, we concentrate on matters of substantive interpretation rather than on details of estimation.

The empirical literature on organizations has stressed the relationship between size and structure. The effect of increasing organizational size on administrative intensity, the fraction in the administrative cadre, has received special scrutiny. [See Scott (1975) for a review of this literature.]

Blau (1970), who has done more than anyone else to advance the study of the internal demography of organizations, made the following argument. Since administrators deal with problems of coordination of divided labor, rational organizations hire and fire administrators according to variations in the need for coordination. The need for coordination varies mainly with the size of the organization. Therefore, the size of an organization and the relative size of its administrative component are related. Blau's model, like other conventional models of administrative intensity, assumes that organizations are closed systems so that the sizes of various personnel components adjust only to internal exigencies. He assumed that adjustment is mechanical and rational and does not involve struggles among personnel components over scarce organizational resources.

We doubt that personnel allocations in organizations depend only on functional needs. Every department in an organization usually claims that it needs more staff than it has. What determines allocations in the face of such conflicting demands? Powerful subunits typically gain staff or at least resist cuts successfully. Less powerful subunits suffer. Thus, a reasonably complete account of personnel demography in organizations must take power and politics into account.

The effects of organizational politics cannot easily be distinguished from the effects of functional rationality in cross-sectional analysis. But, as Freeman and Hannan (1975) pointed out, comparisons of changing allocations in growing and declining organizations permit a direct test of the two views. Suppose that Blau was right, that the size of administrative staffs changes only when the

⟨11⟩ An Example: Organizational Growth and Decline

need for administration changes. Then the rate of change in the administrative staff should be the same (in absolute value) when the organization contracts as when it expands, assuming that the need for administration is proportional to the size of the organization, as Blau argued. In contrast, suppose that Freeman and Hannan were right and that politics is involved in changing the size of the administrative staff. If so, the process of changes in the size of the administrative staff are likely to differ when an organization grows and when it contracts. They suggested two specific differences: (1) response to declining demand for administrators is slower than adjustment to increasing demand because administrators can forestall cuts in their ranks; and (2) the carrying capacity for administrative staff at a given organizational size is higher in decline than in growth. The latter statement implies that organizations with a given size typically employ higher fractions of administrative personnel when they are declining. Freeman and Hannan (1975) argued that the dynamics of the size of the administrative staff exhibit a ratchet pattern, growing when the rest of organization grows but remaining steady (or declining modestly) when the organization declines.

This section presents a simplified analysis of the demography of the administrative staff. We use data on yearly changes in the size of the administrative staff of California school districts over the period 1971–1976. For simplicity we ignore the effects of fluctuations in the sizes of the nonadministrative staff of the school districts. In Section 11.7 we abandon this simplification and analyze the dynamics of all major personnel components.

Let $A_i(t)$ denote the size of the administrative staff for the ith district at t, and let $A_i^*(t)$ denote the upper limit on its size in equilibrium, its carrying capacity. We assume a linear partial-adjustment process:[8]

---

[8] Assumptions of continuity both in time and in the outcome are potentially problematic. It might be argued that most personnel decisions are made at the beginning of a fiscal year and that a discrete-time model with a lag of 1 year is appropriate. Similarly, in view of the small numbers in some categories, one might argue for use of a discrete-state model. However, sizes of categories can change at any time due to resignations, temporary hiring, and movements of personnel between categories. Moreover, part-time appointments are not uncommon in some categories. The

$$\frac{\mathrm{d}A_i(t)}{\mathrm{d}t} = r\left[A_i^*(t) - A_i(t)\right]. \tag{18}$$

Following the previous literature, we assume that the carrying capacity for the administrative staff reflects the organization's "need" for administration and its ability to pay for administration. We assume that the need for administrative services is proportional to student enrollments, $S(t)$, and that ability to pay is proportional to the district's total revenues, $R(t)$. In addition, we assume that each school district has fixed idiosyncratic unobserved characteristics (e.g., local customs and constraints) that affect the level of the administrative staff throughout the study period. We denote the unobserved district-specific factors for the ith district by m_i. For simplicity we assume that the carrying capacity for the administrative staff depends linearly on these three factors:

$$A_i^*(t) = \pi_0 + \pi_1 S_i(t) + \pi_2 R_i(t) + m_i. \tag{19}$$

The linearity of this function implies that an increase in either exogenous variable increases the ceiling on the administrative staff. Equation (19) is consistent with both the rationalist perspective and the political argument. The political argument differs from the rationalist one in claiming that the parameters of (19) differ in growth and decline.

We estimate the model given in (18) and (19) for school districts with growing or declining enrollments. We want to learn whether r and the π's differ in growth and decline. We define growing districts as those whose student enrollments grew 10% or more between 1971 and 1976. Declining districts are defined as those whose enrollments declined 10% or more in the same period. According to this criterion, 182 districts grew and 181 declined between 1971 and 1976. We ignore districts that fall between these categories.[9]

state space of this process is not restricted to the integers. Nonetheless, the process under study does exhibit features that fall midway between discrete and continuous models. We think the model reported here is a useful simplification.

[9]The 10% cutoff gives enough cases in each subgroup to analyze while making sure that the growing and declining districts truly faced different enrollment trends. As one might expect, estimates for the stable districts fall between those for growing and declining districts.

⟨11⟩ An Example: Organizational Growth and Decline 349

Although enrollments tend to jump each September because families are especially likely to move during the summer, they change more or less continuously throughout the school year as well. Students change schools, drop out of school, and move in and out of the area. Our measure of $S(t)$ is daily attendance averaged over the whole school district. It seems fairly plausible to assume that enrollments change linearly between the levels observed at the end of adjacent years. Changes in $R(t)$ are more problematic. To some extent, changes in revenues track changes in enrollments within the year because state aid is tied to average daily attendance. But some forms of revenue jump at discrete points in time, for example, when tax and bond elections are held, or when federal grants begin or expire. Unfortunately we do not know the exact timing of changes in revenues. Lacking any better knowledge of the time path, we assume that revenues also change linearly over the year. With these assumptions, the IE for $A(t)$ has the form of equation (13).

Since we think that the structural parameters do not vary over this short period, we pooled the data for the five 1-year intervals into one analysis (see the discussion of this type of analysis in Chapter 13). We used a method of estimation that is discussed in detail in Chapter 13, Henderson's (1952) approach to weighted generalized least squares (WGLS).[10] We also use the method described in Section 13.3 to calculate standard errors for parameters of the DDE from standard errors of the coefficients in the IEs.

Table 11.1 reports estimates of the coefficients of the IEs for growing and declining districts. Next, we use the methods discussed in the previous section to convert these estimates into estimates for the model in (18) and (19). The first step is to find speeds of adjustment using the relationship in (14a). The estimated speed of adjustment is 0.56 for districts with growing enrollments and 0.45

---

[10] Plots of enrollments versus residuals from GLS regressions show a fan-shaped spread. The variance of the disturbance appears to increase with a district's enrollments, a classic form of heteroscedasticity. We assume that the variance of the disturbance is proportional to enrollments and use the WGLS estimator developed by Nielsen (1978) and used by Nielsen and Hannan (1977). This estimator extends Henderson's (1952) approach to estimation of variance components to this particular problem. Use of this estimator seems to solve the heteroscedasticity problem. The scatter plot of WGLS residuals against enrollments is approximately rectangular.

Table 11.1. Weighted generalized least-squares estimates of the integral equations for a linear partial-adjustment model of administrative growth in growing and declining school districts (standard errors in parentheses)

Independent variable	Growing districts		Declining districts	
Intercept	0.115	(0.024)	0.102	(0.019)
$A(t-1)$	0.570	(0.027)	0.634	(0.026)
$S(t-1)$	0.00080	(0.00011)	0.00032	(0.00010)
$\Delta S(t)$	0.00091	(0.00027)	0.00033	(0.00016)
$R(t-1)$	0.00056	(0.00013)	0.00107	(0.00016)
$\Delta R(t)$	0.00060	(0.00020)	0.00103	(0.00024)
I		182		181
R^2		.957		.962

for districts with declining enrollments. Response is slightly faster in growth, as Freeman and Hannan predicted.

The second step is to estimate the π's in (19). As (14b) and (14c) show, there are two ways to do this, using the estimates of either β_1 or β_2. The two sets of estimates are reported in Table 11.2. The estimates obtained using β_2, the coefficient of $\Delta x(t)$, are larger than those using β_1. The differences between pairs of estimates are large relative to the standard errors of each estimate. For example, a 95% confidence interval around one member of each pair does not include the other member. This difference probably means that some aspect of the model is not specified correctly. Perhaps the adjustment process is not really linear, or changes in $S(t)$ and $R(t)$ are not linear over time. But the most likely misspecification concerns the effects of changes in the sizes of other personnel components, which this model ignores. Indeed, when we include the other personnel components in the model, pairs of estimates of the same parameter do not differ consistently (see Section 11.7). Since our main purpose here is to illustrate the substantive interpretations of a scalar DDE, we did not try to complicate the model to reconcile the two sets of estimates. Instead, we average each pair of estimates, which gives

⟨11⟩ An Example: Organizational Growth and Decline

Table 11.2. Estimates of a linear partial-adjustment model of administrative growth in growing and declining school districts (standard errors in parentheses)

	Growing districts	Declining districts
Speed of adjustment, $\hat{r}$	0.562 (0.047)	0.455 (0.041)
Effects of exogenous variables, $\hat{\pi}$		
Intercept	0.150 (0.031)	0.127 (0.023)
S, Students		
Using $\hat{\beta}_1$	0.0010 (0.0001)	0.0004 (0.0001)
Using $\hat{\beta}_2$	0.0022 (0.0007)	0.0008 (0.0008)
Average	0.0016	0.0006
R, Revenues		
Using $\hat{\beta}_1$	0.0007 (0.0002)	0.0013 (0.0002)
Using $\hat{\beta}_2$	0.0016 (0.0005)	0.0024 (0.0006)
Average	0.0011	0.0018

$$\frac{dA}{dt} = 0.562\left[0.150 + 0.0016\,S(t) + 0.0010\,R(t) - A(t)\right]$$

for growing districts and

$$\frac{dA}{dt} = 0.455\left[0.127 + 0.0006\,S(t) + 0.0021\,R(t) - A(t)\right]$$

for declining districts.

Whether we average or not, the forces governing A^* clearly differ in growth and decline. When enrollments are rising, A^* responds mainly to fluctuations in the size of the student body. But when enrollments are falling, revenues largely determine A^*. This difference has interesting implications. Suppose that enrollments grow at the same pace in rich and poor school districts. Although the administrative staffs in the two districts grow at rates that are not too dissimilar, they respond very differently if enrollments shrink. The carrying capacity for the administrative staff will be lower in the poor district than in the rich district.

The means of both $S(t)$ and $R(t)$ in 1976 are close to 4000 for both growing and declining districts. With enrollments and revenues at this level, A^* is 18.4 for growing districts and 23.6 for declining ones. Thus, A^* is about 25% higher in districts with declining enrollments than in ones with growing enrollments. This difference implies that the time path of decline in the size of the administrative staff lies above the time path of growth—declining districts tend to employ more administrators than comparable growing districts. Of course, this difference is very sensitive to choice of $S(t)$ and $R(t)$. The difference is smaller in poor districts and larger in rich ones.

What do these results mean? The fact that the rate of change in administrative staff differs in growth and decline casts doubt on theories of organizational demography that emphasize the controlling influence of functional needs. But the model used in this section does not include all relevant actors, in particular, the other personnel components. After we discuss the interpretation and solution of linear systems, we present what we regard as a more complete model of the dynamics of administrative growth and decline.

11.4 Linear Systems

Theoretical and empirical work often concerns **coupled** processes, which can be modeled as systems of interdependent equations. We now discuss the interpretation of DDE models for such systems, beginning with a bivariate, coupled, partial-adjustment model:

$$\begin{aligned}\frac{dy_1(t)}{dt} &= r_1 \left[y_1^*(t) - y_1(t) \right], \\ \frac{dy_2(t)}{dt} &= r_2 \left[y_2^*(t) - y_2(t) \right],\end{aligned} \qquad (20)$$

where $y_1^*(t)$ and $y_2^*(t)$ are the target or criterion levels for y_1 and y_2, respectively.

As in the scalar case, we assume that each criterion variable depends linearly on a vector of exogenous variables, $\mathbf{x}(t)$. We also assume that each depends linearly on the other outcome:

$$\begin{aligned}y_1^*(t) &= \alpha_{12} y_2(t) + \boldsymbol{\pi}_1' \mathbf{x}(t); \\ y_2^*(t) &= \alpha_{21} y_1(t) + \boldsymbol{\pi}_2' \mathbf{x}(t).\end{aligned} \qquad (21)$$

Notice that $y_j^*(t)$ *is* the equilibrium of $y_j(t)$, if an equilibrium exists. Thus, in a steady state, $y_1(t)$ depends on $y_2(t)$ and on the values of the causal variables, $\mathbf{x}(t)$. Equation (21) has the same form as a system of simultaneous linear equations.

Next substitute (21) into the partial-adjustment model in (20) and simplify; this gives:

$$\frac{\mathrm{d}y_1(t)}{\mathrm{d}t} = -r_1 y_1(t) + r_1 \alpha_{12} y_2(t) + r_1 \pi_1' \mathbf{x}(t);$$

$$\frac{\mathrm{d}y_2(t)}{\mathrm{d}t} = r_2 \alpha_{21} y_1(t) - r_2 y_2(t) + r_2 \pi_2' \mathbf{x}(t).$$

These equations are easier to manipulate when they are expressed in the form of a negative-feedback model:

$$\frac{\mathrm{d}y_1(t)}{\mathrm{d}t} = c_{11} y_1(t) + c_{12} y_2(t) + \mathbf{b}_1' \mathbf{x}(t),$$
$$\frac{\mathrm{d}y_2(t)}{\mathrm{d}t} = c_{21} y_1(t) + c_{22} y_2(t) + \mathbf{b}_2' \mathbf{x}(t),$$
(22)

where $c_{jj} \equiv -r_j$, $c_{jk} \equiv r_j \alpha_{jk}$, and $\mathbf{b}_j \equiv r_j \pi_j$.

A bivariate partial-adjustment model differs from a scalar model only in specifying that the level of *each* endogenous variable affects the criterion for the other. These effects can also be interpreted in the various ways considered earlier. Suppose that rational utility maximization sets the criteria. Then the model in (21) holds that the optimal level of investment in some quantity, y_1, depends on the current level of investment in y_2. For example, consider the allocation of time between work in the market and other activities. Let $y_1(t)$ and $y_2(t)$ be the weekly hours of work for male and female heads of the family, respectively. According to (21), the optimal labor supply of each spouse depends partly on the current labor supply of the other. This sort of model differs from conventional family labor supply models, which assume that one family member's behavior is affected only by exogenous characteristics of other family members, such as their schooling.

Alternatively, suppose $y_1^*(t)$ and $y_2^*(t)$ refer to two goals of an organization, for example, quality of medical care and quality of scientific production in a university hospital. This model then implies that the target on each dimension shifts with the current level of the other dimension. Even this simple linear model may induce a rather complicated dynamic interdependence among goals and outcomes. Though real organizations probably have even more complex structures of goals, this type of model is a useful starting point for analysis of the behavior of actors with multiple goals. This model has the particular advantage of leaving goals unmeasured and thus avoids serious methodological difficulties that beset comparative studies of *measured* deviations from goals (see Hannan and Freeman, 1977b).

The model may also be applied to interacting subunits. For example, let the y's denote levels of success (e.g., size, income) of two interdependent subunits, such as two ethnic groups, capitalists, and workers. In this sort of application the α's record the intensity and direction of the consequences of the interactions. When α_{12} and α_{21} are both negative, the subunits are said to **compete**. When both are positive, the pattern of interaction is known as **mutualism**. When one is positive and the other negative, the variables often change cyclically.

The bivariate partial-adjustment model is easily generalized to the multivariate partial-adjustment model of change in J coupled outcomes. It is most conveniently written in matrix notation:

$$\frac{d\mathbf{y}(t)}{dt} = \mathbf{R}\left[\mathbf{y}^*(t) - \mathbf{y}(t)\right], \qquad (23)$$

where $\mathbf{R}$ is a J by J diagonal matrix whose jth diagonal element is the speed of adjustment of the jth outcome, and $d\mathbf{y}(t)/dt$, $\mathbf{y}^*(t)$, and $\mathbf{y}(t)$ are J by 1 vectors with representative elements $dy_j(t)/dt$, $y_j^*(t)$, and $y_j(t)$, respectively. An equilibrium exists if $d\mathbf{y}(t)/dt = 0$. It is easy to see from (23) that $\mathbf{y}^*(t)$ is the equilibrium, if one exists.

As in the bivariate case, we assume that the criterion value for the jth outcome, $y_j^*(t)$, depends linearly on the current value of M causal variables *and* on the current values of all other endogenous variables, $y_k(t)$, $k = 1, \ldots, J$, $k \neq j$. We can state this assumption formally as

$$\mathbf{y}^*(t) \equiv \mathbf{A}\mathbf{y}(t) + \boldsymbol{\pi}'\mathbf{x}(t), \qquad (24)$$

where $\mathbf{x}(t)$ is an $M + 1$ by 1 vector of causal variables; $\boldsymbol{\pi}$ is a J by $M+1$ matrix whose jmth element gives the effect of a unit increase in x_m on $y_j^*(t)$; $\mathbf{y}(t)$ is still the J by 1 vector giving the values of the J outcomes at time t; and $\mathbf{A}$ is a J by J matrix whose diagonal elements are zero and whose jkth element gives the effect of a unit increase in $y_k(t)$ on $y_j^*(t)$. Substituting (24) into (23) gives

$$\frac{d\mathbf{y}(t)}{dt} = \mathbf{R}\mathbf{A}\mathbf{y}(t) - \mathbf{R}\mathbf{y}(t) + \mathbf{R}\boldsymbol{\pi}'\mathbf{x}(t),$$

which can be written more compactly as

$$\frac{d\mathbf{y}(t)}{dt} = \mathbf{C}\mathbf{y}(t) + \mathbf{B}\mathbf{x}(t), \qquad (25)$$

where $\mathbf{C} \equiv \mathbf{R}\mathbf{A} - \mathbf{R}$ is a J by J matrix, and $\mathbf{B} \equiv \mathbf{R}\boldsymbol{\pi}$ is a J by $M+1$ matrix. The jth diagonal element of $\mathbf{C}$ is just the negative of the speed of adjustment of the jth variable, so it is easy to go from $\mathbf{B}$ and $\mathbf{C}$ to $\mathbf{R}$, $\mathbf{A}$, and $\boldsymbol{\pi}$—and vice versa.

Multivariate DDEs like (25) have been applied previously to social processes. Two of the most famous applications are Simon's (1957) formalization of Homans' (1950) treatment of social relations in a small group and Richardson's (1960) model of arms races. Doreian and Hummon (1977) describe several other applications.

11.5 Integral Equations for Linear Systems

To estimate the fundamental parameters of a system of J linear DDEs from observed temporal data, it is again necessary to integrate over some time period (e.g., one corresponding to the times that data were collected) in order to obtain an equation in which the dependent variables are observable. The computations necessary to obtain IEs are also useful for studying the stability of equilibria.

There are several approaches to solving a system of linear DDEs like (25). The one we adopt uses a standard trick of mathematicians, namely, we assume that something we *want* to be true *is* true, and then we derive the consequences of our assumption.

In this instance, we would like the solution of a linear system of DDEs to resemble the solution of a linear DDE for a scalar outcome. (It cannot be exactly the same, of course, because of the coupling between outcomes.) In particular, we would like to be able to express each $y_j(t)$ as a linear function of J variables, $z_k(t)$, $k = 1, \ldots, J$:

$$y_j(t) = \sum_{k=1}^{J} v_{jk} z_k(t),$$

where a linear DDE like (8) describes change in each $z_k(t)$:

$$\frac{dz_k(t)}{dt} = \lambda_k z_k(t) + f_k(t),$$

for $k = 1, \ldots, J$. The point to stress is that the rate of change in each $z_k(t)$ is uncoupled from each of the $(J-1)$ other z's.

Matrix notation is essential for finding and expressing the IE for (25). In matrix notation the two equations above are, respectively

$$\mathbf{y}(t) = \mathbf{V}\mathbf{z}(t), \tag{26}$$

$$\frac{d\mathbf{z}(t)}{dt} = \mathbf{\Lambda}\mathbf{z}(t) + \mathbf{f}(t), \tag{27}$$

where $\mathbf{V}$ is a J by J matrix; $\mathbf{\Lambda}$ is a J by J diagonal matrix; and $\mathbf{z}(t)$ and $\mathbf{f}(t)$ are J by 1 vectors.

Since the equations in (27) are uncoupled and (9) is the solution to (8)—see the appendix for the derivation—the solution to (27) can be written immediately:

$$\mathbf{z}(t) = e^{\mathbf{\Lambda}\Delta t}\mathbf{z}(t_0) + e^{\mathbf{\Lambda}t}\int_{t_0}^{t} e^{-\mathbf{\Lambda}s}\mathbf{f}(s)\,ds, \tag{28}$$

where $e^{\mathbf{\Lambda}t}$ is a J by J diagonal matrix with diagonal elements $e^{\lambda_j t}$, $j = 1, \ldots, J$. In addition, if (26) holds,

$$\mathbf{z}(t) = \mathbf{V}^{-1}\mathbf{y}(t). \tag{29}$$

Substituting (29) into (28) gives

$$\mathbf{V}^{-1}\mathbf{y}(t) = e^{\mathbf{\Lambda}\Delta t}\mathbf{V}^{-1}\mathbf{y}(t_0) + e^{\mathbf{\Lambda}t}\int_{t_0}^{t} e^{-\mathbf{\Lambda}s}\mathbf{f}(s)\,ds,$$

which implies that

$$\mathbf{y}(t) = \mathbf{V}e^{\mathbf{\Lambda}\Delta t}\mathbf{V}^{-1}\mathbf{y}(t_0) + \mathbf{V}e^{\mathbf{\Lambda}t}\int_{t_0}^{t} e^{-\mathbf{\Lambda}s}\mathbf{f}(s)\,ds. \tag{30}$$

Expression (30) gives a general rule for solving the system of J linear coupled DDEs in (25), as long as expressions for $\mathbf{\Lambda}$, $\mathbf{V}$, and $\mathbf{f}(t)$ can be found. Finding these is our next task.

⟨11⟩   Integral Equations for Linear Systems   357

At this point we examine another implication of equation (26), namely, that
$$\frac{d\mathbf{y}(t)}{dt} = \mathbf{V}\frac{d\mathbf{z}(t)}{dt}. \tag{31}$$

Substituting (26) and (31) into (25) yields

$$\mathbf{V}\frac{d\mathbf{z}(t)}{dt} = \mathbf{CV}\mathbf{z}(t) + \mathbf{Bx}(t);$$

$$\frac{d\mathbf{z}(t)}{dt} = \mathbf{V}^{-1}\mathbf{CV}\mathbf{z}(t) + \mathbf{V}^{-1}\mathbf{Bx}(t). \tag{32}$$

In order for (27) to be true (as desired), it is necessary that

$$\mathbf{\Lambda} = \mathbf{V}^{-1}\mathbf{CV}; \tag{33}$$

$$\mathbf{f}(t) = \mathbf{V}^{-1}\mathbf{Bx}(t). \tag{34}$$

If (33) is true, **C** is said to be **diagonalizable**. $\mathbf{\Lambda}$ is known as the matrix of **eigenvalues** of **C**; **V** is the matrix of right **eigenvectors** of **C**.[11] The eigenvalues of any J by J matrix such as **C** are the J values of λ satisfying the equation

$$\det(\mathbf{C} - \lambda \mathbf{I}) = 0. \tag{35}$$

Usually (35) is called the **characteristic equation** associated with the matrix **C**. This equation follows from simple algebraic manipulation of (33). Given **C**, one can solve for $\mathbf{\Lambda}$ and **V** using one of the many available algorithms for finding eigenvalues and eigenvectors of a matrix. In addition, if one knows **b** and how $\mathbf{x}(t)$ changes over time, one can determine $\mathbf{f}(t)$. All previously unknown elements for the solution to the system of J linear coupled DDEs in (30) are now specified.

For concreteness, consider again the case in which elements in the vector $\mathbf{x}(t)$ change linearly over time; see (12). Then the IE for (25) is

$$\mathbf{y}(t) = \mathbf{\Gamma}\mathbf{y}(t_0) + \mathbf{\Theta}_1 \mathbf{x}(t_0) + \mathbf{\Theta}_2 \Delta\mathbf{x}(t), \tag{36}$$

[11] It is also possible to define a matrix of left eigenvectors; see Luenberger (1979, pp. 142–144) for a definition and discussion of the differences between and interpretation of left and right eigenvectors.

where

$$\boldsymbol{\Gamma} \equiv \mathbf{V}\, e^{\boldsymbol{\Lambda}\Delta t}\, \mathbf{V}^{-1}; \qquad (37a)$$

$$\boldsymbol{\Theta}_1 \equiv \mathbf{C}^{-1}(\boldsymbol{\Gamma} - \mathbf{I})\mathbf{B}; \qquad (37b)$$

$$\boldsymbol{\Theta}_2 \equiv \mathbf{C}^{-1}\left[\frac{1}{\Delta t}\mathbf{C}^{-1}(\boldsymbol{\Gamma} - \mathbf{I}) - \mathbf{I}\right]\mathbf{B}. \qquad (37c)$$

Since (36) is linear in the observed variables, it can easily be estimated by standard linear regression methods when there are panel data with a fixed interval between waves.

The only difficulty is that the regression coefficients are highly nonlinear functions of the parameters of the underlying dynamic model. Notice, however, that $e^{\boldsymbol{\Lambda}\Delta t}$ is a diagonal, J by J matrix because $\boldsymbol{\Lambda}$ is diagonal. Hence (37a) implies that $\boldsymbol{\Gamma}$ is diagonalizable and has $\mathbf{Q} \equiv e^{\boldsymbol{\Lambda}\Delta t}$ as its matrix of eigenvalues and $\mathbf{V}$ as its matrix of right eigenvectors. Because $\mathbf{Q}$ and $\mathbf{V}$ can be calculated readily from $\boldsymbol{\Gamma}$, and because $\boldsymbol{\Lambda}$ is obtained easily from $\mathbf{Q}$, estimating $\mathbf{C}$ from $\boldsymbol{\Gamma}$ is straightforward. One simply uses the implication of (33) that

$$\mathbf{C} = \mathbf{V}\boldsymbol{\Lambda}\mathbf{V}^{-1}. \qquad (38)$$

Once $\mathbf{C}$ has been estimated, (37b) and (37c) can be manipulated to give estimators of $\mathbf{B}$:

$$\mathbf{B}^{(1)} = (\boldsymbol{\Gamma} - \mathbf{I})^{-1}\mathbf{C}\boldsymbol{\Theta}_1; \qquad (39a)$$

$$\mathbf{B}^{(2)} = \left[\frac{1}{\Delta t}\mathbf{C}^{-1}(\boldsymbol{\Gamma} - \mathbf{I}) - \mathbf{I}\right]^{-1}\mathbf{C}\boldsymbol{\Theta}_2. \qquad (39b)$$

Just as in the scalar case discussed in Section 11.2, there are two distinct estimators for the effects of the exogenous variables.

The method of matrix diagonalization just sketched requires that all eigenvectors of $\mathbf{C}$ (or equivalently, $\boldsymbol{\Gamma}$) be linearly independent. This condition is met whenever all J eigenvalues are distinct. However, even when some eigenvalues are repeated, the eigenvectors may still be independent. Indeed, a broad class of matrices may be diagonalized. Consequently this procedure has wide applicability. For example, it applies even when eigenvalues of $\mathbf{C}$ (or $\boldsymbol{\Gamma}$) have complex roots. For details, see Strang (1976, pp. 207–214, 217–227) or Boyce and DiPrima (1969, pp. 307–311).

11.6 Qualitative Stability

Models based on DDEs specify how a system of variables changes **locally**, that is, in the next instant. This feature makes it easy to apply such models in substantive work. Even when we do not understand the long-run dynamics of a social process, we can sometimes predict the short-term response to certain shocks or interventions. But this ease of modeling pays off substantively only if long-run dynamics can be inferred from short-run adjustments. Consequently, it is important to learn what the parameters of a system of DDEs imply about long-run change.

Questions about the relationship between local and global dynamics have received a great deal of attention from mathematicians during this century. New fields of pure mathematics (qualitative stability theory and catastrophe theory) and applied mathematics (control theory) have emerged from the study of these questions. As we indicate below, it is very easy to relate local and global dynamics for linear systems. Most of the mathematical work concentrates on the more recondite case of nonlinear systems. This section states the main result for linear systems. Section 14.6 briefly sketches results for nonlinear systems.

11.6.1 Equilibria

In the social sciences, the best-known approach to descriptions of the long-run behavior of systems involves investigating the existence and uniqueness of equilibria. As we discussed in Chapter 1, much sociological theory has focused solely on equilibrium conditions. From such a perspective, the most informative way to summarize a dynamic process is to characterize its equilibria. Even those who doubt that most social systems are in equilibrium find it useful to learn whether a social system has any equilibria and, if it does, how the various equilibria differ.

We focus on the following system of J linear equations:

$$\frac{d\mathbf{y}(t)}{dt} = \mathbf{C}\mathbf{y}(t) + \mathbf{B}\mathbf{x}(t). \qquad (40)$$

The vector $\mathbf{y}^e$ is an equilibrium if the system remains at $\mathbf{y}^e$ indefinitely (once $\mathbf{y}^e$ is reached) unless the system is perturbed. In symbolic terms, $\mathbf{y}^e$ is an equilibrium if

$$-\mathbf{C}\mathbf{y}^e = \mathbf{B}\mathbf{x}(t).$$

The equilibria of the system are the solutions of the J algebraic equations,

$$\mathbf{y}^e = -\mathbf{C}^{-1}\mathbf{B}\mathbf{x}(t).$$

This system of equations has a unique solution when $\mathbf{C}$ has full rank, that is, when the rows and columns of $\mathbf{C}$ are linearly independent. One consequence of $\mathbf{C}$'s having full rank is that all of its eigenvalues are nonzero. Therefore, the linear system of DDEs in (40) has a unique equilibrium whenever all of its eigenvalues have nonzero real parts. If the real parts of one or more eigenvalues are zero (see below), the system may or may not have an equilibrium.

11.6.2 Stability of Equilibria

In general, stability is a property of an equilibrium point. Formally, an equilibrium $\mathbf{y}^e$ is said to be **stable** if $\mathbf{y}(t)$, the solution to the system in (40), remains close to $\mathbf{y}^e$ as t approaches infinity. An equilibrium is said to be **asymptotically stable** if $\mathbf{y}(t)$ approaches the equilibrium as t approaches infinity when the initial position of the system is near the equilibrium; it is said to be **globally asymptotically stable** if $\mathbf{y}(t)$ approaches the equilibrium as time unfolds, regardless of the initial position of the system. In the special case of linear systems, one does not have to analyze stability of multiple equilibria because there is a single unique equilibrium.

Although the exogenous variables $\mathbf{x}(t)$ impart time variation to the system, they do not affect stability. Stability depends only on the structure of the endogenous portion of the model. This means that asymptotic stability of a linear system can be analyzed by studying the homogeneous system:

$$\frac{d\mathbf{y}(t)}{dt} = \mathbf{C}\mathbf{y}(t). \tag{41}$$

If the system in (41) is stable, then (40), the system driven by the forcing function, $\mathbf{B}\mathbf{X}(t)$, is stable.

The homogeneous system in (41) clearly has an equilibrium only at zero. Thus determining global asymptotic stability amounts to learning whether the matrix $\mathbf{C}$ implies that $\mathbf{y}(t)$ converges to zero as t approaches infinity. If this result holds for all initial conditions, the system in (41), and by implication the one in (40), is globally asymptotically stable.

⟨11⟩ Qualitative Stability

The question posed in the preceding paragraph can be answered by examining the IE obtained from (30) when $\mathbf{f}(t)$ is zero; from (30) the IE is

$$\mathbf{y}(t) = \mathbf{V}\, e^{\mathbf{\Lambda}\Delta t}\, \mathbf{V}^{-1} \mathbf{y}(t_0), \qquad (42)$$

where (33) holds. Equation (42) shows that the long-run behavior of the system depends on the signs of the eigenvalues of $\mathbf{C}$.

There are several cases to consider. First, suppose that all eigenvalues are real. Equation (42) implies that all $y_j(t)$ tend toward zero only if *all* eigenvalues are negative. If one or more eigenvalues are positive, the system is unstable and grows without bound.

The second case concerns the situation in which two or more roots are complex. Complex eigenvalues appear in conjugate pairs that have the form $\lambda_j = \mu_j + i\omega_j$, where μ_j and ω_j are real and $i = \sqrt{-1}$. Therefore,

$$e^{\lambda_j \Delta t} = e^{(\mu_j + i\omega_j)\Delta t} = e^{\mu_j \Delta t}\, e^{i\omega_j \Delta t}.$$

Since

$$e^{i\omega_j \Delta t} = \cos(\omega_j \Delta t) + i\sin(\omega_j \Delta t),$$

it follows that

$$e^{\lambda_j \Delta t} = e^{\mu_j \Delta t}\left[\cos(\omega_j \Delta t) + i\sin(\omega_j \Delta t)\right].$$

This expression implies that the real parts of the eigenvalues, the μ_j's, govern long-run growth or decline. The complex parts add only an oscillating (or cyclical) component with period ω (see Figure 11.9). Together the two components imply that $y_j(t)$ oscillates, either decaying to zero or growing exponentially, depending on the sign of μ_j. If μ_j is negative for all j, $y_j(t)$ approaches the stable equilibrium at zero through dampened cycles, as Figure 11.2 illustrates. If the real part of any eigenvalue is positive, $y_j(t)$'s asymptotic behavior is characterized by cycles of increasing amplitude, "explosive cycles," as Figure 11.3 illustrates.

Finally, in some cases the real part of one or more eigenvalues is zero. To characterize the asymptotic behavior of such systems requires study of the eigenvectors. When the eigenvectors associated

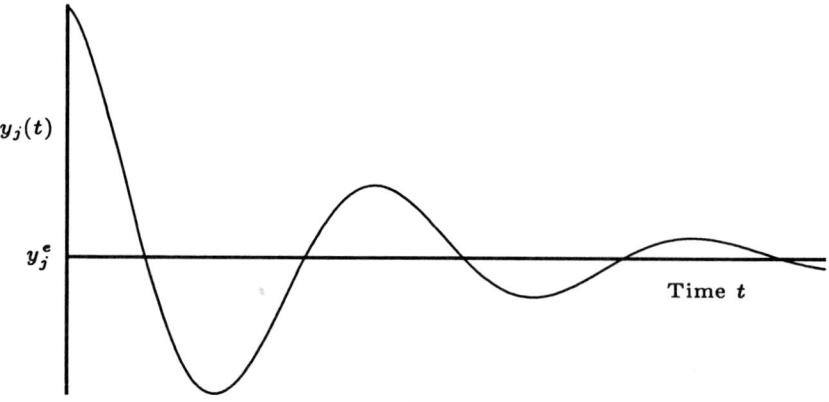

Figure 11.2. Illustrative time path of a member of a stable linear system with cycles.

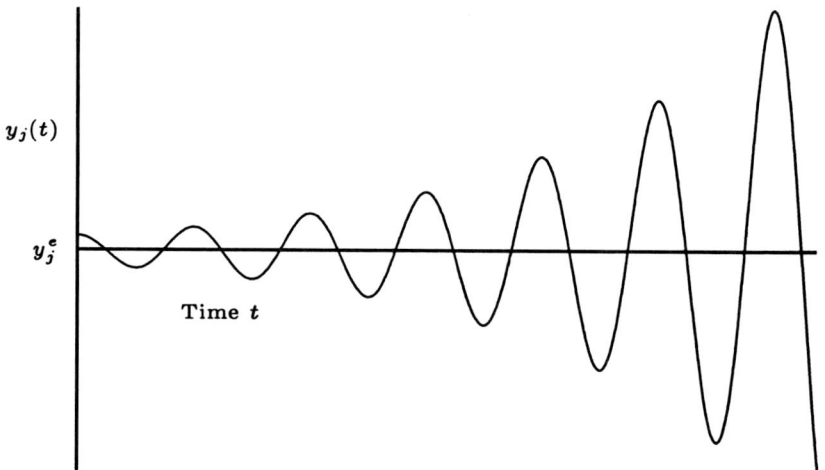

Figure 11.3. Illustrative time path of a member of an unstable linear system with cycles.

with the eigenvalues with zero real parts are linearly independent, $y_j(t)$ does not approach either zero or infinity as time unfolds. Instead it cycles around some center point. Systems that behave in this way are said to be **marginally stable**.

⟨11⟩ Qualitative Stability 363

In sum, the real parts of the eigenvalues determine the asymptotic stability of a linear system, except one that is marginally stable. Indeed, *a necessary and sufficient condition that an equilibrium of a linear system be globally asymptotically stable is that the real parts of all eigenvalues be negative.* Clearly the full set of eigenvalues of a linear system has great substantive importance.

To make this discussion concrete, we return to the bivariate system in (22), which we discussed in Section 11.4. Suppose we know **C** and want to study the stability of the system. The first task is to find the eigenvalues of **C**, that is, those values of λ satisfying the characteristic equation in (35). In general the characteristic equation gives a polynomial in λ whose order is the same as the number of equations in the system. In the bivariate system,

$$\det \begin{pmatrix} c_{11} - \lambda & c_{12} \\ c_{21} & c_{22} - \lambda \end{pmatrix} = 0,$$

implying that

$$(c_{11} - \lambda)(c_{22} - \lambda) - c_{12} c_{21} = 0;$$

$$\lambda^2 - (c_{11} + c_{22})\lambda + (c_{11} c_{22} - c_{12} c_{21}) = 0.$$

This last expression can be written as

$$\lambda^2 - \lambda \operatorname{tr}(\mathbf{C}) + \det(\mathbf{C}) = 0,$$

where

$$\operatorname{tr}(\mathbf{C}) = c_{11} + c_{22};$$

$$\det(\mathbf{C}) = c_{11} c_{22} - c_{12} c_{21}.$$

Recall that the solutions of a second-order polynomial in x, $ax^2 + bx + c = 0$, are

$$x = \frac{-b \pm \sqrt{b^2 - 4ac}}{2a}.$$

This fact implies that the eigenvalues of **C** for a bivariate system are

$$\lambda = \frac{\operatorname{tr}(\mathbf{C}) \pm \sqrt{[\operatorname{tr}(\mathbf{C})]^2 - 4\det(\mathbf{C})}}{2}$$

$$= \frac{(c_{11} + c_{22}) \pm \sqrt{(c_{11} - c_{22})^2 + 4 c_{12} c_{21}}}{2}. \tag{43}$$

Notice that the term whose square root is called for *can* be negative, in which case the eigenvalue has an imaginary component. A *sufficient* (though not a necessary) condition for the eigenvalue to be real is that $c_{11} c_{22} > c_{12} c_{21}$, that is, $\det(\mathbf{C}) > 0$. The *necessary* condition for the eigenvalue to be real is that

$$(c_{11} - c_{22})^2 + 4 c_{12} c_{21} > 0.$$

As we mentioned earlier, if the real part of an eigenvalue is zero, the asymptotic behavior of the system depends on the eigenvectors as well as on the eigenvalues. Equation (38) implies that the eigenvectors for the bivariate system must satisfy

$$\begin{pmatrix} v_{11} & v_{12} \\ v_{21} & v_{22} \end{pmatrix} \begin{pmatrix} \lambda_1 & 0 \\ 0 & \lambda_2 \end{pmatrix} = \begin{pmatrix} c_{11} & c_{12} \\ c_{21} & c_{22} \end{pmatrix} \begin{pmatrix} v_{11} & v_{12} \\ v_{21} & v_{22} \end{pmatrix},$$

which reduces to two pairs of equations:

$$v_{1j} \lambda_j = c_{11} v_{1j} + c_{12} v_{2j},$$

$$v_{2j} \lambda_j = c_{21} v_{2j} + c_{22} v_{2j},$$

for $j = 1, 2$. Rearranging this pair of equations yields

$$(c_{11} - \lambda_j) v_{1j} + c_{12} v_{2j} = 0,$$

$$c_{21} v_{1j} + (c_{22} - \lambda_j) v_{2j} = 0,$$

or

$$(\mathbf{C} - \lambda_j \mathbf{I}) v_j = 0.$$

Since $(\mathbf{C} - \lambda_j \mathbf{I})$ is singular by definition of an eigenvalue, the eigenvector for the jth eigenvalue, λ_j, is not uniquely defined. In particular, one element of each eigenvector can be chosen arbitrarily; the remaining elements in the eigenvector are then determined uniquely. For example, if v_{1j} is chosen to equal $c_{12} \neq 0$, then $v_{2j} = (\lambda_j - c_{11})/c_{12}$.

An interesting special case is the so-called off-diagonal system in which the two feedback terms are zero, $c_{11} = c_{22} = 0$. Assuming that the cross-effects c_{12} and c_{21} are nonzero, there are only two cases to be considered. If the cross-effects have the same sign, the eigenvalues are $\lambda_1 = \sqrt{c_{12} c_{21}}$ and $\lambda_2 = -\sqrt{c_{12} c_{21}}$. Since λ_1 is positive, this system is unstable. But, if the cross-effects have opposite sign, both eigenvalues are imaginary with zero real part. The system is marginally stable.

⟨11⟩ Qualitative Stability

Table 11.3. Stability of a bivariate system: selected examples[a]

Case	c_{11}	c_{12}	c_{21}	c_{22}	tr	tr^2	det	λ_1	λ_2	v_{11}	v_{21}	v_{12}	v_{22}	Q1	Q2
1	−5	2	1	−4	−9	81	18	−3	−6	1	1	2	−1	Y	Y
2	−1	1	−8	5	4	16	3	1	3	1	2	1	4	Y	No
3a	−1	0	0	−1	−2	4	1	−1	−1	1	3	2	1	Y	Y
3b	−1	1	−1	−3	−4	16	4	−2	−2	2	−2	1	1	No	Y
4a	1	0	0	1	2	4	1	1	1	1	3	2	1	Y	No
4b	3	1	−1	1	4	16	4	2	2	2	−2	1	1	No	No
5	1	3	9	−5	−4	16	−32	4	−8	1	1	1	−3	Y	No
6a	0	−4	1	0	0	0	4	2i	−2i	2	−i	−2i	1	Y	b
6b	−1	1	−4	−1	−2	4	5	−1+2i	−1−2i	1	2i	1	−2i	Y	Y
6c	1	1	−4	1	2	4	5	1+2i	1−2i	1	2i	1	−2i	Y	No

[a] Q1 denotes the question, Are the eigenvectors linearly independent? Q2 denotes the question, Is there a stable equilibrium? Answers are denoted by Y (yes) or N (no).
[b] This case is marginally stable; its time path is an ellipse.

11.6.3 Phase-Space Analysis

To this point our treatment of stability has been completely algebraic. Although the algebraic results are essential to determining the asymptotic behavior of the system, they may not give some social scientists much insight into the qualitative patterns of change involved. A geometric analysis helps to fill this gap.

The geometric analysis involves what has come to be known as **phase-space analysis**. Consider the general (possibly nonlinear) bivariate system:

$$\frac{dy_1(t)}{dt} = f(y_1, y_2);$$

$$\frac{dy_2(t)}{dt} = g(y_1, y_2).$$

The solution to this system (if one exists) implies a trajectory or orbit in the three-dimensional space (t, y_1, y_2). As t increases, the pair of solutions trace out a path in the *two-dimensional* space whose coordinates are y_1 and y_2. The y_1–y_2 plane is called the **phase space** of the system.

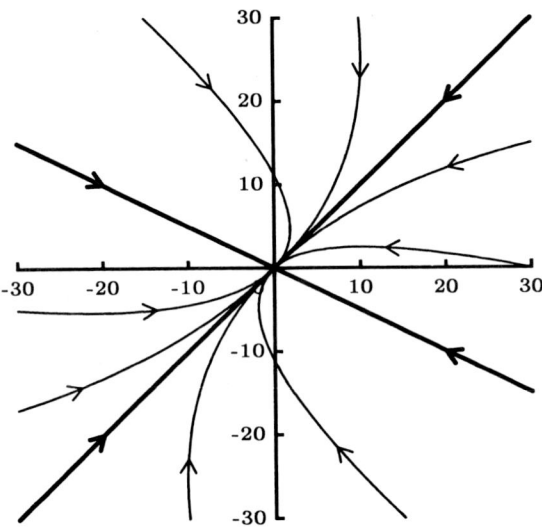

Figure 11.4. Phase-space diagram for a bivariate linear system of DDEs in which $\lambda_1 < \lambda_2 < 0$: $y_1(t)$ versus $y_2(t)$ for case 1 in Table 11.3. Bold lines denote the eigenvectors.

The heuristic value of a phase-space description is the insight that it offers into the time path of changes in sets of variables. This is most easily seen in the bivariate case. The rest of this section considers only the homogeneous linear system in (41) with J equal to two. Let λ_1 and λ_2 denote the two eigenvalues of the system obtained from (43), and let $\mathbf{v}_1$ and $\mathbf{v}_2$ be the associated eigenvectors. Following Braun (1975, pp. 552–566), we consider six main cases. Table 11.3 contains a numerical example of each case (and important subcases), while Figures 11.4 through 11.9 depict the phase-space diagrams corresponding to these cases. Each figure contains half-lines that coincide with the eigenvectors and shows directional arrows that describe the orbits (time paths) from selected starting points to the equilibrium at zero.

Case 1: $\lambda_2 < \lambda_1 < 0$. All directional arrows in Figure 11.4 point toward the equilibrium because the eigenvalues have negative real parts causing the equilibrium to be stable. Notice that the orbits converge on the half-lines. In general the right eigenvectors describe the long-run dynamics (see Luenberger, 1979, pp. 142–144).

⟨11⟩ **Qualitative Stability**

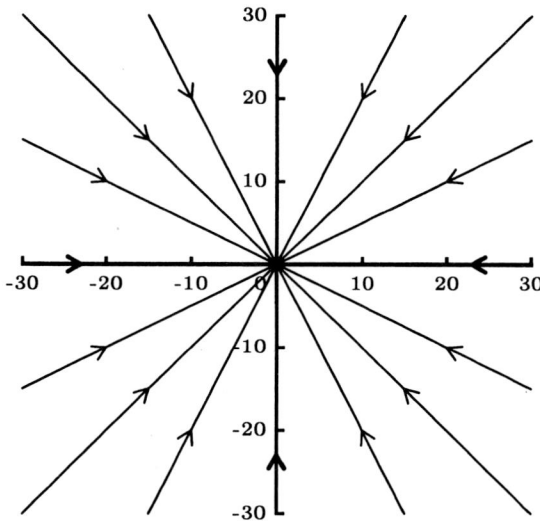

Figure 11.5. Phase-space diagram for a bivariate linear system of DDEs in which $\lambda_1 = \lambda_2 < 0$ and the eigenvectors satisfy equation (44): $y_1(t)$ versus $y_2(t)$ for case 3a in Table 11.3. Bold lines denote the eigenvectors.

Case 2: $\lambda_2 > \lambda_1 > 0$. This case is like the one drawn in Figure 11.4, except that all arrows are reversed, indicating that the system is unstable. Starting at any initial point, the system explodes.

Case 3: $\lambda_1 = \lambda_2 < 0$. If **C** has a double eigenvalue, then it can be shown that either

$$\mathbf{C} = \mathbf{V} \begin{pmatrix} \lambda & 0 \\ 0 & \lambda \end{pmatrix} \mathbf{V}^{-1} \tag{44}$$

or

$$\mathbf{C} = \mathbf{V} \begin{pmatrix} \lambda & 1 \\ 0 & \lambda \end{pmatrix} \mathbf{V}^{-1}. \tag{45}$$

In the first case, all orbits in the phase plane are half-lines pointing at the equilibrium, as in Figure 11.5. In the second case, the solutions converge to the equilibrium along orbits that converge to the half-line proportional to the single eigenvector, as in Figure 11.6.

Case 4: $\lambda_1 = \lambda_2 > 0$. Again there are two cases, which parallel those of Case 3. The qualitative behavior of the system

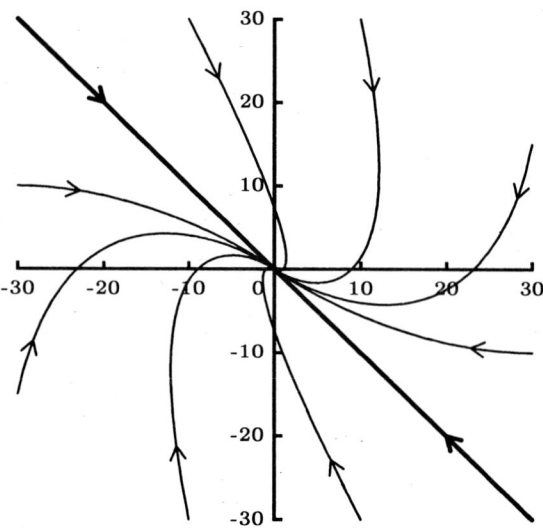

Figure 11.6. Phase-space diagram for a bivariate linear system of DDEs in which $\lambda_1 = \lambda_2 < 0$ and the eigenvectors satisfy equation (45): $y_1(t)$ versus $y_2(t)$ for case 3b in Table 11.3. Bold lines denote the eigenvectors.

is the same as in Figures 11.5 and 11.6, except that all arrows are reversed.

Case 5: $\lambda_1 < 0 < \lambda_2$. Because one eigenvalue is positive, this case has an unstable equilibrium called a saddle point. However, it implies more complicated orbits than the cases considered so far. From some initial position, the system converges toward the equilibrium but then flies away, as illustrated in Figure 11.7.

Case 6: $\lambda_1 = \mu + i\omega$, $\lambda_2 = \mu - i\omega$. As we mentioned earlier, this case gives oscillating change. There are three possible patterns. When μ, the real part of the eigenvalue, is zero, the system continually cycles around the same orbit, with the direction of motion determined by the values of the parameters of the model. This pattern is illustrated in Figure 11.8. When μ is negative, the orbit spirals toward the equilibrium point. This pattern is illustrated in Figure 11.9. Notice that the orbit moves successively through regions in which one variable shifts from positive to negative and then the other shifts sign. As the level of one variable rises, the level of the

⟨11⟩ **Qualitative Stability**

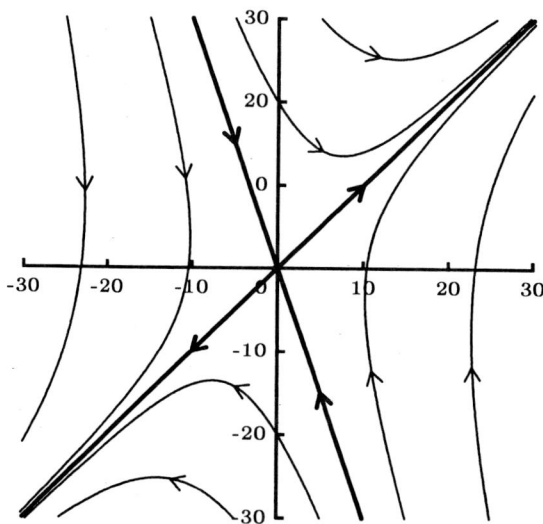

Figure 11.7. Phase-space diagram for a bivariate linear system of DDEs in which $\lambda_1 < 0 < \lambda_2$: $y_1(t)$ versus $y_2(t)$ for case 5 in Table 11.3. Bold lines denote the eigenvectors.

other falls, and vice versa. Finally, if the real part of the root is positive, the system cycles away from the equilibrium, and the distance from equilibrium increases exponentially with time. The phase-space diagram looks exactly like the one in Figure 11.9, except that the arrows point in the opposite direction. As the level of one variable rises, the other falls. But the effects are more than proportional. A small increase in one variable produces a larger decrease in the other, which in turn produces yet a larger increase in the first, and so on. This is an example of cyclical growth that explodes.

We have discussed the phase space of a bivariate system because it is easy to display graphically. The phase space of a system with three or more dimensions is also well defined. The trajectories of a multivariate system trace out a time path in a J-dimensional phase space. Of course, these trajectories cannot be drawn on paper. Sometimes it is useful to analyze three-dimensional spaces visually; for numerous illustrations, see Arnold (1973, p. 140). This can be done by fixing all but two variables and studying the trajectories of these two variables in the phase space. Although such an analysis is

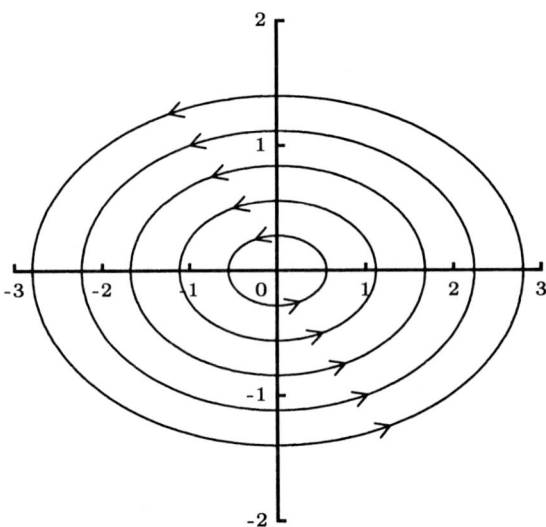

Figure 11.8. Phase-space diagram for a bivariate linear system of DDEs in which $\lambda_1 = +i\omega$, $\lambda_2 = -i\omega$: $y_1(t)$ versus $y_2(t)$ for case 6a in Table 11.3.

clearly an approximation, it can give useful qualitative insight into the local behavior of a portion of the system.

11.7 Organizational Growth and Decline Reconsidered

We now illustrate the use of the multivariate linear partial-adjustment model specified in (23) and (24). The analysis presented in this section, part of continuing research with John Freeman, extends the analysis in Section 11.3. As we mentioned in that section, our goal was to introduce politics and environmental dependence into models of organizational demography. Organizational politics enters the model in Section 11.3 only in the hypothesized difference between growth and decline processes. But surely changes in personnel involve politics more broadly than indicated in this model. In particular, change in the size of every personnel component in an organization is probably affected (at least to some extent) by the size of every other personnel component because various personnel categories compete for a limited budget. Moreover, patterns of competition may differ in favorable and unfavorable environments, that

⟨11⟩   Organizational Growth and Decline Reconsidered   371

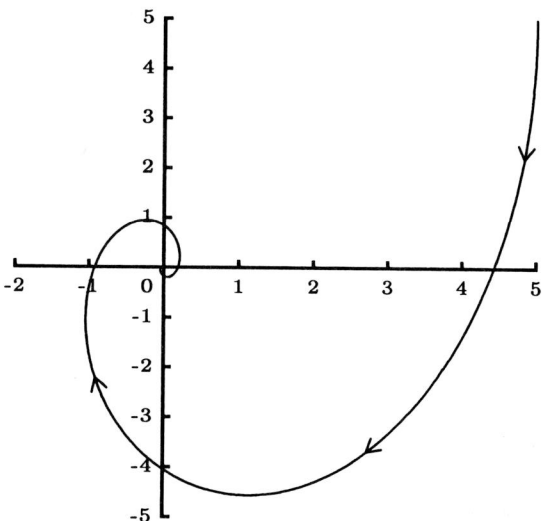

Figure 11.9. Phase-space diagram for a bivariate linear system of DDEs in which $\lambda_1 = \mu + i\omega$, $\lambda_2 = \mu - i\omega$: $y_1(t)$ versus $y_2(t)$ for case 6b in Table 11.3.

is, when student enrollments are growing and declining. The model in Section 11.3 ignores these possibilities.

Freeman and Hannan (1975) proposed a model with limited competition between four personnel components in school districts: administrators, teachers, pupil-service workers, and classified workers. We extend their analysis (see also Hannan and Freeman, 1978; Freeman, Hannan, and Hannaway, 1978; and especially Freeman and Hannan, 1981). When we discuss substantive issues of organizational demography in school districts, we denote the size of these groups at time t by $A(t)$, $T(t)$, $P(t)$, and $C(t)$, respectively. When we discuss the mathematical model of change in the sizes of the groups, we denote their sizes at time t by $y_j(t)$, $j = 1, \ldots, 4$, respectively.

Our starting point is a linear partial-adjustment model:

$$\frac{dy_{ij}(t)}{dt} = r_j \left[y_{ij}^* - y_{ij}(t) \right], \qquad (46)$$

where i denotes the ith school district, $y_{ij}(t)$ the current size of personnel category j in district i, and $y_{ij}^*(t)$ the corresponding carrying capacity. The parameter r_j indicates the speed of adjustment of personnel category j to the gap between its current level and its carrying capacity. When there is no structural inertia, r_j is infinite, and the personnel component adjusts completely in an instant. At the other extreme, when r_j equals zero, the component does not adjust at all. In general, the higher the speed of adjustment r_j, the more rapidly $y_j(t)$ adjusts to $y_j^*(t)$. We contrast this parameter across personnel components and for each component between growth and decline.

Next we consider the carrying capacities, the maximum size that can be sustained under particular conditions. In general, we think that the carrying capacity for any personnel component is determined by three classes of variables: (1) exogenous environmental conditions such as student enrollments $S(t)$, and revenues $R(t)$, (2) unobserved historical factors such as social, political, and cultural characteristics of the environment specific to the ith district, and (3) internal competitive relations, in particular, the sizes of the other personnel components.

As in Section 11.3, we assume that the dependence of the carrying capacity on a vector of variables $\mathbf{x}_i(t)$ is linear in parameters that are constant across districts:

$$y_{ij}^*(t) \equiv \boldsymbol{\pi}_j' \mathbf{x}_i(t) + m_{ij} + \sum_{\substack{k=1 \\ k \neq j}}^{J} \alpha_{jk}\, y_{ik}(t). \tag{47}$$

In our analysis, $\mathbf{x}(t)$ includes $S(t)$ and $R(t)$, which are assumed to change linearly over our observation period (see the discussion of this assumption in Section 11.3). Bioecologists usually call $\boldsymbol{\pi}_j$ in (47) the parameters of the niche of entity j. Time-invariant features of district i that affect the growth of category j are summarized by m_{ij}. Finally, we think that the carrying capacity for category j in district i depends on the size of every other personnel component, $y_k(t)$, $k = 1, \ldots, J$, $k \neq j$. The parameter α_{jk} indicates the manner in which the size of component k affects the carrying capacity for component j. Each coefficient can be positive or zero as well as negative. The α_{jk} are usually called **competition coefficients** even though j and k compete only when both α_{jk} and α_{kj} are negative. We also refer to them as **coupling coefficients** to avoid the connotation that competition always occurs.

⟨11⟩ Organizational Growth and Decline Reconsidered   373

To complete the model, we substitute (47) into (46), which gives

$$\frac{\mathrm{d}y_{ij}(t)}{\mathrm{d}t} = r_j\left[\boldsymbol{\pi}_j' \mathbf{x}_i(t) + m_{ij} + \sum_{k=1}^{J} \alpha_{jk}\, y_{ik}(t)\right], \quad (48)$$

where $j = 1, \ldots, 4$; $i = 1, \ldots, I$; and $\alpha_{jj} = -1$. The system of DDEs in (48), like the systems considered in Section 11.5, has an explicit solution, assuming that the exogenous variables change linearly between waves of observations.

Because the IEs for (48) contain individual-specific effects, we use pooled cross-section and time-series data (the same as in Section 11.3) and WGLS estimators to estimate coefficients of the IEs. Chapter 13 contains a general discussion of these estimators.

We begin by estimating each of the J IEs separately for growing and declining districts. Table 11.4 reports the estimated regression coefficients for the integral equations. The first four rows for each type of district give an estimate of the transpose of what we termed $\boldsymbol{\Gamma}$ in Section 11.5. The eigenvalues and eigenvectors of $\boldsymbol{\Gamma}$ are reported in Tables 11.5 and 11.6, respectively.

For the districts with rising enrollments, all eigenvalues are distinct and real. However, there is a pair of complex eigenvalues for districts with falling enrollments. An eigenvalue with real and complex parts implies cyclical change, as we mentioned earlier. However, the complex portions of these eigenvalues are smaller than the real parts by an order of magnitude and do not appear substantively important. They probably reflect only sampling variability in $\boldsymbol{\Gamma}$. Indeed, when we convert these estimates into estimates of the DDEs, the largest complex part of any coefficient is of the order of 10^{-18}. We round these terms to zero in reporting estimates of parameters of the DDEs.

The estimated DDEs appear in Table 11.7. We follow the partial-adjustment interpretation and translate these findings into speeds of adjustment, coupling coefficients, and effects of exogenous variables on carrying capacities. We turn now to a detailed discussion of findings on these three sets of parameters.

Speed of Adjustment. Previous findings about the speed of adjustment of administrative staff to growth and decline in enrollments have been inconsistent. Freeman and Hannan (1975) predicted and found that adjustment of the administrative staff to

Table 11.4. Weighted generalized least-squares estimates of the integral equations for a linear partial-adjustment model of personnel change in growing and declining school districts[a]

	Dependent variable			
Right-hand side variable	$A(t)$	$T(t)$	$P(t)$	$C(t)$
Growing districts				
$A(t-1)$	0.508*	0.159	−0.012	−0.013
$T(t-1)$	0.030*	0.636*	0.020*	−0.013
$P(t-1)$	−0.031	−0.088	0.712*	−0.495*
$C(t-1)$	−0.001	0.030	−0.002	0.866*
Intercept	0.070	0.314	−0.270	0.526
$S(t)$	0.014	1.043*	−0.048*	0.295
$\Delta S(t)$	0.064*	0.114*	−0.031	0.115
$R(t)$	0.017	0.784*	0.089*	0.487*
$\Delta R(t)$	0.052*	0.781*	0.063*	1.635*
R^2	.958	.992	.906	.949
Declining districts				
$A(t-1)$	0.614	0.400*	0.033	0.402
$T(t-1)$	0.006	0.621*	0.023*	0.070
$P(t-1)$	0.051*	−0.057	0.571	−0.245
$C(t-1)$	0.004*	−0.025	−0.008*	0.745*
Intercept	0.110	0.484	−0.265	0.661
$S(t)$	0.021	0.972*	−0.043*	0.007
$\Delta S(t)$	0.025	0.945*	−0.078	0.572
$R(t)$	0.065*	0.778*	0.061*	0.501*
$\Delta R(t)$	0.093*	0.109*	0.150*	0.997*
R^2	.963	.992	.830	.928

*Significantly different from zero at the .05 level.

[a]Data for 5 years are pooled. For growing districts, $I = 182$; for declining districts, $I = 181$.

Table 11.5. Eigenvalues of $\hat{\Gamma}$, the estimated matrix of endogenous variables, obtained from Table 11.4[a]

Dependent variable	Growing districts	Declining districts
A, Administrators	0.476	$0.547 + 0.060\,i$
T, Teachers	0.846	0.747
P, Pupil-service workers	0.684	$0.547 - 0.060\,i$
C, Classified workers	0.717	0.708

[a] The symbol i denotes $\sqrt{-1}$.

Table 11.6. Right eigenvectors of $\hat{\Gamma}$, the estimated matrix of the endogenous variables, obtained from Table 11.4[a]

	A	T	P	C
Growing districts				
A	−0.409	0.007	−0.055	−0.129
T	0.390	0.18	−0.207	−0.168
P	−0.053	0.050	0.103	0.632
C	−0.069	1.36	0.260	2.06
Declining districts				
A	$-0.337 - 0.973\,i$	−0.173	$-0.337 + 0.973\,i$	0.949
T	$-0.541 + 5.30\,i$	−6.41	$-0.541 - 5.30\,i$	5.98
P	$1.45 + 0.146\,i$	−2.48	$1.45 - 0.146\,i$	1.82
C	$2.37 + 0.996\,i$	34.99	$2.37 - 0.996\,i$	−9.85

[a] The symbol i denotes $\sqrt{-1}$.

changes in enrollments was faster in growth than in decline. But when Hannan and Freeman (1978) estimated a model in which personnel components were interdependent, they found the opposite—adjustment was faster in decline. Neither of the earlier studies incorporated effects of financial resources on carrying capacities. The

Table 11.7. Estimates of parameters in a linear partial-adjustment model of personnel change in growing and declining school districts[a]

Outcome	A	T	P	C	Intercept	S	R
Growing districts							
dA/dt	−0.686	0.053	−0.049	−0.003	0.080	0.0005	0.0005
dT/dt	0.280	−0.458	−0.110	0.041	0.352	0.0196	0.0136
dP/dt	−0.024	0.030	−0.338	0.002	−0.324	−0.0008	0.0011
dC/dt	−0.026	−0.008	−0.629	−0.143	0.047	0.0027	0.0200
Declining districts							
dA/dt	−0.495	0.008	0.089	0.007	0.149	0.0004	0.0012
dT/dt	0.665	−0.475	−0.134	−0.040	0.558	0.0170	0.0178
dP/dt	0.047	0.040	−0.563	−0.012	−0.356	−0.0014	0.0056
dC/dt	0.571	0.108	−0.394	−0.297	0.639	0.0054	0.0138

[a] Entries for S and R are the arithmetic mean of estimates based on the regression coefficients of $S(t-1)$ and $\Delta S(t)$ and $R(t-1)$ and $\Delta R(t)$, respectively.

analysis in Section 11.3, which adds resources to a scalar model of administrative growth, agrees with the earlier findings—adjustment was faster in growth. Table 11.8 reports the estimated speeds of adjustment for the whole system when resources are included. Again we find that adjustment is faster in growth. So the anomalous finding reported by Hannan and Freeman (1978) was apparently spurious, due to the failure to include a measure of financial resources. We conclude that the administrative staff in a school district can indeed stall responses to decline, as predicted.

Interestingly, the speed of adjustment of the teaching staff is nearly the same in growth and decline. This staff appears to follow the dictates of functional needs. However, the least powerful personnel components, pupil-service staff and classified employees, respond to decline more quickly than to growth. Apparently they bear the initial burden of decline.

Competitive Structure. Table 11.9 reports the estimated

Table 11.8. Estimates of the speed of adjustment, r, for growing and declining school districts[a]

Dependent variable	Growing districts	Declining districts
A, Administrators	0.686	0.495
T, Teachers	0.458	0.475
P, Pupil-service workers	0.338	0.563
C, Classified workers	0.143	0.297

[a] Entries are the negative of the feedback coefficients in Table 11.7.

Table 11.9. Estimated coupling coefficients ($\hat{\alpha}_{jk}$) for growing and declining school districts[a]

	A	T	P	C
Growing districts				
A, Administrators	−1.0	0.078*	−0.071	−0.004
T, Teachers	0.611	−1.0	−0.240	0.090
P, Pupil-service workers	−0.072	0.090*	−1.0	0.007
C, Classified workers	−0.181	−0.055	−4.406*	−1.0
Declining districts				
A, Administrators	−1.0	0.016	0.180*	0.014*
T, Teachers	1.40*	−1.0	−0.282	−0.084*
P, Pupil-service workers	0.083	0.070*	−1.0	−0.021*
C, Classified workers	1.92	0.363	−1.33	−1.0

*Corresponding estimate in the IE differs significantly from zero at the .05 level.
[a] $\hat{\alpha}_{jk}$ is the estimated effect of the personnel component in column k on the personnel component in row j. Each $\hat{\alpha}_{jk} = \hat{c}_{jk}/\hat{r}_j$, where $\hat{c}_{jk}$ comes from Table 11.7 and $\hat{r}_j$ comes from Table 11.8.

matrix of competition coefficients for growing and declining districts. With the exception of one coefficient, these estimates imply that coupling between personnel components is stronger in decline than in growth. The absolute values of the estimated coupling parameters

Table 11.10. Estimated carrying capacities for personnel components in growing and declining school districts[a]

Personnel component	Carrying capacity
Growing districts	
A, Administrators	$0.116 + 0.0007\,S + 0.0007\,R$
T, Teachers	$0.769 + 0.0428\,S + 0.0298\,R$
P, Pupil-service workers	$-0.958 - 0.0028\,S + 0.0036\,R$
C, Classified workers	$3.32\ \ + 0.0164\,S + 0.1405\,R$
Declining districts	
A, Administrators	$0.300 + 0.0008\,S + 0.0024\,R$
T, Teachers	$1.17\ \ + 0.0358\,S + 0.0374\,R$
P, Pupil-service workers	$-0.632 - 0.0026\,S + 0.0099\,R$
C, Classified workers	$2.15\ \ + 0.0183\,S + 0.0466\,R$

[a] S denotes student enrollments (average daily attendance); R stands for revenues in thousands of 1967 dollars). Effects on the carrying capacity are found by dividing the corresponding effects in Table 11.7 by the appropriate speed of adjustment in Table 11.8.

tend to be somewhat larger for the sample of declining districts. In addition, only three of the effects for growing districts but six of the effects for declining districts correspond to statistically significant integral coefficients. In both growth and decline, administrative and teaching staffs have a symbiotic relation, that is, each has a positive effect on the carrying capacity of the other. Anything that promotes growth in the number of teachers tends to increase the number of administrators, as Blau's (1970) argument suggests. However, administrative growth also increases the number of teachers, which cannot easily be explained by a rationalist perspective.

Effects of Exogenous Variables. The final set of parameters in the model is the effects of exogenous variables, π_j in equation (47). Table 11.10 reports estimates of the effects of student enrollments and revenues on carrying capacities. For the teaching staff, student enrollments have stronger effects in growth, but revenues have stronger effects in decline. However, the differences between growth and decline are not great. When $S = 4000$ and $R = 4000$

Table 11.11. Eigenvalues of the system of differential equations for personnel change in growing and declining school districts[a]

Dependent variable	Growing districts	Declining districts
A, Administrators	−0.743	−0.597 + 0.109 i
T, Teachers	−0.167	−0.292
P, Pupil-service workers	−0.380	−0.597 − 0.109 i
C, Classified workers	−0.333	−0.345

[a] Each entry is the logarithm of the corresponding entry in Table 11.5.

(close to the means of these variables for both growing and declining districts), T^* is virtually the same in growth and decline, 1 teacher per 14 students. In the case of the pupil-service staff, the estimates also imply that carrying capacities in growth and decline are the same. But the classified staff apparently fares much better when enrollments are rising; its carrying capacity is higher in growing than declining districts.

Given the emphasis of the previous literature on size and structure, the carrying capacity for administrators in growth and decline is particularly interesting. We find that growth and decline processes differ unambiguously for this group. Although the effect of enrollments is approximately the same in growth and decline, revenues have much stronger effects in decline. At any level of S and R, the carrying capacity for adinistrators is much larger in declining districts. For example, when $S = 4000$ and $R = 4000$, it is 5.7 for districts with growing enrollments and 14.1 for districts with declining enrollments.

According to Table 11.11, which reports estimated eigenvalues of the DDEs for growing and declining districts, the real parts of all eigenvalues are negative. In the case of growing districts, all four eigenvalues are real, implying that the system approaches an equilibrium monotonically. The eigenvalues for districts with declining enrollments contain a pair of complex conjugates, implying that the system approaches equilibrium by dampened cycles.

We have found something like the **ratchet effect** predicted by Freeman and Hannan (1975): when student enrollments grow, the administrative staff grows rapidly; when enrollments decline, the administrative staff declines slowly. Moreover, for a given number of students and level of revenues, the carrying capacity for administrators is higher in decline than in growth. Clearly, the growth and decline processes differ. Use of an explicit dynamic model gives insights that can not be seen in the usual static treatment of these issues.

11.8 Conclusions

We think that the linear structural-equation models so often analyzed by sociologists may be viewed profitably as steady-state outcomes of continuous-time models of change. Dynamic analysis, which estimates parameters of such models for systems out of equilibrium, permits deeper sociological insight into social processes than analysis of conventional static, structural-equation models. For example, it allows the effects of exogenous changes on outcomes to be separated from the effects of internal structural arrangements. More generally, it lets us discard the assumption that a social system operates close to an equilibrium.

In this chapter we concentrated on the special case of a linear deterministic differential equation (DDE) model to keep the exposition simple. We reviewed two interpretations of such models, negative feedback and partial adjustment. We showed that such models have potentially rich applications to sociological issues.

We also considered models of change in levels of several interdependent variables. The solutions of such models imply complicated relationships among observable variables. Nevertheless, one can estimate the dynamic parameters from regression estimates of the system of integral equations in many cases.

In addition, we showed that one can understand the qualitative behavior of linear systems by identifying their equilibria and studying the stability of each equilibrium point. For a linear system, stability is determined completely by the signs of the real parts of the eigenvalues of the endogenous part of the model. Therefore, sociologists studying linear change processes should always report and interpret estimated eigenvalues of the matrix of endogenous effects.

Phase-space analysis provides a useful aid in describing the qualitative behavior of systems of DDEs. We have shown that even linear systems may evolve in complex ways over time. Some linear systems move monotonically toward equilibrium points; others cycle toward equilibria; still others cycle endlessly around equilibria. Of course, unstable systems shoot away from equilibrium points. Whenever estimated systems have complex roots, we recommend that sociologists illustrate the behavior of the system with a phase-space diagram. Such diagrams often clarify the nature of the underlying change process and suggest alternative (perhaps nonlinear) specifications for the process.

Appendix

This appendix summarizes the steps involved in solving the linear scalar DDE in (8):

$$\frac{dy}{dt} = cy(t) + f(t),$$

where $f(t)$ is some (as yet unspecified) function of time. Although the procedure for solving this equation can be found in most standard texts on DEs, we include it because such a large portion of the discussion in Part III relies on this result, or on the parallel result for a system of linear DDEs.

We begin by rearranging (8) to give

$$\frac{dy}{dt} - cy(t) = f(t). \qquad (A.1)$$

At this point we take what may seem to be a short detour but is, in fact, the key to solving this DDE. We define

$$e^{-ct} y(t) \equiv u(t).$$

This expression implies that

$$e^{-ct} \left[\frac{dy}{dt} - cy(t) \right] = \frac{du}{dt};$$

$$\frac{dy}{dt} - cy(t) = e^{ct} \frac{du}{dt}. \qquad (A.2)$$

Putting $(A.2)$ into $(A.1)$ gives

$$e^{ct} \frac{du}{dt} = f(t),$$

or
$$du = e^{-ct} f(t)\, dt. \qquad (A.3)$$

Each side of this equation is easily integrated. First, integrate the left-hand side of $(A.3)$:

$$\int_{t_0}^{t} du = u(t) - u(t_0) = e^{-ct} y(t) - e^{-ct_0} y(t_0),$$

and then equate the result with the integral of the right-hand side of $(A.3)$:

$$e^{-ct} y(t) - e^{-ct_0} y(t_0) = \int_{t_0}^{t} e^{-cs} f(s)\, ds.$$

Simple algebraic manipulations give the solution reported in (9):

$$y(t) = e^{c(t-t_0)} y(t_0) + e^{ct} \int_{t_0}^{t} e^{-cs} f(s)\, ds. \qquad (A.4)$$

The general solution in $(A.4)$ can be applied to special cases by replacing $f(s)$ with some specific function and integrating (if possible). We have emphasized the case in which

$$f(t) \equiv \mathbf{b}' \mathbf{x}(t),$$

and $\mathbf{x}(t)$ changes linearly in the interval $[t_0, t]$ [see (12)]. Then the last term in $(A.4)$ becomes

$$e^{ct} \int_{t_0}^{t} e^{-cs} \mathbf{b}' \big[\mathbf{x}(t_0) + \boldsymbol{\kappa}(s - t_0)\big]\, ds$$

$$= e^{ct} \mathbf{b}' \bigg\{ \big[\mathbf{x}(t_0) - \boldsymbol{\kappa} t_0\big] \int_{t_0}^{t} e^{-cs}\, ds + \boldsymbol{\kappa} \int_{t_0}^{t} e^{-cs} s\, ds \bigg\}.$$

Since

$$\int e^{-cs}\, ds = -\frac{1}{c} e^{-cs}$$

and

⟨11⟩ **Appendix**

$$\int e^{-cs} s\,ds = -\frac{cs+1}{c^2} e^{-cs},$$

this expression can be integrated explicitly. It turns out to be

$$-\frac{e^{ct}}{c} \mathbf{b}'\{[\mathbf{x}(t_0) - \boldsymbol{\kappa} t_0][e^{-ct} - e^{-ct_0}]$$

$$+\frac{1}{c}\boldsymbol{\kappa}\left[(ct+1)e^{-ct} - (ct_0+1)e^{-ct_0}\right]\}.$$

Multiplying through by $-e^{ct}$ and letting $\gamma \equiv e^{c\Delta t} \equiv e^{ct-ct_0}$ yields

$$\frac{1}{c}\mathbf{b}'\left\{\mathbf{x}(t_0)[\gamma-1] + \boldsymbol{\kappa} t_0 - \boldsymbol{\kappa} t_0 \gamma - \boldsymbol{\kappa} t - \frac{1}{c}\boldsymbol{\kappa} + \boldsymbol{\kappa} t_0 \gamma + \frac{1}{c}\boldsymbol{\kappa}\gamma\right\}$$

$$= \frac{1}{c}\mathbf{b}'\left\{\mathbf{x}(t_0)[\gamma-1] - \boldsymbol{\kappa}\Delta t + \frac{1}{c}\boldsymbol{\kappa}[\gamma-1]\right\}$$

$$= \frac{1}{c}\mathbf{b}'\left\{\mathbf{x}(t_0)[\gamma-1] + \Delta\mathbf{x}(t)\left[\frac{\gamma-1}{c\Delta t} - 1\right]\right\}.$$

Hence the resulting integral equation is

$$y(t) = e^{c\Delta t} y(t_0) + \frac{e^{c\Delta t}-1}{c}\mathbf{b}'\mathbf{x}(t_0) + \frac{1}{c}\left[\frac{e^{c\Delta t}-1}{c\Delta t} - 1\right]\mathbf{b}'\Delta\mathbf{x}(t),$$

which is equivalent to (13) in Section 11.2.

12
Linear Stochastic Models

The models treated in Chapter 11 do not contain stochastic elements—they have no "noise" or disturbance terms. Few social scientists claim that such models hold exactly. Rather, they defend such simple models as useful approximations to the complex processes that really occur. The desire for simple models, combined with ignorance about true processes, causes us to omit from our models some causal factors that are usually regarded as random noise. The premise justifying the use of *deterministic* models in social research is that random noise has relatively small and unsystematic effects. Given this assumption, the deterministic model may be viewed as a description of the *average* time path of the actual "noisy" process, and the "noise" may be ignored.

Although describing the average of a distribution is a natural starting point, sole reliance on averages is often misleading. The sociological literature shows little awareness of the limitation of deterministic models, especially with regard to the study of dynamics. Therefore, in Section 12.1 we begin by comparing the advantages and disadvantages of deterministic and stochastic models.

Section 12.2 considers implications of adding a stochastic disturbance to a linear deterministic differential equation (DDE), thus yielding a *stochastic differential equation* (SDE). We concentrate on the tractable case of a white-noise disturbance, which converts a scalar DDE into a Markov process. In Section 12.3 we discuss an approach to including both a continuously varying disturbance and a discrete random shock. We suggest that a disturbance that combines white noise with a generalization of the Poisson process considered in Chapter 4 has promise for sociological applications.

Section 12.4 discusses the class of models called diffusion processes. These models specify how transition probability densities evolve over time. Such models have the valuable property of allowing systematic treatment of boundaries, including floors and ceilings on the values that variables can have. We review a variety of boundary specifications in Section 12.5.

Though many substantive models begin by adding a stochastic disturbance to a linear DDE, complete probabilistic description of a process usually requires specifying a diffusion process. Consequently, any practical use of stochastic models raises questions concerning the relationship between diffusion processes and differential equations (DEs) with stochastic disturbances. The relationship is fairly straightforward for the case of linear models; however, subtle problems arise in the case of nonlinear models. We delay discussion of nonlinear stochastic models until Chapter 15.

Finally, in Section 12.6 we discuss ways of developing stochastic models of a system of quantitative outcomes. We note that only a few systems of SDEs may be solved for explicit transition probability densities. Consequently, empirical analysis is far harder.

12.1 Need for Stochastic Models

Deterministic models have one main advantage: simplicity. Often deterministic DEs have explicit solutions while analogous stochastic equations do not. Moreover, estimation and testing in the stochastic framework are complicated.

The main advantage of a stochastic model is realism. As indicated above, real social systems are more complex than our models imply. In addition, real social systems face turbulent environments whose dynamics introduce a large element of chance into social processes. Thus models of social dynamics must almost always contain stochastic elements to be realistic.

Still, sociologists might gladly sacrifice realism for simplicity if the implications of deterministic and stochastic models are largely the same. Most sociologists seem to think that they are, but they are not. If deterministic and stochastic models imply different dynamics for substantively interesting problems, sociologists must rethink the choice between the two types of models.

Deterministic and stochastic approaches can be contrasted directly for the important case of data based on counts. Sociologists often study counted data, for example, the number of members in an organization or social movement, the number of strikes in an industry, the number of levels in an authority structure, or the number of social ties in a network. As we noted in Chapter 3, counted data are treated as discrete at times and continuous at other times. This distinction scarcely matters when counts are large; the addition or deletion of a single unit from a very large count has such a small relative effect on the count that little is lost by assuming continuity. But the magnitude of counts varies greatly across substantive problems. Deterministic and stochastic models agree most closely when counts are large. For example, deterministic and stochastic models of the dynamics of vote counts ordinarily agree more closely when applied to a country's electorate than when applied to the members of a legislature. Furthermore, in the important case of systems of equations, the divergence of deterministic and stochastic models depends on the size of the *smallest* count. More precisely, it is the size of the smallest count compared to the amount of noise in the process that controls the similarity of the two types of models. In turbulent environments stochastic and deterministic models usually do not agree closely, even about the time path of the average count.

Stochastic and deterministic models also differ in the treatment of the disappearance of social units and the disruption of social relationships. Social relationships and social organizations do not last forever. Unless attention is restricted to those that survive, which would usually be a serious substantive error, "deaths" cannot be handled systematically in a deterministic framework. Adoption of a stochastic model seems essential for successful sociological studies of long-run patterns of social change. The ability to model extinction of social forms as a part of the general process of change is a potential benefit of stochastic models that has so far escaped notice in the sociological literature. We develop this issue further below.

Stochastic models are also a better approach to the dynamics of the *variability* in distributions. It is often noted (e.g., see Stinchcombe, 1968, pp. 248–265) that social processes affect the variance of behaviors and attributes of social units as well as the average value. Some social processes may be revealed more clearly in variances than in averages. For example, most social scientists find the shape of the income distribution more interesting than the mean. Similarly, some organizational analysts attend to features of the size distribution of organizations (see Ijiri and Simon, 1977). Hannan and Freeman (1977a) argued that the evolution of the size distribution of organizations tells much about the competitive nature of organizational environments that cannot be observed directly. Many structural processes that are theoretically important but difficult to observe directly seem likely to have testable implications regarding the shapes of distributions.

A deterministic model can explain the shape of a distribution only in a weak sense. Though it can explain change from some assumed initial distribution, it cannot explain how an initial distribution arose in the first place. A stochastic model can explain the evolution of a distribution, even when the initial distribution is uniform. Thus it provides a better way of studying distributional properties of social structure.

Finally, a stochastic perspective facilitates the study of joint changes in quantitative and qualitative variables. Current sociological research has begun to confront problems of modeling linked changes in outcomes such as marital status and earnings, organizational form and size, or type of city government and city crime rate. All analysts seem to agree that models of change in qualitative variables should be stochastic. Can one defend a model of interdependent changes in which some outcomes are stochastic and others are deterministic? We think not. In our opinion there is no satisfactory alternative to stochastic models for this important class of sociological problems. We discuss these matters further in Chapters 15 and 16.

For all of these reasons, we venture into the hazardous terrain of stochastic models of change in metric outcomes, in spite of their technical complexity. In an attempt to keep this discussion at an elementary level, we merely survey the leading issues in the mathematical theory and develop in some detail several models applicable to a wide range of phenomena of sociological interest. For many years no systematic treatment of the relevant theory was available. However, Karlin and Taylor (1981, pp. 157–396) have filled this void. Their treatment is fairly technical but discusses numerous applications from the natural sciences. Readers who wish to pursue the ideas developed below are urged to consult this source.

12.2 Stochastic Differential Equations

In Chapter 11 we discussed sociological applications of DDEs. Three strategies for formulating probabilistic versions of such models have been treated in the literature. The first adds a random disturbance to models like those considered in Chapter 11, which converts DDEs into SDEs. The second considers one or more parameters of models like those in Chapter 11 to be random variables driven by specific stochastic processes. The third treats the initial condition $y(t_0)$ as a random variable. Saaty (1967, Chapter 8) provided a detailed exposition of the three alternatives. Each method converts the outcome, labeled $y(t)$ in Chapter 11, into a stochastic process, which we denote by $Y(t)$. The third strategy does so in a limited way; the process starts at a random point but proceeds deterministically. Because the first and second alternatives have deeper implications and potentially wider applicability, we focus on them. The statistical literature concentrates mainly on the first strategy, the device of introducing a random disturbance into DDEs of the sort considered in the previous chapter; we also emphasize this strategy. The second strategy has many appealing features, but it has not yet been widely applied. In Chapter 15 we do discuss one model constructed by treating parameters as random variables.

The first task is to choose a stochastic process for the noise or disturbance term. Candidates for the disturbance should meet two criteria. They should be stochastic processes that imply realistic behavior for $Y(t)$. They should also be analytically tractable; that is, they should not make it too difficult to describe the behavior of $Y(t)$ analytically. The second requirement is very restrictive for continuous-state outcomes. Only a highly simplified noise process offers any hope of deducing the behavior of $Y(t)$. Therefore, the technical literature concentrates mainly on the simplest possible disturbance: white noise. We focus on white-noise disturbances, too, except in the next section, which considers a more general disturbance.

White noise is a mathematical model for a continuous-state, continuous-time process with **independent increments**. ("Increments" is the term for the changes in an outcome over successive small intervals of time.) White noise has two special features: it consists wholly of instantaneous impulses that are uncorrelated over time, and each impulse is the sum of many independent forces.

⟨12⟩ Stochastic Differential Equations

Consider the problem of modeling fluctuations in ethnic antagonism in social systems. The level of hostility between ethnic groups appears to vary systematically with certain observable features of a community, such as the existence of a split labor market (Bonacich, 1972) or shifts in the degree of overlap of occupational roles among ethnic groups (Hannan, 1979; Nielsen, 1980; Olzak, 1982). Both of these structural factors tend to change slowly. Suppose that one correctly specifies a model relating labor market conditions to the evolution of ethnic hostility. What assumptions should be made about the effects of local and transitory events, for example, chance encounters between members of the various ethnic groups and short-term changes in community structure? It does not seem unreasonable to assume (as a first approximation) that the disturbance consists of uncorrelated impulses, that is, that levels of ethnic antagonism and competition are driven in part by white-noise processes.

The second feature mentioned above, that each shock reflects the influence of many independent forces, implies that white noise, $Z(t)$, has a normal distribution whose mean is zero. This fact is a primary reason for choosing white noise in the first place—a normal distribution has many convenient analytic properties.[1] The assumption that increments in adjacent time intervals are independent (obviously a simplifying assumption) raises some curious analytic questions. It implies that the autocorrelation function $\mathrm{E}[Z(s)Z(t)]$ is zero for $t \neq s$ but nonzero for $t = s$. Clearly the autocorrelation of white noise cannot be an ordinary function. Nor can a random variable $Y(t)$ driven by white noise be an ordinary function of time.

To formalize the peculiar properties of the autocorrelation of white noise, we introduce the **Dirac delta function**, denoted by $\delta(t-s)$. The delta function is zero for all t except $t = s$, where it equals positive infinity; the integral of the delta function over any interval containing t equals unity. Though the delta function is not an ordinary function, treating it as such has given useful results in the study of impulse functions and a variety of physical phenomena.[2] We follow a similar strategy for defining white noise.

---

[1] Clearly one should consider carefully whether a normal distribution is plausible in any particular application.

[2] See Braun (1975, pp. 325–335) for a lucid exposition of the scientific background and interpretation of delta functions.

Standard white noise is a Gaussian (or normal) process with

$$\mathrm{E}\big[Z(t)\,Z(s)\big] = \delta(t-s),$$

where $\delta(t-s)$ is the Dirac delta function. Because of the form of the autocorrelation function, white noise is also called a delta-correlated process.

Though white noise is a useful mathematical concept, it is highly artificial. All realistic processes have some nonzero correlation over time. So in scientific applications, white noise is usually considered to be a convenient approximation to processes in which the autocorrelation of disturbances decreases to zero rapidly as the interval between observations increases. More precisely, white noise provides a good approximation to omitted variables whose serial correlations fall rapidly relative to the rates of change in the other variables in the model. Just as we found in Chapter 9 for qualitative outcomes, the problematic situation is one in which some unobserved factors evolve relatively slowly.

Having discussed the nature of the disturbance, we now consider elementary SDEs. Rather than attempting a general discussion, we concentrate on an important special case called an **Ornstein–Uhlenbeck** (OU) process. This process assumes that increments depend linearly on the current state of the process (which in turn depends on all previous increments). The OU process may be written as a linear DE driven by white noise, $Z(t)$,

$$\frac{\mathrm{d}Y(t)}{\mathrm{d}t} = -r\,Y(t) + \sigma\,Z(t), \tag{1}$$

where $r > 0$. This equation has the same basic form as the linear models treated extensively in Chapter 11.[3] Suppose one ignores the peculiar properties of white noise and simply integrates equation (1) from t_0 to t for each sample path, using the ordinary rules of the calculus. This procedure gives an integral equation (IE) of the form

$$Y(t) = \mathrm{e}^{-r\Delta t}\,y(t_0) + \epsilon(t),$$

---

[3]We continue to denote random variables by upper-case letters and realizations by lower-case letters.

where
$$\epsilon(t) \equiv \sigma \, e^{-rt} \int_{t_0}^{t} e^{ru} \, Z(u) \, du. \tag{2}$$

The classic OU process expresses partial adjustment toward the origin, but one might wish to consider partial adjustment to some nonzero criterion $Y^*(t)$:

$$\frac{dY(t)}{dt} = r\left[Y^*(t) - Y(t)\right] + \sigma Z(t). \tag{3}$$

In the spirit of the discussion in the previous chapter, the criterion can be expressed as a linear combination of observable exogenous factors $\mathbf{x}(t)$:

$$Y^*(t) \equiv \boldsymbol{\pi}'\mathbf{x}(t).$$

Substituting this expression into (3) gives a modified OU process:

$$\frac{dY(t)}{dt} = r\left[\boldsymbol{\pi}'\mathbf{x}(t) - Y(t)\right] + \sigma Z(t). \tag{4}$$

When $\mathbf{x}(t) = \mathbf{x}$, the IE associated with this process is

$$Y(t) = e^{-r\Delta t} \, y(t_0) + \frac{1 - e^{-r\Delta t}}{r} \mathbf{b}'\mathbf{x} + \epsilon(t), \tag{5}$$

where the disturbance $\epsilon(t)$ is still defined by (2) and $\mathbf{b} \equiv r\boldsymbol{\pi}$.

For the stochastic process governing $Y(t)$ in either (1) or (4) to be meaningful, the integral in (2), which is a function of white noise, must be well behaved. This requirement is potentially problematic because of the peculiar structure of $Z(t)$—the fact that $Z(t)$ is delta correlated. Accordingly, substantive interpretation of even the most elementary SDE requires some understanding of the meaning of an integral of a white-noise process.

The integral of white noise is a famous stochastic process in its own right—**Brownian motion**. The process is named after Robert Brown, the English botanist who reported the erratic and turbulent movement of particles suspended in a solution and investigated possible explanations of such behavior. Actually, the first detailed (but nonrigorous) mathematical description of this process concerned a social-scientific application, fluctuations of stock market prices (Bachelier, 1900). Mathematicians often call it a Wiener process, after Norbert Wiener, who first provided a rigorous mathematical formalization of the process. As a comparatively simple and well-studied process, Brownian motion provides a point of entry into the literature on stochastic integrals.

Brownian motion is a stochastic process, $\{B(t); t \geq 0\}$, with the following three properties:[4]

1. **Independence**: $B(t + \Delta t) - B(t)$ is independent of $\{B(s); s \leq t\}$. That is, increments in the process are independent of the entire history of the process, including its current position. This assumption is stronger than the Markov assumption (which permits dependence on the current position of the process) and implies it.
2. **Stationarity**: The distribution of $B(t+\Delta t) - B(t)$ depends only on Δt and does not depend on t.
3. **Continuity (in probability)**:[5]

$$\lim_{\Delta t \downarrow 0} \frac{\Pr\bigl[|B(t+\Delta t) - B(t)| > \epsilon\bigr]}{\Delta t} = 0.$$

If $B(0) = 0$, an increment in the process $B(t) - B(0)$ is *normally distributed* with mean μt and variance $\sigma^2 t$ (see Breiman, 1968, pp. 248–250). Any Brownian-motion process may be transformed into **standard Brownian motion**, which has a mean of zero and variance t, that is, $\sigma^2 = 1$. We use the symbol $W(t)$ to refer to standard Brownian motion with a mean of zero and a variance of 1, and $\sigma W(t)$ to represent a Brownian-motion process with a mean of zero and a variance of $\sigma^2 t$. Without loss of generality we assume that $W(0) = 0$.

The correlation function for a Brownian-motion process starting at time $t_0 = 0$ is

$$\mathrm{E}[B(t)B(s)] = \sigma^2 \min(t,s). \tag{6}$$

---

[4] Most texts on stochastic processes discuss Brownian motion. For instance, see Karlin and Taylor (1975).

[5] Recall that a downward arrow ($\downarrow$) means that Δt approaches 0 from the right; consequently, Δt is always positive.

Notice that the autocorrelation of Brownian motion depends only on the period of overlap between the two segments (both of which begin at $t_0 = 0$). Among other things, the relationship in (6) implies that nonoverlapping segments of a Brownian-motion process are uncorrelated.

Brownian motion has obvious appeal as a specification for the behavior of omitted variables. Normality follows from very elementary (but strong) assumptions, and the first and second moments are uncomplicated functions of elapsed time. However, Brownian motion has some odd properties. Though sample paths (i.e., realizations) of the process are continuous functions of time, Brownian motion is nowhere differentiable nor does it have bounded variation. (It may help to think of the sample path a Brownian-motion process as being infinitesimally jagged.) All these statements hold "almost surely",[6] for a detailed proof, see Doob (1953, p. 393).

Examination of the characteristic function of white noise reveals (e.g., see van Kampen, 1978, pp. 8–9) that

$$W(t) = \int_{t_0}^{t} Z(s)\,\mathrm{d}s, \qquad (7)$$

or, equivalently, that

$$\mathrm{d}W(t) = Z(t)\,\mathrm{d}t. \qquad (8)$$

This means, in some sense, that white noise is the "derivative" of standard Brownian motion. The sense cannot be the usual one, of course, because Brownian motion is not differentiable.

Nevertheless, representing white noise as the derivative of standard Brownian motion has heuristic value because it gives an explicit interpretation of the stochastic integral in (2). This integral, the disturbance associated with $Y(t)$, is a function only of $W(t) - W(t_0)$, an increment in a Brownian-motion process. Consequently, the disturbance term in the OU process is a normally distributed random variable. Clearly the mean of $\epsilon(t)$ is zero because the mean

---

[6]"Almost sure" convergence, also called strong convergence or convergence with probability 1, means that the function in question converges to the criterion (e.g., a continuous function) for all sample paths except a set that has measure (i.e., probability) zero.

of $Z(t)$ is zero. Treating $y(t_0)$ as a fixed constant yields

$$E[Y(t)] = e^{-r\Delta t} y(t_0) + E[\epsilon(t)]$$
$$= e^{-r\Delta t} y(t_0).$$

In the case of the modified OU process in (4), when $\mathbf{x}(t) = \mathbf{x}$, the mean is

$$E[Y(t)] = e^{-r\Delta t} y(t_0) + \frac{1 - e^{-r\Delta t}}{r} \mathbf{b}'\mathbf{x} + E[\epsilon(t)]$$
$$= e^{-r\Delta t} y(t_0) + \frac{1 - e^{-r\Delta t}}{r} \mathbf{b}'\mathbf{x}. \tag{9}$$

Thus the mean of $Y(t)$ for a linear scalar SDE agrees with its deterministic analogue; compare (9) above with equation (10) in Chapter 11. The white-noise process can be ignored in describing the average behavior of $Y(t)$. As we indicate in Section 12.5, this statement must be qualified. It holds only as long as there are no reachable boundaries in the state space of $Y(t)$. Moreover, if the covariates $\mathbf{x}$ are treated as random variables, the average behavior of the process depends on their joint distribution with the white-noise process. Nonetheless, it is comforting to find that linear SDEs agree on average with their deterministic counterparts under at least some circumstances.

Next we calculate the variance and covariance of the OU process. To do so, we must rely on a basic result about integrals defined with respect to Brownian motion. This result can be stated as follows (for a relatively simple proof, see Hoel, Port, and Stone, 1972, p. 144):

$$E\left[\int_{t_0}^{t} f(u)\,dW(u) \cdot \int_{t_0}^{s} g(u)\,dW(u)\right] = \int_{t_0}^{s} f(u)\,g(u)\,du, \tag{10}$$

where $t_0 \leq s \leq t$. In other words, taking expectations (in mean square) converts integrals defined with respect to Brownian motion into ordinary integrals of time. Note that (10) assumes that the intervals of integration overlap at least partially.

From (10) the covariance of the OU process can be shown to be:

$$\text{Cov}[\epsilon(s), \epsilon(t)] = \text{E}[\epsilon(t)\epsilon(s)]$$

$$= \text{E}\left[\sigma\, e^{-rs} \int_{t_0}^{s} e^{ru}\, dW(u) \cdot \sigma\, e^{-rt} \int_{t_0}^{t} e^{ru}\, dW(u)\right]$$

$$= \frac{\sigma^2}{2r}\, e^{-r(t-s)}\left[1 - e^{-2r(s-t_0)}\right], \tag{11}$$

where $s \leq t$. Whereas a Brownian-motion process is delta correlated, the OU process has exponential autocorrelation. The latter is more realistic for most applications. The variance of the OU process, found by setting $s = t$, is

$$\text{Var}[\epsilon(t)] = \frac{\sigma^2}{2r}\left[1 - e^{-2r\Delta t}\right], \tag{12}$$

where $\Delta t \equiv t - t_0$.

In sum, the OU model implies that $Y(t)$ is normally distributed with the same mean as the solution to the analogous deterministic equation and with the variance given in (12).[7] The similarity of this result to standard assumptions in the linear models for panel data often used by sociologists makes application of this model, and the assumption of a white-noise disturbance, very appealing. We rely heavily on this result in developing estimators for the linear partial-adjustment model in the next chapter. Notice that, as long as r is positive (as we have assumed), the variance of the OU process converges to $\sigma^2/2r$ as time unfolds.

Before leaving this subject, we note an important corollary of the basic result in (10). The covariance between two nonoverlapping segments of an OU process is zero (see Hoel, Port, and Stone, 1972, p. 144; Jazwinski, 1970, pp. 99–100); that is,

$$\text{E}\left[\int_a^b f(u)\, dW(u) \cdot \int_c^d g(u)\, dW(u)\right] = 0, \tag{13}$$

when $a \leq b \leq c \leq d$. This fact is fundamental to our strategy for estimating parameters in a scalar OU process, which we present in the next chapter.

---

[7] Indeed, the OU process is the most general continuous-state stochastic process that is a stationary Gaussian Markov process.

To this point we have noted that adding a white-noise disturbance to a scalar DDE like those considered in Chapter 11 implies results that are analogous to those in Chapter 11. The only difference is that the IE has the stochastic disturbance given by (2), whose variance and covariances depend on time. Thus the usual panel regression with normally distributed disturbances (discussed in Chapters 2 and 11) can be considered as a procedure for estimating a scalar SDE with a white-noise forcing function. From a slightly different perspective, this discussion may be viewed as a justification for the procedures proposed by Coleman (1968). He suggested that one estimate parameters of IEs for linear DDEs by using linear regression analysis under the assumption of normally distributed disturbances. The framework discussed so far in this chapter implies that the procedure proposed by Coleman is appropriate for an unbounded linear dynamic model of a scalar outcome driven by a white-noise disturbance.

For example, we might regard the scalar model of growth and decline of the administrative staff in an organization that we discussed in Section 11.3 as being driven by a white-noise disturbance. Since integrated white noise has a normal distribution, the regression procedure that we used would seem to have optimal properties if the disturbance is really white noise. But, because counts cannot be negative, a proper stochastic treatment involves boundary considerations (see Section 12.5). With a boundary at zero, the disturbance is no longer normal, nor does it have mean zero in general. Consequently, models for counted data require a more complex estimation procedure that takes boundary constraints into account.

The results cited in this section tell that the mathematical peculiarities of white noise may be overlooked and standard analytical procedures may be used to obtain meaningful results for the special case of an unbounded scalar *linear* model. However, as we stress in Section 12.6, these procedures do not carry over directly to the case of coupled linear systems. Chapter 15 discusses nonlinear models, which also generate additional complications. Here we merely note that to acknowledge the peculiar mathematical properties of these models, SDEs are usually written in *differential* form.[8]

---

[8]The differential of a function $f(t)$ is defined as
$$\mathrm{d}f(t) \equiv \lim_{\Delta t \to 0} \left[f(t + \Delta t) - f(t) \right].$$

⟨12⟩ *Complicating the Noise Process

$$dY(t) = f[Y(t)]\,dt + g[Y(t)]\,Z(t)\,dt, \qquad (14a)$$

or, given (8),

$$dY(t) = f[Y(t)]\,dt + g[Y(t)]\,dW(t). \qquad (14b)$$

Notice that the constant multiplier of the disturbance in (3), σ, has been replaced with a more general forcing function $g[Y(t)]$, which may depend on the value of Y at time t, $Y(t)$. Equation (14) is defined to be equivalent to the IE[9]

$$Y(t) = y(t_0) + \int_{t_0}^{t} f[Y(s)]\,ds + \int_{t_0}^{t} g[Y(s)]\,dW(s).$$

The extensive statistical literature on SDEs treats properties of sample paths of general stochastic processes, $Y(t)$. We return to these issues in Chapter 15.

12.3 *Complicating the Noise Process

The choice of a white-noise disturbance is widespread but not universal. Some progress has been made with more general disturbances. This section briefly discusses one potentially important extension that permits discontinuous jumps in the disturbance.

Assuming that the disturbance behaves like white noise may be appropriate when environmental influences fluctuate more rapidly than the phenomenon under study. But sometimes portions of the relevant environment change discontinuously and infrequently (e.g., the legal environment of firms and labor unions). If we were to model these processes explicitly, we would use the discrete-state framework of Part II. For consistency with that treatment, we investigate the possibility of including a discrete-state stochastic process in the disturbance. This sort of extension has been proposed in the engineering literature; we follow McGarty's (1974) treatment.

In motivating the choice of white noise for a continuously varying disturbance, we noted that there is little hope of obtaining analytical results if a complicated stochastic process governs the

---

[9] Existence and uniqueness of solutions of SDEs depend on conditions that parallel those for DDEs; see Karlin and Taylor (1981, pp. 373–374).

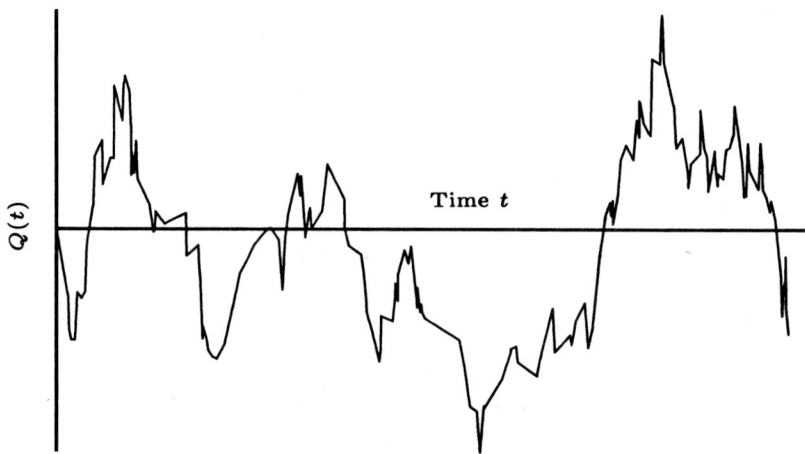

Figure 12.1. Hypothetical sample path of a generalized Poisson process.

disturbance. The same reasoning applies to the specification of a discrete-state disturbance. Once again we restrict attention to processes with independent increments. It turns out that a generalization of the Poisson process discussed in Section 4.4 fits our needs. Recall that if $N(t)$ is a Poisson process, every event increases the level of $N(t)$ by 1, that is, the *step size* is 1. We wish to generalize this model so that the step size becomes a random variable that can be positive or negative. Let the random variable X_n denote the step size of the process at time t_n, where t_n is the time of the nth event. As long as X_n is independent from step to step (the process has no memory), one can form a generalized Poisson process that is still a process with independent increments. Assume that $x_0 = 0$ and that $p(x)$, the probability density of the step size X_n, is independent of n. The generalized Poisson process is defined as

$$Q(t) \equiv \sum_{n=0}^{N(t)} X_n.$$

Figure 12.1 shows a hypothetical sample path of this process.

For empirical work, a particular $p(x)$ must be specified. At least initially, it seems natural to assume that the steps are normally distributed with mean zero and variance σ_x^2. In this case the

⟨12⟩ *Complicating the Noise Process

covariance function of the process (McGarty, 1974, pp. 85–86) is

$$E[Q(t)Q(s)] = \lambda \sigma_x^2 \min(t,s),$$

where λ is the parameter of the underlying Poisson process governing the rate of occurrence of jumps. This expression has the same form as the covariance function for Brownian motion; compare it with equation (6). Because the correlation function of the derivative of the generalized Poisson process is

$$E\left[\frac{dQ(t)}{dt} \frac{dQ(s)}{ds}\right] = \lambda \sigma_x^2 \, \delta(t-s),$$

$dQ(t)/dt$ is a white-noise process. In other words, the generalized Poisson process has the same first and second moments as Brownian motion. Indeed, an independent-increments process is a Brownian-motion process when the state space is continuous, and it is a generalized Poisson process when the state space is at most countable (McGarty, 1974, pp. 87–92). Consequently, an independent-increments process may be factored into a Brownian-motion component and a Poisson component.

Thus, a general noise process for SDEs might be the sum of uncorrelated Brownian-motion and generalized Poisson processes:

$$\eta(t) = \sigma W(t) + Q(t).$$

This general disturbance evolves continuously over time due to $W(t)$ and jumps discontinuously due to $Q(t)$. Nonetheless, it still has mean zero and stationary independent increments. This disturbance appears to be a promising candidate for sociological models. Unfortunately, this extension complicates modeling and estimation. Because we have already discussed discrete-state models at length, we do not consider this form of disturbance further in this book. We note merely that it deserves attention from social scientists.

Below we concentrate on SDEs driven by Brownian-motion disturbances. The next section considers a different perspective on models of change in quantitative outcomes. The remaining sections of this chapter introduce major issues in stochastic models of metric outcomes and cite the relevant literatures. Many of these issues are quite technical and can be skipped on first reading without loss of continuity.

12.4 Diffusion Processes

The temporal evolution of a stochastic quantity may be formalized in two ways. One describes the dynamics of the variable $Y(t)$ itself (the strategy that we have discussed to this point); the second describes the dynamics of the *probability distribution* of $Y(t)$. Since the two strategies give the same results, it is not necessary to employ both of them. Yet it is often instructive to consider both ways of analyzing changes in quantitative outcomes. We suggested earlier that substantive arguments are usually phrased first in the form of a DE. However, if one asks probabilistic questions or introduces certain complications (e.g., maximum and/or minimum values that $Y(t)$ can have; see Section 12.5), the second approach is preferable. Consequently, it is important to understand the exact relationship between SDEs and models of change in probability distributions. So far we have sketched the procedures for using SDEs; now we consider the latter approach.

We consider a general class of continuous-time, continuous-state stochastic processes $\{\,Y(t),\,t* > t_0\,\}$. The term **diffusion process** refers to a Markov process for a metric outcome whose sample paths are almost surely continuous functions of t. It is important to keep in mind that a diffusion process refers not to any *particular* sample path but to the *set* of sample paths. Such processes have been used widely in the physical and biological sciences. They are the natural continuous-state counterparts of the discrete-state processes considered in Part II.

In general one wants to know the probability that a stochastic process at some level y_s at time s is at level y_t at time t, $p \equiv p_{y_s y_t}(s,t)$. This function, called the **transition probability density** of the process, is directly analogous to the discrete-state transition probability $p_{jk}(s,t)$ defined in Section 3.2.2. The process of change can be described by expressing how the transition probability density depends on elapsed time, the level of $Y(t)$, and levels of causal variables.

Usually change in a transition probability density is modeled in terms of two main properties of the process: the **local mean** or **drift** and the **local variance** (sometimes called the **diffusion parameter**). Even though the literature on diffusion processes is quite complex, it is not too difficult to develop an intuitive understanding of these two concepts. Then one can formulate a diffusion process that captures fundamental ideas about some substantive process. When the formulation is not too complicated, implications have sometimes been derived previously and permit empirical analyses. Hence it is worthwhile expending some effort to understand these two concepts even if one does not wish to pursue the technical literature on diffusion processes in depth.

Formally, the local mean (drift) is defined as

$$\mu(y_t) \equiv \lim_{\Delta t \downarrow 0} \frac{\mathrm{E}\big[Y(t+\Delta t) - Y(t) \mid Y(t) = y(t)\big]}{\Delta t}.$$

Roughly speaking, the local mean describes the average change in $Y(t)$ in a small interval of time. Consider the small interval of time between t and $t + \Delta t$ and assume that $y(t) \equiv y_t$ for some set of sample paths. In this interval of time, $Y(t)$ may increase for some sample paths, decrease for others, and perhaps not even change at all for others. If $y(t + \Delta t) = y(t)$ on average, then the local mean is zero. If $y(t + \Delta t) > y(t)$ on average, the local mean is positive. If $y(t + \Delta t) < y(t)$ on average, the local mean is negative. For illustrative purposes, assume that the local mean is known to be positive. One may want to ask, Does the local mean depend on $y(t)$? From the viewpoint of the technical literature, the local mean may increase, decrease, or remain unchanged as $y(t)$ varies. Consequently, when one formulates a model of some sociological process in terms of a diffusion process, one must realize that this is a substantive question to be answered in terms of substantive theory. The technical literature can help only in determining the implications of one's assumptions.

What about the local variance? Formally it is defined as

$$\sigma^2(y_t) \equiv \lim_{\Delta t \downarrow 0} \frac{\mathrm{Var}\big[Y(t)+\Delta t) - Y(t) \mid Y(t) = y(t)\big]}{\Delta t}.$$

Roughly speaking, the local variance describes the variance in the change in $Y(t)$ in a small interval of time. It cannot be negative. If it is exactly zero, $Y(t)$ changes in a deterministic fashion. Hence the local variance is ordinarily strictly greater than zero in diffusion processes. Naturally, a larger value for the local variance means that there is more variability in the change in $Y(t)$ occuring in a small interval of time. Often it greatly simplifies mathematical analyses to assume that the local variance of a process is a constant that does not depend on $y(t)$, but this assumption is not an intrinsic part of the mathematics of diffusion processes. In social-scientific applications, substantive considerations should determine assumptions about the local variance. In Section 15.3 we discuss a diffusion processes in which the local variance does depend on $y(t)$. As we show, it leads to a process familiar to many sociologists.

12.4.1 *Mathematical Representation

To proceed further than the informal overview given above requires mathematical statements about diffusion processes. We state basic equations and results without proof or even much discussion. Our intention is to provide a summary; we urge readers to consult the literature cited for further details.

Usually the transition probability density is derived as the limiting case of a discrete-state birth-and-death process in which the states are made "infinitely small" but "infinitely numerous." For details of this derivation, see Goel and Richter-Dyn (1974, pp. 33–34), Feller (1971, pp. 354–359), or Crow and Kimura (1979, pp. 371–381). We state without proof that this derivation yields the **forward Kolmogorov equation** or **forward diffusion equation** (also often called the Fokker–Planck equation in physical applications):

$$\frac{\partial p}{\partial t} = -\frac{\partial [\mu(y_t) p]}{\partial y_t} + \frac{1}{2} \frac{\partial^2 [\sigma^2(y_t) p]}{\partial y_t^2}. \tag{15}$$

The initial conditions, y_s and s, are called the **backward variables**; y_t and t are called the **forward variables**. The forward diffusion equation is the natural approach to substantive modeling because it takes the initial conditions as given and generates the future of the process.

A similar derivation gives the **backward Kolmogorov equation**,

$$-\frac{\partial p}{\partial s} = \mu(y_s) \frac{\partial p}{\partial y_s} + \frac{1}{2} \sigma^2(y_s) \frac{\partial^2 p}{\partial y_s^2},$$

in which the outcome is treated as given. Though this equation does not appear promising for modeling (because it treats the future as the "initial conditions"), it simplifies certain mathematical problems. Consequently, the backward equation plays a prominent role in mathematical treatments of diffusion processes.

⟨12⟩ Diffusion Processes

Either Kolmogorov equation provides a complete probabilistic description of the evolution of the phenomenon. Each has implications for how the mean and variance of $Y(t)$ (and other moments, if they exist) change over time.

12.4.2 *Steady-State Distribution

If the diffusion process has a steady-state distribution p^*, it may be found by setting $\partial p/\partial t = 0$ in (15):

$$-\frac{\partial[\mu(y_t)\,p^*]}{\partial y_t} + \frac{1}{2}\frac{\partial^2[\sigma^2(y_t)\,p^*]}{\partial y_t^2} = 0.$$

The solution is (Karlin and Taylor, 1981, p. 221):

$$p^* = m(y_t)\left[\alpha\,S(y_t) + \beta\right]. \tag{16}$$

Expression (16) contains two constants, α and β, and two functionals of the diffusion process. The **speed density** $m(y_t)$ is defined as

$$m(y_t) \equiv \frac{1}{\sigma^2(y_t)\,s(y_t)},$$

with

$$s(y_t) \equiv \exp\left[-\int_{y_t} 2\,\frac{\mu(v)}{\sigma^2(v)}\,dv\right].$$

(This notation indicates that the integration is performed over all permissible values of y_t). The **scale measure** $S(y_t)$ is defined as

$$S(y_t) \equiv \int_{y_t} s(v)\,dv.$$

The constants in (16) are chosen to satisfy the constraints that $p^* \geq 0$ and $\int_{y_t} p^*\,dv = 1$.

In the models that we consider, these constraints imply that $\alpha = 0$; hence the stationary distribution in (16) becomes

$$p^* = \frac{\beta}{\sigma^2(y_t)}\exp\left[\int_{y_t} 2\,\frac{\mu(v)}{\sigma^2(v)}\,dv\right]. \tag{17}$$

For example, consider the classic OU process in (1) rewritten in differential form:
$$dY(t) = -r\,Y(t)\,dt + \sigma^2\,dW(t).$$
It can be shown[10] that $\mu(y_t) = -r\,Y(t)$ and $\sigma^2(y_t) = \sigma^2$. Therefore
$$s(y_t) = \exp\left[\frac{rY^2(t)}{\sigma^2}\right]$$
and
$$m(y_t) = \frac{1}{\sigma^2}\exp\left[-\frac{rY^2(t)}{\sigma^2}\right].$$
According to (17),
$$p^* = \frac{\beta}{\sigma^2}\exp\left[-\frac{rY^2(t)}{\sigma^2}\right],$$
which is the density for a normally distributed random variable with a mean of zero and a variance of $\sigma^2/2r$ when $\beta = \sigma\sqrt{r/\pi}$.

With appropriate boundary conditions (see below), the forward diffusion equation also has implications for the distribution of the time until a specified level of Y (e.g., the poverty level of income in a study of earnings) is first reached. This time is usually called the **first passage time**. In Chapter 16 we discuss how the distribution of the first passage time may be used to integrate qualitative and quantitative aspects of some social processes.

Having defined the transition probability density, we can turn to the relationship between the parameters of the diffusion process, $\mu(y_t)$ and $\sigma^2(y_t)$, and the coefficients of SDEs. The relationship is simple in the case of linear SDEs. Let $\{Y(t)\}$ be a Brownian-motion process that starts at zero [i.e., $Y(0) = 0$] and has a mean of μt and a variance of $\sigma^2 t$. Substituting these values into (15) and differentiating, we find that the local drift and variance are $\mu(y_t) = \mu$ and $\sigma^2(y_t) = \sigma^2$, respectively. Consequently, the forward diffusion equation for a Brownian-motion process is
$$\frac{\partial p}{\partial t} = -\mu\frac{\partial p}{\partial y_t} + \frac{1}{2}\sigma^2\frac{\partial^2 p}{\partial y_t^2},$$

---

[10] See equations (9) and (10) in Chapter 15 and the accompanying discussion in Section 15.1.

with the initial condition
$$\lim_{t \downarrow s} p_{y_s y_t}(s,t) = \delta(y_s - y_t),$$
where $\delta(\cdot)$ is the Dirac delta function. This condition is just a formal way of indicating that the probability mass at s is concentrated on the point y_s. To obtain exact results, it is necessary to specify the boundary conditions of the process. For the moment we assume that they are the natural ones, ∞ and $-\infty$, that is,
$$p_{y_s \infty}(s,t) = p_{y_s -\infty}(s,t) = 0.$$
This condition states that the process cannot move an infinite distance in finite time. Subject to these conditions, the partial differential equation can be solved for $p_{y_s y_t}(s,t)$. It turns out that $Y(t)$ [conditional on $Y(0) = 0$] is distributed as $\mathcal{N}(\mu t, \sigma^2 t)$, as we noted for the SDE in Section 12.2 (for details, see Cox and Miller, 1965, pp. 209–210).

The model just considered has neither explicit causal effects nor a restoring force. Causal factors can be included, for example, by letting $\mu(y_t) = \pi' \mathbf{x}$. Consider, for example, the linear partial-adjustment model discussed in the previous chapter. One approach to building a stochastic linear partial-adjustment model, outlined in Section 12.2, adds a stochastic disturbance to the deterministic linear partial-adjustment model; this gives the modified OU model in (4). Alternatively, causal variables can be put in the drift term of a diffusion process. For example, one might assume that the local drift of a diffusion process depends on the difference between the current level and a criterion level but that the local variance is a constant:
$$\frac{\partial p}{\partial t} = -r\left[\pi' \mathbf{x} - y_t\right] \frac{\partial p}{\partial y_t} + \frac{1}{2} \sigma^2 \frac{\partial^2 p}{\partial y_t^2}.$$
This partial differential equation also has a known solution:
$$p_{y_s y_t}(s,t) = \frac{1}{\sqrt{2\pi V^2}} \exp\left[\frac{(y_t - M)^2}{2V^2}\right],$$
where
$$M \equiv e^{-r\Delta t} y_s + \frac{1 - e^{-r\Delta t}}{r} \mathbf{b}' \mathbf{x}; \qquad (18)$$
$$V^2 \equiv \frac{\sigma^2}{2r}\left[1 - e^{-2r\Delta t}\right]. \qquad (19)$$

Note that (18) and (19) agree with (9) and (12), which were obtained by working directly with the SDE in (4). Although the diffusion process and the SDE appear to be quite different models, they are equivalent and have identical implications. There is a direct way to translate from one to the other.

In the two cases just considered, the diffusion equations can be solved for explicit transition probability densities. Given such densities, it is possible to estimate the parameters of the local mean and local variance of the stochastic process $Y(t)$. For example, maximum-likelihood (ML) estimators may be constructed. As we have just indicated, the local mean and variance may depend on exogenous variables as well as on $Y(t)$. The next chapter addresses some of the statistical issues that commonly arise in employing this strategy with panel data on $Y(t)$ and on exogenous variables.

Most diffusion equations, however, do not have explicit solutions. Estimation of parameters in such dynamic models is indirect, involving numerical approximations of the diffusion equations and iterative estimation of the parameters from the approximate solutions (see Chapter 14).

Given the difficulty of obtaining the transition probability density explicitly, it is useful to have a procedure for obtaining just the mean and variance of the stochastic process. As we saw in Section 12.1, knowledge of the first two moments is crucial to comparisons of analogous deterministic and stochastic models. It is straightforward to calculate these moments by solving DDEs; for details, see Goel and Richter-Dyn (1974, pp. 43–44).

12.5 Boundary Behavior

In many of the sociological examples mentioned in this chapter and the previous one, outcomes are counts, for example, the number of members in some social group. We have adopted the common assumption that such measures may be treated as continuous variables when they have reasonably large values. Yet, whether these variables are regarded as discrete or continuous, counts cannot meaningfully be negative. The state space of such processes must be restricted to the nonnegative half-line $[0, \infty)$. In the language of the literature on stochastic processes, there is a boundary

⟨12⟩ **Boundary Behavior**

at zero.[11] A complete specification of a stochastic process must include assumptions about its boundaries. In this section we record several well-known results on the boundary behavior of stochastic processes. Because the subject matter is highly technical, we provide only an informal sketch of the issues. The classic treatment is by Feller (1952). See Karlin and Taylor (1981) for an introduction to the modern approach to analyzing boundary behavior of diffusion processes.

Diffusion equations describe behavior in the interior of the state space of a process, but not on the boundaries. In fact, the diffusion equation for a bounded process is identical to that for the analogous unbounded process. This means that a full description of a diffusion process must include both the diffusion equation *and* a statement about boundary behavior.

The least complicated case, the one used in the last section, involves the "natural" boundaries $(-\infty, \infty)$. This specification may be appropriate whenever negative and positive values of the outcome are meaningful and there is neither a floor nor a ceiling on the process. These conditions hold for profit (or loss) from some exchange, dominance (or dependence) in a system, and antagonism (or cooperation) between ethnic groups or social classes in a society. For such applications, the diffusion equations are solved subject to the initial condition and to the conditions that the boundaries at $-\infty$ and ∞ cannot be reached in finite time. Then, for example, the OU process has a normal probability density, as we noted earlier.

Now suppose there is a boundary at zero because $Y(t)$ is an outcome that rules out negative values for substantive reasons, for example, earnings, group size, and number of ties in a social network. Several kinds of boundaries have been studied. One of the most widely used is the **absorbing boundary**, that is, a value that is held forever once it is reached. Such a boundary is obviously relevant in ecological and demographic analysis. Once the size of any population falls to zero, it has become extinct and cannot recover. A simple specification of this boundary behavior is that

$$p_{0y_t}(s, t) = 0.$$

This says merely that the probability of moving from the boundary at zero at any time s to any nonzero level y_t is zero for every t. In the

---

[11]In general a boundary may occur at any substantively reasonable value.

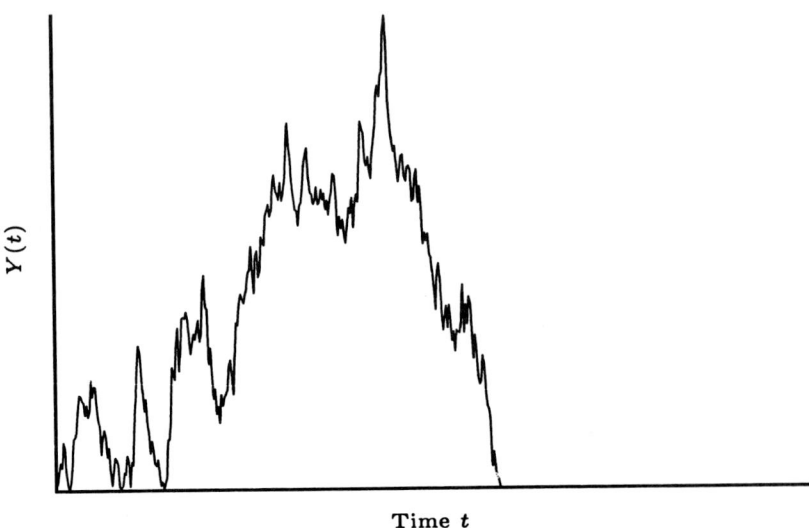

Figure 12.2. A sample path illustrating an absorbing boundary.

case of the modified OU process in (4) with an absorbing boundary at y^*, the solution of the diffusion equation is (for details, see Goel and Richter-Dyn, 1974, Chapter 3):

$$p_{y_s y_t}(s,t) = \frac{1}{\sqrt{8\pi V^2}} \left\{ \exp\left[\frac{(y_t - M)^2}{2V^2}\right] - \exp\left[\frac{(y_t + M)^2}{2V^2}\right] \right\},$$

where M and V^2 are defined in (18) and (19).

The density has two pieces. The first is similar to a normal density; the second gives the probability mass at the boundary. Figure 12.2 shows a typical sample path of such a process. Because there is an explicit solution, it may be used to write a likelihood equation to estimate fundamental parameters of the SDE from panel data.

The statistical literature also gives considerable attention to the case of a **reflecting boundary**. As the name suggests, such a boundary reflects the process from the boundary (zero) back into the interior (the positive half-line), as illustrated in Figure 12.3. The transition probability density for the modified OU processes in (4) with a reflecting boundary at y^* is

$$p_{y_s y_t}(s,t) = \frac{1}{\sqrt{8\pi V^2}} \left\{ \exp\left[\frac{(y_t - M)^2}{2V^2}\right] + \exp\left[\frac{(y_t + M)^2}{2V^2}\right] \right\},$$

⟨12⟩ Boundary Behavior   409

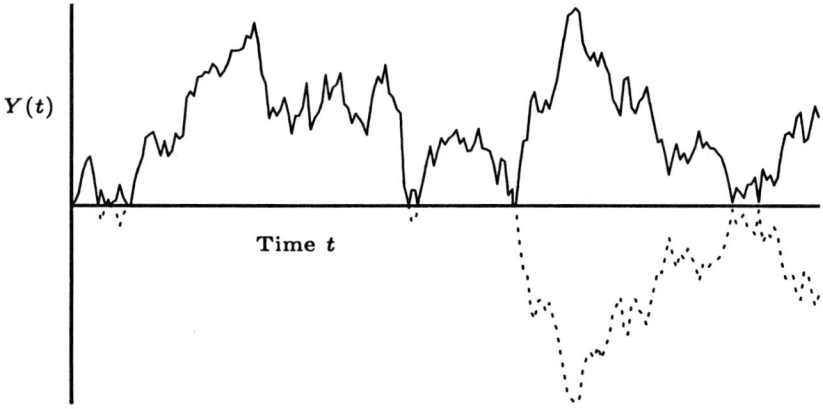

Figure 12.3. A sample path illustrating a reflecting boundary. The dotted segment denotes the path that has been reflected.

where again M and V^2 are defined in (18) and (19).

For many social processes the appropriate specification of a boundary may be some combination of absorbing and reflecting boundaries. Consider fluctuations in hours of work. Individuals may become unemployed for variable periods (temporarily absorbed at zero) but then return to work. It would be extremely useful to specify boundary conditions that let a unit be trapped at zero for a period of random length and then be released to resume its drift. Such a process would combine elements of discrete-state and continuous-state specifications. Work has begun on such models, and the term **sticky boundary** has been applied to such boundaries. Dynkin and Yushkevich (1969, Chapter 4) gave a clear treatment of the strategy of forming models with sticky boundaries and provide results on some discrete-time models. The continuous-time version of this boundary specification may prove useful for a variety of social-scientific applications. Karlin and Taylor (1981, pp. 257–258) gave a brief introduction to this case. Unfortunately, even for the simplest processes (e.g., pure Brownian motion), the diffusion equations do not have explicit solutions. Consequently, development of this approach requires usage of numerical integration in empirical analyses.

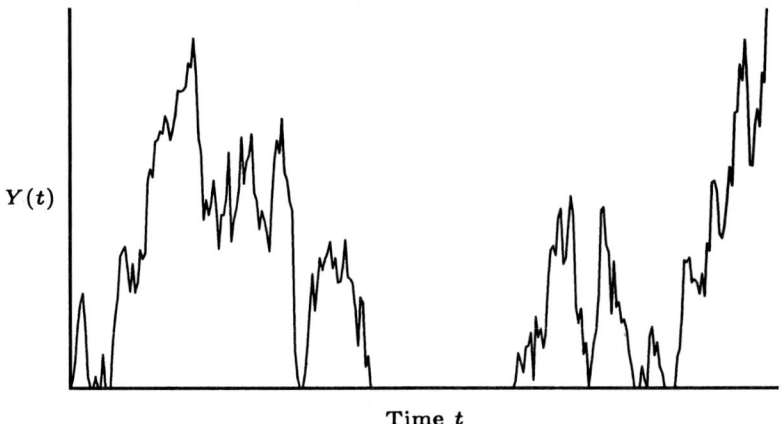

Figure 12.4. A sample path illustrating a sticky boundary.

Even the sticky-boundary formulation may not be general enough for many needs. As the hypothetical sample path of the usual sticky-boundary formulation in Figure 12.4 shows, the process drifts until it hits the boundary, which is zero in this example. In the case of hours of work, individual careers show *jumps* to the boundary as in Figure 12.5. That is, individuals move instantly to unemployment from some reasonably high levels of labor supply. We must combine diffusion processes with some type of discrete-state jump process to capture this feature. We return to this important matter in Chapter 16.

This brief sketch indicates something of the substantive and technical importance of the behavior of continuous-state processes at boundaries. These concerns seem likely to loom large in any serious attempt at stochastic modeling of quantitative outcomes in sociology.

12.6 *Systems of Equations

So far we have discussed scalar processes that parallel the deterministic models in Sections 11.1–11.3. To complete the parallels with Chapter 11, we must also consider systems of SDEs, for example, coupled OU processes. Since there is no analytic difficulty in extending deterministic models from 1 to J outcomes, one might

⟨12⟩ *Systems of Equations

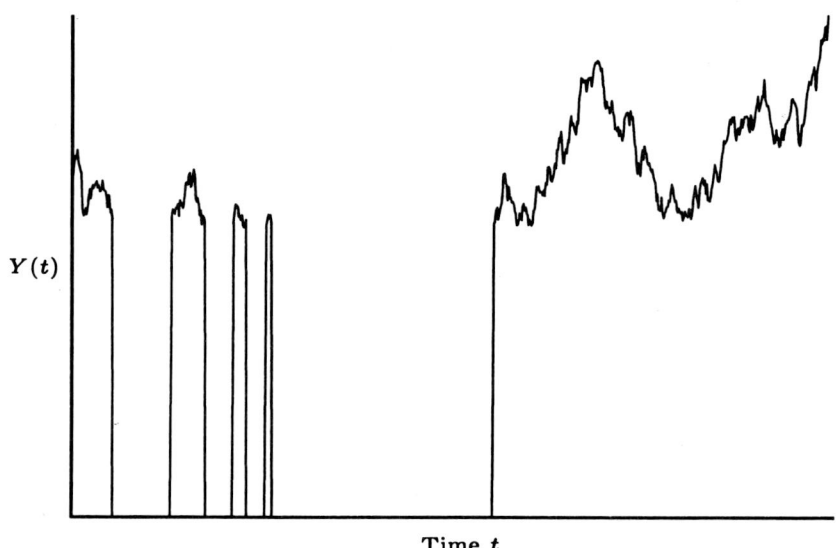

Figure 12.5. A sample path illustrating a sticky boundary with jumps.

imagine that it would be equally straightforward to generalize an OU process from 1 to J outcomes. Unfortunately, this is not the case. Virtually all applications of SDEs and diffusion processes have concentrated on scalar outcomes because it is extremely difficult to obtain explicit transition probability densities for all but the simplest multivariate SDEs and diffusion processes. The main exception is Brownian motion.

12.6.1 A Multivariate Brownian-Motion Process

Consider two statistically independent standard Brownian-motion processes $W_1(t)$ and $W_2(t)$. The random vector $\mathbf{W}(t) \equiv \{W_1(t), W_2(t)\}$ is called a bivariate Brownian-motion process. Its sample path describes motion in a two-dimensional space. Figure 12.6 illustrates a hypothetical sample path.

If the two subprocesses are independent, the transition probability density for the bivariate processs is just the product of the two transition probability densities. More generally, if the random vector $\mathbf{W}(t)$ is a J-dimensional standard Brownian-motion process, its transition probability density is (see Karlin and Taylor, 1981, pp. 291–292)

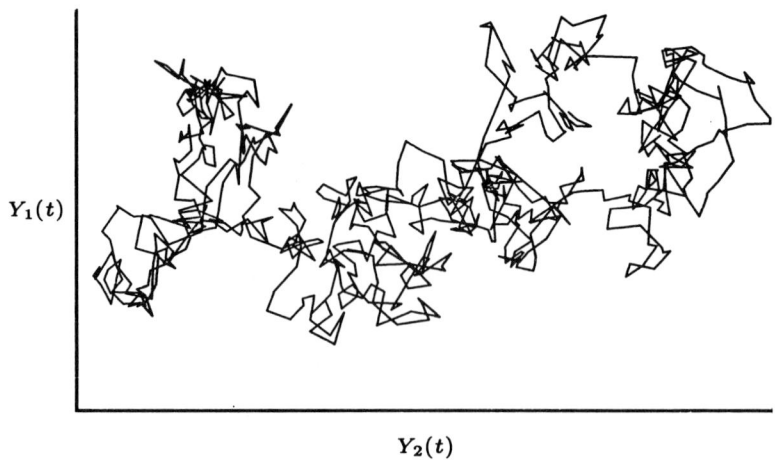

Figure 12.6. Hypothetical sample path for a bivariate Brownian-motion process.

$$p_{\mathbf{w}_0 \mathbf{w}_t}(0, t) = \frac{1}{(\sqrt{2\pi t}\,)^J} \exp\left[-\frac{1}{2t} \sum_{j=1}^{J} \left[\, w_j(0) - w_j(t) \right]^2 \right],$$

where $\mathbf{w}_0$ and $\mathbf{w}_t$ are the realizations of $\mathbf{W}(0)$ and $\mathbf{W}(t)$, respectively, and $w_j(t)$ is the realization of the jth independent Brownian-motion process at time t, $W_j(t)$.

12.6.2 Radial Brownian Motion

A more interesting process can be constructed by defining a new random variable $Y(t)$ that equals the distance of a J-dimensional Brownian-motion process from the origin:[12]

$$Y(t) \equiv \sqrt{W_1(t)^2 + \ldots + W_J(t)^2}, \qquad (20)$$

where $t \geq 0$ and $W_j(t)$ is the jth independent Brownian-motion process at time t. This process is known as the **radial Brownian-motion** or **Bessel process**. Karlin and Taylor (1975, pp. 367–371) showed that $Y(t)$ is a Markov process with continuous sample paths

---

[12] Recall that the distance of any vector from the origin equals the square root of the sum of squares of its elements.

in the sample space $[0, \infty)$. Although this is conceptually a very simple process, it has a complicated transition probability density:

$$p_{y_0, y_t}(0, t) = t^{-1} \exp\left[-\frac{y_0^2 + y_t^2}{2t}\right] y_0^{1-\frac{J}{2}} y_t^{\frac{J}{2}} \mathcal{B}_{\frac{J}{2}-1}(q), \qquad (21)$$

where y_0 and y_t are the realizations of $Y(0)$ and $Y(t)$, respectively;

$$q \equiv \frac{y_0 \, y_t}{t};$$

$\mathcal{B}_m(q)$ is the modified Bessel function

$$\mathcal{B}_m(q) \equiv \sum_{k=0}^{\infty} \frac{1}{k!\, \Gamma(k+m+1)} \left(\frac{q}{2}\right)^{2k+m};$$

and $\Gamma(x)$, $x > 0$, denotes the gamma function

$$\Gamma(x) \equiv \int_0^{\infty} u^{x-1} e^{-u}\, du.$$

In the scalar case, the density in (21) is the same as the transition probability density for Brownian motion reflected at the origin. In higher dimensions, (21) can be evaluated using published tabulations of modified Bessel functions (e.g., see Olver, 1965).

12.6.3 A Special Case of the Multivariate OU Process

The radial Brownian-motion process is interesting mainly because it serves as the foundation for constructing a special multivariate OU process. In the scalar case, the local drift of the standard OU process is $-rY(t)$. In our terminology, this drift expresses partial adjustment (to zero in this case) or negative feedback. In either interpretation the drift reflects the consequences of forces acting to restore the process to some level. In the case of the classic OU process in (1), the process is continually being restored to the origin (zero). The magnitude of the restoring force in the OU process is proportional to the distance of $Y(t)$ from zero.

How can one represent such a restoring force in J-dimensions? The simplest way is to specify that the magnitude of the restoring force is proportional to the distance of the stochastic *vector* from zero. This reasoning suggests that the local drift in a multivariate OU process be set equal to

$$\mu = -\sqrt{Y_1 + \ldots + Y_J(t)^2},$$

where for simplicity the outcomes, $Y_j(t)$, $j = 1, \ldots, J$, are normalized so that $r = 1$ and $\sigma_j^2 = 1$ [compare with equation (1)]. According to this assumption, the subprocesses are coupled because the rate of change in each depends on the current levels of all of the others, but the processes are otherwise independent. In particular, $\sigma_{jk}^2 = 0$ for $k \neq j$. The transition probability density for this special multivariate OU process is (see Karlin and Taylor, 1981, p. 292)

$$p_{y_0,y_t}(0,t) = \frac{y_t^{J-1} e^{-y_t^2}}{1 - e^{2t}} \exp\left[-\frac{(y_0^2 + y_t^2) e^{-2t}}{1 - e^{-2t}}\right]$$
$$\cdot (y_0 y_t e^{-t})^{1-\frac{J}{2}} \mathcal{B}_{\frac{J}{2}-1}(q), \qquad (22)$$

where

$$q \equiv \frac{y_0 y_t e^{-t}}{1 - e^{-2t}},$$

and y_0 and y_t are realizations of $Y(0)$ and $Y(t)$ as defined in (20).

This special version of an OU process goes part of the way toward developing a stochastic parallel to the coupled outcomes discussed in Chapter 11. The subprocesses are indeed coupled because a change in any one dimension alters the distance of the vector from zero and by (22) affects the rate of change in all J dimensions. For example, suppose that a family has J workers and that measurements have been scaled so that the origin is the optimal level of labor supply for all J workers. This model allows any family member's deviation from his or her optimal labor supply to affect the behavior of others. But it does not allow asymmetric effects. Each of the J dimensions receives equal weight in the restoring force. Thus, a given deviation in labor supply has the same effect whether it pertains to the husband, the wife, or a child. In other words, this special model allows only nonspecific or **diffuse coupling**.

12.6.4 Towards a More General Multivariate OU Process

As we explained in Chapter 11, sociologists often think coupling between actors is direct rather than diffuse. Generally the coupling is asymmetric, that is, the effect of actor A's behavior on actor B is not the same as the effect of B's behavior on A. The stochastic analogue to systems of linear DDEs with explicit asymmetric coupling is an OU process in which the local drift of $Y_j(t)$ has the form

$$\mu_j = -r_j \sum_{\substack{k=1 \\ k \neq j}}^{J} \alpha_{jk} Y_k(t).$$

Unfortunately, the transition probability density for this process is unknown. Indeed, the complexity of the special case with diffuse coupling suggests that a tractable expression for the transition probability density may not be found.

There are at least three ways to proceed in developing practical applications of systems of linear SDEs for sociological research. One way is to use the property that increments in Brownian motion are independent to estimate the coefficients of the integral equations implied by the SDEs. Estimates of the coefficients of IEs can be converted to consistent estimates of parameters of the SDEs by the procedures outlined in Chapter 11. A second way is to use discrete approximations of the SDEs, that is, to convert them to stochastic *difference* equations that exactly parallel the original model. We illustrate this approach in a different context in Chapter 14. Both approaches, which are discussed in Chapter 13, are halfway measures, at best. They do not really use the probability structure implied by the process. The third way deals directly with the probability structure by using additional mathematical theory concerning the relationship between parameters of drift-free diffusion processes and analogous diffusion processes with drift. The Cameron–Martin formula (see Strook and Varadhan, 1979) shows that the transition probability density of a process with drift can always be written as an explicit function of the density of the corresponding drift-free process. This may be useful in the present context because complications usually result from the presence of coupling between local drifts. The drift-free version of a J-dimensional OU process is just J-dimensional Brownian motion, which does have a known density, as we noted above. Unfortunately, in the particular applications that we have considered, the transformation implied by the Cameron–Martin formula is very cumbersome. It typically involves complicated stochastic integrals that must be approximated in order to estimate fundamental parameters from empirical data. So this approach also involves approximations, though of a different sort.

This brief discussion suggests that it is difficult to develop full stochastic analogues of the linear systems discussed in the previous chapter, such as the competition model of organizational growth and decline. The precise forms of the disturbance terms—or, from another perspective, the transition probability densities for the corresponding diffusion processes—are unknown. Thus one cannot provide a detailed description of the probability of changes in such outcomes. This impasse reflects partly the greater complexity of stochastic models. But it may also reflect the fact that the study of SDEs is still in its infancy. The literature on the theory and applications of these models has recently begun to grow rapidly.

12.7   Conclusions

What general implications for sociological analysis emerge from this discussion? First, we conclude that it is both feasible and useful for sociologists to formulate stochastic models of change in a metric outcome. This conclusion is apparently a new one; we have remarked earlier on the apparent consensus in sociology to the contrary. We propose that SDEs driven by Brownian-motion disturbances serve as a convenient and powerful vehicle for joining probabilistic arguments to the kinds of substantive concerns discussed in Chapter 11. A good beginning is often a linear SDE, for example, a model based on the Ornstein–Uhlenbeck process, for which analytic results are obtained readily, as long as the boundaries on $Y(t)$ are the natural ones, $(-\infty, \infty)$. In the next chapter we present a strategy for analyzing such models with conventional panel data.

But there are two obstacles to routine use of these types of models in social research. The first is the presence of complicated boundaries in many social processes. If sociologists wish to use SDEs or diffusion processes to model phenomena, they must describe the operation of floor effects, ceiling effects, and other types of boundaries much more systematically than they have in the past. Acknowledging the existence of boundaries on processes implies that

⟨12⟩ **Conclusions**

transition probability densities are more complicated than in analogous unbounded processes, as we have seen. Still, some kinds of boundaries have been studied extensively and can be incorporated in empirical analysis.

The second complication concerns the difficulty in deriving explicit transition probability densities for coupled systems of metric outcomes. This difficulty does not mean that such systems cannot be analyzed empirically. Rather, it means that systems cannot be studied with the same simple tools that suffice in the case of a scalar process.

13

Estimation of Linear Models

How practical is the use of linear stochastic differential equations (SDEs) in sociological research? The answer to this question depends partly on the degree to which conventional data and methods can be adapted to these dynamic models. This chapter shows that available data and methods can indeed be used for dynamic analysis of quantitative outcomes. Moreover, sociologists can use some of the models discussed in Chapter 12 without wholesale methodological retooling. Because we want to emphasize practicality, we focus on simple, direct procedures for estimating parameters of linear SDEs for a scalar outcome. We do not claim that these procedures are optimal. They are simply easy to use and appear to give fairly good estimates of structural parameters.

13.1 Time-Series versus Panel Data

Clearly, *temporal* data—observations on the same units at two or more points in time—are needed to estimate a dynamic model. Sample path data on quantitative outcomes are rarely available. As we indicated in Chapter 2, the two most common observation plans are a time series (repeated measures on a single unit) or a panel (a few repeated measures on many units). A third, less common plan is a multiple time series—repeated measures on a few units. The only difference between a panel and a multiple time series is that panel data contain too few observations per unit to allow meaningful analysis of individuals. For example, social-scientific panels commonly contain only two to five "waves" of observations. It is not informative to analyze separate time series with so few observations on each unit. Because of this difference, we discuss analysis of single time-series and panel data separately. We do not explicitly discuss analysis of multiple time-series data because they only add information to that available in the other two types of data.

Which observation plan is better for studying social dynamics? To highlight the difference between these observation plans, consider the options facing an investigator with a fixed budget. What is gained by sacrificing temporal variation for cross-sectional variation? Suppose available resources permit collection of data on a total of $T = NI$ observations, where I is the sample size (the number of units) and N the number of waves on each sample member. Suppose also that the cost of each observation is the same whether it adds another wave on a given individual or adds another individual at a given wave. If T is fixed by the research budget, how big should N and I be? When $I = 1$ and $N = T$, there is a single time series of length T. When $I = T$ and $N = 1$, there is a cross-section; we do not consider this observation plan further because it precludes any sort of dynamic analysis. When $N = 2$ and $I = T/2$, there is a two-wave panel, which is the temporal observation plan with maximal cross-sectional variation and minimal temporal variation. Usually there are also many other possible combinations of N and I giving the same fixed number of observations, T. To date social scientists have given surprisingly little attention to the principles involved in deciding on the relative sizes of N and I.

Ignoring practical issues such as cost and feasibility, judgments about trade-offs between additional temporal variation and additional cross-sectional variation depend on beliefs about the quality of model specification and on levels of variability in measured causal factors. Assume for the moment that all temporal observation plans yield the same variability in the explanatory variables and there is at least some temporal variation on each unit. Then the choice between cross-sectional and temporal variation is not crucial if models are specified correctly. In this context "good model specification" means that disturbances are uncorrelated with observed variables included in the model and are also uncorrelated from observation to observation. If both of these conditions hold, each replication, over time or over units, constitutes an independent observation. There is no reason to prefer cross-sectional variation over temporal variation (or vice versa) because each replication conveys as much information as any other. For example, given these conditions, an addition of $2N$ observations to a time series yields twice as much information as an addition of N observations.

The silence in the methodological literature about trade-offs between analysis of time-series and panel data may reflect the tacit assumption that social-scientific models are specified well. But in our opinion it is neither realistic nor helpful to think that the world behaves exactly as social-scientific models assume. Careful investigators maintain a healthy skepticism about the quality of their models. They worry about the effects of potential confounding factors—those uncontrolled, unobserved factors that distort relationships among variables included in the model. Because potential confounding factors do not appear explicitly in the model, their effects are incorporated in the disturbance. As we noted above, skepticism about model specification is usually directed at claims that disturbances are independent from observation to observation.

In some research contexts, confounding factors vary more among units at the same point in time than over time. For example, genes vary within populations but not over time for the same person (except for somatic mutations). In other contexts, confounding factors vary mainly over time but not among units at a given time. For example, all firms in a competitive market face similar prices at a given time, but prices vary widely over time. Of course, some confounding factors vary both temporally and cross-sectionally; it is unclear how to control such complex factors by design. Therefore, we focus on those factors that vary in only one dimension.

When confounding factors vary more across units than over time, investigators should try to gather observations for longer time periods on each case rather than on more cases for a shorter time period. We illustrate this point with a simplified discrete-time model. Let $y_i(t)$ denote person i's income at time t, and let $x_i(t)$ denote i's work experience at time t. Assume the true model is

$$y_i(t) = \gamma y_i(t-1) + \beta x_i(t) + \mu_i + \epsilon_i(t),$$

where μ_i is the effect of i's unobserved abilities on income growth and $\epsilon_i(t)$ is a random disturbance that is uncorrelated across time and across cases. If x and μ are positively correlated across cases (a

⟨ 13 ⟩ Time-Series versus Panel Data

plausible assumption), ordinary least-squares (OLS) estimators of γ and β using data from a two-wave panel will be biased. On the other hand, if there are a series of temporal observations on a single case i, an analyst can compute the differences between waves and eliminate the effect of the confounding factor μ_i:

$$y_i(t+1) - y_i(t) = \gamma \big[y_i(t) - y_i(t-1) \big] + \beta \big[x_i(t) - x_i(t-1) \big]$$
$$+ \big[\mu_i - \mu_i \big] + \big[\epsilon_i(t+1) - \epsilon_i(t) \big].$$

Since the third term in brackets on the right-hand side of this equation is zero, OLS estimators of γ and β from data on three or more temporal observations on case i are unbiased.

In general time-series data can be used to minimize biases due to confounding factors (e.g., genes) that vary over cases but not over time. In contrast, a two-wave panel can be used to minimize biases due to confounding factors (e.g., prices) that vary more over time than over units. Panel data on many units at a few waves tell more about between-unit variation than temporal variation. Consequently, such data can be used to minimize biases resulting from unobservables that vary more over time than over units. This reasoning suggests a principle for answering the design question posed initially. Invest in a longer time series if unobserved confounding factors vary mainly among units; invest in a short series on many units if unobserved confounding factors vary mainly over time.

Viewed in this light, a single time series is a risky choice. Findings based on this observation plan depend greatly on the absence of any important confounding factors that vary over time for the units studied. A two-wave panel is also risky because findings based on this observation plan depend greatly on the absence of any important confounding variables that are fixed over time but vary over the units studied. In contrast, risk is minimized by a panel that has both a reasonable sample size I and a reasonable number of waves N because it includes both temporal and cross-sectional variation. It can potentially handle both types of confounding factors. Usage of between-unit variation can help to control the effects of confounding factors that vary mostly over time; usage of temporal variation can help to control the effects of confounding factors that vary mainly over units.

Thus far we have assumed that explanatory variables vary equally in single time-series and panel data. But this is rarely realistic in social research. Usually explanatory variables vary more over people (or other social units) than over time for the same person (or unit). (This is true by definition for time-invariant causal variables like sex and race.) Therefore, a panel usually contains more variability in explanatory factors than a single time series, assuming that NI, the number of waves times the number of units, is the same.

The foregoing discussion may help to explain the widespread skepticism in the social sciences about research findings that depend on a single time series. Since many factors change synchronously in typical field studies, it is extremely hard to isolate the effects of any one of them. Too often reanalysis of a single time series that modifies procedures only slightly yields very different findings. This is not to say that other nonexperimental designs do not lead to erroneous inferences. Rather, we claim that analysis of a single time-series is vulnerable to distortion when clusters of variables change in concert, a common situation. For these reasons we advise that estimation of a dynamic model not be based primarily on the study of a single time series. Multiple time-series or panel data are generally much more useful. Therefore, we concentrate mainly on the use of panel data and comment only briefly on the use of a single time series.

13.2 Two Ways to Estimate a Dynamic Model

Choice of observation plan is only the first of several major methodological decisions that must be made in the course of analyzing a dynamic model empirically. One must also decide how to relate temporal observations (whether a panel or time series) to the underlying continuous-time model. Recall that one cannot analyze SDEs directly because the dependent variable, an instantaneous rate of change, is unobservable. How then does one estimate the parameters of SDEs? One approach, illustrated in Sections 11.3 and 11.7, follows the lead of Coleman (1968): one estimates the parameters of the *integral equation* (IE) associated with the basic model and then solves algebraically for the parameters of the underlying SDE. This method of estimation highlights the connection between the underlying model and the equation used in estimating parameters. It also permits use of standard estimation techniques, namely, linear regression, whenever temporal observations are equally spaced

⟨13⟩ Two Ways to Estimate a Dynamic Model

in time and causal variables change linearly or exponentially with time or are time invariant. Unfortunately, it has several drawbacks that sometimes limit its value sharply.

The first drawback is the difficulty of imposing constraints when estimating *systems* of differential equations (DEs) like (25) in Chapter 11. Sometimes theory implies that some entries in **C**, the matrix of coefficients of the endogenous variables, are zero. No one has yet discovered a way to incorporate such constraints when estimating IEs. Because constraints on elements of **C** cannot be imposed in the estimation phase, estimates of parameters "known" to be zero are typically nonzero. Second, failure to incorporate constraints makes estimates of other parameters inefficient because consistent estimators that make use of constraints have smaller variances than those that do not.

These two limitations have prompted a search for alternative approaches that yield efficient estimators. Most attention has focused on what is called an **exact discrete approximation** to the SDE, which replaces the continuous-time model with a discrete-time analogue. It has the advantage that constraints on parameters may be imposed routinely. Continuous-time modeling is not abandoned because the estimated model is defined as an approximation to the continuous-time model.

Another drawback of the integral-equation strategy has already been noted in Chapter 11: it applies only to models with known solutions. Only a tiny fraction of substantively realistic SDEs can be expressed in terms of an explicit IE. Almost all SDEs with known solutions are linear models for a scalar outcome. As sociologists extend their horizons to include linear systems of linear SDEs or nonlinear models (see Chapters 14 and 15), they must turn to exact discrete approximations, or something similar.

Estimators based on an exact discrete approximation have been developed and applied to time-series data (see Bergstrom, 1976) but not, to our knowledge, to panel data. Such estimators usually allow investigators to impose constraints on fundamental parameters. Extensions to panel applications are not always trivial, however. The conventional approach to an exact discrete approximation requires *equally spaced* observations.[1] But sometimes observations are not

---

[1] Some work in geophysics is concerned with exact discrete approximations

equally spaced in sociological research (see Section 13.8). Moreover, gains in efficiency stemming from the use of constraints may not outweigh approximation errors—discrepancies between the continuous-time model and the discrete approximation. This is especially likely when observations are widely spaced in time.

Neither strategy seems optimal for all applications. We concentrate on the simpler integral-equation strategy in this chapter. In Chapter 14 we show how an exact discrete approximation can be used to estimate parameters in a nonlinear DE.

13.3 Scalar Models

In Chapter 12 we discussed the following simple extension of the Ornstein–Uhlenbeck (OU) process:

$$\mathrm{d}Y(t) = cY(t)\,\mathrm{d}t + \mathbf{b}'\mathbf{x}(t)\,\mathrm{d}t + \sigma\,\mathrm{d}W(t), \qquad (1)$$

where $c < 0$, and $W(t)$ is a standard Brownian-motion process. As we discussed in Chapter 12, this SDE has the solution

$$Y(t) = \mathrm{e}^{(t-t_0)}\, y(t_0) + \int_{t_0}^{t} \mathrm{e}^{c(t-s)}\,\mathbf{b}'\mathbf{x}(s)\,\mathrm{d}s + \epsilon(t), \qquad (2)$$

where

$$\epsilon(t) \equiv \int_{t_0}^{t} \mathrm{e}^{c(t-s)}\,\mathrm{d}W(s)$$

and $y(t_0)$ is the initial condition. The disturbance $\epsilon(t)$ is normally distributed with mean zero, and

$$\mathrm{Var}\bigl[\epsilon(t)\bigr] = \frac{\sigma^2}{2c}\Bigl[\mathrm{e}^{2c(t-t_0)} - 1\Bigr],$$

as we indicated in equation (12) in Chapter 12.[2]

for continuous-time processes observed irregularly; for example, see Andersen and Bloomfield (1974) and Bolt (1978). The methods discussed in these papers might profitably be applied to problems of unequal spacing discussed in Section 13.8.

[2] Notice that r in equation (12) in Chapter 12 equals $-c$.

⟨13⟩ Scalar Models

Henceforth we assume that there are panel data on I units at $N+1$ points in time and that (1) describes all I sample members. We assume that the only sources of interunit heterogeneity are: variation in $\mathbf{x}(t)$, variation in the initial value $y(t_0)$, and variation in unobservable factors. All estimates that we consider condition on the observed initial values in the sample; we do not try to explain this initial distribution. We assume that the disturbances $\epsilon(t)$ are independent and identically distributed.

When estimating (1) from panel data, it is not advisable to relate the outcome at every time point to the initial condition $y(t_0)$ because this complicates the covariances of the disturbances in two ways. First, relating every wave to the initial condition creates heteroscedasticity because the variance of $\epsilon(t)$ depends on $t - t_0$. Moreover, if the time intervals overlap, which occurs when each new wave is related to the same initial condition, the disturbances pertaining to different t's on a given individual i have a nonzero covariance [see equation (11) in Chapter 12]. Consequently, when $\mathbf{x}(t)$ changes linearly over time, we relate the outcome for a given case i at some wave n, t_n, to the level at the previous wave t_{n-1}:

$$Y_i(t_n) = \gamma Y_i(t_{n-1}) + \boldsymbol{\beta}_1'\mathbf{x}(t_{n-1}) + \boldsymbol{\beta}_2'\Delta\mathbf{x}_n + \epsilon_i(t_n), \qquad (3)$$

where

$$\gamma \equiv e^{c\Delta t}, \qquad (4a)$$

$$\boldsymbol{\beta}_1 \equiv \frac{\gamma - 1}{c}\mathbf{b}, \qquad (4b)$$

$$\boldsymbol{\beta}_2 \equiv \frac{\gamma - 1 - \log\gamma}{c^2 \Delta t}\mathbf{b}, \qquad (4c)$$

$$\Delta\mathbf{x}_n \equiv \mathbf{x}(t_n) - \mathbf{x}(t_{n-1}), \qquad (4d)$$

$$\epsilon_i(t_n) \equiv \int_{t_{n-1}}^{t_n} e^{c(t_n-s)}\,\mathrm{d}W(s), \qquad (4e)$$

and $\Delta t \equiv t_n - t_{n-1}$ is the spacing between successive waves of observations. That is, we divide the temporal series on each unit into nonoverlapping segments with some fixed length Δt. Then the variance of $\epsilon_i(t_n)$ is the same for each wave n, and the disturbances for different waves on the same unit are uncorrelated.

Equation (3) can be derived from (2) as follows. According to (2),

$$Y(t_n) = e^{c(t_n - t_0)} y(t_0) + \int_{t_0}^{t_n} e^{c(t_n - s)} \mathbf{b}' \mathbf{x}(s) \, ds$$

$$+ \int_{t_0}^{t_n} e^{c(t_n - s)} \, dW(s);$$

and

$$Y(t_{n-1}) = e^{c(t_{n-1} - t_0)} y(t_0) + \int_{t_0}^{t_{n-1}} e^{c(t_{n-1} - s)} \mathbf{b}' \mathbf{x}(s) \, ds$$

$$+ \int_{t_0}^{t_{n-1}} e^{c(t_{n-1} - s)} \, dW(s).$$

Multiplying the second expression by $e^{c \Delta t} \equiv e^{c(t_n - t_{n-1})}$ and subtracting the result from the first equation yields

$$Y(t_n) = e^{c \Delta t} Y(t_{n-1}) + \int_{t_{n-1}}^{t_n} e^{c(t_n - s)} \mathbf{b}' \mathbf{x}(s) \, ds + \epsilon(t_n).$$

When $\mathbf{x}(t) = \mathbf{x}(t_{n-1}) + \boldsymbol{\kappa}(t - t_{n-1})$, this expression simplifies to (3) for each i.

Notice that equation (3) has a random variable on the right-hand side, $Y_i(t_{n-1})$. Consequently, one cannot assume that the variables on the right-hand side of (3) are fixed, as in the classic linear regression model. However, given the independence of disturbances from period to period, one can rely on generalizations of regression theory to the case of stochastic regressors (e.g., see Johnston, 1972, pp. 267–278). The main consequence of this fact is that one must rely on large-sample theory.

Panel data may be used to estimate the fundamental dynamic parameters in a simple way. The first step consists of obtaining OLS estimates of the linear IE in (3). Given the above assumptions about $\epsilon_i(t)$, OLS estimators of γ and β are consistent and asymptotically efficient (e.g., see Johnston, 1972, pp. 274–278; Malinvaud, 1970, pp. 540–548). Moreover, OLS estimators are the same as the maximum-likelihoood (ML) estimators because the disturbances in (2) are normally distributed. This fact plays a key role in our strategy.

⟨13⟩   Scalar Models

Maximum-likelihood estimators possess a strong invariance property: a monotonic function of an ML estimator is also the ML estimator of the monotonic function.[3] That is, the ML estimator of $f(\alpha)$ is $f(\widehat{\alpha})$, where $\widehat{\alpha}$ is the ML estimator. This implies that the ML estimator of c, the speed of adjustment, can be obtained by simple algebraic manipulations. Since the OLS estimator of γ is the same as the ML estimator, (4a) implies that

$$\widehat{c} = \frac{\log \widehat{\gamma}}{\Delta t} \qquad (5a)$$

is the ML estimator of c. Then, with the ML estimate of c given by (5a), one can estimate **b** in either of two ways:

$$\widehat{\mathbf{b}}^{(1)} = \frac{\widehat{c}}{\widehat{\gamma} - 1} \widehat{\boldsymbol{\beta}}_1; \qquad (5b)$$

$$\widehat{\mathbf{b}}^{(2)} = \frac{\widehat{c}^2 \Delta t}{\widehat{\gamma} - 1 - \log \widehat{\gamma}} \widehat{\boldsymbol{\beta}}_2. \qquad (5c)$$

As we noted in Section 11.2, the two estimators of **b** have the same asymptotic expected value; however, actual estimates sometimes differ considerably in empirical applications. Because of this difference, most analysts take a weighted linear combination of the two estimators as the final estimator of **b**:

$$\widehat{\mathbf{b}} = p\,\widehat{\mathbf{b}}^{(1)} + (1-p)\,\widehat{\mathbf{b}}^{(2)} \qquad (6)$$

where $0 \leq p \leq 1$. Typically p is chosen to be $1/2$.

Finally, given $\widehat{c}$ and $\widehat{\sigma}_\epsilon^2$ (the estimated variance of the disturbance), it is straightforward to calculate the ML estimate of σ, the multiplier of the Brownian-motion disturbance in the DE. So, for this simple case, ML estimation of the fundamental dynamic parameters requires only an OLS regression and some simple calculations.

The results of OLS estimation of (3) also let one estimate the covariance matrix of the fundamental dynamic parameters c and **b**, so that one can test hypotheses about them. Unfortunately, obtaining the covariance matrix for c and **b** is considerably more awkward

---

[3]In general, monotonic transformations of least-squares estimators are consistent but not asymptotically efficient.

than obtaining point estimates of them. To the best of our knowledge, social scientists who have estimated an equation like (3) in order to estimate the dynamic parameters in (1) have not bothered to estimate the standard errors (or covariances) of the dynamic parameters. Instead, they have relied on the standard errors of the estimated coefficients in the IE, that is, the standard errors of $\hat{\gamma}$ and $\hat{\beta}$, in making inferences about causal effects. This practice assumes that the ratios of estimated parameters to standard errors are equal for corresponding coefficients in the IEs and DEs. As far as we know, this assumption has not yet been proved. In fact, based on inspection of the equations expressing the covariance matrix of the dynamic parameters in terms of the covariance matrix of $\hat{\gamma}$ and $\hat{\beta}$ (see below), this assumption is almost certainly false, though the two sets of standards errors may well be monotonically related.

To find the covariance matrix of $\hat{c}$ and $\hat{b}$ from OLS estimation of (3), one makes use of the well-known theorem that

$$\text{Cov}[\hat{c}, \hat{b}] = \text{Cov}[\mathbf{f}(\hat{\gamma}, \hat{\beta})] = \mathbf{J}' \text{Cov}[\hat{\gamma}, \hat{\beta}] \mathbf{J}, \qquad (7)$$

where $\text{Cov}[\hat{\gamma}, \hat{\beta}]$ denotes the covariance matrix of $\hat{\gamma}$ and $\hat{\beta} = (\hat{\beta}_1, \hat{\beta}_2)$, $\mathbf{f}(\cdot)$ is the set of functions expressing $\hat{c}$ and $\hat{b}$ in terms of $\hat{\gamma}$ and $\hat{\beta}$, which comes from equations (5) and (6), and $\mathbf{J}$ is the Jacobian of the function $\mathbf{f}(\hat{\gamma}, \hat{\beta})$. The covariance matrix of parameters in a linear equation estimated by OLS can be found in any standard text (e.g., see Hanushek and Jackson, 1977, p. 119); it is just the inverse of the correlation matrix of the right-hand side variables multiplied by σ_c^2. The Jacobian matrix $\mathbf{J}$ is

$$\mathbf{J} = \begin{pmatrix} \dfrac{\partial c}{\partial \gamma} & \dfrac{\partial c}{\partial \beta_{10}} & \dfrac{\partial c}{\partial \beta_{11}} & \cdots & \dfrac{\partial c}{\partial \beta_{1M}} & \dfrac{\partial c}{\partial \beta_{21}} & \cdots & \dfrac{\partial c}{\partial \beta_{2M}} \\[1em] \dfrac{\partial b_0}{\partial \gamma} & \dfrac{\partial b_0}{\partial \beta_{10}} & \dfrac{\partial b_0}{\partial \beta_{11}} & \cdots & \dfrac{\partial b_0}{\partial \beta_{1M}} & \dfrac{\partial b_0}{\partial \beta_{21}} & \cdots & \dfrac{\partial b_0}{\partial \beta_{2M}} \\[1em] \vdots & \vdots & \vdots & & \vdots & \vdots & & \vdots \\[1em] \dfrac{\partial b_M}{\partial \gamma} & \dfrac{\partial b_M}{\partial \beta_{10}} & \dfrac{\partial b_M}{\partial \beta_{11}} & \cdots & \dfrac{\partial b_M}{\partial \beta_{1M}} & \dfrac{\partial b_M}{\partial \beta_{21}} & \cdots & \dfrac{\partial b_M}{\partial \beta_{2M}} \end{pmatrix}.$$

Differentiation of (5) and (6) yields the elements of $\mathbf{J}$:

⟨13⟩ Scalar Models

$$\frac{\partial c}{\partial \gamma} = \frac{1}{\gamma \Delta t};$$

$$\frac{\partial c}{\partial \beta_{1m}} = \frac{\partial c}{\partial \beta_{2m}} = 0, \quad \text{for all } m = 0, \ldots, M;$$

$$\frac{\partial b_k}{\partial \gamma} = \frac{p\beta_{1k}}{\Delta t(\gamma - 1)} \left[\frac{1}{\gamma} - \frac{\log \gamma}{\gamma - 1} \right]$$
$$+ \frac{(1-p)\beta_{2k}\, c}{\gamma(\gamma - 1 - \log \gamma)} \left[2 - \frac{(\gamma - 1)\log \gamma}{\gamma - 1 - \log \gamma} \right];$$

$$\frac{\partial b_k}{\partial \beta_{1k}} = \frac{p \log \gamma}{\Delta t(\gamma - 1)};$$

$$\frac{\partial b_k}{\partial \beta_{2k}} = \frac{(1-p)c^2 \Delta t}{\gamma - 1 - \log \gamma};$$

$$\frac{\partial b_k}{\partial \beta_{1m}} = \frac{\partial b_k}{\partial \beta_{2m}} = 0, \quad \text{for all } m \neq k.$$

Thus **J** is a matrix whose elements are fairly simple functions of the OLS estimates of γ and $\boldsymbol{\beta}$. Although the matrix multiplication indicated in (7) is tedious to perform by hand, it is easy to do with a computer.

The rest of this chapter builds various practical complications into this simple model. Of course, we cannot exhaust the class of complications that might arise in empirical research. Our choice of complications has been guided by our own experience in using these methods and by judgments about the probable usage of these methods by sociologists.

One complication arises because exogenous variables in sociological applications vary over time in different ways. Recall that the solution of a linear SDE involves terms like

$$\int_{t_0}^{t} e^{c(t-s)}\, \mathbf{b}'\mathbf{f}(\mathbf{x}(s))\, \mathrm{d}s.$$

Elements in $\mathbf{x}(t)$ do not necessarily change *linearly* over time, as we assumed above. If they change exponentially over time, the resulting

IE is also linear in observed variables (see Section 11.2) and can be estimated by OLS as well as by ML. Simple algebraic manipulations of the OLS estimators again let one recover the fundamental dynamic parameters. The case of time-invariant causal variables is, of course, just a special case of linear change; (4) applies directly except that $\Delta x_n = 0$ and $\beta_2 = 0$ for such variables.

The simplicity of the IE for (1) when causal variables change linearly over time makes it tempting to estimate (3) no matter how realistic the assumption of the linear change is. We want to stress that the dynamics of exogenous variables should not be treated mechanically because results on the dynamics of the outcome depend on the postulated dynamics of the exogenous variables. Unless the dynamics of the causal variables are described accurately, one cannot hope to explain change in the outcome. This problem is particularly acute when the observations are spaced widely relative to the typical fluctuations of the exogenous variables. Then (3), the IE obtained under the assumption of linearly changing causal variables, may be a poor approximation to the true IE.

When substantive considerations suggest that the exogenous variables change in more complex nonlinear ways over time, explicit expressions for the IEs are sometimes very complicated or unknown. In this case one can turn to estimation of an exact discrete approximation, an example of which we discuss in Chapter 14.

13.4 Autocorrelation of Disturbances

The complication that dominates most discussions of temporal analysis is autocorrelation of disturbances, which arises because some factors omitted from sociological models are stable over time. If disturbances are autocorrelated, OLS estimators are inefficient, and standard errors are biased toward zero, even when the regression does not contain lagged values of the dependent variable.

The problem is far more serious when the regression equation does contain lagged values of the dependent variable, as in the IEs of all dynamic models considered in Chapter 11. In this situation, autocorrelation confounds the disturbance term with the effects of the lagged dependent variable. Consequently, OLS estimators are biased and inconsistent (Johnston, 1972, pp. 300–320; Malinvaud, 1970, pp. 554–562). When exogenous variables are correlated with the lagged dependent variable, as they usually are, OLS estimates of *all* regression paramaters are biased and inconsistent. So one cannot obtain good estimates of any structural parameters unless autocorrelation is handled properly.

Although one expects autocorrelation to be a common problem in sociological applications, the linear SDEs with a Brownian-motion disturbance, which we discussed in Chapter 12, do not reflect this. Recall that Brownian-motion processes have independent increments. If increments in the disturbance are indeed independent, the disturbances of the IEs are uncorrelated for nonoverlapping temporal observations on the same case. So we must complicate the model discussed in Chapter 12 to allow for the realistic possibility of autocorrelated disturbances.

We know two strategies. The first introduces individual-specific parameters (effects of stable individual characteristics) into the SDE, which is equivalent to assuming that one (or more) time-invariant causal variables are unobserved or omitted from the model. However, this approach assumes that the remainder of the disturbance is white noise. The second complicates the disturbance by relaxing the assumption of independent increments. That is, it lets the noise be "colored", that is, have some general autocorrelation structure. Although the two may be combined, it is useful to contrast the substantive interpretations that fit one rather than the other. The first way, introducing individual-specific effects, fits circumstances in which the omitted causal variables vary across units but are approximately constant for individual units over the observation period. When the omitted variables change greatly over the observed time period but do not vary across units, the second approach is preferable. We discuss the approach based on the first assumption—that potential confounding variables are constant for units over the observation period.

13.5 Pooled Cross-Section and Time-Series Estimators

A useful way of operationalizing the first strategy is to assume that some time-invariant characteristics of units affecting $dY(t)/dt$ are unobservable or omitted from the IE for some other reason. In the study of individual careers, these omitted causal variables might include physiological characteristics, enduring features of personality, status origins, ethnicity, or linguistic styles. In studies of organizations, they might include material infrastructures, stable features of work technology, long-standing political alliances, and cultural settings. We summarize the effects of all such stable omitted variables for the ith sample member by the quantity m_i. Each unit i has its own dynamic process because of m_i, but the remaining parameters are assumed to be the same for all units. This implies a system of I linear SDEs:

$$dY_i(t) = cY_i(t)\,dt + \mathbf{b}'\mathbf{x}_i(t)\,dt + m_i\,dt + \sigma_i\,dW_i(t). \tag{9}$$

This system of equations differs from (1) only in the I individual-specific parameters, m_i, $i = 1, \ldots, I$.

When $\mathbf{x}(t)$ changes linearly over time, the solution of the system of equations in (9) resembles (3):

$$Y_i(t_n) = \gamma Y_i(t_{n-1}) + \boldsymbol{\beta}_1'\mathbf{x}_i(t_{n-1}) + \boldsymbol{\beta}_2'\Delta\mathbf{x}_n + \mu_i + \epsilon_i(t_n), \tag{10}$$

where γ, $\boldsymbol{\beta}$, and $\boldsymbol{\beta}_2$ are defined by (4);

$$\mu_i \equiv \frac{\gamma - 1}{c} m_i. \tag{11}$$

Suppose the model in (9) is correct, but an analyst ignores the unobservable variables whose effects are summarized by μ_i. That is, assume the analyst obtains OLS estimates of

$$Y_i(t_n) = \gamma Y_i(t_{n-1}) + \boldsymbol{\beta}_1'\mathbf{x}_i(t_{n-1}) + \boldsymbol{\beta}_2'\Delta\mathbf{x}_n + \eta_i(t_n), \tag{12}$$

where $\eta_i(t_n) \equiv \mu_i + \epsilon_i(t_n)$. It is well known that OLS estimators of γ are biased and inconsistent in this case. Because each m_i is constant and affects $Y_i(t_n)$ at every wave n, μ_i must be correlated with $Y_i(t_{n-1})$.[4] Therefore, $\eta_i(t_n)$ must be correlated with $Y_i(t_{n-1})$. Ordinary least-squares estimators give credit to $Y_i(t_{n-1})$ for the effect of m_i. As we illustrate in Table 13.1, the bias in $\widehat{\gamma}$ is usually substantial.

Here we have a classic example of the autocorrelation problem. When the effects of the m_i are ignored (and so forced into

---

[4]Although we are treating $y_i(t_0)$ as a fixed initial condition for each individual i, it does vary across sample members and thus may have an empirical correlation with μ_i.

the disturbance), the disturbances become positively autocorrelated. Failure to acknowledge autocorrelation—use of estimators that assume that $\eta_i(t_n)$ is uncorrelated with $Y_i(t_{n-1})$—leads to biased estimation.

The common two-wave panel lacks sufficient information to adjust for autocorrelation. The sociological literature has long given little attention to this problem in panel estimation. As a consequence, many previous sociological applications of panel analysis are suspect. But as long as the effects of omitted variables are stable for individual units, the autocorrelation problem can be solved by using multiwave panels with fixed intervals between waves.[5]

Biometricians (Henderson, 1952, 1953) and econometricians (Kuh, 1959; Balestra and Nerlove, 1966) have proposed estimators for models like (10), which they considered as discrete-time models. Here we extend these estimators to the continuous-time framework. This approach requires the use of *multiwave* panels, that is, panels with observations on the same sample members at three or more times. Clearly, if one has observations at only two times, say t_0 and t_1, one cannot estimate a model with individual-specific effects; there will be fewer sample moments than parameters. If there are three or more waves of observations, *and* the underlying parameters are constant over the observation period, *and* the interval between waves is a constant, one can pool all temporal observations and estimate a single set of parameters. The resulting estimators are often called "pooled cross-section and time-series estimators" to acknowledge the fact that both cross-sectional and temporal variation are used in estimating parameters.

In some research settings it is appropriate to incorporate effects specific to a particular interval of time. When one assumes a discrete-time structure, period-specific effects may be handled formally in exactly the same manner as individual-specific effects. As long as both types of effects enter additively, that is, individual-specific effects and period-specific effects do not interact, no additional complications arise from including both types of effects. This

---

[5]It is important to notice, however, that even if m_i is time-invariant, μ_i will vary from one equation to another if waves are unequally spaced, as (11) indicates. We discuss the situation in which waves are unequally spaced in Section 13.8.

sort of structure does not generalize readily to continuous-time models of change. In the latter context, it is more natural to complicate the model by incorporating jump processes into the noise process, as we proposed in Section 12.3. However, we do not consider this more complicated case here. The following discussion assumes that the only strong threat to correct inference is the presence of omitted variables that vary over sample members but do not vary over time.

Before discussing estimators for pooled models, we must address a basic methodological question: Should the individual-specific components be treated as *fixed* or *random* variables? The two interpretations involve some fairly obvious trade-offs. If one knows the probability distribution of the m_i with confidence, treating the μ_i as random variables achieves considerable economy and statistical power. But, if one is wrong about this distribution, the consequences may be worse than if one treats the m_i as fixed variables and conditions on the observed data. We discuss estimators suitable for each perspective because each seems likely to be preferable in certain contexts.

13.5.1 Fixed-Effects Estimators

If the μ_i are considered fixed, estimation of (10) is simple.[6] As long as the number of waves is greater than two, one can eliminate autocorrelation bias merely by adding a dummy variable for each individual to the model. Naturally a model that contains both an intercept and dummy variables for each individual is not identified. Consequently, we suppress the intercept below.

A discussion of estimators for pooled panel data requires the use of matrix notation. As before, let I be the sample size and N the number of temporal observations on each case after an initial observation at t_0. We assume that there are $M/2$ linearly changing causal variables and that the spacing between observations, $\Delta t \equiv t_n - t_{n-1}$, is the same for all i and all n. It is convenient to organize the data as follows:

---

[6]The simplicity of this case depends strongly on linearity and additivity. In more general models, the fact that the number of so-called incidental parameters m_i goes to ∞ as $I \to \infty$ leads to estimation problems. Chamberlain (1979) reviewed the statistical literature on problems of incidental parameters.

⟨13⟩ **Pooled Cross-Section and Time-Series Estimators** 435

$$\mathbf{y} \equiv \begin{pmatrix} Y_1(t_1) \\ Y_1(t_2) \\ \vdots \\ Y_1(t_N) \\ \vdots \\ Y_I(t_1) \\ Y_I(t_2) \\ \vdots \\ Y_I(t_N) \end{pmatrix}$$

$$\mathbf{Z} \equiv \begin{pmatrix} Y_1(t_0) & x_{11}(t_0) & \cdots & x_{1M/2}(t_0) & \Delta x_{111} & \cdots & \Delta x_{11M/2} \\ Y_1(t_1) & x_{11}(t_1) & \cdots & x_{1M/2}(t_1) & \Delta x_{121} & \cdots & \Delta x_{12M/2} \\ \vdots & \vdots & & \vdots & \vdots & & \vdots \\ Y_1(t_{N-1}) & x_{11}(t_{N-1}) & \cdots & x_{1M/2}(t_{N-1}) & \Delta x_{1N1} & \cdots & \Delta x_{1NM/2} \\ \vdots & \vdots & & \vdots & \vdots & & \vdots \\ Y_I(t_0) & x_{I1}(t_0) & \cdots & x_{IM/2}(t_0) & \Delta x_{I11} & \cdots & \Delta x_{I1M/2} \\ Y_I(t_1) & x_{I1}(t_1) & \cdots & x_{IM/2}(t_1) & \Delta x_{I21} & \cdots & \Delta x_{I2M/2} \\ \vdots & \vdots & & \vdots & \vdots & & \vdots \\ Y_I(t_{N-1}) & x_{I1}(t_{N-1}) & \cdots & x_{IM/2}(t_{N-1}) & \Delta x_{IN1} & \cdots & \Delta x_{INM/2} \end{pmatrix}.$$

Note that $\mathbf{y}$ is NI by 1 and $\mathbf{Z}$ is NI by $M+1$.

We also define an NI by I matrix $\mathbf{D}$, in which the ith column contains a 1 in each of the N rows corresponding to observations on i and 0 in all other rows:

$$\mathbf{D} \equiv \begin{pmatrix} 1 & 0 & \cdot & \cdot & \cdot & 0 & 0 \\ \cdot & \cdot & \cdot & \cdot & \cdot & 0 & 0 \\ 1 & 0 & \cdot & \cdot & \cdot & 0 & 0 \\ 0 & 1 & \cdot & \cdot & \cdot & 0 & 0 \\ \cdot & \cdot & \cdot & \cdot & \cdot & 0 & 0 \\ 0 & 1 & \cdot & \cdot & \cdot & 0 & 0 \\ \cdot & \cdot & \cdot & \cdot & \cdot & 0 & 0 \\ \cdot & \cdot & \cdot & \cdot & \cdot & 0 & 0 \\ 0 & 0 & \cdot & \cdot & \cdot & 0 & 1 \\ \cdot & \cdot & \cdot & \cdot & \cdot & 0 & \cdot \\ 0 & 0 & \cdot & \cdot & \cdot & 0 & 1 \end{pmatrix}.$$

Algebraic expressions for matrices like $\mathbf{D}$ are useful. We can create such expressions using the Kronecker product,[7] which we denote by $\otimes$. Let $\mathbf{I}_I$ denote the I by I identity matrix and $\boldsymbol{\ell}$ denote a N by 1 vector whose entries are ones. Then an alternative definition is

$$\mathbf{D} \equiv \mathbf{I}_I \otimes \boldsymbol{\ell}.$$

These definitions let us rewrite the model in (10) as

$$\mathbf{y} = (\mathbf{Z} \quad \mathbf{D})\begin{pmatrix} \boldsymbol{\alpha} \\ \boldsymbol{\mu} \end{pmatrix} + \boldsymbol{\epsilon}, \qquad (13)$$

where $\boldsymbol{\mu}$ is I by 1, $\boldsymbol{\epsilon}$ is an NI by 1 matrix of random disturbances (integrated Brownian motion), and the $(M+1)$ by 1 parameter vector $\boldsymbol{\alpha}$ is defined as

$$\boldsymbol{\alpha} \equiv \begin{pmatrix} \gamma \\ \beta_1 \\ \beta_2 \end{pmatrix}$$

If the m_i are fixed variables, then all elements of $\boldsymbol{\mu}$ are constants to be estimated.

Ordinary least-squares estimators of the model in (13) solve the normal equations

$$\begin{pmatrix} \mathbf{Z}'\mathbf{Z} & \mathbf{Z}'\mathbf{D} \\ \mathbf{D}'\mathbf{Z} & \mathbf{D}'\mathbf{D} \end{pmatrix} \begin{pmatrix} \boldsymbol{\alpha} \\ \boldsymbol{\mu} \end{pmatrix} = \begin{pmatrix} \mathbf{Z}'\mathbf{y} \\ \mathbf{D}'\mathbf{y} \end{pmatrix}.$$

Simple algebraic operations reveal that this system can be rearranged to eliminate $\boldsymbol{\mu}$:

$$\mathbf{Z}'\mathbf{V}\mathbf{Z}\boldsymbol{\alpha} = \mathbf{Z}'\mathbf{V}\mathbf{y},$$

where

$$\mathbf{V} \equiv \mathbf{I}_{NI} - \mathbf{D}(\mathbf{D}'\mathbf{D})^{-1}\mathbf{D}'$$

[7] The Kronecker product of $\mathbf{A}$, an M by N matrix, and $\mathbf{B}$, a P by Q matrix, equals $\mathbf{C}$, the MP by NQ partitioned matrix that has $a_{ij}\mathbf{B}$ as the ijth partition. See Rao (1965, p. 29) or standard works on linear algebra for more extensive discussions of the Kronecker product and its properties.

⟨13⟩ Pooled Cross-Section and Time-Series Estimators

is an NI by NI symmetric matrix. Since V is idempotent (i.e., $V^2 = V$) and symmetric (i.e., $V = V'$), the normal equations can be rewritten as

$$Z'VVZ\alpha = Z'VVy;$$

or

$$(VZ)'(VZ)\alpha = (VZ)'Vy.$$

These are the OLS normal equations for data transformed by the matrix operator V. Consequently OLS estimation of (13), the model with dummy variables for each individual, is equivalent to OLS estimation of data transformed by V. From the definitions of D and V it follows that

$$V = I_{NI} - \frac{I_I \otimes \ell\ell'}{N}.$$

This is a block-diagonal matrix, that is, it has blocks of nonzero elements on the main diagonal and zeros elsewere. Each block is N by N and has $(N-1)/N$ on the main diagonal and $-1/N$ as off-diagonal elements:

$$\begin{pmatrix} \frac{N-1}{N} & \frac{-1}{N} & \frac{-1}{N} & \cdots & \frac{-1}{N} \\ \frac{-1}{N} & \frac{N-1}{N} & \frac{-1}{N} & \cdots & \frac{-1}{N} \\ \vdots & \vdots & \vdots & & \vdots \\ \frac{-1}{N} & \frac{-1}{N} & \frac{-1}{N} & \cdots & \frac{N-1}{N} \end{pmatrix}.$$

Thus, premultiplication of y and Z by the matrix V subtracts an individual's mean for a variable from every observation on that variable for the individual. For example, it transforms $Y_i(t_n)$ into $[Y_i(t_n) - Y_{i.}]$, where by definition

$$Y_{i.} \equiv \frac{1}{N} \sum_{n=1}^{N} Y_i(t_n).$$

Thus, OLS estimation of the model with individual-specific dummy variables is equivalent to pooled "within-individual" regressions. The latter are usually preferable for computational reasons. Since this method estimates constants for each individual, we call it **least squares with constants (LSC)**, and write the LSC estimators as

$$\widehat{\boldsymbol{\alpha}}_{\text{LSC}} = (\mathbf{Z'VZ})^{-1}\mathbf{Z'Vy}.$$

In this pooled "within-individual" regression, one cannot use LSC to estimate both $\boldsymbol{\mu}$ and coefficients of time-invariant causal variables. The procedure of subtracting individual means eliminates observable time-invariant exogenous variables, like race and sex, from the model. However, coefficients of time-invariant variables can be estimated by the following two-stage procedure. First, use LSC to estimate coefficients of the lagged dependent variable and the time-varying causal variables. Then estimate the new regression equation

$$\mathbf{y}(t_n) - \widehat{\boldsymbol{\alpha}}_{\text{LSC}}\mathbf{y}(t_{n-1}) = \mathbf{X}\boldsymbol{\beta} + \boldsymbol{\varsigma}(t_n),$$

for $n = 1, \ldots, N$. Since the lagged dependent variable has been removed from the right-hand side of this regression, OLS estimators are consistent (though not efficient) even in the presence of $\boldsymbol{\mu}$ in the disturbance. A better alternative is to use Henderson's method, discussed below.

13.5.2 Random-Effects Estimators

If the individual-specific effects (the m_i) are regarded as realizations of a random variable that varies over individuals but not over time, the model can be written as

$$\begin{aligned} \mathbf{y} &= \mathbf{Z}\boldsymbol{\alpha} + \boldsymbol{\eta}; \\ \boldsymbol{\eta} &\equiv \boldsymbol{\mu} + \boldsymbol{\epsilon}. \end{aligned} \quad (14)$$

Different assumptions about $\boldsymbol{\eta}$ lead to different kinds of estimators. We begin with a fairly general set of assumptions:

$$\begin{aligned} \mathrm{E}[\boldsymbol{\mu}] &= 0; \\ \mathrm{E}[\boldsymbol{\epsilon}] &= 0; \\ \mathrm{E}[\boldsymbol{\mu}\boldsymbol{\epsilon}'] &= 0; \\ \mathrm{E}[\boldsymbol{\epsilon}\boldsymbol{\epsilon}'] &= \sigma_\epsilon^2 \mathbf{R}; \\ \mathrm{E}[\boldsymbol{\mu}\boldsymbol{\mu}'] &= \sigma_\mu^2 \mathbf{S}. \end{aligned} \quad (15)$$

Note that these assumptions allow heteroscedasticity and nonzero covariances between the disturbances of different individuals as well as correlation within individuals; **R** and **S** need not be diagonal. These assumptions imply that the model in (14) has the following covariance structure:

$$\Omega \equiv E[\eta\eta'] = \sigma_\epsilon^2 \mathbf{R} + \sigma_\mu^2 \mathbf{S}.$$

Nerlove's Generalized Least-Squares Estimator. Nerlove (1971; see also Balestra and Nerlove, 1966) developed an estimator for a special case of the model discussed above. This model has had a great impact on social-scientific research. It has been used widely in empirical research and has stimulated interest in alternative estimators for panel data on quantitative outcomes. By now the literature on this estimator is voluminous. Some useful methodological papers include Amemiya (1967), Maddala (1971), Wallace and Hussain (1969), and Hannan and Young (1977).

Nerlove assumed the simplest possible form for the disturbance, namely

$$\begin{aligned} E[\epsilon\epsilon'] &= \sigma_\epsilon^2 \mathbf{I}_{NI} \quad (\text{or } \mathbf{R} = \mathbf{I}_{NI}); \\ E[\mu\mu'] &= \sigma_\mu^2 \mathbf{I}_{NI} \quad (\text{or } \mathbf{S} = \mathbf{I}_{NI}). \end{aligned} \qquad (16)$$

That is, Nerlove assumed that elements in ϵ are uncorrelated from observation to observation, that elements in μ are uncorrelated across individuals, and that elements in both ϵ and μ have constant variances σ_ϵ^2 and σ_μ^2, respectively. These assumptions imply that

$$\Omega = \sigma_\mu^2 \mathbf{D}\mathbf{D}' + \sigma_\epsilon^2 \mathbf{I}_{NI}, \qquad (17)$$

where $\mathbf{DD}'$ is a block-diagonal matrix in which each block is N by N and has a 1 in every position.

The conventional way of expressing the variance–covariance matrix of the disturbances in this model uses the intraclass correlation coefficient ρ, where

$$\rho \equiv \frac{\sigma_\mu^2}{\sigma_\mu^2 + \sigma_\epsilon^2} \equiv \frac{\sigma_\mu^2}{\sigma_\eta^2}.$$

Note that ρ is the proportion of the total error variance that is specific to individual sample members; it expresses the correlation among the temporal observations on an individual. For this reason, ρ is often called the **autocorrelation coefficient** for this model. The above definition of ρ lets us write

$$\Omega = (\sigma_\mu^2 + \sigma_\epsilon^2) \begin{pmatrix} A & 0 & \cdots & 0 \\ 0 & A & \cdots & 0 \\ \vdots & \vdots & & \vdots \\ 0 & 0 & \cdots & A \end{pmatrix},$$

where

$$A \equiv \begin{pmatrix} 1 & \rho & \rho & \cdots & \rho \\ \rho & 1 & \rho & \cdots & \rho \\ \vdots & \vdots & \vdots & & \vdots \\ \rho & \rho & \rho & \cdots & 1 \end{pmatrix}.$$

We want an estimator that corrects for autocorrelatation. If Ω is known, use of Aitken's (1935) generalized least-squares (GLS) estimator solves the problem. In this context, the GLS estimator solves the normal equations

$$\begin{pmatrix} Z'\Omega^{-1}Z & Z'\Omega^{-1}D \\ D'\Omega^{-1}D & D'\Omega^{-1}D \end{pmatrix} \begin{pmatrix} \alpha \\ \mu \end{pmatrix} = \begin{pmatrix} Z'\Omega^{-1}y \\ D'\Omega^{-1}y \end{pmatrix}. \quad (18)$$

When Z is fixed, the resulting GLS estimators are best linear unbiased estimators (BLUE). Although Z is not fixed here, the GLS estimators have attractive asymptotic properties even when regressors are stochastic (see Johnston, 1972, for example). Notice that GLS estimation can be interpreted as OLS estimation of the data transformed as follows:

$$\Omega^{-\frac{1}{2}} y = \Omega^{-\frac{1}{2}} Z\alpha + \Omega^{-\frac{1}{2}} \eta. \quad (19)$$

In this respect, the random-effects case parallels the fixed-effects case discussed above.

Given the strong assumptions of Nerlove's model [see (16)], the matrix Ω has a block-diagonal form. Therefore, $\Omega^{-\frac{1}{2}}$ is easy to calculate. It is just (see Nerlove, 1971, p. 370)

$$\Omega^{-\frac{1}{2}} = \begin{pmatrix} G & 0 & 0 & \cdots & 0 \\ 0 & G & 0 & \cdots & 0 \\ \vdots & \vdots & \vdots & & \vdots \\ 0 & 0 & 0 & \cdots & G \end{pmatrix}, \quad (20a)$$

where

$$\mathbf{G} \equiv \frac{1}{\sqrt{1-\rho}}\left[\mathbf{I}_N - \frac{\boldsymbol{\ell}\boldsymbol{\ell}'}{N}\right] + \frac{1}{\sqrt{1-\rho+N\rho}}\left[\frac{\boldsymbol{\ell}\boldsymbol{\ell}'}{N}\right]. \qquad (20b)$$

The form of the GLS transformation in (19) and (20) can be intuitively motivated as follows. The peculiar feature of pooled models is that they use both cross-sectional and temporal variation to estimate causal parameters. The richness of the data lets one choose how to weight one type of variation relative to the other. Out of ignorance, OLS estimation gives every observation equal weight. Generalized least-squares estimation uses ρ to weight the two types of information. To see this, consider the case in which $\rho = 0$. Then $\mathbf{G} = \mathbf{I}_N$, and the transformation in (19) is just an identity transformation; it leaves the data unchanged. Generalized least squares reduces to OLS in which cross-sectional and time-series variation are weighted proportionately to I and N, respectively (see Maddala, 1971). At the other extreme, as ρ approaches unity, $\mathbf{G}$ approaches $\boldsymbol{\ell}\boldsymbol{\ell}'/N$; this transformation averages each sample member's observations over time. The result is a regression on grouped observations in which all of the weight is given to cross-sectional variation. When ρ has a value between 0 and 1, GLS estimation weights temporal variation inversely to ρ. Such a weighting seems appropriate because ρ measures *redundancy* in the temporal series. The more redundancy, the lower the weight attached to temporal variation.

So far we have treated ρ as if it were known a priori. Realistically, sociologists do not have such knowledge. Consequently, we must consider methods of estimating ρ and properties of GLS estimators based on $\widehat{\rho}$.

The most widely used procedure for estimating ρ is based on the fixed-effects estimator discussed in the previous section. To estimate ρ, we need estimates of σ_ϵ^2 and σ_μ^2. Nerlove (1971) suggested using the LSC estimate of σ_μ^2:

$$\widehat{\sigma}_\mu^2 = \frac{1}{I}\sum_{i=1}^{I}(\widehat{\mu}_i - \mu_.)^2,$$

where by definition

$$\mu_. = \frac{1}{I}\sum_{i=1}^{I}\mu_i.$$

An obvious estimator of σ_ϵ^2 is the sum of squared residuals from the LSC regression divided by NI:

$$\hat{\sigma}_\epsilon^2 = \frac{1}{NI} \sum_{i=1}^{I} \sum_{n=1}^{N} [\hat{Y}_i(t_n) - Y_i(t_n)]^2,$$

where $\hat{Y}_i(t_n)$ is calculated from the LSC estimator. Then

$$\hat{\rho}_{\text{LSC}} = \frac{\hat{\sigma}_\mu^2}{\hat{\sigma}_\mu^2 + \hat{\sigma}_\epsilon^2}. \tag{21}$$

Nerlove chose $\hat{\rho}_{\text{LSC}}$ over the ML estimate to avoid negative values, which are not meaningful. Unfortunately, the estimator in (21) is upwardly biased (at least in small samples), and the magnitude of the bias is inversely related to ρ.

To acknowledge the fact that an estimate of ρ is used, we call the resulting estimator of $\boldsymbol{\alpha}$ the modified GLS (MGLS) estimator

$$\hat{\boldsymbol{\alpha}}_{\text{MGLS}} = (\mathbf{Z}'\hat{\boldsymbol{\Omega}}^{-1}\mathbf{Z})^{-1}\mathbf{Z}'\hat{\boldsymbol{\Omega}}^{-1}\mathbf{y}.$$

The MGLS estimator is consistent and asymptotically efficient, even though it uses a biased estimate of ρ. These large-sample properties require only that $\hat{\rho}_{\text{LSC}}$ be a consistent estimator of ρ (Aitken, 1935), which it is.

Henderson's GLS Estimator. An approach developed by Henderson (1953, 1963) yields estimators for a much broader class of stochastic models than the approach just outlined. Henderson's approach also yields GLS estimators for the class of models discussed in this chapter. As we explain below, his GLS estimators have certain advantages over Nerlove's.

It is instructive to begin by returning to the fixed-effects case, relaxing the assumption that the covariance matrix of disturbances is diagonal. That is, we assume that $\mathrm{E}[\boldsymbol{\epsilon}\boldsymbol{\epsilon}'] = \sigma_\epsilon^2 \mathbf{R}$, where $\mathbf{R}$ is a general matrix. This allows disturbances to be heteroscedastic and correlated between individuals. The GLS estimator for this case solves the normal equations

$$\begin{pmatrix} \mathbf{Z}'\mathbf{R}^{-1}\mathbf{Z} & \mathbf{Z}'\mathbf{R}^{-1}\mathbf{D} \\ \mathbf{D}'\mathbf{R}^{-1}\mathbf{Z} & \mathbf{D}'\mathbf{R}^{-1}\mathbf{D} \end{pmatrix} \begin{pmatrix} \boldsymbol{\alpha} \\ \boldsymbol{\mu} \end{pmatrix} = \begin{pmatrix} \mathbf{Z}'\mathbf{R}^{-1}\mathbf{y} \\ \mathbf{D}'\mathbf{R}^{-1}\mathbf{y} \end{pmatrix}.$$

⟨13⟩   Pooled Cross-Section and Time-Series Estimators

If $\mathbf{R}^{-1}$ is known or can be estimated consistently, this estimator can be applied to a wide variety of fixed-effects problems.

Our interest centers mainly on the model in (14), in which μ_i is a random variable. We now work with weaker assumptions about the covariance structure of the individual effects. We use the set of assumptions in (15) including

$$E[\boldsymbol{\mu}\boldsymbol{\mu}'] = \sigma_\mu^2 \mathbf{S},$$

which allows heteroscedasticity and correlation both between and within individuals. Henderson (1953) proved that the GLS estimators for this model are the solutions to the following normal equations:

$$\begin{pmatrix} \mathbf{Z}'\mathbf{R}^{-1}\mathbf{Z} & \mathbf{Z}'\mathbf{R}^{-1}\mathbf{D} \\ \mathbf{D}'\mathbf{R}^{-1}\mathbf{Z} & \mathbf{D}'\mathbf{R}^{-1}\mathbf{D} + \mathbf{S} \end{pmatrix} \begin{pmatrix} \boldsymbol{\alpha} \\ \boldsymbol{\mu} \end{pmatrix} = \begin{pmatrix} \mathbf{Z}'\mathbf{R}^{-1}\mathbf{y} \\ \mathbf{D}'\mathbf{R}^{-1}\mathbf{y} \end{pmatrix}.$$

Defining the estimators in this way has considerable computational advantages (see Henderson, 1971).

The distinctive feature of Henderson's approach is the method of estimating the variance components σ_μ^2 and σ_ϵ^2. His general strategy equates reductions in sums of squares from fitting various submodels (which involve quadratic forms, as we show below) to their expected values in the full model. The solutions to such equations give estimators of the variance components.

Before applying Henderson's method to (14), we need to review some results on the general linear model. We follow Searle (1971a, Chapter 10; see also Searle, 1971b). Consider the model

$$\mathbf{y} = \mathbf{X}\mathbf{b} + \boldsymbol{\epsilon},$$

with $\mathrm{Var}(\mathbf{y}) = \boldsymbol{\Sigma}$. We assume that $\mathbf{X}$ has M columns and full rank.[8] The expectation of a general quadratic form in $\mathbf{y}$, say $\mathbf{y}'\mathbf{Q}\mathbf{y}$, is

$$E[\mathbf{y}'\mathbf{Q}\mathbf{y}] = \mathrm{tr}\{\mathbf{Q}\boldsymbol{\Sigma}\} + E[\mathbf{y}']\mathbf{Q}E[\mathbf{y}].$$

---

[8] Actually, Henderson's procedure works even when $\mathbf{X}$ does not have full rank, which implies that $\mathbf{X}'\mathbf{X}$ cannot be inverted. Searle (1971a,b) gave full details on the use of the generalized inverse to handle this problem.

Some important well-known results when the sample size is I and $\Sigma = \sigma_\epsilon^2 I_I$ include

(a) $\mathbf{Q} = \mathbf{I}_I$, which implies that

$$E[\mathbf{y'y}] = \mathbf{b'X'Xb} + \sigma_\epsilon^2 I;$$

(b) $\mathbf{Q} = \mathbf{X(X'X)}^{-1}\mathbf{X'}$, which means that $\mathbf{y'Qy}$ is the reduction in unexplained sums of squares from fitting the parameters $\mathbf{b}$, which we label $R(\mathbf{b})$. In this case,

$$E[R(\mathbf{b})] = E[\mathbf{y'Qy}] = \mathbf{b'X'Xb} + \sigma_\epsilon^2 \operatorname{tr}\{\mathbf{X(X'X)}^{-1}\mathbf{X'}\}$$
$$= \mathbf{b'X'Xb} + \sigma_\epsilon^2 M. \tag{22}$$

Hence,

$$E[\mathbf{y'y} - R(\mathbf{b})] = \sigma_\epsilon^2 (I - M). \tag{23}$$

This is the well-known formula for the residual sums of squares in a regression with M independent variables (including the constant) and I cases in the sample.

Suppose that the model is mixed, that is, that it contains both fixed and random effects:

$$\mathbf{y} = \mathbf{Xb} + \boldsymbol{\epsilon} = \mathbf{X}_1 \mathbf{b}_1 + \mathbf{X}_2 \mathbf{b}_2 + \boldsymbol{\epsilon},$$

where the rank of $\mathbf{X}_1$ is M_1, the rank of $\mathbf{X}_2$ is M_2, $\mathbf{b}_1$ contains fixed parameters, and $\mathbf{b}_2$ contains random effects that have zero means and zero covariances with all other factors in the model. We let $R(\mathbf{b}_1, \mathbf{b}_2)$ denote the reduction in unexplained sums of squares associated with fitting this model. We let $R(\mathbf{b}_1)$ denote the reduction in unexplained sums of squares from fitting the submodel containing only the M_1 fixed parameters. Finally, we let

$$R(\mathbf{b}_2 \mid \mathbf{b}_1) = R(\mathbf{b}_1, \mathbf{b}_2) - R(\mathbf{b}_1)$$

denote the reduction of unexplained sums of squares from fitting $\mathbf{b}_2$ once $\mathbf{b}_1$ has been fitted.

Equate the reductions in sums of squares with their expectations. The reduction in sums of squares associated with the full model is

$$R(\mathbf{b}_1, \mathbf{b}_2) = \mathbf{y'X(X'X)}^{-1}\mathbf{X'y},$$

and
$$E[R(b_1, b_2)] = \text{tr}\{(X'X)E[bb']\} + \sigma_\epsilon^2 (M_1 + M_2).$$

Similarly,
$$R(b_1) = y'X_1(X_1'X_1)^{-1}X_1'y,$$

and
$$E[R(b_1)] = \text{tr}\{X'X_1(X_1'X_1)^{-1}X_1'X E[bb']\} + \sigma_\epsilon^2 M_1.$$

Therefore,
$$E[R(b_2 \mid b_1)] = \text{tr}\{X_2'[I_I - X_1(X_1'X_1)^{-1}X_1']X_2 E[b_2 b_2']\} + \sigma_\epsilon^2 M_2. \quad (24)$$

Equation (24) shows the general analytic advantage of Henderson's approach for models with both fixed and random effects. Since b_1 does not appear in (24), estimates of random effects do not depend on the fixed effects. Searle (1971a, Chapter 10) discussed this subject at length.

The case that interests us [equation (14)] has only one random factor, μ. That is, the model is $y = Z\alpha + D\mu + \epsilon$ where the rank of D is $I - 1$, that is $M_2 = I - 1$. Cunningham and Henderson (1969) analyzed this case in detail. Since $y'y$ is the sum of squares in the dependent variable and $R(\alpha, \mu)$ denotes the reduction in the unexplained (or error) sums of squares (SSE) from fitting α and μ, the unexplained sums of squares in the full model can be expressed as
$$\text{SSE}(\alpha, \mu) = y'y - R(\alpha, \mu).$$

Expression (23) implies that
$$E[\text{SSE}(\alpha, \mu)] = [NI - M - I + 1]\sigma_\epsilon^2.$$

Hence, an estimator for the first variance component σ_ϵ^2 is
$$\hat{\sigma}_\epsilon^2 = \frac{y'y - R(\alpha, \mu)}{NI - M - I + 1}. \quad (25)$$

To obtain an estimator for the second variance component σ_μ^2, we use equation (24) to obtain

$$E[R(\mu \mid \alpha)] = \sigma_\mu^2 \operatorname{tr}\{D'D - D'Z(Z'Z)^{-1}Z'D\} + \sigma_\epsilon^2(I-1).$$

Therefore, Henderson's estimator of the second variance component is

$$\hat{\sigma}_\mu^2 = \frac{R(\mu \mid \alpha) - \hat{\sigma}_\epsilon^2(I-1)}{\operatorname{tr}\{D'D - D'Z(Z'Z)^{-1}Z'D\}}. \qquad (26)$$

Equations (25) and (26) are the exact formulas for calculating the necessary variance components. In many situations, there are approximations that simplify computation (see Searle, 1971a, pp. 466–470).

Most of the analytic work with Henderson's method assumes that all regressors in Z are fixed. Then Henderson's estimators are BLUE estimators. Unfortunately, little is known about the properties of these estimators when Z contains lagged values of the dependent variable. Although the estimators are consistent and asymptotically unbiased in such cases, we do not know how they compare to other estimators in small samples.

The main advantage of this approach, as we mentioned above, is its generality. It is easy to derive estimators for various situations of considerable practical importance. For example, Nielsen (1978) developed Henderson's GLS estimator for models in which S is diagonal but heteroscedastic (the variance σ_ϵ^2 may not be the same across individuals). We used this estimator in the example of organizational growth and decline processes discussed in Section 11.3. Fuller and Battese (1974) worked out the special case in which there are both period effects and individual effects in a discrete-time model. This estimator has been incorporated in the Statistical Analysis System (1980) package as option "Fuller" in "Time-Series Cross-Section Regressions." Thus, at least one version of this estimator can be applied without developing special computational routines.

Maximum-Likelihood Estimators. Finally, we may form ML estimators for the random-effects model. This is a standard ML regression problem, assuming the μ_i have a multivariate normal distribution. Estimates of γ, β, and ρ may be found by maximizing the log-likelihood function

$$\log \mathcal{L} = -\frac{1}{2} NI \log(2\pi) - \frac{1}{2} \log[\det(\Omega)] - \frac{1}{2} \eta' \Omega^{-1} \eta. \qquad (27)$$

⟨13⟩   **Monte Carlo Studies of Pooled Estimators**   447

Because Ω [see (17)] is a function of two nonnegative terms, σ_η^2 and ρ, it is possible to maximize (27) subject to these constraints. The ML estimators (both unconstrained and constrained) have the good large-sample properties (consistency and efficiency) when the data are indeed multivariate normal. Note that the least-squares estimators are not identical to ML estimators for the cases considered here.

Comparisons. There are three major alternative approaches to the estimation of parameters in dynamic models with individual-specific effects: a marginal likelihood approach (which yields the LSC estimator for the model we considered), GLS, and ML. All three aproaches yield consistent and asymptotically efficient estimators of the coefficients of the lagged endogenous variable and exogenous causal variables. Of the three, we prefer ML in large samples for reasons discussed earlier. The ML estimators have minimum variance under the nonlinear transformations required to go from IEs to DEs. This means that we can use the strategy outlined in Section 13.2 to obtain efficient estimators of the fundamental dynamic parameters. But it is not obvious that the large-sample advantages of ML are retained in small-sized samples.

Throughout this discussion we have relied on large-sample theory. It is important, however, for empirical investigators to have some information about the properties of such estimators in small- and medium-sized samples. There are two key issues: the comparative efficiency of the various consistent estimators in finite samples and the performance of the consistent estimators relative to that of inconsistent estimators (e.g., OLS), which may have smaller mean-squared errors in small samples. We have not yet seen analytical results on these issues. So we consider the results of Monte Carlo experiments on the small-sample properties of the various estimators of the parameters of the IEs. Remember that any bias in estimates of these parameters distorts estimates of the parameters of the underlying DE.

13.6   Monte Carlo Studies of Pooled Estimators

We summarize results from two Monte Carlo simulations that used the same structure. The two studies partially overlap, but also study some different estimators. We concentrate here on the similar cases to facilitate an overall comparison of the estimators under consideration; for more details, see Hannan and Young (1974, 1977) and Tuma and Young (1976). Unfortunately, we did not undertake Monte Carlo studies of Henderson's GLS estimator. Throughout this discussion readers should keep in mind that we are considering the case in which (27) is the correct log-likelihood equation—the data are multivariate normal. If we had used some other distribution, the findings may have been quite different.

13.6.1 Data Generation

Both studies generated data that fit the following model:

$$Y_i(t_n) = \gamma Y_i(t_{n-1}) + \beta X_i(t_n) + \eta_i(t_n),$$

$$\eta_i(t_n) = \mu_i + \epsilon_i(t_n),$$

where $\Delta t = t_n - t_{n-1} = 1$, the components of $\eta_i(t_n)$ have the properties stated in (15) and (16), and both μ and ϵ are normally distributed. The exogenous variable has the structure

$$X_i(t_n) = 0.1 t_n + 0.5 X_i(t_{n-1}) + \nu_i(t_n),$$

where the $\nu_i(t_n)$ are independent normally distributed variables with a mean of zero and a variance of 1. In these respects the simulations followed Nerlove's (1971) procedure. However, they differed from Nerlove's in two main respects.[9] First, we chose the number of individuals, I, to be 50 and the number of time periods, N, to be 5, whereas Nerlove chose 25 and 10, respectively. We chose the former values of I and N because N rarely exceeds 5 in data sets available to sociologists. Second, we studied somewhat different combinations of parameter values. In each combination we set $\sigma_\mu^2 = \sigma_\epsilon^2 = 1$. We selected five values for ρ: 0, .25, .50, .75, and .90. To examine the dependence of estimator quality on the relative strength of the effects of the lagged endogenous and exogenous variables, we chose three combinations of γ and β: $(\gamma, \beta) = (0.3, 1.0), (0.8, 1.0)$, and $(0.8, 0.5)$. In all, we examined 15 combinations of parameter values.

[9]There are two other minor differences. First, we generated pseudo-random variates by Marsaglia's rectangle–wedge–tail algorithm, recommended as best by Knuth (1969), rather than the method described by Nerlove (1971). Second, for each combination of parameter values, we generated 100 sets of data while Nerlove generated 50. The additional data sets give increased confidence about the properties of estimators.

13.6.2 Estimators

We consider the following estimators:

1. **Ordinary Least Squares (OLS).** It is a consistent estimator only when $\rho = 0$.
2. **Least Squares with Constants (LSC).** This is the fixed-effects estimator; it is consistent and asymptotically efficient.
3. **"True" Generalized Least Squares (GLS).** This estimator uses the true (known) value of ρ in (13); it is also a minimum-variance, consistent estimator.
4. **Modified Generalized Least Squares (MGLS).** This estimator is also based on (13) but uses the estimate of ρ found from a first-stage LSC estimator. It is also a consistent and asymptotically efficient estimator.
5. **Unconstrained Maximum Likelihood (UML).** This is the standard ML estimator. It is asymptotically unbiased but inefficient relative to the CML estimator (see below).
6. **Constrained Maximum Likelihood (CML).** This is the standard ML estimator constrained so that $\sigma_\eta^2 > 0$ and $0 \le \rho \le 1$. This estimator is asymptotically unbiased and efficient.

An initial set of parameter estimates must be provided to find both the UML and CML estimates. We compared the unconstrained ML estimates obtained with two types of starting values, the LSC estimates and the true values used to generate the data, for five different parameter combinations (a total of 500 data sets). The two types of initial estimates produced nearly identical final estimates for the four combinations in which $\rho > 0$. For $\rho = 0$ the two sets of parameter estimates differed in only a handful of cases, and by a negligible amount. Therefore, to minimize the cost involved in obtaining the LSC estimates, we used the true parameter values as starting estimates in all remaining ML estimations. We report only the results obtained from using the latter source of initial estimates.

Tuma and Young's (1976) treatment of constraints on $\hat{\sigma}_\eta^2$ and $\hat{\rho}$ departed markedly from Nerlove's (1971). They used an algorithm developed by Gill and Murray (1972a,b) to find the maximum of the likelihood function. The algorithm utilizes a projection method of optimization that permits any feasible linear equality or inequality constraints to be imposed on parameter values. This method does not increase the nonlinearity of the function being optimized or the number of local maxima.

In contrast, Nerlove constrained $\hat{\rho}$ to be positive by maximizing $\log \mathcal{L}$ with respect to $\hat{\sigma}_\eta$ rather than $\hat{\sigma}_\eta^2$. He imposed a nonnegativity constraint on $\hat{\rho}$ by equating it with $\sin^2 \phi$ and maximizing $\log \mathcal{L}$ with respect to ϕ rather than $\hat{\rho}$. As Nerlove acknowledged, this method of applying constraints causes $\log \mathcal{L}$ to have multiple maxima with respect to ϕ because $\sin \phi$ is a periodic function. Murray (1972) warns against employment of trigonometric constraints. Such a procedure can increase the nonlinearity of the function being maximized and cause the matrix of second derivatives of $\log \mathcal{L}$ (which must be negative definite at the maximum of the likelihood function) to become singular or ill conditioned.

We are not aware of any previous evidence indicating the magnitude of the effects of constraints on $\hat{\sigma}_\eta^2$ and $\hat{\rho}$ on ML estimates for the model studied. We do not know whether the mean-squared errors of the constrained estimates of γ and β are appreciably smaller than the unconstrained estimates. Further, we do not know the effects of constraints on $\hat{\sigma}_\eta^2$ and $\hat{\rho}$ on the quality of the estimates of γ and β. Finally, we do not know whether the poor performance of the ML method in Nerlove (1971) results from the small-sample properties of ML estimation of this model or from his implementation of parameter constraints.

Results. Before looking at the mean-squared error and bias of estimators, we comment on the effectiveness and practicality of the ML procedure used. This issue has heightened importance in the present context because Nerlove (1971), in an influential paper, reports that the ML procedure he used failed to converge on most occasions and thus was impractical. Tuma and Young (1976) found that their implementation of the ML method was both successful and practical. Maximum-likelihood estimation converged to a solution for every data set, usually rapidly. On the average, the ML solution was found in 4 to 10 iterations, depending on the particular combination of parameter values. The CML and UML methods required nearly identical numbers of iterations to converge. For both methods several more iterations were usually needed for high values of ρ, especially when ($\gamma = 0.8$; $\beta = 0.5$). These higher numbers of iterations occur together with poor quality of the ML estimates of

⟨13⟩ Monte Carlo Studies of Pooled Estimators

Table 13.1. Mean-squared error of various estimates of γ and β averaged over five values of ρ (based on 500 data sets per estimator)[a]

	$\hat{\gamma}$	$\hat{\beta}$
$\gamma = 0.3$, $\beta = 1.0$		
OLS	6.449	0.348
LSC	0.822	0.239
MGLS	0.226	0.194
CML	0.169	0.182
UML	0.175	0.182
$\gamma = 0.8$, $\beta = 1.0$		
OLS	1.592	0.341
LSC	0.748	0.228
MGLS	0.146	0.198
CML	0.720	0.199
UML	0.722	0.199
$\gamma = 0.8$, $\beta = 0.5$		
OLS	2.420	0.228
LSC	3.865	0.220
MGLS	0.925	0.194
CML	2.352	0.208
UML	2.415	0.218

[a] Entries in this table are multiplied by 100.

γ, β, and σ_η^2, as described more fully below.

It is helpful to know which parameter combinations activate the constraints because the CML and UML estimates are obviously identical otherwise. The constraints that $\hat{\sigma}_\eta^2$ be positive and that $\hat{\rho}$ be less than or equal to 1 were never brought into play (for a similar finding, see Nerlove, 1971). However, the constraint that $\hat{\rho}$ be nonnegative was activated in about 60% of the cases in which $\rho = 0$ or in which $\gamma = 0.8$, $\beta = 1.0$, and $\rho = .90$. The quality of CML and UML estimators is unlikely to differ except for these combinations of parameters.

We begin our assessment of the quality of the estimators by comparing mean-squared errors averaged over the five choices of ρ.[10] These are reported in Table 13.1. Overall, the OLS and LSC estimators are inferior, as expected. The small-sample simulation results agree with the large-sample theory: OLS has the largest mean-squared error in each case. Moreover, these two estimators are notably poor in estimating γ. As we have noted repeatedly, this failure has serious consequences in analysis of continuous-time models. On the basis of these results and additional evidence in Hannan and Young (1977), we advise against the use of OLS and LSC for random-effects models. Henceforth, we direct attention only to the MGLS and ML estimators.

The relative quality of the ML and MGLS estimates in terms of mean-squared error varies according to the size of the ratio of γ, the coefficient of the lagged endogenous variable, and to β, the coefficient of the exogenous variable. In these Monte Carlo studies, ML is superior when the effect of the lagged endogenous variable is small in comparison to the effect of the exogenous variable, while MGLS is best when the opposite is true. If we translate this result into the terms used to describe partial-adjustment models, it means that ML gives better estimates than MGLS when the speed of adjustment is rapid or the time between waves is long, while MGLS is better than ML in the opposite conditions.

We now consider in more detail the performance of the UML and CML estimates, contrasting them to one another and to the best of the least-squares methods, MGLS. We use the measure

$$\% \text{ bias }(\widehat{\theta}) = \frac{100}{I} \sum_{i=1}^{I} \frac{\widehat{\theta}_i - \theta}{\theta},$$

where $\widehat{\theta}_i$ is the estimate for the ith sample. For both γ and β, the percentage biases of the CML and UML estimates are similar across all parameter combinations (see Tables 13.2 and 13.3). Both the ML and MGLS methods display consistently small percentage biases in $\widehat{\beta}$ across all parameter combinations. However, both methods of estimation produce widely varying percentage biases in $\widehat{\gamma}$. For each combination of γ and β, the percentage bias in ML estimates of γ

---

[10]The following tables contain excerpts from Hannan and Young (1977) and Tuma and Young (1976); both of these references contain many additional details.

Table 13.2. Percentage bias in estimators of γ (based on 100 data sets per estimator)[a]

	ρ				
	0	.25	.50	.75	.90
$\gamma = 0.3,\ \beta = 1.0$					
UML	0.0%	3.7	3.9	2.3	0.9
CML	−1.2	3.7	3.9	2.3	0.9
MGLS	−22.4	−12.2	−5.9	−1.5	−0.1
$\gamma = 0.8,\ \beta = 1.0$					
UML	0.2	9.3	13.6	14.2	6.4
CML	−0.8	9.2	13.6	14.2	6.4
MGLS	−7.3	−2.4	0.3	1.9	1.7
$\gamma = 0.8,\ \beta = 0.5$					
UML	−0.4	16.7	21.4	23.4	23.9
CML	−1.5	15.8	21.0	23.3	23.9
MGLS	−19.0	−12.4	−7.7	−1.8	1.9

[a]Entries are rounded off to the nearest tenth of a percent.

tends to become worse as ρ increases. However, for the first two combinations of γ and β, there is a downturn in the percentage bias for high values of ρ. On the other hand, the MGLS estimates of γ are downwardly biased for low values of ρ, but the percent bias decreases monotonically as ρ increases, approaching a negligible percentage bias for $\rho = .90$.

Of course, the mean-squared errors reported earlier depend on the variances of estimators too. However, the variances of the ML and MGLS estimators differ only slightly. The variance falls off sharply as ρ increases for both types of estimators. As this is the only interesting pattern in the variances, we do not report the actual figures (see Tuma and Young, 1976, Tables 4 and 5).

Finally, we look at estimates of ρ. In both UML and CML estimates of ρ, the biases are usually negative and similar (see Table 13.4). The ML and MGLS estimators are optimal at opposite ends of the $[0, 1]$ continuum. Whereas ML estimates of ρ are almost always downwardly biased, the MGLS estimates of ρ, which are actually

Table 13.3. Percentage bias in estimators of β (based on 100 data sets per estimator)[a]

	ρ				
	0	.25	.50	.75	.90
$\gamma = 0.3, \beta = 1.0$					
UML	−0.0%	−0.0	0.1	0.1	−0.0
CML	0.1	−0.0	0.1	0.0	−0.0
MGLS	−0.3	−0.4	−0.3	−0.2	−0.1
$\gamma = 0.8, \beta = 1.0$					
UML	0.0	−1.6	−1.6	−0.4	0.4
CML	0.1	−1.6	−1.6	−0.4	0.4
MGLS	−0.1	−0.3	−0.2	0.0	0.0
$\gamma = 0.8, \beta = 0.5$					
UML	0.0	−2.5	−3.1	−2.8	−1.5
CML	0.2	−2.0	−2.6	−2.6	−1.5
MGLS	−0.9	−1.4	−1.1	−0.5	0.0

[a] Entries are rounded off to the nearest tenth of a percent.

LSC estimates [see (17)], are almost always upwardly biased. And, as we found in our examination of the percentage biases in $\hat{\rho}$, the performance of the ML method tends to be best when MGLS is at its worst, and vice versa. We find that while the bias in ML estimates of ρ is greatest for high values of ρ and least for low values of ρ, just the opposite is true for MGLS.

We conclude that both ML and MGLS perform relatively well with panel data of the size usually available to sociologists ($I = 50$, $N = 5$). They clearly outperform OLS and LSC when the individual-specific effects are normally distributed. It appears that ML does best when γ is small. This implies that ML has the best small-sample properties when systems under study adjust quickly relative to the time between waves of the panel, or, under the alternative interpretation, have strong negative feedback. On the other hand, MGLS appears preferable for systems that adjust more slowly. In light of previous work on these issues, perhaps the most important conclusion is that both ML and MGLS are practical and appear to

Table 13.4. Percentage bias in estimators of ρ (based on 100 data sets per estimator)[a]

	\multicolumn{5}{c}{ρ}
	0	.25	.50	.75	.90
$\gamma = 0.3,\ \beta = 1.0$					
UML	−0.01%	−0.04	−0.05	−0.02	−0.01
CML	0.02	−0.04	−0.05	−0.02	−0.01
MGLS	0.25	0.22	0.14	0.06	0.02
$\gamma = 0.8,\ \beta = 1.0$					
UML	−0.01	−0.17	−0.34	−0.40	−0.10
CML	0.02	−0.17	−0.34	−0.40	−0.10
MGLS	0.32	0.32	0.22	0.09	0.03
$\gamma = 0.8,\ \beta = 0.5$					
UML	−0.01	−0.27	−0.52	−0.73	−0.77
CML	0.02	−0.24	−0.49	−0.72	−0.77
MGLS	0.44	0.48	0.34	0.16	0.05

[a] Entries are rounded off to the nearest hundredth of a percent.

have relatively good small-sample properties.

We can also answer at least partially the question: Should natural constraints on parameters be imposed? Tuma and Young (1976) found, as did Nerlove (1971), that in practice only the nonnegativity constraint on $\hat{\rho}$ is at issue; other natural constraints are never violated. These results show that in terms of the mean-squared error of $\hat{\gamma}$ and $\hat{\beta}$, ML estimation with constraints on $\hat{\rho}$ has a slight advantage over that without constraints. Still, the differences between constrained and unconstrained ML estimates are never large—and always negligible for those parameter combinations in which ML estimates are superior in quality to MGLS estimates. Thus, omitting constraints on $\hat{\rho}$ does not seem to damage seriously the quality of ML estimates of parameters in the model.

13.7 Measurement Error

To this point we have implicitly assumed that all variables in a model are measured with perfect accuracy. This assumption is not realistic. Usually social scientists measure both outcomes and causal variables unreliably. In this section we explore some implications of measurement error when estimating the IE for a model like (1).

Let $Y_i(t_n)$ denote the value of the outcome for a representative case i at time t_n, the nth wave of a panel. Similarly, let x_{i1} stand for i's value on a time-invariant causal variable and $x_{i2}(t_n)$ stand for i's value on a linearly changing causal variable.[11] The assumption that these variables are measured with error can be stated formally as follows:

$$Y_i(t_n) = Y_i^\circ(t_n) + \varsigma_i(t_n),$$

$$x_{i1} = x_{i1}^\circ + \xi_{i1}, \qquad (28)$$

$$x_{i2}(t_n) = x_{i2}^\circ(t_n) + \xi_{i2}(t_n),$$

where a superscript ∘ denotes the observed value of the variable, and the corresponding variable without the superscript represents the true, unobserved value of the variable.

Various assumptions may be made about the nature of measurement errors. We concentrate on the simplest set of assumptions, namely, that these errors are unbiased on average, uncorrelated with all other variables in the model, and have a constant variance. The assumptions about measurement error in the *outcome* can be stated formally as

$$\mathrm{E}[\varsigma_i(t_n)] = 0, \qquad \text{for all } i \text{ and } n;$$

$$\mathrm{E}[\varsigma_i(t_n)\varsigma_v(t_m)] = \begin{cases} 0, & \text{for } v \neq i \text{ or } m \neq n; \\ \sigma_\varsigma^2, & \text{for } v = i \text{ and } m = n; \end{cases}$$

$$\mathrm{E}[\varsigma_i(t_n) Y_v(t_m)] = 0, \qquad \text{for all } i, v, m, \text{ and } n;$$

$$\mathrm{E}[\varsigma_i(t_n) x_{v1}] = 0, \qquad \text{for all } i, v, \text{ and } n;$$

$$\mathrm{E}[\varsigma_i(t_n) x_{v2}(t_m)] = 0, \qquad \text{for all } i, v, m, \text{ and } n.$$

There are comparable assumptions about measurement error in the causal variables. For the *time-invariant causal variable* we assume

---

[11] For simplicity we assume that x_1 and $x_2(t)$ are single variables rather than vectors. It is straightforward to generalize the discussion below to the situation in which each of these is a vector.

⟨13⟩ Measurement Error

that

$$E[\xi_{i1}] = 0, \quad \text{for all } i;$$

$$E[\xi_{i1}\xi_{v1}] = \begin{cases} 0, & \text{if } v \neq i; \\ \sigma_1^2, & \text{if } v = i; \end{cases}$$

$$E[\xi_{i1}x_{v1}] = 0, \quad \text{for all } i \text{ and } v;$$

$$E[\xi_{i1}x_{v2}(t_n)] = 0, \quad \text{for all } i, v, \text{ and } n;$$

$$E[\xi_{i1}Y_v(t_n)] = 0, \quad \text{for all } i, v, \text{ and } n.$$

For the *linearly changing causal variable* we assume that

$$E[\xi_{i2}(t_n)] = 0, \quad \text{for all } i \text{ and } n;$$

$$E[\xi_{i2}(t_n)\xi_{v2}(t_m)] = \begin{cases} 0, & \text{if } v \neq i \text{ or } m \neq n; \\ \sigma_2^2, & \text{if } v = i \text{ and } m = n; \end{cases}$$

$$E[\xi_{i2}(t_n)x_{v1}] = 0, \quad \text{for all } i, v, \text{ and } n;$$

$$E[\xi_{i2}(t_n)x_{v2}(t_m)] = 0, \quad \text{for all } i, v, n, \text{ and } m;$$

$$E[\xi_{i2}(t_n)Y_v(t_m)] = 0, \quad \text{for all } i, v, n, \text{ and } m.$$

To see the consequences of measurement error, one merely substitutes (28) in (3) and investigates covariances across units and waves that result from the unreliability in the observed variables. This substitution yields

$$Y_i^\circ(t_n) + \varsigma_i(t_n) = \gamma Y_i^\circ(t_{n-1}) + \gamma \varsigma_i(t_{n-1}) + \beta_{11} x_{i1}^\circ + \beta_{11} \xi_{i1}$$
$$+ \beta_{12} x_{i2}^\circ(t_{n-1}) + \beta_{12} \xi_{i2}(t_{n-1})$$
$$+ \beta_{22} [x_{i2}^\circ(t_n) - x_{i2}^\circ(t_{n-1})]$$
$$+ \beta_{22} [\xi_{i2}(t_n) - \xi_{i2}(t_{n-1})] + \epsilon_i(t_n).$$

Rearranging the above gives

$$Y_i^\circ(t_n) = \gamma Y_i^\circ(t_{n-1}) + \beta_{11} x_{1i}^\circ$$
$$+ \beta_{12} x_{i2}^\circ(t_{n-1}) + \beta_{22} \Delta x_{in2}^\circ + \phi_i(t_n),$$

where

$$\Delta x_{in2}^{\circ} = x_{i2}^{\circ}(t_n) - x_{i2}^{\circ}(t_{n-1});$$

$$\phi_i(t_n) = \epsilon_i(t_n) - \varsigma_i(t_n) + \gamma \varsigma_i(t_{n-1}) + \beta_{11} \xi_{i1}$$
$$+ \beta_{22} \xi_{i2}(t_n) + (\beta_{12} - \beta_{22}) \xi_{i2}(t_{n-1}).$$

We concentrate on covariances across waves for a given unit. (All covariances across units are zero because of our assumption that all random errors are uncorrelated across units.) Taking expectations of cross-products of the errors for different waves of observations on i tells the covariance structure

$$E[\phi_i(t_n)\phi_i(t_n)] = \sigma_\epsilon^2 + (\gamma^2 + 1)\sigma_\varsigma^2 + \beta_{11}\sigma_1^2$$
$$+ [\beta_{22}^2 + (\beta_{12} - \beta_{22})^2]\sigma_2^2; \qquad (32)$$

$$E[\phi_i(t_n)\phi_i(t_{n-1})] = -\gamma\sigma_\varsigma^2 + \beta_{11}^2\sigma_1^2 + \beta_{22}(\beta_{12} - \beta_{22})\sigma_2^2;$$

$$E[\phi_i(t_n)\phi_i(t_m)] = \beta_{11}^2\sigma_1^2, \quad m < n-1 \text{ or } m > n+1.$$

Thus the covariance matrix Ω has the structure

$$\Omega = \sigma_\phi^2 \begin{pmatrix} A & 0 & 0 & \cdots & 0 \\ 0 & A & 0 & \cdots & 0 \\ \vdots & \vdots & \vdots & & \vdots \\ 0 & 0 & 0 & \cdots & A \end{pmatrix},$$

where

$$\sigma_\phi^2 = \sigma_\epsilon^2 + (\gamma^2 + 1)\sigma_\varsigma^2 + \beta_{11}^2\sigma_1^2 + [\beta_{22}^2 + (\beta_{12} - \beta_{22})^2]\sigma_2^2;$$

$$\mathbf{A} \equiv \begin{pmatrix} 1 & \rho_1 & \rho_2 & \cdots & \rho_2 \\ \rho_1 & 1 & \rho_1 & \cdots & \rho_2 \\ \vdots & \vdots & \vdots & & \vdots \\ \rho_2 & \rho_2 & \rho_2 & \cdots & 1 \end{pmatrix};$$

$$\rho_1 \equiv \frac{-\gamma\sigma_\varsigma^2 + \beta_{11}^2\sigma_1^2 + \beta_{22}(\beta_{12} - \beta_{22})\sigma_2^2}{\sigma_\phi^2};$$

$$\rho_2 \equiv \frac{\beta_{11}^2\sigma_1^2}{\sigma_\phi^2}.$$

⟨ 13 ⟩   Unequally Spaced Observations

Since the IE for the linear partial-adjustment model with individual-specific effects and with measurement error in the outcome has a well defined covariance structure, it can be estimated either by ML or by adapting Henderson's estimator to this specific case.

13.8   Unequally Spaced Observations

In previous sections we have assumed equally spaced panel observations. As long as the length of time between waves in the panel is a constant for all sample members, several approaches to estimation have merit. We have discussed two broad strategies above. Within each, several estimators have good properties. The alternatives are greatly limited when one has panel data with unequally spaced observations. In fact, only one strategy and one estimator currently appears feasible: ML estimation of IEs.

Unequally spaced data arise in two kinds of situations. The first is the conventional multiwave panel in which the interval between waves varies over time but is the same for all sample members. Such variability in the timing of waves may arise from the vagaries of flows of research funds, problems of entry into sites, renewed interest in some earlier panel, and so forth. For example, Meyer's (1975) three-wave panel of finance agencies has a 3-year interval between the first two waves and a 6-year interval between the second and the third. The Sewell panel of Wisconsin high school seniors (e.g., see Hauser and Sewell, 1975), was interviewed in 1957, 1964, and 1976. Exactly the same sort of problems arise in archival research because official sources often gather and release data sporadically. Moreover, scholars using secondary sources must depend on the timing of those who collected the data. The latter may not have been trying to build a temporal data base. As a consequence, the interval between waves may vary considerably.

In the second, more problematic situation the timing of observations varies from one sample member to another. This situation may occur for the reasons discussed above. Some individuals may be "lost" to a panel and only recovered at some later time. However, there is a more systematic reason why the timing of observations may vary across members of a sample. Panel observations may be linked to events generated by a stochastic process. Sometimes retrospective surveys make such links. For example, the Parnes (1975) "mature women panel" contains employment information at marriage, at first birth, and so forth. The panel has marked unequal spacing because the timing of events varies from woman to woman.

As we discuss at greater length in Chapter 16, we think that sociologists ought to study coupled changes in qualitative and quantitative outcomes, such as marital status and earnings. One fruitful approach to such systems involves studying changes in quantitative variables over periods that begin and end with events consisting of changes in the values of qualitative variables. Progress on analyzing coupled changes in quantity and quality requires solving the problem of analyzing unequally spaced panel data.

The first type of unequal spacing is usually handled by analyzing pairs of waves separately. But this solution is generally unsatisfactory because it obviates the possibility of adjusting for individual-specific disturbances. In most sociological applications, estimates of parameters in the underlying continuous-time model depend heavily on the treatment of individual-specific effects.

We have not seen any sociological analysis of data with the second type of unequal spacing in which attention is paid to these methodological problems. Moreover, we have not yet found any systematic treatment of the general problem. So, despite its obvious practical importance and its possible substantive importance, the issue of how to estimate models from unequally spaced data has received surprisingly little attention. We attribute this lacuna to the common preoccupation with discrete-time models in the social sciences. Shifting to a continuous-time perspective suggests solutions to problems of unequal spacing.

We can illustrate a general approach to analyzing unequally spaced data using the simple case of a linear SDE with no individual-specific components, equation (1), which has the solution in (2). The solution in (2) holds for any $\Delta t_i = t - t_{i0}$. So, if the timing of observations varies within the sample, one may write an equation for each Δt_{in}, the length of the period between observations for the ith individual.

One may write an explicit likelihood for this model using the distributional results of Chapter 12. Obviously, the likelihood for any observation is a function of Δt_i. For example, the disturbance in equation (2) is normally distributed with a mean of zero and variance

$$\operatorname{Var}\bigl[\epsilon_i(t)\bigr] = \frac{\sigma^2}{2c}\bigl[e^{c\Delta t_i} - 1\bigr].$$

Since Δt_i is observed for each individual i, it is straightforward, though tedious, to maximize the likelihood with respect to the dynamic parameters, treating Δt_i as part of the observed data. Consequently, when waves of observations are unequally spaced, no new conceptual problems arise. The dynamic parameters can be estimated directly by means of ML.

13.9 Linear Systems

In developing estimators for scalar linear SDEs, we relied on the fact that explicit transition probability densities are known. Unfortunately, we cannot use a similar approach in estimating systems of coupled SDEs because the transition densities are unknown. Nonetheless, it is possible to develop estimators for linear systems of SDEs that do not depend on knowledge of these densities. Indeed, this problem has received considerable attention, beginning with Bartlett and Rajalakman (1953). Other key papers in this research tradition are those of A. W. Phillips (1957), Bergstrom (1966), P. C. B. Phillips (1972, 1974), Wymer (1972), Sargan (1974), and Robinson (1976).

The literature focuses on models of the form

$$d\mathbf{y}(t) = \mathbf{C}\mathbf{y}(t)\,dt + \mathbf{B}\mathbf{x}(t)\,dt + \sigma\,d\mathbf{W}(t),$$

and assumes that $y(t)$ has the following mean-square integral:

$$\mathbf{y}(t) - \mathbf{y}(t_0) = \int_{t_0}^{t} \mathbf{C}\mathbf{y}(s)\,ds + \int_{t_0}^{t} \mathbf{B}\mathbf{x}(s)\,ds + \sigma\bigl[\mathbf{W}(t) - \mathbf{W}(t_0)\bigr].$$

If $x(t)$ is either deterministic and integrable or stochastic and integrable in the mean-square sense, then (see Sargan, 1974)

$$\operatorname{l.i.m.} \mathbf{y}(t) = e^{\mathbf{C}\Delta t}\mathbf{y}(t_0) + \int_{t_0}^{t} e^{(t-s)\mathbf{C}}\,\mathbf{B}\mathbf{x}(s)\,ds$$
$$+ \sigma \int_{t_0}^{t} e^{(t-s)\mathbf{C}}\,d\mathbf{W}(s), \tag{33}$$

where l.i.m. means the limit in the mean-square sense (see Chapter 14). Instead of relating the outcome to the initial condition, as in equation (33), the procedure sketched in Section 13.2 can be used to relate the outcome at one period to the outcome in the previous period:

$$\text{l.i.m. } \mathbf{y}(t_n) = e^{\mathbf{C}\Delta t}\, \mathbf{y}(t_{n-1}) + \int_{t_{n-1}}^{t_n} e^{(t_n-s)\mathbf{C}}\, \mathbf{B}\mathbf{x}(s)\, ds$$

$$+ \sigma \int_{t_{n-1}}^{t_n} e^{(t_n-s)\mathbf{C}}\, d\mathbf{W}(s). \qquad (34)$$

For example, when the x's are fixed, equation (34) reduces to

$$\text{l.i.m. } \mathbf{y}(t_n) = e^{\mathbf{C}\Delta t}\, \mathbf{y}(t_{n-1}) + \mathbf{C}^{-1}\left[e^{\mathbf{C}\Delta t} - \mathbf{I}\right]\mathbf{B}\mathbf{x}$$

$$+ \sigma \left[\mathbf{W}(t_n) - e^{\mathbf{C}\Delta t}\, \mathbf{W}(t_{n-1})\right]. \qquad (35)$$

Using the notation of Chapter 11, this system of linear equations can be expressed as

$$\text{l.i.m. } \mathbf{y}(t_n) = \mathbf{\Gamma}\mathbf{y}(t_{n-1}) + \mathbf{\Theta}\mathbf{x} + \epsilon(t_n). \qquad (36)$$

By the property of independence of increments of Brownian motion, $\epsilon(t_n)$ is independent of each variable on the right-hand side of equation (36), including $\mathbf{y}(t_{n-1})$. Moreover, the system of equations in (36) is recursive. Therefore, OLS estimators of the parameters of the system in (36) are consistent and asymptotically unbiased. Thus one feasible way to estimate $\mathbf{C}$, $\mathbf{B}$, and σ is to apply OLS to (36) to obtain estimates of $\mathbf{\Gamma}$, $\mathbf{\Theta}$, and σ. Using the methods outlined in Chapter 11, the estimated $\mathbf{\Gamma}$ matrix can be diagonalized and elements of $\mathbf{C}$ can be found using the procedure described in Section 11.5. Once $\mathbf{C}$ has been estimated, it is straightfoward to estimate $\mathbf{B}$ and σ, as we showed for the scalar case. We refer to this two-step procedure as the integral-equation approach.

If the model contains individual-specific effects, OLS estimators should be replaced by LSC estimators (for fixed effects) or one of the GLS estimators (for random effects). The procedures for estimating parameters discussed in earlier sections of this chapter apply to the multivariate case.

⟨13⟩ Linear Systems

The integral-equation approach has several potential problems. We have already mentioned that the transition probability density of the system of IEs is unknown. This means that ML estimators cannot be obtained and that the sampling distributions of estimators of parameters of SDEs are unknown. However, Phillips (1972) has developed a minimum-distance estimator that fills this gap at least partly. The minimum-distance estimator avoids the two-step procedure outlined above by estimating the parameters of the system of SDEs directly as nonlinear functions of the observed data. This estimator has desirable asymptotic properties and also performed well in Phillips' (1972) Monte Carlo study of small samples. Unfortunately, this estimator has not, to our knowledge, been studied further.

A second potential problem with estimating the IEs (as well as using Phillips' minimum-distance estimator) is that constraints on **C** and **B** cannot be imposed during estimation. Because each element in $e^{\mathbf{C}\Delta t}$ depends on all elements in **C** in a complicated way, the assumption that a certain element in **C** is zero does not imply that the corresponding element in $e^{\mathbf{C}\Delta t}$ equals zero. Even if an element in **C** is zero in the population, its estimated value is highly unlikely to be zero in any sample. Failure to use a restriction in estimating parameters generally causes estimators to lose efficiency, as we have mentioned before. The inability to use restrictions in the IE approach is troubling to those who wish to obtain efficient estimators of constrained models. Concern with efficient estimation has dominated most discussions of estimation of linear systems of SDEs in ecomometrics. Most of this work can be traced to a proposal by Bergstrom (1966) for using a method of approximation to impose constraints on **C** and **B**.

The spirit of Bergstrom's proposal can be summarized as follows. Instead of estimating the (recursive) system of IEs, (34) or (35), form a discrete approximation to the SDEs, replacing $d\mathbf{y}(t)$ with $\mathbf{y}(t_n) - \mathbf{y}(t_{n-1})$, and $\mathbf{y}(t_n)$ with $[\mathbf{y}(t_n) + \mathbf{y}(t_{n-1})]/2$, and so forth. This gives the approximation

$$\mathbf{y}(t_n) - \mathbf{y}(t_{n-1}) = \mathbf{C}\left[\frac{\mathbf{y}(t_n) + \mathbf{y}(t_{n-1})}{2}\right]\Delta t$$
$$+ \mathbf{B}\left[\frac{\mathbf{x}(t_n) + \mathbf{x}(t_{n-1})}{2}\right]\Delta t + \mathbf{v}(t_n). \quad (37)$$

This discrete approximation is a *nonrecursive* system—the same variables (measured at the same time) appear as both independent and dependent variables in the system. Thus OLS or GLS of estimators of **C** and **B** in (37) are inconsistent. But simultaneous equation estimators, such as two-stage and three-stage least squares, can be used to estimate **C** and **B** consistently. Moreover, constraints on elements of **B** and **C** can be imposed in estimation because **C** and **B** are estimated directly.

Bergstrom's proposal was aimed at efficient estimation since estimators that use constraints are more efficient than estimators that ignore them. However, the choice between estimating the IE and estimating a discrete approximation to the DE involves a complicated trade-off. Estimators from the discrete approximation are asymptotically biased (as the number of observations increases but the spacing between observations remains fixed). Estimators of the IEs are asymptotically unbiased but are inefficient if the model contains constraints on **C** and **B**. It is not obvious which approach is preferable in typical sociological research settings. Does the increased efficiency of the discrete approximation strategy more than offset its asymptotic bias? We do not know which type of estimator has the smaller mean-squared error in general. However, in Phillips' (1972) simulation, his minimum-distance estimator of the IE performed consistently better than a Bergstrom-type three-stage least-squares estimator applied to the discrete approximation. Clearly, more research is needed before we can draw sound conclusions about the utility of the two approaches.

13.10 Conclusions

This chapter emphasized the practical details of estimating continuous-time stochastic models for quantitative outcomes from panel data. To facilitate the use of these models in actual sociological research, we focus on the operationally simple (but limited) method of estimating the IE for a scalar outcome. This method involves solving an SDE subject to initial conditions to obtain an IE. If the disturbance in the dynamic model is an independent Brownian-motion process, the disturbance in the IE is independent and normally distributed. Thus ML estimators of the coefficients of the IE can be obtained by OLS estimation of a linear regression equation using standard equally spaced panel observations. Given such

⟨ 13 ⟩   Conclusions

estimates, one can solve algebraically for the ML estimates of the fundamental dynamic parameters.

A wide variety of social-scientific applications suggest that the disturbance in the IE is not independent of the lagged value of the dependent variable, that is, the disturbance tends to be autocorrelated. Ignoring this problem wreaks havoc with estimates of dynamic parameters. We argued that viewing autocorrelation as a consequence of the presence of stable but unobserved characteristics of individuals is meaningful in many sociological studies. Therefore, we devoted considerable attention to estimating models with such unobserved factors, which may be considered as either fixed or random variables. The relevant estimators are applied to pooled data from equally spaced, multiwave panels. We discussed ML estimators and some least-squares estimators that are not identical to the ML estimators, especially Nerlove's modified generalized least-squares (MGLS) estimator. We also presented Monte Carlo evidence on the small-sample properties of the estimators. We found that both ML and MGLS perform well and that neither is uniformly better over the range of conditions studied. We also discussed Henderson's variant on GLS estimation for mixed models. This method applies to a variety of practical complications such as heteroscedasticity and random measurement error. Unfortunately, we did not include this estimator in our Monte Carlo studies and have not seen any comparisons of its small-sample properties with those of the ML estimators or Nerlove's GLS estimator.

Perhaps the most important practical complication involves unequal spacing of waves of observations. In the case of unequally spaced data, the GLS estimators cannot be used in a straightforward way. But there is no inherent obstacle to the use of ML estimators.

14

Deterministic Nonlinear Models

In this chapter we compare some nonlinear models with the linear differential-equation (DE) models discussed in Chapter 11. Such comparisons afford a deeper understanding of both the utility and limitations of linear models.[1] They also reveal some of the reasons for considering nonlinear generalizations.

14.1 Scalar Models

We begin with a substantive model that has been used fairly widely in the social sciences—a model for the spread of information. Suppose that an item of information diffuses through a population from a single constant source and that individuals cannot transmit it. Under these conditions, the rate of spread depends only on the strength of the source and the number of individuals that have not yet acquired the item. Let $y(t)$ denote the number of individuals who have acquired the item by time t and $N - y(t)$ denote the number who have not. A simple model for the rate of spread is

$$\frac{dy(t)}{dt} = \mu \left[N - y(t) \right],$$

where $\mu > 0$. This model implies that in any fixed period the item is acquired by the same fraction μ of the number still without the item, $N - y(t)$.

---

[1] The term *linear model* denotes a model that is linear in parameters. We have already seen that dynamic linear models give nonlinear time paths in the observable endogenous variables.

⟨14⟩ Scalar Models

The model of diffusion from a constant source bears a striking similarity to the linear partial-adjustment model discussed in Chapter 11 [see equation (4) in that chapter], with N corresponding to $y^*(t)$ and μ to r. However, the linear partial-adjustment model is more general in two respects. First, the ceiling in the diffusion model is fixed at N; the criterion in a linear partial-adjustment model, $y^*(t)$, need not be fixed. The latter may be affected by exogenous variables and may change over time; it is constant only when the exogenous variables affecting it are constant. Second, decline is not possible in the diffusion model. Because the number acquiring the item cannot exceed the population size, $N - y(t)$ cannot be negative. However, decline is well defined in a linear partial-adjustment model. Exogenous changes may lower the criterion in any period. As we discussed in Chapter 11, in such cases a linear partial-adjustment model implies negative exponential adjustment towards the new lower criterion.

14.1.1 State Dependence

Although the model of diffusion from a constant source sometimes fits empirical data well (e.g., see Coleman, Katz, and Menzel, 1966), empirical time paths of diffusion are usually S-shaped. This shape arises when the rate of diffusion is low initially, gradually speeds up, and finally declines as the number who have acquired the item approaches some ceiling. A simple process with an S-shaped time path can be formed by combining diffusion from a constant source with transmission between individuals.[2] At any time t, $y(t)$ persons have acquired the item and $N - y(t)$ have not. Of the $N(N-1)/2$ possible pairs of individuals, $y(t)\left[N - y(t)\right]$ pairs consist of a bearer and a nonbearer. If pairs form at random,[3] the effect of transmission between individuals on the rate of diffusion equals $\nu y(t)\left[N - y(t)\right]$, where ν is a positive constant giving the intensity of transmission between a single pair of individuals. Combining transmission from a single constant source and transmission between pairs of individuals yields

---

[2]For a lucid treatment of these models, see Bartholomew (1973, pp. 298–307).

[3]As this imagery suggests, most of the models discussed in this chapter should be considered as deterministic appproximations to substantively more attractive but complex stochastic models.

$$\frac{\mathrm{d}y(t)}{\mathrm{d}t} = [\mu + \nu y(t)][N - y(t)]. \tag{1}$$

Equation (1) is called a **logistic model.** It is the standard model for diffusion of information.

In line with our previous discussion, we generalize the model in (1) to the case in which N is replaced by a criterion $y^*(t)$:

$$\frac{\mathrm{d}y(t)}{\mathrm{d}t} = [\mu + \nu y(t)][y^*(t) - y(t)]. \tag{2}$$

A noteworthy feature of this model is the way that it generalizes the adjustment process. The linear partial-adjustment model has a constant speed of adjustment, r. But the speed of adjustment in (2) depends on the *current level* (or *state*) of the outcome. Processes with this property are said to be **state dependent.**[4] When ν is positive, the speed of adjustment rises from approximately μ when $y(t)$ is very small to $\mu + \nu y(t)$ when $y(t)$ is large.

The solution of equation (2), subject to the conditions $y_0 \equiv y(t_0)$ and $y^* \equiv y^*(t)$, is the integral equation (IE)

$$y(t) = \frac{y^* e^{(\mu+\nu y^*)t} - \dfrac{\mu(y^* - y_0)}{\nu(y_0 + \mu/\nu)}}{e^{(\mu+\nu y^*)t} + \dfrac{y^* - y_0}{y_0 + \mu/\nu}}. \tag{3}$$

This equation can be estimated from panel or time-series data by nonlinear least squares. [Maximum-likelihood (ML) estimation seems less suitable because there is no random component giving a probability density function.]

A logistic model can also be constructed as a model of population growth in a limited environment.[5] Population growth is generally subject to both physiological and environmental constraints. Let b_0 and d_0 indicate the "natural" birth and death rates determined by physiology alone. The *natural rate of increase* is simply

---

[4] Note that the term *state dependence* has other meanings in other contexts; for example, see Heckman (1978).

[5] The classic statement is by Lotka (1924). For a readable introduction, see Wilson and Bossert (1971, pp. 16–19, 93–104).

the difference between them: $r \equiv b_0 - d_0$. In the absence of environmental limitations, the growth rate can plausibly be assumed to be proportional to the existing size of the reproducing population:

$$\frac{dy(t)}{dt} = r y(t). \tag{4}$$

When r is positive, (4) is commonly called the **exponential** or **Malthusian model** of growth.

When environmental resources are limited, birth and death rates usually vary with the population size $y(t)$. Processes with this property are said to be **density dependent**. For example, the net growth rate of bacteria growing in a flask of nutrients is greatest when the number of organisms in the flask is small and declines as the number becomes large. Clearly, density dependence is a particular kind of state dependence.

The simplest model of density dependence is linear dependence in which the birth rate is $b_0 - k_b y(t)$ and the death rate is $d_0 + k_d y(t)$, where $k_b > 0$ and $k_d > 0$. These assumptions imply that the addition of one member decreases the birth rate by k_b and increases the death rate by k_d, so that the net growth rate is $[b_0 - k_b y(t)] - [d_0 + k_d y(t)]$. Introducing linear density dependence of birth and death rates into the exponential growth model gives

$$\begin{aligned}\frac{dy(t)}{dt} &= y(t) \{[b_0 - k_b y(t)] - [d_0 + k_d y(t)]\} \\ &= y(t) [r - \nu y(t)], \end{aligned} \tag{5a}$$

where $\nu \equiv k_b + k_d$ describes the density dependence. This model has two steady states, zero and

$$y^* \equiv \frac{b_0 - d_0}{k_b + k_d} \equiv \frac{r}{\nu}. \tag{6}$$

Two other parameterizations of this model occur in the literature. Using the above definition of y^*, we can rewrite (5a) as

$$\frac{dy(t)}{dt} = \nu y(t) [y^* - y(t)] \tag{5b}$$

$$= r y(t) \left[1 - \frac{y(t)}{y^*}\right]. \tag{5c}$$

Equation (5b) is the special case of the logistic model in (2) in which $\mu = 0$; (5c) is a common way of stating this model in the literature on population biology.

Since the logistic model in (2) can be solved explicitly, so can (5). For example, setting $\mu = 0$ in (3) gives the solution to (5b):

$$y(t) = \frac{y^*}{1 + \left[\dfrac{y^*}{y_0} - 1\right] e^{-\nu y^* t}}.$$

Solutions corresponding to the parameterizations in (5a) and (5c) can be found by using the relationship in (6). For example, substituting $r = \nu y^*$ in the above expression gives the solution to (5c):

$$y(t) = \frac{y^*}{1 + \left[\dfrac{y^*}{y_0} - 1\right] e^{-rt}}. \tag{7}$$

The logistic model differs from the linear partial-adjustment model because the speed of adjustment to the gap between the target and current levels depends on the current level—compare (5b) and (4) in Chapter 11. Thus the logistic model may be viewed as a linear partial-adjustment model multiplied by $y(t)$. Notice, however, that the analogue of the speed of adjustment, r, in the linear partial adjustment model is denoted by ν in the logistic model.

Rewriting (5c) as

$$\frac{dy}{dt} = r \frac{y(t)}{y^*} \left[y^* - y(t)\right]$$

is helpful for comparing the time paths of the logistic and linear partial adjustment models. When $y(t)$ is close to y^*, the logistic model resembles the linear partial-adjustment model, and the two models agree qualitatively. Although these two models imply similar dynamics near y^*, their time paths have different shapes. The logistic model has an S-shaped path that is symmetric around the point $y^*/2$; the growth rate reaches its maximum at this point, as depicted in Figure 14.1. But the time path of the linear partial-adjustment model is concave (from below) and the growth rate is a maximum near the origin. Thus the two models imply qualitatively different

⟨14⟩ Scalar Models   471

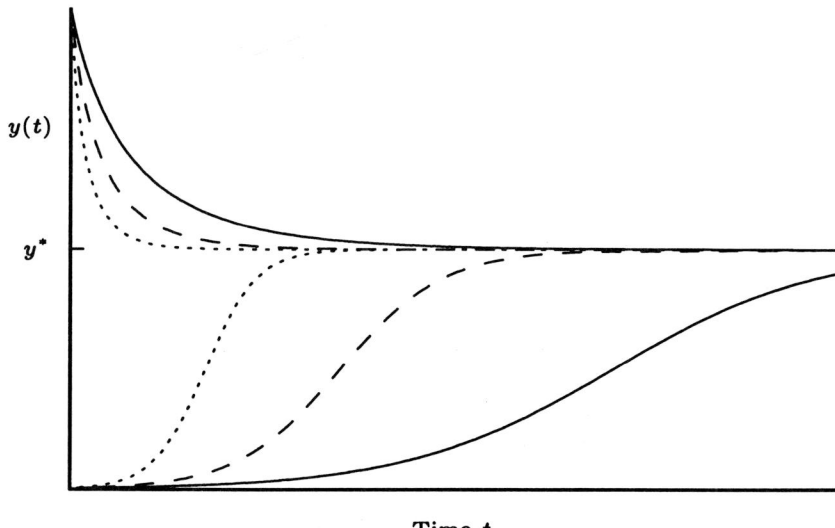

Figure 14.1. Illustrative paths of growth and decline for a logistic model.

dynamics for $y(t)$ far below y^*. In such cases, the logistic model implies lower growth rates than the linear partial-adjustment model. This is illustrated in Figure 14.2.

Social scientists may find it surprising that the linear partial-adjustment and logistic models imply similar dynamics in decline. In fact, both models imply *exponential* decline to the criterion (see Lotka, 1924, p. 68). Thus the choice between the two models does not matter much when $y(t)$ is above y^*.

The version of the model in (5c) provides some additional insight into properties of this model. When $y(t)$ is small, the term in brackets is close to 1, which implies that growth is approximately exponential. As $y(t)$ increases, density dependence slows down the growth rate. When $y(t)$ approaches y^*, the term in brackets in (5c) and the growth rate approach zero. If y^* falls below $y(t)$, the growth rate is negative, and $y(t)$ declines exponentially towards this level.

14.1.2 Time Dependence

There is another useful approach to modeling processes with S-shaped time paths. As we have just seen, the logistic model generalizes the linear partial-adjustment model by letting the speed of

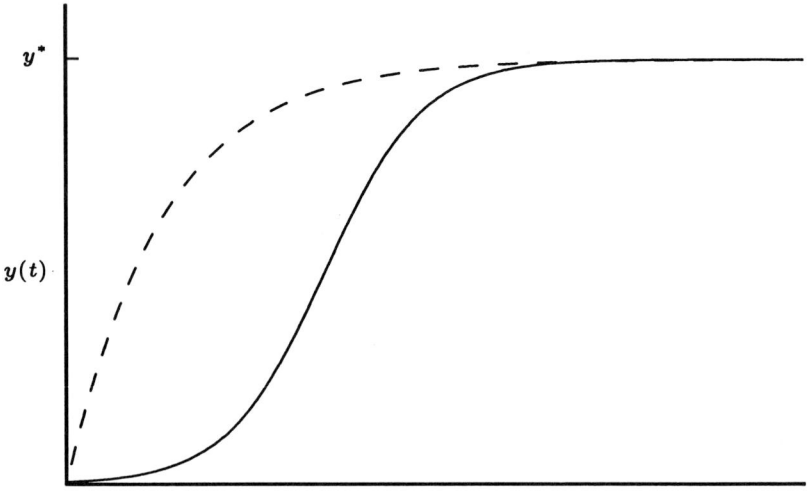

Figure 14.2. A comparison of time paths of logistic and linear partial-adjustment models. The solid curve denotes the logistic model; the dashed curve, the linear partial-adjustment model.

adjustment be state dependent. Sometimes it may be more appropriate to let it be time dependent. One simple form of time dependence gives a well-known model with a long history.

Suppose that the speed of adjustment changes exponentially over time,

$$\frac{dr(t)}{dt} = -\theta\, r(t). \tag{8}$$

We assume that $\theta > 0$ because $y(t)$ grows explosively when this is not the case—even more rapidly than in the Malthusian model. Given the initial condition $r_0 \equiv r(t_0)$, the solution of (8) is

$$r(t) = r_0\, e^{-\theta \Delta t},$$

where $\Delta t \equiv t - t_0$. Substituting this expression into the exponential growth model in (4) yields

$$\frac{dy(t)}{dt} = r_0\, e^{-\theta \Delta t}\, y(t). \tag{9}$$

⟨14⟩ Scalar Models

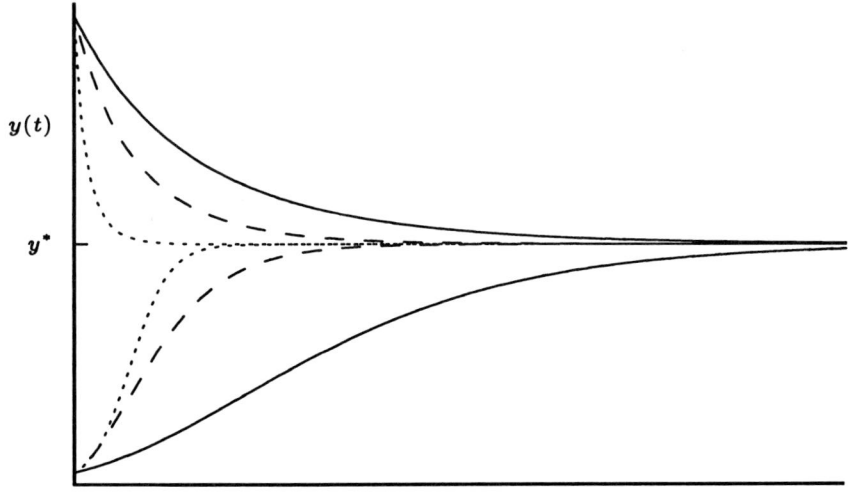

Figure 14.3. Illustrative time paths for a Gompertz model.

Given the initial condition $y_0 \equiv y(t_0)$, the solution of (9) is

$$y(t) = y_0 \exp\left[\frac{r_0}{\theta}\left(1 - e^{-\theta \Delta t}\right)\right]. \tag{10}$$

Equation (10) is called the **Gompertz model** of growth. This model implies S-shaped growth to the ceiling, $y^* = y_0 \exp[r_0/\theta]$, as can be seen by letting $t \to \infty$ in equation (10). Figure 14.3 illustrates the Gompertz model for several combinations of r_0 and θ that imply the same y^*. Unlike the logistic model, the S-shaped growth path of the Gompertz model is not symmetric. This is shown in Figure 14.4, which compares time paths for logistic and Gompertz models constrained to begin at the same level and converge to the same ceiling.

When $y(t)$ has only positive values so that $\log y(t)$ is well defined, the Gompertz growth model can be transformed to show more clearly its relation to the logistic and linear partial-adjustment models. With y^* defined as in the preceding paragraph, it can be shown that the Gompertz model in (10) is also the solution of

$$\frac{dy(t)}{dt} = \theta\, y(t) \log \frac{y^*}{y(t)}. \tag{11}$$

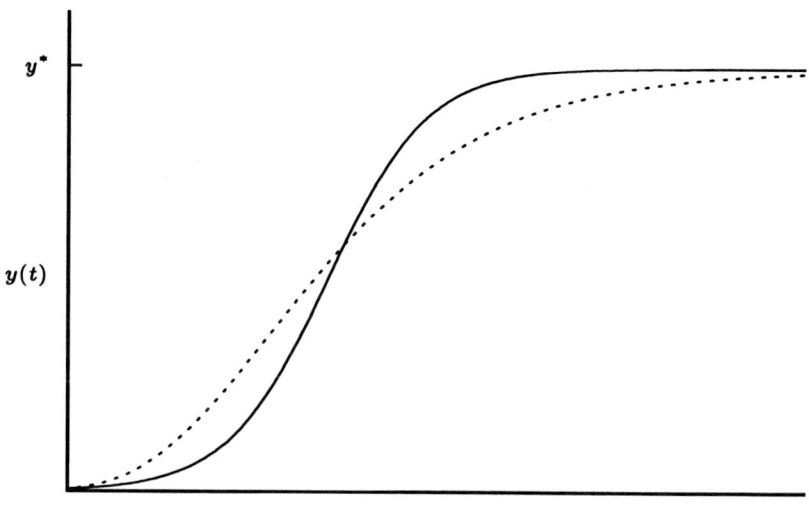

Figure 14.4. A comparison of time paths for logistic and Gompertz models. The solid curve denotes the logistic model; the dotted curve, the Gompertz model.

This suggests that the Gompertz model is a special type of exponential growth model in which the multiplier is

$$r(t) = \theta \log \frac{y^*}{y(t)}.$$

When $y(t)$ is small relative to y^*, this multiplier is large and positive. As $y(t)$ approaches y^*, the multiplier approaches zero. Thus the Gompertz model, like the logistic model, allows a form of state dependence in the growth rate.

Equation (11) can also be rearranged to give

$$\frac{1}{y(t)} \frac{dy(t)}{dt} = \theta \log \frac{y^*}{y(t)},$$

or

$$\frac{d \log y(t)}{dt} = \theta \left[\log y^* - \log y(t) \right].$$

The above equation shows that for positively valued outcomes, the Gompertz model expresses linear partial adjustment in a logarithmic scale. If the speed of adjustment declines exponentially with time, a linear partial-adjustment model describes change in the logarithm of $y(t)$.

Time dependence in sociological models often reflects unobserved causal processes. For example, in fitting the Gompertz model to the distribution of ages at first marriage in a cohort, Hernes (1972) assumed that the rate of marriage declines with age because a person's attractiveness as a mate declines with age. Since change in attractiveness is an unobserved causal process, Hernes found it convenient to assume attractiveness declines exponentially with age, which gives the Gompertz model for age at first marriage. In modeling the spread of violent events, Pitcher, Hamblin, and Miller (1978) assumed that the rate at which individuals become inhibited from engaging in violence declines exponentially. They assumed that individuals gradually learn the costs of participating in violence from observing what happens to those who do. Tilly's (1975) work suggests a different interpretation. This rate may decline in some historical period because repression becomes more efficient or because power-holders concede some disputed issues as time passes. Looked at in this way, time dependence summarizes unobserved actions of those who wield power.

It is often helpful to summarize the effects of unobserved processes as parametric forms of time dependence in rates of change; see the discussion in Section 7.1. When this strategy is successful, it simplifies complicated processes so that their main features can be studied. Still, building models with time dependence should not be an end in itself. Since sociologists seek to explain the processes that govern social structures, they want ultimately to measure the causal factors responsible for time variation in rates. Once causal factors have been measured, they should be incorporated *explicitly* into models. For example, it may be helpful to begin by assuming that responses to collective violence produce exponential decline in rates of initiation of collective violence during certain epochs. However, observations on specific reactions, such as actions by a regime, allow a more meaningful analysis of the process. Of course, movement in this direction requires that the process be reconceptualized as involving a *system* of actors, with equations describing the actions of each actor. A major drawback of the Gompertz model concerns the difficulty in generalizing it to handle systems of interacting units. The logistic model, discussed earlier, does not suffer such limitations, as we discuss at length in Section 14.3.

14.1.3 More General Nonlinear Models

Both the logistic and Gompertz models have known solutions. But what about the general case,

$$\frac{\mathrm{d}y(t)}{\mathrm{d}t} = f(y,t),$$

where $f(y,t)$ denotes a general nonlinear function? Few nonlinear DEs can be solved explicitly. That is, it is seldom possible to write a corresponding IE in terms of a reasonably small number of elementary transcendental functions (logarithms, trigonometric functions, and so forth). Given the ways in which sociologists have studied change, failure to find an explicit solution might seem to be an insurmountable obstacle to quantitative analysis. However, the situation is far from hopeless. For example, qualitative insight about a model can be obtained by identifying its equilibria and analyzing their stability. One can also obtain quantitative information about such models; however, a different strategy of estimation is needed. One such approach involves estimating an exact discrete approximation, as we mentioned in Chapter 13. This approach relies on the fact that a nonlinear function can always be approximated by a sequence of step functions. Use of properly chosen approximations yields useful empirical estimates of parameters in many types of nonlinear deterministic DEs (DDEs).

The rest of this chapter considers elementary issues in qualitative and quantitative analysis of nonlinear DDEs. We turn first to issues concerning nonlinear models of systems. We devote special attention to the famous Lotka–Volterra model for competitive interactions, emphasizing the qualitative behavior implied by this model. We then illustrate the use of an exact discrete approximation with a sociological adaptation of this model. Finally, we discuss stability of nonlinear models and illustrate a simple method of stability analysis.

⟨14⟩ Models of Systems

14.2 Models of Systems

It should come as no surprise to learn that few nonlinear models of systems have known solutions. However, the phase-space analysis introduced in Section 11.6 sometimes allows explicit solutions to be found for complicated models.[6] Instead of analyzing derivatives of variables with respect to time, one analyzes derivatives of one variable with respect to others. Consider, for example, the bivariate nonlinear model:

$$\frac{dy_1(t)}{dt} = f(y_1, y_2);$$
$$\frac{dy_2(t)}{dt} = g(y_1, y_2).$$

Studying the trajectories of this system in the phase plane (i.e., the y_1–y_2 plane) is equivalent to rewriting the above system of equations as

$$\frac{dy_1(t)/dt}{dy_2(t)/dt} = \frac{dy_1}{dy_2} = \frac{f(y_1, y_2)}{g(y_1, y_2)}.$$

Notice that this transformation converts the pair of equations into a scalar equation, which usually can be analyzed more readily than the original nonlinear model. This is the chief computational advantage of this transformation. For example,

$$\frac{dy_1(t)}{dt} = y_2^2,$$
$$\frac{dy_2(t)}{dt} = y_1^2,$$

can be rearranged to give

$$\frac{dy_1}{dy_2} = \frac{y_2^2}{y_1^2}.$$

---

[6] The solutions, however, relate the values of the outcomes to each other and do not describe the time path. For example, a solution might tell how large y_1 is when y_2 has some value but not how rapidly these values are reached.

The latter is a separable equation that can be solved with standard methods for a single equation.

It is difficult to provide any general guidance about the solution and estimation of nonlinear models of systems beyond advising that readers consult one of the many textbooks on systems of DEs. In the next section we concentrate on a few nonlinear models that seem applicable to sociological research. Our detailed discussion of ways of solving and estimating these few nonlinear models may suggest useful strategies for dealing with other nonlinear models.

14.3 Competition Models

In discussing systems of linear DDEs, we emphasized that it is often sociologically important to consider direct linkages between actors. Incorporating such linkages within S-shaped growth models seems valuable. Recall that S-shaped growth may reflect either density dependence or time dependence in growth rates. In this section we consider some density-dependent models for an interdependent system of actors.[7]

14.3.1 Competition for a Single Resource

The classical motivation for a logistic model is the assumption that birth rates and death rates have linear density dependence; see equation (5a). Density dependence reflects constraints due to finite resources. When several populations depend on the same resource, their growth rates must be linked. Growth in one population depletes the resource and thereby retards the growth of others. The linear models discussed in Section 11.4 and illustrated in Section 11.7 incorporate these kinds of constraints. Now we want to include them in nonlinear models. There are several ways of incorporating competitive effects. We begin with one of the simplest of several models developed by the Italian mathematician, Vito Volterra (1927/1978, pp. 122–123; see also Luenberger, 1979, pp. 328–331).

Consider a bounded environment containing J groups,[8] all

---

[7]We do not consider the more difficult task of extending the time-dependent models discussed in Section 14.1.2 to the case of an interdependent system of actors.

[8]The original applications of these models pertained to biotic populations. Since we think that the models apply to all sorts of collections, we use the term *group* instead of *population* in describing the models. The term group

of which consume a single common resource. Let $y_j(t)$ denote the size of group j at time t. Assume that D, the total demand for the resource, is a function of the size of every group, that is, the J by 1 vector $\mathbf{y}(t)$:

$$D[\mathbf{y}(t)] \equiv \sum_{j=1}^{J} a_j\, y_j(t), \qquad (12)$$

where the weight $a_j > 0$ describes the jth group's utilization of the resource.

Since resources consumed by one group are unavailable to others, a reasonable extension of the logistic model in (5) is

$$\frac{dy_j(t)}{dt} = y_j(t)\left\{r_j - c_j\, D[\mathbf{y}(t)]\right\}. \qquad (13)$$

For consistency with the logistic model, r_j, the natural growth rate of group j in the absence of competition for the resource, is assumed to be positive for all j's. The sensitivity of group j to the aggregate resource depletion is measured by c_j. The ratio of the natural growth rate of group j to its sensitivity to resource depletion, r_j/c_j, is called the **fitness factor** of group j.

The equilibria of the system in (13) are the solutions of the system of equations

$$y_j^e\left\{r_j - c_j\, D[\mathbf{y}^e]\right\} = 0,$$

where $j = 1, \ldots, J$. An uninteresting solution is $y_j^e = 0$ for all j's. The interesting equilibria are those in which group size is nonnegative for at least one group; these are found by solving

$$r_j - c_j\, D[\mathbf{y}^e] = 0, \qquad (14)$$

which implies $D[\mathbf{y}^e] = r_j/c_j$. Equation (14) can hold for at most one group if each group has a distinct fitness factor,

$$r_j/c_j \neq r_k/c_k, \qquad (15)$$

for $j \neq k$. Volterra assumed (15) because he believed that the probability of r_j/c_j having the same value for different j is "vanishingly small" (Volterra, 1927/1978, p. 123). Thus Volterra's assumption implies that two or more groups cannot coexist in equilibrium in a system governed by competition for a single common resource.

refers broadly to any social aggregate, for example, a social class, a firm, or a political party, and not just to self-consciously solidary aggregates.

14.3.2 Direct Competition

We think Volterra's model of competition for a single resource does not go far enough in embedding interdependence in the logistic model. It treats only *diffuse* competition. In this respect it is similar to the limited multivariate Ornstein–Uhlenbeck (OU) process discussed in Section 12.6. To appreciate the distinction between diffuse and direct competition, consider the distinction between a classical undominated market with many buyers and sellers and a market with a small number of buyers or sellers, that is, either an oligopoly or a monopsony. In the case of diffuse competition, the behavior of the market can be described without identifying particular buyers and sellers. Market prices summarize the terms of trade quite well. But when the number of buyers and sellers is small, the market relationship has the character of a game in which sequential moves by individual players affect the evolution of the terms of trade. Consequently, one cannot ignore the identities of the participants.

Modeling pairwise linkages is essential in many kinds of sociological studies. As the previous paragraph suggests, it is especially important when a system has few actors, for example, international arms races, ethnic conflicts within nations, and market competition in concentrated industries. It is also important when the number of actors is kept small because competition is restricted by geography or institutional rules. For example, competition between public and private schools for students occurs primarily within local communities.

An important model for direct competition was developed independently by A. J. Lotka (1925) and Volterra (1927/1978). Though the model was designed for studying fluctuations in the sizes of biotic populations, Lotka (1932, reprinted in Scudo and Ziegler, 1978, p. 285) suggested

> [our] treatment ... may find more immediate application in the field of economics. For our variables N_1 and N_2 may be conceived as denoting the size or extent of two (or more) commercial enterprises competing for common sources of supply and for a common market...

This suggestion has been followed only rarely by economists, who have tended to focus on diffuse competition and also to emphasize

⟨14⟩ Competition Models

comparative statics rather than microdynamics.[9] Nonetheless, we think that Lotka's suggestion is a good one. The social sciences appear to offer many opportunities for applications of competition models, as we discussed in Chapter 11.

The Lotka–Volterra model extends the logistic model in (5a) in which the growth rate of each of J units depends only on its own size:

$$\frac{\mathrm{d}y_j(t)}{\mathrm{d}t} = y_j(t)\left[r_j - \nu_j\, y_j(t)\right], \qquad (16)$$

for $j = 1, \ldots, J$. Recasting (16) in the form of a per-capita growth model is conceptually useful:

$$\frac{1}{y_j(t)}\frac{\mathrm{d}y_j(t)}{\mathrm{d}t} = r_j - \nu_j\, y_j(t). \qquad (17)$$

Recall that r_j is the natural rate of increase of group j. According to (17), the per-capita growth rate of group j decreases by ν_j for each 1-unit increase in group j's size. Volterra (1927/1978) suggested that the per-capita growth rate of a group j depends in general *not only* on the size of its own group, $y_j(t)$, *but also* on the size of the other $J - 1$ groups, $y_k(t)$, $k = 1, \ldots, J$, $k \neq j$. The assumption that the per-capita growth rate of group j depends linearly on the size of the other groups leads to the following modification of (17):

$$\frac{1}{y_j(t)}\frac{\mathrm{d}y_j(t)}{\mathrm{d}t} = r_j - \nu_j\, y_j(t) + \sum_{\substack{k=1 \\ k \neq j}}^{J} c_{jk}\, y_k(t) \qquad (18)$$

for $j = 1, \ldots, J$, where c_{jk} is the effect of a 1-unit increase in the size of group k on the per-capita growth rate of group j.

In general, the sign of c_{jk} may be positive or negative. If $c_{jk} > 0$, then the per-capita growth rate of group j rises as $y_k(t)$ increases. Among interacting biological species, this situation arises most often when group k is a source of food for group j. If $c_{jk} < 0$, then the per-capita growth rate of group j declines as $y_k(t)$ increases. For example, in a biological system, group k might be a predator of group j. In the classic form of competition $c_{jk} < 0$ and $c_{kj} < 0$.

[9]One important exception is the evolutionary theory of the firm developed by Nelson and Winter (1982).

Equation (18) can be rearranged to give the growth rate of group j, which can be written in several equivalent ways that parallel the three parameterizations of (5):

$$\frac{dy_j(t)}{dt} = y_j(t)\left[r_j - \nu_j y_j(t) + \sum_{\substack{k=1 \\ k \neq j}}^{J} c_{jk}\, y_k(t)\right] \quad (19a)$$

$$= \nu_j\, y_j(t)\left[y_j^* - y_j(t) + \sum_{\substack{k=1 \\ k \neq j}}^{J} \alpha_{jk}\, y_k(t)\right] \quad (19b)$$

$$= r_j\, y_j(t)\left[1 - \frac{y_j(t)}{y_j^*} + \sum_{\substack{k=1 \\ k \neq j}}^{J} b_{jk}\, y_k(t)\right], \quad (19c)$$

where

$$y_j^* \equiv \frac{r_j}{\nu_j}; \quad (20a)$$

$$\alpha_{jk} \equiv \frac{c_{jk}}{\nu_j}; \quad (20b)$$

$$b_{jk} \equiv \frac{c_{jk}}{r_j}. \quad (20c)$$

These three parameterizations are only some of many that are possible. Since simple expressions relate the c's, α's, and b's to one another [see (20b) and (20c)], c_{jk} in (19a) could, for example, be replaced by $\nu_j\, \alpha_{jk}$ or $r_j\, b_{jk}$. Similarly, α_{jk} in (19b) could be replaced by c_{jk}/ν_j or $b_{jk}\, y_j^*$, and b_{jk} in (19c) could be replaced by c_{jk}/r_j or α_{jk}/y_j^*. If the parameters in the Lotka–Volterra model are just constants, which particular parameterization is chosen is substantively unimportant. But if causal variables are introduced (see Section 14.4.3), the choice does make a substantive difference.

The α's and b's, like the c's in (18) and (19a), indicate the nature of the coupling of the growth of pairs of groups; we refer to all three parameters as *coupling coefficients*.[10] Since ν_j tells the effect of a 1-unit increase in $y_j(t)$ on the growth rate of $y_j(t)$, (20b) means that α_{jk} measures group j's sensitivity to the size of group k *relative* to its sensitivity to its own size. Similarly, since r_j is the intrinsic growth rate of group j, (20c) means that b_{jk} measures group j's sensitivity to the size of group k *relative* to its intrinsic growth rate. Therefore, the magnitudes of the α's and b's in the Lotka–Volterra model are invariant under a change in the scale of y_j. In contrast, the other parameters appearing in (18) and (19)—r_j, ν_j, y_j^*, and c_{jk}—depend on the scale of y_j. Notice, however, that c_{jk}, α_{jk}, and b_{jk} all depend on the scale of y_k.

As derived above, (19) is based on an assumption of linear density dependence among the J groups in the system. It can also be considered an approximation to a more complex system of nonlinear relationships. Lotka (1925) actually developed (19) from this perspective. He argued that the growth rate of each group depends on its own size and the sizes of competing groups in a complex way that can be approximated by (19) when the exact functional dependence is unknown.

Even though the Lotka–Volterra model involves only a modest extension of (5), it does not have a known explicit solution. However, it is easy to find its equilibria; these are found by setting $dy/dt = 0$ in (19). Clearly there is an uninteresting equilibrium at $y_j^e = 0$ for all j. The interesting equilibrium is the one in which y_j^e is nonzero for at least one group. This equilibrium is the solution of the J *linear* equations,

$$y_j^* - y_j^e + \sum_{\substack{k=1 \\ k \neq j}}^{J} \alpha_{jk} y_k^e = 0. \qquad (21)$$

A linear system like (21) has a unique solution whenever the determinant of the matrix of the coupling coefficients (the matrix of the α's with $\alpha_{jj} \equiv -1$) is not zero. Thus, the equilibrium can be determined easily when these parameters are known.

---

[10] In the literature on population biology the α's are usually called *competition coefficients*. We prefer to avoid this term since the interdependencies between groups are not necessarily competitive.

We want to know how the equilibrium depends in general on the values of the parameters. We focus on the case in which $J = 2$:

$$\frac{dy_1(t)}{dt} = \nu_1\, y_1(t)\left[y_1^* - y_1(t) + \alpha_{12}\, y_2(t)\right];$$

$$\frac{dy_2(t)}{dt} = \nu_2\, y_2(t)\left[y_2^* + \alpha_{21}\, y_1(t) - y_2(t)\right].$$

This system has two equilibria: an uninteresting one at $y_1^e = y_2^e = 0$ and another satisfying

$$y_1^* - y_1^e + \alpha_{12}\, y_2^e = 0; \tag{22a}$$

$$y_2^* + \alpha_{21}\, y_1^e - y_2^e = 0. \tag{22b}$$

The solution to (22) is

$$y_1^e = \frac{y_1^* + \alpha_{12}\, y_2^*}{1 - \alpha_{12}\, \alpha_{21}};$$

$$y_2^e = \frac{y_2^* + \alpha_{21}\, y_1^*}{1 - \alpha_{12}\, \alpha_{21}}.$$

In biological applications of the Lotka–Volterra model it is often important to answer the question: is coexistence (i.e., $y_1^e > 0$ and $y_2^e > 0$) possible in equilibrium? According to (22), coexistence implies that

$$y_1^* + \alpha_{12}\, y_2^* > 0;$$

$$y_2^* + \alpha_{21}\, y_1^* > 0;$$

or, rearranging terms,

$$-\frac{1}{\alpha_{21}} < \frac{y_1^*}{y_2^*} > -\alpha_{12}.$$

A substantively more meaningful implication of (22) is that

$$\nu_j > c_{kj}, \tag{23}$$

$j = 1, 2$ and $k \neq j$, which says that an increase in the size of group j reduces its own growth rate more than the growth rate of group k.

Within the context of biological applications of the Lotka–Volterra model, an extensive literature argues that the inequality in (23) is likely to hold if the two groups are dissimilar in their requirements for resources and unlikely to hold if they are very similar. This notion is the foundation of what is called **Gause's principle** or the **principle of competitive exclusion**.

The bivariate Lotka–Volterra model's qualitative behavior is often studied graphically because the equations defining the two outcomes in equilibrium [equation (22)] define straight lines in the phase space. The literature on population biology provides many detailed treatments of such qualitative analyses. Wilson and Bossert (1971) gave a particularly clear introduction to this topic.

Sometimes qualitative analysis is not enough. When there is a need for quantitative results, such as the relative magnitudes of the coupling coefficients, other methods must be used. We turn now to a discussion of a widely used approach to quantitative analysis of such nonlinear systems.

14.4 Exact Discrete Approximations

The lack of an explicit solution for a dynamic model need not detract from its value for theorizing. For example, modern theories of population ecology rely heavily on implications of the Lotka–Volterra model for both dynamic and equilibrium properties of systems. But what about *empirical* analysis? When an explicit IE cannot be found, some numerical approximation must be used.

The technical literature on this topic discusses what is called an "exact discrete approximation" to the DDE (or a "stable difference scheme"). The idea is to approximate the DDE with a difference equation that is convenient for numerical analysis and is "exact," that is, approaches the DDE as the discrete interval in the difference equation becomes infinitesimal. The parameters of the difference equation can be estimated from panel or time-series data. The rules of correspondence between the DDE and the approximating difference equation let estimates of the parameters of the DDE be obtained from the estimated coefficients of the approximation.

In the rest of this section we concentrate on exact discrete approximations to two nonlinear models, the logistic model and the Lotka–Volterra model. We do not attempt to provide a general discussion of the topic of exact discrete approximations because such a discussion requires consideration of issues in numerical analysis and nonlinear estimation that fall beyond the scope of this book.[11] We caution readers that much work remains to be done on this topic, even for the particular cases we consider. Virtually nothing is yet known about the relative quality of different estimation schemes or about ways of testing hypotheses using these schemes.

14.4.1 Logistic Model

Although the IE for the logistic model can be written explicitly [see (7)] and estimated directly by nonlinear least squares, we begin by considering exact discrete approximations to the logistic model. This discussion lays the foundation for understanding exact discrete approximations to the more complex Lotka–Volterra model in (19), for which an explicit solution cannot be written.

Consider the scalar DDE $\mathrm{d}y/\mathrm{d}t = f[y(t)]$. One simple approximation that comes readily to mind is

$$\frac{y(t+n) - y(t)}{n} = f[y(t)],$$

$n > 0$. This approximation is "exact": it obviously approaches the original DDE as $n \downarrow 0$.

In the case of the logistic model in (5a), this method of constructing an exact discrete approximation gives

$$\frac{y(t+n) - y(t)}{n} = y(t)\left[r - \nu y(t)\right],$$

$n > 0$, which can be rearranged to give

$$y(t+n) = y(t)\left\{1 + n\left[r - \nu y(t)\right]\right\}$$
$$= \left[1 + nr\right]y(t) - n\nu y^2(t). \tag{24a}$$

---

[11] For an accessible treatment of numerical analysis of DEs (including illustrative FORTRAN programs), see Gerald (1977). Treatments of estimation issues and engineering applications may be found in Jazwinski (1970) and McGarty (1974). Economic applications as well as theoretical work on continuous-time models may be found in Bergstrom (1976).

⟨14⟩ **Exact Discrete Approximations**

Exact discrete approximations corresponding to (5b) and (5c) can be found from (24a) by using the relationship in (6):

$$y(t+n) = \left[1 + n\nu y^*\right] y(t) - n\nu y^2(t) \tag{24b}$$

$$= \left[1 + nr\right] y(t) - n\frac{r}{y^*} y^2(t). \tag{24c}$$

Equation (24) is linear in form; therefore it can be estimated easily by least squares.

In general one wants the equilibria of both the original DDE and the difference equation used as an approximation to be the same. In other words, one wants $y(t+n) = y(t)$, $n > 0$, if the system is in equilibrium at t. Recall that the logistic model has two equilibria: 0 and y^*. It is clear from (24) that if $y(t) = 0$, then $y(t+n) = 0$, and if $y(t) = y^*$, then $y(t+n) = y^*$. Thus, the difference equation in (24) has two desirable properties: it is exact (i.e., it approaches the DDE as $n \downarrow 0$), and it has the same equilibria as the DDE in (5).

A nonlinear DDE can be approximated exactly by more than one difference equation. This fact is important because one difference equation may be estimated more easily than another, or one may yield estimates closer to the true values. For these reasons, and because it is not yet known which estimation approach is best, we consider still another exact discrete approximation to the logistic model.

Notice that (7), the IE for the logistic model in (5c), has four constants: t_0, y_0, r, and y^*. Let

$$\lambda \equiv e^r\,;$$

$$\theta \equiv \frac{y^*}{y_0} - 1.$$

Substituting these in (7) yields

$$y(t) = \frac{y^*}{1 + \theta \lambda^{-t}}.$$

Similarly, the value of the outcome for a future point in time $t+1$ can be expressed as

$$y(t+1) = \frac{y^*}{1 + \theta \lambda^{-(t+1)}} = \frac{\lambda y^*}{\lambda + \theta \lambda^{-t}}$$

$$= \frac{\lambda y^* y(t)}{y^* + (\lambda - 1) y(t)}. \tag{25}$$

Applying (25) recursively, one obtains

$$y(t+n) = \frac{\lambda^n y^* y(t)}{y^* + (\lambda^n - 1)y(t)} \qquad (26)$$

for $n > 0$.

Subtracting $y(t)$ from both sides of this expression and dividing by n yields

$$\frac{y(t+n) - y(t)}{n} = \left[\frac{\lambda^n - 1}{n}\right] y(t) \left[\frac{y^* - y(t)}{y^* + (\lambda^n - 1)y(t)}\right]. \qquad (27)$$

As $n \downarrow 0$, the left-hand side of (27) approaches $dy(t)/dt$, and the denominator of the right-most term tends to y^*. By L'Hospital's rule,

$$\lim_{n \downarrow 0} \frac{\lambda^n - 1}{n} = \lim_{n \downarrow 0} \lambda^n \log \lambda = \log \lambda \equiv r;$$

therefore the limit of the "discrete derivative" in (27) is

$$\frac{dy(t)}{dt} = r y(t) \left[\frac{y^* - y(t)}{y^*}\right] = r y(t) \left[1 - \frac{y(t)}{y^*}\right],$$

which is identical to (5c). Thus, the difference equation in (26), like the one in (24), is exact.

The difference equation in (26) also has the same equilibria as (5). Putting $y(t) = 0$ in (26) implies $y(t+n) = 0$. Similarly, setting $y(t+n)/y(t) = 1$ in (26) and solving for $y(t)$ yields $y(t) = y^*$.

To use (26) as a basis for estimation, notice that we can rearrange it to give an equation that is linear in form and therefore easily estimated:

$$\frac{1}{y(t+n)} = \left[\frac{1}{\lambda^n}\right] \frac{1}{y(t)} + \left[\frac{\lambda^n - 1}{\lambda^n}\right] \frac{1}{y^*}$$

$$= \beta_1 \frac{1}{y(t)} + \beta_2, \qquad (28)$$

where

$$\beta_1 \equiv \frac{1}{\lambda^n}; \qquad (29a)$$

$$\beta_2 \equiv \left[\frac{\lambda^n - 1}{\lambda^n}\right] \frac{1}{y^*} = \left[1 - \frac{1}{\lambda^n}\right] \frac{1}{y^*} = (1 - \beta_1) \frac{1}{y^*}. \qquad (29b)$$

⟨14⟩ **Exact Discrete Approximations**

One can recover the parameters in the original model because the definition of β_1 implies that $\lambda^n = 1/\beta_1$; hence

$$r \equiv \log \lambda = -\frac{1}{n} \log \beta_1. \tag{30a}$$

Similarly, the definition of β_2 implies that

$$y^* = \frac{1 - \beta_1}{\beta_2}. \tag{30b}$$

Moreover, (6) can be used to find ν when another parameterization of (5) is preferred:

$$\nu = -\frac{\beta_2 \log \beta_1}{n(1 - \beta_1)}. \tag{30c}$$

In sum, social scientists who want to estimate the logistic model in (5) can choose the exact discrete approximation in either (24) or (26) as the basis for their analysis, or they can estimate the IE in (7).

14.4.2 Lotka–Volterra Model

In contrast to the logistic model discussed above, there is no known explicit solution to the Lotka–Volterra model given in (19). Consequently, development of a satisfactory exact discrete approximation to the Lotka–Volterra model seems crucial if social scientists are to use this model as a basis for empirical dynamic analyses.

As in the case of the logistic model, one simple approach is to replace continuous-time derivatives with discrete-time differentials. In the case of the Lotka–Volterra model in (19a), this approach gives

$$\frac{y_j(t+n) - y_j(t)}{n} = y_j(t) \left[r_j - \nu_j y_j(t) + \sum_{\substack{k=1 \\ k \neq j}}^{J} c_{jk}\, y_k(t) \right], \tag{31}$$

for $n > 0$ and $j = 1, \ldots, J$. After rearrangement one obtains

$$y_j(t+n) = \left[1 + n r_j\right] y_j(t) - n \nu_j y_j^2(t) + n \sum_{\substack{k=1 \\ k \neq j}}^{J} c_{jk}\, y_j(t) y_k(t) \tag{32a}$$

for $n > 0$. When (19b) or (19c) is the preferred parameterization of the Lotka–Volterra model, the definitions in (20) can be used to convert (32a) into a suitable exact discrete approximation:

$$y_j(t+n) = \left[1 + n\,\nu_j\,y_j^*\right]y_j(t) - n\,\nu_j\,y_j^2(t)$$

$$+ n\,\nu_j \sum_{\substack{k=1 \\ k \neq j}}^{J} \alpha_{jk}\,y_j(t)\,y_k(t) \tag{32b}$$

$$= \left[1 + n\,r_j\right]y_j(t) - n\,\frac{r_j}{y_j^*}\,y_j^2(t)$$

$$+ n\,r_j \sum_{\substack{k=1 \\ k \neq j}}^{J} b_{jk}\,y_j(t)\,y_k(t). \tag{32c}$$

The approximation in (32) is exact by construction: as $n \downarrow 0$, (31) approaches the original DDE. In addition, the equilibria of the original DDE are also the equilibria of (32). If $y_j(t) = 0$ for all j's, then $y_j(t+n) = 0$, and if (21) holds, then $y_j(t+n) = y_j(t)$ for all j's and $n > 0$.

Notice that (32) defines a set of J linear equations with lagged dependent variables, so it can be estimated easily by least squares. Ayala, Gilpin, and Ehrenfeld (1973) took this approach in an empirical study of the population dynamics of two species of fruit flies.

As in the case of the logistic model, there is more than one possible exact discrete approximation. Leslie (1958) proposed an approximation to the Lotka–Voltcrra model in (19c) that extends the exact discrete approximation to the logistic model given in (26):[12]

---

[12] In fact, Leslie (see also Pielou, 1969) began with the special case of (33) in which $n = 1$ and then attempted to "derive" (33) from this special case. We think that it is preferable to begin with (33) for two reasons. First, the general equation in (33) does *not* follow from recursive application of Leslie's special case. [In this regard it differs from the corresponding approximation to the logistic model: (26) *does* follow from recursive application of (25).] Our second reason is based on results of numerically comparing (32) and (33) and recursive application of Leslie's special case as IEs for the Lotka–Volterra model in (19). For the parameter combinations that we (with Lawrence Wu) examined, both (32) and (33) appear

⟨14⟩ **Exact Discrete Approximations**

$$y_j(t+n) = \frac{\lambda_j^n \, y_j^* \, y_j(t)}{y_j^* + (\lambda_j^n - 1)\left[y_j(t) - y_j^* \sum_{\substack{k=1 \\ k \neq j}}^{J} b_{jk} \, y_k(t)\right]}, \quad (33)$$

where $\lambda_j \equiv e^{r_j}$. To see that (33) gives an exact approximation to the Lotka–Volterra model, subtract $y_j(t)$ from both sides and divide by n. After algebraic manipulation this procedure yields

$$\frac{y_j(t+n) - y_j(t)}{n} = \left[\frac{\lambda_j^n - 1}{n}\right] y_j(t)$$

$$\cdot \frac{y_j^* - y_j(t) + y_j^* \sum_{\substack{k=1 \\ k \neq j}}^{J} b_{jk} \, y_k(t)}{y_j^* + (\lambda_j^n - 1)\left[y_j(t) - y_j^* \sum_{\substack{k=1 \\ k \neq j}}^{J} b_{jk} \, y_k(t)\right]}.$$

As $n \downarrow 0$, this equation approaches

$$\frac{dy_j(t)}{dt} = \log \lambda_j \, y_j(t) \frac{\left[y_j^* - y_j(t) + y_j^* \sum_{\substack{k=1 \\ k \neq j}}^{J} b_{jk} \, y_k(t)\right]}{y_j^*}$$

$$= \log \lambda_j \, y_j(t) \left[1 - \frac{y_j(t)}{y_j^*} + \sum_{\substack{k=1 \\ k \neq j}}^{J} b_{jk} \, y_k(t)\right],$$

which is identical to (19c) since $r_j \equiv \log \lambda_j$.

It can also be shown that the equation in (33) has the same equilibria as the Lotka–Volterra model in (19). Clearly if $y_j(t) = 0$

to be good approximations, and neither performs consistently better than the other. In contrast, recursive application of Leslie's special case often gives extremely unrealistic values in four or five recursions.

for all j's, then $y_j(t+n) = 0$. Showing that $y_j(t+n) = y_j(t)$ when (21) holds is less obvious but requires only simply algebra to prove.

To put (33) in a form that can be estimated readily, invert it:

$$\frac{1}{y_j(t+n)} = \left[\frac{1}{\lambda_j^n}\right]\frac{1}{y_j(t)} + \left[\frac{\lambda_j^n - 1}{\lambda_j^n}\right]\left[\frac{1}{y_j^*} - \sum_{\substack{k=1 \\ k \neq j}}^{J} b_{jk}\frac{y_k(t)}{y_j(t)}\right]$$

$$= \beta_{j1}\frac{1}{y_j(t)} + \beta_{j2} + \sum_{\substack{k=1 \\ k \neq j}}^{J} \gamma_{jk}\frac{y_k(t)}{y_j(t)}, \qquad (34)$$

where

$$\beta_{j1} \equiv \frac{1}{\lambda_j^n}; \qquad (35a)$$

$$\beta_{j2} \equiv \left[\frac{\lambda_j^n - 1}{\lambda_j^n}\right]\frac{1}{y_j^*} = \left[1 - \frac{1}{\lambda_j^n}\right]\frac{1}{y_j^*} = (1 - \beta_{j1})\frac{1}{y_j^*}; \qquad (35b)$$

$$\gamma_{jk} \equiv -(1 - \beta_{j1})b_{jk}. \qquad (35c)$$

Recovering the fundamental parameters proceeds in a fashion paralleling that used in the logistic model. The result is analogous to (30):

$$r_j \equiv \log \lambda_j = -\frac{1}{n}\log \beta_{j1}; \qquad (36a)$$

$$y_j^* = \frac{1 - \beta_{j1}}{\beta_{j2}}; \qquad (36b)$$

$$\nu_j = -\frac{\beta_{j2}\log \beta_{j1}}{n(1 - \beta_{j1})}. \qquad (36c)$$

These relationships plus the definition of γ_{jk} in (35c) give equations for the parameters describing intergroup interdependencies:

$$c_{jk} = -\frac{\gamma_{jk}\log \beta_{j1}}{n(1 - \beta_{j1})}; \qquad (37a)$$

$$\alpha_{jk} = -\frac{\gamma_{jk}\, y_j^*}{1 - \beta_{j1}}; \qquad (37b)$$

$$b_{jk} = -\frac{\gamma_{jk}}{1 - \beta_{j1}}. \qquad (37c)$$

⟨14⟩ **Exact Discrete Approximations**

Thus the Lotka–Volterra model can be estimated from data on $y_j(t)$, $j = 1, \ldots, J$, at a series of discrete points in time using either the exact discrete approximation in (32) or the one based on (33). It is unclear a priori which approximation is preferable; consequently, it seems advisable to employ both and to check for consistency of the results. It should be kept in mind, however, that both approximations assume that n is small—neither is likely to give good results when this assumption does not hold.

14.4.3 Incorporating Causal Factors

The logistic and Lotka–Volterra models in (5) and (19), respectively, and the exact discrete approximations to them discussed above, do not incorporate causal variables. Yet population heterogeneity characterizes virtually all situations studied by social scientists. It is therefore desirable to introduce causal factors into these models so that the effects of such factors on the process of change can be estimated.

Both the logistic and Lotka–Volterra model have several basic forms, each containing two or three fundamental parameters, respectively. Causal factors can be introduced by letting the parameters in any given form depend on these factors. We concentrate on the approach used in previous chapters in Part III; that is, we replace y_j^* with $f_j(\mathbf{x})$, where $\mathbf{x}$ is a vector of exogenous variables.[13] Since neither (5a) nor (19a) includes y_j^* as a fundamental parameter, this approach restricts consideration to (5b) and (5c) in the case of the logistic model and to (19b) and (19c) in the case of the Lotka–Volterra model.

We consider first the parameterizations based on ν_j and y_j^* [(5b) and (19b)]. In the case of the logistic model the first approximation, (24b), becomes

$$y(t+n) = [1 + n\nu f(\mathbf{x})] y(t) - n\nu y^2(t), \qquad (38)$$

while in the case of the Lotka–Volterra model the first approximation, (32b), becomes

---

[13] Another approach is to assume that r_j (or ν_j) is a function of causal variables. For an example of this approach in the case of the logistic model, see Griliches's (1957) classic study of the diffusion of hybrid corn in the United States. For an extension, see Dixon (1980).

$$y_j(t+n) = \left[1 + n\nu_j f_j(\mathbf{x})\right] y_j(t) + n\nu_j \sum_{k=1}^{J} \alpha_{jk} y_j(t) y_k(t). \quad (39)$$

If we retain the specification used in Chapter 11, that is,

$$y_j^* \equiv f_j(\mathbf{x}) = \boldsymbol{\pi}_j' \mathbf{x}, \quad (40)$$

equations (38) and (39) are linear in parameters and can be easily estimated by least squares. In contrast, the second approach to forming an exact discrete approximation [see equations (28) and (34)] does not provide a ready way of estimating (5b) and (19b). To see this, notice that $\lambda_j \equiv \exp[r_j] \equiv \exp[\nu_j y_j^*]$. Consequently, when ν_j and y_j^* are chosen as the fundamental parameters and $y_j^* \equiv f_j(\mathbf{x})$, the parameter β_{j1} in (35a) equals $\exp[-n\nu_j f_j(\mathbf{x})]$. A similar complication arises in the case of β_1 in (29a). This means that (28) and (34) are highly nonlinear and cannot be estimated conveniently. In sum, the first approach to forming an exact discrete approximation seems clearly preferable when (5b) and (19b) are the chosen parameterizations of the logistic and Lotka–Volterra models, respectively.

We turn next to the parameterizations based on r_j and y_j^* [(5c) and (19c)]. In the case of the logistic model the first approximation, (24c), becomes

$$y(t+n) = \left[1 + nr\right] y(t) - nr y^2(t) \frac{1}{f(\mathbf{x})}, \quad (41)$$

while in the case of the Lotka–Volterra model the first approximation, (32c), becomes

$$y_j(t+n) = \left[1 + nr_j\right] y_j(t) - nr_j y_j^2(t) \frac{1}{f_j(\mathbf{x})} + nr_j \sum_{\substack{k=1 \\ k \neq j}}^{J} b_{jk} y_j(t) y_k(t). \quad (42)$$

It is also possible to use the second approach to forming an exact discrete approximation. For the logistic model the second approximation, (28), becomes

$$\frac{1}{y(t+n)} = \beta_1 \frac{1}{y(t)} + (1 - \beta_1) \frac{1}{f(\mathbf{x})}, \quad (43)$$

while for the Lotka–Volterra model the second approximation, (34), becomes

$$\frac{1}{y_j(t+n)} = \beta_{j1} \frac{1}{y_j(t)} + (1 - \beta_{j1}) \frac{1}{f_j(\mathbf{x})} + \sum_{\substack{k=1 \\ k \neq j}}^{J} \gamma_{jk} \frac{y_k(t)}{y_j(t)}. \quad (44)$$

If we retain the specification of y_j^* given in (40), equations (41)–(44) are nonlinear in parameters; they can be estimated by nonlinear least squares but not by ordinary least squares. This complication can be handled by specifying y_j^* in a way that simplifies estimation:

$$y_j^* \equiv f_j(\mathbf{x}) = \frac{1}{\pi_j' \mathbf{x}}. \quad (45)$$

With this specification, (40)–(44) are linear in parameters and can be analyzed by ordinary least squares. This simple solution to the methodological problems presented by (41)–(44) requires careful consideration of its substantive implications. Clearly it is undesirable to switch from the specification of y_j^* in (40) to the one in (45) purely on grounds of methodological convenience.

14.5 An Example: National Expansion of Education

Our illustration of an application of the Lotka–Volterra model consists of Carroll's (1979, 1981) reformulation of Nielsen and Hannan's (1977) organizational model of educational expansion. Nielsen and Hannan noted that most authors view the expansion of schooling in terms of the actions of individual consumers (both potential students and employers) and of the state. Whatever the motivations of these actors, the expansion of schooling also involves organizational processes. Expansion requires that existing organizations grow, that new ones be created, and that resources be reallocated. Therefore, the expansion of schooling should be subject to the usual constraints on organizational growth.

Nielsen and Hannan's model includes three types of constraints on organizational growth: (1) structural inertia—internal and external resistance to change; (2) cohort effects—the effects of numbers of persons eligible to be students; and (3) resource effects—the effects of environmental richness. They argued that primary, secondary, and tertiary levels of educational organizations differ in terms of the complexity of the division of labor and in the cost of each student. These differences imply that the inertia, cohort, and resource effects vary by educational level. Nielsen and Hannan estimated a linear partial-adjustment model in discrete time. A continuous-time analogue is

$$\frac{dy_j(t)}{dt} = r_j \left[y_j^*(t) - y_j(t) \right],$$

$j = 1, \ldots, 3$, where the subscript 1 refers to the primary level, 2 to the secondary level, and 3 to the tertiary level. They assumed that the target level (or carrying capacity) for the jth level is

$$y_j^*(t) = \pi_{0j} + \pi_{1j} R(t) + \pi_{2j} C_j(t),$$

where R denotes the level of resources (measured by gross national product) and C_j is the size of the cohort relevant to the jth level.

Nielsen and Hannan tested hypotheses about both the speeds of adjustment (the r_j's) and the effects of exogenous variables on $y_j^*(t)$. Here we mention only the former. They argued that complexity and per student cost rise with the educational level, and thereby increase structural inertia, which decreases the speed of adjustment:

$$r_1 > r_2 > r_3.$$

Moreover, they argued that speeds of adjustment are higher in less competitive environments. Other things being equal, competition is less intense in environments with abundant resources. Therefore, each educational level is hypothesized to adjust more rapidly in richer countries than in poorer ones.

Panel regressions of a discrete-time model with a 5-year lag estimated for the 1950–1970 period supported these hypotheses, as well as other hypotheses not considered here. However, one problem did arise. Nielsen and Hannan's weighted generalized least-squares (WGLS) estimates of the speeds of adjustment were sometimes negative, which implies that the educational system grows explosively. This implication does not seem realistic.

Carroll (1979, 1981) argued that the Lotka–Volterra model is preferable to the linear partial-adjustment model estimated by

⟨14⟩ An Example: National Expansion of Education

Nielsen and Hannan. His specification differed from that of Nielsen and Hannan in several ways. First, his model lets the growth rate depend on a group's size. Second, his model allows all possible competitive interactions. Nielsen and Hannan specified that enrollments in any level do not affect growth in enrollments in lower levels, for example, that tertiary enrollments do not affect growth in primary enrollments. Such a specification is appropriate to the argument regarding cohort effects due to the supply of eligible students. But higher educational levels may also affect growth in lower levels either by creating a demand for eligible students (e.g., certification of teachers in the tertiary level may increase the demand for primary schools) or through competition for common resources such as state funding. Finally, Carroll used a variant of (19c) as his parameterization of the Lotka–Volterra model rather than (19b), which would be a closer analogue to Nielsen and Hannan's model:

$$\frac{\mathrm{d}y_j(t)}{\mathrm{d}t} = r_j\, y_j(t) \left[1 - \frac{y_j(t)}{y_j^*} + \frac{1}{r_j} \sum_{\substack{k=1 \\ k \neq j}}^{J} c_{jk}\, y_k(t) \right]. \qquad (46)$$

It is important to note that r_j in (46) is not analogous to the r_j in the model estimated by Nielsen and Hannan. The r_j's estimated by the latter authors are more closely comparable to the ν_j's in the Lotka–Volterra model in (19b).

Carroll (1979, 1981) used the second approach to forming an exact discrete approximation to estimate (46). In particular, he estimated (44) from pooled panel data on 64 nations with 5-year intervals between waves (i.e., with $n = 5$). Since plots of residuals in preliminary analyses suggested heteroscedastic disturbances, he used WGLS estimators obtained by Henderson's method; see the description in Section 13.5.

He used two specifications for y_j^*. Following Nielsen and Hannan, he let y_j^* depend additively on resources and cohort sizes. However, nonlinear least-squares estimates of this specification did not always converge.[14] Furthermore, when the iterative procedure did converge, he reported that the estimates tended to be unstable

---

[14] It is not clear why it was so hard to obtain convergence. Presumably high correlations between the explanatory variables are partially responsible.

across small variations in the causal variables included in the model. Consequently, he did not report results for this specification and concentrated instead on the specification in (45). In particular, he assumed that

$$\frac{1}{y_1^*(t)} = \pi_{10} + \pi_{11} \frac{1}{R(t)} + \pi_{12} \frac{1}{P(t)} + \pi_{13} \frac{1}{C_1(t)} + \pi_{14} \frac{1}{R(t)^2},$$

$$\frac{1}{y_2^*(t)} = \pi_{20} + \pi_{21} \frac{1}{R(t)} + \pi_{22} \frac{1}{P(t)}, \quad (47)$$

$$\frac{1}{y_3^*(t)} = \pi_{30} + \pi_{31} \frac{1}{R(t)} + \pi_{32} \frac{1}{P(t)},$$

where R denotes gross national product, a measure of the resource base; P is the size of the national population; and C_1 is the size of the primary-school-age population.[15]

Table 14.1 reports estimates for the coefficients of the right-hand side variables in (34); Table 14.2 reports estimates of the Lotka–Volterra model in (46) with the specification of $f_j(\mathbf{x})$ in (47). Following Carroll, we report three sets of parameters: the intrinsic growth rates, the r_j's; the coupling coefficients, the c_{jk}'s for $k \neq j$; and the π's in (47).

First, consider the estimated intrinsic growth rates. As in Nielsen and Hannan's analysis, the findings support the hypotheses regarding the effect of complexity and per student cost. The intrinsic growth rate for the primary level is roughly twice that of the secondary level, which, in turn, is roughly twice that of the tertiary level.[16]

Estimates of the coupling parameters, the c_{jk}'s, are generally not statistically significant. More precisely, the analogous regression

In addition, the 5-year interval between waves of observations may be too long for the exact discrete approximation to hold closely. The magnitudes of the estimated speeds of adjustment in Table 14.2 (especially for the primary level) suggest that this may be the case.

[15] See Nielsen and Hannan (1977) for a justification of this specification of the effects of the population variables.

[16] In separate analyses of subsamples of rich and poor countries, Carroll (1981) found that the hypothesis concerning the effects of environmental richness is supported for two of the three educational levels.

⟨14⟩ An Example: National Expansion of Education

Table 14.1. Weighted generalized least-squares estimates of the exact discrete approximation in (44) to the Lotka–Volterra model of national expansion of education given by (46) and (47) (standard errors in parentheses) [adapted with permission from Carroll (1979)][a]

	Dependent variable, $1/y_j(t+5)$		
Independent variable	$j = 1$	$j = 2$	$j = 3$
$1/y_j(t)$	0.311 (0.017)	0.563 (0.015)	0.744 (0.033)
$y_1(t)/y_j(t)$	—	−0.005 (0.004)	−0.019 (0.005)
$y_2(t)/y_j(t)$	0.009 (0.017)	—	−0.526 (0.139)
$y_3(t)/y_j(t)$	−0.014 (0.085)	0.171 (0.272)	—
$1/R(t)$	0.060 (0.013)	0.061 (0.104)	−2.28 (5.13)
$1/R^2(t)$	−0.00002 (0.000008)	—	—
$1/P(t)$	0.196 (0.219)	0.017 (0.706)	−11.16 (36.04)
$1/C_1(t)$	0.110 (0.286)	—	—
Intercept	−0.002 (0.006)	0.015 (0.049)	6.56 (1.73)
R^2	.804	.902	.807

[a]Sample size, $I = 64$; $N = 5$.

parameters are not twice their standard errors.[17] The lower educational levels seem, however, to have a strong positive effect on the tertiary level. The only negative effects are those of tertiary enrollments on expansion of the secondary level and of secondary

[17]Recall our earlier warning that nothing is known about testing hypotheses for such models from these exact discrete approximations.

Table 14.2. Estimates of parameters in the Lotka–Volterra model of national expansion of education in (46) and (47) [adapted with permission from Carroll (1979)]

	Dependent variable		
	$\dfrac{dy_1}{dt}$	$\dfrac{dy_2}{dt}$	$\dfrac{dy_3}{dt}$
Speed of adjustment	0.234*	0.115*	0.059*
$y_1(t)$	—	0.001	0.004*
$y_2(t)$	−0.003	—	0.122*
$y_3(t)$	0.005	−0.045	—
Effects of exogenous variables on y_j^*			
$1/R(t)$	0.087*	0.140	−8.91
$1/P(t)$	0.284	0.039	−43.6
$1/C_1(t)$	0.160	—	—
$1/R^2(t)$	−0.00003*	—	—
Intercept	−0.003	0.034	25.6*

*Corresponding regression coefficient is twice its standard error.

enrollments on expansion of the primary level. These negative effects presumably reflect competition for resources.[18] Overall there is some evidence that the size of the eligible student population affects educational expansion and that competition between levels for scarce resources affects the relative growth rates of the three levels.

The π's, the effects of the exogenous variables on y_j^*, are hard to interpret. Because of the unusual functional form for y_j^*, a variable with a negative coefficient has a positive effect on y_j^*. Plots of the estimated functions show that gross national product (GNP) affects y_1^* and y_2^*, the target levels for the primary and secondary enrollments, respectively.

Above we noted that the findings of Nielsen and Hannan sometimes implied unstable dynamics. We comment briefly on the

---

[18]Carroll (1981) also found support for the hypothesis that competitive effects are stronger in poorer countries.

stability of the model implied by the results in Table 14.2. Due to the nonlinearity of the Lotka–Volterra model, it is very difficult to characterize global stability, as we discussed in Section 14.3. The next section shows that local or neighborhood stability (the behavior of the system near a steady state) can be studied directly. Carroll (1979) showed that the estimated system is locally stable. He also plotted the time trajectories implied by the estimates under the assumption that exogenous variables grow exponentially from their 1950 mean values. Though the specification of exponential growth in exogenous variables guarantees explosive growth in the system, the estimated system grows stably for many decades before this happens. Apparently use of this nonlinear model at least partially alleviates the stability problem encountered by Nielsen and Hannan.

14.6 *Qualitative Stability

As we remarked at the beginning of this chapter, most work with nonlinear models of systems focuses on their qualitative behavior, especially their stability. This section gives a brief introduction to stability analysis of nonlinear DEs.

As in the case of a linear model of a system, the first step in studying the qualitative behavior of a nonlinear model is to find its equilibria. This step often requires detailed and laborious analysis when the model is complex. However, for the special cases considered in this chapter, this step is no more complicated than it is for a linear model. For example, the logistic model in (5b) has equilibria at zero and y^*, as we mentioned earlier.

The next step is to characterize the stability of the equilibria. The apparatus for analyzing stability introduced in Chapter 11 applies directly to nonlinear models. Local, asymptotic, and global stability have the same meaning as in Section 11.6.2, but special methods are needed to apply these concepts to nonlinear models.

14.6.1 Linearization

The most common device for studying the local stability of nonlinear models is **linearization**. This technique, often called **Liapunov's first** (or **indirect**) **method**, involves making a linear approximation to the nonlinear model and analyzing the stability of the approximation. Suppose that the scalar process

$$\frac{\mathrm{d}y(t)}{\mathrm{d}t} = f[y(t)] \qquad (48)$$

has an equilibrium at y^e. Although $y(t)$ changes nonlinearly in time, its behavior in a small region near the equilibrium can be approximated well by a linear function that is tangent to f at y^e. It is very useful to rewrite (48) in terms of deviations from the equilibrium point. Any point $y(t)$ can be expressed as $y^e + z(t)$, where $z(t)$ denotes the departure from the equilibrium. Using this metric, we make the following approximation:

$$\frac{dy(t)}{dt} = f[y(t)] \equiv f[y^e + z(t)]$$

$$\approx f[y^e] + \frac{df[y^e]}{dy} z(t) = \frac{df[y^e]}{dy} z(t).$$

The approximation contains the first two terms of a Taylor-series expansion of the function around y^e; hence it is a *linear* approximation. Because $f[y^e] \equiv 0$ by definition, $f[y^e]$ drops out.

A parallel multivariate approximation is used in the case of a system of J equations,

$$\frac{dy_j(t)}{dt} = f_j[\mathbf{y}(t)], \qquad (49)$$

where $\mathbf{y}(t)$ is a vector with elements $y_j(t)$, $j = 1, \ldots, J$. As in the scalar case, f_j is reexpressed in terms of departures from the equilibrium point $\mathbf{y}^e$:

$$f_j[\mathbf{y}(t)] \equiv f_j[\mathbf{y}^e + \mathbf{z}(t)] \equiv f_j[y_1^e + z_1, \ldots, y_J^e + z_J].$$

Again, we form a linear approximation:

$$\mathbf{f}[\mathbf{y}^e + \mathbf{z}(t)] \approx \mathbf{f}[\mathbf{y}^e] + \mathbf{F}(\mathbf{y}^e)\mathbf{z}(t),$$

where $\mathbf{F}(\mathbf{y}^e)$ is the Jacobian matrix

$$\mathbf{F}(\mathbf{y}^e) \equiv \begin{pmatrix} \frac{\partial f_1}{\partial y_1} & \frac{\partial f_1}{\partial y_2} & \cdots & \frac{\partial f_1}{\partial y_J} \\ \frac{\partial f_2}{\partial y_1} & \frac{\partial f_2}{\partial y_2} & \cdots & \frac{\partial f_2}{\partial y_J} \\ \vdots & \vdots & & \vdots \\ \frac{\partial f_J}{\partial y_1} & \frac{\partial f_J}{\partial y_2} & \cdots & \frac{\partial f_J}{\partial y_J} \end{pmatrix}, \qquad (50)$$

⟨14⟩ *Qualitative Stability

where each partial derivative is evaluated at $\mathbf{y}^e$, and $\mathbf{z}(t)$ is the J by 1 vector with elements $z_j(t) \equiv y_j(t) - y_j^e$.

Now consider the DE in (49) in the new metric:

$$\frac{d\mathbf{y}(t)}{dt} \equiv \frac{d[\mathbf{y}^e + \mathbf{z}(t)]}{dt} = \frac{d\mathbf{y}^e}{dt} + \frac{d\mathbf{z}(t)}{dt} \approx \mathbf{f}[\mathbf{y}^e] + \mathbf{F}(\mathbf{y}^e)\mathbf{z}(t). \quad (51)$$

Because $\mathbf{y}^e$ is an equilibrium point, $d\mathbf{y}^e/dt = 0$ and $\mathbf{f}[\mathbf{y}^e] = 0$. Therefore, equation (51) is identical to the linear system

$$\frac{d\mathbf{z}(t)}{dt} = \mathbf{F}(\mathbf{y}^e)\mathbf{z}(t). \quad (52)$$

Here we see the advantage of linearization; analysis of the stability of (52) requires only the simple methods that apply to linear models. As we saw in Section 11.6, stability of a linear model is determined by its eigenvalues. Thus the local stability of the nonlinear model in (49) is determined by the eigenvalues of $\mathbf{F}(\mathbf{y}^e)$, the Jacobian matrix given in (50).

We illustrate this procedure first with the logistic model in (5b). The linearized logistic model is

$$\frac{dz(t)}{dt} = \left.\frac{d\{\nu y(t)[y^* - y(t)]\}}{dy}\right|_{y^e} z(t) = [\nu y^* - 2\nu y^e]z(t).$$

Recall that there are two equilibria, $y^e = 0$ and $y^e = y^*$. At the equilibrium at zero,

$$\frac{dz}{dt} = \nu y^* z(t) = r z(t).$$

This equilibrium point is asymptotically stable if r is negative and unstable if r is positive. For most practical purposes the equilibrium at zero can be considered unstable since r is assumed to be positive in growth models. At the other equilibrium, y^*, the linear approximation equals

$$\frac{dz}{dt} = [\nu y^* - 2\nu y^*]z(t) = -\nu y^* z(t) = -r z(t).$$

This equilibrium point is asymptotically stable when r is positive and unstable when r is negative.

The value of linearization is more apparent when it is applied to a nonlinear model of a system. Consider Volterra's model of diffuse resource competition, given in (13). At most one group can have a nonzero size in equilibrium under Volterra's assumption that each group has a distinct fitness factor r_j/c_j; see Section 14.3.1. But there are J such equilibria, each corresponding to a nonzero value for one of the J groups and zero for all other groups. Are these various equilibria stable?

Since the ordering of groups is arbitrary, we need consider only the case in which the first group has a nonzero equilibrium. The equilibrium point is formed by substituting (12) in (14) and solving for y_1^e when it is assumed that $y_j^e = 0$ for $j > 1$. This yields

$$r_1 - c_1(a_1 y_1^e) = 0,$$

or

$$y_1^e = \frac{r_1}{a_1 c_1}.$$

Putting this equation in (12) implies that

$$D[\mathbf{y}^e] = a_1 y_1^e = \frac{r_1}{c_1}.$$

To find the linearized approximation to Volterra's diffuse resource-competition model in (13), notice first that (13) implies

$$f_j[\mathbf{y}(t)] = \{r_j - c_j D[\mathbf{y}(t)]\} y_j(t)$$
$$= r_j y_j(t) - c_j y_j(t) D[\mathbf{y}(t)].$$

The Jacobian matrix $\mathbf{F}(\mathbf{y}^e)$ involves four kinds of partial derivatives, $\partial f_1/\partial y_1$, $\partial f_1/\partial y_j$, $\partial f_j/\partial y_j$, and $\partial f_j/\partial y_k$, where $j > 1$ and $k \neq j$. Each of these derivatives must be evaluated at the equilibrium point $\mathbf{y}^e = \{r_1/(a_1 c_1), 0, \ldots, 0\}$. It is straightforward to show that

$$\left.\frac{\partial f_1}{\partial y_1}\right|_{\mathbf{y}^e} = r_1 - c_1 D[\mathbf{y}^e] - c_1 y_1^e \frac{\partial D}{\partial y_1}$$
$$= r_1 - c_1 \frac{r_1}{c_1} - c_1 \frac{r_1}{a_1 c_1} a_1 = -r_1;$$

⟨14⟩ *Qualitative Stability

$$\left.\frac{\partial f_1}{\partial y_j}\right|_{y^e} = -c_1 y_1^e \frac{\partial D}{\partial y_j}$$

$$= -c_1 \frac{r_1}{a_1 c_1} a_j = -\frac{a_j}{a_1} r_1 \equiv \mu_j;$$

$$\left.\frac{\partial f_j}{\partial y_j}\right|_{y^e} = r_j - c_j D[\mathbf{y}^e] - c_j y_j^e \frac{\partial D}{\partial y_j}$$

$$= r_j - c_j \frac{r_1}{c_1} \equiv \omega_j;$$

$$\left.\frac{\partial f_j}{\partial y_k}\right|_{y^e} = -c_j y_j^e \frac{\partial D}{\partial y_k} = 0.$$

Substituting these results in (52) gives the linearized version of Volterra's model of competition for a single resource:

$$\frac{d\mathbf{z}(t)}{dt} = \begin{pmatrix} -r_1 & \mu_2 & \mu_3 & \cdots & \mu_J \\ 0 & \omega_2 & 0 & \cdots & 0 \\ 0 & 0 & \omega_3 & \cdots & 0 \\ \vdots & \vdots & \vdots & & \vdots \\ 0 & 0 & 0 & \cdots & \omega_J \end{pmatrix} \mathbf{z}(t). \qquad (53)$$

The Jacobian matrix in (53) has only zeros below the main diagonal. The eigenvalues of a matrix with such a pattern equal the entries on the main diagonal. Therefore, the eigenvalues of the linearized system equal the diagonal elements in (53). Local stability can be inferred directly from the signs of the elements on the main diagonal of this matrix. Since the first element in the main diagonal in (53) is negative, local stability of an equilibrium is determined completely by the signs of the ω_j. The conditions for local stability are

$$w_j \equiv r_j - c_j \frac{r_1}{c_1} < 0,$$

or

$$r_1/c_1 > r_j/c_j,$$

for $j > 1$. That is, stability requires that the group with the nonzero equilibrium level have the largest fitness factor.

Linearization has substantial advantages as a method of analyzing stability because it involves the study of linear equations, which are simple to analyze. Moreover, unless boundary conditions are encountered,[19] it gives clear answers to questions about local stability. Consequently, linearization is almost always a first step in any study of the stability of a nonlinear model of a system.

Often it is valuable to move beyond questions of local stability. Most investigators want to know whether qualitative inferences depend on the initial cconditions rather than on local behavior in the neighborhood of an equilibrium. Linearization cannot tell this. Some more complex technique, such as Liapunov's direct method, must be used instead. For a clear introduction to this complicated subject, see Luenberger (1979).

14.7   *Cyclic Behavior: Predator–Prey Interactions

Our discussion of the Lotka–Volterra model did not illustrate the full range of qualitative behavior possible with nonlinear models of a system. In particular, we did not discuss any cases that imply cyclic time paths of change. This section discusses an important special case of a Lotka–Volterra model that implies cyclic behavior.

When α_{jk} and α_{kj} differ in sign, different qualitative behavior results. The study of predator–prey (or host–parasite) systems began with Volterra's use of a special case of the bivariate model discussed in Section 14.3. He assumed that the prey grows exponentially in the absence of its predator. He also assumed that the prey was the only source of sustenance for the predator, implying that the number of predators declines exponentially to zero when the prey is absent. Letting y_1 and y_2 denote the sizes of the prey and predator, respectively, Volterra's predator–prey model can be expressed as

$$\frac{dy_1(t)}{dt} = r_1\, y_1(t) + c_{12}\, y_1(t)\, y_2(t),$$
$$\frac{dy_2(t)}{dt} = -\nu_2\, y_2(t) + c_{21}\, y_1(t)\, y_2(t), \qquad (54)$$

where r_1, ν_2, and c_{21} are positive and c_{12} is negative.

---

[19]For example, linearization does not answer questions about local stability when any eigenvalue is zero. More advanced methods are needed in such cases.

⟨14⟩ *Cyclic Behavior: Predator–Prey Interactions

This model has an uninteresting equilibrium at $y_1^e = 0$, $y_2^e = 0$. A second, substantively interesting equilibrium, occurs at

$$y_1^e = \frac{\nu_2}{c_{21}};$$

$$y_2^e = -\frac{r_1}{c_{12}}.$$

Is there a stable equilibrium when predator and prey coexist, that is, when $y_1^e > 0$ and $y_2^e > 0$? Again Liapuvnov's first method can provide the answer. The Jacobian matrix $\mathbf{F}$ has four elements:

$$\left.\frac{\partial f_1}{\partial y_1}\right|_{y^e} = r_1 + c_{12}\, y_2^e = r_1 + c_{12}\left(-\frac{r_1}{c_{12}}\right) = 0;$$

$$\left.\frac{\partial f_1}{\partial y_2}\right|_{y^e} = c_{12}\, y_1^e = c_{12}\,\frac{\nu_2}{c_{21}} = \nu_2\,\frac{c_{12}}{c_{21}};$$

$$\left.\frac{\partial f_2}{\partial y_1}\right|_{y^e} = c_{21}\, y_2^e = c_{21}\left(-\frac{r_1}{c_{12}}\right) = -r_1\,\frac{c_{21}}{c_{12}};$$

$$\left.\frac{\partial f_2}{\partial y_2}\right|_{y^e} = -\nu_2 + c_{21}\, y_1^e = -\nu_2 + c_{21}\,\frac{\nu_2}{c_{21}} = 0.$$

Thus the linearized version of (54) is

$$\begin{pmatrix} \frac{dz_1}{dt} \\ \frac{dz_2}{dt} \end{pmatrix} = \begin{pmatrix} 0 & \nu_2\,\frac{c_{12}}{c_{21}} \\ -r_1\,\frac{c_{21}}{c_{12}} & 0 \end{pmatrix} \begin{pmatrix} z_1 \\ z_2 \end{pmatrix}, \qquad (55)$$

where $z_j \equiv y_j^e - y_j$ and $j = 1, 2$. The eigenvalues of $\mathbf{F}(y^e)$ are $\lambda = \pm i\sqrt{r_1 \nu_2}$. Since the eigenvalues are complex, the numbers of predator and prey cycle. As the number of prey rises, the growth rate of the predator increases. The resulting increase in the number of predators causes the growth rate of the prey to become negative. But as the number of prey falls, the growth rate of the predator also falls. In turn, the prey begins to grow again, initiating another cycle. As long as the cycles are bounded and do not reach zero for either population, the process cycles continually around the equilibrium point. We have already depicted such behavior in the phase space in shown in Figure 11.8. The fact that the real part of the roots of this system are zero guarantees that the system neither spirals towards the equilibrium nor spirals away. This is an example of **neutral stability**.

The simple predator–prey model is somewhat unusual because its qualitative behavior can be determined directly. From the linearized equations in (55), we have

$$\frac{dz_1(t)}{dt} = \nu_2 \frac{c_{12}}{c_{21}} z_2(t) = c_{12} y_1^e z_2(t);$$

$$\frac{dz_2(t)}{dt} = -r_1 \frac{c_{21}}{c_{12}} z_1(t) = c_{21} y_2^e z_1(t).$$

Phase-space analysis yields

$$\frac{\frac{dz_1(t)}{dt}}{\frac{dz_2(t)}{dt}} = \frac{dz_1}{dz_2} = \frac{c_{12} y_1^e z_2(t)}{c_{21} y_2^e z_1(t)}.$$

This DE can be rearranged to give

$$\frac{c_{21}}{2 y_1^e} \left[z_1^2(t) - z_{10}^2 \right] = \frac{c_{12}}{2 y_2^e} \left[z_2^2(t) - z_{20}^2 \right],$$

where $z_{j0} \equiv z_j(0)$ for $j = 1, 2$. Replacing $z_j(t)$ with $y_j^e - y_j(t)$ and rearranging yields

$$\frac{c_{21}}{2 y_1^e} \left[y_1^e - y_1(t) \right]^2 - \frac{c_{12}}{2 y_2^e} \left[y_2^e - y_2(t) \right]^2 = \kappa, \quad (56)$$

where κ is a constant that depends on the initial conditions, as well as r_1, ν_2, c_{12}, and c_{21}. Equation (56) defines an ellipse in the y_1–y_2 plane centered around the equilibrium point. The initial positions of the variables determine the distance of the orbit of the ellipse from its center. If the system begins near the equilibrium, it follows a tight cycle around it. If it begins far from the equilibrium, it cycles widely around the equilibrium. In other words, neutral stability implies that each set of initial conditions defines a unique orbit.

⟨14⟩ Conclusions

Neutral stability is precarious. Any slight change in the model, such as introducing weak density dependence in the growth rate of the prey, induces completely different qualitative behavior. Such models are said to be **structurally unstable**. The cyclic variations that appear so often in nature seem unlikely to reflect the actions of such an unstable process. This realization has prompted population biologists to search for structurally stable models that also imply cyclic variation in the numbers of predator and prey. Concise summaries of classes of such models that have been considered, as well as a discussion of the stability properties of these classes of models, can be found in May (1974) and Roughgarden (1979).

14.8 Conclusions

This chapter shows that our general strategy for modeling and estimation may be applied to models that do not have explicit representations as IEs. We illustrated the extension to nonlinear models using a variety of competition models, especially Lotka–Volterra models in which the target levels (or carrying capacities) depend on a set of observable variables. We illustrated how the approach to analyzing stability introduced in Chapter 11 can be used to analyze local stability of fairly complicated nonlinear models. We also showed that use of an exact discrete approximation can permit estimation of parameters of a nonlinear model from panel or time-series data.

The nonlinear models considered in this chapter have considerable potential for sociological analysis and should receive more attention than they have in the past. Indeed, we believe that these models and methods can be adapted to handle a rich variety of substantive situations. There is no need for sociologists interested in studying change to confine their attention to the restrictive case of linear models.

15
Stochastic Nonlinear Models

In this chapter we consider stochastic analogues to some of the continuous-time, continuous-state nonlinear models discussed in the previous chapter. The substantive motivation for these models arises out of issues discussed in Chapter 14; the stochastic modeling structure extends the one introduced in Chapter 12.

In Chapter 14 we saw that deterministic nonlinear models are more complex than the analogous linear models. Indeed, the solution of even the Lotka–Volterra model discussed at length in Chapter 14, which is a fairly simple nonlinear system, cannot yet be expressed exactly in terms of a few common transcendental and nontranscendental functions (i.e., in terms of logarithms, trigonometric functions, and so forth). In the case of stochastic models, the difference in complexity between linear and nonlinear models is far greater.

This chapter may be the last straw for the reader who already doubts that gains in analytic power from stochastic models for quantitative outcomes outweigh increased complexity. Nonetheless, we argue in favor of working toward a stochastic approach. Indeed, we think that the potential gains from adopting a stochastic framework are larger for nonlinear than for linear models. This is certainly true in one important respect. In Chapter 12 we showed that the time path of a linear deterministic model of a scalar outcome and the time path of the mean of the analogous stochastic model agree, unless the outcome is bounded. In general there is no such agreement for nonlinear models. Thus, even the most basic implication

⟨15⟩ Stochastic Nonlinear Models

of a nonlinear model of change depends upon the choice between a deterministic and stochastic formulation.

A simple example illustrates the typical divergence between analogous stochastic and deterministic nonlinear models. In the previous chapter we discussed a model for the spread of some item in a population of fixed size. We saw that when the item spreads both from a constant source and from interaction between units, a useful deterministic model for its dynamics is

$$\frac{dy(t)}{dt} = [\mu + \nu y(t)][N - y(t)],$$

where $y(t)$ is the number of units possessing the item at time t and N the population size. In this model, μ and ν measure the strength of the spread from the constant source and from interaction, respectively. Subject to the initial condition $y(0) = 0$, the solution is

$$y(t) = N\left[\frac{\exp[\nu(N+\theta)t] - 1}{\exp[\nu(N+\theta)t] + N/\theta}\right],$$

where $\theta \equiv \mu/\nu$.

A stochastic analogue to this model is a pure birth process in which the probability of a change from y to $y+1$ in the small interval $[t, t + \Delta t)$ is approximately $\lambda_y \Delta t$ (see Bartholomew, 1973, pp. 298–307). Formally, this means

$$\lim_{\Delta t \downarrow 0} \frac{\Pr[Y(t + \Delta t) = y + 1 \mid Y(t) = y]}{\Delta t} = \lambda_y$$

$$= [\mu + \nu y(t)][N - y(t)].$$

[We use $Y(t)$ rather than $y(t)$ because we are now discussing the outcome of a random process rather than a deterministic one; we continue to use $y(t)$ and y to indicate realizations of $Y(t)$.] This stochastic model has not been solved in general, but it has been solved for some special cases. In particular, for large N and for $Y(t)$ not near zero or N, one can show that (Bartholomew, 1973, p. 304)

$$E[Y(t)] = \frac{(e^X - \theta + 1)N}{e^X + N},$$

where
$$X \equiv \nu(N+\theta)t - \gamma + \psi(\theta-1),$$
γ is Euler's constant $(0.5772\ldots)$, and
$$\psi(z) \equiv \sum_{k=1}^{\infty} \frac{z}{(1+z)k}.$$

Clearly the mean does not equal the solution of the deterministic logistic equation. The deterministic curve lags behind the trajectory of the mean of the stochastic process. The size of the lag depends on N and θ. Even for a model as simple as this one, one cannot presume that the time path of the deterministic model is even near the *average* growth path of the analogous stochastic model. The gap between the two types of models may be large enough to affect qualitative conclusions, as Bartholomew (1973) suggested.

The point of this simple example should be obvious. If the time path implied by a deterministic differential equation (DDE) and the *mean* time path implied by the analogous stochastic differential equation (SDE) differ considerably, one cannot choose to work with the deterministic version just because it is easier, assuming one thinks that exogenous, unobserved shocks affect the rate of change. In our opinion the latter assumption is always plausible. So we must attempt to unravel the complexities of nonlinear SDEs.

15.1 Stochastic Integrals: The Nonlinear Case

Chapter 12 focused on the special class of *linear* SDEs in which the random forcing function does not depend on present or past outcomes of Y. In particular, we emphasized tractable models for a scalar process. These models assume that the local variance $\sigma^2(y_t)$ is a constant and does not depend on the sample path of Y. Often it seems more realistic to assume that the variance of a social process depends on the current level of the outcome $Y(t)$. For example, in modeling competitive interaction among political parties (e.g., Nielsen, 1980), it might be appropriate to specify that the variance of disturbing influences depends on the size of the party. Big random shocks are more likely to disturb small political parties than large, institutionalized parties.

⟨15⟩ Stochastic Integrals: The Nonlinear Case

In this chapter we briefly consider the general case of *nonlinear* SDEs in which the noise process is state dependent. Consider the general SDE given as (14) in Chapter 12:

$$dY(t) = f[Y(t)]\,dt + g[Y(t)]\,dW(t), \tag{1}$$

where $dW(t)$ is white noise (the differential of Brownian motion). As we mentioned at the end of Section 12.2, SDEs are defined mathematically as equivalent to stochastic integral equations. In general, the solution to such an equation contains an integral

$$\int_b^a g[Y(s)]\,dW(s). \tag{2}$$

The problem of defining and interpreting a **stochastic integral** like (2) arises because Brownian motion behaves so erratically. The procedure for measuring the area under a function using ordinary (Riemannian) calculus involves summing areas of rectangles with vanishingly small width. Under the classical assumption of differentiability, it does not matter whether one evaluates each rectangle on the left, on the right, or at any point in between. But it does matter with Brownian motion. Because of jumps in the process, calculations based on evaluating rectangles on the left differ on average from calculations based on evaluating rectangles in the middle or on the right.

Since the early 1960s a literature has developed on the interpretation of stochastic integrals. Much of this literature is extremely technical. Sociologists confronting this literature need some orientation because two different definitions of stochastic integrals are used widely. The two definitions agree about the solutions of linear SDEs, but they disagree about the solutions of nonlinear SDEs. Therefore, we discuss these two definitions and their suitability for sociological analysis. We do not discuss the mathematical theory here; we merely cite major results that seem relevant to social research and give references for further reading. See especially Jazwinski (1970) and Karlin and Taylor (1981).

15.1.1 The Itô Integral

One way to define a stochastic integral, proposed by Itô (1944), builds on the result that an increment in a Brownian-motion process over an interval is independent of its value at the *beginning* of the interval. Itŏ proposed that the random forcing function $g[Y(t)]$ be approximated with a series of step functions:

$$g_n^{(N)} = \begin{cases} 0, & \text{if } t < t_0 \text{ or } t \geq t_N, \\ g[Y(t_{n-1})], & \text{if } t_{n-1} \leq t < t_n, \end{cases}$$

for a given partition of the time axis into N intervals:

$$a \equiv t_0 < t_1 < \cdots < t_N \equiv b.$$

Such an approximation can be formed for any choice of N. The series of step functions can be made to approximate $g[Y(t)]$ as closely as desired by making $\rho \equiv \max(t_n - t_{n-1})$ sufficiently small, which means N sufficiently large. Consider the sequence of step functions $\{g_n^{(N)}\}$ that converge in mean square[1] to $g[Y(t)]$ as $\rho \downarrow 0$ and $N \to \infty$. The Itŏ integral is defined as

$$\int_a^b g[Y(s)]\, dW(s) \equiv \underset{\substack{N \to \infty \\ \rho \downarrow 0}}{\text{l.i.m.}} \sum_{n=1}^N g_n^{(N)} [W(t_n) - W(t_{n-1})], \qquad (3)$$

where l.i.m. denotes the limit in mean square as $N \to \infty$. Note that each term in the sum on the right-hand side of (3) is the product of an increment of Brownian motion and a function of the sample path of Brownian motion, $g[Y(t)]$, evaluated at the beginning of the interval. These two terms are independent because increments in Brownian motion are independent.

The solution to an SDE using Itŏ's definition of the stochastic integral gives results that differ from the classical calculus. The behavior of squared differentials is one important difference. According to Itŏ's calculus, squared differentials of Brownian motion

---

[1] A sequence $\{Y^{(N)}\}$ is said to converge in mean square (or in quadratic mean) to Y if $\mathrm{E}[|Y|^2] < \infty$ for all N, and $\lim_{N \to \infty} \mathrm{E}\{|Y - Y^{(N)}|^2\} = 0$. This form of convergence implies convergence in probability, the so-called plim convergence so widely used in structural-equation analysis. It is slightly weaker than "almost sure" convergence. See Jazwinski (1970, pp. 56–70) for an exposition of the mean-square calculus.

⟨15⟩ **Stochastic Integrals: The Nonlinear Case**   515

behave approximately (in a mean-square sense) like ordinary time differentials:

$$\text{l.i.m.} \left[dW(t) \right]^2 = dt. \tag{4}$$

Because of (4), the Itô calculus gives some surprising results. For example, consider the following simple stochastic integral:

$$\int_0^t W(s) \, dW(s). \tag{5}$$

It can be shown that when $W(0) = 0$, (3) implies

$$\int_0^t W(s) \, dW(s) = \underset{\substack{N \to \infty \\ \rho \downarrow 0}}{\text{l.i.m.}} \sum_{n=1}^N W(t_{n-1}) \left[W(t_n) - W(t_{n-1}) \right]$$

$$= \frac{1}{2} W^2(t) - \frac{1}{2} t. \tag{6}$$

The familiar Riemann integration (of the classical calculus) of the integral in (5) yields only the first term in Itô's solution. The second term reflects the peculiar properties of Brownian motion over any partition and the rules of Itô's stochastic calculus. This simple example illustrates how Itô's calculus typically differs from classical calculus—the solution of the SDE contains a term reflecting the amount of variability in the process.

15.1.2 The Stratonovich Integral

Stratonovich (1966) defined the stochastic integral in a way that yields results in agreement with the classical calculus. Like Itô, he defined a stochastic integral as a mean-square limit of a sequence of step-function approximations to the SDE, but he evaluated the step functions at the *midpoint* of each segment.[2]

$$\int_a^b g[Y(s)] \, dW(s)$$

$$= \underset{\substack{N \to \infty \\ \rho \downarrow 0}}{\text{l.i.m.}} \sum_{n=1}^N g \left[\frac{Y(t_{n-1}) + Y(t_n)}{2} \right] \left[W(t_n) - W(t_{n-1}) \right]. \tag{7}$$

[2]Stratonovich's definition loses the independence property possessed by Itô's definition (see footnote 1) because it evaluates functions of Brownian motion at the midpoint of each partition. This definition complicates probabilistic analysis but simplifies evaluation of the stochastic integral.

The Stratonovich solution to the stochastic integral in (5) is:

$$\int_0^t W(s)\,dW(s) = \text{l.i.m.}\ \frac{1}{2}\sum_{n=1}^N [W(t_n) + W(t_{n-1})][W(t_n) - W(t_{n-1})]$$

$$= \text{l.i.m.}\ \frac{1}{2}\sum_{n=1}^N W^2(t_n) - W^2(t_{n-1})$$

$$= \frac{1}{2}[W^2(t) - W^2(0)]$$

$$= \frac{1}{2}W^2(t), \qquad (8)$$

which agrees with the usual rules of Riemann integration. Thus, Stratonovich's definition of the stochastic integral, unlike Itô's, implies that the solution of this SDE does not depend on the variability of the process.

These two definitions of the stochastic integral differ in two ways. The first is generality. Itô's definition is completely general. It does not even require that $g[Y(t)]$ be a function—it may be a generalized function (or functional). According to Mortensen (1969, p. 207), Stratonovich's definition is "just versatile enough to handle stochastic differential equations." In particular, Stratonovich's definition requires that $g[Y(t)]$ be an *explicit* function of $W(t)$. Itô's calculus has a great advantage from a purely formal perspective. However, the added generality may not be needed very often in empirical social research.

The second difference concerns the relationship of the parameters of SDEs, such as equation (1), to those of the diffusion processes discussed in Section 12.4, which are defined in terms of the local drift $\mu(y_t)$ and the local variance $\sigma^2(y_t)$. Because Itô's definition relies on the independent-increments property of Brownian motion, this relationship is especially simple in Itô's calculus. If $\{Y(t), t > 0\}$ is a Markov process that meets certain regularity conditions (see Doob, 1953, pp. 273–277), then under the Itô calculus,

$$\mu(y_t) = f[Y(t), t]; \qquad (9a)$$

$$\sigma^2(y_t) = g^2[Y(t), t]. \qquad (9b)$$

In other words, the parameters of the SDE may be interpreted directly in terms of the local drift and local variance of the stochastic process, $\{Y(t)\}$, when Itô's calculus is used. In contrast, under the Stratonovich calculus,

$$\mu(y_t) = f[Y(t), t] + \frac{1}{2} g[Y(t), t] \frac{\partial g[Y(t), t]}{\partial y}; \qquad (10a)$$

$$\sigma^2(y_t) = g^2[Y(t), t]. \qquad (10b)$$

Clearly the relationship is more cumbersome with the Stratonovich calculus; compare (9a) and (10a). In particular, one must use information about both the systematic part of the change process, $f(\cdot)$, and the noise portion of the process, $g(\cdot)$, in order to find the local drift with the Stratonovich definition. This makes it awkward to shift back and forth between SDEs and diffusion processes, which is often helpful in deriving substantive implications of models. However, it is also clear from these expressions that one can always transform an Itô solution into a Stratonovich solution, and vice versa (see Wong and Zakai, 1965a,b). This means that the complexity of the relationship between SDEs and diffusion processes in the Stratonovich calculus does not raise any fundamental difficulties.

The main point is simply that the two definitions of the stochastic integral disagree on the fundamental issue of the relationship between SDEs and diffusion equations. Mortensen (1969, p. 279) summarizes the issues as follows:

> the one unambiguous way to specify a Markov process is to specify its transition density, or equivalently the Fokker–Planck (or Kolmogorov) equation obeyed by the transition density. The divergence arises when one wishes to generate the specified process as a solution to a stochastic differential equation forced by the differential of a Wiener (or Brownian motion) process [that is, $dW(t)$]. The divergence boils down to two different ways of associating the coefficients in the Fokker–Planck equation with the coefficients in the SDE, and, respectively, two ways of integrating the stochastic equation.

Most mathematicians prefer the generality of Itô's definition. Mathematical treatments of these issues, which emphasize diffusion processes, usually ignore the Stratonovich definition. Scientists usually construct SDEs as stochastic analogues of existing deterministic models and do not begin with diffusion processes. From this perspective, the choice between the Itŏ and Stratonovich calculi is highly relevant to practice. As we show in the next section, the choice can affect qualitative conclusions. This fact is troubling because there is no agreement on rules guiding the choice between interpretations. Indeed, Mortensen (1969) ended his review of the issues by calling for a "phenomenological approach," choosing the calculus that fits the observable features of the phenomena under study better.

At the present stage of development of these methods, there may be no alternative to a phenomenological approach. However, there is work that suggests some rough guidelines. Suppose one views an SDE driven by white noise as an approximation to some more complex but untractable model. Indeed, most scientists who use SDEs would probably endorse this interpretation of the modeling strategy. It is helpful to consider the nature of this approximation in order to draw conclusions about the substantive meaning of the two stochastic calculi. The literature on the subject proceeds along two main lines. We briefly review the major findings. See Turelli (1977) for a clear exposition of the issues and results, as well as citations to the technical literature.

The two styles of modeling disagree about the source of unrealism in an SDE driven by white noise. One position is that SDEs are used only for analytic convenience and that the behavioral processes actually occur in discrete time. According to this view, the fundamental dynamic relations involve stochastic *difference* equations with uncorrelated disturbances (random forcing functions). The second position does not question the realism of a continuous-time framework. Instead, it argues that realistic noise processes are correlated over time ("colored" rather than "white"). This view holds that the white-noise (or Brownian-motion) specification is chosen because we do not know how to model the correlation structure of the noise process. Put differently, the second perspective proceeds on the presumption that the fundamental dynamic model is a stochastic *differential* equation driven by a **correlated (colored) noise process**.

The discrete-time approach, due to Skorokhod (1958) (see also Kushner, 1974) considers stochastic difference equations that converge to SDEs driven by white noise. The simplest such exact discrete approximation is the sequence of difference equations:

$$Y^{(N)}(t+\rho) - Y^{(N)}(t) = \rho f[Y^{(N)}(t)] \\ + g[Y^{(N)}(t)][W(t+\rho) - W(t)],$$

defined for times $t = t_0, t_0 + \rho, t_0 + 2\rho, \ldots, t_N$, where $\rho = (t_N - t_0)/N$. Skorokhod proved that the sequence $\{Y^{(N)}(t)\}$ converges to the Itô solution as $N \to \infty$ and $\rho \downarrow 0$ (i.e., as the partition of the time axis becomes exceedingly fine). This result suggests that Itô's definition of a stochastic integral should be used in solving an SDE whenever a discrete-time description of a process is more realistic than the analogous continuous-time description.

The "colored-noise" approach, due to Stratonovich (1966) and Wong and Zakai (1965a,b), considers sequences of SDEs

$$\frac{dY^{(N)}(t)}{dt} = f[Y^{(N)}(t)] + g[Y^{(N)}(t)]Z^{(N)}(t),$$

where the sequence $\{Z^{(N)}(t)\}$ converges to white noise $Z(t)$ as $N \to \infty$ and $\rho \downarrow 0$. Stratonovich proved that $\{Y^{(N)}(t)\}$, the sequence of solutions, converges to the Stratonovich solution as $N \to \infty$ and $\rho \downarrow 0$.

This result suggests that the Stratonovich calculus is appropriate whenever the continuous-time description of a process is realistic. It appears that the choice between interpretations hinges at least partly on the realism of continuous-time change processes. Turelli (1977) argued that realistic models for population biology have a discrete-time structure and that the Itô calculus is therefore appropriate. Many other biologists who have written on these issues agree. When population biologists refer to exact models, they usually mean stochastic difference equations. For species with fixed breeding cycles, the natural time unit is surely the fixed (discrete) generation time. But as Crow and Kimura (1970, pp. 5–20) have pointed out, a continuous-time description is more realistic for some biotic systems, for example, bacterial colonies. We have argued throughout the preceding chapters that many (if not most) human social phenomena can change at any time and therefore continuous-time models are more realistic in most sociological applications. Yet, we acknowledge that there are analogues to generation times in some social processes. For example, some institutionalized socialization processes put entrants through a rigidly scheduled ritual sequence. Sociological analysis is likely to need both continuous-time and discrete-time models. It follows that both the Itǒ and Stratonovich calculi may be appropriate in sociological work.

15.2 Geometric Brownian Motion

The rest of this chapter discusses simple nonlinear growth models that illustrate some of the principles of analysis under the Itǒ and Stratonovich calculi. Any of the nonlinear models discussed in Chapter 14 could illustrate the differences between the substantive implications of these two calculi. For clarity, we continue to focus on the simplest nonlinear growth model—exponential growth.

At the beginning of Chapter 12, we mentioned three ways of incorporating randomness in DDEs. In Chapter 12 we emphasized one way, adding a random forcing function to a DDE. The example in this section illustrates a second way, specifying that one or more structural parameters of the behavioral equation are random variables. Though the two ways can lead to the same explicit model, it is valuable to be able to use both of them. Sometimes it is easier to think in terms of models with fixed parameters and a random noise function (the first way). On other occasions it is more suggestive to consider the effects of various types of randomness in parameters, or in some parameters but not others.

The modern treatment of stochastic population growth began with a discrete-time model proposed by Leowontin and Cohen (1969), which was extended to continuous time by Levins (1969). The model has since been extended further by Capocelli and Ricciardi (1974), May (1974), Tuckwell (1974), Feldman and Roughgarden (1975), and others.

Recall that one way in which we developed nonlinear models as generalizations of linear partial-adjustment models in Chapter 14 was by introducing state dependence. State dependence applies in situations in which the size of an increment depends on the level of the outcome. Usually we expect the size of typical increments to increase with the size of the system. For example, year-to-year fluctuations in the gross national product (GNP) of the United States usually exceed the level of GNP in a small nation, not to mention the

⟨15⟩ Geometric Brownian Motion

size of the annual change in GNP in such a country. Similarly, large organizations typically hire and fire many more employees per unit of time than do small organizations. A model based on the assumption of independent increments does not make much sense (even as a baseline model) in such settings. What, then, is a reasonable baseline model of pure noise for a state-dependent process? One reasonable approach is to base the model on the assumption that *percentage* (or fractional) changes are independent. One model with this property is **geometric Brownian motion**.

Suppose that $Y(t)$ is a stochastic outcome that tells the size of some group, the level of productivity of an individual or a system, or some such metric quantity. In the interest of defining a baseline model, we begin by assuming that $Y(t)$ grows exponentially with growth rate $r(t)$:

$$\frac{dY(t)}{dt} = r(t)Y(t), \qquad (11)$$

or that

$$\frac{Y(t)}{y(0)} = \exp\left[\int_0^t r(u)\, du\right].$$

Now suppose that $r(t)$ is a random variable reflecting exogenous conditions. When conditions are unusually favorable, the growth rate rises; when conditions are unfavorable, the growth rate falls. Modeling growth in turbulent environments requires a description of how environments change over time, that is, a specification of the *autocorrelation function* of the environment. When many dimensions of the environment affect the growth rate and these dimensions vary independently, a model with zero autocorrelation is a plausible first approximation.

Recall from Chapter 12 that the lack of any finite autocorrelation in continuous time is the property defining white noise. This suggests that we replace the unknown growth rate $r(t)$ with a white-noise process $\sigma Z(t)$ to construct a baseline model of growth in a turbulent environment:

$$\frac{dY(t)}{dt} = \sigma Z(t) Y(t).$$

Then
$$\frac{Y(t)}{y(0)} = \exp\left[\int_0^t \sigma Z(u)\,\mathrm{d}u\right]$$
$$= \exp\left[\sigma \int_0^t \mathrm{d}W(u)\right]$$
$$= \exp[\sigma W(t) - \sigma W(0)].$$

Without loss of generality, $W(0)$ can be set equal to zero, giving

$$\frac{Y(t)}{y(0)} = e^{\sigma W(t)}. \qquad (12)$$

The right-hand side of (12) defines geometric Brownian motion. It implies that fractional increases (decreases) in the process are independent for nonoverlapping periods. Indeed, it defines a diffusion process confined to the nonnegative real numbers, that is, one with state space $\Omega = [0, \infty)$. Since increments in $W(t)$ are normally distributed, this diffusion generates a *log-normal distribution*. This process has become a standard baseline model in analysis of fluctuations in the value of financial instruments such as stocks and warrants (see the papers in Cootner, 1964). As we indicated above, it has also been used as a baseline model for population growth.

This model can be used without further extension to develop implications for growth in random environments. But incorporation of *explicit* causal factors into baseline stochastic models is a main objective of this book. One way of doing this, which we have already discussed, is to replace standard Brownian motion with Brownian motion with drift. For example, we might specify that the growth rate $r(t)$ is a Brownian-motion process with drift that is an explicit function of observed causal variables. Such specifications are helpful only if implications for transition probability densities of $Y(t)$ can be expressed explicitly in terms of the parameters that relate observed causal variables to the drift. The Itô transformation formula, which we discuss next, makes it possible to do so.

15.3 *The Itô Transformation Formula

Itô's stochastic calculus generalizes the operations of the classical calculus so that they apply to stochastic processes. The most

⟨15⟩ *The Itô Transformation Formula

important generalization concerns the chain rule. Recall that for a deterministic function $\phi[v,t]$,

$$\frac{\partial \phi[v(t),t]}{\partial t} = \frac{\partial \phi}{\partial v}\frac{dv}{dt} + \frac{\partial \phi}{\partial t}.$$

Suppose that the deterministic function $v(t)$ is replaced by a stochastic outcome $V(t)$ that is the solution of the following equation:

$$dV(t) = f[V(t),t]\,dt + g[V(t),t]\,dW(t). \tag{13}$$

We want to study the dynamics of some transform of $V(t)$, say $Y(t) \equiv \phi[V(t),t]$, in terms of the parameters of (13). One standard way to proceed is to express the differential of $V(t)$ in terms of a Taylor-series expansion:

$$dY(t) \equiv d\phi[V(t),t]$$
$$= \phi'_v\,dV(t) + \phi'_t\,dt + \frac{1}{2}\phi''_{vv}\,[dV(t)]^2$$
$$+ \frac{1}{2}\phi''_{vt}\,dV(t)\,dt + \frac{1}{2}\phi''_{tt}\,[dt]^2 + \cdots$$

where $\phi'_v \equiv \partial\phi/\partial v$, $\phi''_{vv} \equiv \partial^2\phi/\partial v^2$, and so forth. One can replace $dV(t)$ with the expression in (13) and make use of the fact given in (4) that $[dW(t)]^2 \approx dt$. Ignoring terms higher than first order yields

$$dY(t) = \phi'_v f[V(t),t]\,dt + \phi'_v g[V(t),t]\,dW(t) + \phi'_t\,dt$$
$$+ \frac{1}{2}\phi''_{vv} g^2[V(t),t]\,dt. \tag{14}$$

Because of the odd properties of Brownian motion, a second-order term involving a second derivative of $\phi[V(t),t]$ with respect to $V(t)$ is retained in this truncation. This term has no parallel in the chain rule for a deterministic function. Just as Itô's stochastic integral contains one more term than its deterministic counterpart, so too does the Itô chain rule. The relationship in (14) is called **Itô's transformation formula** or **Itô's Lemma**.

We use Itô's transformation formula to solve the problem posed at the end of the previous section. In this discussion it is helpful to use different symbols for standard, drift-free Brownian motion and Brownian motion with drift. As in previous discussions, we let $W(t)$ denote standard, drift-free Brownian motion. We denote Brownian motion with drift μ and variance σ^2 by $B(t)$; hence

$$\mathrm{d}B(t) \equiv \mu\,\mathrm{d}t + \sigma\,\mathrm{d}W(t). \tag{15}$$

These definitions let us define **geometric Brownian motion with drift** as

$$Y(t) = y(0)\,\mathrm{e}^{B(t)} = y(0)\,\mathrm{e}^{\mu t + \sigma W(t)}. \tag{16}$$

In order to infer properties of the stochastic process $\{Y(t)\}$, we use Itô's Lemma, with $Y(t) \equiv \phi[V(t)] = \exp[V(t)]$, where $V(t) = B(t)$. Notice that $\partial\phi/\partial v = \partial^2\phi/\partial v^2$ and $\partial\phi/\partial t = 0$ for the exponential transformation. Therefore equation (14) becomes

$$\begin{aligned}\mathrm{d}Y(t) &= \left[\mu + \frac{1}{2}\sigma^2\right]\mathrm{e}^{B(t)}\,\mathrm{d}t + \mathrm{e}^{B(t)}\,\sigma\,\mathrm{d}W(t) \\ &= \left[\mu + \frac{1}{2}\sigma^2\right]Y(t)\,\mathrm{d}t + \sigma Y(t)\,\mathrm{d}W(t).\end{aligned} \tag{17}$$

Comparing (17) with (1) and using the rule in (9), we see that acccording to the Itô calculus,

$$\mu(y_t) = \left[\mu + \frac{1}{2}\sigma^2\right]y_t; \tag{18a}$$

$$\sigma^2(y_t) = \sigma^2 y_t^2. \tag{18b}$$

Consider again the model of exponential growth with a random growth rate $r(t)$. Instead of assuming that the growth rate is white noise, assume that it has some overall trend, which may be positive or negative. In particular, let

$$r(t) \equiv \alpha + \beta Z(t), \tag{19}$$

where α gives the trend in the growth rate. With this definition of $r(t)$, the growth model becomes

$$\begin{aligned}\mathrm{d}Y(t) &= \left[\alpha\,\mathrm{d}t + \beta Z(t)\right]Y(t) \\ &= \alpha Y(t)\,\mathrm{d}t + \beta Y(t)\,\mathrm{d}W(t).\end{aligned} \tag{20}$$

⟨15⟩ *The Itô Transformation Formula

When the model in (20) is interpreted in the Itô sense, the rules of correspondence in (9) imply that

$$\mu(y_t) = \alpha y_t, \tag{21a}$$
$$\sigma^2(y_t) = \beta^2 y_t^2, \tag{21b}$$

for $0 < y < \infty$. Notice the similarity of (18) and (21). Clearly the Itô solution of the growth model in (20) is a geometric Brownian-motion process with drift. Equating terms in (18) and (21) yields

$$\alpha = \mu + \frac{1}{2}\sigma^2 \text{ or } \mu = \alpha - \frac{1}{2}\sigma^2, \tag{22a}$$
$$\beta = \sigma. \tag{22b}$$

Given these identities, an explicit solution (in the Itô sense) to the growth model in (20) can be written in terms of geometric Brownian motion with drift. Replacing μ and σ in (16) with the expressions in (22) gives the solution

$$Y(t) = y(0)\, e^{(\alpha - \frac{1}{2}\beta^2)t + \beta W(t)}. \tag{23}$$

The Stratonovich solution differs from (23). Since the Stratonovich interpretation of a stochastic integral agrees with the usual calculus, it is appropriate simply to integrate the growth model in (20) for each sample path:

$$\int_0^t \frac{dY(s)}{Y(s)} = \int_0^t \alpha\, ds + \int_0^t \beta\, dW(s),$$

or

$$\log \frac{Y(t)}{y(0)} = \alpha t + \beta W(t),$$

$$Y(t) = y(0)\, e^{\alpha t + \beta W(t)}. \tag{24}$$

When the transformation rules in (10) are applied to (20), the local drift and local variance of $Y(t)$ in the Stratonovich sense are found to be

$$\mu(y_t) = \left(\alpha + \frac{1}{2}\beta^2\right) y_t, \tag{25a}$$
$$\sigma^2(y_t) = \beta^2 y_t^2. \tag{25b}$$

Although the two calculi agree that $Y(t)$ has a log-normal distribution for any finite t, they disagree about the value of the mean of $\log Y(t)$ [compare (23) and (24)]. The mean is αt according to the Stratonovich solution, but it is $\left(\alpha - \frac{1}{2}\beta^2\right)t$ according to the Itô solution. The two calculi agree, however, that its variance is $\beta^2 t$ [compare (9b) and (10b)]. Notice that the Stratonovich solution of the SDE implies that $Y(t)$ has the same mean as the corresponding deterministic model. The Itô solution, on the other hand, implies that environmental variability lowers the expected value of $Y(t)$. As can be seen by comparing the two drift terms, (21a) and (25a), the two solutions also differ in their implications for the probability of extinction, that is, that $Y(t) = 0$ for some $t < \infty$. Under the Stratonovich interpretation, the probability of extinction equals unity if $\alpha < 0$, zero when $\alpha > 0$, and one-half when $\alpha = 0$. But under the Itô interpretation, extinction may occur with probability 1 even when the average growth rate is positive (Tuckwell, 1974).

May (1974) argued that one should not make too much of these differences because these models are often used to make only qualitative conclusions about growth. Though the two interpretations give different quantitative results, their qualitative implications agree everywhere, except in a band whose width depends on α and β. Other analysts view the situation differently. Tuckwell (1974) and Capocelli and Ricciardi (1974) suggested that the quantitative differences have considerable substantive importance. They claimed that results of the Stratonovich interpretation appear substantively more reasonable, at least for models of growth of living species. Moreover, Feldman and Roughgarden (1975) showed that the Stratonovich calculus changes all qualitative conclusions for the more complex models on which May has focused, multispecies Lotka–Volterra models. Clearly the differences between the Itô and Stratonovich calculi cannot be side-stepped easily in this context.

15.4 Conclusions

These issues are remote from current sociological practice. But we think that sociological modeling will become more realistic if more emphasis is placed on stochastic processes and if linear models are supplanted with nonlinear models. If we are correct, the issues discussed in this chapter will eventually become central to continued progress in modeling social processes.

⟨ 15 ⟩   Conclusions

We have emphasized that there are two interpretations of the solution to nonlinear SDEs and that the two interpretations disagree about how to relate various quantities to the parameters of SDEs. Choice between the two interpretations is relevant whenever social processes are nonlinear and boundary behavior is substantively important. We think that both conditions apply to many phenomena of sociological interest and that many fundamental social processes are nonlinear and involve important boundaries.

16

Coupled Qualitative and Quantitative Processes

Many systems of interest to sociologists have both qualitative and quantitative features. Often these two kinds of features are interrelated. But as yet there are no standard methods for studying the dynamics of the interdependence of discrete and metric variables. Therefore, social scientists typically consider each aspect alone. Such partial treatment may be a necessary first step in any program of research, and it may give important insights into more complete models. But because partial analyses give only a limited view of the dynamics of social systems, they may also be misleading. Moreover, the lack of formal methods for analyzing the more complex dynamics of coupled qualitative and quantitative variables causes many social scientists to overlook the importance of dynamic relations involving quality and quantity. Inevitably it leads to research practices that do not address many fundamental sociological issues.

Our treatment has largely conformed to sociological convention: we have treated qualitative and quantitative dependent variables separately. However, we have departed from the prevailing practice by treating the two types of variables consistently. We have argued (especially in Chapter 11) that consistency has the advantage of facilitating systematic study of systems of qualitative and quantitative variables. In this chapter we discuss this theme briefly and comment on a variety of sociological applications. We discuss several approaches to modeling and empirical analysis. This discussion is necessarily tentative and preliminary.

Our objective in this chapter is to suggest a wide variety of

⟨16⟩ Quality and Quantity

processes involving coupled qualitative and quantitative outcomes, as well as to sketch alternative modeling strategies.

16.1 Quality and Quantity

A classic problem in sociology pertaining to coupled changes in quantity and quality concerns changes in size and form. The problem can be traced back as far as Herbert Spencer (1864). Spencer noted that the volume of a physical object increases at a faster rate than its external dimensions. He conjectured that this fact exerts a fundamental constraint on evolution. Species presumably cannot evolve to much larger sizes without changing form because a greater volume overburdens the skeletal structure. Spencer raised this observation to the status of a general law and argued that growth always creates differentiation in physical, biological, and social systems. Although Spencer clearly overstated his case, the notion that quantitative variations create qualitative changes is often fruitful. For example, D'Arcy Thompson in the classic *On Growth and Form* (1917) developed a rich set of implications of this simple idea for biological evolution.

Durkheim's (1933) model of the division of labor provides another example. Durkheim argued that population growth increases moral density. Greater moral density raises both the level and scope of economic competition, causing individuals (especially those who fail in competition) to explore new ways of making a living. Eventually a more complex division of labor arises and erodes the competitive pressures. But the more complex division of labor creates ripples of change throughout the various layers of social structure. Durkheim paid particular attention to the impacts of such changes on legal structure, arguing that the resulting social differentiation alters the substantive basis of law (from repressive to restitutive). So the growth of a population creates fundamental qualitative changes in the social structure.

Durkheim's model serves as a prototype for many sociological treatments of the dynamics of size and form. The same kind of argument recurs in many applications. A brief list includes the functionalist theory of normative change (Parsons, 1966), ecological theories of community structure (Hawley, 1950), theories of economic and political modernization (Deutsch, 1961; Almond and Powell, 1966), and more recent theories of change in bureaucratic organizations (Blau, 1970; Scott, 1975).

Many of these arguments can be studied by conventional methods as long as the qualitative dimension is treated narrowly. Consider the relationship between changes in scale and form in growing bureaucracies. One can formalize the process in terms of the relationship between the number of employees in an organization and the *number* of levels in its administrative hierarchy. This is the usual solution. However, the problem of modeling the effects of growth in scale on the *forms* of authority is much harder. If we move away from treating the qualitative dimension as a set of counts (e.g., number of levels, number of rules) and raise questions of variations among a set of forms (e.g., traditional versus bureaucratic forms of authority), models become much more subtle and complex. These issues strain conventional methods.

The problem can be seen more clearly when the unilinear evolutionary imagery of Spencer and Durkheim is abandoned. In Chapter 2 we emphasized the sociological importance of changes in social boundaries. Consider Tilly's (1978) argument that each social system contains a discrete number of organized interests that collectively define the boundary between central and peripheral populations. Over time, interest groups move in and out of the center of the polity as the relative power of populations changes. But Tilly argues that the political process is conflict ridden so that the time path of change is unlikely to be smooth. When the position of some collectivity in the periphery begins to rise, its leaders increase their attempts to penetrate the center. With each rebuff, the level of grievance in the peripheral population rises. If the power and the level of grievance of the rebelling groups continue to rise, the likelihood of explosive collective action (food riots, revolts, and so forth) increases. Eventually the quantitative change in the position of the collectivity and its associated interest group(s) may be translated into a set of discrete collective events.

Collective events often bring a response from the center, in many cases attempts at repression. These may increase levels of grievance in peripheral the population or even destroy its organization. Sometimes the newly powerful interest group may actually penetrate the center. Its power then typically becomes institutionalized and the likelihood of further violent collective action declines, perhaps precipitously.

According to this view, a social movement's history consists of a set of fluctuations in power and levels of grievance, overlaid with an event history—outbreaks of violent acts and attempts at repression. A complete model of the process must relate two kinds of variables. It must specify the effects of the levels of power and grievance on the outbreak of violent events. It must also specify the effects of violent events on the levels of power and grievance over time. In other words, it must model a dynamic system with causal feedback between quantitative and qualitative variables.

16.2 Approaches

We have already mentioned the conventional approach, which is to ignore the coupling between qualitative and quantitative variables and study the process of change in the two kinds of outcomes separately. In subsequent sections we suggest some other strategies.

16.2.1 Fully Quantitative Analysis

Sometimes it is useful to transform a problem involving quantity and quality into a completely quantitative problem. As a first approximation, one may assume that qualitative states reflect points (or intervals) on an underlying metric scale. For example, consider the problem of relating changes in an organization's size and changes in the degree to which its rules are formalized. The latter is often conceptualized and measured as a small set of types of rule systems. Suppose there are four types. Then organizations can be thought of as changing among these four states. If the states are ordered, one might argue that the four states correspond to segments of an underlying continuous variable: the level of formalization. When such an assumption is warranted, one can begin by assigning integers to the four states. If the numerical assignment corresponds to the approximate distance between states, one can analyze changes among the states as diffusion along the underlying metric scale. Thus the problem of modeling links between changes in size and changes in formalization becomes a problem in analyzing coupled diffusion processes [or stochastic differential equations (SDEs)].

Although the approach just sketched may be useful as a first approximation, it relies on the ability to assign a metric to a set of categories in a substantively meaningful way. Cases in which such an assignment is problem free are few. Thus, there is a need for alternative ways of modeling change in coupled qualitative and quantitative variables that do not rely on such strong assumptions about measurement.

Diffusion models with boundaries (see Chapter 12) have some of the characteristics needed for models of coupled qualitative and quantitative outcomes. The behavior of a stochastic process at a boundary introduces some qualitative aspects into otherwise quantitative models. For example, some processes, such as population growth, have a natural boundary at zero. Once the process hits the boundary, the process stops because the population has become extinct. One may apply this idea to a subpopulation as well as to an entire population. Extinction of a subpopulation may bring about a qualitative change in the form of the system. This simple example suggests how the device of including boundaries in a dynamic process of a quantitative outcome can introduce qualitative changes.

This framework can be applied to some of the sociological applications mentioned earlier. Consider, for example, possible boundary specifications for a general trivariate stochastic process involving two metric variables, levels of grievance and power, and one discrete variable, whether a violent collective disturbance is occurring. Figure 16.1 illustrates hypothetical sample paths for these three interdependent variables. Panel (a) shows a diffusion process with a sticky boundary for the level of grievance of some peripheral group, $G(t)$. The boundary at $G^\dagger > 0$ is the threshold at which grievances turn into explosive violence. Violent collective protest occurs whenever $G(t)$ is above this boundary, as depicted by the dotted paths in all three panels of Figure 16 and in particular by the time path for $V(t)$ in panel (b). Violence persists for some random holding time, $u = t_2 - t_1$. In a realistic application the holding time would depend on the nature of the response by the center. Panel (c) shows two possible sample paths of the diffusion of the level of power of the peripheral population, $P(t)$. One sample path jumps to a higher level of power following the violent action. It illustrates collective violence that produces a qualitative change in the power of the interest group. The second sample path jumps to a lower level; perhaps repression has lowered the group's power. An important component of a general model for such a process is the probability process governing the distribution of jumps from the boundary. This process could

⟨16⟩ Approaches

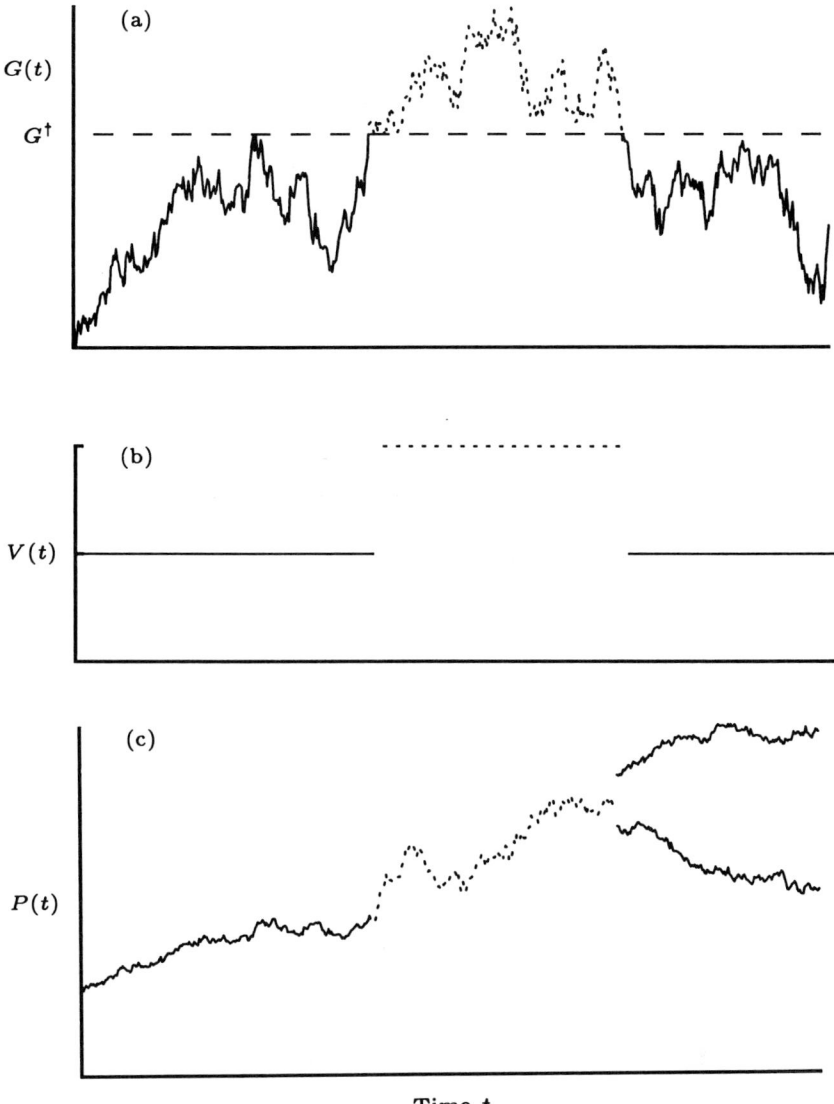

Figure 16.1. Hypothetical stochastic processes for three coupled variables: (a) the level of grievance $G(t)$ of a peripheral group; (b) whether violent collective protest is occurring, $V(t)$; and (c) the level of power of the peripheral group, $P(t)$. Dotted segments denote paths during a violent protest.

reflect substantive arguments about the conditions under which violent protest is a successful strategy (e.g., see Gamson, 1975). Alternatively, one can specify a different process after the jump from the boundary. This modification is appropriate if collective violence tends to change features of organizations such as organizing tactics and the composition of leadership.

While such complex methods may be difficult to implement, we think that they have a practical value by suggesting classes of simpler models that incorporate some of the features of the full process. Section 16.2.3 discusses one way of introducing a variety of complex qualitative behavior at boundaries.

Before moving to a simpler, more feasible strategy, we briefly mention a set of models that resemble those just discussed at least superficially. These are the mathematical models of catastrophes (Thom, 1975); for a nontechnical overview, see Fararo (1978). These models extend geometric or topological theories to explain changes in form, which Thom called morphogenesis. The set of catastrophe points in a space are the points of discontinuity. Most scientific treatments exclude such points. Thom argued that we need more general models that treat both the stable dynamics of systems in the continuous portion of the space *and* the qualitative changes that occur in the regions of discontinuities. Much of the interest in catastrophe theory focuses on the hypothesis that qualitatively distinct catastrophes are limited to a small number identified by Thom. He claimed that by understanding the properties of these catastrophes, it may be possible to unify the treatment of the evolution of forms in many disciplines and at many levels of analysis.

This program has strong appeal. However, a nontrivial application requires an understanding of the topology of the process. It is no accident that Thom's most convincing applications concern problems for which rich quantitative theory already exists. Sociological theories do not seem to be developed nearly well enough for such applications to be part of our discipline's agenda in the near future.

16.2.2 Fully Qualitative Analysis

Another approach is to move in the opposite direction from the simplification sketched at the beginning of Section 16.2.1. Rather than assume that qualitative states denote points on an underlying

⟨ 16 ⟩ Approaches

metric scale, one can collapse all quantitative variables into a set of ordered states. With regard to coupled changes in size and formalization, for example, one might break the size distribution into four or five categories and study changes in the qualitative state space defined by the Cartesian product of the state spaces of the two categorical variables.

We have actually used this kind of simplification to study a problem discussed extensively in Chapter 6: the impact of negative income tax (NIT) treatments on marital stability. Study of the treatments' effects on marital stability is complicated because the treatments also affect labor supply, the average number of hours worked per year. We have argued that NIT effects on labor supply lead to changes in income and independence and thereby alter the marital-dissolution rate. In addition, marital status is known to affect labor supply. Thus, the effect of NIT treatments on labor supply and marital status may partially be *indirect*, reflecting adjustments to changes induced in the other. In order to analyze the *direct* effects of the treatment on either outcome, one must analyze a model that links labor supply and marital status. Since labor supply is a quantitative variable and marriage is qualitative, this problem requires analysis of changes in coupled quantitative and qualitiative variables.

Since much of the observed variation in hours worked reflects movement between the states "employed" and "not employed," one way to proceed is to study the effects of the NIT treatments on changes in a state space defined by employment and nonemployment of husband and wives, and by marital status (married or not married). Tuma, Hannan, and Groeneveld (1980) [see also Groeneveld, Hannan, and Tuma (1983)] reported such an analysis, which we have summarized in Section 9.2. The results indicate that the NIT treatments had a direct effect on the rate of marital dissolution, as well as an indirect effect via changes in employment status. The main point for the present discussion is that much can be learned about the coupled process by converting it to a simpler one involving only qualitative distinctions. Given the relative ease with which such models can be estimated, as we showed in Chapter 9, this kind of approximation is likely to play a prominent role in the initial stages of sociological research on the class of problems discussed in this chapter.

16.2.3 Coupled Discrete and Continuous Processes

A final strategy attempts to remain true to the basic conceptualization of the problem, treating quantitative variables as quantitative and qualitative variables as qualitative. It combines the two main approaches discussed in this book—the style of qualitative analysis discussed in Part II and the kind of quantitative analysis discussed in Part III. Formally, this approach requires specifying bivariate (more generally, multivariate) continuous-time stochastic processes in which the outcome space is a mixture of both discrete and metric variables. Such a model has one or more equations relating hazard functions or transition rates to sets of causal variables and one or more stochastic differential or diffusion equations. Moreover, the two sets of equations are coupled. The hazard functions or transition rates depend on the level of the metric variable(s), and the local mean and local variance of the diffusion equation(s) depend on the value of the discrete variable(s). The diffusion process is then a **switching process**: its parameters switch on and off depending on the states of the qualitative outcome.

Consider again the problem of relating modeling labor supply and marital status jointly. Let $\mathbf{y}(t)$ be a vector of the relevant labor supply variables and $\mathbf{x}(t)$ be a vector of observed causal variables including the NIT treatments. We would like to estimate parameters of the function

$$r(t) = f[\mathbf{y}(t), \mathbf{x}(t)],$$

where $r(t)$ is the rate of marital dissolution at time t. Recall that the survivor function $G(t)$ depends on levels of time-varying variables at all times prior to t:

$$G(t) = \exp\left[-\int_{t_0}^{t} r(s)\,ds\right] = \exp\left[-\int_{t_0}^{t} f[\mathbf{y}(s), \mathbf{x}(s)]\,ds\right].$$

According to this model, the marital dissolution rate fluctuates with changes in the stochastic process describing labor supply.

Suppose the labor supplied in the market by a person is modeled as a diffusion process. To be consistent with economic treatments, we might postulate that the local drift reflects some rational decision-making process, perhaps linear partial adjustment to the optimal level of labor supply. Economic and sociological arguments

⟨16⟩ Approaches   537

imply that the optimal level—hence the local drift—depends on marital status. The local variance might also depend on marital status; for example, married persons might take or be exposed to smaller risks. Thus, in the simplest realistic model, labor supply would be a diffusion process in which parameters in the local drift and local variance switch at dates of changes in marital status.[1]

As in the discussion above and in our treatment of the purely qualitative aspects of marriage and work in Section 9.2, one might introduce coupling as **cross-state dependence**. The rate of change in each outcome (either a transition rate or the time differential in the level of a metric variable) depends on the current level of the other. Though this approach seems natural and appropriate, it is not the only possibility. One might argue that the rate of marital dissolution depends not just on the *level* of husbands' and wives' work efforts but also on the *rate of change* in their work efforts. Similarly one might argue that changes in labor supply depend not (or not only) on current marital status but on the current likelihood of dissolution. We might think of this argument as proposing **cross-rate dependence**. When the rates of change in quantitative and qualititative outcomes are coupled directly in this fashion, models become even more complex. Cross-state dependence involves coupling of unobservable variables [$dy(t)/dt$ and $r(t)$] with observable variables [$y(t)$ and current marital status]. Cross-rate dependence introduces coupling between unobservable variables. Clearly, some cost in complication of analysis results from this shift.

For most substantive problems that we have considered, state dependence fits the substantive arguments reasonably well. When analyses are based on this strategy, the techniques discussed in earlier chapters can be adapted to estimate coupled systems of quantitative and qualitative outcomes. However, one needs quite complete data: full event histories for the qualitative outcome(s) *and* observations on the levels of the quantitative outcomes at the dates of changes in the qualitative variable(s), and preferably more often.

Adapting the techniques discussed in earlier chapters to coupled processes is likely to be far from simple. Analysis of realistic

---

[1] A more complete model might assume that the characteristics of the spouse affect labor supply decisions. We ignore this complexity for the present, assuming that individuals behave the same in all marriages.

continuous-state stochastic processes is complicated enough without introducing switching processes on parameters. Thus, although the approach sketched in this section has considerable appeal as a way to unify the quantitative and qualitative approaches, it is not yet a practical strategy for research. However, we are hopeful that serious applications of the methods and models that we have proposed for simpler problems will pave the way for implementation of the strategy discussed here.

16.3 Conclusions

We think each of the strategies described above has possible payoffs for sociological investigation and hope to see them implemented in a wide variety of contexts. Although any one analysis is unlikely to resolve all of the uncertainties and complexities of the relationship between dynamics of quantity and quality in social organization, the use of these approaches might shed new light on old problems. Moreover, as we have argued above, it will redirect sociological modeling to fundamental substantive problems.

References

AALEN, O. O. (1978) "Nonparametric inference for a family of counting processes." *Annals of Statistics* **6**, 701–726.

AITKEN, A. C. (1935) "On least squares and linear combinations of observations." *Proceedings of the Royal Society of Edinburgh* **55**, 42–48.

ALMOND, G. A., & POWELL, G. B., JR. (1966) *Comparative politics: a developmental approach.* Boston: Little, Brown.

AMEMIYA, T. (1967) "A note on the estimation of Balestra–Nerlove models." Technical Report No. 4, Institute for Mathematical Studies in the Social Sciences, Stanford University.

ANDERSEN, R. S., & BLOOMFIELD, P. (1974) "Numerical differentiation procedures for non-exact data." *Numerische Mathematik* **22**, 157–182.

ARNOLD, V. I. (1973) *Ordinary differential equations* (translated by R. A. Silverman). Cambridge, Massachusetts: MIT Press.

AYALA, F. J. (1978) "The mechanisms of evolution." *Scientific American* **239**, 56–69.

AYALA, F. J., GILPIN, J. G., & EHRENFELD, J. G. (1973) "Competition between species: theoretical models and experimental tests." *Theoretical Population Biology* **4**, 331–356.

BACHELIER, L. (1900) "Theorie de la speculation." *Annales Scientifiques de l'Ecole Normale Supérieure* **3**. [Reprinted in P. Cootner (Ed.), *The random character of stock market prices.* Cambridge, Massachusetts: MIT Press, 1964.]

BALESTRA, P., & NERLOVE, M. (1966) "Pooling cross section and time series data in the estimation of a dynamic model: the demand for natural gas." *Econometrica* **34**, 585–612.

BALTES, P. B., & REINERT, G. (1969) "Cohort effects in cognitive development of children as revealed by cross-sectional sequences." *Developmental Psychology* **1**, 169–177.

BANKS, A. S. (1977) *Political handbook of the world.* New York: McGraw-Hill.

BANKS, A. S., & TEXTOR, R. (1963) *A cross-polity survey.* Cambridge, Massachusetts: MIT Press.

BARNARD, C. I. (1938) *The functions of the executive.* Cambridge, Massachusetts: Harvard University Press.

BARTEL, A. P., & BORJAS, G. J. (1977) "Middle-age job mobility: its determinants and consequences." Working Paper No. 161. New York: National Bureau of Economic Research.

BARTHOLOMEW, D. J. (1957) "A problem in life testing." *Journal of the American Statistical Association* **52**, 350–356.

BARTHOLOMEW, D. J. (1963) "The sampling distribution of an estimate arising in life testing." *Technometrics* **5**, 361–374.

BARTHOLOMEW, D. J. (1973) *Stochastic models for social processes* (2nd ed.). New York: Wiley.

BARTLETT, M. S., & RAJALAKMAN, D. V. (1953) "Goodness of fit tests for simultaneous autoregressive series." *Journal of the Royal Statistical Society* **B15**, 107–124.

BECKER, G. S. (1975) *Human capital* (2nd ed.). New York: Columbia University Press.

BECKER, G. S. (1981) *A treatise on the family.* Cambridge, Massachusetts: Harvard University Press.

BECKER, G. S., LANDES, E., & MICHAEL, R. (1977) "An economic analysis of marital instability." *Journal of Political Economy* **85**, 1141–1187.

BERGSTROM, A. R. (1966) "Non-recursive models as discrete approximations to systems of stochastic differential equations." *Econometrica* **34**, 173–182.

BERGSTROM, A. R. (Ed.) (1976) *Statistical inference in continuous time economic models.* Amsterdam: North-Holland.

BERK, R. A., RAUMA, D., MESSINGER, S. L., & COOLEY, T. F. (1981) "A test of the stability of punishment hypothesis." *American Sociological Review* **46**, 805–828.

BERKSON, J. (1944) "Application of the logistic function to bioassay." *Journal of the American Statistical Association* **39**, 357–365.

BIELBY, W. T., HAUSER, R. M., & FEATHERMAN, D. L. (1977) "Response errors of nonblack males in models of intergenerational transmission of socioeconomic status." *American Journal of Sociology* **82**, 1242–1288.

References

BILLINGSLEY, P. (1961) *Statistical inference in Markov processes.* Chicago: University of Chicago Press.

BISHOP, Y. M. M., FIENBERG, S. E., & HOLLAND, P. W. (1975) *Discrete multivariate analysis: theory and practice.* Cambridge, Massachusetts: MIT Press.

BLALOCK, H. M., JR. (1970) "Estimating measurement error using multiple indicators and several points in time." *American Sociological Review* **35**, 101–117.

BLAU, P. M. (1964) *Exchange and power in social life.* New York: Wiley.

BLAU, P. M. (1970) "A formal theory of differentiation in organizations." *American Sociological Review* **35**, 201–218.

BLAU, P. M., & DUNCAN, O. D. (1967) *The American occupational structure.* New York: Wiley.

BLUMEN, I., KOGAN, M., & MCCARTHY, P. J. (1955) *The industrial mobility of labor as a probability process.* Cornell Studies in Industrial and Labor Relations No. 6. Ithaca: Cornell University Press.

BOAG, J. W. (1949) "Maximum likelihood estimates of the proportion of patients cured by cancer therapy." *Journal of the Royal Statistical Society* **B11**, 15–53.

BOLT, B. (1978) "Summary value smoothing of physical time series with unequal intervals." *Journal of Computational Physics* **29**, 357–369.

BONACICH, E. (1972) "A theory of ethnic antagonism: the split labor market." *American Sociological Review* **37**, 547–559.

BONACICH, E. (1975) "Abolition, the extension of slavery and the position of free blacks: a study of split labor markets in the United States, 1830–1863." *American Journal of Sociology* **81**, 601–628.

BOYCE, W. E., & DIPRIMA, R. C. (1969) *Elementary differential equations* (2nd ed.). New York: Wiley.

BOX, G. E. P., & JENKINS, G. M. (1976) *Time series analysis: forecasting and control* (2nd ed.). San Francisco: Holden-Day.

BRAUN, M. (1975) *Differential equations and their applications: an introduction to applied mathematics.* New York: Springer-Verlag.

BREIMAN, L. (1968) *Probability.* Reading, Massachusetts: Addison-Wesley.

BRESLOW, N. E. (1974) "Covariance analysis of censored survival data." *Biometrics* **30**, 89–99.

BRITTAIN, J., & FREEMAN, J. H. (1980) "Organizational proliferation and density-dependent selection." In J. Kimberly and R. Miles (Eds.), *The organizational life cycle*, pp. 291–338. San Francisco: Jossey-Bass.

BUMPASS, L. L., & SWEET, J. A. (1972) "Differentials in marital instability: 1970." *American Sociological Review* **37**, 754–766.

CAMPBELL, D. T. (1963) "From description to experimentation: interpreting trends as quasi-experiments." In C. W. Harris (Ed.), *Problems in measuring change*, pp. 212–242. Madison: University of Wisconsin Press.

CAPOCELLI, R. M., & RICCIARDI, L. M. (1974) "A diffusion model for population growth in a random environment." *Theoretical Population Biology* **5**, 28–41.

CARROLL, G. R. (1979) "Dynamics of national educational expansion: an extension of the Nielsen–Hannan model." Mimeographed. Department of Sociology, Stanford University.

CARROLL, G. R. (1981) "Dynamics of organizational expansion in national educational systems." *American Sociological Review* **46**, 585–599.

CARROLL, G. R. (1982) *Publish and perish: a dynamic analysis of environmental selection in the American local newspaper industry from 1800 to 1975.* Unpublished Ph. D. Dissertation, Stanford University.

CARROLL, G. R., & DELACROIX, J. (1982) "Organizational mortality in the newspaper industries of Argentina and Ireland: an ecological approach." *Administrative Science Quarterly* **27**, 169-199.

CARROLL, G. R., HANNAN, M. T., TUMA, N. B., & WARSAVAGE, B. (1978a) "Alternative estimation procedures for event-history analysis: a Monte Carlo study." Technical Report No. 70, Laboratory for Social Research, Stanford University.

CARROLL, G. R., HANNAN, M. T., TUMA, N. B., & WARSAVAGE, B. (1978b) "The impact of measurement error in the analysis of log-linear rate models." Technical Report No. 69, Laboratory for Social Research, Stanford University.

CHAMBERLAIN, G. (1979) "Heterogeneity, omitted variables bias, and duration dependence." Discussion Paper No. 691, Harvard Institute of Economic Research, Harvard University.

CHASE-DUNN, C. (1975) "The effects of international economic dependence on development and inequality." *American Sociological Review* **40**, 720–738.

CHIANG, C. L. (1968) *Introduction to stochastic processes in biostatistics.* New York: Wiley.

ÇINLAR, E. (1975) *Introduction to stochastic processes.* Englewood Cliffs, New Jersey: Prentice-Hall.

COHEN, J. E., & SINGER, B. (1979) "Malaria in Nigeria: constrained continuous-time Markov models for discrete-time longitudinal data on human mixed-species infections." In S. Levin (Ed.), *Lectures on mathematics in the life sciences*, vol. 12, pp. 69–133. Providence: American Mathematical Society.

COHEN, L. E., & LAND, K. C. (1979) "Social change and crime rate trends: a routine activities approach." *American Sociological Review* **44**, 588–607.

COLEMAN, J. S. (1964a) *Introduction to mathematical sociology*. New York: Free Press.

COLEMAN, J. S. (1964b) *Models of change and response uncertainty*. Englewood Cliffs, New Jersey: Prentice-Hall.

COLEMAN, J. S. (1968) The mathematical study of change. In H. M. Blalock, Jr. and A. Blalock (Eds.), *Methodology in social research*, pp. 428–478. New York: McGraw-Hill.

COLEMAN, J. S. (1973) *The mathematics of collective action*. Chicago: Aldine.

COLEMAN, J. S. (1981) *Longitudinal data analysis*. New York: Basic Books.

COLEMAN, J. S., BLUM, Z. D., SØRENSEN, A. B., & ROSSI, P. H. (1972) "White and black careers during the first decade of labor force experience." *Social Science Research* **1**, 243–270.

COLEMAN, J. S., KATZ, E., & MENZEL, H. (1966) *Medical innovation: a diffusion study*. New York: Bobbs-Merrill.

CONVERSE, P. (1976) *The dynamics of party support: cohort-analysis of party identification*. Beverly Hills: Sage Publications.

COOTNER, P. (Ed.) (1964) *The random character of stock market prices*. Cambridge, Massachusetts: MIT Press.

CORCORAN, M. (1979) "Work experience, work interruption, and wages." In G. J. Duncan and J. N. Morgan (Eds.), *Five thousand American families: patterns of economic growth*, vol. VI, pp. 47–103. Ann Arbor: Institute for Social Research.

COX, D. R. (1962) *Renewal theory*. London: Methuen.

COX, D. R. (1972) "Regression models and life tables." *Journal of the Royal Statistical Society* **B34**, 187–220.

COX, D. R. (1975) "Partial likelihood." *Biometrika* **62**, 269–276.

COX, D. R., & MILLER, H. D. (1965) *The theory of stochastic processes*. London: Methuen.

CRANO, W. D., KENNY, D. A., & CAMPBELL, D. T. (1972) "Does intelligence cause achievement? A cross-lagged panel analysis." *Journal of Educational Psychology* **63**, 258–275.

CROW, J. F., & KIMURA, M. (1970) *An introduction to population genetics theory*. New York: Harper and Row.

CUNNINGHAM, E. P., & HENDERSON, C. R. (1968) "An iterative procedure for estimating fixed effects and variance components in mixed model situations." *Biometrics* **24**, 13–25.

CUSHING, J. M. (1977) *Integrodifferential equations and delay models in population dynamics.* New York: Springer-Verlag.

DAVIS, J. A. (1978) "Studying categorical data over time." *Social Science Research* **7**, 151–179.

DEMPSTER, A. P., LAIRD, N., & RUBIN, D. (1977) "Maximum likelihood from incomplete data via the EM algorithm." *Journal of the Royal Statistical Society* **39B**, 1–38.

DEUTSCH, K. W. (1961) "Social mobilization and political development." *American Political Science Review* **55**, 493–514.

DHRYMES, P. (1970) *Econometrics: statistical foundations and applications.* New York: Harper and Row.

DIEKMANN, A., & MITTER, P. (1983) "The 'sickle hypothesis'. A time dependent Poisson model with applications to deviant behavior and occupational mobility." *Journal of Mathematical Sociology* **9**, 85–101.

DIPRETE, T. A. (1981) "Unemployment over the life cycle: racial differences and the effect of changing economic conditions." *American Journal of Sociology* **87**, 286–307.

DIXON, R. (1980) "Hybrid corn revisited." *Econometrica* **48**, 1451–1461.

DOOB, J. L. (1953) *Stochastic processes.* New York: Wiley.

DOREIAN, P., & HUMMON, N. P. (1976) *Modeling social processes.* Amsterdam: Elsevier.

DOREIAN, P., & HUMMON, N. P. (1977) Estimates for differential equation models of social phenomena. In D. R. Heise (Ed.), *Sociological Methodology 1977*, pp. 180–208. San Francisco: Jossey-Bass.

DRAZGA, L. S. (1978) *Stochastic models for conflict and decision-making: an application to conformity behavior.* Unpublished Ph. D. Dissertation, Stanford University.

DUNCAN, O. D. (1966) Methodological issues in the analysis of social mobility. In N. Smelser and S. M. Lipset (Eds.), *Social structure and social mobility in economic development*, pp. 51–97. Chicago: Aldine.

DUNCAN, O. D. (1969) "Some linear models for two-variable panel analysis." *Psychological Bulletin* **72**, 177–182.

DUNCAN, O. D. (1972) Unmeasured variables in linear models for panel analysis. In H. L. Costner (Ed.), *Sociological Methodology 1972*, pp. 36–82. San Francisco: Jossey-Bass.

DUNCAN, O. D. (1975) *Introduction to structural equation models.* New York: Academic Press.

DUNCAN, O. D., FEATHERMAN, D. L., & DUNCAN, B. (1972) *Socioeconomic background and achievement.* New York: Seminar Press.

DUNCAN, R. P., & PERRUCCI, C. C. (1976) "Dual occupation families and migration." *American Sociological Review* **41**, 252–261.

DURKHEIM, E. (1933; original 1893) *The division of labor in society* (translated by G. Simpson). Glencoe, Illinois: Free Press.

DURKHEIM, E. (1951; original 1897) *Suicide* (translated by J. A. Spaulding and G. Simpson). Glencoe, Illinois: Free Press.

DUVERGER, M. (1968) La sociologie des partis politiques. In G. Gurvitch (Ed.), *Traite de sociologie,* vol. II (3rd ed.), pp. 22–45. Paris: Presses Universitaires.

DYNKIN, E. B., & YUSHKEVICH, A. A. (1969) *Markov processes: theorems and problems* (translated by J. S. Wood). New York: Plenum.

EFRON, B. (1977) "The efficiency of Cox's likelihood function for censored data." *Journal of the American Statistical Association* **72**, 557–565.

ELANDT-JOHNSON, R. C., & JOHNSON, N. L. (1980) *Survival models and data analysis.* New York: Wiley.

EMERSON, R. (1962) "Power-dependence relations." *American Sociological Review* **27**, 31–41.

ERDELYI, A. (Ed.) (1954) *Tables of integral transforms,* Vols. I and II. New York: McGraw-Hill.

ESMER, Y. (1979) "Political mobilization and economic development: a confirmatory factor analysis." In J. W. Meyer and M. T. Hannan (Eds.), *National development and the world system: educational, economic and political change, 1950–1970,* pp. 117–127. Chicago: University of Chicago Press.

FARARO, T. J. (1978) "An introduction to catastrophes." *Behavioral Science* **23**, 291–317.

FEIGL, P., & ZELEN, M. (1965) "Estimation of exponential survival probabilities with concomitant information." *Biometrics* **21**, 826–838.

FELDER, H. E. (1975) "Job search: an empirical analysis of the search behavior of low income workers." Research Memorandum No. 25, Center for the Study of Welfare Policy, Menlo Park, California: SRI International.

FELDMAN, M., & ROUGHGARDEN, J. (1975) "A population's stationary distribution and chance of extinction in a stochastic environment with remarks on the theory of species packing." *Theoretical Population Biology* **7**, 197–207.

FELLER, W. (1952) "The parabolic differential equations and the associated semi-groups of transformations." *Annals of Mathematics* **55**, 468–519.

FELLER, W. (1971) *An introduction to probability theory and its applications* vol. II (2nd ed.). New York: Wiley.

FIENBERG, S. E., & MASON, W. M. (1978) "Identification and estimation of age-period cohort models in the analysis of discrete archival data." In K. F. Schuessler (Ed.), *Sociological Methodology 1979*, pp. 1–67. San Francisco: Jossey-Bass.

FLINN, C., & HECKMAN, J. J. (1982) "New methods for analyzing individual event histories." In S. Leinhardt (Ed.), *Sociological Methodology 1982*, pp. 99–140. San Francisco: Jossey-Bass.

FONER, A., & KERTZER, D. (1978) "Transitions over the life course: lessons from age-set societies." *American Journal of Sociology* **83**, 1081–1104.

FORM, W. H., & MILLER, D. C. (1949) "Occupational career patterns as a sociological instrument." *American Journal of Sociology* **54**, 317–329.

FREEMAN, J. H., CARROLL, G. R., & HANNAN, M. T. (1983) "The liability of newness: age dependence in organizational death rates." *American Sociological Review* **48**, 692–710.

FREEMAN, J. H., & HANNAN, M. T. (1975) "Growth and decline processes in organizations." *American Sociological Review* **40**, 215–228.

FREEMAN, J. H., & HANNAN, M. T. (1981) "Effects of resources and enrollments on growth and decline in school districts: evidence from California and New York." Technical Report No. 81-B1, Institute for Research on Educational Finance and Governance, Stanford University.

FREEMAN, J. H., & HANNAN, M. T. (1983) "Niche width and the dynamics of organizational populations." *American Journal of Sociology* **88**, 1116–1145.

FREEMAN, J. H., HANNAN, M. T., & HANNAWAY, J. (1978) "The dynamics of school district administrative intensity: effects of enrollments and finances in five states." Final report on Contract HEW-76-0177. Cambridge, Massachusetts: Abt Associates.

FULLER, W., & BATTESE, G. (1974) "Estimation of linear models with crossed-error structure." *Journal of Econometrics* **2**, 67–78.

References

GAMSON, W. (1975) *The strategy of social protest.* Homewood, Illinois: Dorsey Press.

GERALD, C. F. (1977) *Applied numerical analysis* (2nd ed.). Reading, Massachusetts: Addison-Wesley.

GHEZ, G. R. & BECKER, G. S. (1975) *The allocation of time and goods over the life cycle.* New York: National Bureau of Economic Research.

GILL, P. F., & MURRAY, W. (1972a) "The implementation of two modified Newton algorithms for unconstrained optimization." National Physical Laboratory Report NAC 24.

GILL, P. F., & MURRAY, W. (1972b) "Two methods for the solution of linearly constrained and unconstrained optimization problems." National Physical Laboratory Report NAC 25.

GINSBERG, R. B. (1971) "Semi-Markov processes and mobility." *Journal of Mathematical Sociology* **1**, 233–262.

GLENN, N. (1977) *Cohort analysis.* Beverly Hills: Sage Publications.

GOEL, N., & RICHTER-DYN, N. (1974) *Stochastic models in biology.* New York: Academic Press.

GOLDBERGER, A. S. (1964) *Econometric theory.* New York: Wiley.

GOLDBERGER, A. S. (1971) "Econometrics and psychometrics: a survey of communalities." *Psychometrika* **36**, 83–107.

GOLDBERGER, A. S. (1973) "Efficient estimation in over-identified models: an interpretative analysis." In A. S. Goldberger and O. D. Duncan (Eds.), *Structural Equation Models in the Social Sciences,* pp. 131–152. New York: Seminar Press.

GOMPERTZ, B. (1825) "On the nature of the function expressive of the law of human mortality." *Philosophical Transactions of the Royal Society* **115**, 513–583.

GOODMAN, L. A. (1968) "Analysis of cross-classified data: independence, quasi-independence, and interactions in contingency tables with or without missing entries." *Journal of American Statistical Association* **63**, 1091–1131.

GOODMAN, L. A. (1972a) "A modified multiple regression approach to the analysis of dichotomous variables." *American Sociological Review* **37**, 28–46.

GOODMAN, L. A. (1972b) "A general model for the analysis of surveys." *American Journal of Sociology* **77**, 1035–1086.

GOODMAN, L. A. (1973) "Causal analysis of data from panel studies and other kinds of surveys." *American Journal of Sociology* **78**, 1135–1191.

GRANGER, C. W. J. (1969) "Investigating causal relations by econometric models and cross-spectral methods." *Econometrica* **37**, 424–438.

GRANOVETTER, M. S. (1974) *Getting a job: a study of contacts and careers.* Cambridge, Massachusetts: Harvard University Press.

GRILICHES, Z. (1957) "Hybrid corn: an exploration in the economics of technological change." *Econometria* **25**, 501–522.

GRIZZLE, J. E., STARMER, C. F., & KOCH, G. G. (1969) "Analysis of categorical data by linear models." *Biometrics* **28**, 489–504.

GROENEVELD, L. P., HANNAN, M. T., & TUMA, N. B. (1983) *Seattle-Denver Income Maintenance Experiment final report, Volume I, Part 5: marital stability.* Washington, D. C.: Government Printing Office.

GROENEVELD, L. P., TUMA, N. B., & HANNAN, M. T. (1980) "The effects of NIT programs on marital stability." *Journal of Human Resources* **15**, 654–674.

GROSS, A. J., & CLARK, V. A. (1975) *Survival distributions.* New York: Wiley.

HANNAN, M. T. (1979) "The dynamics of ethnic boundaries in modern states." In J. W. Meyer and M. T. Hannan (Eds.), *National development and the world system: educational, economic and political change, 1950–1970*, pp. 253–275. Chicago: University of Chicago Press.

HANNAN, M. T., & CARROLL, G. R. (1981) "Dynamics of formal political structure: an event-history analysis." *American Sociological Review* **46**, 19–35.

HANNAN, M. T., & FREEMAN, J. H. (1977a) "The population ecology of organizations." *American Journal of Sociology* **82**, 929–964.

HANNAN, M. T., & FREEMAN, J. H. (1977b) "Obstacles to comparative studies." In P. S. Goodman and J. M. Pennings and Associates (Eds.), *New perspectives on organizational effectiveness*, pp. 103–131. San Francisco: Jossey-Bass.

HANNAN, M. T., & FREEMAN, J. H. (1978) "Internal politics of growth and decline." In M. Meyer and Associates (Eds.), *Environments and organizations*, pp. 177–199. San Francisco: Jossey-Bass.

HANNAN, M. T., & TUMA, N. B. (1979) "Methods for temporal analysis." *Annual Review of Sociology* **5**, 303–328.

HANNAN, M. T., TUMA, N. B., & GROENEVELD, L. P. (1976) "The impact of income maintenance on the making and breaking of marital unions: an interim report." Center for the Study of Welfare Policy, Research Memorandum No. 28. Menlo Park, California: SRI International.

References

HANNAN, M. T., TUMA, N. B., & GROENEVELD, L. P. (1977a) "Income and marital events: evidence from an income maintenance experiment." *American Journal of Sociology* **82**, 1186–1211.

HANNAN, M. T., TUMA, N. B., & GROENEVELD, L. P. (1977b) "A model for the effect of income maintenance on rates of marital dissolution: evidence from the Seattle and Denver income maintenance experiments." Center for the Study of Welfare Policy, Research Memorandum No. 44. Menlo Park, California: SRI International.

HANNAN, M. T., TUMA, N. B., & GROENEVELD, L. P. (1978) "Income and independence effects on marital dissolution: results from the Seattle and Denver income maintenance experiments." *American Journal of Sociology* **84**, 611–633.

HANNAN, M. T., & YOUNG, A. A. (1974) "Estimation of pooled cross-section and time series models: preliminary Monte Carlo results." Paper presented at Conference on Policy Research in Education: Methods and Implications, University of Wisconsin, Madison.

HANNAN, M. T., & YOUNG, A. A. (1977) "Estimation in panel models: results on pooling cross-sections and time series." In D. R. Heise (Ed.), *Sociological Methodology 1977*, pp. 52–83. San Francisco: Jossey-Bass.

HANUSHEK, E., & JACKSON, J. (1977) *Statistical methods for social scientists*. New York: Academic Press.

HASTINGS, N. A. J., & PEACOCK, J. B. (1974) *Statistical Distributions*. London: Butterworth.

HAUSER, R. M. (1977) "A structural model of the mobility table." *Social Forces* **56**, 919–953.

HAUSER, R. M., KOFFEL, J. N., TRAVIS, H. P., & DICKINSON, P. J.. (1975) "Temporal change in occupational mobility: evidence from men in the United States." *American Sociological Review* **40**, 279–297.

HAUSER, R. M., & SEWELL, W. H. (1975) *Education, occupation and earnings*. New York: Academic Press.

HAUSMAN, J. A., HALL, B. H., & GRILICHES, Z. (In press) "Econometric models for count data with an application to the patents R&D relationship." *Econometrica*.

HAWLEY, A. (1950) *Human ecology: a theory of community structure*. New York: Ronald Press.

HECKMAN, J. J. (1978) "Simple statistical models for discrete panel data developed and applied to test the hypothesis of true state dependence against the hypothesis of spurious state dependence." *Annals de l'INSEE* **30–31**, 227–269.

HECKMAN, J. J. (1979) "Sample selection bias as a specification error." *Econometrica* **47**, 153–161.

HECKMAN, J. J. (1981) "Statistical models for discrete panel data." In C. Manski and D. McFadden (Eds.), *Structural analysis of discrete data with econometric applications*, pp. 114–178. Cambridge, Massachusetts: MIT Press.

HECKMAN, J. J., & SINGER, B. (1982a) "Population heterogeneity in demographic models." In K. C. Land, & A. Rogers (Eds.), *Multidimensional mathematical demography*, pp. 567–599. New York: Academic Press.

HECKMAN, J. J., & SINGER, B. (1982b) "The identification problem in econometric models for duration data." In W. Hildenbrand (Ed.), *Advances in econometrics*. Cambridge: Cambridge University Press.

HECKMAN, J. J., & WILLIS, R. J. (1976) "Estimation of a stochastic model of reproduction: an econometric approach." In N. E. Terleckyj (Ed.), *Household production and consumption*, pp. 99–138. New York: National Bureau of Economic Research.

HEISE, D. R. (1970) "Causal inference from panel data." In E. F. Borgotta and G. W. Bohrnstedt (Eds.), *Sociological Methodology 1970*, pp. 3–27. San Francisco: Jossey-Bass.

HENDERSON, C. R. (1952) "Specific and combining ability." In J. W. Gowens (Ed.), *Heterosis*, pp. 352–370. Ames, Iowa: Iowa State College Press.

HENDERSON, C. R. (1953) "Estimation of variance and covariance components." *Biometrics* **9**, 226–251.

HENDERSON, C. R. (1963) "Selection index and expected genetic advance." In *Statistical genetics in plant breeding*. National Research Council Publication No. 982. Washington, D. C.: National Academy of Sciences.

HENDERSON, C. R., JR. (1971) "Comment on 'The use of error components models in combining cross section and time series data.'" *Econometrica* **39**, 397–402.

HERBST, P. G. (1963) "Organizational commitment: a decision process model." *Acta Sociologica* **7**, 34–46.

HERNES, G. (1972) "The process of entry into first marriage." *American Sociological Review* **37**, 173–182.

HIBBS, D. A., JR. (1977) "On analyzing the effects of policy interventions: Box–Jenkins and Box–Tiao versus structural equation models." In D. R. Heise (Ed.), *Sociological Methodology 1977*, pp. 137–179. San Francisco: Jossey-Bass.

References

HOEL, P. G., PORT, S. C., & STONE, C. J. (1972) *Introduction to stochastic processes.* Boston: Houghton Mifflin.

HOEM, J. M. (1972) "Inhomogeneous semi-Markov processes, select actuarial tables, and duration-dependence in demography." In T. N. E. Greville (Ed.), *Population dynamics.* New York: Academic Press.

HOEM, J. M. (1983) "Weighting, misclassification, and other issues in the analysis of survey samples of life histories." Stockholm Research Reports in Demography, No. 11, Section for Demography, Department of Statistics, University of Stockholm.

HOGAN, D. P. (1978) "The variable order of events in the life course." *American Sociological Review* **43**, 573–586.

HOLLAND, P. W., & LEINHARDT, S. (1977) "A dynamic model for social networks." *Journal of Mathematical Sociology* **5**, 5–20.

HOLT, J. D. (1978) "Competing risk analyses with special reference to matched pair experiments." *Biometrika* **65**, 159–165.

HOMANS, G. C. (1950) *The human group.* New York: Harcourt, Brace & Co.

HORVATH, W. J. (1968) "A statistical model for the duration of wars and strikes." *Behavioral Science* **13**, 18–28.

HOWARD, R. A. (1971) *Dynamic probability systems, vol. II: semi-Markov and decision processes.* New York: Wiley.

HUMMON, N. P., DOREIAN, P., & TEUTER, K. (1975) "A structural control model of organizational change." *American Sociological Review* **40**, 813–824.

HUNTINGTON, S. P. (1968) *Political order in changing societies.* New Haven: Yale University Press.

HUTCHINSON, G. E. (1957) "Concluding remarks." *Cold Spring Harbor Symposium on Quantitative Biology* **22**, 415–427.

IBRDWT (various years) *International Bank for Reconstruction and Development World Tables.* Washington, D. C.: International Bank for Reconstruction and Development.

IJIRI, Y., & SIMON, H. A. (1977) *Skew distributions and the sizes of business firms.* Amsterdam: North-Holland.

INVERARITY, J. (1976) "Populism and lynching in Louisiana, 1889–1896: a test of Erickson's theory of the relationship of boundary crises and repressive justice." *American Sociological Review* **41**, 262–279.

ITŌ, K. (1944) "Stochastic integral." *Proceedings of Imperial Academy of Tokyo* **20**, 519–524.

JAZWINSKI, A. H. (1970) *Stochastic processes and filtering theory.* New York: Academic Press.

JOHNK, M. D. (1964) "Erzung von betaverteiler und gammaverteiler zufallzahlen." *Metrika* **8(2)**, 5–15.

JOHNSON, N. L., & KOTZ, S. (1970) *Continuous univariate distributions*, vol. II. New York: Houghton Mifflin.

JOHNSTON, J. (1972) *Econometric methods* (2nd ed.). New York: McGraw-Hill.

JÖRESKOG, K. G. (1970) "A general method for the analysis of covariance structures." *Biometrika* **57**, 239–251.

JÖRESKOG, K. G., & SORBOM, D. (1976) "Statistical models and methods for analysis of longitudinal data." In D. J. Aigner and A. S. Goldberger (Eds.), *Latent variables in socioeconomic models*, pp. 285–325. Amsterdam: North-Holland.

JORGENSON, D. W. (1961) "Multiple regression analysis of a Poisson process." *Journal of the American Statistical Association* **56**, 235–245.

JOVANOVICH, B. (1979a) "Job matching and the theory of turnover." *Journal of Political Economy* **87**, 972–990.

JOVANOVICH, B. (1979b) "Firm specific capital and turnover." *Journal of Political Economy* **87**, 1246–1260.

KALBFLEISCH, J. D., & PRENTICE, R. L. (1978) "Marginal likelihoods based on Cox's regression and life model." *Biometrika* **60**, 267–278.

KALBFLEISCH, J. D., & PRENTICE, R. L. (1980) *The statistical analysis of failure time data*. New York: Wiley.

KAPLAN, E. L., & MEIER, P. (1958) "Nonparametric estimation from incomplete observations." *Journal of the American Statistical Association* **53**, 457–481.

KARLIN, S., & TAYLOR, H. M. (1975) *A first course in stochastic proceses* (2nd ed.). New York: Academic Press.

KARLIN, S., & TAYLOR, H. M. (1981) *A second course in stochastic processes*. New York: Academic Press.

KEIDING, N. (1975) "Maximum likelihood estimation in the birth-and-death process." *The Annals of Statistics* **3**, 363–372.

KELLEY, J. (1973) "Causal chain models for the socioeconomic career." *American Sociological Review* **38**, 481–493.

KENDALL, M. G., & BUCKLAND, W. R. (1971) *A dictionary of statistical terms* (3rd ed.). Edinburgh: Oliver and Boyd.

KENNY, D. A. (1973) "Cross-lagged and synchronous common factors in panel data." In A. S. Goldberger and O. D. Duncan (Eds.), *Structural equation models in the social sciences*, pp. 153–167. New York: Seminar Press.

KENNY, D. A. (1975) "Cross-lagged panel correlation: a test for spuriousness." *Psychological Bulletin* **82**, 345–362.

KNUTH, D. E. (1969) *The art of computer programming*, vol. II. Cambridge, Massachusetts: Addison-Wesley.

KNUTH, D. E. (1979) *TEXand METAFONT: new directions in typesetting*. Bedford, Masschusetts: American Mathematical Society and Digital Press.

KNUTH, D. E. (1984) *The TEXbook*. Reading, Massachusetts: Addison-Wesley.

KOHN, M. L., & SCHOOLER, C. (1978) "The reciprocal effects of the substantive complexity of work and intellectual flexibility: a longitudinal assessment." *American Journal of Sociology* **84**, 24–52.

KUH, E. (1959) "The validity of cross-sectionally estimated behavior equations in time series applications." *Econometrica* **39**, 341–358.

KUSHNER, H. J. (1974) "On the weak convergence of interpolated Markov chains to a diffusion." *Annals of Probability* **2**, 40–50.

LANCASTER, A. (1972) "A stochastic model for the duration of a strike." *Journal of the Royal Statistical Society* **A135**, 257–271.

LAND, K. C. (1970) "Mathematical formalization of Durkheim's theory of the causes of the division of labor." In E. F. Borgotta and G. W. Bohrnstedt (Eds.), *Sociological Methodology 1970*, pp. 257–282. San Francisco: Jossey-Bass.

LAND, K. C., & FELSON, M. (1976) "A general framework for building dynamic macro social indicator models: including an analysis of changes in crime rates and police expenditures." *American Journal of Sociology* **82**, 565–604.

LAZARSFELD, P. F. (1940) "Panel studies." *Public Opinion Quarterly* **4**, 122–128.

LAZARSFELD, P. F. (1948) "The use of panels in social research." *Proceedings of the American Philosophy of Sociology* **92**, 405–410.

LAZARSFELD, P. F., BERELSON, B. R., & GAUDET, H. (1944) *The people's choice*. New York: Duell, Sloan and Pearce.

LEOWONTIN, R. C., & COHEN, J. E. (1969) "On population growth in a randomly varying environment." *Proceedings of the National Academy of Sciences* **62**, 1056–1060.

LESLIE, P. H. (1958) "A stochastic model for studying the properties of certain biological systems by numerical methods." *Biometrika* **45**, 16–31.

LEVINS, R. (1969) "The effect of random variations of different types on population growth." *Proceedings of the National Academy of Sciences* **62**, 1061–1065.

LIPSET, S. M. (1960) *Political man*. Garden City, New York: Doubleday.
LIPSET, S. M. (1963) *The first new nation*. New York: Basic Books.
LOFTIN, C., & MCDOWELL, D. (1982) "The police, crime, and economic theory: an assessment." *American Sociological Review* **47**, 393–401.
LORD, F. M., & NOVICK, M. R. (1968) *Statistical theory of mental test scores*. Reading, Massachusetts: Addison-Wesley.
LOTKA, A. (1925) *Elements of mathematical biology*. New York: Dover.
LOTKA, A. (1932) "The growth of mixed populations: two species competing for a common food supply." *Journal of the Washington Academy of Sciences* 21: 461–469. [Reprinted in F. M. Scudo and J. R. Ziegler (Eds.), *The golden age of theoretical ecology: 1923–1940*. New York: Springer-Verlag, 1978.]
LUENBERGER, D. G. (1979) *Introduction to dynamic systems: theory, models, and applications*. New York: Wiley.
MACURDY, T. E. (1981) "An empirical model of labor supply in a life cycle setting." *Journal of Political Economy* **89**, 1059–1085.
MADDALA, G. S. (1971) "The use of variance components models in pooling cross-section and time series data." *Econometrica* **39**, 341–358.
MADDEN, C. H. (1957) "Some temporal aspects of the growth of cities in the United States." *Economic Development and Cultural Change* **6**, 143–170.
MALINVAUD, E. (1970) *Statistical methods of econometrics* (2nd. ed., translated by A. Silvey). Amsterdam: North-Holland.
MANTON, K. G., & STALLARD, E. (1980) "A stochastic compartment model representation of chronic disease dependence: techniques for evaluating parameters of partially unobserved age inhomogeneous stochastic processes." *Theoretical Population Biology* **18**, 57–75.
MANTON, K. G., STALLARD, E., & VAUPEL, J. W. (1983) "Alternative estimates of the heterogeneity of mortality risks among the aged." Mimeographed, Duke University.
MARCH, J. G., & SIMON, H. A. (1958) *Organizations*. New York: Wiley.
MAY, R. M. (1974) *Stability and complexity in model ecosystems* (2nd ed.). Princeton: Princeton University Press.
MAYER, T. F. (1972) "Models of intragenerational mobility." In J. Berger, M. Zelditch, Jr., and B. Anderson (Eds.), *Sociological theories in progress*, vol. II, pp. 308–357. Boston: Houghton Mifflin.
MAYER, T. F., & ARNEY, W. R. (1974) "Spectral analysis and the study of social change." In H. L. Costner (Ed.), *Sociological Methodology 1973–1974*, pp. 305–355. San Francisco: Jossey-Bass.

References

MCGARTY, T. (1974) *Stochastic systems and state estimation*. New York: Wiley.

MCGINNIS, R. (1968) "A stochastic model of social mobility." *American Sociological Review* **33**, 712–722.

MENDENHALL, W., & LEHMAN, E. H. JR. (1960) "An approximation to the negative moments of the positive binominal useful in life testing." *Technometrics* **2**, 227–242.

MENKEN, J., TRUSSELL, J., STEMPEL, D., & BABAKOL, O. (1981) "Proportional hazards life table models: an illustrative analysis of socio-demographic influences on marriage dissolution in the United States." *Demography* **18**, 181–200.

MEYER, J. W. (1980) "The world polity and the authority of the nation state." In A. Bergesen (Ed.), *Studies of the modern world-system*, pp. 109–137. New York: Academic Press.

MEYER, J. W., & HANNAN, M. T. (EDS.) (1979) *National development and the world system: educational, economic, and political change, 1950–1970*. Chicago: University of Chicago Press.

MEYER, M. (1975) "Leadership and organizational structure." *American Journal of Sociology* **81**, 514–542.

MICHELS, R. (1959; original 1915) *Political parties: a sociological study of the oligarchical tendencies of modern democracy* (translated by E. Pane and C. Pane). New York: Dover.

MILLER, R. G., & HALPERN, J. (1981) "Regression with censored data." Technical Report No. 86, Division of Biostatistics, Stanford University.

MILLS, J. P. (1926) "Table of the ratio: area to bounding ordinate for any portion of normal curve." *Biometrika* **18**, 395–400.

MINCER, J. (1974) *Schooling, experience, and earnings*. New York: National Bureau of Economic Research.

MOLOTCH, H. (1977) "The city as a growth machine: toward a political economy of place." *American Journal of Sociology* **82**, 309–332.

MORRISON, P. M. (1970) "Movers and stayers: an analysis based on two longitudinal data files." Technical Report P-4409, The Rand Corporation, Santa Monica, California.

MORTENSEN, R. (1969) "Mathematical problems of modeling stochastic nonlinear dynamic systems." *Journal of Statistical Physics* **1**, 271–296.

MURRAY, W., (Ed.) (1972) *Numerical methods for unconstrained optimization*. New York: Academic Press.

NELSON, J. F. (1981) "Multiple victimization in American cities: a statistical analysis of rare events." *American Journal of Sociology* **85**, 871–891.

NELSON, R., & WINTER, S. (1982) *An evolutionary theory of economic change.* Cambridge, Massachusetts: Harvard University Press.

NELSON, W. (1972) "Theory and application of hazard plotting for censored failure data." *Technometrics* **14**, 945–965.

NERLOVE, M. (1971) "Further evidence on the estimation of dynamic economic relations from a time series of cross-sections." *Econometrica* **39**, 359–382.

NERLOVE, M., & PRESS, S. J. (1973) *Univariate and multivariate log-linear and logistic models.* Santa Monica, California: Rand Corporation.

NIELSEN, F. (1978) *Linguistic conflict in Belgium: an ecological approach.* Unpublished Ph. D. Dissertation, Stanford University.

NIELSEN, F. (1980) "The Flemish movement in Belgium after World War II: a dynamic analysis." *American Sociological Review* **45**, 76–94.

NIELSEN, F., & HANNAN, M. T. (1977) "The expansion of national educational systems: tests of a population ecology model." *American Sociological Review* **42**, 479–490.

NIELSEN, F., & ROSENFELD, R. A. (1981) "Substantive interpretations of differential equation models." *American Sociological Review* **46**, 159–174.

OAKES, D. (1977) "The asymptotic information in censored survival data." *Biometrika* **64**, 441–448.

OLVER, F. W. J. (1965) "Bessel functions of integral order." In M. Abramowitz and I. A. Stegun (Eds.), *Handbook of mathematical functions,* pp. 355–436. New York: Dover.

OLZAK, S. (1982) "Ethnic mobilization in Quebec." *Ethnic and Racial Studies* **5**, 253–275.

PAIGE, J. M. (1975) *Agrarian revolution: social movements and export agriculture in the underdeveloped world.* New York: Free Press.

PALMER, G. L. (1954) *Labor mobility in six cities.* New York: Social Science Research Council.

PANEL ON YOUTH. (1973) *Youth: transition to adulthood.* Washington, D. C.: Office of Science and Technology, Executive Office of the President.

PARKER, R. N. (1981) "Structural constraint and career earnings patterns." *American Sociological Review* **46**, 844–892.

PARNES, H. S. (1975) "The national longitudinal surveys: new vistas for labor market research." *American Economic Review* **65**, 244–249.

PARSONS, T. (1966) *Societies: evolutionary and comparative perspectives.* Englewood Cliffs, New Jersey: Prentice-Hall.

PELZ, D. C., & ANDREWS, F. M. (1964) "Causal priorities in panel study data." *American Sociological Review* **29**, 836–848.

References

PETO, R., & PETO, J. (1972) "Asymptotically efficient rank invariant test procedures." *Journal of the Royal Statistical Society* **A135**, Part II, 185–207.

PHILLIPS, A. W. (1957) "The estimation of parameters in systems of stochastic differential equations." *Biometrika* **46**, 67–76.

PHILLIPS, D. T., & BEIGHTLER, C. S. (1972) "Procedure for generating gamma variates with non-integer parameter sets." *Journal of Statistical Computation and Simulation* **1**, 197–208.

PHILLIPS, P. C. B. (1972) "The structural estimation of a stochastic differential equation system." *Econometrica* **40**, 1021–1042.

PHILLIPS, P. C. B. (1974) "The estimation of some continuous time models." *Econometrica* **42**, 803–824.

PIELOU, E. C. (1969) *An introduction to mathematical ecology.* New York: Wiley-Interscience.

PITCHER, B. L., HAMBLIN, R. L., & MILLER, J. L. L. (1978) "The diffusion of collective violence." *American Sociological Review* **43**, 23–35.

PRENTICE, R. L., & KALBFLEISCH, J. D. (1979) "Hazard rate models with covariates." *Biometrics* **35**, 25–39.

PRENTICE, R. L., KALBFLEISCH, J. D., PETERSON, A. V., JR., FLOURNOY, N., FAREWELL, V. T., & BRESLOW, N. E.. (1978) "The analysis of failure times in the presence of competing risks." *Biometrics* **34**, 541–554.

PULLUM, T. W. (1977) "Parameterizing age, period, and cohort effects: an application to U. S. delinquency rates, 1964–1973." In K. F. Schuessler (Ed.), *Sociological Methodology 1978*, pp. 116–140. San Francisco: Jossey-Bass.

PYKE, R. (1961a) "Markov renewal processes: definitions and preliminary properties." *Annals of Mathematical Statistics* **32**, 1231–1242.

PYKE, R. (1961b) "Markov renewal processes with finitely many states." *Annals of Mathematical Statistics* **32**, 1243–1259.

RAO, C. R. (1965) *Linear statistical inference and its applications.* New York: Wiley.

RICHARDSON, L. F. (1960) *Arms and insecurity.* Pittsburgh: Boxwood Press.

ROBINSON, P. M. (1976) "The estimation of linear differential equations with constant coefficients." *Econometrica* **44**, 751–764.

ROBINS, P. K., TUMA, N. B., & YAEGER, K. E. (1980) "Effects of the Seattle and Denver income maintenance experiments on changes in employment status." *Journal of Human Resources* **15**, 545–573.

ROGOSA, D. (1979) "Causal models in longitudinal research: rationale, formulation, and interpretation." In J. R. Nesselroade and P. B. Baltes (Eds.), *Longitudinal research in human development: design and analysis*, pp. 263–302. New York: Academic Press.

ROGOSA, D. (1980a) "A critique of cross-lagged panel analysis." *Psychological Bulletin* **88**, 245–258.

ROGOSA, D. (1980b) "Time and time again: some analysis problems in longitudinal research." In C. Bidwell and D. M. Windham (Eds.), *The analysis of educational productivity, Volume II: issues in macroanalysis*, pp. 153–201. Cambridge, Massachusetts: Ballinger.

ROSENFELD, R. A. (1978) "Women's intergenerational occupational mobility." *American Sociological Review* **43**, 36–46.

ROSENFELD, R. A. (1980) "Race and sex differences in career dynamics." *American Sociological Review* **45**, 583–609.

ROUGHGARDEN, J. (1979) *Theory of population genetics and evolutionary ecology: an introduction.* New York: Macmillian.

RUBINSON, R. (1976) "The world economy and the distribution of income within states: a cross-national study." *American Sociological Review* **41**, 638–659.

RYDER, N. B. (1965) "The cohort as a concept in the study of social change." *American Sociological Review* **30**, 843–861.

SAATY, T. L. (1967) *Modern nonlinear equations.* New York: McGraw-Hill.

SARGAN, J. D. (1974) "Some discrete approximations to continuous time stochastic models." *Journal of the Royal Statistical Society* **B36**, 74–90.

SARTORI, G. (1976) *Parties and party systems*, vol. I. Cambridge: Cambridge University Press.

SCOTT, W. R. (1975) "Organizational structure." *Annual Review of Sociology* **1**, 1–20.

SCUDO, F. M., & ZIEGLER, J. R., (Eds.) (1978) *The golden age of theoretical ecology: 1923–1940.* New York: Springer-Verlag.

SEARLE, S. R. (1971a) *Linear models.* New York: Wiley.

SEARLE, S. R. (1971b) "Topics in variance components estimation." *Biometrics* **27**, 1–76.

SEWELL, W. H., HAUSER, R. M., & FEATHERMAN, D. L. (1976) *Schooling and achievement in American society.* New York: Academic Press.

SHORTER, E., & TILLY, C. (1970) "The shape of strikes in France." *Comparative Studies of Society and History* **13**, 60–86.

SILCOCK, H. (1954) "The phenomenon of labour turnover." *Journal of the Royal Statistical Society* **A117**, 429–440.
SIMON, H. A. (1957) *Models of man.* New York: Wiley.
SIMON, H. A. (1962) "The architecture of complexity." *Proceedings of the American Philosophical Society* **106**, 467–482.
SIMON, H. A. (1978) "Rationality as process and as product of thought." *American Economic Review Papers and Proceedings* **68**, 1–16.
SINGER, B. (1980) "Individual histories as the focus of analysis in longitudinal surveys." *Journal of Economics and Business* **49**, 273–305.
SINGER, B. (1981) "Estimation of nonstationary Markov chains." In S. Leinhardt (Ed.), *Sociological Methodology 1981*, pp. 319–337. San Francisco: Jossey-Bass.
SINGER, B., & COHEN, J. E. (1980) "Estimating malaria incidence and recovery rates from panel surveys." *Mathematical Biosciences* **49**, 273–305.
SINGER, B., & SPILERMAN, S. (1974) "Social mobility models for heterogeneous populations." In H. L. Costner (Ed.), *Sociological Methodology 1973–1974*, pp. 256–401. San Francisco: Jossey-Bass.
SINGER, B., & SPILERMAN, S. (1976a) "The representation of social processes by Markov models." *American Journal of Sociology* **82**, 1–54.
SINGER, B., & SPILERMAN, S. (1976b) "Some methodological issues in the analysis of longitudinal surveys." *Annals of Economic and Social Measurement* **5**, 447–474.
SJOBERG, G. (1963) "Rise and fall of cities: a theoretical perspective." *International Journal of Comparative Sociology* **4**, 107–120.
SKOCPOL, T. (1979) *States and social revolutions in France, Russia, and China.* Cambridge: Cambridge University Press.
SKOROKHOD, A. V. (1958) "Limit theorems for Markov processes." *Theoretical and Applied Probability* **3**, 202–246.
SNYDER, D., & TILLY, C. (1972) "Hardship and collective violence in France, 1830–1960." *American Sociological Review* **37**, 520–532.
SØRENSEN, A. B. (1975) "The structure of intragenerational mobility." *American Sociological Review* **40**, 456–471.
SØRENSEN, A. B. (1977) "Estimating rates from retrospective questions." In D. R. Heise (Ed.), *Sociological Methodology 1977*, pp. 209–223. San Francisco: Jossey-Bass.
SØRENSEN, A. B., & HALLINAN, M. T.. (1976) "A stochastic model for change in group structure." *Social Science Research* **5**, 43–61.
SØRENSEN, A. B., & HALLINAN, M. T.. (1977) "A reconceptualization of school effects." *Sociology of Education* **50**, 273–289.

SØRENSEN, A. B., & TUMA, N. B. (1981) "Labor market structures and job mobility." *Research in Social Stratification and Mobility* **1**, 67–94.

SPENCER, H. (1866–1867) *Principles of biology*. New York: Appleton.

SPILERMAN, S. (1970) "The causes of racial disturbances: a comparison of alternative explanations." *American Sociological Review* **35**, 627–649.

SPILERMAN, S. (1972a) "The analysis of mobility processes by the introduction of independent variables into a Markov chain." *American Sociological Review* **37**, 277–294.

SPILERMAN, S. (1972b) "Extensions of the mover-stayer model." *American Journal of Sociology* **78**, 599–626.

SPILERMAN, S. (1977) "Careers, labor market structure, and socioeconomic achievement." *American Journal of Sociology* **83**, 551–593.

STEVENSON, W. B. (1982) "The high and low frequency of change in organizational hierarchies." Paper presented at the Seventy-Seventh Annual Meeting of the American Sociological Association, San Francisco, California, September 6–10.

STINCHCOMBE, A. L. (1965) "Social structure and organizations." In J. G. March (Ed.), *Handbook of organizations*, pp. 142–193. Chicago: Rand-McNally. pp. 142–193.

STINCHCOMBE, A. L. (1968) *Constructing social theories*. New York: Harcourt, Brace, Jovanovich.

STRANG, G. (1976) *Linear algebra and its applications*. New York: Academic Press.

STRATONOVICH, R. L. (1966) "A new form of representing stochastic integrals and equations." *Journal of SIAM Control* **4**, 362–371.

STROOK, D. W., & VARADHAN, S. R. S. (1979) *Multidimensional diffusion processes*. New York: Springer-Verlag.

TAKACS, L. (1962) *Introduction to the theory of queues*. New York: Oxford University Press.

TARTER, M. E. (1979) "Trigonometric maximum likelihood estimation and application to the analysis of incomplete survival information." *Journal of the American Statistical Association* **74**, 132–139.

TAYLOR, C. L., & HUDSON, M. C. (1971) *World handbook of political and social indicators*, vol. II. Ann Arbor: University of Michigan Press.

THEIL, H. (1969) "A multinomial extension of the linear logit model." *International Economic Review* **10**, 251–259.

THEIL, H. (1970) On the estimation of relationships involving qualitative variables." *American Journal of Sociology* **76**, 103–154.

References

THOM, R. (1975) *Structural stability and morphogenesis* (translated by D. H. Fowler). Reading, Massachusetts: Benjamin.

THOMAS, G. M., RAMIREZ, F. O., MEYER, J. W., & GOBALET, J. G. (1979) "Maintaining national boundaries in the world system: the rise of centralist regimes." In J. W. Meyer and M. T. Hannan (Eds.), *National development and the world system: educational, economic and political change, 1950–1970*, pp. 85–116. Chicago: University of Chicago Press.

THOMPSON, D'A. W. (1917) *On growth and form*. Cambridge: Cambridge University Press.

TILLY, C. (Ed.) (1975) *The formation of nation states in western Europe*. Princeton: Princeton University Press.

TILLY, C. (1978) *From mobilization to revolution*. Reading, Massachusetts: Addison-Wesley.

TILLY, C., TILLY, L., & TILLY, R. (1975) *The rebellious century 1830–1930*. Cambridge, Massachusetts: Harvard University Press.

TRUSSELL, J., & HAMMERSLOUGH, C. (1983) "A hazards-model analysis of the covariates of infant and child mortality in Sri Lanka." *Demography* **20**, 1–27.

TRUSSELL, J., & RICHARDS, T. (In press) "Correcting for unobserved heterogeneity in hazard models using the Heckman–Singer procedure." In N. B. Tuma (Ed.), *Sociological Methodology 1985*. San Francisco: Jossey-Bass.

TSIATIS, A. (1975) "A nonidentifiability aspect of the problem of competing risks." *Proceedings of the National Academy of Sciences* **72**, 20–22.

TSIATIS, A. (1981) "A large sample study of Cox's regression model." *Annals of Statistics* **9**, 93–108.

TUCKWELL, H. C. (1974) "A study of some diffusion models of population growth." *Theoretical Population Biology* **5**, 345–357.

TUKEY, J. W. (1977) *Exploratory data analysis*. Reading, Massachusetts: Addison-Wesley.

TUKEY, J. W. (1980) "We need both exploratory and confirmatory." *The American Statistician* **34**, 23–25.

TUMA, N. B. (1972) *Stochastic models of social mobility: a comparative analysis and an application to job mobility of Mexican-American men*. Unpublished Ph. D. Dissertation, Michigan State University.

TUMA, N. B. (1973) "Incorporating independent variables into stochastic models of social mobility." Paper presented at the Sixty-Eighth Annual Meeting of the American Sociological Association, New York, New York, August 27–30.

Tuma, N. B. (1976) "Rewards, resources and rate of mobility: a nonstationary multivariate stochastic model." *American Sociological Review* **41**, 338–360.

Tuma, N. B. (1978) "Effects of labor market structure on job-shift patterns." Paper presented at the Seventy-Third Annual Meeting of the American Sociological Association, San Francisco, California, September 4–8, 1978.

Tuma, N. B. (1979) *Invoking RATE* (2nd ed.). Menlo Park, California: SRI International.

Tuma, N. B. (1980a) "When can interdependence in a dynamic system of qualitative variables be ignored?" In K. F. Schuessler (Ed.), *Sociological Methodology 1980*, pp. 358–391. San Francisco: Jossey-Bass.

Tuma, N. B. (1980b) "Further results on the effects of the Seattle and Denver Income Maintenance Experiments on changes in employment staus." Menlo Park, California: SRI International.

Tuma, N. B. (1982) "Nonparametric and partially parametric approaches to event-history analysis." In S. Leinhardt (Ed.), *Sociological Methodology 1982*, pp. 1–60. San Francisco: Jossey-Bass.

Tuma, N. B., & Hannan, M. T. (1978) "Approaches to the censoring problem in analysis of event histories." In K. F. Schuessler (Ed.), *Sociological Methodology 1979*, pp. 209–240. San Francisco: Jossey-Bass.

Tuma, N. B., Hannan, M. T., & Groeneveld, L. P. (1979) "Dynamic analysis of event histories." *American Journal of Sociology* **84**, 820–854.

Tuma, N. B., Hannan, M. T., & Groeneveld, L. P. (1980) "The effects of the Seattle and Denver Income Maintenance Experiments on marital dissolution conditional on spouses' employment statuses." Technical Memorandum SD.28. Menlo Park, California: SRI International.

Tuma, N. B., & Robins, P. K. (1980) "A dynamic model of employment behavior." *Econometrica* **48**, 1031–1052.

Tuma, N. B., Robins, P. K., & Smith-Donals, L. G. (1980) "Effects of the Seattle and Denver income maintenance experiments on changes in employment status: analysis of six years of data." Menlo Park, California: SRI International.

Tuma, N. B., & Smith-Donals, L. G. (1980a) "Husband-wife interactions and changes in employment status." Menlo Park, California: SRI International.

Tuma, N. B., & Smith-Donals, L. G. (1980b) "Differential labor force responses of husbands and wives on an NIT program:

a comparison of blacks, whites, and chicanos." Paper presented at the Seventy-Fifth Annual Meeting of the American Sociological Association, New York, New York, August 27–31.

TUMA, N. B., & YOUNG, A. A. (1976) "Constrained and unconstrained maximum-likelihood estimation of a variance components model of cross-sections pooled over time." Technical Report No. 60, Laboratory for Social Research, Stanford University.

TURELLI, M. (1977) "Random environments and stochastic calculus." *Theoretical Population Biology* **12**, 140–178.

UNDY (various years) *United Nations Demographic Yearbook.*

UNSY (various years) *United Nations Statistical Yearbook.*

UNYITS (various years) *United Nations Yearbook of International Trade Statistics.*

VAN KAMPEN, N. G. (1978) "An introduction to stochastic process for physicists." In L. Garrido, P. Selgar, and P. J. Shephard (Eds.), *Stochastic processes in nonequilibrium systems*, pp. 2–23. Berlin: Springer-Verlag.

VIGDERHOUS, G. (1977) "Forecasting sociological phenomena: applications of Box–Jenkins methodology to suicide rates." In K. F. Schuessler (Ed.), *Sociological Methodology 1978*, pp. 20–51. San Francisco: Jossey-Bass.

VOLTERRA, V. (1978; original 1927) "Variations and fluctuations in the number of coexisting animal species." In F. M. Scudo and J. R. Ziegler (Eds.), *The Golden Age of Theoretical Ecology: 1923–1940*, pp. 65–236. New York: Springer-Verlag.

WALLACE, T. D., & HUSSAIN, A. (1969) "The use of error components models in combining cross section and time series data." *Econometrica* **37**, 55–77.

WALLERSTEIN, I. (1966) "The decline of the party in single-party African states." In J. LaPalombara and M. Weiner (Eds.), *Political parties and political development*, pp. 201–214. Princeton: Princeton University Press.

WASSERMAN, S. S. (1977) *Stochastic models for directed graphs.* Unpublished Ph. D. Dissertation, Harvard University.

WHEATON, B., MUTHEN, B., ALWIN, D. F., & SUMMERS, G. F. (1977) "Assessing reliability and stability in panel models." In D. R. Heise (Ed.), *Sociological Methodology 1977*, pp. 84–136. San Francisco: Jossey-Bass.

WHITE, H. C. (1970) *Chains of opportunity: systems models of mobility in organizations.* Cambridge, Massachusetts: Harvard University Press.

WILSON, E. O., & BOSSERT, W. H. (1971) *A primer of population biology.* Stamford, Connecticutt: Linauer Associates.

WINSBOROUGH, H. H. (1978) "Statistical histories of the life cycle of birth cohorts: the transition from schoolboy to adult male." In K. E. Taeuber, L. L. Bumpass, and J. A. Sweet (Eds.), *Social demography,* pp. 231–259. New York: Academic Press.

WONG, E., & ZAKAI, M. (1965a) "On the convergence of ordinary integrals to stochastic integrals." *Annals of Mathematical Statistics* **36**, 1560–1564.

WONG, E., & ZAKAI, M. (1965b) "On the relation between ordinary and stochastic differential equations." *International Journal of Engineering* **3**, 213–229.

WYMER, C. R. (1972) "Econometric estimation of some stochastic differential equation systems." *Econometrica* **40**, 565–578.

Author Index

A

Aalen, O. O., 59, 74, 539
Aitken, A. C., 440, 442, 539
Almond, G. A., 190, 529, 539
Alwin, D. F., 37, 563
Amemiya, T., 439, 539
Andersen, R. S., 424, 539
Andrews, F. M., 33, 556
Arney, W. R., 39, 554
Arnold, V. I., 369, 539
Ayala, F. J., 490, 539

B

Babakol, O., 31, 555
Bachelier, L., 392, 539
Balestra, P., 433, 439, 539
Baltes, P. B., 192, 540
Banks, A. S., 308, 540
Barnard, C. I., 10, 540
Bartel, A. P., 195, 540
Bartholomew, D. J., 140, 230, 282, 467, 511, 512, 540
Bartlett, M. S., 461, 540
Battese, G., 446, 546
Becker, G. S., 5, 6, 193–195, 216, 540, 547

Beightler, C. S., 146, 557
Berelson, B. R., 18, 553
Bergstrom, A. R., 423, 461, 463, 464, 486, 540
Berk, R. A., 22, 540
Berkson, J., 298, 540
Bielby, W. T., 38, 540
Billingsley, P., 311, 541
Bishop, Y. M. M., 24, 541
Blalock, H. M., Jr., 37, 541
Blau, P. M., 5, 44, 346, 347, 378, 530, 541
Bloomfield, P., 424, 539
Blum, Z. D., 20, 44, 213, 543
Blumen, I., 30, 31, 156, 174, 175, 324, 541
Boag, J. W., 117, 541
Bolt, B., 424, 541
Bonacich, E., 389, 541
Borjas, G. J., 195, 540
Bossert, W. H., 468, 485, 564
Box, G. E. P., 39, 541
Boyce, W. E., 358, 541
Braun, M., 366, 389, 541
Breiman, L., 392, 541
Breslow, N. E., 251, 254, 541, 557

Brittain, J., 340, 541
Buckland, W. R., 47, 552
Bumpass, L. L., 25, 542

C

Campbell, D. T., 33, 542, 543
Capocelli, R. M., 520, 526, 542
Carroll, G. R., 31, 146, 224, 240, 307, 312, 313, 495–501, 542, 546, 548
Chamberlain, G., 262, 263, 434, 542
Chase-Dunn, C., 309, 542
Chiang, C. L., 113, 542
Çinlar, E., 113, 542
Clark, V. A., 43, 61, 548
Cohen, L. E., 22, 543
Cohen, J. E., 26, 27, 29, 305, 520, 559, 542, 553
Coleman, J. S., 20, 21, 26, 30–32, 34, 44, 106, 107, 110, 111, 156, 158, 208, 213, 268, 332, 334–336, 343, 344, 396, 422, 467, 543
Converse, P., 192, 543
Cooley, T. F., 22, 540
Cootner, P., 522, 543
Corcoran, M., 6, 543
Cox, D. R., 31, 96, 100, 113, 193, 232, 235, 236, 239, 247, 263, 278, 405, 543
Crano, W. D., 33, 543
Crow, J. F., 402, 519, 543
Cunningham, E. P., 445, 544
Cushing, J. M., 334, 544

D

Davis, J. A., 36, 544
Delacroix, J., 31, 224, 542
Dempster, A. P., 184, 544
Deutsch, K. W., 529, 544
Dhrymes, P., 120, 122, 544
Dickinson, P. J., 24, 549

Diekmann, A., 230, 544
DiPrete, T. A., 31, 544
DiPrima, R. C., 358, 541
Dixon, R., 493, 544
Doob, J. L., 393, 516, 544
Doreian, P., 22, 35, 39, 355, 544, 551
Drazga, L. S., 106, 544
Duncan, B., 5, 44, 545
Duncan, O. D., 5, 19, 34, 35, 37, 44, 331, 541, 544, 545
Duncan, R. P., 25, 545
Durkheim, E., 529, 530, 545
Duverger, M., 308, 545
Dynkin, E. B., 409, 545

E

Efron, B., 239, 247, 545
Ehrenfeld, J. G., 490, 539
Elandt-Johnson, R. C., 43, 545
Emerson, R., 5, 545
Erdelyi, A., 100, 545
Esmer, Y., 38, 545

F

Fararo, T. J., 534, 545
Farewell, V. T., 254, 557
Featherman, D. L., 5, 38, 44, 540, 545, 558
Feigl, P., 89, 545
Felder, H. E., 89, 545
Feldman, M., 520, 526, 546
Feller, W., 140, 402, 407, 546
Felson, M., 22, 553
Fienberg, S. E., 24, 192, 541, 546
Flinn, C., 31, 546
Flournoy, N., 254, 557
Foner, A., 8, 546
Form, W. H., 20, 546
Freeman, J. H., 35, 224, 340, 346, 347, 350, 354, 370, 371, 373, 375, 376, 379, 387, 541, 546, 548

Author Index

Fuller, W., 446, 546

G

Gamson, W., 190, 534, 547
Gaudet, H., 18, 553
Gerald, C. F., 486, 547
Ghez, G. R., 6, 547
Gill, P. F., 449, 547
Gilpin, J. G., 490, 539
Ginsberg, R. B., 95, 194, 547
Glenn, N., 192, 547
Gobalet, J. G., 307, 310, 315, 316, 318, 321, 561
Goel, N., 402, 406, 408, 547
Goldberger, A. S., 25, 34, 344, 547
Gompertz, B., 210, 547
Goodman, L. A., 24, 298, 311, 547
Granger, C. W. J., 38, 39, 548
Granovetter, M. S., 258, 548
Griliches, Z., 19, 493, 548, 549
Grizzle, J. E., 25, 548
Groeneveld, L. P., 5, 21, 31, 32, 106, 108, 119, 166, 168, 171, 235, 263, 272, 304, 322, 323, 326, 535, 548, 549, 562
Gross, A. J., 43, 61, 548

H

Hall, B. H., 19, 549
Hallinan, M. T., 30, 35, 268, 559
Halpern, J., 120, 555
Hamblin, R. L., 475, 557
Hammerslough, C., 31, 561
Hannan, M. T., 5, 7, 21, 22, 31, 32, 35, 47, 106, 108, 119, 140, 146, 166, 168, 171, 224, 235, 240, 263, 272, 304, 307, 312, 313, 322, 323, 326, 346, 347, 349, 350, 354, 371, 373, 375, 376, 379, 387, 389, 439, 448, 452, 495–498, 500, 501, 535, 542, 546, 548, 549, 555, 556, 562
Hannaway, J., 371, 546
Hanushek, E., 310, 428, 549
Hastings, N. A. J., 221, 549
Hauser, R. M., 24, 38, 44, 310, 459, 540, 549, 558
Hausman, J. A., 19, 549
Hawley, A., 529, 550
Heckman, J. J., 6, 31, 129, 184, 185, 195, 310, 468, 546, 549, 550
Heise, D. R., 36, 550
Henderson, C. R., 349, 433, 438, 442, 443, 445, 446, 448, 459, 465, 497, 544, 550
Henderson, C. R., Jr., 443, 550
Herbst, P. G., 32, 33, 550
Hernes, G., 475, 550
Hibbs, D. A., Jr., 39, 550
Hoel, P. G., 394, 395, 551
Hoem, J. M., 95, 121, 551
Hogan, D. P., 9, 20, 551
Holland, P. W., 24, 110, 268, 541, 551
Holt, J. D., 254, 255, 551
Homans, G. C., 355, 551
Horvath, W. J., 247, 551
Howard, R. A., 68, 95, 96, 100, 551
Hudson, M. C., 308, 560
Hummon, N. P., 22, 35, 39, 355, 544, 551
Huntington, S. P., 314, 315, 321, 551
Hussain, A., 439, 563
Hutchinson, G. E., 340, 551

I

IBRDWT, 308, 551
Ijiri, Y., 387, 551
Inverarity, J., 28, 551
Itô, K., 513, 514, 551

J

Jackson, J., 310, 428, 549
Jazwinski, A. H., 395, 486, 513, 514, 551
Jenkins, G. M., 39, 541
Johnk, M. D., 146, 552
Johnson, N. L., 43, 58, 210, 211, 221, 545, 552
Johnston, J., 426, 430, 440, 552
Jöreskog, K. G., 28, 37, 552
Jorgenson, D. W., 89, 552
Jovanovich, B., 194, 552

K

Kalbfleisch, J. D., 232, 247, 248, 254, 552, 557
Kaplan, E. L., 52, 54, 552
Karlin, S., 113, 387, 392, 397, 403, 407, 409, 411, 412, 414, 513, 552
Katz, E., 467, 543
Keiding, N., 113, 552
Kelley, J., 22, 552
Kendall, M. G., 47, 552
Kenny, D. A., 33, 34, 543, 552, 553
Kertzer, D., 8, 546
Kimura, M., 402, 519, 543
Knuth, D. E., 448, 553
Koch, G. G., 25, 548
Koffel, J. N., 24, 549
Kogan, M., 30, 31, 156, 174, 175, 324, 541
Kohn, M. L., 22, 38, 553
Kotz, S., 58, 211, 221, 552
Kuh, E., 433, 553
Kushner, H. J., 518, 553

L

Laird, N., 184, 544
Lancaster, A., 80, 553
Land, K. C., 22, 339, 543, 553
Landes, E., 193, 540
Lazarsfeld, P. F., 18, 23, 24, 33, 34, 38, 331, 553
Lehman, E. H. Jr., 140, 555
Leinhardt, S., 110, 268, 551
Leowontin, R. C., 520, 553
Leslie, P. H., 490, 491, 553
Levins, R., 520, 553
Lipset, S. M., 190, 315, 554
Loftin, C., 39, 554
Lord, F. M., 334, 554
Lotka, A., 468, 471, 480, 481, 483, 554
Luenberger, D. G., 357, 366, 478, 506, 554

M

MaCurdy, T. E., 6, 554
Maddala, G. S., 439, 441, 554
Madden, C. H., 190, 554
Malinvaud, E., 426, 430, 554
Manton, K. G., 177, 185, 554
March, J. G., 10, 554
Mason, W. M., 192, 546
May, R. M., 509, 520, 526, 554
Mayer, T. F., 26, 31, 33, 39, 554
McCarthy, P. J., 30, 31, 156, 174, 175, 324, 541
McDowell, D., 39, 554
McGarty, T., 397, 399, 486, 555
McGinnis, R., 31, 555
Meier, P., 52, 54, 552
Mendenhall, W., 140, 555
Menken, J., 31, 555
Menzel, H., 467, 543
Messinger, S. L., 22, 540
Meyer, J. W., 7, 9, 22, 307, 310, 315, 316, 318, 321, 555, 561
Meyer, M., 22, 459, 555
Michael, R., 193, 540
Michels, R., 190, 555
Miller, D. C., 20, 546
Miller, H. D., 96, 113, 193, 278, 405, 543

Miller, J. L. L., 475, 557
Miller, R. G., 120, 555
Mills, J. P., 57, 555
Mincer, J., 195, 555
Mitter, P., 230, 544
Molotch, H., 9, 555
Morrison, P. M., 89, 555
Mortensen, R., 516–518, 555
Murray, W., 121, 449, 450, 547, 555
Muthen, B., 37, 563

N

Nelson, J. F., 22, 555
Nelson, R., 480, 556
Nelson, W., 59, 556
Nerlove, M., 310, 433, 439–442, 448–451, 455, 465, 539, 556
Nielsen, F., 35, 338, 341, 349, 389, 446, 495–498, 500, 501, 512, 556
Novick, M. R., 334, 554

O

Oakes, D., 239, 556
Olver, F. W. J., 413, 556
Olzak, S., 389, 556

P

Paige, J. M., 7, 556
Palmer, G. L., 28, 556
Panel on Youth, 6, 556
Parker, R. N., 39, 556
Parnes, H. S., 459, 556
Parsons, T., 529, 556
Peacock, J. B., 221, 549
Pelz, D. C., 33, 556
Perrucci, C. C., 25, 545
Peterson, A. V., Jr., 254, 557
Peto, J. 54, 557
Peto, R., 54, 557
Phillips, A. W., 461, 557
Phillips, D. T., 146, 557
Phillips, P. C. B., 461, 463, 464, 557
Pielou, E. C., 490, 557
Pitcher, B. L., 475, 557
Port, S. C., 394, 395, 551
Powell, G. B., Jr., 190, 529, 539
Prentice, R. L., 232, 247, 248, 254, 552, 557
Press, S. J., 310, 556
Pullum, T. W., 192, 557
Pyke, R., 95, 557

R

Rajalakman, D. V., 461, 540
Ramirez, F. O., 307, 310, 315, 316, 318, 321, 561
Rao, C. R., 436, 557
Rauma, D., 22, 540
Reinert, G., 192, 540
Ricciardi, L. M., 520, 526, 542
Richards, T., 185, 561
Richardson, L. F., 355, 557
Richter-Dyn, N., 402, 406, 408, 547
Robins, P. K., 6, 106, 109, 268, 298, 299, 557, 562
Robinson, P. M., 461, 557
Rogosa, D., 34, 39, 558
Rosenfeld, R. A., 24, 35, 338, 341, 556, 558
Rossi, P., 20, 44, 213, 543
Roughgarden, J., 509, 520, 526, 546, 558
Rubin, D., 184, 544
Rubinson, R., 309, 558
Ryder, N. B., 191, 558

S

Saaty, T. L., 388, 558
Sargan, J. D., 461, 558
Sartori, G., 307, 308, 558
Schooler, C., 22, 38, 553
Scott, W. R., 12, 346, 530, 558

Scudo, F. M., 480, 558
Searle, S. R., 443, 445, 446, 558
Sewell, W. H., 44, 459, 549, 558
Shorter, E., 22, 558
Silcock, H., 175, 177, 180, 559
Simon, H. A., 10, 13, 355, 387, 551, 554, 559
Singer, B., 20, 21, 26, 27, 29, 31, 87, 105, 106, 184, 185, 281, 305–307, 311, 542, 550, 559
Sjoberg, G., 190, 559
Skocpol, T., 7, 559
Skorokhod, A. V., 518, 519, 559
Smith-Donals, L. G., 6, 268, 269, 562
Snyder, D., 22, 28, 559
Sorbom, D., 37, 552
Sørensen, A. B., 20, 30, 31, 35, 44, 94, 118, 140, 152, 213, 217, 235, 245, 257, 268, 543, 559, 560
Spencer, H., 529, 530, 560
Spilerman, S., 6, 20, 21, 25–27, 29–31, 87, 94, 105, 106, 111, 177, 281, 305–307, 559, 560
Stallard, E., 177, 185, 554
Starmer, C. F., 25, 548
Stempel, D., 31, 555
Stevenson, W. B., 39, 560
Stinchcombe, A. L., 124, 190, 224, 335, 386, 560
Stone, C. J., 394, 395, 551
Strang, G., 358, 560
Stratonovich, R. L., 515, 519, 560
Strook, D. W., 415, 560
Summers, G. F., 37, 563
Sweet, J. A., 25, 542

T

Takacs, L., 114, 560
Tarter, M. E., 52, 560
Taylor, C. L., 308, 560

Taylor, H. M., 113, 387, 392, 397, 403, 407, 409, 411, 412, 414, 513, 552
Teuter, K., 35, 551
Textor, R., 308, 540
Theil, H., 298, 560
Thom, R., 534, 561
Thomas, G. M., 307, 310, 315, 316, 318, 321, 561
Thompson, D'A. W., 529, 561
Tilly, C., 7, 20, 22, 23, 28, 475, 530, 558, 559, 561
Tilly, L., 23, 561
Tilly, R., 23, 561
Travis, H. P., 24, 549
Trussell, J., 31, 185, 555, 561
Tsiatis, A., 69, 239, 254, 561
Tuckwell, H. C., 520, 526, 561
Tukey, J. W., 79, 561
Tuma, N. B., 5, 6, 21, 26, 30–32, 46, 47, 106, 108, 109, 119, 140, 146, 156, 158, 166, 168, 171, 177, 180, 194, 195, 216, 218, 220, 235, 240–243, 245, 246, 257, 258, 263, 268, 269, 272, 278, 279, 284, 298, 299, 304, 322, 323, 326, 448–450, 452, 453, 455, 535, 542, 548, 549, 557, 560–562, 563
Turelli, M., 518, 519, 563

U

UNDY, 308, 563
UNSY, 308, 563
UNYITS, 308, 563

V

van Kampen, N. G., 393, 563
Varadhan, S. R. S., 415, 560
Vaupel, J. W., 185, 554
Vigderhous, G., 39, 563
Volterra, V., 478–481, 504, 506, 563

Author Index

W

Wallace, T. D., 439, 563
Wallerstein, I., 316, 563
Warsavage, B., 146, 240, 542
Wasserman, S. S., 110, 563
Wheaton, B., 37, 563
White, H. C., 116, 392, 563
Willis, R. J., 6, 550
Wilson, E. O., 468, 485, 564
Winsborough, H. H., 9, 564
Winter, S., 481, 556
Wong, E., 517, 519, 564
Wymer, C. R., 461, 564

Y

Yaeger, K. E., 298, 299, 557
Young, A. A., 439, 448–450, 452, 453, 455, 549, 563
Yushkevich, A. A., 409, 545

Z

Zakai, M., 517, 519, 564
Zelen, M., 89, 545
Ziegler, J. R., 480, 558

Subject Index

A

Aalen estimator, 59–60
Administrative intensity, 334
Age dependence, 190
"Almost sure" convergence, 393
Alternating renewal and loss (ARL) model, 108–109
Alternating renewal (AR) model, 106
Attrition, 322
Autocorrelation
 bias, 37–38, 430, 433
 coefficient, 440
 of disturbances, 430–431
 function, 521

B

Bessel
 function, modified, 413
 process, 412
Binomial model, 92, 107–108
Birth and death model, 112–114
Boundaries of diffusion processes, 406–410, 531–534
 absorbing, 407–408
 natural, 407
 reflecting, 408–409
 sticky, 409
Brownian motion, 391–393
 correlation function, 392
 with drift, 404–405, 524–526
 geometric, 520–522, 524–526
 multivariate, 411–412
 radial, 412–413
 standard, 392

C

Cameron–Martin formula, 415
Carrying capacity, 340
Catastrophe theory, 534
Censoring, 47, 118–145, 151–154
 left, 128–135
 right, 122–128
Change in causal (exogenous) variables
 exponential, 325
 linear, 208–215, 324
Characteristic equation, 357
Cohort analysis, 191–192
Competing risks, 68
Competition, 354, 478–485

573

Competition coefficients, *see* Coupling, coefficients
Conditional survivor function, 68–70
  Kaplan–Meier estimator, 69–70
  relation to survivor function, 69
Conditional transition probability, 66–67
  relation to transition probability, 66
Continuous-time versus discrete-time modeling, 79–88
Core matrix, 97
Counted data, 386
Coupled qualitative and quantitative processes, 528–538
Coupling
  coefficients, 372, 482–483
  diffuse or indirect, 414, 478–480
  direct, 352-354, 480–483
Criterion, *see* Target level
Cross-lag correlations, 33
Cross-rate dependence, 537
Cross-sectional analysis, 297–304
Cross-state dependence, 537
Cycles, 506–509

D

Delta-correlated data, 391
Density dependence, 469–471, 478 ff.
Design, *see* Observation plan
Differential equations
  deterministic (DDE)
    for a scalar outcome, 333–341, 466–476
    solution of, *see* Integral equations
    systems of, 352–355, 477–509
  stochastic (SDE)
    relationship to diffusion processes, 404–406, 517–520
    for a scalar outcome, 388–397
    systems of, 410–416
Diffusion of information, 466–467, 511–512
Diffusion parameter, *see* Local variance
Diffusion process, 400–406
Dirac delta function, 389
Disappearance of social units, *see* Extinction
Discrete-time approach, *see* Continuous-time versus discrete-time modeling
Duration dependence, 192–195
Dynamic analysis
  need for, 4–8, 11–14
  obstacles to, 14–15

E

Educational expansion, 495–501
Eigenvalues, 357–370
Eigenvectors 357–370
Embedding problem, 27, 305–306
Employment status, 268–276, 298–301
Episode, *see* Spell
Equilibrium, 8–11, 49, 297–304, *see also* Stability
Estimation
  least squares
    generalized (GLS), 439–441, 442–446
    modified generalized (MGLS), 441–442
    ordinary (OLS), 426–430
    weighted generalized (WGLS), 446
    with constants (LSC), 438
  maximum-likelihood (ML), 119 ff., 426–430, 446–447
  moment, 140
  partial-likelihood (PL), 235–264

Subject Index

Event, 45
Event-count analysis, 304–305
Event-history analysis, 28–33, 43–77
  event-history data 45–48
  terms for populations of event histories, 49–77
Event sequence analysis, 303–304
Event transition probability, 68
  relation to conditional transition probability, 68
Exact discrete approximation, 423–424, 463–464, 485–495
Experience dependence, 195–196
Exploratory data analysis 29, 79–82
Extinction, 386

F

Fit of models, 321–327
Fitness factor, 479
First passage time, 404
Flow diagram, 102–104
Fokker–Planck equation, *see* Kolmogorov or diffusion equation, forward

G

Gamma function, 177–178, 221
Gause's principle, 485
Gompertz model, 132, 210, 221, 473–475
Growth models, 110–112
  exponential, 469
  random, 521–522, 524–526
  state dependent, 468–470
  time dependent, 471–476

H

Hadamard product, 97
Hazard function, 57–65
  cumulative (integrated), 59–65
  plots of, 60, 63–65, 74, 76

  for the nth event, 58–59
  relation to survivor function, 59
Henderson's method, 442–446
Heterogeneity, *see* Population heterogeneity, Unobserved heterogeneity
Heteroscedasticity, 438, 442
History, dependence on, 191
Holding time, 47
  distribution function, 70–71
  relationship to survivor function, 70–71

I

Independent increments, 388
Individual-specific effects, 432–434
Instantaneous transition rate, 71–77, 88–91
  cumulative (integrated), 73
  estimation, 135–138
  relation to conditional survivor function, 72
  relation to conditional transition probability, 72
  relation to hazard function, 72
  relation to transition probability, 72
Integral equations
  deterministic
    scalar, 341–345, 381–383
    systems, 355–357
  stochastic, 512–520
    comparison between Itô and Stratonovich, 516–520
    Itô, 513–515
    Stratonovich, 515–516
Inverse Gaussian distribution, 230
Itô transformation formula, 522–526

J

Jacobian matrix, 428

Job shift, 54–55, 60–65, 67, 73–77, 179–183, 216–218, 244–247, 256–259

K

Kaplan–Meier estimator, 52–54
Kolmogorov or diffusion equation
  forward, 402
  backward, 402
Kronecker product, 436
K strategy, 340–341

L

Laplace transform, 100
Latent states, 32–33
Latent variables, 37–38, 69
Least squares, see Estimation
Liapunov's first method, see Linearization
Linear deterministic models
  scalar case, 331–352, 381–383
  systems of, 352–380
Linearization, 501–506
Local drift, see Local mean
Local mean, 400–401
Local variance, 400–402
Logistic model, 468–471, 486–489, 503
Log-linear analysis, 298–304
Log-logistic model, 230
Log-normal distribution, 230, 522
Loss (L) model, 106–107
Lotka–Volterra model, 480–485, 489–495, 504–505

M

Makeham model, 221
Marital
  stability, 165–175, 199–208
  status, 193–194, 268–276, 303–304, 322–327
Markov model, 92–94
Matrix diagonalization, 357–358

Mean number of events, 51
Mean square
  convergence in, 514
  limit in, 514
Measurement error, 145–151, 455–459
Model of coupled dichotomous variables, 110, 267 ff.
Mover–stayer model, 156, 174–175
Multiwave panel design, see Observation plan
Multinomial model, 92
Mutualism, 354

N

Negative-feedback model, 334–336
Negative income tax (NIT) program, 165–175, 199–208, 268–276, 298–304, 322–327
Niche parameters, 340
Noise
  colored, 431, 518
  white, 388, 390, 393
Nuisance function, 234, 250–254

O

Observation plan
  event count, 19–20
  event history, 21–22
  event sequence, 20
  multiple time series, 22
  multiwave panel, 433
  panel, 18–19, 22, 23–24, 418–422
    equally spaced waves, 423
    unequally spaced waves, 459–461
  sample path, see event history, above
  time series, 22, 418–422
Organizational growth and decline, 326–352, 370–380

Organizational mortality, 223–229
Operational time, 93–95
Ornstein–Uhlenbeck process
   covariance of, 394–395
   modified, 405, 408, 429
   multivariate, 413–416
   standard, 390–391, 404
   variance of, 394–395
Oscillations, 361

P

Panel analysis of qualitative outcomes, 23–27, 305–307
   contingency-table strategy, 24–25
   regression strategy, 25–26
   continuous-time strategy, 26–27
Panel analysis of quantitative outcomes, 33–38, 418–465
   identification problem, 35–36
Partial-adjustment model
   bivariate, 353
   multivariate, 354–355, 497
   scalar, 337–338, 468
Partial likelihood, *see* Estimation
Persistence of initial conditions, 338
Phase-space analysis, 365–370
Poisson process, 90, 110–111, 136
   generalized, 398–399
Pooled cross-section and time-series estimators, 431–455
Political change, 307–321
Population heterogeneity, 30–31, 155–186, *see also* Unobserved heterogeneity
Predator–prey model, 506–509
Proportional rates, 233–235
Pure decline (bounded growth) model, 112
Pure growth model, *see* Poisson process

R

Rayleigh model, generalized, 61, 221, 230
Ratchet pattern, 379
Rate dependence, 268
r strategy, 340–341

S

Sample path, 48
Sample-selection bias, 129, 133
Scale measure, 403
Self-transition, 92
Semi-Markov model, 94–101, 104–114
   mean of the waiting time, 99
   mean of the number of events in a period, 99–100, 105, 109, 111
   state probabilities, 101
   survivor function, 98
   transition probabilities, 100
   two-state semi-Markov model, 104–105
Sickle model, 230
Size and form, 529–530
Spacing between observations, 306–307, 423
Speed density, 403
Speed of adjustment, 337, 468, 472
Spell, 47
Stability, qualitative, 359–370, 501–509
   asymptotic, 360, 363
   global, 360
   marginal, 362
   neutral, 508
State dependence, 195, 268, 467–471
State probabilities, 49
State space, 45

Steady-state distribution, 49, 298–302, 359–360, 403–406
Stochastic difference equations, 518–520
Stochastic models, need for, 385–387
Structural-equation models, 331
Survivor function, 51–52
  Kaplan–Meier estimator, 52–54
  survivor function for the nth event, 52
Switching process, 536

T

Target level, 336, 339–341
Ties in times of events, 247–248
Time dependence, 31–32, 187–264
Time-series analysis, 38–39
Time stationarity, 93, 101
Transition probability, 50–51
  density, 400
Transition rate, *see* Instantaneous transition rate

U

Unions, labor, 224—229
Unobserved heterogeneity, 174–186, 475–476, *see also* Population heterogeneity

W

Waiting time, 47
  distribution function, 55–57
Weibull model, 61, 211, 221
Wiener process, *see* Brownian motion

QUANTITATIVE STUDIES IN SOCIAL RELATIONS
(Continued from page ii)

J. Ronald Milavsky, Ronald C. Kessler, Horst H. Stipp, and William S. Rubens, **TELEVISION AND AGGRESSION**: *A Panel Study*

Ronald S. Burt, **TOWARD A STRUCTURAL THEORY OF ACTION**: *Network Models of Social Structure, Perception, and Action*

Peter H. Rossi, James D. Wright, and Eleanor Weber-Burdin, **NATURAL HAZARDS AND PUBLIC CHOICE**: *The Indifferent State and Local Politics of Hazard Mitigation*

Neil Fligstein, **GOING NORTH**: *Migration of Blacks and Whites from the South, 1900–1950*

Howard Schuman and Stanley Presser, **QUESTIONS AND ANSWERS IN ATTITUDE SURVEYS**: *Experiments on Question Form, Wording, and Context*

Michael E. Sobel, **LIFESTYLE AND SOCIAL STRUCTURE**: *Concepts, Definitions, Analyses*

William Spangar Peirce, **BUREAUCRATIC FAILURE AND PUBLIC EXPENDITURE**

Bruce Jacobs, **THE POLITICAL ECONOMY OF ORGANIZATIONAL CHANGE**: *Urban Institutional Response to the War on Poverty*

Ronald C. Kessler and David F. Greenberg, **LINEAR PANEL ANALYSIS**: *Models of Quantitative Change*

Ivar Berg (Ed.), **SOCIOLOGICAL PERSPECTIVES ON LABOR MARKETS**

James Alan Fox (Ed.), **METHODS IN QUANTITATIVE CRIMINOLOGY**

James Alan Fox (Ed.), **MODELS IN QUANTITATIVE CRIMINOLOGY**

Philip K. Robins, Robert G. Spiegelman, Samuel Weiner, and Joseph G. Bell (Eds.), **A GUARANTEED ANNUAL INCOME**: *Evidence from a Social Experiment*

Zev Klein and Yohanan Eshel, **INTEGRATING JERUSALEM SCHOOLS**

Juan E. Mezzich and Herbert Solomon, **TAXONOMY AND BEHAVIORAL SCIENCE**

Walter Williams, **GOVERNMENT BY AGENCY**: *Lessons from the Social Program Grants-in-Aid Experience*

Peter H. Rossi, Richard A. Berk, and Kenneth J. Lenihan, **MONEY, WORK, AND CRIME**: *Experimental Evidence*

Robert M. Groves and Robert L. Kahn, **SURVEYS BY TELEPHONE**: *A National Comparison with Personal Interviews*

N. Krishnan Namboodiri (Ed.), **SURVEY SAMPLING AND MEASUREMENT**

QUANTITATIVE STUDIES IN SOCIAL RELATIONS

Beverly Duncan and Otis Dudley Duncan, SEX TYPING AND SOCIAL ROLES: *A Research Report*

Donald J. Treiman, OCCUPATIONAL PRESTIGE IN COMPARATIVE PERSPECTIVE

Samuel Leinhardt (Ed.), SOCIAL NETWORKS: *A Developing Paradigm*

Richard A. Berk, Harold Brackman, and Selma Lesser, A MEASURE OF JUSTICE: *An Empirical Study of Changes in the California Penal Code, 1955–1971*

Richard F. Curtis and Elton F. Jackson, INEQUALITY IN AMERICAN COMMUNITIES

Eric Hanushek and John Jackson, STATISTICAL METHODS FOR SOCIAL SCIENTISTS

Edward O. Laumann and Franz U. Pappi, NETWORKS OF COLLECTIVE ACTION: *A Perspective on Community Influence Systems*

Walter Williams and Richard F. Elmore, SOCIAL PROGRAM IMPLEMENTATION

Roland J. Liebert, DISINTEGRATION AND POLITICAL ACTION: *The Changing Functions of City Governments in America*

James D. Wright, THE DISSENT OF THE GOVERNED: *Alienation and Democracy in America*

Seymour Sudman, APPLIED SAMPLING

Michael D. Ornstein, ENTRY INTO THE AMERICAN LABOR FORCE

Carl A. Bennett and Arthur A. Lumsdaine (Eds.), EVALUATION AND EXPERIMENT: *Some Critical Issues in Assessing Social Programs*

H. M. Blalock, A. Aganbegian, F. M. Borodkin, Raymond Boudon, and Vittorio Capecchi (Eds.), QUANTITATIVE SOCIOLOGY: *International Perspectives on Mathematical and Statistical Modeling*

N. J. Demerath, III, Otto Larsen, and Karl F. Schuessler (Eds.), SOCIAL POLICY AND SOCIOLOGY

Henry W. Riecken and Robert F. Boruch (Eds.), SOCIAL EXPERIMENTATION: *A Method for Planning and Evaluating Social Intervention*

Arthur S. Goldberger and Otis Dudley Duncan (Eds.), STRUCTURAL EQUATION MODELS IN THE SOCIAL SCIENCES

Robert B. Tapp, RELIGION AMONG THE UNITARIAN UNIVERSALISTS: *Converts in the Stepfathers' House*

QUANTITATIVE STUDIES IN SOCIAL RELATIONS

Kent S. Miller and Ralph Mason Dreger (Eds.), COMPARATIVE STUDIES OF BLACKS AND WHITES IN THE UNITED STATES

Douglas T. Hall and Benjamin Schneider, ORGANIZATIONAL CLIMATES AND CAREERS: *The Work Lives of Priests*

Robert L. Crain and Carol S. Weisman, DISCRIMINATION, PERSONALITY, AND ACHIEVEMENT: *A Survey of Northern Blacks*

Roger N. Shepard, A. Kimball Romney, and Sara Beth Nerlove (Eds.), MULTIDIMENSIONAL SCALING: *Theory and Applications in the Behavioral Sciences,* Volume I — Theory; Volume II — Applications

Peter H. Rossi and Walter Williams (Eds.), EVALUATING SOCIAL PROGRAMS: *Theory, Practice, and Politics*